BIBLICAL RESEARCHES

IN

PALESTINE,

AND IN THE ADJACENT REGIONS.

A

JOURNAL OF TRAVELS IN THE YEAR

1838.

BY E. ROBINSON AND E. SMITH.

DRAWN UP FROM THE ORIGINAL DIARIES, WITH HISTORICAL ILLUSTRATIONS,

BY

EDWARD ROBINSON, D. D. LL. D.

PROFESSOR OF BIBLICAL LITERATURE IN THE UNION THEOLOGICAL
SEMINARY, NEW YORK.

WITH NEW MAPS AND PLANS.

IN TWO VOLUMES.

VOL. I.

PUBLISHED BY CROCKER AND BREWSTER,

No. 47 Washington Street.

LONDON—JOHN MURRAY.

1856.

TO THE

REV. MOSES STUART,

PROFESSOR OF SACRED LITERATURE IN THE ANDOVER THEOLOGICAL SEMINARY,

THIS WORK,

THE FRUIT OF STUDIES BEGUN IN THE BOSOM OF HIS FAMILY,

IS RESPECTFULLY INSCRIBED,

AS A TOKEN OF GRATEFUL ACKNOWLEDGEMENT ON THE PART OF A

PUPIL AND FRIEND.

ADVERTISEMENT.

THE former edition of the BIBLICAL RESEARCHES IN PALESTINE having been for several years out of print, both in the United States and in England, the work is now again issued, in a condensed form, in two volumes; with an additional supplemental volume, the fruit of a second visit to the Holy Land in A. D. 1852.

This compression of the original work has been effected, partly by a different style of printing, and partly by the omission of portions of the former Appendix and Notes. The Text remains unchanged; except the few corrections necessarily incident to such a work. The chief portions thus omitted are: the Memoir on the Maps; the Essay on the Pronunciation of the Arabic; and the Arabic Lists of Names of Places. These latter are important to the scholar; but not to the general reader. It has therefore been thought best, to have these Lists carefully corrected and enlarged, and then printed as a separate work at Beirût, under the personal supervision of the Rev. Eli Smith, D. D.

For a like reason, no Arabic type has been used in the Index of Names; care being taken to have the corresponding system of notation fully carried out in that Index. The reader will find more on this topic in the Preface to the new volume.

In respect also to the Maps and Plans, the reader is in like manner referred to the Preface to the new volume.

VOL. I.—A*

The corrections and additions to the original work are few, but not unimportant. Notes have been added at the end of Vol. I, on the position of Israel at Sinai, on Jebel Serbâl, and on the Sinaitic Inscriptions. Ancient *Geba* is now identified with Jeba'; *Gibeah* of Benjamin is recognised at Tuleil el-Fûl; while *Ophrah, Ephron,* and *Ephraim,* as being probably one and the same, are fixed at Taiyibeh. The historical evidence is also given of the identity of *Eleutheropolis* with Beit Jibrîn; and a new marginal note enumerates the reasons for not seeking *Kadesh-barnea* in the high western desert.

The publication of the BIBLICAL RESEARCHES was received with unexpected favour. In 1842, the Royal Geographical Society of London awarded to it their Patron's Gold Medal. The voice of approbation and kindness came up from the scholars of Great Britain and Germany, from the Old world, as well as from the New; and the volumes have been permitted to take rank as a standard work in relation to the Holy Land. All this was wholly unanticipated by the author, and demands his grateful acknowledgments.

Not unmindful of the obligations thence resulting, the author now lays before the Christian public the present work, comprising the observations made during his *two* visits to the Holy Land. It is his completed work; it constitutes a connected whole; and is therefore issued in a permanent form.

May the Great Head of the Church cause these volumes still further to subserve the high interests of Biblical learning and religious truth!

NEW YORK, *July*, 1856.

PREFACE

————•◆•————

THE occasion, the motives, and the manner of the journey, of which these volumes contain the history, are sufficiently detailed at the beginning and close of the introductory Section. It remains here only to speak of the form, in which the materials have been wrought up.

It was my original plan, to present to the public only the results of our researches in Palestine, without any reference to personal incidents. But the advice of friends, whose judgment I could not but place above my own, was averse to such a course. I have therefore everywhere interwoven the personal narrative; and have endeavoured so to do it, as to exhibit the manner in which the Promised Land unfolded itself to our eyes, and the processes by which we were led to the conclusions and opinions advanced in this work. In all this there is at least one advantage for the public. As we venture to hope, that these volumes contain a considerable amount of new information upon the historical topography of Palestine, this course will enable the reader better to judge of the opportunities for observation enjoyed by the travellers, as well as of the credibility of their testimony and the general accuracy of their conclusions. In all these particulars, we have no desire to shun the closest scrutiny.

A similar doubt existed for a time, in respect to the form of narrative to be adopted; whether a full and regularly arranged account of each object in succession, as in the works of Pococke and Niebuhr; or a daily journal, like those of Maundrell and

Burckhardt. I chose the latter, for a reason similar to that already assigned, viz. that in this way the reader is better able to follow the process of inquiry and conviction in the traveller's own mind. It is, however, an evil necessarily incident to this form, that remarks upon one and the same object sometimes occur in different places, instead of being brought together as parts of a whole. Thus, in regard to the Horeb of the present day, the probable place of the giving of the law, the order of time has led me first to speak of it as it appeared on our approach; again, as we measured the plain and took bearings of the mountains around; and then, once more, in connection with our visit to its summit. In like manner, at Beit Jibrîn, the ancient Eleutheropolis, which we examined at two different times, various objects of interest are naturally described under each visit. Yet it seems to me, that this is not an evil of sufficient magnitude, to counterbalance the general advantages of the journal form.

Another more important change of the original plan, arose during the progress of the work, which has had the effect, not only to enlarge the size, but also to increase the labour of preparation more than fourfold. I mean the introduction of historical illustrations, and the discussion of various points relating to the historical topography of the Holy Land. My first purpose was merely to describe what we saw, leaving the reader to make his own application of the facts. But as I proceeded, questions continually arose, which I could not pass over without at least satisfying my own mind; this sometimes led to long courses of investigation; and when I had thus arrived at satisfactory conclusions, it seemed almost like a neglect of duty towards the reader, not to embody them in the work. Most of these were topics relating to the geography of the Bible, and intimately connected with its interpretation; and I remembered too, that they had never been discussed by any one, who had himself visited the Holy Land.

One branch of these historical investigations, which I cannot but consider as important for the future geographer and traveller, presents a field comparatively untrodden. I refer to the mass of topographical tradition, long since fastened upon the Holy Land by foreign ecclesiastics and monks, in distinction from the ordinary tradition or preservation of ancient names among the native population. The general view which I have taken of this subject, and the principles on which we acted in our inquiries, are sufficiently exhibited in the beginning of Sec. VII. This view has been silently carried out in the subsequent parts of the work; and the attempt made to point out, in most cases, not only what is truth and what is mere legendary tradition, but also to show how far the latter reaches back.[1]

As here presented to the public, these volumes may therefore be said to exhibit an historical review of the Sacred Geography of Palestine, since the times of the New Testament; pointing out under each place described, how far and in what period it has hitherto been known. This applies however, in strictness, only to the parts of the country examined by us; although these include, in a certain sense, nearly the whole of Palestine west of the Jordan.

A point to which we gave particular attention, was the orthography of Arabic names, both in Arabic and Roman letters. In respect to the former, my companion, Mr Smith, had already made some preparation for our journey, by obtaining the names of places in many of the provinces and districts, written by educated natives. These lists were afterwards verified and corrected from various sources, as well as by himself on visiting the respective districts. The remaining names were written down by him from the pronunciation of the Arabs, with great care, and according to the established rules of the language. In the region of Mount Sinai and Wady Mûsa, we had the benefit of Burckhardt's orthography, which was found to be usually, though not always, correct. It is worthy of remark, that Burckhardt is hitherto the only Frank traveller in Syria, who has, to any extent, given us Arabic names written with Arabic letters.[2]

In this connection, we could not but feel the want of a regular system of orthography for the same names, when written with Latin letters. Scarcely a trace of such a system can be said to have existed hitherto, except in individual works. The subject was brought before the general meeting of the Syrian

---

A paragraph on the different epochs of this tradition has been transferred from this place to the beginning of Sec. VII. p. 254.

[2] The names written in Arabic letters on the great map of Palestine by Jacotin, and also those in the Travels of Scholz, are so very incorrect, as to form no exception to the above remark.

mission at Jerusalem; and after long consideration, it was re-
solved to adopt, in general, the system proposed by Mr Pickering for the Indian languages,[1] with such modifications as might
be necessary in adapting it to the oriental tongues. Two motives led to a preference of this system; first, its own intrinsic
merits and facility of adaptation; and secondly, the fact, that it
was already extensively in use throughout Europe and the
United States, in writing the aboriginal names in North America and the South Sea Islands; so that by thus adopting it for
the oriental languages, a uniformity of orthography would be
secured among the missions, and also in the publications, of the
American Board.[2]

In furtherance of the same general object, my friend took
pains to exhibit, in a short but very clear Essay, the principles
which govern the pronunciation of the spoken Arabic at the
present day.[3] This was highly acceptable to Arabic scholars.
It was printed in the Appendix to the last volume; and was
there followed by the Lists of Arabic names of places above
referred to, which are more fully described at the beginning of
Sec. IX. The Arabic orthography of all the names occurring
in the text, was likewise given in an alphabetical Index at the
close of the work.

The maps were drawn, under my own inspection, by Kiepert,
a young scholar of great talent and promise in Berlin. In the
parts of the country visited or seen by us, they were constructed
almost solely from our own routes and observations and the information we were able to collect, brought into connection with
known and fixed points. The other portions were supplied from
the best authorities, viz. the form and shores of the gulfs of the
Red Sea, from the chart of Capt. Moresby; the country south
of Wady Mûsa and parts of Sinai, so far as known, from Laborde, with corrections from Burckhardt and Rüppell; the
coast of Palestine, as far north as to 'Akka, and the country
around Nazareth, from the great map of Jacotin, compiled from

---

[1] "Essay on a uniform Orthography for the Indian Languages of North America. By John Pickering." Cambr. N. E. 1818. —The Indian languages of North America and of the Islands of the Pacific, have mostly been reduced to writing according to this simple system.

[2] In a few Arabic names and words already common in European languages, we have preferred to follow the usual orthography; as Saladin, Ramleh, Wady, etc.
[3] Some slight changes in the tenses have here and further on been introduced.

surveys made during the French expedition in A. D. 1799; the positions on the coast being corrected from later astronomical observations.[1] The small portion given of the country east of the Jordan, was reconstructed from the routes and observations of Burckhardt, compared with those of Seetzen, Irby and Mangles, and a few others of less importance. The whole of Mount Lebanon north of Sidon, was drawn from manuscript maps of Prof. Ehrenberg of Berlin, and of the Rev. Mr Bird formerly of the American Mission in Syria, kindly communicated to me for that purpose. The map of the former was used by Berghaus; those of the latter had never been brought before the public.

In the construction of the maps, it was a main principle, to admit no name nor position on mere conjecture, nor without some sufficient positive authority. Where a place was known to exist, though its position was not definitely ascertained, it was marked as uncertain. The operation of this principle was, to exclude a multitude of names, ancient and modern, which figure at random on most maps of Palestine. For what is the advantage of multiplying names, if we know not where they belong? On the other hand, I would fain hope, that very much was gained in truth and correctness. The orthography upon the maps, for the most part, was reduced to our system. In respect to several names, however, along the coasts of the Red Sea, as well as a very few others, this was not in my power; and they were given in the current orthography.

This is all I have to say respecting the work, as here presented to the public. We wish it to be regarded merely as a beginning, a first attempt to lay open the treasures of Biblical Geography and History still remaining in the Holy Land; treasures which have lain for ages unexplored, and had become so covered with the dust and rubbish of many centuries, that their very existence was forgotten. Were it in our power again to travel through that Land of Promise, with the experience acquired during our former journey and from the preparation of this work, and furnished too with suitable instruments, I doubt not we should be able to lay before the Christian world results far more important and satisfactory. But this high priv-

---

1) The great map of Jacotin is valuable only in the parts actually visited by the French engineers, viz. along the coast as far as to 'Akka, the region of Nazareth, and around Mount Tabor. The other parts are worthless, being apparently mere fancy sketches.

ilege, I at least can never more hope to enjoy. My companion, however, returns to the seat of his labours in Beirût, taking with him instruments of the best kind, in the hope of being able during his occasional journeys to verify or correct our former observations, and also to extend his examination over other parts of the country. I trust that I may yet be the medium of communicating many of his further observations to the public; and that in this way, if God will, we may still be active together, in promoting the study and illustration of the Holy Scriptures. Should my life be spared, I hope to be enabled to use all the materials thus collected by us both, for the preparation of a systematic work on the physical and historical geography of the Holy Land.

The manuscript of this work was wholly prepared in Berlin; where, in the unrestricted use of that noble institution, the Royal Library, and of the very valuable private collections of Ritter, Neander, and Hengstenberg, I had access to all the literary means I could desire. For all these privileges, and for other aid from many friends, my best thanks are due. How much I owe besides to the advice and unwearied kindness of RITTER, I need not say to those who know him; the many months of cherished intercourse to which his friendship admitted me, will ever remain among the brightest recollections of my life.

The manuscript was completed in August 1840. Soon after that time, the intervention of the European powers caused Palestine once more to revert to the sway of the Sultan; and the Egyptian dominion over it came to an end. But I see no reason to change anything I have written; and the work may stand as a record of the aspect of the land, during the period of its subjection to the ruler of Egypt.

It gives me pleasure to be able to add, that the whole of the manuscript was looked through by my companion Mr Smith; and thus received the benefit of his corrections.

With humble gratitude to God, I here bring this work to a close. It is the fruit of studies and plans of life running back for nearly twenty years; and for the last four years, it has occupied, more or less exclusively, well nigh all my waking hours. May He, who has thus far sustained me, make it useful for the elucidation of His truth!

NEW YORK, *June* 1841.

ORTHOGRAPHY AND PRONUNCIATION OF ARABIC NAMES AND WORDS.

Throughout the whole work an attempt has been made to imitate the native pronunciation in European characters, according to certain definite principles. For the full development of the system, the reader is referred to Dr Smith's Essay on the Pronunciation of the Arabic, printed in the former edition of this work, Vol. III. App. pp. 89–111. The following summary exhibits the powers given to the different Roman consonants and vowels, as used for this purpose.

As, however, such a system is of little importance to the general reader, it is fully carried out only in the first Index; to which the scholar is in all cases referred, for the correct representation of the Arabic forms and pronunciation.

CONSONANTS.

b	represents	ب	Be.
d	. . . . .	د	Dâl.
ḍ	. . . . .	ض	Ḍâd.
dh	. . . . .	ذ	Dhâl; like *th* in *this, then.*
ḍh	. . . . .	ظ	Ḍha; rarely ض Ḍâd.
f	. . . . .	ف	Fe.
g	. . . . .	ج	Jim hard, as in Egypt.
gh	. . . . .	غ	Ghain, pron. best like *g* hard.
h	. . . . .	ه	He.
ḥ	. . . . .	ح	Ḥa.
j	. . . . .	ج	Jim soft, as in Syria.
k	. . . . .	ك	Kâf.
ḳ	. . . . .	ق	Ḳâf guttural.
kh	. . . . .	خ	Khe; sounded nearly like the Swiss-German *ch.*
l	. . . . .	ل	Lâm.
m	. . . . .	م	Mîm.
n	. . . . .	ن	Nûn.
r	. . . . .	ر	Re; rolling, and stronger than the English *r.*
s	. . . . .	س	Sin; always sharp, as in *son.*
ṣ	. . . . .	ص	Ṣâd.

sh	represents	ش	Shîn.
t	. . . . .	ت	Te.
ṭ	. . . . .	ط	Ṭa.
th	. . . . .	ث	The; always sharp, as in *thick, thing.*
w	. . . . .	و	Wâw.
y	. . . . .	ى	Ye.
z	. . . . .	ز	Ze; very rarely ظ Ḍha.
(')	. . . . .	ع	'Ain; a sound not known in western languages.
(')	. . . . .	ء	Hamza with Alef (ا) in the middle of a word. Hamza with Alef at the beginning of a word, is represented only by the vowel.

No letter is written double, except it be doubled (i. e. have a Teshdîd) in the original.

When two Roman letters stand for one in the original, they are not written twice at the end of a word, though the Arabic letter have a Teshdîd. So too *Haj* for *Hajj.*

The ARTICLE before the solar letters is written as pronounced; and is in all cases connected with its noun or adjective by a hyphen (-); as *el-Kuds, er-Ramleh, esh-Sheikh.*

VOWELS.

a stands for Fathah, and has the sounds of *a* in *hat*, Germ. *Mann,* and *what.*

â stands for Fathah prolonged by ا, and has the same sounds lengthened, as in *hare, father, call.*

ai stands for a Fathah followed by ى, and has the sound of *ai* in Italian and German, or of the English *i* in *pine.*

âi stands for a prolonged Fathah followed by ى, and has the sound of the two letters combined in a diphthong.

au stands for a Fathah followed by و, and has the sound of *au* in Italian and German, or of the English *ow* in *how.*

e stands for Fathah and Kesrah, and has the sound of *e* in *led.*

ei stands for a Fathah followed by ى, and has the sound of *ei* in *vein.*

i stands for Kesrah, and has the sound of *i* in *pin.*

î stands for Kesrah prolonged by ى, and has the sound of *i* in *machine.*

o stands for Dümmeh, and has the sound of *o* in *police.*

ö stands for Dümmeh, and has the sound of the German *ö*, nearly equivalent to the French *eu.*

ô stands for a Fathah followed by ‎و‎ , and has the sound of *o* in *note*.

u stands for Dümmeh and Kesrah, and has the sound of short *u* in *full*.

ü stands for Dümmeh, and has the sound of *ü* in German, the same as the French *u*.

û stands for Dümmeh prolonged by ‎و‎ , and has the sound of long *u* in Italian and German, or of the English *oo*.

ŭ stands for Fathah, and has the English sound of *u* in *tub*.

y stands for ‎ى‎ at the end of a word, and has the sound of *y* in *fully*.

MEASURES, WEIGHTS, AND MONEY.

I. The Measure of Distance is usually reckoned by *hours*, the length of which varies with the kind of animal, and also according to the nature of the ground. As a general average the following specification in miles has been found most correct and convenient:

	Geog. M.	Stat. M.	Rom. M.	Germ. M.
1 Hour, with Camels =	2	2⅕	2¼	⅓
1 " with Horses or Mules =	2.4	2⅘	3	⅖

In 1852 we travelled with our own horses, and often without luggage; so that an average rate in that year may be reckoned at about 3 English statute miles the hour.

Note. The measures of heights are sometimes given in French feet. The French foot contains 144 lines, of which 135 are equal to an English foot. The proportion of the English foot to the French is therefore as 15 to 16.

II. The common Measure of Land is the *Feddân* (yoke), which is very indefinite and variable. In general it may be compared with the English *acre* and German *Morgen*.

III. Corn Measures are the following:

1 *Ardeb* is equivalent, very nearly, to five English bushels.

1 *Ruba'* is the twenty-fourth part of an *Ardeb*.

1 *Mid* (measure) in Palestine contains twelve *Ruba's*.

IV. Weights.

> 1 *Rutl* or pound is in general about a quarter of an ounce less than the English pound avoirdupois; but it is sometimes also reckoned only at 12 oz.
>
> 1 *Ukkah* (called by the Franks *Oke*) is about 2¾ lbs English.
>
> 1 *Kuntâr*, or hundred-weight, contains 100 *Rutls*.

MONEY.

Money is everywhere reckoned by *Piastres;* but the value of these is fluctuating, and has greatly depreciated since about 1820.

> 1 *piastre* contains 40 *Fuddâhs*, called in Turkish *parahs*.
>
> 10 piastres were equivalent in 1838 to 1 Austrian florin.
>
> 20   "   "   "   to 1 Austrian or American dollar.
>
> 21   "   "   "   to 1 Spanish pillared dollar.
>
> 100   "   "   "   about 1 pound sterling.
>
> 1 *Kis* or purse is 500 piastres, or about $25 or 5£ sterling.

At Constantinople in 1838 the Spanish dollar (colonnato) was worth 23 piastres, and the other coins in proportion.

In 1852 the American and Austrian dollar was current in Smyrna and in Palestine at 24 piastres. This was the regular rate of exchange then followed by the Austrian steamers.

*** For the Measures, Weights, and Moneys of Egypt, to which those of Syria are similar, see Lane's Modern Egyptians, II. p. 370 sq. edit. 1.

FOR THE READER.

Throughout Vols. I and II, a reference is given, at the bottom of each page, to the corresponding pages of the first edition.—In this way the many references made in various works to the first edition, are rendered available also for the present edition.

CONTENTS.

SECTION I.

INTRODUCTION.—GREECE AND EGYPT.

Pages 1–33.

Original plan of the journey; arrangement with Rev. Eli Smith, 1. His qualifications, 1, 2.—Departure from New-York, 2. England and Germany; early winter, 2. Trieste, steamers, embarkation, 2, 3. Ancona, the Adriatic, Corfu, 3, 4. Theaki, *Ithaca*, 4. Patras, 5. Coast of Maina, 5, 6. Approach to Attica, 6.

GREECE. The Piræus, 6.—*Athens*, 6. Acropolis and Areopagus, 7. Paul's preaching, 7, 8. The Pnyx and Demosthenes, 8. The Academy, Hymettus and its honey, 9. Sunrise at the Parthenon, 9, 10. Character of the Greek people, 10, 11. —Correspondence with Mr Smith, 11. Syra, 11, 12. *Crete*, Canéa, 12, 13. Approach to *Alexandria*, 13.

EGYPT. Escape from quarantine, 13, 14. Landing, motley crowd, 14. Lodgings, 14. Ancient city, 15. Column of Diocletian, 15. Mode of travelling, 15, 16. The canal and boats, 16. The Nile and its waters, 17. Voyage, 17. Lodgings at Cairo, difficulties, 17, 18. Habîb Effendi and his audience, 18. Arab procrastination, 18. Voyage up the Nile, its characteristics, 18, 19. To Thebes, 19. *Thebes*, 20. Its architecture, 21. Tombs of the Kings, 21. Sculptures, e. g. Shishak, 22. Climate, 23. Return to Cairo, 23. The city, 23, 24. Roda, Old Cairo, 24. *Heliopolis*, 24. Mounds of the Jews, 25. Pyramids of Gizeh, 25–27. Sakkâra, mummy-pits, 27. *Memphis*, its mounds, 27.—Muhammed 'Aly, 27. His conscriptions, 28. Forced civilization, 28. The people made slaves, as of old by Pharaoh, 28, 29. Safety in travelling, 29. Imitated by the Sultan, 30. Important changes to be expected in the East, 31.

Long cherished purpose of the journey, 31. Instruments, 32. Journals, 32. Books and Maps, 32, 33.

VOL. I.—B*

SECTION IV.

FROM MOUNT SINAI TO 'AKABAH.

Pages 145–172.

SECTION V.

FROM 'AKABAH TO JERUSALEM.

Pages 173-220.

SECTION VI.

JERUSALEM.—INCIDENTS AND FIRST IMPRESSIONS.

Pages 221–250.

SECTION VII.

JERUSALEM.—TOPOGRAPHY AND ANTIQUITIES.

Pages 251–364.

SECTION VIII.

JERUSALEM.—HISTORY, STATISTICS, ETC.

Pages 365–433.

SECTION IX.

EXCURSION FROM JERUSALEM TO BETHEL, ETC.

Pages 434–465.

SECTION X.

EXCURSION TO 'AIN JIDY, THE DEAD SEA, THE JORDAN, ETC.

Pages 466-580.

NOTES.

CONTENTS.

SECTION I.

THE following work contains the description of a journey, which had been the object of my ardent wishes, and had entered into all my plans of life for more than fifteen years. During a former residence of several years in Europe, from A. D. 1826 to 1830, I had hoped that a fit opportunity for such a journey would have presented itself; but for much of that time Syria was the seat of war and commotion; and this, combined with other circumstances, dissuaded me from making the attempt. In the year 1832, the Rev. Eli Smith, American missionary at Beirût, made a visit to the United States; having recently returned from a long journey with the Rev. Mr. Dwight to Armenia and Persia. He had in former days been my pupil and friend; and a visit to the Holy Land naturally became a topic of conversation between us. It was agreed that we would, if possible, make such a journey together at some future time; and the same general plan was then marked out, which we have since been permitted to execute. A prominent feature of the plan was, to penetrate from Mount Sinai by 'Akabah to Wady Mûsa, and thence to Hebron and Jerusalem; not knowing at the time that any part of this route had been already explored; though it has since become almost a highway for travellers. I count myself fortunate in having been thus early assured of the company of one, who, by his familiar and accurate knowledge of the Arabic language, by his acquaintance with the people of Syria, and by the experience gained in former extensive journeys, was so well qualified to alleviate the difficulties and overcome the obstacles which usually accompany oriental travel. Indeed, to these qualifications of my companion, combined with his taste for geographical and historical researches, and his tact in eliciting and sifting the information to be obtained from an Arab population, are mainly to be ascribed the more important and interesting results of our journey. For I am well aware, that had I been compelled to travel with an ordinary uneducated interpreter, I should naturally have undertaken much less than we together have actually accomplished ; while many points of interest would have been overlooked, and many inquiries would have remained without satisfactory answers.[1]

Embarking with my family at New-York, July 17th, 1837, we had a favourable voyage across the Atlantic, and landed at Liverpool on the eighteenth day. We passed on to London ; stopping for a few days in Leamington and its charming environs ; and also a few days amid the calm dignity of Oxford and its scholastic halls. In London it was now the season when " all the world is out of town ;" yet some veterans in oriental travel were still there ; and I received many hints of information, which were afterwards of great use to me. After a few weeks, we proceeded by Antwerp and Brussels to Cologne ; and thence by easy land-journeys up the glorious Rhine to Frankfort ; and so by Weimar and Halle to Berlin. Here I had hoped to learn much from Ritter, as to many points of inquiry lying out of my own department ; but he was absent, himself engaged in exploring the classic soil of Greece and its remoter islands.

Leaving my family with their friends in Germany, I set off from Berlin on the 13th Nov. by way of Halle ; where Gesenius, Tholuck, and Roediger, suggested many topics of importance in respect to the researches on which I was about to enter. My course was now by Vienna to Trieste. The whole journey was exceedingly uncomfortable, a constant succession of cold storms of rain and snow, heavy roads, and all the discomforts and dreariness of an early winter. During the whole interval from Berlin to Trieste, the sun appeared only on two days ; and then but for a short time. I entered Trieste in a driving snow-storm, which abated for a time only to change its character and return with new vehemence in another form, as a furious Levanter, accompanied by torrents of rain. The next morning, Nov. 30th, all traces of winter had disappeared, except the snows along the summits of the Friulian Alps. The brilliant sky of Italy was again cloudless ; and balmy breezes, as of spring, were playing upon the bright waters of the Adriatic. It was an almost instantaneous change from winter in its rudest forms, to the brightness and deliciousness of May. I could not but hail the

---

[1] The results of Mr. Smith's journey to Armenia, above alluded to, have been given to the public in the work entitled,   *Researches in Armenia, etc., by Messrs. Smith and Dwight.* Bost. 1833. Lond. 1834.

i. 2, 3

change with gratitude, and regard it as a favourable omen; and from that time onward the progress of my journey was never retarded for an hour, nor scarcely for a moment rendered uncomfortable, by any unfavourable state of the weather.

I had chosen the route by Trieste as the shortest; and was gratified to find that it had been recently rendered still shorter by the arrangement of the steamers of the Austrian Lloyd to run twice a month, both to Constantinople and Alexandria. In London I had made diligent inquiry; but was unable to learn, with certainty, that any steamer was running from Trieste to the Levant. In Berlin too I had made similar inquiries, especially at the embassies of England, Austria, and Bavaria, with no better success; but finally obtained the desired information at the Post Office. This route also afforded two important advantages over the Danube route from Vienna to Constantinople; first, because I could thus pass a fortnight at Athens, and yet reach Egypt at the allotted time; and further, because I could thus enter Egypt from Greece without quarantine; while all persons coming to Egypt from any part of the Turkish empire, were subjected to a quarantine of three weeks.

On the 1st of December I embarked at Trieste; having been joined almost at the last moment by two young countrymen, who continued to be my companions in Egypt, and one of them also in the Holy Land. Our vessel was the Giovanni Arciduca d'Austria, under the command of Capt. Pietro Marasso, one of the most intelligent and gentlemanly commanders, whom it has been my fortune to meet with. Seven months afterwards, I found this steamer plying between Syra and Alexandria; and Capt. Marasso in command of the Mahmoudie, a larger vessel running between Syra and Constantinople.—It was a lovely sunset as we glided out of the harbour of Trieste; a flood of golden light was poured upon the glassy waters and upon the eastern mountain, sprinkled with white cottages and country seats, from which it was reflected back upon the city and shipping below. We passed swiftly by the gulf of Capo d'Istria; saw the lights of Isola and the light-house of Pirano; and then in darkness laid our course for Ancona.

The next morning was bright and beautiful; before us was the Italian coast, over which towered the snow-capped ridges of the Apennines. At 9 o'clock we cast anchor in the rock-bound and picturesque harbour of Ancona; where we lay till towards evening, and then pursued our way along the Adriatic. The next day we were plunging against a head wind through the midst of the broadest part of the sea; where the islands and coasts on each side were only occasionally visible. Monte Gargano alone, on the Italian coast, was seen the whole day. But

the morning of the 4th was brilliant and exciting. At sunrise
we were in the channel of Otranto, abreast of the little island
Saseno and Cape Linguetta ; while before us on the left the eye
rested in fascination upon the lofty summits of the Acroce-
raunian mountains, the terror of ancient mariners, wild, dark,
desolate peaks, as if scathed and blasted by lightning ; whence
their name. The sun was now rising over them in splendour.
The Albanian coast continues onward in high rocky ridges ;
desolate, but picturesque. For a long distance there was no
trace of human habitations. Afterwards, a few miserable villages
were seen clinging to the rocky side of the mountains ; but no
appearance of tillage, and hardly of vegetation. In the afternoon we approached the island of Corfu, and passing onward
through the enchanting scenery of its channel, dropped our anchor at evening in its harbour, between the little island of Vido
and the city. The whole region, the island, the harbour, and
the opposite Albanian coast, are exceedingly picturesque ; and
in the impression which they make, reminded me strongly of
the bay of Naples ; though every thing here is on a much smaller
scale.

We remained at Corfu until the evening of the following day,
Dec. 5th. We went on shore, visited the various quarters of the
city, enjoyed the prospect from the light-house on the high rock
of the citadel, and mingled with the people. They were the first
specimen we saw of a Greek population ; and I must do the
Greek nation the justice to say, that they were also the worst.
The streets were thronged with ragged, cut-throat looking fellows,
—fierce, rugged, weather-worn visages, who might well have sat
for Byron's pictures. Our old friends, the Lazzaroni of Naples,
are gentlemen in comparison. And yet these Corfuites might
afford to look down upon some boat-loads of wild Albanian
peasants, which we saw in the harbour. The government of the
Ionian Islands, under the direction and influence of the English Lord High Commissioner, has established many schools, in
which the Scriptures are read. Mr. Lowndes, the intelligent
missionary of the London Missionary Society, is the general su-
perintendent of all these schools throughout the Islands, and had
just returned from a tour, in which he had visited eighty schools.
No religious instruction is given in them, beyond the reading
of the Scriptures. According to the estimate of Mr. Lowndes, who
had resided twenty-two years in Corfu, the city contains about
16,000 inhabitants ; and the whole island about 35,000. Other
estimates vary much from this.

Leaving Corfu at sunset, we saw during the evening the
islands of Paxos and Anti-Paxos ; and passed at night through
the channel between Santa Maura and Theaki, the ancient

i. 5, 6

Ithaca. We of course lost the sight of Sappho's Leap on the western coast of the former. The morning found us some distance S.E. of the latter island ; of which we had a distinct, though not a close view ; yet enough to awaken all our classic feelings, and call up vividly before us Ulysses and the great "Father of Song." Both these islands, as also Cephalonia, present the aspect of dark, high, rocky mountains, with little appearance of fertility.

We entered the bay of Patras, and anchored in its roadstead for some hours. The bay is shut in by mountains, which exclude the winds. The weather was warm and sunny, like a day of June. Patras is a large straggling village with about 7000 inhabitants, lying at the foot of the western slope of Mount Voda, the ancient Panachaicon. Above the village is a dismantled fortress ; from which there is a fine prospect of the bay and its shores. The plain of Patras is fertile and tolerably well tilled. On the north of the bay is the ancient Ætolia ; here one sees the modern Missilonghi on the coast ; and further east the mouth of the Eurotas ; and far in the N. E. the snowy summits of Œta and Parnassus. An hour or more N. E. of Patras is the narrow entrance to the gulf of Lepanto, defended by two fortresses on low opposite points ; and just beyond is the town of Lepanto on the northern coast.—From Patras the mail is usually sent by land to Athens, across the isthmus of Corinth ; and travellers also often take this route.

Towards evening we were again upon our way ; and passed during the night along the coast of Arcadia. The next morning, soon after sunrise, we were running close in shore and near to Navarino and Modon ; and then, rounding the islands of Sapienza and Cabrera, we struck across the bay of Koron to the coast of Maina. Here the frowning peaks of Pentedaktylon, the ancient Taygetus, rose in majesty before our view, the loftiest and most rugged summits of the Peloponnesus. These mountains, the backbone of ancient Laconia, are still inhabited by a brave and high-spirited people, the Mainotes ; who boast that they are of pure Spartan descent, and that they have never been conquered. The events of recent years, however, seem to call in question the latter of these assertions ; while a sprinkling of Slavic words and names of places, are thought by scholars versed in these matters, to indicate some infusion of Slavic blood. We passed quite near to the coast, and could see many of their villages, mere clusters of stone hovels with square towers intermingled, for the purpose of defence in the frequent feuds between families and neighbours, which were formerly so common. The stern hand of a regular government has lessened the number of these feuds, and destroyed many of these private castles. The

i. 7, 8

people are turning their attention more to the arts of peace and civilization. They have demanded teachers; and a missionary station had just been established among them by the American Board, under the patronage of the fine old Mainote Bey, Mavromichalis, with every encouragement and prospect of success.

In the afternoon we turned the high rocky point of Cape Matapan, and struck across the Laconian gulf to the northward of Cerigo towards Cape Malio. This latter cape we passed at evening; and bore away during the night for Hydra. In the morning of Dec. 8th, we were abreast of this island at some distance from it; and could see on our right the little island of St. George, and the remoter ones of Zea and Thermia. Cape Colonna was also visible, and the island Helena beyond; while before us lay Mount Hymettus, upon which a cloud was discharging its snows. As we advanced, the Acropolis and then Mount Pentelicus opened upon the view; and rounding the promontory of Mynichia, we cast anchor at 11½ o'clock in the oval land-locked basin of the Piræus. We were somewhat astonished to find fiacres in waiting, apparently of German manufacture; and in one of them we were soon on our way along a Macadamized road to the city of Athens, a distance of six English miles.

This drive was accompanied by sad feelings. The day was cloudy, cold, and cheerless. The plain and mountains around, the scenes of so many thrilling associations, were untilled and desolate; and on every side were seen the noblest monuments of antiquity in ruins, now serving to mark only the downfall of human greatness and of human pride. Nor did the entrance to the city tend to dissipate these feelings. Small dwellings of stone, huddled together along narrow, crooked, unpaved, filthy lanes, are not the Athens which the scholar loves in imagination to contemplate. Yet they constitute, with a few exceptions, the whole of modern Athens. Even in its best parts, and in the vicinity of the court itself, there is often an air of haste and shabbiness, which, although not a matter of wonder under the circumstances in which the city has been built up, cannot fail to excite in the stranger a feeling of disappointment and sadness. This however does not last long. The force of historical associations is too powerful not to triumph over present degradation; and the traveller soon forgets the scenes before him, and dwells only on the remembrance of the past.

We found a welcome home in the hospitable mansions of Messrs King and Hill, American missionaries; and rejoiced to learn that their exertions in behalf of education and religious instruction are duly acknowledged by the Greek people, and are

i. 8, 9

bearing good fruit. The clergy, as is well known, are in general opposed to such labours; and the government to a great degree indifferent; except in respect to the female schools of Mrs. Hill, which the government has so far encouraged, as to furnish at its own cost a certain number of pupils, to be afterwards employed as teachers in national female schools.

It would not become me to enter into any details respecting the antiquities of Athens. Greece was not the object of my journey; nor had a visit to Athens made part of my original plan. I was therefore not prepared to investigate its remains, any further than I could gather information on the spot from the excellent works of Col. Leake and Dr. Wordsworth.[1] Yet no one can visit Athens without receiving a profound impression of its ancient taste and splendour; and the record of this impression in my own case, is all that I can give.

The most striking feature in Athens is doubtless the Acropolis. It is a mass of rock, which rose precipitously in the midst of the ancient city, and is still accessible only on its N. W. part. On the oblong area of its levelled surface were collected the noblest monuments of Grecian taste; it was the very sanctuary of the arts, the glory, and the religion of ancient Athens. The majestic Propylæa, the beautiful Erechtheum, and the sublime Parthenon, all built of the purest marble, though now ruined and broken down, still attest the former splendours of the place, and exhibit that perfect unity of the simple, the sublime, and the beautiful, to which only Grecian taste ever attained. In this respect, there is no other spot like it on earth. Rome has nothing to compare with it; and the vast masses of Egyptian architecture, while they almost oppress the mind with the idea of immensity, leave no impression of beauty or simplicity.

My first visit in Athens was to the Areopagus, where Paul preached.[2] This is a narrow naked ridge of limestone rock, rising gradually from the northern end, and terminating abruptly on the south, overagainst the west end of the Acropolis, from which it bears about north; being separated from it by an elevated valley. This southern end is fifty or sixty feet above the said valley; though yet much lower than the Acropolis. On its top are still to be seen the seats of the judges and parties, hewn in the rock; and towards the S. W. is a descent by a flight of steps, also cut in the rock, into the valley below. On the west of the ridge, in the valley between it and the Pnyx, was the ancient market, and on the S. E. side, the later or new market. In which of these it was that Paul

---

[1] Leake's Topogr. of Athens. Wordsworth's Athens and Attica.   [2] See the narrative in Acts 17, 16 sq.

i. 10, 11

"disputed daily," it is of course impossible to tell; but from either, it was only a short distance to the foot of "Mars Hill," up which Paul was probably conducted by the flight of steps just mentioned. Standing on this elevated platform, surrounded by the learned and the wise of Athens, the multitude perhaps being on the steps and in the vale below, Paul had directly before him the far famed Acropolis with its wonders of Grecian art; and beneath him, on his left, the majestic Theseium, the earliest and still most perfect of Athenian structures; while all around other temples and altars filled the whole city. Yet here, amid all these objects of which the Athenians were so proud, Paul hesitated not to exclaim: "God, who made the world and all things that are therein,—He being Lord of heaven and earth, dwelleth not in temples made with hands!" On the Acropolis, too, were the three celebrated statues of Minerva; one of olive wood; another of gold and ivory in the Parthenon, the master-piece of Phidias; and the colossal statue in the open air, the point of whose spear was seen over the Parthenon by those sailing along the gulf. To these Paul probably referred and pointed, when he went on to affirm, that "the Godhead is not like unto gold, or silver, or stone, graven by art and man's device." Indeed it is impossible to conceive of any thing more adapted to the circumstances of time and place, than is the whole of this masterly address; but the full force and energy and boldness of the Apostle's language, can be duly felt, only when one has stood upon the spot. The course of the argu-ment too is masterly; so entirely adapted to the acute and susceptible minds of his Athenian audience.

Directly overagainst the Areopagus, and in full view of the place thus consecrated by the labours of the great Apostle of the Gentiles, is another spot still more distinctly marked, and hardly less interesting, as being the undoubted scene of the patriotic exertions of the great Athenian orator. On the east-ern slope of the longer hill, wheh runs parallel to the Areopagus in the west, lies the Pnyx, the place where the assemblies of the Athenian people were held in the open air. It is a semi-circular area; the rock on the upper part having been cut away to the depth of eight or ten feet; and the lower part being in some places built up in a straight line with cyclopean walls. At the highest point, in the middle of the arc, a square mass of the rock is left projecting into the area, with steps to ascend it on the sides. Here was the spot, the very *Bema*, on which Demosthenes stood, when he addressed the Athenian people in those strains of fervid eloquence, which

> "Shook th' arsenal, and fulmined over Greece,
> To Macedon, and Artaxerxes' throne."

i. 11, 12

The exactness of this locality cannot well be drawn in question. It is true, that the *Bema* stood originally on the summit of the ridge, some yards above the present spot, whence the orator could see the Piræus and its fleets ; but its position had been changed long before the days of Demosthenes.[1]

One afternoon we rode with Mr. Hill to the supposed site of the Academy, where Plato taught his ' words of wisdom.' There is nothing to mark the site definitely. It lies N. E. of the city in the plain, beyond the Cephisus, which is here a brawling brook, much used for irrigating the adjacent fields and gardens The whole tract is covered with olive groves. We returned by the hill of Kolonos, the scene of the Œdipus Coloneus of Sophocles ; where once stood a temple of Neptune. This hill affords a noble view of Athens and its environs. It was a splendid afternoon ; and the atmosphere had all that perfect clearness and transparency for which the climate of Attica is remarkable ; far surpassing in this respect the sky of Italy or of any other country known to me. Remote objects were seen with the utmost distinctness ; the island of Hydra seemed to be hardly ten miles off ; though its real distance is more than forty English miles. The sun went down while we were yet upon the hill, pouring a flood of transparent glory over the landscape ; and as the reflection of his last beams lingered upon the Parthenon, and slowly ascended the dark sides of Mount Hymettus beyond, they were followed by hues of brilliant purple, which also climbed the heights of Hymettus, and spread themselves abroad upon the sky.

Another day we rode with the same friend to the ancient quarries on the side of Hymettus ; and then to a farm near the foot of the mountain. Hymettus was of old celebrated for its honey ; and large quantities of it are still collected in the neighbourhood. On the farm we visited, there were about two hundred hives of bees ; and the people were then engaged in gathering the honey. This was a second harvest (in December) ; the first and greater one being in August. We were gratified in being able to taste the honey of Hymettus, at its fountain-head ; though I cannot award to it the palm of superior excellence, which both the ancient and modern Athenians have claimed for it. It is dark coloured, and has a very strong flavour of thyme ; being indeed chiefly collected from this plant, which thickly covers the whole slope of the mountain.

On one of the last mornings of our stay in Athens, I went

---

[1] German scholars have since raised the question, whether the Pnyx was on this spot. See F. G. Welcker, Der Felsaltar des höchsten Zeus, oder des Pelasgikon, bisher genannt die Pnyx, nach der Entdeckung des Prof. Ulrichs in Athen ; in Phil. und hist. Abhandl. der. Acad. der Wiss. in Berlin, aus dem Jahre 1852.

very early to the Acropolis, to see the sun rise over Mount
Hymettus. The morning was clear and cold; a frost, for the
first time, had left slight traces of ice in the streets. I was
alone upon the Acropolis, in the midst of the solemn grandeur
of its desolations. Seating myself within the ruins of the
Parthenon, where the eye could command the whole horizon
through the columns of the eastern portico, I waited for the
rising sun. The whole sky was so resplendent, that for a long
time I could not determine the point where the orb of day
would appear. The sunlight already lay upon the eastern plain
and on the northern mountains, falling between Hymettus and
Pentelicus. Small fleecy clouds came floating on the north
wind; and, as they hovered over Hymettus and met the rays of
the sun, were changed to liquid gold. At length the first
beams fell upon the Parthenon, and lighted up its marbles and its
columns with a silvery splendour. It was one of those moments
in the life of man, that can never be forgotten.

We remained seventeen days in Athens; the next steamer
having been delayed two days beyond the regular time. The
weather during this interval was variable; frequent storms of
high wind with rain, and the mountains sometimes thinly
covered with snow; and then again intervening days like the
loveliest of June. A morning cloud, however small, on Mount
Hymettus was the sure prognostic of rain in the course of the
day. The thermometer fell only once below the freezing point;
and this was regarded as the severest cold of the winter. We
had planned an excursion to Argos, where some of our American friends were then residing; intending to cross the gulf to
Nauplia, and return by way of Corinth and its isthmus. But a
storm hindered us at the time appointed, and for some days
afterwards; and I was compelled to rest satisfied with the view
of the acropolis of Corinth, as seen from the acropolis of
Athens. Similar circumstances prevented also a proposed excursion to the summit of Mount Pentelicus and the plain of
Marathon.

I had of course no extensive opportunity to observe the people of Greece; nor, in any case, would this be the proper place
to dwell upon their political circumstances. But as the result
of my own observation, coupled with information received from
many quarters, I must do the inhabitants of the kingdom of
Greece the justice to say, that although burdened with a foreign
government, in which as a people they have no voice, this little
nation of 800,000 souls, in the short period of their existence as
a state, have in a good degree shaken off their former degradation, and have raised themselves, as to independence of character, integrity, and intellectual and moral enterprise, to a standing

i. 14 15

considerably above any other portions of their countrymen, and especially above those who still remain under the Turkish dominion. The people have an ardent desire for instruction and for free institutions ; and although they may not yet be ripe for the latter, yet it is to be hoped that the influence of some of the larger continental powers, however strongly exerted, will not be mighty enough to quench these aspirations.[1]

During our stay at Athens I was able to have communication with my friend, the Rev. Eli Smith, who was then in Smyrna. I would gladly have joined him there, that so we might have proceeded together to Egypt. But the business of which he had charge, would not permit of his leaving immediately ; and then too there was a quarantine of three weeks between Smyrna and Alexandria. Of course it was more pleasant and profitable to spend these three weeks under the warmer sun and amid the wonders of Egypt, than to be shut up within the walls of a miserable lazaretto at Syra or Alexandria. It was arranged therefore with Mr. Smith, with the unanimous and hearty assent of his missionary brethren in Smyrna and Athens, that he should meet me at Cairo in the last days of February ; and so leaving him to enjoy the quarantine alone, we set our faces directly towards Egypt.

We embarked at the Piræus on the evening of Dec. 25th, on board the steamer Baron Eichhof ; and at sunrise next morning were off the north end of Syra, surrounded by a splendid array of picturesque islands, the Cyclades of former days. Behind us lay Jura, Zea, and Thermia. In the N. W. were visible the lofty mountains on the southern end of Negropont, capped with snow ; and in the S. W. were Serfo and Sifanto. Near at hand on our left were the large islands of Andros and Tinos, the former with snowy mountains ; and before us, Mycone, Delos, and Great Delos. As we rounded the northern point of Syra, we came in sight of Naxos, Paros, and Anti-Paros ; and could also see the high land of Nikeria over the southern extremity of Tinos. In a direction a little further to the south, I looked long for Patmos ; but in vain. At 8 o'clock we cast anchor in the fine bay of Syra, on the eastern side of the island ; which has of late years acquired celebrity as the chief commercial port of Greece, and the central point of meeting for all the various lines of French and Austrian steamers.

We passed here a very agreeable and very busy day, chiefly in the society of our kind American friends, the Rev. Dr. Robertson and his family, who afterwards removed to Constantinople, and

---

[1] After the above was written, I had the pleasure of learning from Prof. Ritter, that he too was led to the same conclusion respecting the relative intellectual and moral standing of the Greek people, in and out of the kingdom of Greece.

i. 16, 17

have since returned to the United States. We visited their schools and printing establishment; and also the flourishing schools of the English Church Missionary Society, under the care of Messrs Hildner and Wolters.—The old town of Syra lies on the sides of a conical hill at some distance from the shore, and contains 5000 inhabitants. The new town, which sprung into existence during the Greek revolution, lies upon the shore below; and is supposed to contain a population of 18,000 souls. Ship-building is here carried on extensively. The expenses of living are said to be greater in this town, than anywhere else in the Levant; chiefly because all articles of necessity or luxury must be brought from a distance; the island itself furnishing almost nothing.

We embarked again the same evening, Dec. 26th, for Alexandria, on board the steamer Prince Metternich, which was lying in quarantine. A thunder storm which passed over the harbour, delayed our departure until after midnight. At sunrise we were abreast of the small island Polykandro on our left; having on our right Sifanto, Argentiera, Polino, and Milo; while behind Polykandro we could see Sikyno and Nio, and far in the S. E. the high volcanic island of Santorin, which Ritter had explored so thoroughly a few months before. At 10 o'clock Crete was visible, but was indistinct, and covered with clouds. At evening we cast anchor in the harbour of Canéa, on the north coast of the island near its western end. This city contains about 6000 inhabitants, and lies like an amphitheatre around a small inner circular port, at the foot of a large bay setting up between the capes Spada and Meleka; the land rising gradually from the water on all sides. Back of the city Mount Mélessa rises to the height of several thousand feet, and was then covered with deep snow; while far in the east, near the middle of the island, was seen the majestic and loftier form of Mount Ida, also white with snows, and glittering in the last beams of the setting sun.

The little port of Canéa is formed by an artificial mole, with a fortress on each side of the entrance. Here for the first time we beheld mosks and minarets, the latter crowned by the crescent; showing us that we had here entered a territory subject to the Muslim rule. It was now near the close of the fast of Ramadân; and the minarets were lighted up by rows of small lamps thickly suspended from the external galleries, producing a pleasing effect in the darkness of evening. Indeed the whole effect of the lights of the city at evening, rising on every side, was fine and imposing.

Crete was now under the dominion of the Pasha of Egypt; and at that time presented the rather singular anomaly even in

i. 17, 18

oriental quarantines, that while Egypt itself had no quarantine against Greece, yet Crete had a quarantine against both Greece and Egypt. We were not permitted to land at Canéa ; but some American missionary friends, to whom we had letters, kindly came off in a boat the next morning, and gratified us by a short visit along side. Mr. Benton and his family had then been established in Canéa about a year, with very encouraging prospects of usefulness and success.

We left Canéa again at 11 o'clock A. M. Dec. 28th, and pursued our way along the northern coast of Crete. A strong N. E. wind had set in, which was contrary to us and raised a heavy sea ; so that our progress was slow, and the motion of the vessel very uncomfortable. Clouds likewise gathered upon the island ; permitting us only occasional glimpses of the coast and the lofty brow of Ida. The next morning we were off the eastern end of Crete, which was just visible in a low line beneath the clouds which rested on it ; and in the N. E. we could distinguish the high islands of Caso and Scarpanto. The N. E. wind was now more favourable, and our progress more rapid ; but the weather was still cold and the motion uncomfortable. The next day, Dec. 30th, was warmer ; and a heavy shower from the S. W. left a strong wind from that quarter, with much motion. Early in the afternoon we began to meet vessels which had left Alexandria with the change of wind. At 3 o'clock the column of Diocletian began to appear ; then the tall masts of the Egyptian fleet, which was lying in the harbour ; afterwards the Pasha's palace and other buildings ; and finally the low coast. At 5 o' clock we gained the narrow entrance of the western port, following a pilot, who led the way in his small boat. He refused to come on board, saying we were to be in quarantine,—a piece of news which somewhat alarmed our captain ; as he had left the port only a few days before *in pratique*, and had since been in no port against which there was a quarantine. Half an hour afterwards we cast anchor near the city, in the midst of the huge men of war which composed the Egyptian fleet. A boat with Frank health officers soon ran along side. The officers came on board with all due precautions, and instituted a very strict scrutiny as to the passengers and letters ; to the great surprise of our captain, who had never experienced any thing of the kind before. The result of the scrutiny was in our favour ; and all of a sudden the chief health officer, a friend of the captain, threw his arms around the latter ; and the deck resounded with their mutual kisses and congratulations. We were not uninterested spectators of this scene ; and joined heartily in the rejoicings of the moment. We now learned that the last French steamer, which arrived just a week before us, and in which we at first had thought of taking passage, had by some negligence received on board at Syra the letters and packages from Constantinople and Smyrna, without their having first been fumigated at the health office. In consequence of this, the vessel had been put in quarantine at Alexandria for twenty days, and her passengers for seven days; from which the latter were freed only the day after our arrival. We of course were grateful for this escape from confinement in an Egyptian lazaretto.

It was now too late to go on shore and look up lodgings in a strange city. We waited until morning, and then landed with the captain at the custom house. The moment we set foot on shore, we needed no further conviction, that we had left Europe and were now in the oriental world. We found ourselves in the midst of a dense crowd, through which we made our way with difficulty,—Egyptians, Turks, Arabs, Copts, Negros, Franks; complexions of white, black, olive, bronze, brown, and almost all other colours; long beards and no beards; all costumes and no costume; silks and rags; wide robes and no robes; women muffled in shapeless black mantles, their faces wholly covered except peep-holes for the eyes; endless confusion, and a clatter and medley of tongues, Arabic, Turkish, Greek, Italian, French, German, and English, as the case might be; strings of huge camels in single file with high loads; little donkeys, bridled and saddled, each guided by a sore-eyed Arab boy with a few words of sailor English, who thrusts his little animal *nolens volens* almost between your legs;—such is a faint picture of the scene in which we found ourselves on landing in Alexandria.

We made our way at length to the Frank quarter, in the S. E. part of the city, through narrow, crooked, dirty streets and lanes, running between dead walls or ill built houses with flat roofs. The Frank quarter is near the eastern port, and consists of a broad street or place, surrounded by large houses in the Italian style. We paid our respects to Mr Gliddon, consul of the United States, to whom I had an official letter; and he immediately sent his Kawwâs or Janizary to procure us lodgings, and to pass our luggage at the custom-house. During our stay in Alexandria, and afterwards in Cairo, we were greatly indebted to the courtesy and kind offices of Mr Gliddon; and I take pleasure in this opportunity of tendering to him my grateful acknowledgments.

It was now the third day of the great festival of the Muhammedans, (the lesser Bairam of the Turks,) which follows the fast of Ramadân, and continues three days. All was of course joy and rejoicing among the population; bands of jugglers were exhibiting their feats in the open places of the streets; the ships of war in the harbour were gaily decked with flags and

i. 20, 21

streamers; and at noon the thunder of their cannon proclaimed a salute in honour of the day. This was the first and only Muhammedan festival, which we had an opportunity of seeing.

Of ancient Alexandria, that renowned city, which contained 600,000 inhabitants, and was second only to Rome itself, scarcely a vestige now remains. The hand of time and the hand of barbarism have both swept over it with merciless fury, and buried its ancient glory in the dust and in the sea. Her illustrious schools of theology, astronomy, and various other sciences; her noble library, unique in ancient history;[1] her lighthouse, one of the seven wonders of the world; all have utterly vanished away, and 'the places thereof know them no more.' Her former site, thickly strown with fragments of bricks and tiles, showing that even the materials of her former structures have perished, has been dug over, and the foundations of her edifices turned up, in search of stones to build the modern navy-yard and other works of the Pasha. The only surviving remains of the ancient city are, a few cisterns still in use; the catacombs on the shore west of the city; the granite obelisk of Thothmes III, with its fallen brother, brought hither from Heliopolis, and usually called Cleopatra's needles; and the column of Diocletian, more commonly known as Pompey's pillar. This last is upon the highest part of the ancient site, between the modern city and Lake Mareotis. There it stands, towering in loneliness and desolation, the survivor of that splendour which it was intended to heighten; while near at hand the straggling and neglected tombs of a Muhammedan cemetery only serve to render the desolation more mournful.[2] The catacombs are nearly filled with earth, and are difficult to be explored. They consist of halls and apartments with niches for the dead, and with ornaments in the Greek style of architecture. But they are chiefly interesting as being the first Egyptian sepulchres which the traveller meets.[3] The population of the modern city is reckoned by the best judges at about 40,000 souls.

If the traveller feels on landing in Alexandria, that he has now entered the borders of the oriental world, he is not less strongly reminded of the same fact, when he comes to leave that city, and set off for the interior of Egypt. Until now he has had all the conveniences of travel which exist in Europe and America; he has had only to await the departure of a steamer, and betake himself on board with bag and baggage, without further thought or care. But travelling in Egypt and Syria, is

[1] The foundations of the ancient Library are supposed to have been recently discovered. See Brugsch Reisebericht aus Aegypten, Berlin, 1855, p. 9.

[2] See Note I, at the end of the volume.

[3] See also Brugsch, Reisebericht aus Aegypten, p. 11.

i. 21, 22

quite a different thing. Here are neither roads, nor public conveyances, nor public houses ; and the traveller is thrown back wholly upon his own resources. In Egypt he must hire a boat for himself, unless he can find a companion to share it with him ; he must provide his own bed and cooking utensils, and also his provisions for the journey, except such as he can procure at the villages along the Nile ; and withal and above all he must have a servant, who can at the same time act as cook, purveyor, and interpreter. He will soon find himself very much in the power of this important personage, who will usually be able neither to read nor write ; and the discomforts and vexations of this relation of dependence will probably continue more and more to press upon him, until he has himself learned something of the Arabic language, or is fortunate enough (as I was) to fall in with a companion to whom the language is familiar. If the traveller has time, he will do well to purchase the chief necessaries at Alexandria. He needs them just as much during the voyage to Cairo, as afterwards ; and he will thus save time and avoid care in the latter city.

Most travellers, on arriving at Alexandria, suppose they have only to take a boat directly from that city along the canal and the Nile to Cairo ; and it may be some days before they learn, that at 'Atfeh, where the canal leaves the Nile, they will be compelled to hire another boat ; the canal being there shut off from the river by a dam with sluices, but without locks. At this point every thing which passes between Alexandria and Cairo has to be transhipped ; to the great inconvenience of the public and the special annoyance of travellers just arrived in the country.[1] The boats on the canal and river are much the same ; long, narrow and sharp, with a low cabin at the stern in which one can rarely stand erect ; and usually having two low masts with immense lateen sails, their long yards turning around the top of the mast as on a pivot. The cabins for the most part will accommodate only two persons to sit (cross-legged) and sleep in. If a party consists of more, a larger boat will be necessary ; which enhances the expense and commonly the length of the voyage.

It was on a delightful morning, Jan. 5th, 1838, that we found ourselves floating for the first time on the bosom of the mighty Nile. In Alexandria we had almost daily showers of rain ; and during the night that we had lain by at 'Atfeh, a heavy shower had fallen, clearing the atmosphere, and leaving behind it a fine north wind, which was driving us onward cheerily against the powerful current. It was a moment of excitement ; indeed a new emotion was awakened by the first day's sail upon this

----

[1] This has since been remedied by means of locks.
i. 23, 24

noble stream, so closely associated with the earliest and choicest recollections of childhood and manhood. It was a glorious sight to look upon the mighty river, rolling its waters for nearly fifteen hundred miles, without a single tributary, through a region which but for it would be a desert; and rendering this desert by its waters the garden of the world. The Rosetta branch of the Nile, where we came upon it, reminded me strongly of the Rhine at Cologne, in its general breadth and current, and in the general character of its banks. The water of the Nile is celebrated for its deliciousness; and is deserving of its fame in this respect. Strangers are apt to drink too freely of it at first; and not unfrequently experience a slight attack of dysentery in consequence. The water is slightly turbid; but becomes clear by filtering through the porous jars of the country; or on being left to stand in jars, the sides of which have been rubbed with almond-paste.

We had been told in Alexandria that we should probably reach Cairo in three days; but our fine wind lasted only for one day; and it was not until after a voyage of five days in all, that we landed at Búlak, the port of Cairo. For a whole day previous, we had seen the great pyramids, towering upon the southern horizon. Several other travellers, about the same time, had still longer passages. Our luggage and ourselves were speedily mounted on donkeys; and we were soon cantering along the straight road that leads to the gate of Cairo, two English miles distant. This gate opens on the middle of the N. W. side of the great place or square el-Ezbekiyeh; not far from which, on the southern side, lies the Frank quarter. Here we found lodgings in a hotel which had formerly been kept by an Italian; but was now nominally under English management.

At Cairo we had fallen, for the present, on evil times. Mr. G. R. Gliddon, the American consul, was absent in the United States. The English vice-consul, to whom I had been particularly addressed, was at first absent; and on his return found himself honoured or burdened by a new appointment, which for the time overwhelmed him with a chaotic mass of business; so that he hardly knew which way to turn. Messrs. Lieder and Kruse, missionaries of the Church Missionary Society, to whom I had letters from the society in London, and who afterwards rendered us most important services, were at the time confined to their houses by illness. Mr Gliddon senior had been so kind as to place at our disposal the Janizary of the American consulate, both during the time of our stay in Cairo, and for our further voyage on the Nile; yet this did not help us much at present; for Mustafa spoke nothing but Arabic; and we could therefore communicate with him usually only through our other servant. He went with us up the Nile, and we found him at all times honest, faithful, and kind hearted.

Left thus alone, as strangers in this great city, we determined to leave it as soon as possible for Upper Egypt, hoping for better auspices on our return. We visited therefore at present only the bazars ; the slave market with its abominations ; the tombs of the Memlûks, fine specimens of Saracenic architecture now falling to decay ; the citadel ; and the charming orange-gardens connected with the Pasha's palace at Shubra. As we wandered one day with our servant through the citadel, looking at the apartments of the Pasha, and entering the halls of audience and public business, we stumbled into the room where Habîb Effendi, governor of Cairo and minister of the interior, was transacting the usual routine of matters which came before him. He sat munching in one corner of the room, with several persons around him ; and there were other similar groups in various parts of the hall. As persons were continually passing in and out, we did not hesitate to gratify our curiosity ; and were retiring, when the governor sent the dragoman of the English consulate after us, inviting us to take coffee with him. As we were still utter strangers in Egypt, and had no friend with us who was *au fait* in such matters, we declined the invitation as politely as we could, on the ground that we had seen his Excellency was very much engaged. The occurrence is not worth mentioning, except as illustrating the mighty change which has taken place in the feelings and conduct of Muhammedans towards Frank Christians.

The weather was fine and the air balmy, all the time we were at Cairo. There had been however several rainy days shortly before ; and especially on Christmas day a violent storm of wind and rain. The thermometer, at sunrise, ranged between 44° and 54° of Fahrenheit.

The indolence and procrastinating habits of the Egyptians and Arabs, are well known. They seem indeed to have a different version of the good old English maxim ; and act as if it were to be read exactly the reverse, viz. "Never to do to-day what can be put off till to-morrow." Under the circumstances in which we were placed, it was of course a slow and wearisome matter to make the necessary preparations ; and it was therefore not until the evening of Jan. 19th, that we were again upon the Nile, ploughing its current with a fine breeze from the north, under the brilliant light of an African moon.

A voyage upon the Nile at this season, can never be otherwise than interesting. The weather is usually pleasant, and the traveller is surrounded by scenes and objects striking in themselves, and closely associated with all that is great and

i. 26, 27

venerable in the records of the ancient world. The gleaming
waters of the mighty river, rushing onward in ceaseless flow ;
the pyramids, those mysterious monuments of gray antiquity,
stretching in a range along the western shore from Gîzeh upwards beyond Sakkârah and Dashûr ; the frequent villages along
the banks, each in the bosom of its own tall grove of graceful
palm trees ; the broad valley, teeming with fertility, and shut
in on both sides by ranges of naked, barren mountains, within
which the desert is continually striving to enlarge its encroachments ; all these are objects which cannot be regarded but with
lively emotion. Nor is this wholly a scene of still life. The
many boats with broad lateen sails, gliding up and down ; the
frequent water wheels, *Sâkieh*, by which water is raised from the
river to irrigate the fields ; the more numerous *Shadûfs*, who
laboriously ply their little sweep and bucket for the same end ;[1]
the labourers in the fields ; the herds of neat cattle and buf-
faloes ; occasional files of camels and asses ; large flocks of
pigeons, ducks, and wild geese ; and, as one advances, the occasional sight of crocodiles sleeping on a sand-bank, or plunging
into the water ; all these give a life and activity to the scene,
which enhances the interest and adds to the exhilaration. Yet
if the traveller set foot on shore, the romance of his river voyage
will quickly be dissipated. He will find the soil becoming an
almost impalpable powder under his feet, through which he may
wade his way to the next village ; and this village too he will
find to be only the squalid abode of filth and wretchedness ; mud
hovels, not high enough to stand up in, built on mounds accumulated in the course of centuries from the ruins of former
dwellings.

The voyage from Cairo to Thebes, about 500 miles, varies
much as to time, according to the wind ; but is accomplished, on
the average, in about twenty days. It takes from three to six
days more to reach the first cataract at Aswân, 140 miles further.
We left Cairo intending to visit Thebes, and to reach the cataract
if our time would permit. At first the winds were very favourable.
We pressed forward day and night ; and on the twelfth day had
accomplished more than three quarters of the distance to Thebes.
But the wind now changed to the south ; and the only mode of
advancing further was by tracking. In this slow and very tedious manner, with only a few intervals of sailing, we reached
Thebes on the nineteenth day from Cairo. Since that time,
in eleven days, I have crossed the Atlantic from New-York to
Liverpool. All hope of reaching the cataract was now abandoned ; and we set to work in earnest to employ, in the best
manner, the few days we had to devote to the ruins of Thebes.

[1] See Note II, end of the volume.

i. 27, 28

I am not about to write a description of these wonderful remains of high antiquity. Wilkinson has devoted half his work to them, without exhausting the subject in any part. The chief points of interest on the western shore, are the Memnonium, the temples of Medînet Habû, the statue of Memnon and its companion, the tombs of the kings, and the tombs in the hill of Sheikh Abd-el-Kûrneh. On the eastern shore are the temple of Luksor, and the temple or rather immense cluster of temples of Karnak.

It is impossible to wander among these scenes, and behold these hoary yet magnificent ruins, without emotions of astonishment and deep solemnity. Every thing around testifies of vastness, and of utter desolation. Here lay once that mighty city, whose power and splendour were proverbial throughout the ancient world. The Jewish prophet, in reproaching great Nineveh, breaks forth into the bitter taunt: "Art thou better than populous No [Thebes], that was situate among the rivers, the waters round about it; whose rampart was the sea, and her wall from the sea?"[1] Yet even then Thebes had been "carried away into captivity; her young children dashed in pieces at the top of all her streets; they had cast lots for her honourable men, and all her great men were bound in chains." Subsequently she was again plundered by Cambyses, and destroyed by Ptolemy Lathyrus. Her countless generations have passed away, leaving their mighty works behind, to tell to wanderers from far distant and then unknown climes the story of her greatness and her fall. The desert hills around are filled with their corpses, for which they vainly strove to procure an exemption from the dread decree: "Dust thou art, and unto dust shalt thou return." For twenty-five centuries they have indeed slept securely in their narrow abodes; from which they are now daily wrested, to be trampled into dust and scattered to the winds.

The character of Egyptian architecture, as exhibited in the temples at Thebes and elsewhere, is heavy and vast; with nothing of that lightness, and harmonious proportion, and beautiful simplicity, which distinguish the Athenian temples. Yet this very vastness, coupled with the associations of the place, produces a strong impression of sublimity. All is gloomy, awful, grand. The most striking specimens of this gigantic architecture, are the great colonnade at Luksor, which we first visited by moonlight; and especially the grand hall at Karnak, "one hundred and seventy feet by three hundred and twenty-nine, supported by a central avenue of twelve massive columns, sixty-six feet high (without the pedestal and abacus), and twelve in diameter; besides one hundred and twenty-two of smaller or

---

[1] Nah. 3, 8. See Note III, end of the volume.

i. 20, 30

rather less gigantic dimensions, forty-one feet nine inches in height, and twenty-seven feet six inches in circumference, distributed in seven lines on either side of the former."[1] Nor were the decorations of these temple-palaces on a scale less imposing. The two colossal statues of Amenoph (usually called of Memnon), seated majestically upon the plain, once guarded the approach to the temple-palace of that king. They are sixty feet high, including the pedestal.[2] The temple has perished ; Memnon has long ceased to salute the rising sun ; and the two statues now sit in lonely grandeur, to tell what Thebes once was. The stupendous statue of Remeses II, in the Memnonium, a single block of Syenite granite, now prostrate and shattered, still "measures from the shoulder to the elbow twelve feet ten inches ; twenty-two feet four inches across the shoulders ; and fourteen feet four inches from the neck to the elbow."[3] This enormous mass is nearly three times as large as the solid contents of the largest obelisk. How it could ever have been transported from Upper Egypt and erected here, is a problem which modern science cannot solve ; nor is there much less difficulty in accounting for the manner of its destruction.

The tombs of the Kings are situated among the barren mountains, which skirt Thebes upon the west ; in a narrow valley where desolation sits enthroned. Not a tree nor shrub is to be seen ; not a blade of grass or herbage ; not even a trace of moss upon the rocks ; but all is naked and shattered, as if it had been the sport of thunders and lightnings and earthquakes ever since the creation. The tombs are entered by narrow portals in the sides of this valley, from which a corridor usually leads by a slight descent to halls and apartments on either side, all decorated with paintings in vivid colours, representing scenes drawn from the life of the deceased monarch, and from Egyptian mythology, or sometimes also from the occupations of common life. In this respect these tombs afford the finest illustrations of the manners and customs of the ancient Egyptians. In the chief apartment is usually a large sarcophagus. Here "the kings of the nations, all of them, lay in glory, every one in his own house ;" but "they have been cast out as an abominable branch."[4] The tombs of the priests and private persons are found in the sides of the hills adjacent to the city. They are

---

[1] Wilkinson's Mod. Egypt, II. p. 248.
[2] Ibid. II. p 160.
[3] Ibid. II. p. 143.
[4] Is. 14, 18, 19. From these or similar tombs is drawn apparently the imagery of the Hebrew prophet, Ez. 8, 8–10 : "Then said he unto me, Son of man, dig now in the wall: and when I had digged in the wall, behold a door. And he said unto me, Go in, and behold the wicked abominations that they do here. So I went in and saw ; and, behold, every form of creeping things, and abominable beasts, and all the idols of the house of Israel, portrayed upon the wall round about." There is, however, no direct evidence that Egyptian sepulchres were made the seat of idolatrous rites or mysteries.

i. 30, 31

on a smaller scale ; but are often decorated with equal skill and beauty, with scenes drawn from common life.[1]

The walls of all the temples at Thebes are covered with sculptures and hieroglyphics, representing in general the deeds of the kings who founded or enlarged those structures. Many of these afford happy illustrations of Egyptian history. To me the most interesting was the scene which records the exploits of Sheshonk, the Shishak of the Scriptures, who made a successful expedition against Jerusalem in the fifth year of king Rehoboam, B. C. 971.[2] These sculptures are on the exterior of the S. W. wall of the great temple of Karnak. They represent a colossal figure of this monarch advancing, and holding in his hand ten cords, which are attached to as many rows of captives, one above another, behind him. These he presents to the deity of the temple. The upper rows, behind the middle of his back, contain each twelve or fourteen captives ; the lower ones extend under his feet, and have more. The heads and shoulders of the captives are complete ; while the bodies have merely the form of a *cartouch* with hieroglyphics, containing perhaps the name or character of the individual.[3] In front of the high cap of the monarch, is a cartouch with his name ; and behind him, above the rows of captives, the wall is covered with hieroglyphics.

The period in which Thebes enjoyed the highest prosperity, was probably coeval with the reigns of David and Solomon, the earliest Jewish kings. From the language of the prophet Nahum already quoted, who lived, according to Josephus, under king Jotham about B. C. 750, and perhaps for some time later, we learn that the city had already, in or before his day, been sacked, apparently by a foreign conqueror.[4] This event may not improbably stand in connection with the expedition of Tartan, alluded to by the cotemporary prophet Isaiah.[5] Profane history is silent in respect to it, and speaks only of the capture of the city by Cambyses, 525 B. C., and of its final destruction by Ptolemy Lathyrus, after a siege of three years, 81 B. C. From this overthrow it never recovered ; and in the time of Strabo, as at present, its site was occupied by several villages.[6] The pre-

---

[1] See Note IV, end of the vol.

[2] 1 Kings 14, 25 sq. 2 Chr. 12, 2-9.

[3] In one of these cartouches Champollion and Rosellini profess to read the words, *Yuda Hamelk*, 'King of Judah ;' and they consider this captive as the personification of the conquered kingdom of Judah. But Wilkinson has doubts. Indeed, it is hardly probable, that all these individuals should represent different nations or tribes, as the same theory assumes. They are

too numerous. To me most of them seemed to have Jewish features, with short peaked beards. Champollion reads also the names *Beth-horon* and *Mahanaim*. See Champollion's Grammaire Egyptienne, p. 160. Rosellini Monumenti Storici, II. p. 79 sq. Wilkinson's Manners and Cust. of the Anc. Egyptians, I. p. 136.

[4] Jos. Ant. 9. 11. 3.

[5] Ch. 20.

[6] Strabo 17. 1. 46. p. 815.

i. 32, 33

servation of its magnificent remains, so far as this is not dependent on the purity and uniformity of the atmosphere, must be ascribed, not to any respect or veneration on the part of the people of the land ; but solely to the circumstance, that no other city has risen in the vicinity, to abstract and absorb in its own buildings the materials of the Theban structures.

During our stay at Thebes, and during our whole voyage up and down the river, the weather was uncommonly fine and uniform, and of a temperature like the month of June in the milder parts of Europe and America. The thermometer ranged at sunrise from 40° to 60° ; and at 3 P. M. from 68° to 82° Farenheit. The atmosphere was sometimes hazy, and the sky cloudy ; but we experienced no frost ; although this sometimes occurs. The common report that rain *never* falls in Upper Egypt, is incorrect. One evening as we lay at Kineh, Feb. 4th, there was a slight shower ; the thermometer standing at the time at 77° F. with a strong south wind. The valleys too, in the mountains around Thebes, bear evident traces of occasional and violent rain.[1]

We arrived at Thebes in the afternoon of Feb. 7th ; and left it again on our return on the morning of Feb. 11th. The downward voyage was slow and tedious ; our boat being unfortunately too large to be propelled rapidly with oars, or even to float with the current against a strong head-wind. We stopped for a day at the temple of Dendera ; and visited the dilapidated tombs in the mountains back of Siout, where we also enjoyed the noble prospect from the summit. Another day was given to the very remarkable tombs of Beni Hassan, which are among the most ancient in Egypt. We finally reached Cairo on the morning of Feb. 28th ; where I had the satisfaction of meeting my future companion, Mr Smith, who had arrived three days before. Here in the hospitable dwelling of Mr Lieder and the welcome society of valued friends, I soon forgot the discomforts of the voyage ; and was able to survey, under better auspices than formerly, the city and its interesting environs.

Cairo is one of the best built cities of the east ; the houses are of stone, large, lofty, and solid. The streets are narrow and often crooked ; and the houses sometimes jut over them upon each side, so as almost to meet above. Its original name in Arabic was *el-Kâhirah ;* but it is now universally called *Musr,* as were the former capitals of Egypt. The population is estimated at about 250,000 souls. In 1835 the plague made fearful ravages

---

[1] On this point there can be no better authority than Wilkinson. " Showers," he says, " fall *annually* at Thebes ; perhaps on an average four or five in the year ; and every eight or ten years, heavy rains fill the torrent-beds of the mountains, which run to the banks of the Nile. A storm of this kind did much damage to Belzoni's tomb some years ago." Mod. Egypt, p. 75, ed. I.

i. 33, 34

in Cairo, sweeping off not less than 80,000 of its inhabitants ; but at the time of our visit, the population was supposed to have again reached its usual number. Here, as in Alexandria, donkeys with Arab boys take the place of cabs and fiacres. A full and most perfect description of the city and its inhabitants is given in the admirable work of Mr. Lane.[1]

During the twelve days that we now remained at Cairo, we were of course much occupied with the preparations for our future journey in the desert. Yet we took time, and made several excursions from the city to places in the neighbourhood. One was to the island of Roda just below Musr el-Atikeh or Old Cairo, on which Ibrahim Pasha had caused pretty gardens to be laid out, partly in the Italian and partly in the English style. On the south end of this island is the famous Nilometer, now half in ruins, dating back at least as far as A. D. 860, and exhibiting pointed arches even at that early period. Although of no utility at present, it is carefully guarded ; and we found difficulty in obtaining admission, not having procured the ordinary permit in Cairo. At Musr el-Atikeh are the remains of a Roman fortress, marking the site of the Egyptian Babylon, on which was afterwards built the city of Fostát, the former Arab capital of Egypt.[2] Passing eastward over the immense field of rubbish on which Fostát once stood, we entered the broad valley or desert plain, which skirts the western base of Jebel Mukattem, to the southward of Cairo. In this desert spot is one of the largest cemeteries of the city. Here, amid the thousands of humbler sepulchres, the Pasha has erected a splendid edifice with two domes, to cover the tombs of his family and himself. We were admitted at once, and passed without hindrance through the carpeted halls and among the highly ornamented tombs. Those of the Pasha's wife and his two sons, Ismail and Tussum, are the most conspicuous. In a corner distant from these, we were shown the spot reserved by the Pasha for his own last abode.— Between this and the city, the whole way is full of tombs and sepulchral enclosures.

On another day we rode out to the site of ancient Heliopolis, about two hours N. N. E. from Cairo. The way thither passes along the edge of the desert ; which is continually making its encroachments so soon as there ceases to be a supply of water for the surface of the ground. The water of the Nile soaks through the earth for some distance under this sandy tract ; and is everywhere found on digging wells eighteen or twenty feet deep. Such wells are very frequent in parts which the inunda-

[1] See Note V, end of the volume.
[2] Wilkinson's Mod. Egypt, I. p. 274. Edrisi says expressly, that it was called
i. 35 36

Babylon by the Greeks; p. 302, ed. Jaubert.

tion does not reach. The water is raised from them by wheels turned by oxen, and applied to the irrigation of the fields. Wherever this takes place, the desert is quickly converted into a fruitful field. In passing to Heliopolis we saw several such fields in the different stages of being reclaimed from the desert; some just laid out, others already fertile. In returning by another way, more eastward, we passed a succession of beautiful plantations wholly dependent on this mode of irrigation. The site of Heliopolis is marked by low mounds, enclosing a space about three quarters of a mile in length, by half a mile in breadth; which was once occupied partly by houses and partly by the celebrated temple of the Sun. This area is now a ploughed field, a garden of herbs; and the solitary obelisk which still rises in the midst, is the sole remnant of the former splendours of the place. This was that On of the Egyptians, where the father of Joseph's wife was priest.[1] The Seventy translate the name On by Heliopolis, City of the Sun; and the Hebrew prophet calls it, in the same sense, Bethshemesh.[2] The city suffered greatly from the invasion of Cambyses; and in Strabo's time it was a mass of splendid ruins.[3] In the days of Edrisi and Abdallatif, the place bore the name of 'Ain Shems;[4] and in the neighbouring village Matarîyeh is still shown an ancient well bearing the same name. Near by it is a very old sycamore, its trunk straggling and gnarled, under which legendary tradition relates that the holy family once rested.

Farther to the N. E., towards Belbeis, are several ruined towns on lofty mounds, traditionally called *Tell el-Yehûd,* 'Mounds of the Jews.' If there is any historical foundation for this name, which is doubtful, these mounds can only be referred back to the period of the Ptolemies, in the centuries immediately before the Christian era, when great numbers of Jews resorted to Egypt and erected a temple at Leontopolis. It was in the same age, and for these Jews, that the Greek version of the Old Testament was made.[5]

Our most important excursion was to the pyramids, situated about six miles west of el-Gizeh, which lies on the left bank of the Nile, opposite Old Cairo. Crossing the river at that place, we proceeded on a direct course to the pyramids; although at other seasons of the year, when the river is higher, a considerable

[1] Gen. 41, 45. Sept. ib. Ex. 1, 11. Ezek. 30. 17. Herodot. 2. 3, 59.
[2] Jer. 43, 13.
[3] Strabo 17. 1. 27.
[4] Edrisi, p. 306 sq. ed. Jaubert. Abdallatif Relat. de l'Égypte, par de Sacy, p. 180 sq.
[5] Wilkinson's Mod. Egypt, I. p. 297.

Niebuhr's Reisebeschr. I. p. 213. Joseph. Antiq. 13. 3. 1, 2, 3. c. Apion. 2. 5.—The name of Theodotus, bishop of Leontopolis in Egypt, occurs among the signatures of the second council of Constantinople, A. D. 553. Harduin Acta Concilior. III. p. 52. Comp. le Quien Oriens Christ. Tom. II. p. 554.

circuit is necessary, in order to cross the Bahr Yûsuf, the canal which runs parallel to the Nile. Even now the water in it was so deep, that we could not well pass it on donkeys; but were carried over on the shoulders of Arabs from the adjacent villages. The pyramids, as seen from the river against the horizon, appeared enormously large; as we approached, their apparent magnitude continually diminished; and was nowhere less, than as seen from the foot of the rocky terrace on which they stand. This terrace is about one hundred and fifty feet above the plain; and the pyramids are thus seen only against the sky, without any surrounding objects from which the eye can judge of their relative magnitude. They seem here to be composed of small stones, and to have no great elevation. But as we approached their base, and became aware of the full size of the stones, and looked upward along their mountain sides to the summit, their huge masses seemed to swell into immensity, and the idea of their vastness was absolutely overpowering. They are probably the earliest, as well as the loftiest and most vast of all existing works of man upon the face of the earth; and there seems now little room to doubt, that they were erected chiefly, if not solely, as the sepulchres of kings. Vain pride of human pomp and power! Their monuments remain unto this day, the wonder of all time; but themselves, their history, and their very names, have been swept away in the dark tide of oblivion.

We followed the usual course of visitors. We explored the dark passages of the interior; mounted to the summit of the great pyramid; and admired the mild features of the gigantic Sphynx, the body of which is again nearly covered by the drifting sand. We also visited several of the adjacent tombs; and examined those which had then recently been cleared from the sand, under the direction of Col. Vyse.—The ascent of the great pyramid is less difficult, than a visit to its interior. The top is now a square platform of thirty-two feet on each side, at an elevation of four hundred and seventy feet above the base.[1] The view from it is very extensive; in front, Cairo and numerous villages, with their groves of slender palm trees; in the rear, the trackless Libyan wastes; on the south, the range of smaller pyramids extending for a great distance along the margin of the desert; and then in boundless prospect, north and south, the mighty river, winding its way through the long line of verdure, which it has won by its waters from the reluctant grasp of the desert upon either side. The platform is covered with the names of travellers, who have resorted hither in different ages from various and distant lands; and have here stood as upon a common and central point in the history of the world. Here too we

[1] Wilkinson's Mod. Egypt, I. p. 330, 340.
i. 38. 39

found an American corner, with the names both of living and departed friends.

We left the great pyramids the same evening, and proceeded southwards along the edge of the desert to Sakkâra, where we slept ; and the next morning visited the tombs in the neighbouring cliffs and the great necropolis around the adjacent pyramids. The whole tract here was anciently a cemetery. Pits leading to the chambers of death have been opened in every direction ; and the ground is everywhere strewed with the bones and cerements of mummies. Such a field of dead men's bones, I have nowhere else seen. There can be little doubt, that all this long tract, from the pyramids of Gîzeh to those of Dashûr, was once the great necropolis of ancient Memphis, which lay between it and the Nile.[1]

We now bent our course towards Mitraheny, near the river, where are the large mounds which mark the site of ancient Memphis.[2] These mounds of rubbish, a colossal statue sunk deep in the ground, and a few fragments of granite, are all that remain to attest the existence of this renowned capital. In Strabo's time, although partly in ruins, it was yet a populous city, second only to Alexandria ; and in the days of Abdallatif there were still extensive ruins.[3] In this instance the abodes of the dead have proved to be more lasting than the habitations of the living. But the total disappearance of all the ancient edifices of Memphis is easily accounted for, by the circumstance, that the materials of them were employed for the building of adjacent cities. Fostât arose out of the ruins of Memphis ; and when that city was in turn deserted, these ruins again migrated to the more modern Cairo.—We crossed the river, and having visited the ancient quarries near Tûra, from which the stones were cut for the pyramids, we returned to Cairo along the eastern bank.

A few words on the political and social condition of Egypt under its famous ruler, Muhammed 'Aly, may close this introductory section. This extraordinary man, with native talents which in other circumstances might have made him the Napoleon of the age, has accumulated in Egypt a large amount of wealth and power ; but he has done it only for himself,—not for the country, nor even for his family. He has built up an army

---

[1] Two of the pyramids of Dashûr are built of brick. We had often occasion to see both the ancient and modern bricks of Egypt. They are unburnt, and are made of the mud of the Nile, mingled with chopped straw to bind it together; on the same principle that hair is sometimes used in making mortar. Compare the narrative in Ex. 5, 7 sq.—In this necropolis, half an hour north of the village of Sakkâra, the ancient Serapæum, or temple of Apis, has been recently discovered by M. Mariette. See Brugsch, ib. p. 27.

[2] In Arabic *Menf*, in Hebrew *Moph*, Hos. 9, 6. Also under the name of *Noph*, Is. 19, 13. Jer. 2, 16.

[3] Strabo 17. 1. 32. Abdallatif Relation de l'Egypte, par de Sacy, p. 184 sq. Abdallatif was born A. D. 1161.

and fleet, not by husbanding and enlarging the resources of Egypt, but by draining them almost to exhaustion. The army consists chiefly of levies torn from their families and homes by brutal force. We saw many gangs of these unfortunate recruits on the river and around Cairo, fastened by the neck to a long heavy chain which rested on their shoulders. Such is the horror of this service among the peasantry, and their dread of being thus seized, that children are often mutilated in their fingers, their teeth, or an eye, in order to protect them from it.[1] Yet the country is now so drained of able-bodied men, that even these unfortunate beings are no longer spared. In the companies of recruits which were daily under drill around the Ezbekiyeh, we saw very many who had lost a finger, or their front teeth ; so that an English resident proposed in bitter irony to recommend to the Pasha, that his troops should appear only in gloves. Indeed, it is a notorious fact, that this drain of men for the army and navy has diminished and exhausted the population, until there are not labourers enough left to till the ground ; so that in consequence large tracts of fertile land are suffered to lie waste.

The same line of policy, or impolicy, has been pursued in the introduction of manufactures and schools of science. The sole object of the Pasha has been, not to benefit the nation, but to augment his own wealth, and increase the capability of the instruments of his power. With barbarian eagerness, he has overlooked the planting of the seed, and grasps only after the ripe fruit. Not a step has been taken for the education and improvement of the people at large ; but all the schools established are intended solely to train up young men for his own service. The workmen in the manufactories in like manner labour only by compulsion, and are recruited by force in the same manner as the soldiers. When once a manufactory of any article has been established by the Pasha, it is made a complete monopoly ; and the people must purchase from him that article at his own price, or go without. Thus, not a family in Egypt dares to spin and weave the cotton stuffs which they wear upon their own bodies.

The people of Egypt, formerly the owners as well as the tillers of the soil, would seem to be an object of peculiar and wanton oppression to the government, or at least to its subordinate ministers. Whenever requisitions are made upon the

---

[1] "There is now (in 1834) seldom to be found, in any of the villages, an able-bodied youth or young man, who has not had one or more of his teeth broken out, (that he may not be able to bite a cartridge,) or a finger cut off, or an eye put out or blinded, to prevent his being taken for a recruit." Lane's Modern Egyptians, I. p. 246.

i. 41, 42

people by the former, the latter are sure to extort nearly the double. By a single decree, the Pasha declared himself to be the sole owner of all the lands in Egypt ; and the people of course became at once only his tenants at will, or rather his slaves. It is interesting to compare this proceeding with a similar event in the ancient history of Egypt under the Pharaohs.[1] At the entreaty of the people themselves, Joseph *bought* them and their land for Pharaoh, so that "the land became Pharaoh's ;" but he gave them bread in return, to sustain them and their families in the time of famine. "Only the land of the priests he bought not ;" but the modern Pharaoh made no exception, and stripped the mosks and other religious and charitable institutions of their landed endowments, as mercilessly as the rest. Joseph also gave the people seed to sow, and required for the king only a fifth of the produce, leaving four fifths to them as their own property ; but now, though seed is in like manner given out, yet every village is compelled to cultivate two thirds of its lands with cotton and other articles solely for the Pasha ; and also to render back to him, in the form of taxes and exactions in kind, a large proportion of the produce of the remaining third. And further, not only is every individual held responsible for the burdens laid upon himself ; but also, as the inhabitant of a village, he is bound to make good in part or in whole, as the case may be, the delinquency or arrears of every other inhabitant. Sometimes, too, a village which has paid up all its own dues, is compelled to make good the arrears of another village. As might be expected in such a state of things, there is among the peasantry an utter depravation of morals and degradation of character.[2]

Of Muhammed 'Aly himself, it is universally admitted in Egypt, that while he is energetic and severe, he is yet by nature neither cruel nor revengeful. The people in general do not ascribe their oppression so much to the Pasha, as to his subordinate agents. They suppose, that if the murmurs of the peasantry could reach his ear, the immediate and pressing evils would be remedied.[3] In one respect, the energy of Muhammed 'Aly deserves all praise ; although the severity by which it is attended may not always be the most justifiable. He has rendered the countries under his sway secure ; so that travellers, whether Orientals or Franks, may pass in their own dress throughout Egypt and Syria, and also among the Bedawin of the adjacent deserts, with the same degree of safety as in many parts of civilized Europe.—How different might have been the state of Egypt, had he

[1] Gen. 47, 18–26.
[2] Compare Lane, I. p. 156 sq.
[3] Wilkinson's Mod. Egypt, II. p. 553

adapted his measures to the true policy of the country; and, instead of aggrandizing himself by grasping rapacity and foreign conquest, had made Egypt what it ought to be, an agricultural nation, and diffused the blessings of personal freedom and education among the people! Under such a policy, the extreme fertility of the soil and its capacity for the production of almost every article of consumption and commerce, would soon have enlarged the resources of the country to an unlimited extent; and given to Egypt once more a name and rank among the nations of the earth.

In one point of view, the innovations of the present ruler of Egypt open up a cheering prospect. His whole line of policy has been obviously founded on a conviction and tacit acknowledgment of the superiority of European arts and arms. The discipline of his troops, the organization of his fleet, the establishment of schools and manufactories, have all sprung from this principle; and are an attempt on his part to procure, by a forced process, advantages, which can only result from a gradual and general development and improvement. True, he might as well expect to reap where he has not sown; or command the fruit to spring ripe from the tree, without the intervention of blossoms. Yet one good effect has resulted from his measures; this same conviction of European superiority has spread from the ruler among the people; and, in consequence, the stronghold of Muhammedan prejudice and contempt towards European Christians, is fast breaking down and vanishing away. Then too, from the example of Egypt, a similar conviction has been forced upon the ruler of the Turkish empire; and the like effects are rapidly developing themselves in his dominions. Even now, Franks in their own dress may wander alone through all the streets of Cairo and Constantinople, and of other oriental cities, as freely as in London or New-York, without hindrance or molestation; where fifteen years ago they would have been followed with curses, and perhaps with stones. If they travel in the interior, they are everywhere received with courtesy, and usually with kindness. Such at least was the result of our inquiries and experience.—A still more important consequence of this state of things has been, that the Egyptian government, and recently that of Turkey also, have placed their native Christian subjects on an equal footing with the Muhammedans, as to civil rights and justice; and have done away, or at least forbidden, the hereditary and wanton oppressions exercised by the latter.[1]

---

[1] After the above paragraphs were written, Sultan Mahmûd descended to the tomb; and the battle of Nizib and the defection of the Turkish fleet demonstrated the comparative strength and weakness of the Egyptian and Turkish governments at the time. Yet I see no reason for changing any of the views expressed in the text.—For the best books on Egypt, see Note VI, end of the volume.

i. 44, 45

All these things mark important changes as having already taken place in the oriental character and feelings ; and new causes are daily springing into operation, which will necessarily render these changes not only permanent, but progressive. The introduction of steam-navigation in the Levant and on the Nile and Black Sea, is bringing the power of European civilization into still closer contact with the east, and cannot but augment its influence a thousand fold. Already the oriental churches are in parts beginning to awake from their slumber ; and the whole fabric of Muhammedan prejudice and superstition is sapped and tottering to its fall. In all human probability, the coming generation will behold changes and revolutions in the oriental world, of which few now have any conception. Then may the Egyptian people be freed from the oppressions under which they now groan,—a bondage more galling than that inflicted by their ancestors upon the Israelites of old ; then may Egypt cease to be, what she so long has been, "the basest of kingdoms."

In respect to our further journey, it may be proper to remark, that I entered upon it without the slightest anticipation of the results to which we were providentially led. My first motive had been simply the gratification of personal feelings. As in the case of most of my countrymen, especially in New England, the scenes of the Bible had made a deep impression upon my mind from the earliest childhood ; and afterwards in riper years this feeling had grown into a strong desire to visit in person the places so remarkable in the history of the human race. Indeed in no country of the world, perhaps, is such a feeling more widely diffused than in New England ; in no country are the Scriptures better known, or more highly prized. From his earliest years the child is there accustomed not only to read the Bible for himself ; but he also reads or listens to it in the morning and evening devotions of the family, in the daily village-school, in the Sunday-school and Bible-class, and in the weekly ministrations of the sanctuary. Hence, as he grows up, the names of Sinai, Jerusalem, Bethlehem, the Promised Land, become associated with his earliest recollections and holiest feelings.—With all this, in my own case, there had subsequently become connected a scientific motive. I had long meditated the preparation of a work on Biblical Geography ; and wished to satisfy myself by personal observation, as to many points on which I could find no information in the books of travellers. This indeed grew to be the main object of our journey, the nucleus around which all our inquiries and observations clustered. But I never thought of adding any thing to the former

i. 45, 46

stock of knowledge on these subjects; I never dreamed of any
thing like discoveries in this field. Palestine had for centuries
been visited by many travellers; and I knew that Schubert had
just preceded us, to explore the country in its physical aspects,
its botany and geology; and we could hope to add nothing to
what he and others had observed.

Under the influence of these impressions, we carried with us
no instruments, except an ordinary surveyor's and two pocket
compasses, a thermometer, telescopes, and measuring tapes;
expecting to take only such bearings and measurements as
might occur to us upon the road, without going out of our way
to seek for them. But as we came to Sinai, and saw how much
former travellers had left undescribed; and then crossed the
great desert through a region hitherto almost unknown, and
found the names and sites of long-forgotten cities; we became
convinced that there "yet remained much land to be possessed,"
and determined to do what we could with our limited means
towards supplying the deficiency. Both Mr Smith and myself
kept separate journals; each taking pencil-notes upon the spot
of every thing we wished to record, and writing them out in full
usually the same evening; but we never compared our notes.
These journals are now in my hands; and from them the following work has been compiled. On thus comparing them for the
first time, I have been surprised and gratified at their almost
entire coincidence. My own notes were in general more full in
specifications of time, the course, the features of the country,
and personal incidents; while those of my companion were
necessarily my sole dependence in respect to Arabic names and
their orthography, and chiefly so as to all information derived
orally from the Arabs. The bearings also were mostly taken by
Mr Smith; since it often required a great deal of questioning
and cross-examination, in order to extract the necessary information from the Arabs as to distant· places and their names.
This department therefore naturally fell to him; while I contented myself usually with taking the bearings of such places as
were already known to us. It is only since my return, that I
became aware of the value of the materials thus collected, in a
geographical point of view, from the judgment passed on them
by eminent geographers; and I look back with painful regret on
the circumstances, which prevented me from taking along more
perfect instruments, and from obtaining a more exact knowledge
of the observations necessary for the trigonometrical construction
of a map.

With books we were better supplied. First of all we had our
BIBLES, both in English and in the original tongues; and then
RELAND'S *Palæstina*, which next to the Bible is the most

i. 47, 48

important book for travellers in the Holy Land. We had also RAUMER'S *Palästina*, BURCKHARDT'S *Travels in Syria and the Holy Land*, the English compilation from LABORDE'S *Voyage en Arabie Petrée*, and the *Modern Traveller* in Arabia, Palestine, and Syria. Were I to make the journey again, considering the difficulty of transporting books, I should hardly add much to the above list, excepting perhaps a compendious History of the Crusades, and the volumes of RITTER'S *Erdkunde*, containing Palestine in the second edition. At Jerusalem we had access to the works of Josephus, and of several travellers.—We had with us LABORDE'S large Map of Sinai and Arabia Petræa; and also BERGHAUS' Map of Syria, the best undoubtedly up to that time, but whch was of little service to us in the parts of the country we visited.

i. 48

SECTION II.

FROM CAIRO TO SUEZ.

THE preparations for a journey of some thirty days through the desert, occupied a good deal of time. A tent was to be purchased and fitted up; water-skins were to be procured and kept full of water, which was to be changed every day in order to extract the strong taste of the leather; provisions were to be laid in for a whole month, as we could hope to obtain little either at Suez or at the convent; besides all the numerous smaller articles which are essential to the traveller's progress and health, even if he renounce all expectations of convenience and comfort. In all these purchases we were greatly indebted to the faithful services of our Janizary Mustafa, whom we remember with gratitude.

We chose a large tent with a single pole. This was folded into two rolls, for which we had sacks; so that it was easily packed and loaded, and suffered little damage on the way. We had large pieces of painted canvass to spread upon the ground under our beds; and found these more convenient than poles or bedsteads; as the mattresses could be rolled up in them during the day, and thus be protected from dust or rain. At a later period, when we came to travel with horses and mules in Palestine, we left our mattresses behind, taking only blankets and other covering, which might by day be thrown over our saddles. Indeed, if he choose, the traveller can very well do without either bed or tent, provided he has cloaks and covering enough to protect him from the night-chill. But to us it was important to keep a tolerably full record of our observations; and for this a tent and lights were necessary. Our provisions consisted chiefly of rice and biscuit. The latter is bulky; and at a later period we substituted for it flour, from which our servants made unleaven-

ed bread ; this was baked in thin cakes upon an iron plate, and
proved quite palatable and not unwholesome. Flesh may be
obtained occasionally from the Arabs upon the way. With
coffee, tea, sugar, butter, dried apricots, tobacco, wax-candles,
etc. we were well supplied. We found the dried apricots quite
a luxury in the desert ; and a timely distribution of coffee and
tobacco among the Arabs is an easy mode of winning their
favour and confidence. We had wooden boxes, like those of the
Mecca pilgrims, for packing many of the articles ; but after-
·wards abandoned them for small sacks and larger saddle-bags of
hair-cloth, like those of the Bedawîn. These proved to be more
advantageous, as diminishing the bulk of the loads, and thus
removing a source of expense and a cause of grumbling among the
camel-drivers and muleteers. We took also a supply of charcoal,
which proved of essential service.

We hired two Egyptian servants, who continued with us
all the way to Beirût. The elder, whom we knew only by the
name of Komeh, (although that seemed not to be his real name,)
was a fine resolute fellow, faithful and trust-worthy in all he
undertook, and ready to stand by us to the last drop of blood.
He spoke nothing but Arabic ; had formerly been sent with a
missionary family to Abyssinia, as their guide and purveyor ;
and had also been at Mecca ; for which reason he was sometimes
dignified with the title of Hajji Komeh. The younger, Ibrahim,
spoke a little English, and answered our purpose well enough as
a helper to the other.

It was for a time quite a matter of deliberation with us,
whether we should take any arms. We knew that the country
was entirely safe, and arms unnecessary, as far as 'Akabah, and
also in Palestine ; but as to the desert tracts between, we were
not so sure. We might very probably come in contact with the
lawless hordes that roam through those wastes ; and then the
mere *show* of arms would protect us from annoyance and
vexations, which might be attempted if we were known to be
wholly unarmed. On this ground we purchased two old muskets
and a pair of old pistols, in which our servants and Arab guides
usually took great pride ; and we afterwards had reason to believe
that we had acted wisely. It will of course be understood, that
we never had a thought of actually using these weapons for personal defence against the Arabs ; for this, we knew, would only
bring down tenfold vengeance on our heads.

The time has gone by when it was necessary for a Frank to
assume the oriental dress in any part of Egypt or Syria. It
may sometimes be convenient to do so, if he is to reside long in
the country ; but in the case of the mere traveller, it now only
excites the ridicule of the natives. A person in a Frank dress,

with a long beard, they hold to be a Jew. We usually wore the
Tarbûsh or red cap of the country, as a matter of convenience ;
but in the desert a broad-brimmed hat of light materials is desirable. We also took with us each a common Arab cloak, to
throw over our Frank dresses in case of suspicious appearances
at a distance ; but we were never called to use them on any
occasion of this kind.

In consequence of an application from Mr Gliddon senior,
we received from the Pasha a Firmân, or properly speaking a
Bûyuruldy, for our protection ; and the English vice-consul,
Dr Walne, was so kind as to procure for us a letter from Habîb
Effendi to the governor of 'Akabah, and another from the Greek
convent in Cairo to that in Mount Sinai. At the English consulate we also found Bedawin from Sinai ; many of whom are
continually in Cairo with their camels, and are much employed
in transporting coals from thence to Suez, for the steam-vessels
on the Red Sea. We had wished to obtain Tuweileb as our
guide, who has of late years become so well known among travellers ; but he was not then in Cairo. We therefore, with the
help of the English dragoman, made a contract for camels and
attendants with Beshârah, who had formerly accompanied Laborde, and was now grown into a man of weight in his tribe,
though not a regular Sheikh. After a long talk and some
clamour, the bargain was completed for three dromedaries and
five camels, at the rate of one hundred and ninety piastres each,
from Cairo to 'Akabah ;[1] it being also agreed that Tuweileb
should accompany us from the convent. The contract was immediately written down by an ordinary scribe upon his knee, and
signed and sealed in a very primitive manner. Most of the
Arabs of the towns have each his signet-ring, either worn on the
finger or suspended from the neck ; the impression of which
serves as a signature ; but the poor Bedawy of the desert commonly has little to do with such matters, and has therefore no
seal. Instead of it, Beshârah presented one of his fingers to the
dragoman, who besmeared the tip of it with ink, and then
gravely impressed it upon the paper ; which to him was then
doubtless just as binding as if sealed with gold or jewels. He
proved a very faithful and obliging conductor, and fulfilled his
contract honourably. He was of the Aulâd Sa'îd or Sa'îdiyeh,
one of the three divisions of the Tawarah Arabs which have the
right of taking travellers to the convent, and are reckoned as

---

[1] The Spanish pillared dollar, or *colonnato*, was then regularly worth in Egypt
and Syria 21 piastres ; while all other
dollars, Austrian, Italian, or American,
were valued at 20 piastres. In Constantinople, the Spanish dollar fluctuated be-
i. 52, 53

tween 22 and 23 piastres ; and the others
were usually current at about 21 piastres.
The most acceptable coin among the Arabs
were the small gold pieces of nine piastres ; though they also took the larger gold
coins without difficulty.

its Ghafîrs or protectors. Tuweileb, he said, was his brother; which probably meant no more, than that he belonged to the same tribe.

We engaged our animals quite to 'Akabah, in order to avoid the trouble of making a new bargain at the convent; and found the arrangement to be a convenient one.—The only difference between the camel and the dromedary is, that the latter is trained for riding, and the former for burdens. The distinction, at the most, is the same as between a riding-horse and a pack-horse; but among the Bedawîn, so far as our experience went, it seemed to amount to little more, than that the one had a riding-saddle, and the other a pack-saddle.

There are three principal routes from Cairo to Suez, viz. the Derb el-Haj, Derb el-'Ankebîyeh, and Derb el-Besâtin. The first leads from Cairo to the Birket el-Haj, a small lake a few miles northeastward of Heliopolis, and four hours from Cairo, where the pilgrims of the great Mecca caravan or Haj assemble; thence its course is to the south of east to 'Ajrûd. The second, the usual route of the Tawarah Arabs, proceeds from Cairo directly eastward to 'Ajrûd, and falls into the Haj-route a day's journey before reaching that place.[1] The third takes a southern direction from Cairo, by the village el-Besâtin and around the end of Jebel el-Mukattem, and passing south of this mountain and then north of Jebel Gharbûn and Jebel 'Atâkah, it also falls into the Haj-route several hours west of 'Ajrûd. A branch of the same road passes south of both these latter mountains through Wady Tawârik to the coast some distance below Suez.—A fourth and longer road north of the Haj-route, called Derb el-Bân, leaves the region of the Nile at Abu Za'bel, and proceeding towards 'Ajrûd, falls into the main trunk before reaching that fortress.

It had been our wish to take a still more circuitous route from Cairo to Suez, descending the eastern branch or canal of the Nile beyond Belbeis as far as to the province Shûrkiyeh, and thence along the valley of the ancient canal to the head of the gulf of Suez. Our object in taking this route would have been to make inquiries and observations personally in relation to the land of Goshen and the Exodus of the Israelites. But the season was already too far advanced, and our time was limited; so that we were compelled to take the usual and shortest route, the Derb el-'Ankebîyeh. This was travelled by Burckhardt in 1816, and has not been described since.

Monday, March 12th, 1838. This was the day fixed for our departure from Cairo. We had directed the Arabs to come in

---

[1] Called also Derb et-Tawarah; Wilkinson's Mod. Egypt, I. p. 302. Handb. p. 207.

good season, hoping to make an early start and reach Suez on the third day. Accordingly at six o'clock A. M. the camels were already at our door, filling the narrow street with their cries, or rather growls. The time spent in packing and arranging so many articles, and in procuring others that were still wanting, was very considerable ; and then it was found that another camel would be necessary. Our servants had fixed the number at five for themselves and the luggage ; but they had reckoned upon the strong heavy camels of Egypt, which carry a load of 600 *Rätl* of twelve ounces ; while the camels of the Bedawin are more slender and usually carry only two thirds as much. In consequence of all these delays, and the clamour and wrangling of the Arabs in loading the camels, it was one o'clock P. M. ere we bade adieu to our excellent friends, and set our faces toward the desert. Passing out at the Shubra gate as the nearest, we kept along near the wall towards the Bâb en-Nûsr or gate of Victory on the east side of the city, and at length halted near Kâid Beg, not far from the splendid but now neglected tombs of the Memlûk kings. Here the camels were unloaded, while the men went to the city for provisions and provender. At their return the luggage was re-arranged, and the loads of the camels adjusted for the whole journey ; as this could not be done so well in the narrow streets of the city. All this caused a delay of several hours. The Rev. Mr Lieder, who had accompanied us thus far, here bade us farewell ; as did also the faithful Mustafa.

Mounting again at five o'clock we proceeded on our way, having on the left a desert plain apparently once tilled ; and on the right the Red Mountain and low ridges connected with Jebel el-Mukattem. In thirty-five minutes we crossed Wady Liblâbeh, the broad shallow bed of a torrent, and entered among low hills of sand and gravel, strewed with pebbles of flint, coarse jasper, and chalcedony, and also with frequent specimens of petrified wood ; the latter probably brought hither in some way from the petrified forest on the S. S. E. of the Red Mountain.[1] In one place we saw the petrified trunk of a tree, eight or ten feet long, broken in several pieces. The path was a mere camel track. We rode on until 7.05 P. M. and then pitched our tent for the night in Wady en-Nehedein. All these Wadys of the desert are mere water-beds, or slight depressions in the surface, by which the water flows off in the rainy season ; while at all other times they are dry. Yet in uneven or mountainous regions, the same name, Wady, is applied to the deepest ravines and broadest valleys. Here the Wadys all descend N. or N. W. to the borders of the Nile ; but many of them probably run together before leaving the desert.

[1] See Wilkinson's Mod. Egypt, I. p. 800.

i. 55, 56

Our Arabs, as they walked by our side, were full of song and glee, at the idea of being once more free from the city and abroad upon their native wastes. To me also it was a new and exciting feeling, to find ourselves thus alone in the midst of the desert, in the true style of oriental travel ; carrying with us our house, our provisions, and our supply of water for many days ; and surrounded by camels and the wild ' sons of the desert,' in a region, where the eye could find nought to rest upon but desolation. It was a scene which had often taken possession of my youthful imagination; but which I had not dared to hope would ever be realized. Yet all was now present in reality ; and the journey which had so long been the object of my desires and aims was actually begun.

The evening had already closed in, and the moon was shining brightly, when we halted for the night. The tent was soon pitched ; a fire kindled ; and as it was now too late to let the camels browse, they were made to lie down around the tent, and were fed with a small quantity of beans in a bag drawn over the nose. To secure them for the night they are usually fastened one to another ; or a halter is tied round one of the fore legs as it lies folded together, in order to prevent the animal from rising. It was too late, and the situation too new, to think of much comfort in this our first night in a tent ; and therefore arranging our beds, each as he best could, we soon laid ourselves down to rest.

Tuesday, March 13th. Rising early and taking a slight breakfast, we were again upon our way at 6¾ o'clock, A. M. We crossed in succession Jerf el-Mukâwa, Wady Abu Hailezôn, Wady Ansûry ; and at 12.20 reached Wady el-'Ankebiyeh er-Reiyâneh, " the wet," which gives name to the road.[1] The way continued much the same as yesterday. The ridges on the right, extending eastward from Jebel el-Mukattem, became gradually lower and broken up into small hills, like those upon the left. Specimens of petrified wood were abundant; and among the pebbles with which the ground was strewed, jaspers and chalcedonies were still common. A less pleasing sight was the frequent carcasses and skeletons of camels, which had broken down and died by the way. The day was clear, with a cold wind from the N. N. E., the thermometer at 10 o'clock standing at 59 F. so that we were glad to ride all day in our cloaks.—In Wady el-'Ankebiyeh, on the left of the road, our guides pointed out the spot where (as they said) an unsuccessful attempt was made to bore for water a few years since. Water, they said, was found in small quantities, but soon disappeared. Rüppell mentions this or a similar attempt, as having been made

---

[1] The relative distances of all these points are specified very exactly in the Itinerary of our journey; see at the end of the volume.

i. 56, 57

in Wady Gandali on the southern route, at a point three hours
southward from the direct road.[1]

On the low rise of ground beyond this Wady, lay the petrified trunk of a tree eighteen feet long, broken in several pieces;
but the specimens of petrified wood extend no further. At 1
o'clock, P. M. the mountains of 'Aweibid and 'Atâkah came in
sight at a great distance before us. The road passes between
them. We now descended into Wady el-'Ankebîyeh el-'Ate-
shâneh, "the dry," and soon after passed a mass of black stones
on the left, looking at a distance like the small crater of an
extinct volcano. Wady el-'Eshrah and Wady el-Furn soon
followed; and then we entered upon an immense plain, called
by Burckhardt el-Mukrih, but which our Arabs named differently in various parts, after the Wadys that run across it. This
plain is skirted on the south by a low ridge running from
west to east called Mukrih el-Weberah; beyond which is seen
the higher mountain, Jebel Gharbûn. At 4.55 we encamped
near some hills on the left, in a tract called el-Mawâlih, from a
salt-hill a little further east, whence our Arabs brought us
specimens of very good salt. From this point 'Aweibid bore E.
3° S.; 'Atâkeh, east end as here seen, E. 15° S.; Jebel Gharbûn E. 29° S.

The camels were now turned loose for a time, to browse on
the scanty shrubs and herbs which they might find; and were
then fed as before with a few beans or a little barley. This was
their whole sustenance day after day; except the few mouthfuls
which they could occasionally snatch upon the march. The
peculiar gait of the camel causes a long rocking motion, which
to the rider is monotonous and tiresome. They lie down for the
rider to mount; but it requires some little practice in a novice,
not to be thrown over the animal's head, when he awkwardly
rises upon his hinder legs first. During the march, it is not
usual to make them lie down; but the driver stoops and presents his shoulders for the rider to mount upon.—We now had
time to arrange matters more to our mind within our tent; so
that on encamping hereafter, it was the work of only a few
minutes to put everything in order. It usually took an hour or
two to prepare dinner; during which interval and afterwards,
we had time to make observations, and write out in full the
pencil-notes of the day.

The desert which we were now crossing, is not sandy; but
its surface, for the most part, is a hard gravel, often strewed
with pebbles. Numerous Wadys or shallow water-courses inter-
sect its surface, all flowing towards the N. and N. W. In all

---

[1] Reise in Abyss. I. p. 101, 102.

i. 58, 59

these Wadys there are usually to be found scattered tufts of herbs, or shrubs; on which the camels browse as they pass along, and which serve likewise as their pasturage when turned loose at night. During the rainy season also, and afterwards, the inhabitants of Belbeis and the Shŭrkiyeh, as probably did the Israelites of old, still drive their mingled flocks of sheep and goats for pasturage to this quarter of the desert. During the present year there had been no rain; and the whole aspect of the desert and its Wadys was dry and parched. The rains usually fall here in December and January; and extend sometimes into March or even April.[1]

We found to-day upon the shrubs an insect, either a species of black locust or much resembling them, which our Bedawin called *Faras el-Jundy*, ‘soldier's horses.’[2] They said these insects were common in Mount Sinai, of a green colour; and were found on date trees, but did them no injury.

Wednesday, March 14th. We set off at 6.20 A. M. and travelled most of the day over the great plain on which we had entered yesterday. At 9 o'clock we reached Wady Jendal, at a point about three miles south of Dâr el-Hŭmra, the first station on the Haj-route, marked by a single acacia tree standing alone in this wide waste. Further on we saw, on that route, the tomb of a Sheikh, who had died on his pilgrimage, a mere pyramid of stones.[3] Crossing Wady Athîleh, we were at 10.35 directly south of Bir el-Bŭtr, indicated by reddish mounds of sand thrown up in digging a well. According to Burckhardt this well was begun about seventy years ago by command of 'Aly Bey; but on reaching the depth of eighty feet without finding water, it was abandoned.[4] At 12.55 we came to Wady Hufeiry, a broad, shallow depression, which as our guides said runs down to Belbeis. It is the last Wady we passed, running in that direction; and probably receives on the way many of those we had already crossed. In it, our road and that of the Haj come together; and the plain is covered with parallel tracks. The camels of loaded caravans are usually fastened one behind another in single file, and thus make one deep track or footpath; but in the Haj and in a small party like ours, they are left to choose their own way, and seldom follow each other in a line; so that many parallel tracks are thus formed.—In all the Wadys yesterday and to-day we found many tufts of the strong scented herb 'Abeithirân, apparently

---

[1] Brown had rain for 4½ hours in March; see his Travels, c. xiv. p. 175. In the middle of April, 1831, heavy rain fell for two days in and around Suez; Rüppell's Reise in Abyssinien, I. p. 104.

[2] Compare the language in Rev. 9, 7.

[3] For this tomb, see also Handb. for Egypt, p. 208.

[4] Le Père of the French Expedition says these wells were begun in A. D. 1676. Deser. de l'Egypte, Et. Mod. T. I. p. 33. Comp. Handb. for Egypt, p. 208.

the *Santolina fragrantissima* of Forskal,[1] somewhat resembling wormwood both in appearance and smell. The camels cropped it with avidity.

We were now approaching Jebel 'Aweibid, and began to ascend the gentle slope which extends from it towards the W. and S. W. Here on the left are many small heaps of stones and marks of graves, which we reached at 2.10. They are called Rejûm esh-Shawâghiriyeh, and mark the spot where a robbery was committed not many years ago on a caravan of Arabs of that name, who were carrying coffee from Suez to Cairo. Most of them were murdered. The Shawâghiriyeh are a tribe of Bedawin, who have taken up their abode at Kâid Beg, and own quite a number of camels. This affair is not improbably the same referred to by Burckhardt as having happened in 1815.[2] At 3.20 we came to the junction of the southern or Besâtin route. Near the same point is the watershed between the Nile and the gulf of Suez. The road here passes along a broad valley between Jebel 'Aweibid on the north, and the western ridges of Jebel 'Atâkah on the south. We encamped five minutes after four o'clock in the Wady Seil Abu Zeid, which runs towards the Red Sea. Here the camels found more pasture. The day had been cold and clear, and was followed by a fine star-light evening. The north star stood in brightness over the east end of 'Aweibid; from which a range of lower hills extends eastward towards 'Ajrûd.

During these two days we had seen several instances of the *mirage*, (Arabic Serâb,) presenting all around us the appearance of lakes of water, with islands and shores distinctly marked. One instance especially to-day among the hills on our right, was so strikingly natural, that we could scarcely resist giving credit to the impression thus made upon the senses.

With our Arabs we had come to be on a very good footing. Beshârah, our chief guide, proved to be active, good natured, and obliging; he had brilliant white teeth, and spoke with great rapidity and an animation almost like the excitement of anger. He had made the contract for all our camels; though he himself was the owner of but one. At setting off, we had besides him six men and two boys; but one or two of the former disappeared on the way. Most of them were owners each of one or two camels. One of the oldest, Ahmed, had been quite a traveller in his day; and liked much to relate his adventures and tell stories of the olden time. He was better acquainted with the country off our route than Beshârah. It was something new to them to find a Frank traveller

[1] Flora Egyptiaco-Arabica, p. 147. Compare the same work, p. lxxiv. i. 61, 62

[2] Travels in Syria and the Holy Land, p. 462.

speaking their own language fluently ; and my companion took care to cultivate this favourable impression by often dismounting and walking and talking with them. At night they always gathered around a fire made of shrubs or dry camel's dung ; but slept on the ground among their camels, without any other covering than they often wore by day ; the thermometer usually falling during the night on an average from 60° to 45° F. Our servants also slept in the open air ; but they were provided with blankets.

Thursday, March 15th. As we were preparing to set off, a small caravan of camels passed by on their way to Cairo ; and not far from our tent, we saw tracks of gazelles upon the sand. These were almost the only signs of life we had yet met with in the desert. Starting at 6.05 A. M. we followed down for a time the Wady Seil Abu Zeid, and soon passed the bed of a torrent coming down from the right, in which were several stunted acacia trees, the first we had seen upon our route. The carcass of a dead horse lay by the way-side ; and during the day we saw two others, said to have belonged to Mughá-ribeh pilgrims in the late caravan of the Haj, which had left Cairo about the 20th of January. The Wady now bends more to the N. E. under the range of low sand-hills which extends east from Jebel 'Aweibid ; while the path continues straight onward over low hills, connected with the foot of Jebel 'Atákah on the south. The whole region, mountains and hills, is of limestone, and is entirely destitute of vegetation. Gradually we came in sight of another and still higher summit of Jebel 'Atákah in the S. E., a collection of dark cliffs of limestone, naked of vegetation, and thickly strewed with pebbles of flint. Passing a small heap of stones, we found it had a name, although it did not mark a grave. Indeed the Bedawin give a name to every object and almost every spot in the desert, at least upon their more frequented routes ; in order that in travelling they may be able to designate the scene of any event, or the place where they were at a given time. At 8 o'clock we crossed Wady Emsháש, a broad torrent-bed coming down from the right, and sweeping round eastward to join Wady Abu Zeid ; after which it gives name to the whole. It then passes down on the north side of 'Ajrúd to the sea ; having in it a well of tolerable water, Bir Emshásh, about two miles west of the fortress.[1]

Soon afterwards we saw three Arabs sitting under a very old acacia, while their dromedaries were browsing near them. Our guides supposed them to be the Pasha's post. Muhammed

---

[1] Burckhardt's Travels in Syria, p. 464.

'Aly has established at least three lines of dromedary posts, by which letters and despatches are transmitted to and from the government as occasion may require ; and of which the foreign consuls are also permitted to avail themselves.   Between Cairo and Alexandria there is a regular daily line.   Between Cairo and Damascus, and Cairo and Mecca, the communication is frequent, but not regular.

Our course hitherto all the way from Cairo, had been nearly due east ; but we now, at 9¼ o'clock, turned E. S. E. around a small hill called el-Muntūla'.   Here the road which leaves the Nile at Abu Za'bel, comes in from the left.   This hill was formerly a favourite place of look-out for Arab robbers ; and the top is covered with heaps of stones commemorating the robberies and murders which have been committed in the vicinity.   Even so late as 1816, Burckhardt was compelled to wait three days in the fortress of 'Ajrūd, to avoid being plundered by a party of 'Amrân, who were lying in wait not far off.[1] But now the strong arm of the Pasha has swept off all such intruders, and the whole way is perfectly safe.   The road here begins to descend rapidly through a rough, stony, narrow pass, also called el-Muntūla',[2] which was formerly considered very dangerous ; as is indicated by the name el-Mukhâfeh (fear) which it likewise bears.   The pass gradually widens, and we had a glimpse of 'Ajrūd.   We thought too that the Red Sea lay in sight before us, but it turned out to be only the *mirage*.   At the foot of the pass we met several camels and a donkey ; and further on, a man riding on a donkey, with a camel for his luggage and two young gazelles in its panniers ; their small heads and languishing eyes being alone visible.   Not long after we met also a large caravan of Egyptian camels in single file, loaded with coffee and merchandise for Cairo.   Their stout heavy frames contrasted strongly with the thin and meager appearance of our poor animals.   We now dismounted from our camels and ascended a hill on the right, from which we had a wide prospect over the plain into which the valley opens, the fortress of 'Ajrūd on the left, and Suez on the right in the S. E. with the Red Sea beyond.   The atmosphere to-day seemed specially adapted to produce the *mirage ;* for as we looked towards Suez it seemed wholly surrounded by water ; while lakes and ponds apparently stretched from the sea far up towards the north upon the desert plain.   This plain, which we

[1] Travels in Syria, p. 627.

[2] Pococke writes " Haraminteleh," and strangely enough suggests that the ancient canal might pass this way; Descr. of the East, I. p. 131.   This has given occasion i. 63, 64   to the hardly less strange suggestion of Rennell, that this is "just where we should look for *Heroum* or Heroopolis;" Geogr. Syst. of Herodot. II. p. 64.

now overlooked, is not far from ten miles square ; extending
with a gentle slope from 'Ajrûd to the sea west of Suez, and from
the hills at the base of 'Atâkah to the arm of the sea north of
Suez. But it retains the same general character as the desert
we had passed. Hills and mountains and the long narrow strip
of salt water were indeed around and before us ; but not a tree,
nor scarcely a shrub, and not one green thing, was to be seen in
the whole circle of vision.

'Ajrûd is the next station on the Haj-route after Dâr el-
Hûmra. It is a square fortress with a well of bitter water two
hundred and fifty feet deep, built for the accommodation and
protection of the pilgrims on their way to and from Mecca.[1]
Near by it is a mosk with a saint's tomb, also enclosed with
walls. The fortress stands on the south side of Wady Emshâsh,
along which on the north a range of low hills stretches from
west to east. The Haj-route passes by the castle on the south,
and continues its course directly towards the mountains which
lie east of the line of the gulf, and constitute the ascent to the
high plain of the eastern desert. Two summits were pointed
out to us in this range of mountains, between which the road
passes on towards 'Akabah ; the northern one called Mukhsheib,
and the southern er-Râhah, as belonging to the more southern
chain of that name.

Before reaching 'Ajrûd our road separated from that of the
Haj, turning more southeast ; and we passed the fortress at
11.40, leaving it about twenty minutes distant on our left.
From 'Ajrûd to Suez is reckoned four hours. Crossing the
plain, which is everywhere intersected by water-courses, we came
at 2.50 to Bir Suweis, the well of Suez, one hour from the
town. Here are two deep wells, surrounded by a square massive
building of stone with towers at the corners, erected in the seventeenth century, as appears from an inscription. The water is
brackish, and is carried to Suez on asses and camels only for
cooking and washing, being too salt to be drank. Even where
it flows upon the ground round about the building, it produces
no vegetation, causing only a saline efflorescence. In Niebuhr's
time the water was drawn up by hand ; but is now raised by
wheels turned by oxen, and runs into a large stone trough outside, where animals drink and water-skins are filled.[2] Here our
camels were watered for the first time. They had been fed in

---

[1] Burckhardt's Travels in Syria, etc. p.
628. Edrisi mentions 'Ajrûd about the
middle of the twelfth century. Rüppell
singularly enough writes the name *Hadgi
Routh;* Reise in Abyssinien, I. p. 135.
The Arabic orthography has been fixed at

least ever since the days of Edrisi ; pp. 328,
329, ed. Jaubert.

[2] Reisebeschr. I. p. 217. These would
seem to be the wells mentioned by Edrisi
under the name el-'Ajúz, between 'Ajrûd
and Kolzum ; p. 329, ed. Jaubert.

Cairo with green clover ; and had not drank, it was said, for twelve days before our departure. Yet they now drank little, and some of them none at all.

We reached Suez (Arabic *Suweis*) at 3.50, and pitched our tent outside of the walls on the north of the town, near the shore ; having first reconnoitered the interior and found no spot so clean and convenient among all its open places ; to say nothing of the annoyance and risk to which we should have been exposed from idlers.—From the gate of Cairo to Suez we reckoned 32¼ hours of march, equivalent to 64½ geogr. miles, or somewhat less than 75 statute miles.[1]   Our whole time, including the stops at night, was 71¾ hours, or nearly three whole days.   The India mails had just before been carried across in twenty-two hours ; and the Pasha is said to have once crossed on horseback in thirteen hours, by having relays of horses stationed on the way.[2]

We paid our respects to the English vice-consul, Mr. Fitch, to whom we had letters ; and of whose kindness we retain a grateful remembrance.[3]   He had been only five weeks in the place ; and his chief business was the agency for the Bombay steamers, which were to arrive and depart every month.   At his invitation we attended his *soirée ;* where however we met only three other persons, and these in his employ.   They were three brothers Manucli, natives of the place and members of the Greek church.   One of them, Nicola, had been for many years English agent at Suez, until recently superseded by the vice-consul ; under whom he now acted as dragoman and fac-totum.   We found him to be a very intelligent and well informed man ; and obtained from him satisfactory information on many points of inquiry connected with this region.   At the suggestion of the vice-consul, he procured for us a letter from the governor of Suez to the governor of 'Akabah ; which however we found to be of little importance.[4]

Suez is situated on the angle of land between the broad head of the gulf, the shore of which here runs nearly from east to west, and the narrow arm which runs up northward from the eastern corner of the gulf.   It is poorly walled on three sides ;

---

[1] See Note VII, at the end of the volume.

[2] In 1839 three stations were established on the road between Cairo and Suez, for keeping relays of animals, and to serve also as inns for travellers passing between Europe and India; see Kinnear's Cairo, etc. p. 61.—At present (1856) the route is traversed with vans, which take from 14 to 16 hours.   Seven station houses are built along the way, about 10 or 11 miles apart.   The mail route lies between the Haj-route and ours, and joins the former at Dâr el-Hâmra.   See Handb. for Egypt, pp. 205, 206.

[3] This gentleman died a year afterwards at Alexandria.

[4] An English hotel has since been established at Suez for the benefit of passengers in the steam-vessels.

i. 66, 67

being open to the water on the east, or rather northeast, where is the harbour and a good quay. Here were lying quite a number of the Red Sea craft, vessels of considerable size, with neat white bottoms, but with only one mast and sail, and no deck except over the cabin. The timber and materials for all vessels built here, have usually been brought from the Nile on camels.[1] Within the walls are many open places, and several Khâns built around large courts. In the large open space connected with the building occupied by the consulate, a beautiful tame gazelle was running about, belonging to the governor, whose house was adjacent to the same court. The houses in general are poorly built. There is a bazar, or street of shops, which we found tolerably furnished with provisions and stuffs, mostly from Cairo. The inhabitants consist of about twelve hundred Muhammedans and one hundred and fifty Christians of the Greek church. The geographical position of Suez is in Lat. 29° 57′ 30″ N. and Long. 32° 35′ E. from Greenwich.[2]

The transit of the productions and merchandise of the east from the Red Sea to the Nile, has always made this an important point, and caused the existence of a city in the vicinity ; though Suez itself, as a town, is of modern origin,[3] and has been greatly aided by the concourse of pilgrims who annually embark here for Mecca. The present arrangements for making it the point of communication between Europe and India by means of steam-navigation on the Red Sea, may probably give to it an impulse, and somewhat enlarge its population ; but it can never well become any thing more than a mere place of passage, which both the traveller and the inhabitant will hasten to leave as soon as possible. The aspect both within and without is too desolate and dreary. Not a garden, not a tree, not a trace of verdure, not a drop of fresh water ; all the water with which Suez is supplied for personal use, being brought from the fountain Nâba', three hours distant across the gulf, and so brackish as to be scarcely drinkable.

About ten minutes or one third of a mile north of the town, is a lofty mound of rubbish, in which a few substructions are visible, and frequent fragments of pottery. It is called Tell Kolzum. This is doubtless the site of the former city Kolzum, so often mentioned by Arabian writers as the port where fleets were built on the Red Sea. It was the successor of the Greek Klysma ; Kolzum being merely the Arabic form of the same name.[4]

---

[1] Niebuhr Reisebeschr. I. p. 218. Compare Wilken's Gesch. der Kreuzzüge, III. ii. p. 223.

[2] Wilkinson's Handb. for Egypt, p. 209.

[3] See Note VIII, at the end of the volume.

[4] Klysma (Κλύσμα) is mentioned in this place by Cosmas Indicopleustes so late as about A. D. 530 ; see Montfaucon's Collectio nova Patrum, T. II. p. 194. In the council of Constantinople, A. D. 553, the name of Stephanus, bishop of Clysma,

The earlier city of Arsinoe or Cleopatris is supposed to have stood somewhere in the vicinity ; and may perhaps have occupied the same spot.[1]

The gulf of Suez, as seen from the adjacent hills, presents the appearance of a long strip of water, setting far up like a large river through a desert valley of twenty or thirty miles in width ; the shores skirted sometimes by arid plains, and sometimes interrupted by naked mountains and promontories on either side. The whole configuration reminded me strongly of the valley of the Nile on a larger scale ; except that there the noble river bears fertility on its bosom, and scatters it abroad in lavish profusion ; while here desolation reigns throughout. The gulf becomes narrower towards Suez, and terminates in a line of coast extending from the town westward nearly to Jebel 'Atâkah, a distance of six or eight miles. Further south, this mountain runs quite down to the sea, forming the promontory called Râs 'Atâkah ; beyond which opens the broad mouth or plain of Wâdy Tawârik ; and then follows Jebel Deraj or Kulâlah, and the long chain of African mountains. On the east side of the gulf, the parallel ridge of mountains, called er-Râhah, is here twelve or fifteen miles distant from the coast. Around the head of the gulf, extensive shoals stretch out southward far into the sea, and are left bare at low water ; except a narrow winding channel like a small river, by which light vessels come quite up to the town. We saw these shoals twice while the tide was out. They extend a mile and a half or two miles below Suez ; are quite level and hard, thinly covered with seaweed ; and are composed apparently of sand mingled perhaps with coral. We saw persons walking upon them quite near the southern extremity. Larger vessels and the steamers lie off in the road below these shoals, more than two miles distant from the town.

The desert plain back of Suez, which has been mentioned above as extending west as far as to 'Atâkah and north to 'Ajrûd, is composed for the most part of hard gravel ; and is apparently of no recent formation, but as old as the adjacent hills and mountains. Just at Suez a narrow arm of the sea runs up northwards, for a considerable distance, from the northeast corner of the gulf ; in which, when we saw it, the water extended up about two miles ; but the depression or bed of it continues beyond the mounds of the ancient canal, and as far as

---

appears among the signers ; Harduin Acta Concilior. III. p. 52. For Kolzum see Edrisi Geogr. I. p. 331, 333, ed. Jaubert. Abulfeda in Busching's Magazin, IV. p. 196. Comp. Bochart's Phaleg, II. c. 18.

[1] The following bearings were taken

I. 69, 70

from Tell Kolzum : Jebel Mukhsheib N. 65° E. Tâset Sûdr S. 41° E. Jebel 'Atâkah, north peak, N. 72° W. Extreme point of Râs 'Atâkah, S. 26° W. End of the shoal running out from the eastern shore, S. 1° W.

the eye can reach. Opposite Suez this arm is about eleven hundred and fifty yards wide according to Niebuhr ;[1] but higher up and opposite Tell Kolzum, it is broader, and has several low islands or sand-banks, which are mostly covered at high water. It is here and around the northern part of this arm, that there are evident traces of a gradual filling up of this part of the Red Sea. I am not aware of any circumstances, which go to show that the *level of the sea* itself has been changed ; but the change, if any, has been brought about solely by the drifting in of sand from the northern part of the great desert plain, which here extends to the eastern mountains. This plain is ten miles or more wide. Burckhardt crossed it in 1812 in six hours from the wells of Mab'ûk at the foot of the mountains to the mounds of the canal ; and says it was full of " moving sands which covered the plain as far as he could discern, and in some places had collected into hills thirty or forty feet in height."[2] Such it was as we also saw it on our left in passing around the head of the bay ; and this sand, driven by the strong northeast wind which often prevails, is continually carried towards and into the water, and the process of filling up is still going on. There can be little room for doubt, that the islands above Suez were formed in this manner ; since in former days vessels probably lay at Kolzum, which they now cannot reach. Around the head of the inlet, there are also obvious indications, that the water once extended much further north, and probably spread itself out over a wide tract towards the northeast. The ground bears every mark of being still occasionally overflowed ; and our Arabs said it was often covered by the sea, especially in winter, when the south winds prevail. The soil of this part is a fine sand like that of the adjacent desert, only rendered more solid by the action of the waves. In some parts it was covered with a saline crust, and occasionally exhibited strips white with shells. Whether the shoals south of Suez were formed in the same manner, it is more difficult to decide ; though they would seem now to have a firmer consistence.

We were told that the tide rises at Suez and upon these shoals about *seven* English feet. According to the French measurements, the average rise of the tides in their time was $5\frac{1}{2}$ Paris feet, though it sometimes exceeded 6 feet. Niebuhr found it to be only $3\frac{1}{4}$ feet.[3] It must obviously vary much with the direction of the wind ; since a strong wind from the northern quarter would have the effect to drive the tide out and prevent its return ; while a south wind would produce the contrary re-

---

[1] Reisebeschr. I. p. 253.   Mod. I. p. 90. Niebuhr Beschr. von Arab.
[2] Travels in Syria, etc. p. 454.   p. 421 sq.
[3] Le Père in Descr. de l'Egypte, Et.

sults. Opposite Suez there is a ferry; and higher up, at Tell Kolzum, a ford, which is sometimes used at low water, leading over two of the sandy islands. Niebuhr's guides passed this ford on foot, and the water came scarcely up to their knees.[1] An island just below the ford is called Jezirat el-Yehûdiyeh, "Jews' Island;" but, although we inquired particularly, we could not learn that the ford itself is called Derb el-Yehûd or Jews' road, as reported by Ehrenberg.[2] There is also another ford south of Suez, near the edge of the shoals, where a long narrow sand-bank extends out from the eastern shore. Here at low tides the Arabs sometimes wade across the channel; the water being then about five feet deep, or, as they said, coming up to the chin.

The road which we travelled from Cairo to Suez is the shortest and most direct of all those between the two points; and like all the rest (except the southern one) is wholly destitute of water as far as to 'Ajrûd. On the Besâtin route west of Jebel Gharbûn are the shallow pits of Gandali (or Gandelhy), in which a small quantity of tolerable water collects. On the more southern and longer branch of this route, through Wady Tawârik, is the well of 'Odheib ('ödheib, sweet water) near the shore south of Râs 'Atâkah, about eight hours from Suez. Here is also a small mound of rubbish with fragments of pottery, indicating a former site.[3] But the shortest route of all between Suez and the borders of the Nile, lies to the northward of all these roads, and passes nearer to the valley of the ancient canal. Caravans proceeding from Suez in this direction, stop the first night at Rejûm el-Khail, a mere station in the desert without water; and the next day reach Râs el-Wâdy, a considerable village on the border of Wady Tûmilât, some distance northeast of Belbeis. This Wady is the western part of the broad valley of the canal, which more to the eastward is called Wady Seba' Biyâr (Seven Wells). The water of the Nile flows up into it during the annual inundation, sometimes as far as to the salt lakes called Temsah (Crocodile Lakes), as marked on the maps; which lakes indeed are said on the great French map to have water only at these periods. This inundation of course renders the valley a tract of fertile land, on which are scattered many villages and traces of ancient sites. By taking a direction more to the right from Rejûm el-Khail, a day's journey brings the traveller to the well of Abu Suweirah, situated in the northern part of the same great Wady, a little northwest of the

[1] Reisebeschr. I. p. 252.
[2] See his map in Naturgesch. Reisen, Abth. I. Berlin, 1828.
[3] Le Père in Descript. de l'Egypte, Et. Mod. I. p. 46. This route serves also as a medium of communication between Suez i. 72, 73

and Upper Egypt; a branch of it passing directly from Wady Tawârik through a side valley to the Nile near Tebbin, some distance above Cairo.—For other names of this valley, see Note IX, at the end of the volume.

Crocodile Lakes.[1] A more direct course from Suez to the latter place, is prevented by salt marshes, in which the camels sink or slip. Our Arabs, who had themselves been this route and gave us this information, said these marshes were made by a canal cut thus far from the Red Sea and then neglected ; though now a hill (as they said) separates them from the sea. These are doubtless the well-known marshes or Bitter Lakes of the ancients, which the French found to be from forty to fifty feet (12 to 15 metres) below the usual level of the gulf of Suez ; while the broad tract of sand, which now separates them from the gulf, is only about three feet above the same level. A higher bank or swell of ground at their western extremity, separates them in like manner from the Crocodile Lakes, and forms the utmost limit of the inundations of the Nile.[2]

The bearing of the preceding details upon one of the most remarkable events of Biblical History, will be obvious ; I mean the Exodus of the Israelites and their passage through the Red Sea. I propose to bring together in this place all I have to say on this subject ; premising such information as we were able to obtain relative to the land of Goshen, and the probable route of the Israelites on leaving Egypt.

We were quite satisfied from our own observation, that they could not have passed to the Red Sea from any point near Heliopolis or Cairo in three days, the longest interval which the language of the narrative allows. Both the distance and the want of water on all the routes, are fatal to such an hypothesis. We read, that there were six hundred thousand men of the Israelites above twenty years of age, who left Egypt on foot.[3] There must of course have been as many women above twenty years old ; and at least an equal number both of males and females under the same age ; besides the "mixed multitude" spoken of, and very much cattle. The whole number therefore probably amounted to two and a half millions, and certainly to not less than two millions. Now the usual day's march of the best appointed armies, both in ancient and modern times, is not estimated higher than fourteen English, or twelve geographical miles ;[4] and it cannot be supposed that the Israelites, en-

[1] See Note X, end of the volume.
[2] Rozière in Descr. de l'Egypte, Antiq. Mem. I. p. 137. Le Père and Du Bois-Aymé, ib. Et. Mod. I. p. 21 sq. 187 sq. Comp. Ritter's Erdkunde, Th. II. 1818, p. 232 sq. A valuable abstract of the results contained in the great French work, is given by Mr Maclaren in the Edinburgh Philosophical Journal, 1825, Vol. XIII. p. 274. See further in Note XI, end of the volume.
[3] Ex. 12, 37. 38. Compare Num. 1, 2. 3. 45. 46, where a year later the number is given at 603,550.
[4] Rennell's Compar. Geogr. of Western Asia, I. p. liv. I am informed by Prussian

cumbered with women and children and flocks, would be able to accomplish more. But the distance on all these routes being not less than sixty geographical miles, they could not well have travelled it in any case in less than five days.

The difficulty as to water might indeed have been obviated, so far as the Israelites were concerned, by taking with them a supply from the Nile, like the caravans of modern days. But Pharaoh appears to have followed them upon the same track with all his horses and chariots and horsemen; and this could not have taken place upon any of the routes between Cairo and the Red Sea. Horses are indeed often taken across at the present day; but then a supply of water must be provided for them, usually about two water-skins for each horse. Six of these water-skins are a load for a camel; so that for every three horses, there must be a camel-load of water. Still they not unfrequently die; and we saw the carcasses of several which had perished during the recent passage of the Haj. Flocks of sheep and goats might pass across; but for neat cattle this would be impossible, without a like supply of water.

LAND OF GOSHEN.

The preceding considerations go far to support the usual view of scholars at the present day, that the land of Goshen lay along the Pelusiac arm of the Nile, on the east of the Delta, and was the part of Egypt nearest to Palestine.[1] This tract is now comprehended in the modern province esh-Shŭrkiyeh, which extends from the neighbourhood of Abu Za'bel to the sea, and from the desert to the former Tanaitic branch of the Nile; thus including also the valley of the ancient canal. If the Pelusiac arm, as is commonly assumed, were navigable for fleets in ancient times, the Israelites were probably confined to its eastern bank; but if we are at liberty to suppose, that this stream was never much larger than at present, then they may have spread themselves out upon the Delta beyond it, until restrained by larger branches of the Nile.[2] That the land of Goshen lay upon the waters of the Nile, is apparent from the circumstance, that the Israelites practised irrigation; that it

officers of rank, that the usual march of their armies is three German miles a day, equal to twelve geographical miles of sixty to the degree. Forced marches are reckoned at five German miles a day. In either case the whole army rests every fourth day.

[1] The usual arguments from Scripture and the early writers, on which this opinion i. 75, 76

rests, may be found in Rosenmueller's Bibl. Geogr. III. p. 246 sq. Gesenius' Thesaur. Ling. Heb. p. 307. Amer. Bibl. Repos. Oct. 1832. p. 744. A view of the various earlier theories respecting the position of Goshen, is given in Bellermann's Handb. der bibl. Literatur, IV. p. 191 sq. Gesenius, l. c.

[2] See Note XII, end of the volume.

was a land of seed, figs, vines, and pomegranates ; that the
people ate of fish freely ; while the enumeration of the articles
for which they longed in the desert, corresponds remarkably
with the list given by Mr Lane as the food of the modern
Fellàhs.[1] All this goes to show, that the Israelites, when in
Egypt, lived much as the Egyptians do now ; and that Goshen
probably extended further west and more into the Delta than
has usually been supposed. They would seem to have lived
interspersed among the Egyptians of that district, perhaps in
separate villages, much as the Copts of the present day are
mingled with the Muhammedans. This appears from the circumstance of their borrowing "jewels of gold and silver " from
their Egyptian neighbours ; and also from the fact, that their
houses were to be marked with blood, in order that they might
be distinguished and spared in the last dread plague of the
Egyptians.[2]

The immediate descendants of Jacob were doubtless nomadic
shepherds like their forefathers, dwelling in tents ; and probably
drove their flocks for pasture far up in the Wadys of the desert,
like the present inhabitants of the same region.[3] But in process of time they became also tillers of the soil, and exchanged
their tents for more fixed habitations. Even now there is a
colony of the Tawarah Arabs, about fifty families, living near
Abu Za'bel, who cultivate the soil and yet dwell in tents. They
came thither from Mount Sinai about four years before the
French invasion. This drove them back for a time to the
mountains of the Teràbìn, east of Suez ; but they had acquired
such a taste for the good things of Egypt, that like the Israelites they could not live in the desert, and soon returned after
the French were gone. " Now," said our Arabs, " though we
acknowledge them as cousins, they have no right to dwell among
us ; nor could they live in our barren mountains after enjoying
so long the luxuries of Egypt."

The land of Goshen was " the best of the land ; "[4] and
such too the province esh-Shùrkiyeh has ever been, down to the
present time. In the remarkable Arabic document translated
by De Sacy,[5] containing a valuation of all the provinces and
villages of Egypt in the year 1376, the province of the Shùrkiyeh

---

[1] Deut. 11, 10. Num. 20, 5.—Num. 11,
5, " We remember the fish we did eat in
Egypt freely ; the cucumbers, and the
melons, and the leeks, and the onions, and
the garlic."—Manners and Customs of the
Mod. Egyptians, I. p. 242, "Their food
consists of bread made of millet or of
maize, milk, new cheese, eggs, small salted
fish, cucumbers and melons, and gourds
of a great variety of kinds, onions and
leeks, beans, chick-peas, lupins," etc. etc.
[2] Ex. 11, 2. 12, 12. 13. 22. 23, etc.
[3] See above, p. 41.
[4] Gen. 47, 6 " in the best of the land,
. . . in the land of Goshen."
[5] Abdallatif's Relation de l'Egypte, par
De Sacy, p. 583.

comprises 383 towns and villages, and is valued at 1,411,875 *dinars;* a larger sum than is put upon any other province, with one exception. During my stay in Cairo, I made many inquiries respecting this district ; to which the uniform reply was, that it was considered as the best province in Egypt. Wishing to obtain more definite information, I ventured to request of Lord Prudhoe, with whom the Pasha was understood to be on a very friendly footing, to obtain for me, if possible, a statement of the valuation of the provinces of Egypt. This, as he afterwards informed me, could not well be done ; but he had ascertained that the province of the Shŭrkiyeh bears the highest valuation and yields the largest revenue. He had himself just returned from an excursion to the lower parts of this province, and confirmed from his own observation the reports of its fertility. This arises from the fact that it is intersected by canals, while the surface of the land is less elevated above the level of the Nile, than in other parts of Egypt ; so that it is more easily irrigated. There are here more flocks and herds than anywhere else in Egypt ; and also more fishermen. The population is half migratory, composed partly of Fellâhs, and partly of Arabs from the adjacent deserts and even from Syria ; who retain in part their nomadic habits, and frequently remove from one village to another. Yet there are very many villages wholly deserted, where many thousands of people might at once find a habitation. Even now another million at least might be sustained in the district ; and the soil is capable of higher tillage to an indefinite extent. So too the adjacent desert, so far as water could be applied for irrigation, might be rendered fertile ; for wherever water is, there is fertility.

ROUTE OF THE ISRAELITES TO THE RED SEA.

From the land of Goshen as thus defined to the Red Sea, the direct and only route was along the valley of the ancient canal. The Israelites broke up from their rendezvous at Rameses "on the fifteenth day of the first month, on the morrow after the passover ; "[1] and proceeded by Succoth and Etham to the sea. Without stopping to inquire as to the identity of Rameses with Heroopolis, or the position of the latter place, it is enough for our purpose, that the former town (as is generally admitted) lay probably on the valley of the canal in the middle part, not far from the western extremity of the basin of the Bitter Lakes. Nor is it necessary to discuss the point, whether this basin anciently formed a prolongation of the gulf of the Red Sea, as is supposed by some ; or, as is more probable, was

[1] Ex. 12, 37. Num. 33, 3.

i. 78, 79

covered with brackish water, and separated from the Red Sea, as now, by a tract of higher ground. Nothing more is needed for our present purpose, even admitting that a communication existed from this basin to the sea, than to suppose that the inlet, if any, was already so small, as to present no important obstacle to the advance of the Israelites.[1]

From Rameses to the head of the gulf, according to the preceding data, would be a distance of some thirty or thirty-five miles; which might easily have been passed over by the Israelites in three days. A large portion of the people were apparently already collected at Rameses, waiting for permission to depart, when the last great plague took place. From the time when Pharaoh dismissed Moses and Aaron in the night of the fourteenth day of the month (according to the Jewish reckoning), until the morning of the fifteenth day, when the people set off, there was an interval of some thirty hours, during which these leaders could easily reach Rameses from the court of Pharaoh, whether this were at Memphis, or, as is more probable, at Zoan or Tanis.[2]

The first day's march brought them to Succoth, a name signifying "booths," which might be applied to any temporary station or encampment. Whether there was water here is not mentioned; and the position of the place cannot be determined. On the second day they reached Etham "in the edge of the wilderness."[3] What wilderness? The Israelites after passing the Red Sea are said in Exodus to have gone three days' march into the desert of Shur; but in Numbers, the same tract is called the desert of Etham.[4] It hence follows, that Etham probably lay on the edge of this eastern desert, perhaps not far from the present head of the gulf, and on the eastern side of the line of the gulf or canal. May it not have stood upon or near the strip of land between the gulf and the basin of the Bitter Lakes?[5] At any rate, it would seem to have been the point, from which the direct course of the Israelites to Sinai would have led them around the present head of the gulf and along its eastern side. From Etham they "turned" more to the right; and instead of passing along the eastern side, they marched down the western side of the arm of the gulf, to the vicinity of Suez. This movement, apparently so directly out of their course, might well give Pharaoh occasion to say, "they are entangled in the land, the wilderness hath shut them in;"

---

[1] See Note XIII, end of the volume.
[2] The Psalmist places the scene of the miracles of Moses in the region of Zoan. Ps. 78, 12. 43.
[3] Ex. 13, 20. Num. 33, 6.

[4] Ex. 15, 22. Num. 33, 8.
[5] This view would be supported by the Egyptian etymology which Jablonsky assigns to the name Etham, viz. *ATIOM*, "Border of the Sea."

and lead him to pursue them with his horsemen and chariots, in the hope of speedily overtaking and forcing them to return.[1]

The position of Migdol, Pi-haheroth, and Baal-Zephon, cannot of course be determined; except that they probably were on or near the great plain back of Suez. If the wells of 'Ajrûd and Bîr Suweis were then in existence, they would naturally mark the sites of towns; but there is no direct evidence either for or against such an hypothesis. That this point, so important for the navigation of the Red Sea, was already occupied by a town, perhaps Baal-Zephon, is not improbable. A few centuries later several cities lay in the vicinity; and these must have had wells, or there were more fountains than at present. In this plain, the Israelites would have abundant space for their encampment.

PASSAGE OF THE RED SEA.

The question here has respect to the part of the sea where the passage took place. This many writers and travellers have assumed to be the point at the mouth of Wady Tawârik, south of Râs 'Atâkah; principally perhaps because it was supposed that the Israelites passed down that valley. But according to the preceding views, this could not well have taken place; and therefore, if they crossed at that point, they must first have passed down around Râs 'Atâkah and encamped in the plain at the mouth of the valley.

The discussion of this question has often been embarrassed, by not sufficiently attending to the circumstances narrated by the sacred historian; which are, in the main points, the following. The Israelites, hemmed in on all sides,—on their left and in front the sea, on their right Jebel 'Atâkah, and behind them the Egyptians,—began to despair of escape, and to murmur against Moses. The Lord now directed Moses to stretch out his rod over the sea; and the Lord caused the sea to flow (Heb. *go*) by a strong east wind all that night, and made the sea dry; and the waters were divided. And the children of Israel went into the midst of the sea upon the dry (ground); and the waters were a wall unto them on their right hand and on their left. The Egyptians pursued and went in after them; and in the morning watch, the Lord troubled the host of the Egyptians. And Moses stretched out his hand over the sea, and the sea returned to his strength when the morning appeared, and the Egyptians fled against it; and the waters returned and covered all the host of Pharaoh.[2]

In this narration there are two main points, on which

---

[1] Ex. 14, 2. 3 sq.   [2] Ex. 14, 11. 12. 21—28.

i. 81, 82

the whole question may be said to turn. The first is, *the means* or instrument with which the miracle was wrought. The Lord, it is said, caused the sea to go (or to flow out) *by a strong east wind.* The miracle therefore is represented as mediate ; not a direct suspension of, or interference with the laws of nature, but a miraculous adaptation of those laws to produce a required result. It was wrought by natural means supernaturally applied. For this reason we are here entitled to look only for the natural effects arising from the operation of such a cause. In the somewhat indefinite phraseology of the Hebrew, an east wind means any wind from the eastern quarter ; and would include the N. E. wind, which often prevails in this region. Now it will be obvious from the inspection of any good map of the gulf,[1] that a strong N. E. wind acting here upon the ebb tide, would necessarily have the effect to drive out the waters from the small arm of the sea which runs up by Suez, and also from the end of the gulf itself, leaving the shallower portions dry ; while the more northern part of the arm, which was anciently broader and deeper than at present, would still remain covered with water. Thus the waters would be divided, and be a wall (or defence) to the Israelites on the right hand and on the left. Nor will it be less obvious from a similar inspection, that in no other part of the whole gulf, would a N. E. wind act in the same manner to drive out the waters. On this ground, then, the hypothesis of a passage through the sea opposite to Wady Tawârik, would be untenable.

The second main point has respect to the interval of *time* during which the passage was effected. It was night ; for the Lord caused the sea to go (out) "all night ; " and when the morning appeared, it had already returned in its strength ; for the Egyptians were overwhelmed in the morning watch. If then, as is most probable, the wind thus miraculously sent, acted upon the ebb tide to drive out the waters during the night to a far greater extent than usual, we still cannot assume that this extraordinary ebb, thus brought about by natural means, would continue more than three or four hours at the most. The Israelites were probably on the alert, and entered upon the passage as soon as the way was practicable ; but as the wind must have acted for some time before the required effect would be produced, we cannot well assume that they set off before the middle watch, or towards midnight. Before the morning watch or two o'clock, they had probably completed the passage ; for the Egyptians had entered after them, and were destroyed before the morning appeared. As the Israelites numbered more than two

---

[1] Especially Niebuhr's Tab. XXIV, in his Beschr. von Arabien.

millions of persons, besides flocks and herds, they would of course be able to pass but slowly. If the part left dry were broad enough to enable them to cross in a body one thousand abreast, which would require a space of more than half a mile in breadth (and is perhaps the largest supposition admissible), still the column would be more than two thousand persons in depth ; and in all probability could not have extended less than two miles. It would then have occupied at least an hour in passing over its own length, or in entering the sea ; and deducting this from the largest time intervening before the Egyptians must also have entered the sea, there will remain only time enough, under the circumstances, for the body of the Israelites to have passed at the most over a space of three or four miles. This circumstance is fatal to the hypothesis of their having crossed from Wady Tawárik ; since the breadth of the sea at that point, according to Niebuhr's measurement, is three German or twelve geogr. miles, equal to a whole day's journey.[1]

All the preceding considerations tend conclusively to limit the place of passage to the neighbourhood of Suez. The part left dry might have been within the arm which sets up from the gulf, which is now two thirds of a mile wide in its narrowest part, and was probably once wider ; or it might have been to the southward of this arm, where the broad shoals are still left bare at the ebb, and the channel is sometimes forded. If similar shoals might be supposed to have anciently existed in this part, the latter supposition would be the most probable. The Israelites would then naturally have crossed from the shore west of Suez in an oblique direction, a distance of three or four miles from shore to shore. In this case there is room for all the conditions of the miracle to be amply satisfied.

To the former supposition, that the passage took place through the arm of the gulf above Suez, it is sometimes objected, that there could not be in that part space and depth enough of water, to cause the destruction of the Egyptians in the manner related. It must however be remembered, that this arm was anciently both wider and deeper ; and also, that the sea in its reflux would not only return with the usual power of the flood tide, but with a far greater force and depth, in consequence of having been thus extraordinarily driven out by a N. E. wind. It would seem moreover to be implied in the triumphal song of Moses on this occasion, that on the return of the sea, the wind was also changed, and acted to drive in the flood upon the Egyptians.[2] Even now caravans never cross the ford above

[1] Niebuhr's Reisebeschr. I. p. 251.   [2] Ex. 15, 10; comp. verse 8.
i. 84, 85

Suez; and it is considered dangerous, except at quite low water.[1]

Our own observation on the spot, led both my companion and myself to incline to the other supposition, that the passage took place across shoals adjacent to Suez on the south and south-west. But among the many changes which have occurred here in the lapse of ages, it is of course impossible to decide with certainty as to the precise spot; nor is this necessary. Either of the above suppositions satisfies the conditions of the case; on either the deliverance of the Israelites was equally great, and the arm of Jehovah alike gloriously revealed.

[1] In 1799, Gen. Bonaparte in returning from 'Ayûn Mûsa attempted the ford. It was already late and grew dark; the tide rose, and flowed with greater rapidity than had been expected: so that the General and his suite were exposed to the greatest danger, although they had guides well acquainted with the ground. See Note of Du Bois-Aymé, Descr. de l'Egypte, Antiq Mem. I. p. 127 sq.

i. 86

SECTION III.

FROM SUEZ TO MOUNT SINAI.

Friday, March 16th, 1838.—Having seen all that Suez offers to the notice of the traveller, we were glad to leave it again this day. We took the longer route around the head of the arm or inlet, in order to examine the make of the land; though most persons send only their camels round, and themselves cross at the ferry. Setting off at 1 o'clock P. M. we passed to the left of Tell Kolzum, and taking a course N.½E. reached at 2.35 the mounds of the ancient canal. The ground all the way is a hard gravelly plain, slightly elevated above the water, and sloping gently towards it. The banks of the ancient canal are very distinct, here five or six feet high, and running parallel to each other thirty or forty yards apart, as far as the eye can reach in a northerly direction.[1] The route of the Haj crosses them at a point still further north. We now turned E. S. E. descending to the lower level or bed of the inlet, where the ground soon began to bear every mark of being occasionally overflowed ; the flood tide evidently at some seasons extending far up to the northward. The bottom was fine sand, like the drift sand of the desert, hardened by the action of the water, and covered in some places with a saline efflorescence. Here we silently glided out of Africa into Asia, without knowing the precise line of division. At 3 o'clock, Suez bearing S. 25° W. we again changed our course to S. by E. which we kept for the rest of the day.

In half an hour more we came to low hills of sand and gravel, connected with the desert on our left. Among these hills, tracts of low land of the character just described run up to

[1] See in Note XI, end of the volume.

i. 87, 88

the N. E. and E. for a great distance ; showing that the upper part of this arm once spread itself out into a large bay, in which these hills we·e islands, if they then existed.   One such apparent inlet towards the N. E. was very large and distinctly marked.   We were nowhere able to see the water on our right ; and could not determine how far up it extended at the time ; partly from the lowness of the ground, and partly on account of the *mirage*, which gave to the whole tract in that direction the appearance of a lake.   At 3.55 we left the low lands entirely, and came again upon a gravelly plain ; from which, half an hour after, the town bore due west, about an hour distant.   At ten minutes past 5 o'clock we encamped upon this desert plain, Suez bearing from us N. N. W.

The nature of the tract we had thus passed over, strongly indicates, that the arm of the gulf which now runs up north of Suez, was anciently not much wider at its entrance than at present ; while further north it spread itself out into a broader and deeper bay.   Parallel to the gulf on the east runs the long range of mountains called er-Râhah, which seem to be little more than an ascent to the high plateau of the interior desert.   They are some four or five hours distant from the shore of the gulf ; and the tract between is here a gravelly desert plain, sometimes interrupted by low ridges and hills, running in various directions.

The place where we encamped was about an hour and a half distant from Suez ; and probably it was in this vicinity that the children of Israel came out upon the eastern shore.   Here, at our evening devotions, and near the spot where it was composed and first sung, we read, and felt in its full force, the magnificent triumphal song of Moses : " The Lord hath triumphed gloriously ; the horse and his rider he hath thrown into the sea." We then laid us down in peace and slept ; for the Lord caused us also to dwell here in safety.

Saturday, March 17th.   At 6.20 we were again upon our camels, refreshed and invigorated by the balmy air of the morning.   The weather of yesterday had been fine ; and it continued so through this and many succeeding days.   Our course all day varied between S. by E. and S. S. E. nearly parallel to the coast, but for the most part at some distance from it.   At 7 o'clock we crossed the track leading from the ferry of Suez to the fountain Nâba', or, as it was called by our Arabs, el-Ghŭrkŭdeh, from which that town is supplied with water for drinking.   From this point the fountain was apparently three miles distant.   Some of our Arabs went with a camel for water ; while we kept on our way, sending one of our servants with them to see that the skins were well rinsed.   According to his report, the fountain is a mere excavation in the plain at the foot of a range of sand-hillocks, a basin eight or ten feet in diameter and six or eight feet deep, with stone steps to go down into it. In this basin the water, which is quite brackish, boils up continually and stands two or three feet deep, without any outlet ; furnishing enough to supply two hundred camel-loads at once. About twenty camels were then there, taking loads of water for Suez.

Half an hour afterwards a very gradual ascent lay before us, which terminated at 8 o'clock in a steep descent. From the brow of the latter we had a wide view of the sea and of the low plain before us, in which a few stunted palm trees marked the situation of 'Ayûn Mûsa, the fountains of Moses. On the west of the sea, the barren peaks of 'Atâkah and Deraj rose lofty and dark ; and between them was spread out the broad plain of Wady Tawârik. On our left, further to the south, a single peak in the range of er-Râhah formed a sort of land-mark, which we had already seen from Suez ; it is called Tâset Sŭdr, lying at the head of the Wady of that name. We reached 'Ayûn Mûsa half an hour afterwards. Here I counted seven fountains, several of them mere recent excavations in the sand, in which a little brackish water was standing. Others were older and more abundant ; but the water is dark-coloured and brackish, and deposits a hard substance as it rises ; so that mounds have been formed around these larger springs, on the top of which the water flows out and runs down for a few yards, till it is lost in the sand. We did not remark that the water was warm, as reported by Monconys and others. The Arabs call the northernmost spring sweet ; but we could not perceive that it differed much from the others. One of them has a small rude drain laid with stones, a few paces long, which the French have dignified with the name of a Venetian aqueduct.[1] About twenty stunted untrimmed palm trees, or rather palm bushes, grow round about in the arid sand. A patch of barley, a few rods square, was irrigated from one or two of the more southern fountains. The barley was now in the ear ; and we counted six men busy in frightening away the little birds called *Semmânch ;* thus showing the value attached to the only spot of cultivation in the vicinity of Suez, to which place they belonged. There were also a few cabbage plants. Near the fountains is a low mound of rubbish with fragments of tiles and pottery, and some foundations visible on

---

[1] See Monge in Descr. de l'Egypte, Et. Mod. I. p. 409 sq. Laborde's Map.—M. Monge speaks of this aqueduct as extending down to the sea so as to form a watering-place for ships. We were not at the

time aware of this hypothesis, and did not therefore examine the coast. But there is nothing around the springs which indicates it. See also Marmont's Voyage, Tom. IV. p. 153, Brux. 1837.

i. 89, 90

the top, apparently marking the site of a former village.[1] Râs
'Atâkah bore from here S. 70° W.

Immediately south of these fountains, the path rises over
sand-hills. At 9.35 we crossed Wady er-Reiyâneh running towards the sea; as do all the following Wadys. An hour further
on, a path branched off to the left, towards the mountain at
the head of Wady Sûdr, where the Arabs Terâbin have their
chief encampment. We came to Wady Kûrdhiyeh at 11.35;
not a plain as Burckhardt says;[2] for the Bedawin usually give
names only to the Wadys, and not to the plains between. The
road continues over a gravelly tract of several hours in extent.
At 12¼ o'clock a path went off more to the right, which leads
along the shore to the fountain Abu Suweirah near the mouth
of Wady Wardân, and so to the warm springs of Jebel Hammâm. Soon after 1 o'clock we crossed Wady el-Ahtha coming
down through the plain. All these Wadys are mere depressions in the desert, with only a few scattered herbs and shrubs,
now withered and parched with drought. Along these plains
we first saw scattered rocks of coral formation; which we afterwards found also in the adjacent hills. At 4.10 we encamped
near the middle of Wady Sûdr, a broad tract on a level with
the plain, along which the mountain-torrents sweep down to
the sea. It is covered with drift sand, which accumulates in
mounds around the shrubs and low trees. Here were a few
stunted tamarisk trees, and many herbs and shrubs; so that
our camels found better pasture than heretofore. The peak
Tâset Sûdr bore nearly east, at the head of the Wady.[3]

The former mountain is so called (Cup of Sûdr) from a fountain near it which runs towards Wady Sûdr. Here are the
head-quarters of the Terâbin, who dwell chiefly in the mountains er-Râhah, but visit also the fountain Abu Suweirah, and
claim the whole territory from opposite Suez to Wady Ghüründel. They are poor and few, not numbering in all more than
twenty-five tents or some forty families. These Terâbin are regarded by the Tawarah as strangers here, a colony from the
main tribe of the same name, which occupies the country south
of Gaza, and is very rich in flocks and herds. Their territory
as above described, besides the two fountains just mentioned,
includes also those of Mab'ûk, Nâba' and 'Ayûn Mûsa in the
north; as well as those of Hawârah and Wady Ghüründel in
the south.

With our Tawarah guides, we had every reason to be satis-

---

[1] M. Monge regards this as the former
site of a pottery, where earthen vessels
were manufactured on the spot, in order to
carry away water; Descr. de l'Egypte, l. c.

[2] Travels in Syria, etc. p. 470.

[3] The northernmost peak of Jebel 'Atâkah bore N. 34° W. The northern end of
Jebel Deraj or Kubilah, N. 89° W. Southern end of the same S. 53° W.

fied. They were good natured obliging fellows, ready and desirous to do for us everything we wished, so far as it was in their
power. Beshârah had the command, and took charge of the
arrangements for encamping at night and setting off in the
morning ; but in other respects all seemed to be much on a footing. They walked lightly and gaily by our side ; often out-
stripping the camels for a time, and then as often lagging behind ; and they seldom seemed tired at night. Like all the
Tawarah they wore turbans, and not the *Kefiyeh* of the northern and eastern deserts. Shoes and stockings are luxuries which
neither their poverty nor their habits permit them to indulge
in ; and their sandals were of the rudest and most primitive
kind, made of the thick skin of a species of fish caught in the
Red Sea. Some of the men had old muskets with match-locks ;
the barrels mostly very long and apparently of Turkish or
western manufacture ; while the stocks and locks were ruder,
and evidently made among themselves. Several of our Arabs,
and others whom we saw with camels, carried in their hands a
small stick or staff about three feet long, having a crook at the
top with an oblong head parallel to the staff, and cut in a peculiar form. This is only worth mentioning, as presenting a
remarkable instance of the permanency of oriental customs ;
for this very stick, precisely in the same form, appears in the
hands of figures sculptured on the walls of the Theban temples.[1]

We had paid at Cairo one hundred piastres in advance for
each of our camels, with the express agreement that nothing
more was to be demanded until the end of the journey ; yet on
arriving at Suez, Beshârah came to us in quite a humble mood,
saying that all the money received at Cairo had been paid out
for necessaries and for former debts, and that now they had
nothing wherewith to buy provisions and fodder. To us it was
a matter of indifference, whether we gave them money then or
afterwards, so long as we took care not to advance them their
full pay ; and we therefore yielded to their entreaty in this
respect. It was of course our wish and endeavour in all things
to deal with them kindly, and treat them as men ; and in this
way we won their confidence and received from them kindness
in return. Travellers often complain of the obstinacy of the
Bedawin, and of the impositions attempted by them ; and probably not without reason ; but the fault, I apprehend, most frequently lies on the side of the traveller himself. He cannot
usually converse with his guides except through an interpreter,
who is to them an object of suspicion or contempt ; and the

[1] See Rosellini Monumenti Storici, Plates XLII, CXXI, CXXII, CXXXIV, and
several others.

i. 92. 93

traveller thus becomes himself suspected, and suspects them in turn, until even their most harmless movements are distorted and ascribed to hostile motives. Not unfrequently too, the stranger undertakes to carry his point by threats and violence ; and he may thus succeed for the moment ; but he will find in the end, that instead of friends, he has made enemies ; and he will leave behind no good name, either for himself or for his countrymen who may come after him. Kind words and a timely appeal to their palates and stomachs, are a cheaper and far more efficacious means of carrying a point with the Bedawîn, than hard words and browbeating. Had we adopted the latter course with our guides, I doubt not we should have found them as wilful and obstinate as they have sometimes been represented.

Sunday, March 18th. We remained encamped all day in Wady Sûdr. We had determined, before setting off from Cairo, always to rest on the Christian Sabbath, if possible ; and during all our journeys in the Holy Land, we were never compelled to break over this rule but once. Strange as it may at first seem, these Sabbaths in the desert had a peculiar charm ; and left upon the mind an impression that can never be forgotten.

We had made no agreement with our Arabs on this point ; leaving it to time and circumstances to open the way for such an arrangement. On mentioning to them yesterday our wish to lie by for to-day, they made no objection, and were quite ready to gratify us. The poor fellows set no value on time ; and when a bargain is once made, whether they spend ten days or fifteen upon the way, is a matter of no importance to them. We gave them rice for their dinner, and thus afforded them quite a feast. One of them had sore eyes ; and we were glad for his sake and our own, that we had brought with us a supply of eye-water.

About noon three men on camels came up and stopped near us for the rest of the day and night. One was a young monk, a sort of noviciate in the convent of Mount Sinai ; another a Greek priest from Philippopolis ; and the third a Wallachian pilgrim ; all on their way to the convent. They kept near us during several of the following days.

Monday, March 19th. We rose early and set off with the rising sun ; which, throwing its mellow beams across the gulf, gave us a distinct view of the dark face of 'Atâkah, and of the more southern Kulâlah (as our Arabs called it) with its long ridge, and of the broad Wady Tawârik between these two mountains. Keeping on our way over the same great plain, we reached at 9¼ o'clock the north side of Wady Wardân, a broad strip like Wady Sûdr, marked by torrent-beds and drifts of sand. In it towards the sea-shore is the fountain Abu Suweirah, which usually affords a small quantity of sweet water ; but dries up when the rains fail for a season. Here was the scene of an interesting story of Arab warfare, related by Burckhardt.[1] The mountains on the east still bore the general name er-Râhah; but different parts were now named after the Wadys which descend from them; as Tâset Sŭdr, Jebel Wardân, and the like. Near the head of Wady Wardân, a range of hills comes off from these mountains in a S. W. direction; while near the mouth of the same Wady a low chain of sand-hills begins on the right, and runs towards the S. E. These unite about four hours from Wady Wardân, and terminate the great plain. At 12 o'clock we entered among the hills, the road winding for a time under the eastern side of two high hills or banks of sand and pebbles; and after twenty-five minutes crossed a ridge where we had the first view of Jebel Hammâm, bearing south. The way continued among hills of limestone formation, all equally destitute of vegetation, and some of them exhibiting an abundance of crystallized sulphate of lime. Twenty minutes further brought us to the small Wady el-'Amârah, having in it a few scattered shrubs. At 2½ o'clock we passed a large square rock lying near the foot of the hill on our right. It is called Hajr er-Rukkâb, "Stone of the Riders," and is mentioned by Niebuhr. Fifteen minutes beyond this, we came to the fountain Hawârah, lying to the left of the road on a large mound, composed of a whitish rocky substance formed apparently by the deposites of the fountain during the lapse of ages. No stream was now flowing from it; though there are traces of running water round about. The basin is six or eight feet in diameter, and the water about two feet deep. Its taste is unpleasant, saltish, and somewhat bitter; but we could not perceive that it was very much worse than that of 'Ayûn Mûsa; perhaps because we were not yet connoisseurs in bad water. The Arabs however pronounce it bitter, and consider it as the worst water in all these regions. Yet when pinched they drink of it; and our camels also drank freely. Near by the spring were two stunted palm trees; and round about it many bushes of the shrub Ghŭrkŭd, now in blossom.[2] This is a low bushy thorny shrub, producing a small fruit which ripens in June, not unlike the barberry, very juicy and slightly acidulous. The Ghŭrkŭd seems to delight in a saline soil; for we found it growing around all the brackish fountains which we afterwards fell in with, during our journeys in and around Palestine. In the midst of parched deserts, as in the Ghôr south of the Dead Sea, where the heat

---

[1] Page 471. I shall recur to the same story further on, in speaking of the character of the Tawarah.
[2] *Peganum retusum*, Forsk. Flora. Æg. i. 96. 97

Arab. p. LXVI. More correctly *Nitraria tridentata* of Desfontaines; Flora Atlant. I. 372. Comp. Gesenius' Note on Burckhardt, p. 1082.

was intense and the fountains briny, the red berries of this plant often afforded us a grateful refreshment.

The fountain of Hawârah is first distinctly mentioned by Burckhardt. Pococke perhaps saw it; though his language is quite indefinite.[1] Niebuhr passed this way; but his guides did not point it out to him; probably because the Arabs make no account of it as a watering-place. Since Burckhardt's day it has generally been regarded as the bitter fountain Marah, which the Israelites reached after three days' march without water in the desert of Shur.[2] The position of the spring and the nature of the country tally very exactly with this supposition. After having passed the Red Sea, the Israelites would naturally supply themselves from the fountains of Nâba' and 'Ayûn Mûsa; and from the latter to Hawârah is a distance of about sixteen and a half hours, or thirty-three geographical miles; which, as we have seen above, was for them a good three days' journey. On the route itself there is no water; but near the sea is now the small fountain Abu Suweirah, which may then have been dry or not have existed; and in the mountains on the left is the "Cup of Sûdr," several hours from the road and probably unknown to the Israelites. I see therefore no valid objection to the above hypothesis. The fountain lies at the specified distance, and on their direct route; for there is no probability that they passed by the lower and longer road along the sea-shore. We made particular inquiries, to ascertain whether the name Marah still exists, as reported by Shaw[3] and others; but neither the Tawarah Arabs, nor the inhabitants of Suez, nor the monks of the convent, so far as we could learn, had ever heard of it. Travellers have probably been led into error by the name of Wady el-'Amârah; or possibly by el-Mûrkhâh, a fountain nearly two days' journey further south, on the lower route to Mount Sinai and Tûr.

Burckhardt suggests that the Israelites may have rendered the water of Marah palatable, by mingling with it the juice of the berries of the Ghûrkûd.[4] The process would be a very simple one, and doubtless effectual; and the presence of this shrub around all brackish fountains, would cause the remedy to be always at hand. But as the Israelites broke up from Egypt on the morrow of Easter, and reached Marah apparently not more than two or three weeks later, the season for these berries would hardly have arrived. We made frequent and diligent inquiries, whether any process is now known among the Bedawin for thus sweetening bad water, either by means of the juice of

[1] Travels, I. p. 139. fol.
[2] Ex. 15, 23 sq. Num. 33, 8.
[3] Travels, 4to. p. 314.
[4] Travels in Syria, p. 474.

berries, or the bark or leaves of any tree or plant ; but we were invariably answered in the negative.[1]

Proceeding on our way, in half an hour we had on our left a small plain or basin, called Nukeia' el-Fûl, in which water stands after abundant rains, causing a soil of rich loam, which produces a luxuriant vegetation. This was testified by the large stalks of an abundance of weeds now dry. On some portions of it the Terâbîn sow wheat and barley after the rains, and reap a good crop. It was the only spot of soil known to our Arabs in these parts. A few goats were feeding upon the herbs on the hills around, watched by females. From them we obtained a supply of milk, for which we paid in bread instead of money, as being far more acceptable. These were the first flocks we had seen since leaving Cairo ; and we afterwards saw the few tents of the owners, Terâbîn Arabs, pitched near the head of Wady Ghûrûndel. We reached this latter Wady at 4¼ o'clock ; it comes down as a broad valley from the mountains on the left, and runs from N. E. to S. W. to the sea south of Râs Hammâm. The mountain at its head is called Râs Wâdy Ghûrûndel, a continuation of the chain er-Râhah, which here bends off towards the S. E. and E. where it afterwards receives the name et-Tîh, and extends across the peninsula to the gulf of 'Akabah. Thus far our course all day had been about S. S. E., but we now turned down the Wady S. W. and encamped after half an hour in a deep and narrow part of its bed.

Wady Ghûrûndel is deeper and better supplied with bushes and shrubs than any we had yet seen ; and like Sûdr and Wardân it bore marks of having had water running in it the present year. The Ghûrkûd is very frequent. Straggling trees of various kinds are found in it ; the most common of which is the Tûrfa, a species of tamarisk, *Tamarix Gallica mannifera* of Ehrenberg, on which our camels browsed freely ; and also mimosas or acacias, called by the Arabs Tûlh and Seyâl. A few small palm trees are scattered through the valley. We saw many of the wood-ticks mentioned by Burckhardt ; but they did not trouble us. About half an hour below our encampment, the Arabs procured water, as they said, from fountains with a running brook. It was brackish, and of the same general character as that of all the preceding fountains, though less disagreeable than that of Hawârah. We kept it over night in our leather-bottles, and it did not change its taste ; though the Arabs said it would grow worse, as Burckhardt also testifies.

---

[1] It is perhaps hardly necessary to remark, that the Hebrew original, like the English version, has here only the general word for " tree ; " and therefore all spec-
i. 98 99

ulations as to the name of any particular plant can only rest on air. See Lord Lindsay's Letters, 1st edit. I. p. 263 sq.

When the rains fail for two or three years, the brook ceases to flow ; but water is always to be found by digging a little below the surface.

This Wady is now commonly regarded as the Elim of Scripture, to which the Israelites came after leaving Marah, and found twelve wells of water and seventy palm trees.[1] There is nothing improbable in this supposition, if we admit 'Ain Hawârah to be Marah. The fountains of Wady Ghûrûndel are two and a half hours, or nearly half a day's journey for the Israelites, distant from Hawârah ; and are still one of the chief watering places of the Arabs. The main objection which might here be urged, is the distance from this point to the next station, where the Israelites " encamped by the Red Sea ; "[2] a fixed and definite point, as we shall see in the sequel. But this objection may perhaps be evaded.

Beyond Wady Ghûrûndel the mountains, or at least a more mountainous tract, may be said to commence. On the right along the coast in the S. W. is the high mountain called Jebel Hammâm, from the hot sulphur springs at its northern end. On the left the continuation of er-Râhah appears, with several spurs running down from it S. W. along the south side of Ghûrûndel and extending almost to Jebel Hammâm. The whole region is of limestone formation. Wady Ghûrûndel does not extend up through the mountains on the left towards Gaza, as was reported to Burckhardt ; but near its head another valley, called Wady Wûtâh, comes into it from the east ; where the latter runs up between the Tih on the N. E. and a mountain ridge in front of it, called also Wûtâh. Here is quite a retired valley hemmed in by mountains, from the head of which a pass leads over to the plain er-Ramleh ; the whole forming a shorter but more difficult route from Ghûrûndel to Mount Sinai.

Tuesday, March 20th. Niebuhr travelled down Wady Ghûrûndel to the sea, about two and a half hours from our encampment ; and then an hour and a half along the shore of the bay called Birket Hammâm Far'ôn to the hot springs ; which he and many travellers have described.[3] Thence the way passes

---

[1] Ex. 15, 27. Num. 33, 9. We found nowhere any trace of a valley called 'Alun or Ghulim, as reported by Gesenius on the authority of Ehrenberg ; see Gesenius Lex. Hebr. Man. art. אֵילִם

[2] Num. 33, 10.

[3] The following account of these springs is by Russegger, who passed this way a few months after us : "These hot sulphur springs break out from the strata of lower chalk, nearly on a level with the sea, at the foot of the mountain. The largest of them has a temperature of 55° 7 Reaum. that of the air being 26° 3 Reaum. The water deposites a great deal of common salt mixed with sulphur ; and the latter is also found sublimated on the walls of the many caverns connected with the fountains and penetrated by their hot vapours." See Berghaus' Annalen der Erdk. März 1839, p. 422. Leonhard's Jahrbuch für Mineralogie, 1839, p. 174.

up Wady Useit. But the direct road from our encampment in Ghŭrŭndel leads over the high ground between that Wady and Useit. We took this course ; and mounting our camels at 6.10 soon turned out of Wady Ghŭrŭndel by a sort of gully, and began to ascend the low ridge before us. On our right was Jebel Hammâm, extending along the coast towards the south, black, desolate, and picturesque. At 6¾ o'clock we came out upon the higher tract or plain ; and soon had a view of Jebel Serbâl, which, as here seen in the direction of its ridge, appeared like a lofty rounded peak, bearing S. E. by S. Twenty minutes further on was a heap of stones called Hŭsân Abu Zenneh, upon which one of our Arabs kicked a quantity of dirt, crying out, as he said was their custom, " Feed the horse of Abu Zenneh." It marked the place where a horse once died, owned by a person of that name. After another fifteen minutes, we passed the small Wady Um Suweilih, where a branch of the lower road came in from Abu Suweirah. Here was a single acacia or Tŭlh tree. At 7.55 we struck a small branch Wady, and followed it down for half an hour to Wady Useit or Wuseit. This valley resembles Ghŭrŭndel, though not so large ; and has a few small palm trees and a little brackish water standing in holes. The ground in many parts is covered with a white crust apparently nitrous. This Wady runs from E. S. E. to W. N. W., and passing along the northern end of Jebel Hammâm reaches the sea at the bay Hammâm Far'ôn. Here the main branch of the lower road by Abu Suweirah and the hot springs, comes into ours.

Thus far our course was about S. E. ; but now turning S. E. by S. we crossed a plain of some extent which takes its name from the small Wady el-Kuweiseh, which we reached at 10 o'clock. On the plain our Arabs pointed out the recent tracks of a hyæna. As we passed on, we had on the right Jebel Hammâm ; and on the left other smaller ridges, spurs running out from et-Tîh. The former mountain is lofty and precipitous, extending in several peaks along the shore ; consisting apparently of chalky limestone mostly covered with flints, which give to the whole mountain a dark aspect, except where the chalk is seen. Its precipices extend quite down to the sea, and cut off all passage along the shore from the hot springs to the mouth of Wady et-Taiyibeh, except a foot-path for men high up on the mountain. This circumstance renders it certain, that the Israelites must of necessity have passed inside of this mountain by the road we were now following, to the head of Wady Taiyibeh ; for no other road exists, or can exist, in this direction.

Wady Thâl or Athâl followed at 10¾ o'clock ; running from east to west with shrubs and acacias and a few palm trees ; and
i. 101. 102

also some holes with brackish water, like Wady Useit; the
ground being likewise covered with a nitrous crust.   The mountain at the head of this valley takes the name of Râs Wâdy
Thâl; and is strictly not a part of Jebel et-Tih, being divided
from it by the Wady Wûtâh above mentioned.   Wady Thâl
finds its way down through Jebel Hammâm to the sea by a deep
and narrow ravine; but on the south of it there is still no road
along the shore.   Proceeding now on a course nearly south, and
passing round the end of a spur running out S. E. from Jebel
Hammâm, we came after a few rods to a small heap of stones under a bank by the roadside, with a few rags scattered around,
which the Arabs regard as the tomb of a female saint, 'Oreis
Themmân, or Bride of Themmân.   Burckhardt says, the Arabs
are in the habit of saying a short prayer here; but ours did not.
Crossing a low hill we came at 11¾ o'clock to Wady Shubeikeh,
running here nearly south, the bed of which we followed.   This
valley has several branches, which unite further down; and from
this junction of the many, comes the name Shubeikeh, "net."
While passing down this Wady, our sharp-eyed Arabs discovered
two gazelles upon the high ridge on the right; and it was
amusing to see with what eagerness both old and young immediately set off in pursuit.   They always try to approach the game
by a circuit on the side opposite the wind; and having only guns
with match-locks they must get within shot without disturbing
the animal.   This time they came back unsuccessful.   The
beautiful animals had seen them before they started, and bounding gracefully over the hills, had not suffered them to come near.
But it made quite an incident in the usual monotony of the way.
Here too, as in very many other instances, we could not but be
struck with the likeness which the Bedawin bear to the American Indians in many of their habits; especially in the unerring
sagacity with which they trace and recognise the shadowy footsteps of persons, and even of camels, upon the surface of the
deserts.

Passing the junction of the several branches of Wady Shubeikeh, we soon came, at 12¼ o'clock, to an open place, where
Wady Humr comes down from the E. S. E., and joining the
Shubeikeh, the two then form Wady et-Taiyibeh, which passes
down S. W. through the mountains to the sea shore, two hours
distant from this spot.[1]   Here the two roads to Mount Sinai
separate; the upper and shorter one, which we took, turning to
the left up Wady Humr; while the lower and easier one goes
down Wady Taiyibeh to the sea.   This latter Wady is described
as a fine valley inclosed by abrupt rocks, with many trees, and a

---

[1] Burckhardt, p. 625. Lepsius calls it also Wady Shubeikeh; Briefe aus Aeg. p. 349.

little brackish water like the preceding Wadys. Where it
reaches the sea there is a high promontory on the north; while
on the south the mountains retire, leaving a sandy plain with
many shrubs, extending southwards for an hour and a half along
the shore. Then the mountains come down again to the sea for
about the same distance, admitting a passage around them only
at low water, while at other times travellers must cross over
them; as was the case when Burckhardt passed. Beyond the
mountains, towards the south, a large plain opens along the
shore, in which at an hour's distance is the bitter fountain el-
Mŭrkhâh. Burckhardt describes it as a small pond in the sandstone rock, near the foot of the mountains which skirt the plain
on the east. The taste of the water is bad; owing partly to the
weeds, moss, and dirt, with which the pond is filled; but chiefly,
no doubt, to the saline nature of the soil around it. Our Arabs
however said it was better than the water of Hawârah. Next to
Ghŭrŭndel, it is the principal watering place of the Arabs on
this road. Burckhardt also mentions a reservoir of rain water in
Wady edh-Dhafary, half an hour S. E. by S. from el-Mŭrkhâh.
An hour or more south of this latter fountain (el-Mŭrkhâh), the
road to Sinai separates from that to Tûr; the latter keeping
along the coast; while the former enters the mountains through
Wady Shellâl, and so continues through Wady Mukatteb to
Wady Feirân, where there is water and also cultivation.[1]

It has been already remarked, that the Israelites must have
passed from Ghŭrŭndel inside of Jebel Hammâm to the head of
Wady et-Taiyibeh; and it must also have been on the plain at
the mouth of this valley, that they again encamped by the Red
Sea.[2] The nature of the country shows conclusively, that if
they passed through this region at all, they must necessarily
have taken this course, and had their encampment at this place.
From Ghŭrŭndel to the head of Taiyibeh we found the distance
to be six hours, making eight hours or sixteen geographical miles
to its mouth; a long day's journey for such a multitude. This
is the objection which might be urged against the identity of
Ghŭrŭndel and Elim; and might lead us to place Elim perhaps
in Wady Useit. Still, as Ghŭrŭndel is one of the most noted
Arab watering places, and the Israelites very probably would
have rested there several days; it would not be difficult for them
for once to make a longer march and thus reach the plain near
the sea. Besides, in a host like that of the Israelites, consisting of more than two millions of people, with many flocks, it can
hardly be supposed that they all marched in one body. More
probably the stations as enumerated refer rather to the head-

[1] See in general Burckhardt's Travels in   [2] Num. 33, 10.
Syria, etc. p. 623 sq.
    i. 104, 105

quarters of Moses and the elders, with a portion of the people
who kept near them ; while other portions preceded or followed
them at various distances, as the convenience of water and
pasturage might dictate.   Water, such as it is, they would find
in small quantities throughout this tract ; and they probably
continued to practise the method of sweetening it which they
had been taught at Marah ; for we hear no more complaint of
bad water.   But how they could have obtained a *sufficiency* of
water during their whole stay in the peninsula and their subsequent wanderings in the desert, even where no want of water is
mentioned, is a mystery which I am unable to solve ; unless we
admit the supposition, that water was anciently far more abundant in these regions, than at present.   As we saw the peninsula,
a body of two millions of men could not subsist there a week,
without drawing their supplies of water, as well as of provisions,
from a great distance.

From their encampment at the mouth of Wady et-Taiyibeh,
the Israelites would necessarily advance into the great plain,
which, beginning near el-Mûrkhâh, extends with a greater or
less breadth almost to the extremity of the peninsula.   In its
broadest part, northward of Tûr, it is called el-Kâ'a.   This
desert plain, to which they would thus necessarily come, I take
to be the desert of Sin, the next station mentioned in Scripture.[1]
From this plain they could enter the mountains at various points,
either by the present nearer route through the Wadys Shellâl
and Mukatteb, or perhaps by the mouth of Wady Feirân itself.
Their approach to Sinai was probably along the upper part of
this latter valley and Wady esh-Sheikh ; but the two subsequent
stations, Dophkah and Alush, are mentioned so indefinitely, that
no hope remains of their ever being identified.[2]   The same is
perhaps true of Rephidim, to which we shall recur again in the
sequel.

We were for a time quite at a loss, which of the roads to
take from the head of Wady et-Taiyibeh to Sinai.   We wished
much to see the celebrated inscriptions in Wady Mukatteb on
the lower road ; and we wished just as much to visit the mysterious monuments of Sûrâbit el-Khâdim near the upper one.
As we knew, however, that similar inscriptions existed along this
latter route, though not in such multitudes, we decided to take
it ; and turning into Wady Humr at a quarter past noon, we
proceeded up that valley on a course E. S. E.[3]   The mountains

[1] Ex. 16, 1. Num. 33, 11.
[2] Num. 33, 12. 13.
[3] Burckhardt gives the name of Taiyibeh to our Wady Shubeikeh ; and that of
Shubeikeh to the lower part of Wady

Humr.   We had his book with us, and
were aware of this difference on the spot ;
but all our guides knew no other application of these names than that given in the
text.   I would not fail, however, here and

around the head of Wady et-Taiyibeh, where we now were, abound in salt ; and our Arabs brought us several pieces of it, beautifully white. Wady Humr is broad, with precipitous sides of limestone, from one hundred to one hundred and fifty feet high. We here found the heat very oppressive, occasioned by the reflection of the sun from the chalky cliffs ; although the thermometer in the shade rose only to 80° F. Water had evidently been running here not long before ; and the herbs and shrubs were fresher than usual.

After two hours the valley opens out into a wide plain ; another broad Wady called Ibn Sŭkr comes in obliquely from the east ; while almost in front rises the high dark pyramidal peak of Sarbût el-Jemel, which had been in sight occasionally ever since we left Wady Ghŭrŭndel. This mountain is of limestone and is connected by low ridges with et-Tih, or rather with Jebel Wŭtâh, which runs in front of et-Tih and parallel to it. A ridge also apparently runs off from Sarbût el-Jemel towards the S. W. and bounds the plain in that quarter. We struck across the plain towards the S. E. corner of the pyramidal mountain, which rose naked and desolate before us, seeming to cut off all further progress. Indeed it was not till we arrived almost at its foot, that we perceived the opening of a Wady coming down through the ridge, which we entered and turned the S. E. point of the mountain at 3.25. We now proceeded up through this mountain gorge, with lofty walls of rock two or three hundred feet high on each side, still bearing the name of Wady Humr. The southern mountain is called Um ez-Zuweibin, from a heap of stones in the road. Here we first entered the sandstone region ; the wall upon our right being of that material ; while that on the left was still apparently chiefly limestone. After about an hour we came (at 4½ o'clock) to a sharp turn at right angles in the valley, which then turns short again and passes on in the same direction as before. At the last of these corners, on the right, we found several rude drawings on the rocks, and also some of the famous Sinaite inscriptions, like those of Wady Mukatteb. One large block, which had fallen from the cliff above, was covered with them, mostly short, and beginning with the usual initial letters, like those copied by Burckhardt and others. On another smaller stone are rude drawings of camels or horses ; for it was hard to tell which. One rider is armed with a spear, and before him stands a man with sword and shield. Is the former perhaps a knight? On one stone were two crosses ; but in this instance they were

elsewhere, to bear testimony to the extreme general accuracy of this lamented traveller, in his topographical details and descriptions. His orthography of Arabic names is not always so exact ; yet it is all we have hitherto had.

i. 107, 108

evidently later than the neighbouring inscriptions. The spot is one where travellers would be likely to rest during the heat of the midday sun. Burckhardt mentions the drawings, but not the inscriptions.[1]

A little beyond this place our Arabs expected to find rain water among the rocks ; and scattered themselves, running off into the different openings of the mountains, to seek for it. They were not very successful, finding but little, and that strongly impregnated with camel's dung. Yet our Arabs seemed to drink it with gusto. We now found ourselves in fact straitened for water. What we had brought from the spring Nâba' near Suez, had become much worse than at first ; and since then we had met with none fit to fill the empty water-skins. We had got tolerably accustomed to a *leathery* taste in the water we carried ; but had not yet learned to relish that which was briny and bitter, or which smacked of camel's dung. This however was the only time we were thus straitened ; nor did we now suffer much inconvenience. We encamped at 5.10 in Wady Humr, after a long day's march of eleven hours, near the place where the high rocks on either side terminate. The valley has several trees and many shrubs, so that the camels found good pasturage. The only trees throughout this region are the Tŭrfa, properly a tamarisk, with long narrow leaves and without thorns, the same on which the manna (Arabic *Monn*) is elsewhere found ; and the *Tŭlh* or *Seyâl*, said by the Arabs to be identical, a species of very thorny acacia, producing a little gum arabic of an inferior quality.[2] This the Arabs sometimes gather and sell, when not too lazy. But all these trees are here small and stunted, for the want both of soil and of water.

Wednesday, March 21st. We set off at 6.20, still following up Wady Humr, E. S. E. The rocks on our right became lower ; while on our left the high mountain Jebel Wŭtâh rose almost from the bank of the Wady. This is strictly a spur of Jebel et-Tih, connected with it at the eastern end, and thence running westward parallel with it, having the retired Wady Wŭtâh between. In less than an hour, the rocks ceased on the right ; and at 7.15 a road turned off on that side to Wady en-Nŭsb, across an uneven sandy plain called Debbet en-Nŭsb. This road is often taken by the Arabs and by travellers on account of the fine spring of water in that valley ; but it is longer, and returns after some hours into the direct road. One or two of our men with a camel were sent round by this route, in order to fill the water-skins ; and they brought us a load of better water

---

[1] Page 476.
[2] This tree is the *Mimosa Sejal* of Forskal; Flora Æg. Arab. p. 177. By later
botanists it is known as *Acacia gummifera*, and is called by Abdallatif *Tŭlh;* Sprengel Hist. Rei Herbar. I. p. 270.
ii. 109, 110

than we had found since leaving the Nile. Wady Humr now
spreads out into a broad plain sprinkled over with herbs, extending round the east end of Jebel Wŭtâh quite to et-Tih. At 8
o'clock the valley became narrower between sand-hills for half an
hour; but then opened again as before. At 9 o'clock we reached
the head of the Wady or plain, whence we ascended for twenty
minutes a rocky slope covered with sand.

From this spot we had a wide view over the surrounding
country. On our left was the Tih, a long, lofty, level, unbroken
ridge, the continuation of er-Râhah, stretching off eastward as
far as the eye could reach, apparently of limestone. On our
right and before us, along the foot of the Tih, lay an uneven
sandy plain, several miles in breadth, full of low broken ridges
and water-courses. This sandy plain extends, as we afterwards
found, through the whole interior of the peninsula, almost to the
eastern coast. It lies between the Tih and the proper mountains of the peninsula, which rose on our right in fantastic shapes
and wild confusion. Those adjacent to the plain are of sandstone, cut up by deep valleys and ravines, into which the shallow
Wadys which descend from the Tih across the plain, enter and
find their way down to the sea. Further south is a belt of
grünstein and porphyry ; and then the centre of the peninsula
is occupied by large masses of granite, constituting the proper
mountains of Sinai itself. We could here see the pass leading
over between et-Tih and Jebel Wŭtâh into Wady Wŭtâh, and
so down to Wady Ghŭrŭndel. It bore from us N. 20° W.
In the long ridge of the Tih itself, which our Arabs said takes
this general name from the high desert on its northern side, they
pointed out two passes, through which caravan roads lead from
Sinai to Gaza and Hebron. The westernmost (still some hours
east of where we stood) is called er-Râkineh, and the other el-
Mureikhy. Between them is a third, called el-Wŭrsah, used
only by the Arabs, being too steep and difficult for loaded caravans. From it a Wady of the same name descends southwards
across the plain to Wady Nŭsb, and is probably the Warsân
mentioned by Niebuhr.[1] Still further east, Jebel et-Tih divides
into two ridges, which then run nearly parallel, at the distance
of several hours from each other, to the gulf of 'Akabah. So far
as we could learn, the southern branch is at first called edh-
Dhŭlŭl, and the northern one in its western part, el-'Ŏjmeh.
A road leads from Sinai by a pass over the southern ridge to the
head of Wady ez-Zŭlakah and 'Ain ;[2] and thence by another
pass over the northern ridge to Gaza and Hebron.

[1] Reisebeschr. I. p. 231.
[2] This pass is mentioned by Laborde,
who asserts it to be the *only* pass or road
i. 110, 111

leading over et-Tih. Voyage en Arab.
Petr. p. 63. Engl. ed. p. 226. Sir F.
Henniker passed by way of er-Râkineh;

Proceeding over this plain in a direction E. S. E. before coming upon the sand we crossed several shallow Wadys, studded with shrubs, all flowing towards Wady Nŭsb. One of them, at 10 o'clock, was called Wady Beda'. Beyond this, on the right, are three springs of brackish water, called el-Mâlih. Crossing a low ridge at 10.45, we got our first view of the granite peaks around Sinai, still indistinct and nameless ; bearing S. S. E. while Serbâl at the same time bore S. by E. Here we came upon the great sandy tract, which we had seen before, called by the Arabs Debbet er-Ramleh, and also, according to Burckhardt, Raml el-Mûrâk, extending eastward further than the eye could reach. Among the sandstone mountains on our right, the site of Sûrâbit el-Khâdim had already been pointed out to us ; and at 11¼ o'clock we turned off to the right on a course nearly south to visit it ; leaving our servants and loaded animals to follow the direct road to the head of Wady el-Khŭmileh, and encamp a short distance within that valley.

In about half an hour we descended into a broad sandy valley, called Seih en-Nŭsb, which runs S. W. along the mountains and enters them obliquely, having several branches coming in also from the east and S. E. In one of these we crossed about noon the other road, coming up from the fountain in Wady Nŭsb, of which the Seih is the principal head. This path passes on eastward up a sandy hill called el-Mûrâk, and joins the direct road still upon the plain. Our way led across the same hill of sand, but further to the right ; and we found the ascent very toilsome from the depth and looseness of the sand ; there being no trace of a path. Descending again we reached a broad sandy valley, called Wady Sûwuk, running from S. E. to N. W. within the skirts of the mountains into Wady Nŭsb. On the further side of this valley we left our camels at half past 1 o'clock, and crossing on foot a ridge of deep sand towards the west into a rocky ravine, we began the difficult ascent of the mountain at its S. E. end.

The mountain may be some six or seven hundred feet high ; and is composed entirely of precipitous sandstone rock, mostly red, but alternating occasionally with strata of different shades. A track leads up the toilsome and somewhat dangerous ascent, along the face of the precipice at the head of the ravine, marked only by small heaps of stones. Climbing slowly and with difficulty to the top, we found ourselves at the end of three quarters of an hour upon a level ridge, connected with a tract of high table land of sandstone formation, much resembling the Saxon Switzerland, and like it intersected in every direction by deep

as also Breydenbach and Fabri in 1484.—   given in Note XXIV, at the end of the
A special Itinerary of all these routes is   volume.

precipitous ravines ; while higher peaks of irregular and fantastic form lay all around us. A short distance westward, on this ridge, with a deep chasm upon either side, are situated the singular and mysterious monuments of Sûrâbit el-Khâdim.

These lie mostly within the compass of a small enclosure, one hundred and sixty feet long from east to west by seventy feet broad, marked by heaps of stones thrown or fallen together, the remains perhaps of former walls or rows of low buildings. Within this space are seen about fifteen upright stones, like tombstones, and several fallen ones, covered with Egyptian hieroglyphics ; and also the remains of a small temple, whose columns are decorated with the head of Isis for a capital. At the eastern end is a subterranean chamber excavated in the solid rock, resembling an Egyptian sepulchre. It is square ; and the roof is supported in the middle by a square column left from the rock. Both the column and the sides of the chamber are covered with hieroglyphics ; and in each of the sides is a small niche. The whole surface of the enclosure is covered with fallen columns, fragments of sculpture, and hewn stones strewn in every direction ; over which the pilgrim can with difficulty find his way. Other similar upright stones stand without the enclosure in various directions, and even at some distance ; each surrounded by a heap of stones, which may have been thrown together by the Arabs. These upright stones both within and without the enclosure, vary from about seven to ten feet in height ; while they are from eighteen inches to two feet in breadth, and from fourteen to sixteen inches in thickness. They are rounded off on the top, forming an arc over the broadest sides. On one of these sides usually appears the common Egyptian symbol of the winged globe with two serpents, and one or more priests presenting offerings to the gods ; while various figures and cartouches cover the remaining sides. They are said to bear the names of different Egyptian kings ; but no two of them to have the name of the same monarch. According to Major Felix, the name of Osir-tisen I. is found on one of them, whom Wilkinson supposes to have been the patron of Joseph. Not the least singularity about these monuments is the wonderful preservation of the inscriptions upon this soft sandstone, exposed as they have been to the air and weather during the lapse of so many ages. On some of the stones they are quite perfect ; on others both the inscription and the stone itself have been worn away deeply by the tooth of time.

This spot was first discovered by Niebuhr in 1761, who, inquiring for the inscriptions of Wady el-Mukatteb, was brought by his guides to this place as one of still greater interest and wonder ; or rather, as it would seem, from ignorance on their

i. 113-115

part of the real object of his inquiries.[1] The next Frank visiter appears to have been the French traveller Boutin in 1811, who was afterwards murdered in Syria ; and he was followed by Rüppell in 1817.[2] Many other travellers have since been here on their way to Sinai. So Lord Prudhoe and Major Felix ; and after them Laborde and Linant, who have given drawings and views of the place and several of the monuments.[3] All these travellers, with the exception of the two Englishmen, have pronounced this to be an ancient Egyptian cemetery, and these monuments to be tombstones, connected with a supposed colony near the copper mines in Wady en-Nūsb. That these upright stones resemble the tombstones of the west in form, is true ; and this would seem to be the chief circumstance which has given rise to the hypothesis. There is nothing of the kind in Egypt ; nor can they well be sepulchral monuments, unless excavated tombs exist beneath them ; which there is every reason to believe is not the case. What then could have been the intent of these temples and these memorial stones in the midst of solitude and silence ? in this lone and distant desert, with which they would seem to have no possible connection ? This is a point wrapped in the darkness of time, which the hand of modern science has not yet unveiled.

An ingenious hypothesis was mentioned to me by the English nobleman named above, viz. that this was perhaps a sacred place of pilgrimage for the ancient Egyptians, just as the mountain near Mecca is to the Muhammedans at the present day ; and to it the Egyptian kings made each his pilgrimage and erected a column with his name. A slight historical ground for such an hypothesis, may perhaps be found in the fact, that Moses demanded permission for the Israelites to go three days' journey into the desert in order to sacrifice ;[4] a demand which seems to have caused no surprise to the Egyptians, as if it were something to which they were themselves accustomed. Still all this can claim to be nothing more than conjecture. Yet this lone spot, although inexplicable, is deeply interesting ; it leads the beholder back into the gray mists of high antiquity ; and fills him with wonder and awe as he surveys here, far from the abodes of life, the labours of men unknown for an object alike unknown.[5]

From the high tract about Surábit el-Khádim, there is a

[1] Reisebeschr. I. p. 285.

[2] Burckhardt's Travels in Syria, etc. p. 573. Rüppell's Reisen in Nubien, etc. p. 267.

[3] The most exact description is by Rüppell, as cited in the preceding note.

[4] Ex. 8, 27. 28. [23. 24. Heb.] The object of this journey was to be a 'festival' (חג), corresponding to the modern *Haj* of the Muhammedans. Ex. 10, 9.

[5] Lepsius, who visited the spot in 1845, regards these monuments as having been erected in connection with the working of copper mines; Br. aus Aeg. p. 337 sq. See i. 115, 116

wide view of the surrounding country.[1] We saw no traces of mines around the place, as mentioned by Laborde; but our Arabs said that towards the west in Wady Sûhau, a branch of Wady en-Nûsb, was found the stone from which *el-Kuhal* is made and carried to market. We suppose this to be antimony; though we saw none of it.[2]

After spending an hour and a quarter among these monuments, we descended again by the same rugged path, and returned to our camels in Wady Sûwuk. From this point to the fountain of Nûsb is a distance of about two and a half hours; and the Wady Nûsb, having collected its numerous branches, then finds its way through the mountains to the western gulf, or rather to the great plain along the coast. In the valley a flock of sheep and goats were feeding, tended by two young girls, whose tents were not far off. The owner of the flock soon made his appearance; and after some chaffering we bought a kid, intending to give our Arabs a good supper. Mounting at 4¾ o'clock, we proceeded S. E. up Wady Sûwuk to its head. One of the Arabs led the kid by a string, and as the poor animal trotted nimbly by their side, they were elated at the thought of the savoury meat in prospect. As we passed along the valley, our sharp-sighted guides discovered a *Beden* or mountain goat (related to the Steinbock of the Alps) among the rocks on our left. One of them immediately started in pursuit; but as he could approach only on the windward side, the goat scented him, and dashed lightly along the side and up the face of the precipice, presenting a graceful object against the sky with his long recurved horns and bounding leaps. The Arab began to mount after him with great agility, but was called back by his companions. At the head of the valley is a steep and rugged pass, which our camels mounted with difficulty; and here we saw the first strata of grünstein. On reaching the top, we found ourselves upon the western ridge of Wady el-Khůmileh, a broad sandy tract, thus far a mere arm of the great plain extending towards the S. E. into the mountains. Our tent stood below in the valley; and passing down by a gradual descent, we reached it at three quarters past 5 o'clock. The Greek priests who had kept near us since Sunday, had passed on some distance beyond; and we saw them no more until we reached the convent.

The poor kid was now let loose, and ran bleating into our

---

also Wilkinson's Mod. Egypt, II. p. 405. Handb. for Egypt, p. 216.

[1] The pass of Wütah bore N. 30° W.; er-Râkineh N. 20° E.; Mount Serbâl S. 16° E., and Mudhu'in, a peak in the cluster of Sinai, S. 33° E.

[2] Ancient copper mines, with tablets and hieroglyphic inscriptions near, are still found in Wady Mughâra; see Lepsius Briefe, p. 336. Bartlett's Forty Days in the Desert, p. 44 sq.

i. 116, 117

tent, as if aware of its approaching fate. All was activity and bustle
to prepare the coming feast ; the kid was killed and dressed with
great dexterity and despatch ; and its still quivering members
were laid upon the fire and began to emit savoury odours, particularly gratifying to Arab nostrils. But now a change came
over the fair scene. The Arabs of whom we had bought the kid,
had in some way learned that we were to encamp near ; and
naturally enough concluding that the kid was bought in order to
be eaten, they thought good to honour our Arabs with a visit,
to the number of five or six persons. Now the stern law of Bedawin hospitality demands, that whenever a guest is present at a
meal, whether there be much or little, the first and best portion
must be laid before the stranger. In this instance the five or six
guests attained their object, and had not only the selling of the
kid, but also the eating of it ; while our poor Arabs, whose
mouths had long been watering with expectation, were forced to
take up with the fragments. Besharah, who played the host,
fared worst of all ; and came afterwards to beg for a biscuit, saying he had lost the whole of his dinner.

Thursday, March 22nd. Starting at 6½ o'clock, we continued down Wady Khumileh on a S. E. course. It is wide,
with many shrubs and with rocks of sandstone on each side. In
fifteen minutes we came to a rock on the right hand covered with
Sinaitic inscriptions, figures of camels, mountain goats, and the
like. Five minutes further is another large rock on the same
side with inscriptions, and several crosses apparently of the same
age. Here are also inscribed the names of several travellers ; one
is *Palerne*, 1582, perfectly fresh. The Wady gradually contracts
and grows deeper ; and at 8 o'clock we came to the spot where
it turns a sharp angle to the W. N. W. through a narrow ravine,
and passes by itself to the sea, as our Arabs said, (probably under another name,) receiving Wady Mukatteb on the way. We
still kept on the same course, ascending a branch Wady for
twenty minutes to a small plain, forming the water-shed between
it and a similar short Wady running S. E. to the Seih. On this
little plain is a lone Arab burial ground, called Mūkberat esh-
Sheikh Ahmed, where all the Bedawin, who die in the vicinity,
are buried. A few stones rudely piled together, or set up singly,
serve to mark the graves ; and there was one new grave. All
around was silence and solitude, with nothing to disturb this
wild abode of the dead.

Half an hour more brought us to Wady es-Seih, which here
comes down from the S. E. and turning more to the W. runs on
to join Wady Khumileh further down. The sandstone rocks had
already begun to give place to grünstein and porphyry. Passing up Wady Seih we came at 9 o'clock to an open place among

precipitous hills of porphyry and granite, disintegrated and shattered, where several Wadys unite and flow off through Wady Seih.   Here the mountains begin to assume features of grander and sterner desolation. We entered the mouth of Wady el-Bürk on a course S. by W. for half an hour, when it turned S. S. E. Here at the angle are a few short inscriptions, quite near the ground. The valley is narrow, and its bed covered with *debris* from the adjacent mountains,—loose stones and fragments of rocks spread over the surface and rendering the way difficult and painful for the camels. These rocks are chiefly granite and porphyry, intermixed with grünstein. This valley, as well as the open place we had passed, had an unusual number of Seyâl trees, the largest we had yet seen.

In this valley the camel of my companion gave out ; and he was compelled to mount another, after its load had been distributed among the rest. The camel belonged to Beshârah, who had paid eleven Spanish dollars for it the year before ; a low price, as the animal probably had been already broken down. We were told that many camels had died in the peninsula the present year, owing chiefly to the excessive drought ; there having been but little rain (or according to the Arab mode of speech, *none*) for now two seasons. There was of course great distress among all the Bedawin, as we had occasion enough to learn afterwards for ourselves. The wearied camel was left in charge of a boy to follow at a slower pace ; and we proceeded on our way. The occurrence detained us for nearly half an hour.

A side valley called Ibn Sükr came in from the left at 10.45, in which there is good water at a little distance. Half an hour further on, a rude stone wall or breast-work crossed the valley, marking the scene of one of the most important events in the history of the Tawarah. The story was told us with great animation by Beshârah, who was himself present at the time. Formerly the carrying of goods between Cairo and Suez belonged of right to the Tawarah, or, in occidental phrase, was a monopoly of theirs. But several years ago the merchants began to employ also the Ma'âzeh and Haweitât, to the great annoyance of the Tawarah, inasmuch as it took from them a source of support and distressed them. To recompense themselves for this outrage, the tribes all combined, and plundered a large caravan of several hundred camels laden with coffee and other merchandise, between Suez and Cairo, bringing home to their mountains a rich booty of coffee, wares, and camels. The Pasha sent to demand back the plunder. They meantime had revelled in their spoils, and eaten up or disposed of the whole ; and their laconic answer was : "We were hungry and have eaten." The Pasha immediately despatched a force of two or three thousand men against them.

i. 119-121

The Arabs gathered at this place and built a wall, expecting the troops to come along the valley. But the latter divided and climbed along the tops of the mountains on each side in order to get round the Arabs ; who of course were compelled to meet them on these heights ; and they now pointed out to us the places on the summits of these rugged ridges, where the battle was fought. Almost as a matter of course, the Tawarah were routed with little slaughter ; the troops marched to the convent ; the chief Sheikh came and surrendered ; and peace was granted on condition of their paying the expenses of the war. Since that time, the Tawarah have remained in quiet subjection to the Pasha.[1]

We reached the top of the pass at the head of Wady Bŭrk at a quarter past noon ; and immediately descended along a gully for twenty-five minutes, when we reached Wady 'Åkir, which, coming down from before us, here entered the mountains on our right, flowing off into the great Wady Feirân. This valley we now followed up on a course S. E. by S. Here the coloquintida (colocynthus) was growing, with its yellow fruit already ripe.[2] At first the valley is narrow, but gradually grows wider. At 1¼ o'clock, the mouth of Wady Kinch was pointed out, coming in from the S. E. through the ridge on our left. Above this point the Wady we were in loses the name 'Åkir, and takes that of el-Lebweh, from a pass before us at its head. The two Wadys Lebweh and Kinch are parallel to each other ; both spread out into wide plains ; the ridge between them in some parts almost disappears ; so that in several places they run together and form one great sloping plain several miles in breadth, covered with tufts of herbs, chiefly 'Abeithirân, but no trees ; furnishing abundant pasturage in seasons when rain falls. In the upper part of the plain of Wady Kinch there is water ; and Sheikh Sâlih, the head Sheikh of the Tawarah, with a part of his tribe, was encamped not far off, in sight of our road. The two valleys separate again ; and near the pass at the head of el-Lebweh is a sharp isolated peak on the left, called Zub el-Bahry.

The pass itself is a mere continuation of the plain, a broad water-shed, rising very gradually on one side and descending as gradually on the other. Burckhardt has noticed this as a peculiar conformation of the mountain ranges of the peninsula ; " the valleys reaching to the very summits, where they form a plain, and thence descending on the other side."[3] But the

---

[1] Laborde relates the same story, as having occurred several years before his journey in 1828. He makes it refer to the caravan of the Haj on its return from Mecca. This is probably an error. Voy-age en Arab. Petr. p. 72. Engl. p. 264.

[2] *Cucumis colocynthus* of Linnæus; in Arabic *Handhal*.

[3] Travels in Syria, etc. pp. 483, 484. Burckhardt gives the name el-Lebweh to

i. 121, 122

same general feature exists in the great Wady el-'Arabah, and in various parts of Palestine. We reached the plain at the top of the ascent at 3¼ o'clock, where is a small Arab cemetery. The surface soon begins to slope towards the south, and opens out to an extensive plain with many shrubs, forming the head of Wady Berâh and surrounded by peaks of moderate height. A long, high, dark-looking mountain was pointed out to us, called ez-Zebir, bearing S. about two hours distant; on the top of which there was said to be table land and pasturage for camels. Passing down the plain on the same course as before (S. E. by S.) we came at 4 o'clock to its S. E. part, where it contracts between noble granite cliffs; and entering Wady Berâh for a short distance, we encamped at 4.15 on its western side. The rocks on both sides of this valley presented everywhere surfaces so well adapted for inscriptions, that leaving my companions to follow down the right side, I struck across to the left. Here on a large rock I found four short inscriptions in the usual unknown character. Over the longest of them was a cross, evidently of the same date. Just by our tents was also a huge detached rock covered with similar inscriptions much obliterated. Here were two crosses, apparently of later date, or else retouched.

This evening our Arabs again brought us good water from a spring in the small Wady Retâmeh, which enters the Berâh opposite our encampment. They had shown themselves every day more and more obliging; and commonly took as active a part in pitching the tent and arranging the luggage for the night, as our servants. In all these matters, our resolute Komeh was master and director, and made the Arabs do his bidding. He found the less difficulty in this, as being cook and purveyor he knew how to distribute the fragments in his department with great nicety and discrimination; so that it was an object of some importance to a hungry Bedawy to keep on good terms with him.

Among the many plants we had noted on this and the preceding days, some of the most frequent besides the 'Abeithirân were the *Retem*, a species of the broom plant *Genista rætam* of Forskal,[1] with small whitish variegated blossoms, growing in the water-courses of the Wadys; the *Kirdhy*, a green thorny plant with small yellow flowers, which our camels cropped with avidity; the *Silleh*, apparently the *Zilla myagrioides* of Forskal;[2] the *Shih* or *Artemisia Judaica* of Sprengel; and the *'Ajram*, from which the Arabs obtain a substitute for soap, by pounding it when dry between stones, and mixing it with the water in which they wash their linen.

the pass at the head of Wady Bûrk; but our Arabs on being questioned were very positive that this was not the case, and said that Lebweh was the name of three i. 122–124

different passes at and near the head of the Wadys Lebweh and Kineh.
[1] Flora Ægypt. Arab. p. 214.
[2] Ibid. p. 121.

Friday, March 23d. We set off again at 6.25 down Wady Berâh, our course being S. S. E. ½ E. We had ever wished to set off earlier in the morning, than we had yet been able to do. The Arabs were never in a hurry to break up; and this morning especially they were occupied with Beshârah's camel, which had come up late at evening, and was now sent home to their encampment. As we were approaching Sinai, and no longer needed to carry a load of water, this caused us little inconvenience. But let us rise as early as we would, we found it difficult to start under an hour and a half or two hours. It was decidedly a saving of time, on the whole, to breakfast before setting off, rather than stop on our way for that purpose; and this with the delay of packing the utensils and tent, and loading the camels, always made our departure later than the time appointed.

As we proceeded down the valley, the rocks on the right presented several inscriptions in the same unknown writing. Indeed we found them at almost every point where the overhanging or projecting rocks seemed to indicate a convenient resting place. The mountains on either side continued of the same character as those we had passed yesterday, chiefly porphyry and red granite, with an occasional vein of gray granite. The rock was mostly of a coarse texture, much disintegrated and often worn away by the weather, like sandstone. Not unfrequently thin perpendicular veins apparently of grünstein or porphyry were to be seen, projecting above the granite and running through the rocks in a straight line over mountains and valleys for miles, and presenting the appearance of low walls. They reminded me strongly of the stone fences of New England.

At a quarter past 7 o'clock the Wady spread out into a plain, where the peak of Jebel Mûsa was first pointed out to us bearing S. E. while the left hand peak of Serbâl bore S. W. Ten minutes later Wady 'Ôsh, a side valley, entered the Berâh from the left, in which sweet water is found at some distance. Opposite its mouth, on our right, was an old cemetery, apparently no longer used by the Arabs. The heaps of stones which mark the graves are larger than usual, and our guides referred them back to the times of the Franks; as the Bedawin do every thing of which they know nothing themselves. They seem to have a general impression, not perhaps a distinct tradition, that the country was once in the possession of Frank Christians. At 7¾ o'clock Wady el-Akhdar came in from the N. E. It was said to begin near Jebel et-Tîh where there is a spring of the same name, 'Ain el-Akhdar; and uniting here with the Berâh, it passes on S. W. to join Wady esh-Sheikh. The united valley after this junction takes the name of Wady Feirân. The point where the Berâh and Akhdar unite, is a broad open space

covered with herbs and surrounded by low hills. Here is a fine
view of Mount Serbâl which rose in full majesty upon our right
at the distance of twelve or fifteen miles, being separated from
us only by a low ridge or tract beyond which lies Wady Feirân.
As thus seen, it presents the appearance of a long, thin, lofty
ridge of granite, with numerous points or peaks, of which there
are reckoned five principal ones ; the whole being strictly what
the Germans call a *Kamm*. We saw it now in the bright
beams of the morning sun, a grand and noble object, as its ragged peaks were reflected upon the deep azure beyond.

Thus far we had followed the same route which Burckhardt
took in 1816 ; but from this point he turned into the Akhdar,
and then crossed higher up to Wady esh-Sheikh, which he then
followed to Mount Sinai. We kept the more direct and usual
road, crossing the Akhdar, and continuing on a S. S. E. course
up the short ascent of Wady Soleif to the top or water-shed,
which we passed at 8¼ o'clock ; and then descending along a
Wady still called Soleif towards Wady esh-Sheikh. Here we
met Sheikh Tuweileb, on foot, the same who was to be our
future guide, returning it was said to his family. At three quarters past 8 o'clock we reached Wady esh-Sheikh, one of the
largest and most famous valleys of the peninsula. It takes its
rise in the very heart of Sinai, whence it issues a broad valley at
first in an eastern direction, and then sweeping round to the
north and west, it passes down towards Serbâl. We found it
here running from N. E. to S. W. After receiving the Akhdar
it takes the name of Feirân, and as such is well watered, has
gardens of fruit and palm trees, and receiving many branches runs
to the northward of Serbâl quite down to the sea. The lower
and easier road from Wady et-Taiyibeh to Sinai enters the
Feirân from the head of Wady Mukatteb, and follows it up
through Wady esh-Sheikh almost to the convent. From the
point where we now were, this road is long and circuitous ;
while a shorter one strikes directly towards the convent, ascending in part by a narrow and difficult pass. We took the latter ;
and crossing Wady esh-Sheikh proceeded on a course S. E. by
S. up the broad Wady or rather sloping plain, es-Seheb, thickly
studded with shrubs, but without trees. Here and around Wady
esh-Sheikh are only low hills, lying between the rocky mountains
behind us and the cliffs of Sinai before us ; and forming as it
were a lower belt around the lofty central granite region. Over
these hills, low walls of porphyry or grünstein, like those above
described, run in various directions, stretching off to a great distance.

This plain of Seheb had been last year the scene of threatened war between the different tribes of the Tawarah ; growing

i. 126. 127

out of a dispute as to the right of conducting travellers to and from the convent. The story had some reference to Lord Lindsay and his party ; and I shall give it, as we heard it, at the close of the present Section, in speaking of the divisions and character of the Tawarah.

We came to the top of the plain at a quarter before 11 o'clock, where is a short but rough pass, full of *debris*, having on the right a low sharp peak called el-'Orf. From this point to the base of the cliffs of Sinai there is a sort of belt or tract of gravel and sand, full of low hills and ridges, sinking down towards the foot of the cliffs into the Wady Soláf, which runs off west along their base to join Wady esh-Sheikh. The black and frowning mountains before us, the outworks as it were of Sinai, are here seen to great advantage, rising abrupt and rugged from their very base eight hundred to a thousand feet in height, as if forbidding all approach to the sanctuary within. On the west of the pass, which is here hardly distinguishable, the cliffs bear the name of Jebel el-Haweit. Descending S. S. E. across the belt, we came at 12.15 to Wady Soláf, which has its head not very far to the left, near a spring called Ghûrbeh, where some tamarisks and other trees were visible. Here the road from Tûr falls into ours from the S. W., having come up through Wady Hibrân, and crossed over the ridge that separates the waters flowing to that valley from those of Wady esh-Sheikh ;[1] the one running on the north and the other on the south of Serbâl. The same ridge also forms the connecting link between Serbâl and the more central Sinai. This road enters Wady Soláf an hour and a half below.

We now turned up Wady Soláf a little, along the base of the mountains on a S. E. course, passing in fifteen minutes the mouth of a very narrow valley or chasm, Wady Rŭdhwâh, coming down from the S. S. W. through the cliffs ; from it a steep pass was said to lead S. W. over the mountains, to a place called Bûghâbigh with water and gardens at or near the head of Wady Hibrân. Leaving the Soláf at 12¾ o'clock, we began gradually to ascend towards the foot of the pass before us, called by our Arabs Nŭkb Hâwy, " Windy Pass," and by Burckhardt Nŭkb er-Râhah from the tract above it.[2] We reached the foot at a quarter past 1 o'clock, and dismounting commenced the slow and toilsome ascent along the narrow defile, about S. by E. between blackened shattered cliffs of granite some eight hundred feet high, and not more than two hundred and fifty yards

---

[1] Here and elsewhere, in speaking of running waters, I mean of course the waters of the rainy season as they flow off. At this time there was very little (if any) running water in the peninsula. We saw none.

[2] Page 596.

apart ; which every moment threatened to send down their ruins
on our heads.   Nor is this at all times an empty threat ; for the
whole pass is filled with large stones and rocks, the debris of
these cliffs.   The bottom is a deep and narrow water-course,
where the wintery torrent sweeps down with fearful violence.
A path has been made for camels along the shelving piles of
rocks, partly by removing the topmost blocks, and sometimes by
laying down large stones side by side, somewhat in the manner
of a Swiss mountain road.   But although I had crossed the
most rugged passes of the Alps, and made from Chamouny the
whole circuit of Mont Blanc, I had never found a path so rude
and difficult as that we were now ascending.[1]   The camels toiled
slowly and painfully along, stopping frequently ; so that although
it took them two hours and a quarter to reach the top of the
pass, yet the distance cannot be reckoned at more than one
hour.   From a point about half way up, the east end of Jebel
ez-Zebîr bore N. 42° W. and two peaks at its western end,
called el-Benât, N. 60° W.   Higher up the path lies in the bed
of the torrent and became less steep.   As we advanced, the
sand was occasionally moist, and on digging into it with the
hand, the hole was soon filled with fine sweet water.   We tried
the experiment in several places.   Here too were several small
palm trees, and a few tufts of grass, the first we had seen since
leaving the borders of the Nile.   Burckhardt mentions a spring
called Kaneitar in this part of the pass ;[2] but it was now dry ;
at least we neither saw nor heard of any.   In the pass we
found upon the rocks two Sinaite inscriptions ; one of them
having over it a cross of the same date.

It was half past 3 o'clock when we reached the top, from
which the convent was said to be an hour distant ; but we found
it two hours, as did also Burckhardt.[3]   Descending a little into
a small Wady, which has its head here and runs off through a
cleft in the western mountains apparently to Wady Rûdhwâh,
we soon began to ascend again gradually on a course S. E. by S.
passing by a small spring of good water ; beyond which the
valley opens by degrees and its bottom becomes less uneven.
Here the interior and loftier peaks of the great circle of Sinai
began to open upon us, black, rugged, desolate summits ; and
as we advanced, the dark and frowning front of Sinai itself
(the present Horeb of the monks) began to appear.   We were
still gradually ascending, and the valley gradually opening ; but
as yet all was a naked desert.   Afterwards a few shrubs were

---

[1] Pococke speaks of this pass as "a
narrow vale which has a gentle ascent
with water and palm trees in it." Travels I. fol. p. 142.
    i. 129, 130

[2] Page 597.

[3] Page 596. Burckhardt travelled in
the other direction, from the convent down
the pass.

sprinkled round about, and a small encampment of black tents
was seen on our right, with camels and goats browsing, and a
few donkeys belonging to the convent.   The scenery through
which we had now passed, reminded me strongly of the mountains around the Mer de Glace in Switzerland.   I had never seen
a spot more wild and desolate.

As we advanced, the valley still opened wider and wider with
a gentle ascent, and became full of shrubs and tufts of herbs,
shut in on each side by lofty granite ridges with rugged shattered peaks a thousand feet high, while the face of Horeb rose
directly before us.   Both my companion and myself involuntarily
exclaimed : "Here is room enough for a large encampment !"
Reaching the top of the ascent, or water-shed, a fine broad plain
lay before us, sloping down gently towards the S. S. E. enclosed
by rugged and venerable mountains of dark granite, stern, naked,
splintered peaks and ridges, of indescribable grandeur ; and terminated at the distance of more than a mile by the bold and
awful front of Horeb, rising perpendicularly in frowning majesty,
from twelve to fifteen hundred feet in height.   It was a scene of
solemn grandeur, wholly unexpected, and such as we had never
seen ; and the associations which at the moment rushed upon
our minds, were almost overwhelming.   As we went on, new
points of interest were continually opening to our view.   On the
left of Horeb, a deep and narrow valley runs up S. S. E. between
lofty walls of rock, as if in continuation of the S. E. corner of
the plain.   In this valley, at the distance of nearly a mile from
the plain, stands the convent ; and the deep verdure of its fruit
trees and cypresses is seen as the traveller approaches ; an oasis
of beauty amid scenes of the sternest desolation.   At the S. W.
corner of the plain the cliffs also retreat, and form a recess or
open place extending from the plain westward for some distance.
From this recess there runs up a similar narrow valley on the
west of Horeb, called el-Leja, parallel to that in which the convent stands ; and in it is the deserted convent el-Arba'in, with
a garden of olive and other fruit trees not visible from the plain.
A third garden lies at the mouth of el-Leja, and a fourth further
west in the recess just mentioned.   The whole plain is called
Wady er-Râhah ; and the valley of the convent is known to the
Arabs as Wady Shu'eib, that is, the vale of Jethro.   Still advancing, the front of Horeb rose like a wall before us ; and one
can approach quite to the foot and touch the mount.   Directly
before its base is the deep bed of a torrent, by which in the
rainy season the waters of el-Leja and the mountains around the
recess, pass down eastward across the plain, forming the commencement of Wady esh-Sheikh, which then issues by an opening through the cliffs of the eastern mountain, a fine broad

valley, affording the only easy access to the plain and convent.
—As we crossed the plain our feelings were strongly affected, at
finding here so unexpectedly a spot so entirely adapted to the
Scriptural account of the giving of the law. No traveller has
described this plain, nor even mentioned it except in a slight and
general manner ; probably because the most have reached the
convent by another route without passing over it ; and perhaps
too because neither the highest point of Sinai (now called Jebel
Mûsa), nor the still loftier summit of St. Catharine, is visible
from any part of it.[1]

As we approached the mountain our head Arab, Beshârah,
became evidently quite excited. He prayed that our pilgrimage
might be accepted, and bring rain ; and with great earnestness
besought, that when we ascended the mountain, we would open
a certain window in the chapel there, towards the south, which
he said would certainly cause rain to fall. He also entreated
almost with tears, that we would induce the monks to have compassion on the people, and say prayers as they ought to do for
rain. When told that God alone could send rain, and they
should look to him for it, he replied : " Yes, but the monks have
the book of prayer for it ; do persuade them to use it as they
ought."[2] There was an earnestness in his manner which was
very affecting, but cannot be described. Just after crossing
Wady esh-Sheikh, we passed at the mouth of Wady Shu'eib,
a burial ground much venerated by the Arabs. Here Beshârah
repeated a few words of prayer, the first time we had known
him or any of our Arabs pray since leaving Cairo.

From the Wady esh-Sheikh to the convent is a distance of
twenty-five minutes, by a difficult path along the rocky bed of
the narrow valley. We had come on in advance of the loaded
camels, and reached the convent at half past 5 o'clock. Under
the entrance were many Arabs in high clamour, serfs of the convent, who were receiving a distribution of some kind of provision
from above ; we did not learn what. The only regular entrance
at present is by a door nearly thirty feet (or more exactly 28
feet 9 inches) from the ground ; the great door having been
walled up for more than a century. On making known our

---

[1] Monconys appears to have come by
the same route in A. D. 1647, " par un
chemin très rude, où les chameaux tra-
vaillaient beaucoup." He says the convent is seen from the top of the ascent,
"dans le fond d'une grande campagne
verte qui commence en cet endroit. Elle
a une lieue et demi de long, et un grand
quart de lieue de large." Tom. I. p. 214.
Morison describes the plain as being
" d'une lieue de longueur, mais d'une lar-
geur peu considérable ;" Relation Histo-
i. 132, 133

rique, p. 91. These notices, although exaggerated, are the most distinct mention
of the plain that I have been able to find.
Of Shaw's account I can make nothing ;
p. 314, 4to.

[2] " They [the Arabs] are persuaded,
that the priests of the convent are in possession of the Taurât, a book sent down
to Moses from heaven, upon the opening
and shutting of which depend the rains of
the peninsula." Burckhardt, p. 567.

arrival, a cord was let down with a demand for our letters ; and we sent up the one we had received from the branch convent in Cairo. This proving satisfactory, a rope was let down for us ; in which seating ourselves, we were hoisted up one by one by a windlass within to the level of the door, and then pulled in by hand. The superior himself, a mild-looking old man with a long white beard, received us with an embrace and a kiss, and conducted us to the strangers' rooms. While these were preparing, we seated ourselves in the adjacent piazza, upon antique chairs of various forms, which have doubtless come down through many centuries ; and had a few moments of quiet to ourselves, in which to collect our thoughts. I was affected by the strangeness and overpowering grandeur of the scenes around us ; and it was for some time difficult to realize, that we were now actually within the very precincts of that Sinai, on which from the earliest childhood I had thought and read with so much wonder. Yet, when at length the impression came with its full force upon my mind, although not given to the melting mood, I could not refrain from bursting into tears.

We were soon put in possession of our rooms, and greeted with kindness by the monks and attendants. The priests and pilgrim, who passed us on the way, had arrived some hours before us. Almonds were now brought, with coffee and date brandy ; and the good monks wondered when we declined the latter. Our servants and baggage arrived later ; and having been drawn up in like manner, the former were installed in the kitchen near our rooms, under the auspices of an old man of more than eighty years, our chief attendant. Supper was prepared in an adjoining room, chiefly of eggs and rice, with olives and coarse bread ; the superior making many apologies for not giving us better fare, inasmuch as it was now Lent, and also very difficult to obtain camels to bring grain and provisions from Tûr and elsewhere. Indeed such had been the lack of rain for several years, and especially the present season, that all food and pasturage was dried up ; and camels were dying of famine in great numbers. Beshârah, on the way, heard of the death of a dromedary of his at home ; and the one which we left behind on the road, died a few days afterwards. It was well that we were to stop some days at the convent ; for our camels were nearly worn out, and quite unable to go on. Yet it was for a time somewhat doubtful, whether we should be able to procure others in their stead.

The rooms we occupied were small and tolerably neat ; the floor was covered with carpets which had once been handsome, though now well worn ; and a low divan was raised along three sides of the room, which served as a seat by day and a place to spread our beds at night. Here all travellers have lodged, who

i. 133, 134

have visited the convent for many generations ; but they have
left no memorials behind, except in recent years. The inscriptions pasted upon the walls, which Burckhardt mentions in 1816,[1]
commemorating the visits of Rozières, Seetzen, and others, no
longer remain ; for the walls have been since painted or washed
over, and all traces of them destroyed. Instead of them an
album is now kept, which does little credit to some of those,
whose names figure in it most conspicuously. Father Neophytus,
the superior, came to us again after supper ; and as my companion could speak modern Greek with some fluency, we found
peculiar favour in the eyes of the good old man, to whom the
Arabic was almost an unknown tongue. We had been furnished with a letter of introduction in Arabic from the agent of
the convent in Suez, one of the brothers Manueli, and now presented it ; but they were obliged to send for the Ikonomos, who
deals with the Arabs, to read it. When he came, it was only to
say, that as we spoke Greek it was useless to read an Arabic
letter.

The geographical position of the convent, as determined by
Rüppell in A. D. 1826, is Lat. 28° 32' 55" N. and Long. 31°
37' 54" E. from Paris, or 33° 58' 18" E. from Greenwich.[2]
The elevation above the sea, according to Schubert's observations, is 4725. 6 Paris feet ; according to Russegger, 5115 Paris
feet. The number corresponding to Rüppell's other measurements, would be about 4966 Paris feet.[3]

Saturday, March 24th. We felt as if we had now a place
of rest for a time. Our Arabs with their camels had dispersed
to their homes ; and Beshârah was to return after three days to
learn when we wished to depart for 'Akabah. We found enough
to do for this day, in writing up our journals and examining the
vicinity of the convent.

The valley of Shu'eib runs up from the plain S. E. by S.
and forms a *cul de sac*, being terminated not far beyond the
convent by a mountain less lofty and steep than those on the
sides, over which a pass leads towards Sherm on the coast of the
eastern gulf. The valley is so narrow at the bottom, that while
the eastern wall of the convent runs along the water-course, the
main body of the building stands on the slope of the western
mountain, so that the western wall lies considerably higher than
the eastern. The mountains on either side tower to the height
of a thousand feet above the valley.

The convent is an irregular quadrangle, 245 French feet

---

[1] Page 552.
[2] Rüppell's Reisen in Nubien, etc. p.
292. Berghaus' Memoir zu seiner Karte
von Syrien, pp. 28, 30.
[3] For Schubert's measurements, where
i. 135, 136

not specified in his work, I am indebted to
a manuscript copy. For Russegger's, see
Berghaus' Annalen der Erdkunde, Feb. u.
März 1839, p. 425 sq.

long by 204 broad ;[1] enclosed by high walls, built of granite blocks, of which there is no lack here, and strengthened with small towers in various parts ; in one or two of which there are small cannon. One portion of the eastern wall was now threatening to tumble down ; and workmen were already preparing the materials for rebuilding it. Another portion was rebuilt with great solidity by the French when in Egypt, by order of General Kleber, who sent workmen from Cairo for that purpose ; and the monks retain a very grateful feeling towards that nation in consequence. The space enclosed within the walls is cut up into a number of small courts, by various ranges of buildings running in all directions, forming quite a labyrinth of narrow winding passages, ascending and descending. Some of the little courts are ornamented with a cypress or other small trees, and beds of flowers and vegetables ; while many vines run along the sides of the buildings. Every thing is irregular, but neat ; and all bears the marks of high antiquity ; being apparently the patch-work of various by-gone centuries. In the court near the strangers' rooms is a large well ; but the water for drinking is usually taken from the fountain of Moses near the church, and is very pure and fine.

The garden joins the convent on the north, extending for some distance down the valley ; and is in like manner enclosed with high walls ; which however it would not be very difficult to scale. In the course of the morning the superior invited us to walk through it, showing us the way himself along a dark and partly subterranean passage under the northern wall of the convent. This is closed by an iron door, now left open all day for the free ingress and egress of the inmates and visitors. The garden, like the convent, lies along the slope of the western mountain, and is formed into several terraces, planted with fruit trees. At its southeast corner, near the high entrance of the convent, the wall is mounted on the inside by a stile, with a ladder to let down outside, forming a way of entrance to the garden and convent. By this way ladies are introduced, when they happen to wander as travellers into this solitary region. There is another similar entrance to the garden through a small building on the wall in the northwest part, which is easier and more used ; the wall having here a slight inclination, and being ascended by the help of a rope. At present the passages are left open during the day ; but are strictly shut up at night.

The garden was now suffering from drought ; but it looked beautifully verdant in contrast with the stern desolation that reigns all around. Besides the tall dark cypresses which are seen from afar, it contains mostly fruit trees ; few vegetables being

[1] Journal of the Prefect of the Franciscans, in 1722.

cultivated in it. Indeed, the number and variety of fruit trees is surprising, and testifies to the fine temperature and vivifying power of the climate, provided there be a supply of water. The almond trees are very large, and had been long out of blossom. The apricot trees are also large, and like the apple trees were now in full bloom ; or rather, were already in the wane. There are also pears, pomegranates, figs, quinces, mulberries, olives, and many vines ; besides other trees and shrubs in great variety. The fruit produced is said to be excellent. The Arabs are now on good terms with the monks, and do not rob the gardens ; but the long want of rain had made them less productive. This garden, although under the immediate care of the monks, is not well kept, and has nothing ornamental about it ; nor is it well irrigated. Still it is a gem in the desert.

As we were walking up and down in the garden, we were met by Sheikh Husein, the former guide of Laborde and other travellers, who was now head Sheikh of his tribe, the Aulâd Sa'id, and had come to the convent on business. He was a fine-looking intelligent man in middle life, and enjoyed great consideration and influence among the Tawarah and at the convent. We were glad to meet him and answer his inquiries, so far as we could, in respect to the many Frank travellers whom we had known ; all of whom he seemed to remember with kindness. Nor was he less disposed to answer our many questions, relative to the parts of the peninsula with which he was best acquainted. We learned on this occasion, that the Arabs are not now, as formerly, wholly excluded from the convent and its precincts ; but the Sheikhs and chief men are freely admitted into the garden, where business is often transacted with them ; and sometimes also into the convent itself. A number of the serfs likewise live within the garden walls. But the ordinary mode of communicating with the common Arabs, is from the high door, or through a small hole in the wall lower down.

In the afternoon we went out through the garden to examine more particularly the plain which we had crossed yesterday. Taking our station on the highest part of the plain, or watershed, and looking towards the convent, we found the general direction of the plain and valley of the convent to be S. E.$\frac{1}{2}$S. or more exactly S. 41° E. The mountain on the left or N. E. of the plain, called Jebel el-Furcia', is long and high, with table land on the top and pasturage for camels. It extends northward along the pass by which we ascended, and southward to Wady esh-Sheikh at the southeast corner of the plain. South of this Wady, the mountain which overhangs the convent on the east, is called Jebel ed-Deir, and also Mountain of the Cross.[1] The mountain

---

[1] This is the mountain called Episteme by Pococke and others. A cross now i. 138, 139

on the west of the pass and plain is called Jebel es-Seru or es-
Surey ; but south of the cleft running down to Wady Rûdhwâh
it takes for a time the name of Sülsül Zeit ; and then at its
southern end near the recess, that of el-Ghûbshch. Along the
plain this mountain is somewhat lower than the opposite or
eastern one, and its top more broken into ragged peaks ; while
over it and through the breaks in its ridge is seen a much higher
ridge, further west, called Jebel Tinia. This western side of the
plain is quite irregular, from the spurs and points of the mountain which jut out into it. On the west of the recess above
mentioned is Jebel el-Humr, connected by a lower ridge or *col*
with el-Ghûbshch, over which a pass leads to Wady Tûlâh, and
so to the head of Wady Hibrân. Jebel Humr runs up for some
distance along the western side of el-Leja ; and then more to
the south, and further back, lies the lofty summit of Jebel Kâtherin, or St. Catharine.

The name of Sinai is now given by the Christians in a general
way to this whole cluster of mountains ; but in its stricter sense
is applied only to the ridge lying between the two parallel valleys
Shu'eib and el-Leja. It is the northern end of this ridge, which
rises so boldly and majestically from the southern extremity of
the plain ; and this northern part is now called by the Christians,
Horeb ; but the Bedawin do not appear to know that name.
From this point the high ridge extends back about S. E. by S.
for nearly or quite three miles, where it terminates in the higher
peak of Jebel Mûsa, which has commonly been regarded as the
summit of Sinai, the place where the law was given.

The Arabs of the present day have no other name for the
whole cluster of mountains in the peninsula, than Jebel et-Tûr.
It is possible that they may sometimes add the word Sina (Tûr
Sina) by way of distinction; but this certainly is not usual.[1]

We measured across the plain, where we stood, along the
water-shed, and found the breadth to be at that point 2700
English feet or 900 yards ; though in some parts it is wider.
The distance to the base of Horeb, measured in like manner, was
7000 feet, or 2333 yards. The northern slope of the plain, north
of where we stood, we judged to be somewhat less than a mile
in length by one third of a mile in breadth. We may therefore
fairly estimate the whole plain at two geographical miles long,
and ranging in breadth from one third to two thirds of a mile ; or
as equivalent to a surface of at least one square mile. This space

stands upon it, and there is said once to
have been a convent there; whence its
present name.

[1] The supposed Ibn Haukal about the
eleventh century writes *Tûr Sina';* see
Ouseley's Ebn Haukal p. 29.—Edrisi and
Abulfeda have only *Jebel Tûr* and *et-Tûr ;*
see Edrisi ed. Jaubert, p. 332. Abulfed.
Arabia, in Geogr. vet. Scriptores Minores
ed. Hudson, Oxon. 1712. Tom. III. p. 74
sq.

is nearly doubled by the recess so often mentioned on the west, and by the broad and level area of Wady esh-Sheikh on the east, which issues at right angles to the plain, and is equally in view of the front and summit of the present Horeb.

The examination of this afternoon convinced us, that here was space enough to satisfy all the requisitions of the Scriptural narrative, so far as it relates to the assembling of the congregation to receive the law. Here too one can see the fitness of the injunction, to set bounds around the mount, that neither man nor beast might approach too near.[1] The encampment before the mount, as has been before suggested, might not improbably include only the head-quarters of Moses and the elders, and of a portion of the people; while the remainder, with their flocks, were scattered among the adjacent valleys.

The reader will I hope pardon these topographical details in a region so interesting. They will help him the better to understand the map, and prevent the necessity of many repetitions.— It was late when we returned to the convent; we found the entrances to the garden closed; and were again drawn up through the high door in the wall.

Sunday, March 25th. Having expressed a desire to attend the service in the great church this morning, we were welcomed to it, with the remark, that this was something unusual with travellers. We had already been invited to breakfast afterwards with the fraternity in the refectory. The service commenced in the church at 7 o'clock, and continued an hour and a half. It was simple, dignified, and solemn, consisting in great part in the reading of the Gospels, with the touching responses and chants of the Greek ritual. The associations of Sinai came strongly in aid of the calm and holy influence of the service; and every thing tended to awaken in the breast feelings of veneration and devotion. The antique yet simple grandeur of the church is also imposing. The monks seemed each to have his particular seat or stall; and two very old men struck me in particular, who chanted the responses and *Kyrie eleison* with great simplicity and apparent fervour. The service included also the high mass, or consecration of the sacrament of the Lord's supper. But the monks did not commune; only one stranger, a Greek from Tûr, partook of it. Just at the close of the service, Father Neophytus, the prior, as a mark of special favour, called us of his own accord into the sacristy and showed us the relics of St. Catharine; whose body the monks suppose to have been transported by angels from Alexandria to the summit of the mountain which now bears her name. The relics

---

[1] Exod. 19, 12. 13.

i. 141. 142

consist of a skull and hand, set in gold and embossed with jewels.

We now repaired to the refectory, and were seated at the long table next below the priests ; the lay brethren and pilgrims taking their seats still further down. The table was neat, and without a cloth ; some of the larger vessels were of tinned copper ; but the plates, spoons, basins, mugs, and porringers for drinking, were all of pewter. An orange and half a lemon lay by each plate, with a portion of coarse bread. After a grace, a large basin of soup or stew, made of herbs and a species of large shell-fish, was set on ; from which each helped himself at will. This with a few plates of olives and raw beans soaked in water till they sprout, formed the whole repast. The good monks seemed to eat with relish ; and some of the very old ones set away their plates with the remains of these tid-bits in drawers beneath the table. During the meal the young monk or deacon, whom we had met with on the way, read from a small pulpit a sermon or homily in modern Greek, in praise of Chrysostom. On rising from the meal a taper was lighted on a small table at the head of the room, around which all gathered, and a prayer was said over a piece of bread and a very small cup of wine. These were then carried around to all standing ; every one (including ourselves) breaking off a morsel of the bread and tasting the wine. This was explained to us as a sort of love-feast, a mere symbol of the enjoyment of wine, of which the monks are not permitted by their rules to drink. The ceremony however has no reference to the sacrament of the Lord's supper; as has been erroneously supposed by some travellers.[1] After this, on leaving the room, each one received separately the benediction of the superior ; and we all retired to the adjacent ancient piazza, where coffee was handed round ; the deacon following and continuing his reading the whole time.—There was a simplicity and seriousness during the whole repast and its accompaniments, which were quite pleasing.

After an hour or two the superior came and took us to visit the different parts of the interior of the convent. We now saw the great church with more attention. It is massive and solid, dating from the time of the emperor Justinian, about the middle of the sixth century ; although it has since received many additions and repairs. The alcove over the altar exhibits in mosaic a large picture of the Transfiguration, said to be of the same date with the church itself; and also portraits of Justinian and his wife. This has been copied by Laborde. There are many paintings of saints, great and small ; and the church

[1] See Incidents of Travel in Arabia Petræa, etc. by Mr. Stephens.

i. 142–144

is richly furnished with silver lamps suspended around the altar
and in various parts. The floor is very neatly paved with marble
of different colours, wrought into figures ; and was said to have
been laid only some sixty or seventy years ago.[1] The ceiling
had been quite lately repaired. Back of the altar we were
shown the chapel covering the place where the burning bush
is said to have stood, now regarded as the most holy spot in the
peninsula ; and as Moses put off his shoes in order to approach
it, so all who now visit it must do the same. The spot is
covered with silver, and the whole chapel richly carpeted. Near
by, they show also the well from which (as they say) Moses
watered Jethro's flocks. Besides the great church, there are
twenty-four chapels[2] in different parts of the convent ; some of
which formerly belonged to the Latins ;[3] and some also earlier
to the Syrians, Armenians, and Copts. At present all are in
the hands of the Greeks. Several were opened for us, but they
contain nothing remarkable ; and the daily masses which were
formerly read in them, are now neglected. We understood, that
mass was at present read only occasionally on festival days in
some of the more important ones. Not far from the great church
stands also a Muhammedan mosk, large enough for two hundred worshippers ; a curious memorial of the tolerance or policy
of former tenants of the monastery. It has now fallen into dis-
use, the convent being rarely visited by Muslim pilgrims.[4]

We were now taken up and down through several of the little courts and many winding corridors ; the whole convent indeed being a labyrinth of blind passages. The cells of the monks
are in different parts, along these corridors. They are small
and mean, and wholly without comfort ; being furnished simply
with a mat and rug, spread upon a raised part of the floor for a
bed, and perhaps a wooden chair, but no table. Shops, or rather
places for working in the open air, we saw in several parts, with
tools rude and more ancient than the arms that now wield them.
They make use of hand-mills ; but have also a larger mill turned
by a donkey. The archbishop's room, as it is called, is large
and better than the rest, having been once tolerably furnished.
It is hung with several portraits ; one a likeness of the present
archbishop, who was also until recently patriarch of Constanti-
nopl   In this room is kept a beautiful manuscript of the four

[1] Pococke was told the same in 1738 ; Travels, I. p. 150. fol.

[2] Burckhardt says twenty-seven ; the Prefect of the Franciscans, seventeen.

[3] When Monconys was here, A. D. 1647, there was still a Roman Catholic chapel near the strangers' rooms, in which one of his companions celebrated Latin mass ; Voyages I. p. 237. Sicard saw it i. 144, 145

in 1715, with a picture of Louis XIV ; Nouv. Memoires des Miss. dans le Levant, I. p. 8. Pococke also speaks of it in 1738 ; Travels I. p. 154. fol.

[4] According to some old Arabic records preserved in the convent and read by Burckhardt, this mosk appears to have existed before A. H. 783, or A. D. 1381. Travels in Syria, etc. p. 543.

Gospels, written on vellum in double columns with letters of gold ; the form of the letters being the same as in the Alexandrine manuscript. The Gospel of John stands first ; and there seemed to be no date. It was said to have been presented to the convent by an emperor Theodosius ; perhaps the third of that name in the eighth century.[1] We were also shown a copy of the Greek Psalter written on twelve duodecimo pages by a female. The hand was neat ; but needed a microscope to read it.—Near this room is the small church said (like so many others) to have been built by Helena.

The library is in another quarter, in a room furnished with shutters, which like the door are very rarely opened. The printed books are mostly in Greek and very old ; the library being rich in *Incunabula*, but possessing very few modern books, except some copies of the Scriptures from the British and Foreign Bible Society, presented by a missionary. These rest here now in the same undisturbed quiet, which the Aldine Septuagint has enjoyed for centuries. I made an estimate of the whole number of books by counting the shelves and the volumes on two or three ; and found it in this way to be about fifteen hundred volumes. Burckhardt makes fifteen hundred Greek books, and seven hundred Arabic manuscripts ; which latter he examined without finding any thing of much value.[2] The library is utterly neglected ; private reading forming no part of the duties or pleasures of these worthy fathers.

With evident reluctance, the superior conducted us to the tomb, or rather charnel-house of the convent, situated near the middle of the garden. We inferred from his conversation, that travellers who have visited it, have sometimes wounded the feelings of the monks by their remarks, or by exhibiting disgust or horror at the ghastly spectacle. The building is half subterranean, consisting of two rooms or vaults ; one containing the bones of priests and the other those of lay monks. The dead bodies are first laid for two or three years on iron grates in another vault ; and then the skeletons are broken up and removed to these chambers. Here the bones are laid together in regular piles, the arms in one, the legs in another, the ribs in a third, etc. The bones of priests and laymen are piled separately in the different vaults ; except the skulls, which are thrown promiscuously together. The bones of the archbishops, whose bodies are always brought hither with their clothing and property after death, are kept separately in small wooden boxes. The skeleton of one saint was pointed out to us ; and also those of two ascetics, who are said to have lived as hermits in the adjacent moun-

---

[1] Tischendorf in 1844 was unable to get sight of this manuscript; Reise I. p. 240.
[2] Page 551.

tain, wearing shirts of mail next the body, and binding themselves together by the leg with an iron chain, parts of which are
here preserved.[1] This is emphatically the house of Death,
where he has now sat enthroned for centuries, receiving every
year new victims, until the chambers are nearly filled up with
this assembly of the dead. It must be a solemn feeling, one
would think, with which the monks repair to this spot, and look
upon these relics of mortality, their predecessors, their brethren,
their daily companions, all present here before them in their last
earthly shape of ghastliness ; with whom too their own bones
must so soon in like manner be mingled piecemeal, and be gazed
upon perhaps like them by strangers from a distant world. I
know of no place where the living and the dead come in closer
contact with each other ; or where the dread summons to prepare for death, rises with a stronger power before the mind. Yet
the monks seemed to regard the whole as an every-day matter,
to which their minds have become indifferent from long habit,
if not from levity. There was a stillness in their manner, but
no solemnity.

In the afternoon we were left undisturbed to the enjoyment
of our own thoughts, and our own more private exercises of devotion. Thus passed to us the Christian Sabbath amid this
stern sublimity of nature, where the Jewish Sabbath was of old
proclaimed to Israel. We were here in the midst of one of the
oldest monastic communities on earth ; where however all we
saw and heard tended only to confirm the melancholy truth, that
through the burden of human infirmity, even the holiest and
most spirit-stirring scenes soon lose by habit their power to ele-
vate and calm the soul.

The prior returned to us in the evening, as we sat at tea,
and accepted the cup we proffered him, on condition that it
should be without milk ; it being now the fast of Lent, during
which the tasting of every animal substance is strictly avoided.
A tea-spoon which had been dipped in milk, was sent out to be
washed for his use ; but in order to be on the safe side, he chose
even then to stir his tea with the handle of the spoon.

Monday, March 26th. Our plan had been laid to devote
this and the following day to the ascent of Jebel Mûsa and St.
Catharine ; and the superior had taken us into such favour, as
to announce his intention of accompanying us at least for the
first day. This, he said, was an honour he had never shown to
any traveller, except a French archbishop ; whose name and

---

[1] As Burckhardt heard the story, these
were two "Indian princes;" p. 564. Monconys in 1647 has it, "two sons of a king
of Ethiopia," I. p. 235 ; and Neitzschitz
i. 147. 148

in 1634, "two brothers, sons of an emperor of Constantinople," Welt-Beschauung,
p. 168. So also Van Egmond and Heyman about A. D. 1720 ; Reizen II. p. 174.

title however we found in the album as a Romish bishop *in partibus* from Syria.[1] Nor was this civility on the part of the superior perhaps quite so disinterested, as he was willing to have it appear; for it came out, that he wished to take along two younger monks, new comers, in order to make them acquainted with the holy places, so that they might hereafter accompany travellers and pilgrims as guides; there being at present only one monk besides the prior who knew them all, and he old and infirm. It was arranged that we should to-day visit Jebel Mûsa and the more northern brow of Horeb; sleep at the convent el-Arba'in; and thence ascend St. Catharine to-morrow. Accordingly, the provisions and other things for the night were sent round through the valley to el-Arba'in, while we took with us over the mountain only such articles as were necessary for the day. We made in all a larger party than was desirable; ourselves and servants, the superior with the two noviciates and pilgrim who had passed us on the way, (the two former, it seemed, being the persons to be initiated as future guides,) and two Arabs of the Jebeliyeh, serfs of the convent, who carried the articles we took with us. The convent has the monopoly of providing guides and attendants for all persons visiting the sacred places; and employs for this purpose its own serfs, paying them a trifle in grain or bread, and charging to travellers a much higher rate. There are two regular Ghafirs for travellers, or guides general; one an old man, 'Aid, who was with us only to-day, and the other Muhammed, quite a youth. Several Arab children also followed us up the mountain, with no other motive than to get a bit of bread for their pains.

We had risen early in order to set off in good season; but the variety of preparation and some dilatoriness on the part of the superior, delayed us until a late hour. We at length issued from the northwest entrance of the garden at 7¼ o'clock, and turning to the left, passed along above and back of the convent. The route ascends through a ravine on the south of the convent, running up obliquely through the perpendicular wall of the mountain; and the course from the convent almost to the head of this ravine is due south. The path leads for some time obliquely across the debris; and where it begins to grow steep, has been in part loosely laid with large stones, like a Swiss mountain road; which stones serve too as a sort of steps. In some places likewise there are more regular steps, but merely of rough stones in their natural state. It is usually reported that there were once regular steps all the way to the summit; but this, like so

---

[1] The prior forgot, it seems, that he had accompanied Schubert and his party in like manner to the summit of the mountain the year before; see Schubert's Reise, II. p. 312.

many other stories, would seem to be only an exaggeration of
travellers. At least every appearance at present testifies to the
contrary. In many parts steps would be unnecessary; and then
there is no trace of them. In other places where they are most
regular, some are six inches high and others nearly or quite two
feet. Hence, any attempt to estimate the height of the mountain from the pretended number of the steps, as has been done
by Shaw and others, can only be futile. After twenty-five minutes we rested at a fine cold spring under an impending rock;
the water of which is said to be carried down to the convent by
an aqueduct. It is called Ma'yan el-Jebel, the Mountain spring.
At 8.25 we reached a small rude chapel, still in the ravine, dedicated to the Virgin of the Ikonomos. Here the monks lighted
tapers and burnt incense, as they did in all the chapels to which
we came afterwards. The superior, being sixty-five years of age
and somewhat heavy, had to rest often; and this made our progress slow. Here and at all the subsequent holy places, while
we rested, he related the legend attached to each spot.

The story belonging to this chapel was as follows : In former
days, he said, the monks were so annoyed with fleas, and had
so few pilgrims, that they determined to abandon the convent.
They all went in procession to make their last visit to the holy
places of the mountain; and when near the top, the Virgin
suddenly appeared to them, bidding them not to depart, for pilgrims should never fail, fleas should disappear, and the plague
should never visit them. At the same time that they thus saw
the Virgin higher up the mountain, she appeared also to the Ikonomos on this spot. When the monks returned home, they
found a caravan of pilgrims actually arrived; the plague has
never since been here; and (according to them) fleas do not
exist in the convent; though in this latter particular, our own
experience did not exactly justify so unconditional a praise of
the Virgin.[1]

The path now turns nearly west and passes up out of the ravine by a steep ascent. At the top is a portal which we reached at
8¾ o'clock; and ten minutes afterwards another, through which
is the entrance to the small plain or basin, which here occupies the
top of the lofty ridge between the valley of the convent and that
of el-Leja. At these portals, in the palmy days of pilgrimage,

[1] The old travellers of the fifteenth and
sixteenth centuries, Tucher, Breydenbach,
F. Fabri, Wormbser, and others, relate
the same story, almost as if they copied
one from another; and make it refer to
"serpents, toads, and other poisonous rep-
tiles and vermin." But de Suchem in
A. D. 1336-50, heard it of "gnats, wasps,
and fleas;" though without any proces-
i. 150, 151 .

sion or vision; and so powerful was the
protection afforded in those days, that although these insects were very trouble-
some without the walls of the convent,
yet if brought within, they died immediately; p. 66 sq. Reissb. des heil. Landes,
p. 840. William of Baldensel (A. D.
1336) professes to have seen them die
when thus brought in, with his own eyes.

priests were stationed to confess pilgrims on their way up the mountain; and all the old travellers relate that no Jew could pass through them. At this point we saw for the first time the peak of Sinai or Jebel Músa on our left, and the higher summit of St. Catharine in the southwest beyond the deep valley el-Leja. At 9 o'clock we reached the well and tall cypress tree in the plain or basin, where we rested for a time; the prior distributing to all a portion of bread. After this allowance, the Arab children who had thus far hung about us, went back. Burckhardt speaks of this well as a stone tank, which receives the winter rains. We understood it at the time to be a well of living water, and such is its appearance, being of very considerable depth and regularly stoned up in the usual form of a deep well. Near by is a rock with many Arabic inscriptions, recording the visits of pilgrims. The lone cypress tree with its dark foliage is quite an interesting addition to this wild spot.[1]

This little plain is about twelve or thirteen hundred feet above the valleys below, extending quite across the ridge; and from it towards the west a path descends to the convent el-Arba'in in Wady el-Leja. On the right, clusters of rocks and peaks from two to four hundred feet higher than this basin, extend for nearly two miles towards the N. N. W. and terminate in the bold front which overhangs the plain er-Râhah north of the convent. This is the present Horeb of Christians. On the left, due south from the well, rises the higher peak of Sinai, or Jebel Músa, about seven hundred feet above the basin and nearly a mile distant. A few rods from the well, where the ascent of Sinai begins, is a low rude building containing the chapels of Elijah and Elisha. Here was evidently once a small monastery; and the older travellers speak also of a chapel of the Virgin. In that of Elijah the monks show near the altar a hole just large enough for a man's body, which they say is the cave where the prophet dwelt in Horeb.[2] Tapers were lighted and incense burnt in both these chapels. The ascent hence is steeper, though not difficult. There are steps for a great part of the way, merely rough stones thrown together; and in no part of the ascent of the whole mountain are they hewn, or cut in the rock, as is said by Burckhardt.[3]

In Niebuhr's time there were here two large trees; and the Prefect of the Franciscans in Cairo in 1722, mentions also here, "two cypress trees and two olive trees." The latter also speaks of the well as a "collection of water made by the winter snows and rains." The journal of this Prefect is first mentioned by Pococke (I. p. 147. fol.) and was afterwards translated into English and published by Clayton, bishop of Clogher, in a Letter to the Society of Antiquaries, Lond. 1753. It is also appended to the recent editions of Maundrell's Journey to Jerusalem, etc.

[2] 1 Kings 19, 8. 9. The elevation of this building above the convent in the valley below, is given by Schubert at 1400 Paris feet.

[3] Page 565.

Leaving the chapels at half past 9 o'clock, we ascended slowly, not failing to see the track of Muhammed's camel in the rock by the way ; and reached the summit of Jebel Mûsa at twenty minutes past ten. Here is a small area of huge rocks, about eighty feet in diameter, highest towards the east, where is a little chapel almost in ruins, formerly divided between the Greeks and Latins ; while towards the S. W. about forty feet distant stands a small ruined mosk. The summit and also the body of this part of the mountain are of coarse gray granite.[1] On the rocks are many inscriptions in Arabic, Greek, and Armenian, the work of pilgrims. In the chapel are the names of many travellers ; and I found here a pencil note of Rüppell's observations, May 7th, 1831 ; marking the time 12.15 ; Barom. 21' 7.6'' ; Therm. 13¼° R. or 62° F. At half past ten o'clock my thermometer stood in the chapel at 60° F.—The height of this peak above the sea, according to the observations of Rüppell, compared with simultaneous ones at Tûr, is 7035 Paris feet ; and its elevation above the convent el-Arba'in about 1670 feet.[2] From it the peak of St. Catharine bears S. 44° W. a thousand feet higher ; and Râs es-Sûfsâfeh, the highest among the peaks near the front of Horeb, N. 22° W.[3]

My first and predominant feeling while upon this summit, was that of disappointment. Although from our examination of the plain er-Râhah below, and its correspondence to the Scriptural narrative, we had arrived at the general conviction that the people of Israel must have been collected on it to receive the law ; yet we still had cherished a lingering hope or feeling, that there might after all be some foundation for the long series of monkish tradition, which for at least fifteen centuries has pointed out the summit on which we now stood, as the spot where the ten commandments were so awfully proclaimed. But Scriptural narrative and monkish tradition are very different things ; and while the former has a distinctness and definiteness, which through all our journeyings rendered the Bible our best

---

[1] Pococke correctly remarks, that the "north part of Sinai [Jebel Mûsa] is of red granite for above half way up ; all the rest being a granite of a yellowish ground, with small black grains in it, and the mountain at a distance appears of two colours ; " I. p. 147. fol. This difference of colour is especially striking as seen from the valley el-Leja.

[2] Rüppell's Reise in Abyssinien, I. pp. 118, 124. I follow here Rüppell's measurements throughout, because they alone are founded on corresponding observations on the sea-coast at Tûr. Schubert gives the height of Sinai at 6796.4 Paris feet,

i. 153, 154

or 2071 feet above the convent in Wady Shu'eib ; Russegger at 7097 Paris feet, or 1982 feet above the same convent.

[3] Other bearings from Jebel Mûsa were as follows : Um Lauz, a peak beyond Wady Sebâ'iyeh, N. 40° E. Um 'Alawy, connected with smaller peaks running towards the eastern gulf, N. 73° E. Abu Mas'ûd, west of Wady Wa'rah S. 36° E. Jebel Humr, S. 87° W. Jebel Tinia, or Sûnr et-Tinia, N. 62° W. Jebel Fureia', north end, N. 23° W. Jebel ed-Deir N. 21° E. Jebel ez-Zebîr, east end, N. 85° W. el-Benât, or el-Jauzeh, N. 45° W. Island of Tirân, S. 31° E.

guide-book, we found the latter not less usually and almost
regularly to be but a baseless fabric. In the present case, there
is not the slightest reason for supposing that Moses had any
thing to do with the summit which now bears his name. It is
three miles distant from the plain on which the Israelites must
have stood ; and hidden from it by the intervening peaks of the
modern Horeb. No part of the plain is visible from the summit ;
nor are the bottoms of the adjacent valleys ; nor is any spot to
be seen around it, where the people could have been assembled.
The only point in which it is not immediately surrounded by
high mountains, is towards the southeast, where it sinks down precipitously to a tract of naked gravelly hills. Here, just at its
foot, is the head of a small valley, Wady es-Sebâ'iyeh, running
toward the northeast beyond the mount of the Cross into Wady
esh-Sheikh ; and of another not larger, called el-Wa'rah, running southeast to the Wady Nûsb of the gulf of 'Akabah ; but
both of these together hardly afford a tenth part of the space contained in er-Râhah and Wady esh-Sheikh.[1] In the same direction is seen the route to Sherm ; and, beyond, a portion of the
gulf of 'Akabah and the little island Tirân ; while more to the
right and close at hand is the head of el-Leja among the hills.
No other part of the gulf of 'Akabah is visible ; though the
mountains beyond it are seen.[2]

Towards the southwest and west tower the ridges of St. Catharine and Tinia, cutting off the view of the gulf of Suez and
the whole western region ; so that neither Serbâl on the right,
nor the loftier Um Shaumer towards the left, are at all visible
from this peak of Sinai.[3] Indeed in almost every respect the
view from this point is confined, and is far less extensive and
imposing than that from the summit of St. Catharine. Only
the table land on the mountain of the Cross, is here seen nearer
and to better advantage across the narrow valley of Shu'eib.
Neither the convent from which we had come, nor that of el-
Arba'in, both lying in the deep valleys below, were visible. To
add to our disappointment, old 'Aid, the head-guide, who had
been selected expressly in order to tell us the names of the

[1] See more in Note XIV, end of the
volume.
[2] Brown speaks of having seen the
whole length of the gulf of 'Akabah from
Sinai ; but this is an impossibility. Travels, chap. XIV. p. 179.
[3] Yet Laborde professes to have seen
from it Serbâl, Um Shaumer, and the
mountains of Africa beyond. It must
have been with 'the mind's eye.' Voyage
en Arab. Pet. p. 68. Engl. p. 252. A
similar exaggerated account is given by
Russegger ; see Berghaus' Annalen, März

1839, p. 420 sq. Rüppell correctly remarks : "The prospect from the peak of
Sinai is limited in the east, south, and
west, by higher mountains ; and only towards the north, one looks out over a
widely extended landscape ;" Reise in
Abyssinien, I. p. 118. Burckhardt was
prevented by a thick fog from seeing even
the nearest mountains ; Travels, etc. p.
566.—The statements of this note have
sometimes been questioned ; but I must
again assert their entire accuracy, which
is also manifest from the list of bearings.
i. 154, 155

mountains and objects around, proved to know very little about them, and often answered at random. In short, the visit to the summit of Jebel Mûsa, was to me the least satisfactory incident in our whole sojourn at Mount Sinai.

We remained upon the summit nearly two and a half hours. Leaving it at 12¾ o'clock, we returned to the cypress tree and well near the chapel of Elijah. From this point a path leads south of west over the little plain, and descends partly by steps to the convent el-Arba'ín in Wady el-Leja. We determined, however, to visit the northern brow of Horeb, which overlooks the plain er-Râhah ; and took a route towards the N. N. W. in order to reach it. As we left the well for this purpose at 1¼ o'clock, the clouds which had been gathering for some time, threatened to drench us with a shower of rain. The drops began to fall thinly but heavily ; and for a while we hoped that Beshârah's entreaties for rain might have been fulfilled ; even at the expense of our being counted as prophets by the Arabs, and getting a wet skin for ourselves. But the clouds soon passed away, and the desert remained parched and thirsty as before.

The path was wild and rugged, leading over rocks and winding through ravines among low peaks. In fifteen minutes we came to a small round basin among the hills, with a bed of soil full of shrubs ; where also were a hollyhock and hawthorn, and evident traces of an artificial reservoir for water, which was said formerly to have been carried down to the convent. Here stands a small chapel of St. John the Baptist. Not far off are the cells of several anchorites cut in the rock. Twenty minutes further is another larger basin, surrounded by twelve peaks, and the bottom enclosed by a low wall ; showing that it was once tilled as a garden. At 2 o'clock we reached a third basin, still deeper and more romantic, surrounded by a like number of higher peaks, one of which is Râs es-Sûfsâfeh, the highest in this part of the mountain. A narrow fissure runs out northward from this basin towards the plain, through which the mountain may be ascended. Here a willow and two hawthorns were growing, with many shrubs ; and in all this part of the mountains were great quantities of the fragrant plant *Ja'deh*, which the monks call hyssop. Here is a small chapel dedicated to the Virgin of the Zone. Near by we found a pair of horns of the Beden or Ibex, left behind perhaps by some hunter.

While the monks were here employed in lighting tapers and burning incense, we determined to scale the almost inaccessible peak of es-Sûfsâfeh before us, in order to look out upon the plain, and judge for ourselves as to the adaptedness of this part of the mount to the circumstances of the Scriptural history. This cliff rises some five hundred feet above the basin ; and the

i. 156, 157

distance to the summit is more than half a mile. We first attempted to climb the side in a direct course ; but found the rock so smooth and precipitous, that after some falls and more exposures, we were obliged to give it up, and clamber upwards along a steep ravine by a more northern and circuitous course. From the head of this ravine, we were able to climb around the face of the northern precipice and reach the top, along the deep hollows worn in the granite by the weather during the lapse of ages, which give to this part, as seen from below, the appearance of architectural ornament.

The extreme difficulty and even danger of the ascent, was well rewarded by the prospect that now opened before us. The whole plain er-Râhah lay spread out beneath our feet, with the adjacent Wadys and mountains ; while Wady esh-Sheikh on the right, and the recess on the left, both connected with, and opening broadly from er-Râhah, presented an area which serves nearly to double that of the plain. Our conviction was strengthened, that here or on some one of the adjacent cliffs was the spot, where the Lord "descended in fire" and proclaimed the law. Here lay the plain where the whole congregation might be assembled ; here was the mount that could be approached and touched, if not forbidden ; and here the mountain brow, where alone the lightnings and the thick cloud would be visible, and the thunders and the voice of the trump be heard, when the Lord "came down in the sight of all the people upon Mount Sinai." We gave ourselves up to the impressions of the awful scene ; and read with a feeling that will never be forgotten, the sublime account of the transaction and the commandments there promulgated, in the original words as recorded by the great Hebrew legislator.[1]

Between es-Sûfsâfeh and the plain are still some lower peaks, overhanging the latter more directly, which we were desirous to visit ; but the time did not permit. Descending therefore to our companions, who were in no hurry, we returned to the second basin above mentioned, and thence at 3.45 took a path more to the right. At 4 o'clock we came to a small church on the western brow of the ridge, dedicated to St. Pantelcemon. The chapel of St. Anne mentioned by Pococke and other travellers, we did not see. Hence a long and in some parts steep descent, about southwest, brought us at a quarter past 5 o'clock to the convent el-Arba'in, where we were to lodge.

This monastery is said to have received its name, el-Arba'in, "the Forty," from the circumstance that the Arabs once took it by surprise, and killed the forty monks who were its inmates. Hence it is called by the older travellers the convent of the

---

[1] Exod. 19, 9-25. 20, 12-1.

Forty Saints or Martyrs.[1] Tradition has forgotten the time
when this event took place ; but the story probably refers to the
massacre of forty hermits around Sinai near the close of the
fourth century.[2] A large plantation of olive trees extends far
above and below the monastery along the valley, which is narrow
like that of Shu'eib, but longer and less desert. Just around
the buildings is also a garden of other fruit trees, in which apple
and apricot trees were in blossom ; and not far off is a small
grove of tall poplars, here cultivated for timber. In this garden
too was a rill of water ; which however was lost after a few rods.
The convent, as such, has been deserted for several centuries ;
yet two or three of the monks usually reside here for a time
every summer ; though even this custom had been neglected for
the last three years. A family of Jebeliyeh, or serfs, was here to
keep the garden. As we entered, the sweet voice of a prattling
Arab child struck my ear, and made my heart thrill, as it recalled
the thoughts of home.—The elevation of this spot above the sea,
was found by Rüppell to be 5366 Paris feet.[3]

A large room, the best in the building, though lighted only
by the door, was assigned to us, in which our beds were already
spread on a layer of fragrant herbs. A fire was lighted in a
corner ; and we found it quite comfortable, although the thermometer stood at 65° F. Indeed an Arab has no idea of passing a night without fire at any season. The superior and his
monks occupied a room in another part of the building. The
good father spent the evening in our apartment, and was very
social and communicative. He had borne the walk of to-day so
well, that he was determined to accompany us to-morrow to the
summit of St. Catharine. We had here a curious instance of
the respect in which he is held by his Arab serfs. He had pulled
off his shoes and was sitting with bare feet, (for he like the other
monks wore no stockings,) when the old guide 'Aid came in to
bid good night, and perceiving his situation suddenly kneeled
down and kissed his toe. Indeed, it seemed to be quite an occasion of festivity with these Arabs, to meet the patriarchal old
man so far abroad out of the convent walls.

Tuesday, March 27th. We started from our fragrant couch
at early dawn, in order to set off in good season for the mountain. But here, as in so many other cases where aught was de-

---

[1] Quaresmius II. p. 996. Tucher of
Nürnberg relates this story in A. D.
1480; as also Baumgarten in 1507, lib. I.
c. 24. These travellers found the convent deserted, as now, except by two or
three monks.—The monks themselves, as
I have since learned, sometimes refer the
name to the Forty Martyrs of Armenia.
i. 159. 160

[2] See further on, under the head of
" Sinai in the early Christian ages."

[3] Reise in Abyssinien, I. p. 124. From
a comparison with Schubert's measurements, it would appear that el-Arba'in
lies about 400 Paris feet higher than the
other convent. This difference, however,
seems to me to be too great.

pending on Arabs, we found it impossible to 'keep the word of promise' to our hopes. Old 'Aid, the guide, gave out at starting; and his place had to be supplied by a youth, Sâlim, who overtook us on the way, and proved a better guide than the old man. We thought too we perceived some slight symptoms of abatement in the good superior's zeal for undertaking the more arduous task which awaited us to-day; and at our suggestion he concluded to remain and await our return.

At length we issued from the garden at ten minutes past 6 o'clock, and proceeded S. W. by S. up a ravine which comes down from the side of St. Catharine, called Shŭk Mûsa, 'Cleft of Moses,' from a deep rent in the mountain at its head. At ten minutes from the convent and before beginning to ascend, the path passes between two large rocks, both having Sinaite inscriptions, and one of them quite covered with them. These Burckhardt did not see; for he says expressly, that there are none in el-Leja higher up than the rock of Moses, which lies at some distance below el-Arba'in. We found none afterwards. The ravine soon becomes narrow and precipitous, and the way exceedingly difficult; the path leading over stones and rocks in their natural state, which have never been removed nor laid more evenly. Indeed, we could not discover all day the slightest trace, that any path had ever existed here with steps, or laid stones, like that which leads up Jebel Mûsa. At 7.25 we reached the fine cold spring called Ma'yan esh-Shunnâr, 'Partridge fountain;' it having been discovered, as they say, by the fluttering of one of these birds, when the monks were bringing down the bones of St. Catharine from the mountain. It is on a shelf of rock under the left-hand precipice, about a foot in diameter and depth, with fine cold water never increasing nor diminishing. The water percolates through some fissure in the rock into a natural reservoir below, where it is found in considerable quantity. Several hawthorn trees (Arab. Za'rûr) were growing in the vicinity. Directly above this spot is the deep cleft properly called Shŭk Mûsa. The path now turns S. W. by W. passing up a very steep ascent for a time; and then across loose debris to the top of the main ridge, which runs up towards the summit, here bearing S. S. W. This ridge we reached about 8½ o'clock; and here the view opened towards the west over the deep valleys below.

We now kept along the western side of the ridge, beneath the brow, where the mountain side slopes rapidly down into the depths below, and is covered like the Wadys with tufts of herbs and shrubs, furnishing abundant pasturage for the flocks of the Bedawin, as well as for the troops of gazelles and mountain goats (Beden) which haunt these wild retreats. The Ja'deh or hys-

sop was here in great plenty ; and especially the fragrant *Za'ter*,
a species of thyme, *Ocymum zatarhendi* of Forskal.[1] This vegetation extends quite up to the foot of the highest peak, an
immense pile of huge blocks of coarse red granite thrown promiscuously together. Climbing this mass of rocks with difficulty on the south side, we reached the summit at a quarter
past 9 o'clock. This consists of two small knolls or elevations
of the rocks ; one towards the east on which stands a rude
chapel ; the other towards the west a few feet higher. According to the latest observations of Rüppell, similar to those on
Sinai, the height of this mountain is 8063 Paris feet above the
sea, or about 2700 feet above the convent el-Arba'in.[2] Its elevation therefore is 1030 feet greater than that of Jebel Mûsa.
The sky was perfectly clear, and the air cool. A cold northwest
wind swept fitfully over the summit. The thermometer stood
in the shade at 43° F. In the sun it rose at first to 52° ; but
as the gust grew strong, it sunk to 48° F.

During the ascent, I had found myself unwell ; and reached
the top in a state of great exhaustion. While my companion
was busy in cross-examining the guides as to the mountains and
places in view, I sought out a sunny and sheltered spot among
the rocks, where I lay down and slept sweetly for half an hour,
and awoke greatly refreshed.

The chief motive which led us to ascend Jebel Kâtherîn, was
the hope of obtaining a more distinct and extensive view of the
region of Sinai and of the peninsula. Nor were our hopes disappointed. The mountain indeed has little of historical interest ; there being not the slightest probability that it had any connection with the giving of the law to Israel. But the prospect
is wide and magnificent, comprehending almost the whole peninsula. The chief interruption of the view is by Um Shaumer,
bearing S. 20° W., a sharp granite peak, said by Burckhardt to
be inaccessible, and perhaps the highest point in the peninsula.
Jebel Mûsa, lying N. 44° E. was far below us, and appeared
only as an inferior peak. Towards the southeast the large Wady
Nûsb was seen (S. 62° E.) running towards the eastern gulf ;
of which also a much larger portion was visible around Sherm,
than from Jebel Mûsa, with the island Tîrân bearing S. 35° E.
The northern part of this gulf could not be traced ; though the
Arabian mountains beyond it were very distinct. A mountain
which our guides called Râs Muhammed, bore S. 9° E. in the
general direction of the cape of that name ; around which, and
to the right of Um Shaumer, almost the whole course of the gulf

[1] Flora Æg. Ar. p. 109, 110.
[2] Reise in Abyssinien, I. pp. 121, 124.
Russegger gives the height of St. Catha-
i. 162, 163

rine at 8168 Paris feet. Schubert did not
ascend this mountain.

of Suez was visible, with the African mountains beyond ; a sil-
very thread of waters stretching far up through a naked desert.
Two of these African mountains were very distinct ; one, ez-
Zeit, bearing S. 56° W. and the other the cone of Jebel Ghârib,
bearing S. 77° W. called by our guides the mountain of the
'Abâbideh. Between the western gulf and the mountains of
Sinai, the great plain el-Kâ'a was spread out, extending beyond
Tûr ; and north of that place along the shore was seen the low
range of limestone mountains, among which lies the sounding
hill Nakûs. Nearer at hand were many dark peaks ; and among
them that of Madsûs, just beyond the gardens of Bûghâbigh,
bearing N. 78° W. and a peak of Jebel Haweit, N. 45° W.
Near this last rises Wady Kibrin, which runs off to Wady Hibrân. More distant in the same direction rose the rugged cliffs
of Serbâl, lying between N. 57° W. and N. 70° W. while farther
to the right were seen Sarbût el-Jemel, el-Benât, and ez-Zebir.
In the north, the great sandy plain er-Ramleh was seen stretching far along the base of the high level ridge of et-Tih ; and we
were shown the point where this mountain separates into two
parallel ridges, bearing from us about north. Towards the eastern quarter, between us and the whole length of the gulf of
'Akabah, the eye wandered over a sea of mountains, black, abrupt,
naked, weather-worn peaks ; a fitting spot where the very genius
of desolation might erect his horrid throne.—Below us, just at
the western foot of St. Catharine, a valley called Um Kûrâf
was seen running northwards ; while another, ez-Zuweitin,
having a succession of gardens, passes down from the right near
the base of el-Humr, to join it. The Wady thus formed is
called Tûlâh, and runs down between the mountains of Seru
N. 15° W. and Tinia N. 26° W. apparently joining the Rûdhwâh and so flowing off to Wady Solâf. Jebel el-Humr was below us in the direction N. 3° E. Jebel Tinia was also called by
our guides Sûmr et-Tinia.[1]

We found that our guides of to-day and yesterday, both old
and young, knew very little of distant mountains and objects ;
while they were familiarly acquainted with those near at hand.
It was only after long and repeated examination and cross-ques-
tioning, that my companion could be sure of any correctness as
to more remote objects ; since at first they often gave answers at

---

[1] Other bearings from Jebel Kâtherin were the following: Jebel ed-Deir, N. 35° E. Um Lauz, N. 41° E. Um 'Alawy, N. 62° E. el-Habeshy, further distant, N. 66° E. Urk ez-Zâgherah, a long ridge beyond Um 'Alawy, north end, N. 87° E.; south end, S. 80° E. Abu Mas'ûd, be-tween the Wadys Nûsb and Wa'rab, S. 30° E. Zebir, another peak of St. Catha-rine near at hand, S. 12° E. Muheirid el-Kunâs, S. 6° E. and el-'Odhu, S. 10' W. both connected with Um Shaumer. Fera' Suweid, S. 25° W. and es-Sik, S. 77° W.; dark peaks nearer St. Catharine. el-Benât, N. 45° W. ez-Zebir, west end, N. 40' W.; east end, N. 31° W.

i. 163–165

random, which they afterwards modified or took back. The young man Sâlim was the most intelligent of the whole. After all our pains, many of the names we obtained were different from those which Burckhardt heard ; although his guides apparently were of the same tribe.—A tolerably certain method of finding any place at will, is to ask an Arab if its name exists. He is sure to answer Yes ; and to point out some spot at hand as its location. In this way, I have no doubt, we might have found Rephidim, or Marah, or any other place we chose ; and such is probably the mode in which many ancient names and places have been discovered by travellers, which no one has ever been able to find after them.[1]

Of the two, the ascent of St. Catharine is much to be preferred to that of Jebel Mûsa. The view is far more extensive and almost unlimited, affording to the spectator a good general idea of the whole peninsula ; of which he learns little or nothing from Sinai. The ascent indeed is longer and more laborious ; but it also repays the toil in a much higher degree. Our whole visit here to day was one of satisfaction and gratification ; not, as yesterday, of disappointment. The time generally necessary for the ascent of Jebel Mûsa may be estimated at an hour and a half ; and for St. Catharine from two and a half to three hours. We were longer on the way.

After remaining for two and a half hours on the summit, we left at 11¾ o'clock, and reached the convent of the Forty Martyrs at a quarter past one. Here we found the superior still waiting in order to conduct us around through Wady el-Leja to the convent, and show us the holy places on the way. The distance is reckoned an hour and a half, and may be thus divided : forty minutes to the mouth of el-Leja ; twenty-five minutes along the front of Horeb to Wady Shu'eib ; and twenty-five minutes to the convent in that valley. This is a sort of household path for the monks, which they have travelled for centuries ; and along which, as a matter of convenience, they have gathered together all the holy places they know of in connection with Sinai.

After stopping about half an hour at el-Arba'in, we proceeded slowly down the valley, without seeing the chapel and grot of St. Onuphrius, which are said by Pococke to be near the north end of the olive plantation. In about twenty minutes we came to the rock which they say Moses smote, and the water gushed out. As to this rock one is at a loss, whether most to admire the credulity of the monks or the legendary and discrepant reports of travellers. It is hardly necessary to remark, that there is not

[1] So, for example, Marah, Capernaum, Bethsaida, Chorazin, etc.
i. 165, 166

the slightest ground for assuming any connection between this narrow valley and Rephidim ; but on the contrary, there is every thing against it. The rock itself is a large isolated cube of coarse red granite, which has fallen from the eastern mountain. Down its front, in an oblique line from top to bottom, runs a seam of a finer texture, from twelve to fifteen inches broad, having in it several irregular horizontal crevices, somewhat resembling the human mouth, one above another. These are said to be twelve in number ; but I could make out only ten. The seam extends quite through the rock, and is visible on the opposite or back side ; where also are similar crevices, though not so large. The holes did not appear to us to be artificial, as is usually reported ; although we examined them particularly. They belong rather to the nature of the seam ; yet it is possible that some of them may have been enlarged by artificial means. The rock is a singular one ; and doubtless was selected, on account of this very singularity, as the scene of the miracle.

Below this point are many Sinaite inscriptions along the rocks in the valley. Having Burckhardt's Travels with us, we compared some of his copies with the originals, and found them tolerably exact.[1] Where Wady el-Leja opens out into the recess that runs in west from the plain er-Râhah, there is on the left a garden ; and further down on the right another, having a great number and variety of fruit trees. This Burckhardt says is called, by way of eminence, el-Bostân, ' the Garden ; ' a name which we did not hear. These gardens mark the sites of former convents, now fallen to ruin ; that towards the west once bearing the name of St. Peter and St. Paul, and the other that of St. Mary of David. Over the mountain towards the west among the gardens which we saw from St. Catharine in Wady Zuweitin or Tûlâh, was formerly another small convent of St. Cosmas and Damian, visited by Pococke ;[2] but of which we heard nothing. Overagainst the mouth of el-Leja, in the northern part of the recess, we, like all travellers, were pointed to the spot where the earth opened and swallowed up Korah, Dathan and Abiram, with their followers ; the good fathers of the monastery, as a matter of convenience, having transferred the scene of that event from the vicinity of Kadesh to this place.[3]

Farther eastward in front of Horeb, a hole in a granite rock level with the sand, is shown as the mould in which Aaron cast

---

[1] Not so Pococke's copies, in which there is hardly a trace of resemblance ; nor are those of Niebuhr much better.

[2] Travels, I. pp. 149, 153. fol. In a cell or perhaps convent in this valley, the Abbot Johannes Climacus, known as a writer, lived for forty years, in the latter part of the sixth century. The name of the valley in Greek was then Θωλά, Thola. See in Max. Biblioth. vet. Patrum, Tom. X. p. 386 sq. Acta Sanctorum, Jan. Tom. I. p. 963, col. 1.

[3] Num. c. 16, compared with Num. 13, 26.

the golden calf. Burckhardt has exaggerated this story a little
at the expense of the monks, making them show the head of the
golden calf itself transmuted into stone. The small elevation or
point between the channels of the Wadys Sheikh and Shu'eib,
they also show as the place where Aaron was standing, when the
people danced around the golden calf in the plain, and Moses
descended behind him from the mountain. Just at the foot of
the adjacent corner of Horeb is a rock, marking the spot where
Moses threw down and broke the tables of the law. These the
monks and Arabs both believe are still buried there unto this
day ; and the Arabs often dig around the spot in the hope of
finding them.[1]

As we advanced up the valley towards the convent, we were
followed by quite a throng of Arab women and children of the
Jebeliyeh, begging various articles of the superior, and kissing
his hand and the hem of his garment, as if rejoiced to meet him
without the walls. The old man dealt kindly with them, and
distributed his little gifts with patriarchal dignity and grace.
We reached the convent at 4¾ o'clock, exceedingly fatigued, and
glad to find a quiet home. The Ikonomos undertook to pay our
Arab attendants in barley, charging us at the rate of seven piastres a day for each guide. As the poor fellows would probably
get much less than this in their barley, we sent them a trifling
bakhshish or present in money, with which they went away delighted.

Wednesday, March 28th. We had fixed on Thursday as
the day of our departure ; and were to-day of course very busy
with our journals and letters. Beshârah arrived in the afternoon,
saying that the camels would be here at night or in the morning ;
and that Tuweileb would go with us to 'Akabah, according to
the contract.

The good superior, Father Neophytus, continued his attentions, although it was a day on which he was peculiarly occupied in the duties of the convent. All the morning until 12
o'clock the monks were at prayers ; and the same was to be the
case at night from ten o'clock until two ; this being a particular
regulation of the convent during certain days in Lent. After
dinner we were invited to visit the superior at his room. We
found him in the midst of a little establishment by himself ; a
small court, a work-bench with a few joiner's tools, a sitting-room,
kitchen, and two or three small chambers. His sitting-room,
like the one we occupied, was furnished with low divans and carpets, rather old and worn ; in a recess stood a low desk and trunk ;
and on the opposite side were a closet and cupboard. Several

[1] Burckhardt has transferred this legend to the summit of Sinai; p. 567.
i. 168, 169

Greek books, mostly devotional, were scattered on a shelf and in the window. The room was very small. Oranges from Egypt sliced with sugar were presented to us ; and also coffee, prepared by the young deacon.

As this was to be our last day at the convent, the superior made us several presents as memorials of our visit to Sinai, remarkable rather for the value which he set upon them, than for any intrinsic worth. An engraving of the convent and mountain was curious as a specimen of perspective drawing (or rather nonperspective) a century ago ; and this and some beautiful white corals from Tûr, and a skin of sweetmeats for our journey, were the chief articles. The latter contained a mixture of dates and almonds, highly prized, and usually prepared (he said) only as presents to Pashas and persons of rank.

In accordance with a former promise, the old man likewise put into our hands a small quantity of the manna of the peninsula, famous at least as being the successor of the Israelitish manna, though not to be regarded as the same substance. According to his account, it is not produced every year ; sometimes only after five or six years ; and the quantity in general has greatly diminished. It is found in the form of shining drops on the twigs and branches (not upon the leaves) of the Tûrfa, *Tamarix Gallica mannifera* of Ehrenberg, from which it exudes in consequence of the puncture of an insect of the coccus kind, *Coccus manniparus* of the same naturalist.[1] What falls upon the sand is said not to be gathered. It has the appearance of gum, is of a sweetish taste, and melts when exposed to the sun or to a fire. The Arabs consider it as a great delicacy, and the pilgrims prize it highly ; especially those from Russia, who pay a high price for it. The superior had now but a small quantity which he was keeping against an expected visit from the Russian consul general in Egypt. Indeed, so scarce had it become of late years, as to bear a price of twenty or twenty-five piastres the pound.

Of the manna of the Old Testament, it is said : "When the dew that lay was gone up, behold, upon the face of the desert a small round thing, small as the hoar-frost on the ground;—and it was like coriander seed, white ; and the taste of it was like wafers with honey ;[2]—And the people gathered it, and ground it in mills, and beat it in a mortar, or baked it in pans, and made cakes of it ; and the taste of it was as the taste of fresh oil. And when the dew fell upon the camp in the night, the manna fell upon it."[3] Of all these characteristics not one is applicable to the present manna. And even could it be shown to be the same, still a supply of it in sufficient abundance for the daily

---

[1] See Note XV, end of the volume. [2] Ex. 16, 14. 31. [3] Num. 11, 8. 9.

consumption of two millions of people, would have been no less
a miracle.

The superior also procured for me a pair of the sandals usually worn by the Bedawin of the peninsula, made of the thick
skin of a fish which is caught in the Red Sea. The Arabs
around the convent called it *Tûn ;* but could give no farther
account of it, than that it is a large fish, and is eaten. It is a
species of Halicore, named by Ehrenberg *Halicora Hemprichii.*[1]
The skin is clumsy and coarse, and might answer very well for
the external covering of the tabernacle, which was constructed at
Sinai ;[2] but would seem hardly a fitting material for the ornamental sandals belonging to the costly attire of high-born dames in
Palestine, described by the prophet Ezekiel.[3]

It will not be supposed that all these things were presented
to us without the hope of a recompense. Indeed, some of them,
as the manna and sandals, were a matter of purchase on our
part ; and as to the rest, we knew very well that a *present* of
money was expected to an amount greater than the value of the
articles.

Thursday, March 29*th, Forenoon.* This being the day appointed for our setting off, we held ourselves ready at an early
hour ; but it was nearly eleven o'clock before Tuweileb arrived
with the camels. After a long talk in the garden in presence of
the superior, it was agreed, that as Beshârah had now no camel,
Tuweileb should take his place in the contract, and conduct us to
'Akabah. Three of the men also, who had come with us from
Cairo, concluded to go no further ; and we found that we were
to have an entirely new set of camels, which proved to be better
than the former ones. The 190 piastres to be paid for each
camel from Cairo to 'Akabah, the Arabs divided among themselves as follows : 40 from Cairo to Suez ; 80 from Suez to the
convent ; and 70 from the convent to 'Akabah. Yet there would
seem to be no regular price for any of these routes; for an
English traveller the year before had paid at the rate of 40 piastres to Suez ; 100 thence to the convent ; and 60 from the convent to 'Akabah.

We parted from Beshârah with regret. He had served us
faithfully and well ; was ever active and vigilant ; and had
always manifested some independence and self-respect. We
made him a small additional present on account of the camel he
had lost in our service ; and promised to put him into our book,
if we made one. As he said he should return immediately to

---

[1] See Ehrenberg's Symbola Phys. *Mam-*
malia, Decas II. Text fol. K.   Also ibid.
Zootomica, Dec. I. Tab. 3, 4, 5.   According to this writer, the Arabs on the coast
call this fish *Naka* and *Lottâm.*
i. 171, 172

[2] Ex. 25, 5.   26, 14. al. The Hebrew
word is תַּחַשׁ, usually translated *badger ;*
though, as it would seem, without sufficient reason in this case.
[3] Ez. 16, 10.

Cairo, we entrusted letters to his care, with a promise of reward on their being delivered ; but it was many months ere they reached the places of their destination.

Tuweileb was an older man than Besharah ; he had travelled more, was better acquainted with the routes and with the country in general, and knew more of the habits and usual wants of Frank travellers. He was, however, less active ; was apparently growing old ; and had seen his best days. Yet we found him throughout faithful, trustworthy, and kind ; although for a great part of the time he was with us, he was labouring under ill health. We cheerfully add our testimony in his favour, to that of former travellers.

Our residence of five and a half days in the convent turned out to be rather an expensive one. The community provided us with various articles which we needed on our further journey ; as bread, dried fruits, almonds, candles, and the like ; but would set no price upon them. These we could estimate ; but to do the 'proper thing' as to our lodgings and entertainment, and a fit 'remembrance' to all the inmates, from the superior down to the servants, was a matter requiring more nicety and tact. With the aid of our Komeh, who was skilled in these matters, we made out to get through the business to the apparent satisfaction of all parties, except the good superior. He had exerted himself perhaps unusually to pay us friendly attentions ; and possibly he expected from us too much in return. His manner was still and resigned ; but his countenance was fallen and beclouded. A civil speech, however, with the dexterous application of a couple of dollars in addition, wrought a sudden change ; the cloud cleared away, his eyes lighted up, and his whole countenance assumed an expression of more than wonted benignity.

During our journey to the convent, it had been a part of our plan, or rather our wish, to make an excursion to Jebel Serbâl, in order to examine for ourselves, whether this mountain has any claim to be regarded as the Sinai of Scripture ; as Burckhardt suggests was perhaps anciently the case.[1] But after we reached the convent, and perceived the adaptedness of that region to the circumstances of the historical narrative, this wish became less strong ; and afterwards the want of time and the information given us by Sheikh Husein and Tuweileb respecting the district of Serbâl, led us to abandon the idea of visiting it. Tuweileb had spent several weeks around the mountain the preceding season ; and both assured us, that nowhere in the vicinity of it, is there any valley or open spot like the plain er-Râhah, or even like Wady esh-Sheikh. From the northeast side of Serbâl the Wadys run down to Wady Feirân ; but they are comparatively

Travels, etc. page 609.

narrow and rocky. On its southwest side still narrower Wadys run out to the great plain el-Kâ'a, at the distance of an hour or more. There is water in plenty on both sides of the mountain ; and a path, laid in part with steps, leads along the eastern and southern sides to the summit. The route from the convent to Serbâl goes down Wady Sheikh ; or else by the Nŭkb Hâwy and down Wady Solâf. The distance from the convent to Feirân near the foot of Serbâl by this latter route, is nine or ten hours. The mountain itself is a long ridge with five principal peaks. Burckhardt ascended the easternmost, which with the one adjacent he supposed to be the highest. Rüppell in 1831 ascended the second from the west, by a path along the northern side of the mountain ; he regards this as the highest, and took observations upon it to ascertain its elevation. From these its height was found to be 6342 Paris feet above the sea ; or 976 feet higher than the convent el-Arba'in.[1] Hence it turns out that Serbâl is more than 1700 feet lower than St. Catharine ; although as it rises alone and magnificently from the midst of far inferior ridges, its *apparent* elevation is not much less than that of the former mountain.

On both the summits ascended by Burckhardt and Rüppell, these travellers found inscriptions in the usual unknown character ; and also in the valleys leading to the mountain. In a Wady on the southwest side of the ridge, near its eastern end, are the remains of a large and well built convent, from which a path is said to lead up the mountain. These circumstances would seem to indicate, that Serbâl was anciently a place of pilgrimage of some kind ; but whether because it was perhaps regarded as the Sinai of Scripture, or only in connection with this convent and the episcopal see of Pharan ; or more probably as a sacred place of the heathen inhabitants of the peninsula ; it may be now difficult to determine.[2]

The weather during our residence at the convent, as indeed during all our journey through the peninsula, was very fine ; with the slight exception already mentioned on Jebel Mûsa. At the convent, the thermometer ranged only between 47° and 67° F. The winter nights are said here to be cold ; water freezes as late as February ; and snow often falls upon the mountains. But the air is exceedingly pure, and the climate healthy ; as is testified by the great age and vigour of many of the monks. And if in general few of the Arabs attain to so great an age, the cause is doubtless to be sought in the scanti-

---

[1] Reise in Abyss. I. pp. 128, 124.
[2] See generally, Burckhardt's Travels, etc. p. 606 sq. Rüppell's Reise in Abys-i. 174, 175

sinien, I. p. 125 sq.—See more in Note XVI, end of the volume.

ness of their fare and their exposure to privations; and not in
any injurious influence of the climate.

In closing this Section of our Journal, I throw together here
all that remains to be said upon the Sinai of the Old Testament,
Sinai in the early Christian ages, the present convent, and also
upon the Arab inhabitants of the peninsula.

SINAI OF THE OLD TESTAMENT.

We came to Sinai with some incredulity, wishing to investigate the point, whether there was any probable ground beyond
monkish tradition, for fixing upon the present supposed site.
The details of the preceding pages will have made the reader
acquainted with the grounds, which led us to the conviction, that
the plain er-Râhah above described is the probable spot where
the congregation of Israel were assembled, and that the mountain impending over it, the present Horeb, was the scene of the
awful phenomena in which the law was given. We were satisfied after much examination and inquiry, that in no other quarter
of the peninsula, and certainly not around any of the higher
peaks, is there a spot corresponding in any degree so fully as this
to the historical account, and to the circumstances of the case.
I have entered above more fully into the details, because former
travellers have touched upon this point so slightly ;[1] and because,
even to the present day, it is a current opinion among scholars,
that no open space exists among these mountains.[2] We too
were surprised as well as gratified to find here, in the inmost
recesses of these dark granite cliffs, this fine plain spread out
before the mountain ; and I know not when I have felt a thrill
of stronger emotion, than when in first crossing the plain, the
dark precipices of Horeb rising in solemn grandeur before us, we
became aware of the entire adaptedness of the scene to the
purposes for which it was chosen by the great Hebrew legislator.
Moses doubtless, during the forty years in which he kept the
flocks of Jethro, had often wandered over these mountains, and
was well acquainted with their valleys and deep recesses, like the
Arabs of the present day. At any rate, he knew and had visited
the spot to which he was to conduct his people ;[3] this *adytum*
in the midst of the great circular granite region, with only a
single feasible entrance ; a secret holy place shut out from the
world amid lone and desolate mountains.

---

[1] Comp. above, pp. 104–107, 117. See
also more in Notes XIV, XVI, at the end of
the volume.

[2] Compare Winer's Bibl. Realwörterb.
art. *Sinai.*

[3] Ex. 3, 1.

The Israelites probably approached Sinai by the Wady Feirân ; and entered the plain through the upper part of Wady esh-Sheikh. At least there is no conceivable reason, why they should have passed to the south of Mount Serbâl, and taken the circuitous and more difficult route near Tûr, and through the Wady Hibrân, as has sometimes been supposed. From the desert of Sin, which I have above taken to be the great plain along the shore, to Sinai, three stations are marked, Dophkah, Alush, and Rephidim,[1] equivalent to four days' journey for such a host ; and this accords well with the distance of twenty-six to twenty-eight hours as usually travelled by camels.[2]

The names of Horeb and Sinai are used interchangeably in the Pentateuch, to denote the mountain on which the law was given ; and this circumstance has naturally occasioned difficulty to commentators. The most obvious and common explanation is, to regard one (Sinai) as the general name for the whole cluster, and the other (Horeb) as designating a particular mountain ; much as the same names are employed by the Christians at the present day.[3] So too the Arabs now apply the name Jebel et-Tûr to the whole central granite region ; while the different mountains of which it is composed, are called Jebel Kâtherin, Jebel Mûsa, etc. On looking at the subject during our sojourn at the convent, I was led to a similar conclusion ; applying the names however differently, and regarding Horeb as the general name, and Sinai as the particular one. Two circumstances seem to favour this conclusion. One is, that before and during the march of the Israelites from Egypt to the place where the law was given, the latter is called only Horeb ; just as the Arabs now speak of going from Cairo to Jebel et-Tûr ; while during the sojourn of the Hebrews before the mountain, it is spoken of (with one exception) only as Sinai ; and after their departure, it is again referred to exclusively as Horeb. The other and main fact is, that while the Israelites were encamped at Rephidim, Moses was commanded to go on with the elders before the people, and smite the rock in Horeb, in order to obtain water for the camp. The necessary inference is, that some part of Horeb was near to Rephidim ; while Sinai was yet a day's march distant.[4]

The position of Rephidim itself can be conjectured only from the same passages to which reference has just been made. If we admit Horeb to be the general name for the central cluster of mountains, and that the Israelites approached it by the great

[1] Num. 33, 12-15.
[2] Burckhardt's Travels, pp. 598, 602, 618, 621, 622.
[3] Gesenius' Notes to Burckhardt's Travels, p. 1078. Rosenmüller Bibl. Geogr. i. 176-178

III. p. 115. Winer's Bibl. Realwörterb. art. Horeb.
[4] Ex. 17, 1. 5. 6. 19, 1. 2. See also Note XVII, end of the volume.

Wady esh-Sheikh, then Rephidim must have been at some point in this valley not far from the skirts of Horeb, and about a day's march from the particular mountain of Sinai. Such a point exists at the place where Wady esh-Sheikh issues from the high central granite cliffs. We did not visit the spot; but Burckhardt in ascending Wady esh-Sheikh towards the convent, thus describes it: "We now approached the central summits of Mount Sinai, which we had had in view for several days. Abrupt cliffs of granite from six to eight hundred feet in height, whose surface is blackened by the sun, surround the avenues leading to the elevated platform to which the name of Sinai is specifically applied. These cliffs enclose the holy mountain on three sides, leaving the east and northeast sides only, towards the gulf of 'Akabah, more open to the view. We entered these cliffs by a narrow defile about forty feet in breadth, with perpendicular granite rocks on both sides. [In this defile is the Seat of Moses, so called.] Beyond it the valley opens, the mountains on both sides diverge, and the Wady esh-Sheikh continues in a south direction with a slight ascent."[1] The entrance to this defile from the west, is five hours distant from the point where Wady esh-Sheikh issues from the plain er-Râhah. This would correspond well to the distance of Rephidim; and then these blackened cliffs would be the outskirts of Horeb. I am not aware of any objection to this view, except one which applies equally to every part of Wady esh-Sheikh and the adjacent district, viz. that neither here nor in all this tract is there at the present day any special want of water. There is a well near the defile itself; and an hour above it a spring called Abu Suweirah, which we visited; besides others in various quarters. This difficulty I am not able to solve; except by supposing, that as the people appear to have remained for some time at Rephidim, the small supply of water was speedily exhausted.

It was during the encampment at Rephidim that Amalek came and fought with Israel.[2] It is not necessary here to look for a wide open plain, on which the battle might take place according to the rules of modern warfare. The Amalekites were a nomadic tribe, making an irregular attack upon a multitude probably not better trained than themselves; and for such a conflict the low hills and open country around this part of Wady esh-Sheikh would afford ample space.

After the departure of the Israelites from Mount Sinai, there is no account, either in Scripture or elsewhere, of its having been visited by any Jew; except by the prophet Elijah, when he fled from the machinations of Jezebel.[3] This is the

---

[1] Travels, etc. p. 488.　　　[2] Ex. 17, 8.　　　[3] 1 Kings 19, 3–8.

more remarkable; as this region had been the seat of the revelation of their law, to which they clung so tenaciously; and because from the splendour and terrors of that scene, the inspired Hebrew poets were wont to draw their sublimest images.

SINAI IN THE EARLY CHRISTIAN AGES.

No very distinct notices of Sinai appear in the earliest Christian writers. Dionysius of Alexandria, about A. D. 250, mentions, that these mountains were the refuge of Egyptian Christians in times of persecution; where they were sometimes seized as slaves by the Saracens or Arabs.[1] The legend of St. Catharine of Alexandria, who first fled to Sinai, and whose body after martyrdom at Alexandria is said to have been carried by angels to the summit of the mountain that now bears her name, is laid in the beginning of the next or fourth century, about A. D. 307.[2] In the third and fourth centuries also, ascetics and anchorites took their rise in Egypt; and were soon followed by communities of monks in desert places. There is no mention of the first introduction of these holy persons and communities into the peninsula of Mount Sinai; but it is natural to suppose, that a region with so many historical associations, and so well adapted to their purposes by its loneliness and desolation, would not be overlooked by them, nor long remain untenanted.

Accordingly we find, from various writings preserved among the remains of monastic piety and learning, that during the fourth century this mountain was already the seat of many anchorites; who, although residing in separate cells, had regular intercourse with each other, and gathered in small communities around the more distinguished ascetics and teachers. The earliest of these fathers of whom I find mention at Sinai, was the Abbot Silvanus, an Egyptian anchorite, who retired for some years to this mountain apparently about A. D. 365; and went afterwards to Gerar, where he became the head of a large community of ascetics.[3] At Sinai he had a garden which he tilled and watered; and although he was the superior of several anchorites, yet he is said to have lived alone with only his disciple Zacharias.[4]

A fuller notice of Sinai about the same period, is found in the little tract of Ammonius, a monk of Canopus in Egypt; who, after visiting the holy places in Palestine, returned by way of Mount Sinai, in company with other Christians who made

---

[1] Euseb. Hist. Ecc. 6. 42.
[2] Baronius Annal. A. D. 307. xxxiii.
[3] Tillemont Mémoires pour servir à l'Histoire Ecclesiast. X. p. 448 sq. Cotelier Ecclesiae Graecae Monumenta, I. p. 563 sq.
i. 180. 181.
[4] Tillemont l. c. p. 451. Cotelier l. c. p. 680.

the same pilgrimage. They reached Sinai in eighteen days from
Jerusalem by way of the desert. This visit appears to have
taken place in or about A. D. 373.[1] The pilgrim found many
anchorites living here under a superior named Doulas, a man of
uncommon piety and meekness. They subsisted only on dates,
berries, and other like fruits, without wine, or oil, or even bread.
Yet for the sake of strangers and guests, a few loaves were kept
by the superior. They passed the whole week in the silence
and solitude of their cells, until the evening of Saturday; when
they assembled in the church and continued all night together
in prayer. In the morning of the Lord's day they received the
sacrament, and then returned to their cells.

A few days after the arrival of Ammonius, the Saracens,
whose chief had lately died, made an attack upon these holy
men. Doulas and those with him retired into a tower; but all
who could not reach this place of safety, were killed. The
Saracens attacked the tower, and were near to take it; when,
according to Ammonius, the top of the mountain appeared all
in flame, and frightened the barbarians from their purpose.
They fled; and the fathers descended to seek and bury the
slain. They found thirty-eight corpses; twelve of which were
in the monastery Gethrabbi,[2] and others in Chobar and Codar.
Two hermits, Isaiah and Sabbas, were found still alive, though
mortally wounded; making up in all the number of forty killed.[3]
At the same time, a similar massacre of Christian anchorites
took place at Raithou, situated on the coast of the Red Sea,
two days' distance from Sinai. This place was regarded as the
Elim of the Scriptures; and corresponds to the modern Tûr.[4]

Somewhat more definite and equally mournful, is the narrative of Nilus; who himself resided many years at Sinai from
about A. D. 390 onwards, and was present at a second massacre
of the ascetics during a similar incursion of the Saracens.[5] He

[1] This tract of Ammonius is found in
the work of Combefis, *Illustrium Christi
Martyrum læti Triumphi*, Paris 1660.
8vo. p. 88 sq. A very exact abstract of it
is given by Tillemont, Mémoires pour servir à l'Hist. Ecc. VII. p. 573 sq. The
date given in the text is that assigned by
Tillemont, l. c. p. 782 sq.

[2] Nilus writes this name *Bethrambe;*
Nili Opera quæd. p. 89. Is the Chobar
(Χοβάρ) in the text perhaps a corruption
for *Horeb?*

[3] The Greeks and Latins solemnize the
14th of January as the day on which these
martyrs were killed; see Acta Sanctorum,
Jan. Tom. I. p. 961. Tillemont, l. c.
VII. p. 573.—It was perhaps from these
forty martyrs, that the convent el-Arba'in,

'the Forty,' received its name. Not improbably it may have been the Gethrabbi
of the text. Comp. Quaresmius Elucid.
Terr. Sanct. II. p. 996.

[4] Raithou ('Ραϊθοῦ) is also mentioned
by Cosmas Indicopleustes, (about A. D.
535,) as the probable site of Elim; Topogr. Christ. in Montfaucon's Coll. nov.
Patrum, II. p. 195. The place occupied
by the convent near Tûr is still called
Raithu by the Greeks; Rüppell's Reisen
in Nubien, etc. p. 181. Sicard in Nouv.
Mem. des Miss. dans le Levant, 1715.
Tom. I. p. 20.

[5] Nilus himself wrote an account of this
massacre in Greek; see *Nili Opera quæ-
dam, ed. P. Possino*, Gr. et Lat. Paris,
1639. The Latin version is also printed
i. 181 182

relates, that these holy men had fixed their cells upon the mountain at the distance of a mile or more from each other, in order to avoid mutual interruption during the week; although they occasionally visited each other. On the eve of the Lord's day they descended to the holy place of the Bush, where was a church and apparently a convent; or at least a place where stores were laid up for the winter. Here they spent the night at prayers; received the sacrament in the morning of Sunday; and after passing some time in spiritual conversation returned to their cells. One morning, the 14th of January, as they were about to separate, they were attacked by a party of Saracens, who drove them all into the church, while they plundered the repository of stores. Then, bringing them out, the barbarians killed the superior Theodulus and two others outright; reserved several of the younger men as captives; and suffered the rest to escape up the sides of the mountains. Among these last was Nilus; his son Theodulus was among the captives. The Saracens now withdrew, taking the captives with them, and killing eight other anchorites in various places. Nilus and his companions in flight descended at night and buried the dead bodies; and afterwards retired to Pharan (Feirân). The council or senate of this city immediately sent messengers to the king of the Saracens; who disavowed the outrage and promised reparation. Meantime Theodulus had been sold and brought to Elusa; where he was redeemed by the bishop of that city, and ultimately recovered by his father.

In the middle of the fifth century, we find a letter from the emperor Marcian to the bishop Macarius, the archimandrites, and monks in Mount Sinai, "where are situated monasteries beloved of God and worthy of all honour," warning them against the dangerous tenets and practices of the heretic Theodosius, who had fled to these mountains, after the council of Chalcedon, A. D. 451.[1] Nearly a century later, A. D. 536, among the subscriptions at the council of Constantinople, appears the name of Theonas, a presbyter and legate of the holy Mount Sinai, the desert Raithou (Tûr), and the holy church at Pharan.[2]

The tradition of the present convent relates, that it was established by the emperor Justinian A. D. 527, on the place where a small church had been built by Helena long before. The main fact of this tradition, the building of the great church, is supported by the testimony of Procopius the historian, who

in the Acta Sanctorum, Jan. Tom. I. p. 953 sq. See too a very complete summary of this tract of Nilus, in Tillemont Mémoires pour servir à l'Histoire Eccl. Tom. XIV. p. 189 sq.

i. 183, 184

[1] Harduin Acta Concilior. II. col. 665, compared with col. 685.
[2] Harduin Acta Conc. II. col. 1281, 1304.

flourished about the middle of the same century. He relates
that Mount Sinai was then inhabited by monks, "whose whole
life was but a continual preparation for death;" and that in
consideration of their holy abstinence from all worldly enjoyments, Justinian caused a church to be erected for them, and
dedicated it to the holy Virgin.[1] This was placed not upon the
summit of the mountain, but far below; because no one could
pass the night upon the top, on account of the constant sounds
and other supernatural phenomena which were there perceptible.[2] At the foot or outmost base of the mountain, according to
Procopius, the same emperor built a strong fortress, with a se-
lect garrison, to prevent the inroads of the Saracens from that
quarter into Palestine.

More explicit is the testimony of Eutychius, patriarch of
Alexandria in the latter half of the ninth century; which apparently as yet has never been referred to, but which shows that
the present tradition has come down with little variation since
that age. He relates that Justinian caused a fortified convent
to be erected for the monks of Sinai, including the former tower
and chapel, in order to protect them from the incursions of the
Ishmaelites. This accords with the appearance of the building
at the present day; and is probably the same work which Procopius has confounded with a fortress.[3]

Towards the close of the same (sixth) century, Sinai was
visited by Antoninus Martyr; who found in the recently erected
convent three abbots, who spoke the Syrian, Greek, Egyptian
and Besta (Arabic?) languages. A chapel was already built
upon the summit, and the whole region was full of the cells and
dwellings of hermits. On a part of Mount Horeb or mountain
of the Cross, the Saracens or Ishmaelites (Antoninus calls them
by both names) at that time venerated an idol, apparently connected with the worship of the morning star, which was common
among the Saracens.—It appears then, that these Saracens, the

[1] This is doubtless the church now
standing; which, however, bears the name
of the Transfiguration.

[2] Procop. de Ædificiis Justiniani, 5. 8.
We did not notice the Greek inscription
over the gate leading to the garden, given
by M. Letronne in the Journal des Savans, Sept. 1836, p. 358. Burckhardt
speaks only of one in modern Arabic
characters, with the same contents. Both
inscriptions refer the building of the convent to Justinian in the thirtieth year of
his reign, A. D. 527. But in that year
Justinian first ascended the throne; and
the inscription is doubtless therefore the
work of a later age, and founded on a false

tradition. As to the chapel said to have
been built by Helena, there is not the
slightest historical hint that she was ever
in the region of Mount Sinai, or caused
any church to be erected there.—A copy
of both inscriptions is given by Lepsius;
Briefe, p. 440 and Plate.

[3] Eutychii Annales, ed. Pococke, II. p.
160. The whole passage is so curious,
that a full translation of it is given in
Note XX, at the end of the volume. Not
improbably the "Arabic document" mentioned by Burckhardt, (p. 545,) as preserved in the convent, may be a manuscript of the work of Eutychius.

supposed descendants of the Nabatheans, had continued to inhabit the peninsula, notwithstanding the intrusion of the monks and Christians. They differed probably in few respects from the Arabs of the present day.

During the earlier centuries of this monastic possession of the peninsula, the seat of the bishop appears to have been at Pharan or Faran, the present Feirân ; where was likewise a Christian population and a senate or council so early as the time of Nilus, about A. D. 400. About this time too Naterus or Nathyr is mentioned as its bishop. The bishop Macarius spoken of above probably had his seat there ; and before the middle of the sixth century there is express mention of Photius as bishop of Pharan.[1] About the same time, A. D. 535, Pharan is mentioned by Cosmas as the location of Rephidim.[2] Theodorus of the same see was famous in the Monothelitic controversy, and was denounced by two councils ; that of the Lateran, A. D. 649, and that of Constantinople, A. D. 680. The town of Faran or Feirân was situated in the Wady of that name, opposite to Jebel Serbâl. Rüppell found here the remains of a church, the architecture of which he assigns to the fifth century ; and Burckhardt speaks of the remains of some two hundred houses, and the ruins of several towers visible on the neighbouring hills.[3] With the episcopal city the monasteries around Serbâl and Sinai stood of course in intimate connection ; until at length the growing importance and influence of the convent established by Justinian, appears to have superseded the claims of Faran, and to have caused the chief episcopal seat to be transferred within its own walls, at least before the close of the tenth century. The death of Jorius, " bishop of Mount Sinai," is recorded in A. D. 1033.[4] At this time Sinai as an episcopal see stood directly under the patriarch of Jerusalem, as an archiepiscopate ; that is, without the intervention of a metropolitan ; and although the name of Faran still appears as a bishopric, yet all further notices of its importance are wanting.[5]

After the Muhammedan conquests, when the Saracens of the peninsula would seem to have exchanged their heathen worship for the tenets of the false prophet, the anchorites and inmates of the monasteries appear to have continued to live on in the

---

[1] Le Quien Oriens Christ. III. col. 753. Comp. Tillemont Mémoires, etc. X. p. 453.

[2] Cosmas Indicopl. Topogr. Christ. in Montfaucon Coll. nov. Patrum, II. p. 195.

[3] Rüppell's Reisen in Nubien, etc. p. 263. Burckhardt's Travels, etc. p. 616 ; also Lepsius' Briefe, p. 333 sq. Bartlett, Forty Days in the Desert, p. 53 sq. See more on Pharan in Note XVIII, at the end of the volume.

i. 185-187

[4] Le Quien, l. c. col. 754.

[5] See the *Notitia ecclesiastica* of Nilus, A.D. 1151, and that appended to the history of William of Tyre, Gesta Dei per Francos, p. 1045. These are given in full by Reland, Palæst. pp. 219, 220, 228.— Jacob de Vitry in the beginning of the twelfth century speaks of Sinai as the only suffragan see under the metropolitan of Petra, i.e. Kerak ; Gesta Dei, etc. p. 1077.

same state of inquietude, and sometimes perhaps of danger.
Near the close of the sixth century, and during the seventh, the
well known monkish writers, Johannes Climacus and Anastasius
Sinaita, flourished here. About the middle of the tenth century
the monks of Sinai are reported to have all fled for their lives to
a mountain called Latrum.[1] In the beginning of the eleventh
century, the convent was again in a flourishing state, and was
visited by great numbers of pilgrims. At this time the celebrated St. Simeon resided here as a monk ; who understood the
Egyptian, Syriac, Arabic, Greek, and Latin languages ; and who
in A. D. 1027 came to Europe and was hospitably entertained
by Richard II, duke of Normandy. He brought with him relics
of St. Catharine, and collected alms for the convent ; but afterwards founded an abbey in France, where he died.[2] In A. D.
1116, King Baldwin I. of Jerusalem made an excursion to the
gulf of 'Akabah, and expressed the intention of visiting Mount
Sinai ; he was persuaded not to do so by messengers from the
monks, in order that they might not by his visit be exposed to
suspicion and danger from their Mussulman masters.[3]

All the circumstances hitherto detailed, seem to render it
probable, that from about the beginning of the fourth century
onwards a very considerable Christian population existed in the
peninsula. The remains of the many convents, chapels, and
hermitages, which are still visible in various quarters, go to
show the same thing ; and add weight to the tradition of the
present convent, that at the time of the Muhammedan conquest,
six or seven thousand monks and hermits were dispersed over
the mountains.[4] That pilgrimages to these holy spots, so
sacred in themselves, and as the abodes of holy men, should
then be frequent, was in that age almost a matter of course ;
and these are continued more or less even to the present day.

With these early pilgrimages the celebrated Sinaite inscriptions have been supposed to stand in close connection. Several
of them have been mentioned above as occurring on our way to
Sinai ; and they are found on all the routes which lead from the
west towards this mountain, as far south as Tûr. They extend
to the very base of Sinai, above the convent el-Arba'in ; but are
found neither on Jebel Mûsa, nor on the present Horeb, nor on
St. Catharine, nor in the valley of the convent ; while on Serbâl
they are seen on its very summits. Not one has yet been found
to the eastward of Sinai. But the spot where they exist in the

---

[1] Baronius Annal. A.D. 956, viii.
[2] See Mabillon Acta Sanctor. Ord. Benedict. Sæc. VI. P. I. p. 374. Ejusd. Annales Ord. St. Benedict. lib. 56. c. 35, 36.
Hist. Literaire de France, Tom. VII. p. 67.

[3] Albert. Aq. 12. 22, in Gesta Dei per
Francos. Wilken Gesch. der Kreuzzüge,
II, p. 403.
[4] Burckhardt's Travels, etc. p. 546.

greatest number is the Wady Mukatteb, 'Written Valley,' through which the usual road to Sinai passes before reaching Wady Feirân. Here they occur by thousands on the rocks, chiefly at such points as would form convenient resting-places for travellers or pilgrims during the noon-day sun ;[1] as is also the case with those we saw upon the other route. Many of them are accompanied by crosses, sometimes obviously of the same date with the inscription, and sometimes apparently later or retouched. The character is everywhere the same ; but until recently it has remained undeciphered, in spite of the efforts of the ablest paleographists. The inscriptions are usually short ; and most of them exhibit the same initial characters. Some Greek inscriptions are occasionally intermingled.

These inscriptions are first mentioned by Cosmas, about A. D. 535. He supposed them to be the work of the ancient Hebrews ; and says certain Jews, who had read them, explained them to him as noting " the journey of such an one, out of such a tribe, in such a year and month ; " much in the manner of modern travellers.[2] Further than this, the most recent decipherers have as yet hardly advanced. When the attention of European scholars was again turned upon these inscriptions by Clayton, bishop of Clogher, about the middle of the last century,[3] they were still attributed by him and others to the Hebrews on their journey to Sinai. Since that time they have usually been regarded as probably the work of Christian pilgrims on their way from Egypt to Mount Sinai, during the fourth century. At any rate, the contents of them were already unknown in the time of Cosmas ; and no tradition appears to have existed respecting their origin. As to the character, Gesenius supposed it to belong to that species of the Phenician, or rather Aramæan, which, in the first centuries of the Christian era, was extensively employed throughout Syria, and partially in Egypt ; having most affinity with that of the Palmyrene inscriptions. Prof. Beer of Leipzig, on the other hand, who has quite recently deciphered these inscriptions for the first time, regards them as exhibiting the only remains of the language and character once peculiar to the Nabathæans of Arabia Petræa ; and supposes, that if at a future time stones with the writing of the country shall be found among the ruins of Petra, the character will prove to be the same with that of the inscriptions of Sinai. Accord-

---

[1] Burckhardt's Travels, etc. 620.

[2] Cosmas Indicopl. Topogr. Christ. in Montfaucon's Collect. nov. Patrum, II. p. 205.

[3] See his Letter to the Society of Antiquaries, published under the title : "Journal from Grand Cairo to Mount Sinai," i. 188–190

etc. Lond. 1753. This is the Journal of the Prefect of the Franciscans in Cairo, already referred to. The bishop offers in his letter, to bear any proper portion of the expense which might arise from sending a person to copy these inscriptions. p. 4.

ing to this view, they may not improbably turn out to have been made by the native inhabitants of the mountains.[1]—Still, it cannot but be regarded as a most singular fact, that here in these lone mountains an alphabet should be found upon the rocks, which is shown by the thousands of inscriptions to have been once a very current one, but of which perhaps elsewhere not a trace remains.[2]

THE MODERN CONVENT.

After the times of the crusades, the first notices of Mount Sinai and the present convent are from Sir John Maundeville, William de Baldensel, and Ludolf de Suchem, who all visited this region in the first half of the fourteenth century. The latter traveller (A. D. 1336–50) found here more than four hundred monks, under an archbishop and prelates ; including lay brethren, who did hard labour among the mountains, and went with camels from Elim to Babylon (Tûr to Fostât), carrying charcoal and dates in large quantities to market. In this way the convent obtained a scanty support for its own inmates, and for the strangers who came to visit them.[3]

Burckhardt found among the archives of the convent the original of a compact between the monks and the Bedawîn, made in the year A. H. 800 or A. D. 1398 ; from which it appears that at that time, besides the great convent, six others were still existing in the peninsula, exclusive of a number of chapels and hermitages. In the fifteenth century there was an inhabited convent at Feirân. From another document two and a half centuries later (A. H. 1053, A. D. 1643) it appears, that all these minor establishments had been already abandoned, and that the great convent alone remained ; still holding property at Feirân, Tûr, and in other fertile valleys.[4] This accords with the testimony of travellers in the fifteenth and sixteenth centuries, who speak only of deserted convents besides that of Sinai.[5] In this monastery in A. D. 1484, Felix Fabri relates, that there were then said to be eighty monks, although he did not see half that number. In Belon's time, about A. D. 1546, the number was reduced to sixty ;[6] and Helffrich, in A. D. 1565, found the convent temporarily abandoned. A century later Von Troilo

---

[1] Such is now (1856) understood to be actually the case.

[2] See more in Note XIX, end of the volume.

[3] Itin. Terr. Sanct. p. 65. Reissb. des heil. Landes, Ed. 2, p. 839.—Ritter refers this passage to the Jebeliyeh or serfs of the convent. But it speaks expressly and only of lay brothers ; and moreover the serfs were never entrusted with such matters. See Geschichte des Petr. Arabiens, in Abhandl. der Berl. Acad. 1824, Hist. phil. Cl. p. 222.

[4] Burckhardt's Travels, etc. p. 547 sq. 617.

[5] So Tucher, A. D. 1479; Breydenbach and Fabri, 1484 ; and many others.

[6] Observatt. Paris 1588, p. 282.

found seventy monks. At present the number varies between twenty and thirty ; though we found only twenty-one, of whom six were priests, and fifteen lay brethren ; but two or three new members apparently arrived with us. The present inmates are chiefly from the Greek islands ; and remain here for the most part only a few years. The affiliated or branch convent at Cairo has a prior and forty or fifty monks.[1]

All the earlier travellers to Sinai without exception speak of this as the convent of St. Catharine ; and of the monks as belonging to the order of St. Basil. Burckhardt on the other hand says the monastery is dedicated to the Transfiguration ; which is at least true of the church. Rüppell again calls it the convent of the Annunciation, on what authority I know not. Nor am I able to affirm which of all these statements is most correct.

The last archbishop who resided in the convent, is said to have been Kyrillos, who died here in A. D. 1760.[2] Since that time it has been found advisable for this prelate to pass his life abroad, in order to avoid the rapacious exactions of the Arabs on the occasion of his accession and entrance into the convent. Long before that period the great gate of the convent had been walled up in self-defence, being opened only to admit a new archbishop ; and even this seems not to have taken place since A. D. 1722.[3] The present archbishop is the ex-patriarch of Constantinople ; and were he to visit the convent, the great gate (it was said) would have to be thrown open and remain so for six months ; during which time the Arabs would have the right to come at will and eat and drink ; and many thousand dollars would not cover the expense.

The archbishop is elected by a council of the monks, which manages in common the affairs of this convent and the branch at Cairo. This prelate is always selected from the priests of the monastery ; and having then been consecrated as bishop by the patriarch of Jerusalem, (in consequence of the ancient connection,) he becomes one of the four independent archbishops of the

[1] It is this branch convent that gives letters of introduction to travellers visiting Sinai from Cairo. For want of such a letter, Niebuhr in 1762 was refused admission to the convent at Sinai ; but we were there told that a letter is not now indispensable, all who come being received. Still it is better to have one. See Niebuhr's Reisebeschr. I. p. 244.

[2] Burckhardt, p. 549.

[3] Burckhardt says not since A. D. 1709 ; but the Prefect of the Franciscans, who was here in 1722, relates that it had been open that very year. This writer also i. 191–193.

seems to be the first, who speaks of the traveller's being drawn up to the high door or window. The same is mentioned by Van Egmond and Heyman about the same time. Von Troilo, A. D. 1666, describes the entrance as low, and defended by double iron doors, which were kept fastened night and day. He likewise mentions a high window, through which the monks let down food in a basket for the Arabs by a cord, but gives no hint that travellers were drawn up the same way. Reisebeschreibung, Dresd. 1676, pp. 379, 380.

Greek church ; the others being at Cyprus, Moscow, and Ochrida in Roumely. Were he present, he would have but a single voice in the management of the affairs of the convent, as a member of the council. While residing at a distance, he has no authority or connection with it, except to receive money and presents from its revenues.—The prior or superior, both here and at Cairo, is elected in like manner by the council. The present superior at Sinai, Father Neophytus, was originally from Cyprus, and had been here eighteen years.

The monks of Sinai lead a very simple and also a quiet life, since they have come to be on good terms with their Arab neighbours. Five centuries ago Ludolf de Suchem describes their life in terms which are equally applicable to them at the present day. " They follow very strict rules ; live chaste and modestly ; are obedient to their archbishop and prelates ; drink not wine but on high festivals ; eat never flesh ; but live on herbs, pease, beans, and lentiles, which they prepare with water, salt, and vinegar ; eat together in a refectory without a table cloth ; perform their offices in the church with great devotion day and night ; and are very diligent in all things ; so that they fall little short of the rules of St. Antony."[1] To this day the same rules continue ; they eat no flesh and drink no wine ; but their rules were made before the invention of distilled liquors, and therefore do not exclude date brandy. Yet they all seem healthy and vigorous ; and those who remain here, retain their faculties to a great age. The lay brother who waited on us, had seen more than eighty years ; one of the priests was said to be over ninety ; and one had died the year before at the age of one hundred and six. A great portion of their time is nominally occupied in religious exercises. They have (or should have) regularly the ordinary prayers of the Greek ritual seven times in every twenty-four hours. Every morning there is a mass about 7 o'clock ; and on Saturdays two, one at 3 A. M. and the other at the usual hour. During Lent the exercises on certain days are much increased ; on the Wednesday which we spent there, the monks were at prayers all the morning until 12 o'clock ; and again during the night from 10 till 4 o'clock.

The pilgrims have of late years greatly fallen off ; so that not more than from twenty to sixty now visit the convent annually. These, according to the superior, are chiefly Greeks, Russians, and English ; a few Armenians and Copts ; and only now and then a Mussulman. The good father probably regards all visitors as pilgrims. Yet so late as the last century, regular caravans of pilgrims are said to have come hither from Cairo and from Jerusalem ; and a document preserved in the convent,

[1] Itin. Terræ S. p. 63. Reissbuch, Ed. 2, p. 839.

mentions the arrival in one day of eight hundred Armenians from Jerusalem, and at another time, of five hundred Copts from Cairo.[1]

Besides the branch at Cairo, the convent has many *metochia* or farms, in Cyprus, Crete, and elsewhere. The Greek parish in Tûr is also a dependency ; but not that of Suez. The convent has one priest in Bengal, and two in Golconda, in India. The gardens and olive groves in the vicinity all belong to it ; as also extensive groves of palm trees near Tûr ; but its chief revenues are derived from the distant *metochia*. The gardens and orchards in the peninsula are not now robbed by the Arabs ; but owing to the great drought of the two preceding years, they were less productive. In a few weeks the convent would have consumed all the productions of its own gardens, and expected to become dependent on Egypt for every thing. Their grains and legumes they always get from Egypt. Of these they were now consuming at the rate of about one thousand *ardebs*[2] a year, or nearly double the common rate, in consequence of the drought and scarcity, which rendered the Arabs much more dependent than usual upon the convent for bread. The date gardens near Tûr commonly bring them in about three hundred ardebs of fruit ; and if properly managed, might yield five hundred.

The inmates of the convent have now for many years lived for the most part in peace and amity with the Bedawîn around them. Occasional interruptions of the harmony indeed occur ;[3] but of late, and especially since the time of scarcity and famine, the consideration and influence of the monks among the Arabs would seem to be greatly on the increase. This is further enhanced by the awe in which the latter stand of the Pasha of Egypt ; and the certainty, that any injustice practised by them against the convent, would in the end recoil upon their own heads.

Among the tribes or clans of the Tawarah, three are by long custom and perhaps compact, *Ghafîrs*, or protectors of the convent ; and hold themselves responsible for its safety and that of every thing which belongs to it. These are the Dhuheiry, 'Awârimeh, and 'Aleikât. In return, the individuals of these clans are entitled to a portion of bread whenever they visit the convent. They formerly received also a cooked dish on such occasions ; besides five and a half dollars each in money annu-

---

[1] Burckhardt, p. 552.
[2] The *ardeb* is equivalent very nearly to five bushels English. Lane's Mod. Egypt. II. p. 371. ed. 1.
[3] So late as A. D. 1828, during Laborde's visit, a pilgrim was wounded in the thigh by a ball aimed at a monk by a

i. 194–196

Bedawy from the rocks above the convent; Voyage, etc. p. 67. Engl. p. 243. A monk who accompanied the prefect of the Franciscans to the top of Sinai in 1722, was seized and beaten by the Arabs. The older travellers are full of similar accounts, and speak of the Arabs only as monsters.

ally, and a dress for each male ; but all these are no longer
given. When in Cairo, they are likewise entitled to receive from
the branch convent there, two small loaves every morning and a
cooked dish every day at noon ; and formerly they had in addition four loaves every evening, which however had been stopped
the present year. Besides all this, they have the exclusive privilege of conveying travellers and pilgrims to and from the convent.

It may be well supposed, that to satisfy all these claims in
addition to the partial support of their own serfs, must draw
largely upon the temporal resources of the convent. Yet the
monks find it advisable to stop these many Arab mouths with
bread, rather than expose themselves to their noisy clamour, and
perhaps to the danger of sudden reprisals. The bakehouse of
the convent is of course upon a large scale. At the time of our
visit, they complained of not being able to obtain camels to
bring their supplies of grain from Tûr ; and from this cause,
perhaps, the best bread we saw was coarse and mingled with
barley. That distributed to the Arabs is always of a very inferior
quality. Their date brandy was said to be no longer distilled in
the convent, as was formerly the case.

ARABS OF THE PENINSULA.

The following account of the Bedawîn who inhabit the peninsula of Sinai, was derived chiefly from themselves ; and if it be
less complete than that of Burckhardt, it may yet serve to fill
out the notices given by that traveller.[1]

The tribes reckoned to the proper Tawarah, the Bedawîn of
Jebel Tûr or Sinai, are the following :

I. *The Sawâlihah*, the largest and most important of all the
divisions of these Arabs, and comprising several branches which
themselves constitute tribes ; viz. 1. *The Dhuheiry ;* of whom
again a subdivision or clan are the *Aulâd Sa'id* or *Sa'idiyeh*, to
whom our guides belonged. The Aulâd Sa'id occupy the best
valleys among the mountains, and are respected, and seem to
have most connection with the convent. Their present Sheikh
Husein has been mentioned above. 2. *The 'Awârimeh.* 3. *The
Kûrrâshy*, whose head Sheikh Sâlih has long been the principal
Sheikh of the Tawarah in all foreign relations, being the person
to whom the Pasha addresses his orders relative to the peninsula.
The Sawâlihah for the most part occupy the country west and
northwest of the convent. The pasturing places of the tribe are
in general common to all its branches ; but the valleys where
date trees grow and tillage exists, are said to be the property of
individuals. They consider themselves as the oldest and chief

---

[1] Travels, etc. p. 557 sq.

inhabitants of the peninsula. All the branches regard each other as cousins, and intermarry. Their tradition is, that their fathers came hither from the borders of Egypt about the time of the Muhammedan conquest. The Kŭrrâshy, however, are said to be descendants of a few families, who early came among them as fugitives from the Hejâz. Hence it is, perhaps, that the two first branches are Ghafîrs of the convent ; and the Kŭrrâshy not.—Each of the branches is subdivided into smaller clans. Burckhardt speaks of the *Rahamy* as a branch ; but they were not named to us.

II. *The 'Aleikât* are also an old tribe ; but much weaker than the Sawâlihah, being indeed few in number. Intermarriages occasionally take place between them and the latter tribe ; but they are not in general approved of. The 'Aleikât are also Ghafîrs of the convent. They encamp chiefly around the western Wady Nŭsb ; and extend their pasturage as far as to the Wadys Ghŭrŭndel and Wŭtâh.

III. *The Muzeiny* came into the peninsula at a later period ; and are still regarded as intruders by the Sawâlihah, who do not intermarry with them. Our Arabs of the Aulâd Sa'îd held them in great contempt. The story of their introduction to the penin- sula, as related by our guides, was as follows : The whole terri- tory of the Tawarah originally belonged to the Sawâlihah and 'Aleikât, and was equally divided between them ; the former having possession of the western part of the peninsula, and the latter of the eastern. During a famine, a war arose between the two tribes, in which the former in a night attack near Tûr, killed all but seven men of the 'Aleikât. To celebrate this victory, they assembled around the tomb of Sheikh Sâlih in Wady esh- Sheikh, and sacrificed a camel. Just at this time, seven men of the Muzeiny came to them from their country Harb on the road to the Hejâz, and proposed to settle with them in the peninsula on equal terms ; saying they had fled from home because they had shed blood, and feared the avenger. The Sawâlihah replied, that if they would come as serfs, they were welcome ; if not, they might depart. They chose to depart ; and on their way fell in with the remnant of the 'Aleikât. Forming a league with these, they together fell upon the Sawâlihah at night, as they were assembled among the Tŭrfa trees to feast upon the camel ; and a great slaughter was the consequence. The war continued for many years ; but at last peace was made between the con- tending parties by foreign mediation. The 'Aleikât now gave to the Muzeiny half of their portion of the peninsula and of their general rights ; and admitted them to intermarriage. Those rights the Muzeiny still enjoy ; but having increased very much in number, while the 'Aleikât have remained few and feeble, they

i. 197–199

now occupy all the eastern part of the peninsula and the whole Tawarah portion of the shore of the gulf of 'Akabah, living very much by fishing ; while the 'Aleikât, as is said above, have withdrawn to the vicinity of the western Wady Nŭsb. The Muzeiny stand in no connection with the convent.[1]

IV. *Aulâd Suleimân*, consisting of only a few families in the neighbourhood of Tûr.

V. *Beni Wâsel*, also only a few families dwelling among the Muzeiny in and around Sherm.

These five tribes constitute the proper Bedawin of Mount Sinai or Jebel Tûr, whence their name Tawarah in the plural, from the form Tûry in the singular. They stand connected under one head Sheikh ; at present Sheikh Sâlih of the Kŭrrâshy, as said above. They form a single body when attacked by other Bedawin from abroad ; but have occasionally bloody quarrels among themselves.

VI. To the Arab inhabitants of the peninsula must also be reckoned the *Jebelîyeh*, or serfs of the convent. The Tawarah do not of course acknowledge them as .Bedawin ; but call them Fellâhs and slaves. Their very existence was almost unknown out of the peninsula, until the full account which Burckhardt for the first time gave of them.[2]

The tradition of the convent respecting these vassals, as related to us by the superior, is as follows : When Justinian built the convent, he sent two hundred Wallachian prisoners, and ordered the governor of Egypt to send two hundred Egyptians, to be the vassals of the monastery, to serve and protect it. In process of time, as the Arabs came in and deprived the convent of many of its possessions, the descendants of these vassals became Muslims, and adopted the Arab manners.[3] The last Christian among them, a female, the superior said, died about forty years ago in the convent of the Forty Martyrs.[4] These serfs are under the entire and exclusive control of the convent, to be sold, or punished, or even put to death, as it may determine. They are not now to be distinguished in features or manners from the other Bedawin. A portion of them still encamp

---

[1] The Muzeiny and Sawâlihah are said to have since become reconciled, and now act together.

[2] Most of the early travellers appear to have known nothing of these Jebeliyeh. Belon merely mentions the 'slaves' of the convent; Observatt. p. 286. Paulus' Sammlung, etc. I. p. 224. Van Egmond and Heyman, (about A. D. 1720,) give a short but correct account of them; Reizen, II. p. 165. This was copied by Büsching, Erdbeschr. XI. i. p. 605. Ritter's construction of the language of Ludolf de

Suchem has been noted above, p. 129, note 3. The testimony of Eutychius mentioned in the next note, has been hitherto entirely overlooked.

[3] The substance of this tradition is corroborated as far back as the ninth century by the testimony of Eutychius, patriarch of Alexandria; Annales II. p. 167 sq. The passage is curious, and is translated at length in Note XX, at the end of the volume. Compare p. 125, above.

[4] Or, as Burckhardt was told, in A. D. 1750. P. 564.

among the mountains in the vicinity of the convent; and have charge of its gardens in the neighbourhood. Some of them also attend by turns in the convent itself; where they perform menial offices, and lodge in the garden. Most of those who thus live around the convent, are in a great measure dependent upon it for support. When they work for the convent, as they often do in the garden and elsewhere, they are paid at a certain rate, usually in barley. They too have the exclusive privilege of conducting visitors to the summits of the neighbouring mountains; for which they are paid in the same manner. But this right does not extend to conducting strangers on their journey to and from the convent. Every other day, those who apply, receive bread; each man five small loaves about as large as the fist, and of the coarsest kind; each woman less; and children one or two loaves. Of course none can regularly apply, except such as live quite near. The young and middle aged men looked well and hardy; but there were old men and sick persons and children, who came around the convent, the very pictures of famine and despair. These miserable objects, nearly naked, or only half covered with tatters, were said to live very much upon grass and herbs; and even this food now failing from the drought, they were reduced to mere skeletons.

Other portions or clans of these vassals are distributed among the gardens which the convent has now, or formerly had, in possession in different parts of the peninsula. Thus the *Tebna* are settled in the date gardens of Feirân; the *Bezia* in the convent's gardens at Tûr; and the *Satla* in other parts.

On inquiring of the superior as to the number of these vassals, he said he could not tell; but would give us the estimate he had formed about seven years before, when he had an opportunity to see them all together. At that time Sheikh Sâlih of the Kŭrrâshy, the head Sheikh of the Tawarah, who has always shown himself unfriendly to the convent, laid claim to the Jebeliyeh as his serfs, and undertook to enforce obedience to his demands. They were all greatly affrighted, and fled to a rendezvous in the mountains of et-Tih, a distance of five days' journey. The superior went thither in person with another monk, to invite them back; but they refused to come without security against further molestation. He then went and laid the matter before the governor of Suez, producing the Firmâns of the convent (of which they have many) containing express mention of the Jebeliyeh as their serfs. Sheikh Sâlih was now summoned, but could bring forward no authority whatever in support of his claim. The result was, that he was thrown into prison and fined; and the Jebeliyeh returned to their former mode of life. At that time, the superior said, he judged the

i. 200–202

whole number collected to be between fifteen hundred and two thousand souls.   But this estimate is probably by far too large.

Within a few years, the superior had baptized two of these serfs, who had embraced Christianity ; and no objection had been made by any one.

The Arabs of the Tawarah pretend to claim the whole territory of the peninsula as far north as to the Haj road leading from Suez to 'Akabah ; but they are in actual possession only of the part lying south of the chain of the Tih.   The tract north of this chain, including the northern desert, is inhabited by the *Terâbîn*, the *Tiyâhah*, and the *Haiwât*, allied tribes, who together are stronger than the Tawarah.   The Terâbin have been already mentioned as occupying the mountains er-Râhah and encamping around Tâset Sûdr ; and connecting towards the north with the tribe of the same name near Gaza.   A small branch of them also occupy the eastern coast of the peninsula, along the gulf of 'Akabah, between the ridges of et-Tih.   The Haiwât encamp upon the eastern part of the higher plateau north of et-Tih, towards 'Akabah.   The Tiyâhah roam over the district intervening between the Haiwât and western Terâbin, and extend their wanderings northward towards Gaza.   The pastures of the Wadys along the northern side of et-Tih are said to be good, and extend quite across the peninsula.   Between the Tawarah and the Terâbîn, Tuweileb said, there is an oath of friendship, to endure " as long as there is water in the sea, and no hair grows in the palm of the hand."

In former times and down to the last century, the convent had also its protectors among all these northern tribes, and likewise among the 'Alawin, Haweitât and other tribes towards Gaza and Hebron.   In those days many, if not most, of the pilgrims came by way of Gaza ; and none but the protectors had the right of conveying them.   But as most visitors now come only from Egypt, this right has become restricted to the Tawarah ; the connection with other protectors has been dropped ; and visitors arriving from any other quarter may bring with them, as guides, Arabs of any tribe.   But they may depart only with guides from the Tawarah.

The Tawarah are regarded as among the poorest of all the Bedawin tribes ; nor can it well be otherwise.   Their mountains are too desolate and sterile ever to furnish more than the scanty means of a precarious existence.   Their flocks and camels are comparatively few, and the latter feeble ; asses are not common ; horses and neat cattle are entirely unknown, and could not subsist in their territory.   Their scanty income is derived from their flocks, from the hire of their camels to transport goods and coals between Cairo and Suez, and from the sale of the little charcoal which they burn, and the gum arabic which they gather and bring to market, together with their dates and other fruits. But this is scarcely sufficient to buy clothing and provisions for their families; since all their grain must be purchased in Egypt, not a particle being raised in the peninsula. And when, as now, the rains fail, and dearth comes upon the land, and their camels die off, then indeed despair and famine stare them in the face.

The entire population of the peninsula, as far north as to the Haj route, is estimated by Burckhardt at not over four thousand souls. The calculation made out by Rüppell amounts to about seven thousand, which he regards as at least a fourth part too large. I am not able to add any new data for an estimate; but should regard that of Burckhardt as more probably correct.[1]

I have remarked above, that only two of the divisions of the Sawâlihah, viz. the Dhuheiry and Awârimeh, together with the tribe 'Aleikât, stand in the relation of Ghafirs or protectors to the convent; while the other division of the former tribe, the Kûrrâshy, as also the tribe Muzeiny, do not enjoy this privilege. Yet the tradition is, that long ago the Kûrrâshy shared in this right by sufferance, although not fully entitled to it; or, as our Arabs said, "not written in the book of the convent." But they lost the privilege in the following manner, according to the Arab story. One night seven of their leaders entered the convent secretly by a back way; and in the morning presented themselves armed to the monks, demanding to be "written in the book." The monks, affrighted, said: "Very well; but it must be done in the presence of witnesses from among the other protectors." Witnesses were sent for; and on their arrival, being ordered to put aside their arms, were drawn up into the convent. By a private understanding with the monks, however, they had arms concealed in the bags they brought with them. The monks were secretly armed; and upon a given signal, all fell upon the Kûrrâshy and killed six outright. The remaining one was thrown from the convent walls and killed. Since that time the Kûrrâshy have had no claim to any connection with the convent.

Still, it is obvious, that privileges like those which the protectors enjoy, must ever be an object of longing and jealousy to tribes of half savage Bedawîn, who can see no reason why they should be excluded from them. Hence the Kûrrâshy and Muzeiny are often in league against the convent and its protectors; and at all times cherish towards them an unfriendly spirit. An instance of this kind occurred no longer ago than the preceding

---

[1] Burckhardt, p. 560. Rüppell's Reisen in Nubien, p. 198. i. 203–205

year, in reference to Lord Lindsay and his party on their departure from the convent. His Lordship has alluded to the circumstance in his Letters; and I therefore feel at liberty to relate
the story as we heard it from the Arabs on the spot. The Kûrrâshy and Muzeiny, wishing to break down the monopoly of the
protectors, applied to carry the party from the convent to 'Akabah. As soon as this became known, the three tribes of the
protectors assembled in Wady Scheb (near Wady esh-Sheikh)
under their Sheikhs Mûsa and Muteir; while the two former
tribes also collected in Wady el-Akhdar under their Sheikhs
Sâlih and Khudeir. The decision of the travellers was waited
for with anxiety. If they concluded to take those who were not
protectors, it was to be the signal for the protectors to fall upon
the others in deadly conflict. But they decided for the protectors, and then the other party declared, that they would appeal to the Pasha. Here, however, the convent in Cairo interfered, and the appeal was never made. Subsequently to this a
French traveller took one of the Muzeiny as guide to 'Akabah,
against the counsel and influence of the convent; the Arab having gained over the dragoman of the traveller by a present. But
by the advice of the convent, the protectors took no further re-
venge, than to procure for him a sound drubbing at 'Akabah.

There seems, however, a strong probability, that this matter
will not be definitely settled without blood; for the two tribes
above mentioned are continually renewing their attempts to share
in the privileges of the protectors. We ourselves came near falling into the hands of the Muzeiny at Cairo, while we were yet
ignorant of the whole subject. By some oversight, Khudeir their
Sheikh was introduced to us at the British consulate, to furnish us
with camels for our journey to the convent; but he failed to come
at the time appointed, in consequence (as we understood) of the
interference of the branch convent.

In such quarrels among the Bedawin, the Pasha of Egypt
does not interfere, unless he is appealed to. About thirty years
ago, during a war between the Tawarah and the Ma'âzeh inhabiting the mountains west of the Red Sea, a party of the former
of about forty tents were encamped in Wady Sûdr. The Ma'âzeh
made up an expedition of two hundred dromedaries, nine horsemen, and a company of fifty Mughreby horsemen, to plunder this
encampment. Passing Suez in the night, they found the Tawarah had removed to Wady Wardân; and fell upon them as the
day dawned. Most of the men escaped; the women, as is the
Bedawin custom, were left untouched; and only two men, including the Sheikh, were killed. The Sheikh, an old man, seeing
escape impossible, sat down by the fire; when the leader of the
Ma'âzeh came up, and cried out to him to throw down his tur-

i. 205; 206

ban and his life should be spared. The spirited Sheikh, rather than do what, according to Bedawîn notions, would have stained his reputation ever after, exclaimed : "I shall not uncover my head before my enemies;" and was immediately killed by the thrust of a lance. Fifteen dromedaries, many camels, some slaves, and much clothing and furniture were carried off; for the encampment was rich.[1] The Tawarah waited three months ; and then collected a company of five hundred dromedaries and one hundred footmen, making in all a party of six hundred armed men. Passing Suez secretly, they surprised the Ma'àzeh in the night, killed twenty-four men including the Sheikh, and took seventy dromedaries, one hundred camels, and much other booty. The Sheikh was killed by mistake ; for they had agreed to spare him, because he was a good and generous man, and had not been consenting to the expedition against them. Two other expeditions against the Ma'àzeh followed ; in which more than twenty men were killed, and a great booty taken. The Ma'àzeh then sent a present of three dromedaries to Shedîd, Sheikh of the Haweitât residing at Cairo, begging him to bring about a peace with their enemies. He laid the case before Muhammed 'Aly ; who, sending for the two parties, made peace between them, which has continued ever since.

The Tawarah regard the 'Abâbideh of Upper Egypt as enemies ; and used formerly to cross the gulf in boats and steal camels from them. At present nothing of the kind is done ; but the enmity continues. A short time since, one of the Tiyâhah went by land to the country of the 'Abâbideh, and stole fifteen dromedaries ; but the Pasha compelled him to restore them.

The Tawarah never go to law before the Egyptian tribunals. The Sheikh of each tribe or division acts as judge, in the true style of ancient patriarchal simplicity. Minor quarrels are generally settled by the parties between themselves. But when not, they bring the case before the judge, each putting into his hands a pledge ; and he who loses the cause, forfeits his pledge to the judge as his fee ; while that of the other party is restored. When the judge has given his decision, the party who gains, executes the sentence for himself. Their mode of trial was described, both by the Arabs and by the superior, as being wonderfully just. Bribery and partiality are unknown among them.—If two persons quarrel, a third may step in and make them kiss each other. Thenceforward they are to all appearance friends as before ; although the case may still remain to be tried ; and perhaps months may elapse before it is brought to an issue.

The following are some of the peculiarities of Bedawin law ;

[1] This story is in part related by Burckhardt, p. 471. The incident of the Sheikh's death is derived from him.

i. 206-208

a law not of statute but of prescription, and as binding as the
common law of England. If a Bedawy owes another, and refuses
to pay, the creditor takes two or three men as witnesses of the
refusal. He then seizes or steals, if he can, a camel or something
else belonging to the debtor, and deposits it with a third person.
This brings the case to trial before the judge ; and the debtor
forfeits the article seized.—The Bedawin in their quarrels avoid
beating each other with a stick or with the fist, as disreputable ;
this being the punishment of slaves and children, and a great
indignity to a man. If it takes place, the sufferer is entitled to
very high damages. Their code of honour allows blows to be
given only with the sword or with a gun ; and by these the
sufferer feels himself far less aggrieved. In a quarrel of this
kind, where swords have been used, if the case be brought to
trial, a fine is imposed upon the party least wounded, large
enough to counterbalance the excess of blows or injury received
by the other party. The degree of offence, or provocation, or
claim, is of no account ; it being taken for granted that nothing
can justify a quarrel, and that all such occurrences must be tried
on their own simple merits.

If one person assaults and wounds another, who remains pas-
sive, friends step in and act as mediators. They first persuade
the wounded man to agree to a truce of a month or more, during
which time the parties leave each other in quiet. At the expira-
tion of this term, the mediators on examination fix upon the
sum which the injured man ought to receive as damages ; for
example, two thousand piastres. This he agrees to accept, on
condition that one of them becomes surety for it. But now one
friend comes after another, and entreats him to remit for his
sake a certain portion of this sum. In this way the fine will be
reduced perhaps to two hundred piastres. The parties are now
brought together ; and the injured man gives up to the offender
perhaps one hundred more. In this way he actually receives not
more than one hundred piastres ; and if the reconciliation be
sincere, he may very probably give up even that. If both parties happen to be wounded, a balance of injuries is struck. The
instrument of offence is forfeited by law to the person injured.

If in such quarrels, or in any other way, a person be killed,
it is the right and duty of the nearest relative of the deceased, to
slay the murderer or his nearest relative, wherever he may be
found. But in general, those who are likely to suffer in this
way, flee the country for a year or two ; and in the mean time
persons of influence interfere to appease the relatives of the deceased, and induce them to accept a considerable sum of money
from the offender, as the fine of blood. The feud is then usually
made up, and the offender is free to return. This is the ancient

blood-revenge of the Hebrews, which was so firmly fixed in all
their habits of life, that even the inspired lawgiver did not choose
to abolish it directly ; but only modified and controlled its influence by establishing cities of refuge. Nothing of this kind exists
among the Arabs.[1]

The simplest form in which these rules appear, is in their
application to the same clan or tribe. But the same principles
are also applied to quarrels and murders which take place between individuals of different tribes ; unless the tribe of the
aggressor take his part and adopt the quarrel as their own. In
that case war ensues.

The strict honesty of the Bedawin among themselves is proverbial; however little regard they may have to the right of
property in others. If an Arab's camel dies on the road, and he
cannot remove the load, he only draws a circle in the sand round
about, and leaves it. In this way it will remain safe and untouched for months. In passing through Wady Sa'l on our way
to 'Akabah, we saw a black tent hanging on a tree ; Tuweileb
said it was there when he passed the year before, and would
never be stolen. Theft, he said, was held in abhorrence among
the Tawarah ; but the present year the famine was so great, that
individuals were sometimes driven to steal food. He had just
returned from Egypt with a camel load of grain for his family,
which he had put into one of their magazines as a place of safety ;
but it had all been stolen. Burckhardt relates, that he was
shown in Wady Humr a point upon the rocks, from which one
of the Tawarah, a few years before, had cast down his son headlong, bound hand and foot, for an offence of the very same kind.[2]

The following trait was communicated to us by the superior
of the convent. If a Bedawy discovers his wife or his daughter
in illicit intercourse, he turns away and conceals the fact from
every one, not even letting the guilty parties know that he has
seen them. Months afterwards he will marry off his daughter ;
or after a longer time perhaps divorce his wife ; living with them
mean time as if nothing had happened, and assigning some other
reason for the measure he adopts. One motive for this conceal-
ment is, to avoid personal disgrace ; and another, to prevent the
impossibility of the offender's ever being married.

We made many inquiries in the peninsula and among the
tribes which we fell in with further north, but could never hear
of a Bedawy among them all, who was able to read. Even
Sheikh Salih, the head Sheikh of all the Tawarah, has not this
power ; and whenever a letter is addressed to him, or an order

---

[1] The chief passages in the Old Testament respecting the Hebrew blood-revenge are: Ex. 21, 13. Num. 35, 9 sq.
Deut. 19, 4 sq. Josh. 20, 1 sq. See also Joseph. Ant. 4. 7. 4.
[2] Page 475.

i. 209–211

from the government, he is obliged to apply to the convent to have it read. Among the Tawarah this ignorance seems rather to be the result of habit and want of opportunity; but among the tribes of the northern deserts, we found it was accounted disreputable for a Bedawy to learn to read. They rejoice in the wild liberty of their deserts, as contrasted with towns and cities; and in like manner take pride in their freedom from the arts and restraints of civilized life.

The Muhammedanism of all these sons of the desert, sits very loosely upon them. They bear the name of followers of the false prophet; and the few religious ideas which they possess, are moulded after his precepts. Their nominal religion is a matter of habit, of inheritance, of national prescription; but they seemed to manifest little attachment to it in itself, and live in the habitual neglect of most of its external forms. We never saw any among them repeat the usual Muhammedan prayers, in which other Muslims are commonly so punctual; and were told indeed that many never attempt it; and that very few among them even know the proper words and forms of prayer. The men generally observe the fast of Ramadân, though some do not; nor do the females keep it. Nor is the duty of pilgrimage more regarded; for according to Tuweileb, not more than two or three of all the Tawarah had ever made the journey to Mecca.—The profaneness of the Bedawin is excessive and almost incredible. " Their mouth is full of cursing ; " and we were hardly able to obtain from them a single answer that did not contain an oath.

We asked the superior of the convent whether the Bedawin would feel any objection to professing Christianity? His reply was : " None at all ; they would do it to-morrow, if they could get fed by it." It is this indifference of dark and unregulated minds, that lies in the way of all moral and intellectual improvement among them. The convent might exert an immense influence over them for good, if it possessed in itself the true spirit of the Gospel. Were a missionary to go among the Tawarah and perhaps other tribes, speaking their language and acquainted with their habits, he would doubtless be received with kindness ; and were he to live as they live, and conform to their manners and customs in unimportant things, he would soon acquire influence and authority among them. In all our intercourse with them, we found them kind, good natured, and accommodating ; although, as might be expected, great beggars. But no very permanent impression can well be hoped for upon them, so long as they retain their wandering and half savage life ; and this mode of life must necessarily continue, so long as the desert is their home. To introduce civilization among them, their in-

veterate predilection for the desert and its wild fascinations must
first be overcome; and they then be transplanted to a kindlier
soil, where they may become wonted to fixed abodes, and to the
occupations of a more regular life. But it may be doubtful,
whether such a course is possible through any mere human
agency; at least, it would be no light matter, thus to overturn
habits and a mode of life, which have come down to them
through nearly forty centuries unchanged.

i. 213

SECTION IV.

Thursday, March 29th, 1838. *Afternoon.* About noon our luggage and then ourselves were let down from the high window of the convent ; and after a vast amount of scolding and clamour among the Arabs about the division of the loads, we mounted at 1 o'clock and bade adieu to the friendly monastery. Burckhardt has remarked, that every Arab who is present at the departure of a stranger from the convent, is entitled to a fee ; [1] but we did not find this to be the case, although our intended departure was known throughout the mountains. A number of the Jebeliyeh indeed collected around us ; but they were the old and sick and lame and blind, who came as beggars, and not to claim a right. We escaped their importunity by leaving Komeh behind us, to distribute a few piastres among them after our departure. Just at setting off, I bought a stick of a boy for a trifle, to serve as a staff or to urge on my camel. It was a straight stick with shining bark, very hard and tough ; and I learned afterwards, that our Arabs regarded it as cut from the veritable kind of tree, from which the rod of Moses had been taken. It did me good service through the desert, and in all our subsequent wanderings in Judea and to Wady Mûsa ; but did not stand proof at last against the head of a vicious mule on our way to Nazareth.

We reached the entrance of Wady esh-Sheikh in twenty-five minutes, and turned into it between the high cliffs of el-Furei'a on the left, and the mountain of the Cross on the right, leaving Horeb behind us. The valley is here a quarter of a mile in width ; and our course in it was E. N. E. At a quarter past two we were opposite the mouth of Wady es-Sebâ'iyeh, which

[1] Page 491.

here comes in as a broad valley from the south, having its head
near the southeast base of Jebel Mûsa, and thence sweeping
around to the east of the mountain of the Cross. A little before
reaching this point, a small Wady called Abu Mâdhy comes down
from the mountain on the right; at the head of which is water.
Wady esh-Sheikh now bends round to the N. N. E. and afterwards to the north, and spreads out into a broad plain tufted
with herbs and shrubs affording good pasturage. At 2½ o'clock
we lost sight of Horeb. Jebel Mûsa and St. Catharine had
nowhere been visible. We now had Jebel Furei'a on our left;
on the top of which there is table land with water, and pasturage for camels. After another hour we passed the mouth of the
small Wady el-Mûkhlefch, which enters from the right, and
came immediately (at 3½ o'clock) to the tomb of Sheikh Sâlih,
one of the most sacred spots for the Arabs in all the peninsula.
It is merely a small rude hut of stones; in which the coffin of
the saint is surrounded by a partition of wood hung with cloth,
around which are suspended handkerchiefs, camels' halters, and
other offerings of the Bedawin. The history of this saint is uncertain; but our Arabs held him to be the progenitor of their
tribe, the Sawâlihah; which is not improbable. Once a year,
in the latter part of June, all the tribes of the Tawarah make a
pilgrimage to this tomb, and encamp around it for three days.
This is their greatest festival.[1] We dismounted and entered
the building; at which our guides seemed rather gratified, and
prided themselves on the interest we took in their traditions.

We here left Wady esh-Sheikh, which now bends more to
the northward, and at an hour and a half from this place issues
from the dark cliffs forming the outworks of the central granite
region, at the point near which I have above supposed Rephidim
to have been situated. Crossing some low hills running out
from the eastern mountain, we came in half an hour on a course
N. E. by N. to the well Abu Suweirah, in the lower part of the
small Wady es-Suweiriyeh which comes down from the northeast. The well is small, but never fails; and near by are two
small enclosed gardens. Passing on a little further, we encamped at 4.10 in the narrow Wady.

The exchange we had made at the convent both as to men
and camels, proved on the whole to be advantageous; except
perhaps in the case of one old man, Heikal, who turned out to
be the very personification of selfishness. His two camels were
among the best; and he always contrived that they should have
the lightest loads. Tuweileb was a man of more experience
and authority than Beshârah; though less active. All were at
once ready to lend a hand at pitching the tent, and making the

[1] Burckhardt, p. 489.

i. 215, 216

necessary preparations for the evening repast. After dinner Tuweileb paid us a visit in our tent; and this practice he continued regularly all the time he was with us. He was always sure of a cup of coffee; and in these visits was more open and communicative than anywhere else, giving us freely all the information he possessed on the points to which we directed our inquiries.

The road we had now entered upon, is the usual one from the convent to 'Akabah, and the same followed by Burckhardt in A. D. 1816, in his unsuccessful attempt to reach the latter place. Times have now changed, after the lapse of more than twenty years; and we and others found no difficulty in doing what that enterprising traveller was unable to accomplish.

Friday, March 30th. The thermometer at sunrise stood at 38° F. the coldest morning I had experienced since entering Egypt in the beginning of January; and only at one other time, a few days later, did we have a like degree of cold. In the course of the day, however, as we passed through valleys shut in by rocks and desolate mountains, we found the heat caused by the reflection of the sun's rays to be very oppressive.

Starting at five minutes before 6 o'clock, and proceeding up the little valley N. E. by E. we came in twenty-five minutes to its head; from which we ascended for twenty minutes further by a rocky pass to the top of a ridge, which here forms the water-summit between the waters flowing into Wady esh-Sheikh and so to the gulf of Suez, and those running to the gulf of 'Akabah. From near the top of the pass, Jebel Kâtherin bore S. S. W.$\frac{1}{4}$W. We now turned E. by S. for half an hour along the top of a low ridge between two small Wadys; that on the left called 'Örfân, which runs into Wady Sa'l; and that on the right el-Mûkhlefeh, running to Wady ez-Zûgherah. These two large Wadys, S'al and Zûgherah,[1] pass down at the opposite ends of the high black ridge el-Fera'; but run together before reaching the sea, which they enter at Dahab. At 7.10 we turned E. N. E. and crossing a tract of broken ground, descended by a branch of Wady 'Örfân. This latter unites with several others and takes the name of Wady Sa'l ten minutes after; although it is still not the main Wady of that name. Our general course was now east, apparently towards the middle of the long dark ridge of Fera'.

From this point Jebel Habeshy bore southeast, lying to the south of Wady Zûgherah, between that valley and Wady Nûsb; which also unites with the Zûgherah further down. Nearly behind us were now seen the peaks of Um Lauz, Um 'Alawy,

---

[1] Wady ez-Zûgherah appears to be the valley called by Laborde Wady *Zackal,* by which he descended to the eastern gulf.

and Râs el-Ferûsh, seeming like outposts of Sinai on this part.
Indeed, on crossing the low pass soon after setting off this morning, we had left the upper granite region of Sinai, which on this
side is comparatively open and unguarded ; the peaks just mentioned lying further south. The sides of Wady Sa'l which we
were now descending, are here only low hills of disintegrated
granite, similar to the low belt around Sinai in the northwest.
The valleys are wide and shallow, and have many tufts of herbs,
chiefly 'Abeithirân. At 8 o'clock a conspicuous mountain came
in sight on the left, bearing north, and called Râs esh-Shûkeirah
from a valley of that name. It is a spur of the southern ridge
of the Tih, running off southeast from it. The road from the
convent to 'Ain passes near this mountain, leaving it on the
right ; while in crossing the southern Tih, it leaves the part
called edh-Dhûlûl to the left; and then strikes the head of
Wady ez-Zûlakah (called also ez-Zûrânîk), which it follows down
to 'Ain.[1]

Half an hour afterwards this open country terminated ; we
reached the dark barrier of el-Fera' which bounds it on the east
and seems to cut off all further progress. But the Wady we
were following, here enters the mountain by a narrow cleft, and
continues for six hours to wind its way among dark and naked
ridges and peaks through scenes of the sternest desolation. The
ridge Fera' extends on the right from this point to Wady
Zûgherah ; on the left it takes the name of el-Munciderah. The
valley, still a branch of Wady Sa'l, is narrow and winds exceedingly ; yet the general course is nearest east. The high and
desolate mountains which thus shut it in, are chiefly of grünstein, with some slate and veins of porphyry ; the higher peaks
as we advanced being sometimes slightly crested with sandstone.
Shrubs and herbs indeed are scattered in the bottom of the
valley ; but the mountains are destitute of vegetable life, and
the blackness of the rocks renders the valley gloomy.

After half an hour more (at 9 o'clock) the main branch of
Wady Sa'l comes in from the W. N. W. through which passes
up a route from en-Nuweibi'a to Suez, crossing the great sandy
plain er-Ramleh, and reaching the head of the western Wady
Nûsb in two days from this point. It strikes this latter Wady
at the tomb of Sheikh Habûs, which lay on our left in going to
Surâbit el-Khâdim. The first day's journey crosses Wady
Akhdar and stops at a station without water, called el-Humeit.
—At 10.15 another tributary came in from the northwest called
es-Sa'l er-Reiyâny, " the wet," in which there is water some

---

[1] This is the Wady Salaka of Rüppell.   neither Tuweileb nor any of our Arabs
Both he and Laborde also speak of it, or   knew this name ; although the former was
of a part of it, as Wady Saffran ; but   the guide of both these travellers.
i. 218. 219

distance above. The Seyâl or Tûlh trees began now to appear, and continued till we left the valley. Many of them are of considerable size, with thin foliage and a multitude of thorns. From them gum arabic is sometimes gathered. According to Tuweileb, all these trees, as also the Tûrfa, are public property; and whoever will, may gather both gum and manna.

We had now entered the territory of the Arabs Muzeiny. At 1.50 the valley opened out to a wide plain; the mountains on the left disappeared; and we could look out over the great sandy plain already described, quite to the southern ridge of the Tîh. It bore here the same character as where we saw it at the head of Wady Nûsb, an even, unbroken, precipitous chain, showing horizontal layers of rock, and perfectly barren. Wady Zûlakah and all the waters which connect with 'Ain, lie north of this ridge, between it and the northern Tîh. From this point our course was northeast. At ten minutes past 2 o'clock Wady esh-Shûkeirah came in from the west, having its head in the fork between Râs esh-Shûkeirah above mentioned and the southern Tîh. Soon afterwards we saw a black tent hanging on a tree, which Tuweileb said was there when he passed this way last year, and would never be taken away except by the rightful owner.[1] The plain of Wady Sa'l here connects on the north with the great sandy plain reaching to et-Tîh; while the Wady itself sweeps off to the southeast and again entering the mountains goes to join Wady Zûgherah in the direction of Dahab. We left the plain of the Sa'l at 2.40, ascending a low ridge called 'Ôjrat el-Fûras, the top of which we reached at 3 o'clock; and again descending we encamped half an hour later in a small valley tributary to Wady Mûrrah, in the midst of an open, undulating, desert region, with hills of grünstein on the right, capped with sandstone. Our day's journey had not been a long one; but the heat had been very oppressive, pent up as we were so long within the naked walls of Wady Sa'l, and exposed to both the direct and reflected rays of an unclouded sun.

This evening Tuweileb gave us some account of himself, and of the kindness he had experienced from M. Linant. He was now about sixty years old and obviously in the wane of his strength. His wife had died not long before, leaving him two children, a boy of some twelve years of age, and a girl about eight. These children were now in our train. On inquiring of their father, how he came to take them on such a journey, he said they were alone at home, and he had intended to leave them so; but on his coming away, they cried to go with him, and he said, "No matter, get upon the camels and come along." He had thus brought with him two spare camels, which were not in

[1] See above, p. 142.

our employ, and were said to have been broken down. The children were bright and active. The boy usually watched the camels when they were turned loose to feed. The little girl had fine eyes and a pleasing face. She usually wore only a long flowing shirt, but had a blanket for the night and for cooler days ; and commonly rode all day bare-headed under a burning sun. She at first stood in great fear of the strangers ; nor did her shyness towards us ever fully wear off.

During the preceding year, Tuweileb had spent a fortnight in and near the great plain el-Kâ'a, not far from Mount Serbâl, pasturing his camels, without a drop of water for himself or them. He drank the milk of the camels ; and they, as well as sheep and goats, when they have fresh pasture, need no water. In such case they will sometimes go for three or four months without it. Others had told us, that the camel needs water once in every three days in summer, and every five days in winter ; but this is probably when the pastures are dry, or when they are fed on provender.

Saturday, March 31st. We set off at 5.50, and continuing down the little Wady towards the northeast for twenty-five minutes, reached the main branch of the Wady Mûrrah. This comes from the northwest, where it rises near et-Tîh, and passes off in a southeast direction to join Wady Sa'l. We crossed it on a very oblique course, going E. N. E. till 6.55 ; when we left the Wady and passed over hills of drift sand, which our guide called el-Burka'. Among these it required all Tuweileb's sagacity and experience to keep the proper road ; and here apparently Burckhardt's guide missed the way and kept on further down Wady Mûrrah.[1] Our course was now northeast over a sandy region full of low ridges and hills of sandstone of various colours. At 7.50 we came out upon an open sandy plain extending to the foot of the Tîh, here an hour or more distant, and still retaining its character of a regular wall, composed of strata of sandstone, with layers apparently of limestone or clay towards the top. At 8 o'clock we began to cross the heads of several small Wadys called Ridhân esh-Shûkâ'a. At 8.15 our course was again E. N. E. and half an hour later Mount St. Catharine was visible, bearing S. W. by W. In another half hour a high mountain was seen across the eastern gulf, called Jebel Taurân, bearing E. by S. At half past 9 o'clock we descended a little into another Wady or shallow water-course called el-Ajeibeh, coming from the foot of et-Tîh, and flowing off to Wady Mûrrah. We crossed it very obliquely E. by N. and emerged from it after twenty-five minutes, keeping on the same course. None

---

[1] Travels, page 493.

i. 221, 222

of all these Wadys bore any marks of water during the present year.

Opposite this point the chain of et-Tih bends more northeast and sinks down into lower hills. At three quarters past ten, our guides pointed out the place of the fountain 'Ain el-Hŭdhera through a pass N. N. E. with several low palm trees around it; and soon after, we came upon another series of connected Wadys, called Mawârid el-Hŭdhera, or "paths" to this fountain. Our course led us to the right of el-Hŭdhera; but at 11.10 we stopped in a valley, at the point where our road came nearest to it; and all the camels were sent up the valley to be watered at the fountain, which was said to be more than half an hour distant towards et-Tih. Meantime we lay down upon the sand and slept. After a while, some of the men came back with five of the camels; saying the path was so rugged and difficult that their camels could not reach the spring. The others however succeeded; and after a delay of nearly three hours, returned, bringing a supply of tolerably good water, though slightly brackish. It is the only perennial water in these parts. These Arabs, being out of Tuweileb's sight, had probably turned their camels loose at the fountain to feed; and had themselves followed our example, and refreshed themselves with a nap. From this point a high mountain, said to lie in the fork of Wady Zŭgherah and Wady Nŭsb, bore S. S. W. ½ S.

Burckhardt has already suggested, that this fountain el-Hŭdhera is perhaps the Hazeroth of Scripture, the third station of the Israelites after leaving Sinai, and either four or five days' march from that mountain.[1] The identity of the Arabic and Hebrew names is apparent, each containing the corresponding radical letters; and the distance of eighteen hours from Sinai accords well enough with the hypothesis. The determination of this point is perhaps of more importance in Biblical history, than would at first appear; for if this position be adopted for Hazeroth, it settles at once the question as to the whole route of the Israelites between Sinai and Kadesh. It shows that they must have followed the route upon which we now were, to the sea and so along the coast to 'Akabah; and thence probably through the great Wady el-'Arabah to Kadesh. Indeed, such is the nature of the country, that having once arrived at this fountain, they could not well have varied their course, so as to have kept aloof from the sea and continued along the high plateau of the western desert.

We were again upon our way at 2¼ o'clock, approaching now the southern chain of the Tih. Our general course was E.

[1] Num. 11, 35. 33, 17. Comp. 10, 33.—Burckhardt, p. 495.

N. E. At 2.40 there was a narrow pass and a slight descent among hills of sandstone. Here on the rocks at the left were several Arabic inscriptions with crosses, marking them as the work of pilgrims ; and lower down along the descent were many rude drawings of animals. The route now winds much among sandstone hills and ridges, itself very sandy ; and at 3 o'clock we came out into a large open tract or plain called el-Ghôr, extending far to the southeast and connecting apparently with the great sandy plain which skirts the Tîh further to the west. We had now reached the line of the southern chain of the Tîh ; which here sinks down into precipitous isolated hills and masses of sandstone rock, rent to the bottom by narrow sandy valleys or clefts, through which the route passes, neither ascending nor descending except slightly. We may call these hills the fragments of the Tîh. Entering among these cliffs, we came without perceptible ascent at 3¼ o'clock to the point which divides the waters of Wady Mûrrah and Sa'l from those which run northwards to Wady Wetîr. Here we struck the head of Wady Ghûzâleh, which we followed down northeast, having perpendicular walls of sandstone on each side, and so narrow that in some places it might be closed by a gate. At the end of another fifteen minutes we emerged from these hills or fragments of the Tîh, into an open sandy plain, with hills upon the left, and on the right at some distance Jebel es-Sûnghy, a long ridge running from northwest to southeast and forming a sort of continuation of this part of the Tîh towards the eastern coast. In this mountain, on the other side, rises the Wady of the same name. At 3.50 the middle of the ridge bore east. At 4 o'clock we left the bed of Wady Ghûzâleh running off north to join Wady Wetîr ; and crossing a sandy tract on the right for fifteen minutes we struck Wady er-Ruweihibîyeh[1] coming down from the northeast and flowing by a short turn into Wady Ghûzâleh. We ascended this valley till half past 4 o'clock and then encamped in it for the night and for the next day. It is one of the prettiest Wadys we had found ; the sand ceased as we entered it, and the bottom is of fine gravel. The valley is broad ; the sides are rugged naked cliffs, where sandstone, grünstein, and granite, all appear alternately. It is everywhere dotted with herbs ; and many Seyâl trees scattered in it give it almost the appearance of an orchard.

The country we had passed through this day is a frightful desert. In some of the Wadys there were herbs and shrubs ; in others none ; while the sandy plains and ragged sandstone hills were without a trace of vegetation. As we emerged from the narrow part of Wady Ghûzâleh, the aspect of the country

[1] Wady Rahab of Burckhardt, p. 496.

i. 224, 225

changed; and it was evident that we had passed the southern range of the Tih. We were now among another net of Wadys, which drain the mountainous region between the two parallel ridges of that mountain. The most central and frequented spot in this region is the fountain and Wady called el-'Ain, lying several hours distance to the northwest of our present encampment; where there is living water and a brook and luxuriant vegetation, resembling apparently Wady Feirân, though without cultivation.[1] The water is said not to be so good as that of el-Hûdhera. From that point the great Wady Wetîr runs down eastward by a winding course to the gulf, forming the great drain into which all the Wadys of the region from the north and south empty themselves. A road already mentioned leads from the convent to el-'Ain, crossing the southern Tih at a point considerably further west than our route, and then following down Wady Zûlakah. From 'Ain a route goes off northwards to Gaza and Hebron, crossing the northern ridge of the Tih; and another keeps down Wady Wetîr to the gulf, and so along the coast to 'Akabah.

Sunday, April 1st. We remained all day encamped. In the afternoon I wandered away into a lone side valley and wrote a letter. Scarcely ever have I had such a sense of perfect solitude. No human eye was there; and no sound save that of the wind among the rocks. Just as I was about to return, a wild looking Arab with his gun stood suddenly before me. I might have been startled, had I not recognised him at once as one of our own men, a good natured fellow, who had come to look for me on account of my long absence.

Monday, April 2d. We started at 5½ o'clock. The morning was bright and beautiful; the sky serene; and the air of the desert fresh and invigorating. We proceeded up the valley N. E. by E. A little bird sat chirping on the topmost twig of one of the Seyâl trees; and reminded me strongly of the notes of the American robin on my own green native hills. What a contrast to this desert! in which we had only once seen a blade of grass since we left the region of the Nile. In twenty minutes we came out on an open plain at the head of Wady er-Ruweihibiyeh. This plain consists of sandstone only partially covered with earth; the surface declines slightly towards the northeast and its waters flow off in that direction to Wady es-Sûmghy. At 6.25 we struck a small Wady descending northeast along the northwestern extremity or base of Jebel Sûmghy. The rocks here still exhibited alternate specimens of sandstone, grünstein, and granite. Twenty-five minutes further, the Wady entered very obliquely among the cliffs, which on this side form the

---

[1] Rüppell's Reisen in Nubien, p. 255 sq.

commencement of the mountainous tract extending without much change of character to the coast. The cliffs were dark; and as we advanced, seemed to be chiefly of gray granite, with an occasional intermixture of porphyry and grünstein. Nothing could be of a more barren and uninviting aspect. At a quarter past 7 o'clock we left the Wady running on in the same direction to join Wady es-Sŭmghy further down, and turned at right angles into a branch Wady coming from the southeast. Here we ascended gradually for a few minutes, and then crossing the low water-shed descended towards Wady Sŭmghy, which we reached at 8 o'clock. This is a wide valley coming from the southwest. It is joined at this point from the south by another broad Wady or plain called el-Mŭkrih; and the united valley flows off N. N. E. It is quite wide, and has many Seyâl trees, from which gum arabic is collected in summer. All the trees of this species which we had seen since leaving the convent, were larger than those on the western side of the peninsula, and might compare with apple trees of a moderate size.

Our course now lay down Wady Sŭmghy N. N. E. The cliffs on each side are high and irregular, and occasionally capped with sandstone. After half an hour we had a distant view of the northern ridge of the Tîh, in which a high point bore N. 15° E. The shrubs in this valley were greener than we had seen before; indicating that more rain had fallen in this quarter than elsewhere. At 9.40 we left the Sŭmghy, and turned short towards the right into a side valley, which after a rather steep ascent of forty minutes brought us at 10.20 by a narrow pass to the top of a sharp ridge. Here is the head of Wady es-Sa'deh, which runs under the same name quite down to the sea.[1] We now followed down this valley on a general course E. N. E. between abrupt cliffs, alternately of granite and grünstein, from three hundred to five hundred feet in height, sometimes tipped with sandstone. The cliffs grew higher as we advanced, and contracted the valley more and more, often presenting at the frequent turns grand and imposing bulwarks. For a moment at 11.10 we had a distant glimpse of the sea for the first time; but it speedily vanished. Fifteen minutes further a large tributary came in from the right; and at 11.35 the whole valley was contracted between enormous masses of rock to the width of only ten or twelve feet. This romantic pass is called el-Abweib, "the little door." At 12¼ o'clock Wady es-Sa'deh at length opened from the mountains towards the shore upon a large bed of gravel, apparently brought down by its torrents. Here, just

---

[1] The short valley by which we ascended is the Wady Boszeyra (Büseiráh) of Burckhardt. Our Arabs did not know this name; but reckoned the whole to Wady es-Sa'deh.

i. 227, 228

at the left, is a thin ridge or stratum of chalk. The shore is still nearly a mile distant; and near it, directly in front, is the brackish fountain en-Nuweibi'a, with a few low palm trees, belonging to the Muzeiny. The descent towards the shore over the bed of gravel is very considerable.[1]

The first view of the gulf and its scenery from the spot where we now stood, if not beautiful, (for how can a desert be beautiful?) was yet in a high degree romantic and exciting. The eastern gulf of the Red Sea is narrower than the western; but it is the same long blue line of water, running up through the midst of a region totally desolate. The mountains too are here higher and more picturesque than those that skirt the gulf of Suez; the valley between them is less broad; and there is not the same extent of wide desert plains along the shores. Towards the south the gulf seemed to be some ten geographical miles in breadth. Immediately at our left, a broad gravelly plain, having also drift sand upon it, extended out into the sea for a great distance; while on the opposite coast a like projection appeared to reach out to a less extent; so that between the two the breadth of the gulf at this point was very much diminished. Further north it widens again, as before. The western mountains are mostly precipitous cliffs of granite, perhaps eight hundred feet in height, and in general a mile or more distant from the shore; though bays occasionally set quite up to their foot. From them a slope of gravel usually extends down to the sea. Opposite to Wady es-Sa'deh the mountains of the eastern coast are higher than those of the western; but further north they are lower. The general line of the western coast runs N. N. E. as far as to the remarkable cape Râs el-Burka', which terminates the view in that direction.

We now turned to the left along the coast, descending gradually to the gravelly plain above mentioned; and passing along it half way between the mountain and the sea. We found it everywhere much cut up by water-courses and gullies from Wady Wetir, which spread themselves widely over the plain, as the waters of the rainy season rush from that Wady towards the shore. This important Wady, the mouth of which we passed at a quarter past one, serves (as I have said above) to drain the whole region between the two ridges of the Tih; and brings down occasionally immense volumes of water, as is evident from the traces left upon the plain. Here for the first time we saw trunks of trees thus brought down. The road taken by Rüppell and Laborde in going from 'Akabah to Sinai, passes up this

---

[1] This point of the coast was reached by Seetzen in A. D. 1810, by nearly the same route. Hence he proceeded south-wards along the shore of the gulf. Zach's Monatl. Corresp. XXVII. p. 64.

valley to el-'Ain, about a day and a half distant; and thence through Wady Zûlakah to the convent.

At 1½ o'clock we were opposite to el-Wâsit, a small fountain near the shore, with a number of palm trees, marking the boundary between the Muzeiny and the few families of Terâbîn who inhabit this region. Having crossed the projecting plain, we came at a quarter past two o'clock to a small grove of palm trees on the slope near the shore, and a well called Nuweibi'a of the Terâbin, to distinguish it from the other. Here were traces of a recent encampment of these people; and we expected to find at least some fishermen who frequent the coast; but none appeared. Traces of former dwellings, or perhaps magazines, were also visible, formed of rude stones laid together without cement; such as are not unfrequent among the Arabs of the peninsula. Every three or four of the palm trees are enclosed by a mound forming a reservoir, into which the torrents from the mountains had been turned. The well is eight or ten feet deep; the water naturally brackish; and now, from long standing, it emitted an odour of sulphuretted hydrogen. The camels were watered here, and seemed thirsty. The Arabs also filled their water skins, saying we should find no more water so good until we reached 'Akabah. The shrub Ghürküd grows here in abundance.—After a detention of an hour, we again set off. Many heaps of large shells were seen as we passed along; showing how very abundant shell-fish must be upon this coast. After three quarters of an hour, we encamped at 4 o'clock on the shore, at the head of a bay which sets up near to the mountains.

Tuesday, April 3d. Our road for the whole day lay along the shore, with high mountains at our left, composed chiefly of dark gray granite with now and then a crest of sandstone upon the top of the ridge. We were mounted and upon our way at half past 5 o'clock. The rising sun threw his mellow beams upon the transparent waters of the gulf; and the eastern mountains, lighted up by his rays, presented a fine picture of dark jagged peaks and masses. At the end of an hour the path passed close to the rocks, which are here sandstone. Ten minutes further a small Wady came down from the mountains, for which our guides knew no name; around it were low hills of conglomerated granite. At 7¼ o'clock we passed the small Wady Um Hâsh of Burckhardt; a line of chalk was visible at the foot of the hills, which were crested with sandstone. Just at the edge of the water is an isolated rock called Mürbüt Ka'ûd el-Wâsileh, on which in former times a watchman was stationed to observe all comers from the north. On seeing any one, it was his duty to ride to Nuweibi'a and make report. Half an hour

i. 230, 231

further we passed the mouth of another Wady, called Muwâlih by Burckhardt, with a wide plain of gravel at its mouth.

We now had before us the high ridge running from southwest to northeast, which terminates in the cape Râs el-Burka' or Àbu Burka', the "Veil cape," so called from its white appearance when seen at a distance. Along the southern side of this ridge lies a wide bay, to the shore of which we came at ten minutes past 8 o'clock. At 9¼ o'clock, we neared the southwest end of the ridge of the promontory; and at 10 o'clock doubled the point of the cape, where it juts into the sea and only admits a very narrow path along its base. This point is considerably lower than the ridge further back; it is a hill covered with drifts of white sand, apparently driven up from the sea, and looking at a distance like a chalky cliff. After passing the cape, we saw immediately the northern branch of the Tih, presenting the same general appearance of a wall of horizontal strata as the southern branch, and terminating in a high headland which Burckhardt calls Râs Um Haiyeh; though Tuweileb knew no other name for it than et-Tih. As far as to this headland, the general course of the shore was still N. N. E.

We now had a fine beach on our right, and recreated ourselves by walking along the shore and picking up the curious shells, which everywhere abound. The transparent green of the water was very inviting; indeed, nothing could look purer than the waves as they rolled in over the clean white sand. I could not resist the temptation; and lingering behind the company, took a hasty but very refreshing bath. The mountains here retreat a little, leaving a plain of some width between them and the water. At 11½ o'clock we came to a well of bad brackish water, marked by a few palm trees, and called, like so many others, Abu Suweirah. From this point we began to approach more nearly the end of the northern Tih; which comes tumbling down towards the sea in immense masses apparently of yellow sandstone; but is intercepted by a range of granite cliffs between it and the shore, running from S. S. W. to N. N. E. which again are capped with red sandstone. We reached the southwest end of these cliffs at 1 o'clock. A steep slope of gravel extends from them down to the water; on a part of which three gazelles were feeding, which on seeing us bounded off fleetly and gracefully.

At half past two o'clock Wady el-Muhâsh came down through the cliffs, having before it an immense bed of gravel. Looking up through its gap, we could see the masses of the Tih on the right beyond. This is probably the spot where Burckhardt's guide, old 'Aid, so resolutely went for water.[1] An hour

[1] Travels, p. 503.

afterwards, at 3½ o'clock, we were opposite the end of the Tih, or Râs Um Haiyeh, which does not project into the sea, though a bay flows up to its foot. Its height is about the same as the cliffs near Nuweibi'a. Further north the mountains become lower. We now entered again upon a wide gravel slope lying before Wady Mukübbeleh north of et-Tih, the mouth of which we passed at 4 o'clock. It is here broad; but one can look up through it far into the mountains, where it is quite narrow. Three quarters of an hour further on, a rocky promontory at the head of a bay (the Jebel Sherâfeh of Burckhardt) presented a very narrow and difficult pass; in traversing which one of the camels fell and came near rolling into the sea. The animal had to be unloaded in order to rise; and several of the things were wet. Meantime we had gone on and encamped at 5 o'clock in the broad Wady el-Huweimirât, which here comes down from the northwest, and was full of herbs.

The shore during the whole journey of to-day, was strewed with innumerable shells of every variety and size, from the smallest up to those weighing several pounds. They were however mostly broken and of no further value. Occasionally the sandy beach was paved or rather incrusted, with a conglomerate of debris and shells, evidently formed by the action of the sea-water. The shore was everywhere dotted with small tracks, which the Arabs said were made by a species of shell-fish, that comes upon the land every night and returns to the sea in the morning. We afterwards saw many crabs of various species running briskly upon the shore. One curious little animal was very frequent; a species of shrimp or minute lobster, that had taken possession of convolute shells, in which he had made himself at home; and protruding his head and legs, ran about in great numbers, carrying his shell with him. He was evidently a foreigner; for though his body had grown to the shape of the shell, yet the shells were all old and some of them broken. The little fellow was not in any way attached to his shell; and when drawn out, would run away. Some also had outgrown their shells.

From the headland of the Tih northwards, the general direction of the western coast is northeast to its extremity. This of course contracts the breadth of the gulf more and more the nearer it approaches 'Akabah; as the eastern coast apparently continues nearly on a straight line. Immediately beyond the valley in which we encamped, are two promontories running out for some distance into the sea; not high, but terminating in rocks; so that loaded camels cannot easily pass around them. The southernmost, called el-Mudâreij, is the shortest and most difficult; and between them is a broad valley.

i. 233, 234

The mountains on the opposite or eastern coast, were here low; and a narrow sloping plain seemed to intervene between them and the sea. A place called Hakl, the first station of the Haj after 'Akabah (mentioned also by Edrisi) was visible near the coast, bearing S. E. ½ S. It is in a Wady called el-Mebrūk, having many palm trees. Here the route of the Haj turns more inland. The tract of mountains between Hakl and 'Akabah is inhabited by the Arabs 'Amrân; while those further south are the seat of the tribe called Mesâ'îd, a subdivision (*Fendeh*) of the Haweitât.

Wednesday, April 4th. The promontories before us compelled us to take a back route, so as to cross their ridges higher up. We set off at a quarter after six, passing up Wady el-Huweimirât for ten minutes N. N. W. and then turning into a narrower side Wady on a course northeast. Twenty minutes more brought us to the foot of a steep pass leading over to the next valley. The path is very narrow, ascending along the face of the sandstone rock, and seemed to be in part artificial. One camel again fell, and began to give out. We reached the top at 6.50, and descended gradually to the broad valley between the two promontories; where we stopped at a quarter past 7 for twenty minutes, to adjust the loads, and leave the tired camel free. The poor animal was however too far gone, and died the same night.

This Wady our Arabs called also el-Huweimirât, although not connected with the former one of that name.[1] It descends rapidly to the sea, which is not far off; and Burckhardt appears to have followed down this valley and passed around the second promontory, which he describes as composed of black basaltic cliffs, into which the sea has worn several small creeks like little lakes, full of fish and shells. Here Laborde found a bed of oysters. It seems also to have been in this valley, that Burckhardt on his return was attacked by robbers. Our guides preferred to avoid this promontory also by a back route. Crossing therefore the Wady, we continued on the same course up a side valley; and came at 7.55 to the top of another pass, from which the descent was more steep and rugged than anything we had yet met with. This brought us at 8¼ o'clock into Wady Merâkh,[2] which we followed down E. N. E. to the sea. It is broad and barren; and further down another large branch joins it from the northwest bearing the same name. The two open broadly together upon the sea, over an immense slope of gravel, forming quite a promontory. We came out upon the slope at half past

[1] In like manner Burckhardt apparently gives the name Mezârik to both; though incorrectly.

[2] Wady Emrag of Rüppell; the name being less corrupted than is often the case with that traveller.

nine. Towards the sea is a palm tree, and a little further north another. There was said also to be brackish water in the vicinity. Here some fishermen were encamped in two or three black tents, with a few goats. One of them brought us a Beden (as he called it) which he had shot; we bought it for five piastres, instead of the twenty which he asked; but it turned out to be a gazelle. We were now in the territory of the Haiwât; that of the Tawarah and Terâbin extending only to the northern Tih.

This is doubtless the spot where Burckhardt was stopped on his way to 'Akabah, and compelled to turn back. As seen from here, every thing corresponds to his description;[1] the line of date trees around the castle of 'Akabah bearing N. E. by E.; the promontory of Râs Kureiyeh (as he calls it); and the little island with ruins which his guides told him of, but which he did not see; having probably looked for it (as I did at first) further out in the gulf, while it lies close in near the shore and directly under the eye. Burckhardt however calls the place not Wady Merâkh, but Wady Tâba'; and in general the names he mentions in this vicinity are so different from those we heard, or so differently applied, that for a long time we knew not what to make of it. We knew that old 'Aid, Burckhardt's guide, must have been well acquainted with the country; and as there was no reason to suspect any deception on his part, we were inclined to distrust the accuracy of Tuweileb's information. On mentioning the discrepancy to Tuweileb, he said at once that 'Aid knew better than he, and would not tell a lie. Yet on his inquiring in our presence of the Arabs encamped on the spot, they confirmed the account which Tuweileb had already given. I am inclined therefore to charge the error to Burckhardt himself, or rather to the circumstances in which he was placed; for he says expressly, that for the two days he was in these parts he found no opportunity to take any notes.[2] It is not surprising, that in such a multitude of new names, not noted at the time, some should have been forgotten and others applied to wrong places. We here took leave for the present of this accomplished and lamented traveller; whose book hitherto had been our constant companion.[3]

Turning now to the left we descended obliquely on a north-east course across the gravel slope, and at 9.40 reached the shore of a little bay with a sandy beach. At 10 o'clock we were op-

---

[1] Page 509.

[2] Page 517.

[3] Old 'Aid, it seems, was quite a noted character in the peninsula. Tuweileb had known him, and all our Arabs had heard of him. They also knew Hamd, the other

i. 236, 237

faithful and intrepid attendant of Burckhardt, who was of their clan, the Aulâd Sa'id. He was still living as a poor man in Cairo; where he made it his business to procure fodder for camels.

posite the little island above mentioned, which we judged to be
a good quarter of a mile distant from the shore. It is merely a
narrow granite rock some three hundred yards in length, stretching from northwest to southeast with two points or hillocks, one
higher than the other, connected by a lower isthmus. On it are
the ruins of an Arabian fortress with a battlemented wall running
around the whole, having two gateways with pointed arches.
This is without any doubt the former citadel of Ailah, mentioned
by Abulfeda as lying in the sea. In A. D. 1182 it was unsuccessfully besieged with ships, by the impetuous Rainald of
Chatillon; and in Abulfeda's time (about A. D. 1300) it was
already abandoned, and the governor transferred to the castle on
the shore.[1] The ruins therefore cannot well be referred to a
period later than the twelfth century. Our Arabs called this
island only el-Kurey, or el-Kureiyeh; the diminutive of a word
which signifies a village, but which they also apply to the ruins
of such a place. The Arabs of the eastern coast, according to
Lieut. Wellsted, give it the name of Jezîrat Far'ôn, 'Pharaoh's
Island.'[2] From the castle of 'Akabah it bears W. S. W.

Continuing our course we came in twenty minutes to the
little Wady el-Kureiyeh, coming down from the left, so called
from the island before it. Then followed the sand and stones of
Wady el-Mezârik, which we passed at 10¾ o'clock. Here low
hills of sandstone and chalk interrupted the granite for a time.
Further on, in the broad plain of Wady Tâba', we came at half
past 11 o'clock to a brackish well, with many palm trees.
Among the latter was one tree of the species called *Dôm*, the
Theban palm, so frequent in Upper Egypt. Here was also a
large square hole dug in the ground, walled up with rough
stones, like a cellar; in it had once been a well, but the bottom
was now covered with young palm trees. Higher up in the valley there was said to be better water.

Beyond this valley or plain, the granite rocks come down to
the shore again, forming a long black promontory, called by
Burckhardt Râs Kureiyeh, and by our guides Elteit; but the
Arabs at 'Akabah gave it the name of Râs el-Musry, and said
that Elteit was the name of a valley on the eastern coast. Ten
minutes brought us to the side of this promontory running E. N.
E. Our way led along its base; and we turned the extremity
at a quarter past noon. Hence the little island bore S. 65° W.

[1] Wilken Gesch. der Kreuzzüge III. ii.
p. 222. Abulfed. Arab. in Geogr. vet.
Scriptores, ed. Hudson, Oxon. 1712. Tom.
III. p. 41. Schultens Ind. Geogr. in Vit.
Salad. art. *Aila*. Rommel's Abulfeda, p.
78, 79. See more under *Ailah*, further
on.

[2] This island has been described by
Lieut. Wellsted, Travels, II. pp. 140, 142
sq.; also by Laborde and by Rüppell, Rei-
son in Nubien, p. 252. Both these travellers have given views of the ruins; that
of Laborde is more elegant, that of Rüppell more correct.

while the shore before us continued northeast. Just beyond this point, a valley called Wady el-Musry is said to come in; but we did not take note of it at the time. The mountains on the left here retire from the coast; and near it are only low hills of conglomerated sand and gravel, almost of the consistence of rock, and extending beyond the head of the gulf. We now began to see the opening of the great valley el-'Arabah. The mountains on the east of it are high and picturesque; and a low spot in them marks the place of Wady el-Ithm. At 2 o'clock, we passed a small rock on the shore, with a heap of stones upon it, called Hajr el-'Alawy, 'Stone of the 'Alawy.' This, Tuweileb said, was the ancient and proper boundary of the Tawarah in this quarter, separating them from the 'Alawin; and here in former days, both men and beasts entering the territory of the Tawarah paid a tribute. At length, at a quarter past 2 o'clock, we reached the northwest corner of the gulf, and entered the great Haj road, which comes down from the western mountain and passes along the shore at the northern end of the sea. Just at this point we met a large caravan of the Haweitât coming from the eastern desert, whence they had been driven out by the drought. They were now wandering towards the south of Palestine, and had with them about seventy camels and many asses, but no flocks. These were the first real Arabs of the desert we had seen; not wearing the turban like the Tawarah, but decorated with the *Kefiyeh*, a handkerchief of yellow, or some glaring colour thrown over the head, and bound fast with a skein of woollen yarn; the corners being left loose and hanging down the sides of the face and neck. They were wild, savage, hungry-looking fellows; and we thought we had much rather be with our mild Tawarah than in their power. Tuweileb held a parley with them, which detained us fifteen minutes.

From this point, which we left at 2½ o'clock, the north shore of the gulf runs southeast almost in a straight line nearly to the castle of 'Akabah. The general course of Wady el-'Arabah, taken about the middle, is here N. N. E. Its width at this end is about four geographical miles; farther north it is wider. The mountains on either side are high; those on the west fifteen to eighteen hundred feet, and those on the east two thousand to twenty-five hundred feet. The valley was full of sand-drifts as far as the eye could reach; and seemed to have little or no acclivity towards the north. The torrents, which in the rainy season stream into it from the adjacent mountains, flow along its western side, so far as they are not absorbed by the sand; and enter the sea at the northwest corner. There is no appearance of a water-course in any other part of the valley. Along the shore from this point nearly to the castle, the waters of the gulf

i. 239, 240

have cast up an unbroken bank of sand and gravel which is
higher than the level of the Wady, and would prevent the passage of any stream. On the north of the path, towards the
western side, a large tract has the appearance of moist marshy
ground, seemingly impregnated with nitre, and looking as if
water had recently been standing upon it; which sinking or dry-
ing away, had left an incrustation on many portions of the surface. This tract is mostly naked of vegetation; yet the parts
in the vicinity are full of shrubs, chiefly of the Ghŭrkŭd; and
seen from a distance, the ground appears as if covered with a
luxuriant vegetation. This however vanishes on a nearer approach. We looked in vain in the western part of the valley for
traces of ruins of any kind; we had hoped to find something by
which to fix a site for Ezion-geber. Towards the eastern side
and around the castle is a large grove of palm trees, extending
both ways for some distance along the shore.

At 3.40 we reached the end of the straight part of the shore,
which here takes a direction due south for perhaps half an hour;
when it again curves around S. S. W. to the general line of the
eastern coast. At this point the extensive mounds of rubbish,
which mark the site of Ailah, the Elath of Scripture, were on
our left. They present nothing of interest, except as indicating
that a very ancient city has here utterly perished. We did not learn
that they have now a name. Further east than these, beyond a
gully coming down from the eastern mountain, are the ruins of
an Arab village, mere walls of stone once covered probably with
flat roofs of palm leaves, like the dwellings now just around the
castle. Many of the palm trees are here enclosed in reservoirs,
in order to retain the water of the rainy season around them.
At 3.50 we reached the castle, and entered the huge portal
from the northwest through strong and massive doors heavily
cased with iron; the whole passage-way being lined with many
Arabic inscriptions.

The castle is an oblong quadrangle of high thick walls, with
a tower or bastion at each of the four corners.[1] All around the
wall on the inside is a row of chambers or magazines one story
high, with a solid flat roof, forming a platform around the interior of the castle. On this platform are erected in several parts
temporary huts or chambers, covered with the stalks of palm
leaves, and occupied apparently by the garrison as dwellings.
We did not learn the time when the fortress was built; the
date is doubtless contained in some of the numerous inscriptions;
but we were so much taken up with other matters, that this
point was overlooked. Burckhardt says it was erected, as it now
stands, by the Sultan el-Ghûry of Egypt in the sixteenth century.

[1] A view of the castle of 'Akabah is given by Rüppell and by Laborde.
i. 240–242

This is not improbable; though I am not aware of the authority
on which the assertion rests. The garrison consisted at this
time of thirty-three undisciplined soldiers, Mugháribeh or Western Africans, as they were called, but actually Bedawin from
Upper Egypt. In command of these were a captain of the gate,
a gunner, a Wakil or commissary, and over all a governor.

As we entered the fortress, the governor was sitting in the
open air on a small platform under the windows of a room near
the southwest corner of the court. He received us with apa-
thetic civility, invited us to sit upon his platform, ordered coffee,
and meantime read the letters which we had brought from Habíb
Effendi and the governor of Suez. He was a young man, who
had been here only four or five months; his predecessor having
been recalled, it was said, on account of incivility to former
travellers. There was therefore in his whole demeanour towards
us, now and afterwards, an air of studied endeavour, not indeed
to please and gratify us, but so to conduct as to avoid complaint
and future censure. The room before which he was sitting, was
assigned to us; it seemed to be his usual hall of audience, with
coarse gratings for windows, but no glass. Here our luggage
was deposited, and we spread our beds; and as the walls of the
room were of stone and the floor of earth, and cold, we escaped
the usual annoyance from bugs and fleas, for which the place is
famous. Scorpions are also said to be in plenty here; but we
saw none of them. They are caught by cats, of which there are
great numbers in the castle, as we found at night to our cost.—
Our Tawarah with their camels betook themselves for the night
without the walls.

We were yet sitting and chatting with the governor, when it
was discovered that the palm leaf roof of one of the huts overagainst us had caught fire; and suddenly it burst out into a
terrific blaze, rising along and above the wall of the castle. All
was now confusion and clamour and hurrying to and fro; the
governor forgot his pipe, his slippers, and his dignity, and rushed
eagerly among the crowd, distributing his orders, to which no
man listened; while to heighten the alarm, it was now announced
that the powder magazine of the fortress was directly under the
flames. Fortunately there was nothing but stone-work in the
vicinity, and water in plenty was near; so that the fire was soon
extinguished with little damage, after vast clamour and uproar
among the Arabs. We were not able to satisfy ourselves, whether
the story of the powder had any foundation or not.

We now withdrew to our room, and endeavoured to make
use of the time for writing; but the idea of our wishing to be
alone was incomprehensible to our new friends; and we might
as well have set ourselves down in the middle of the court. My
i. 242, 243

companion wishing to speak with the governor by himself, sought him out in his private room, and found him less reserved and more friendly than he had been in public. Indeed, it is well understood, that all the officers mentioned above are only spies upon each other; and the governor had regulated his demeanour in public accordingly. Meantime, as our spokesman was absent, our own apartment was left more in quiet.

In the evening we were invited by the governor to coffee in his private room, up one flight of stairs near the southwest bastion. The room was small and entirely naked, with a floor of earth and a roof of the stalks of palm leaves. In one corner was a wooden bench or platform about three feet high, on which were his carpet and cushions; in another part a little basin or hearth for making coffee; and these with one or two mats on the floor made up the furniture. We were admitted to his divan; others who came in, took their places on the mats or squatted down on their feet. This *soirée* was well meant, but proved to be rather tedious.

In coming by the way of 'Akabah, it had been our plan to proceed directly to Wady Mûsa, either along the 'Arabah, or through the eastern mountains, and thence to Hebron; and we had been habitually led to look upon this place as perhaps the most critical point in our whole journey. The country between it and Wady Mûsa, including the 'Arabah, is in possession of the 'Alawin, a branch or clan of the great tribe Haweitât; who of course have the right of conducting all travellers passing through their territory. They are a lawless tribe, standing in no good repute among their neighbours; and their Sheikh Husein has of late years become especially notorious among travellers, as faithless and mean-spirited.[1] We therefore anticipated difficulty and much petty annoyance and imposition, both here and on our way to Hebron; though we knew that the fear of the Pasha would exempt us from all open attempts upon our persons or property. We had never thought of taking any other route. We now learned, however, that Husein and his tribe were encamped at the distance of two days' journey from 'Akabah, near Ma'ân; and that it would require at least four days' time to get him here; besides the delay that would be incident to making a bargain and other preparations for the further journey. If therefore we sent for him, we must be content to wait here pent up in the fortress for five or six days, without employment or interest, and exposed to perpetual annoyance from Arab curiosity and official impertinence.

[1] This is the same person whom Schubert calls "Emir Salem of Gaza, the great Sheikh of the Araba;" Reise. etc. II. p. 394. We heard nothing of any such name or attributes.

i. 243-245

The idea of such a loss of time was insupportable ; and we looked about for some way of escaping at a less expense from this castle, which we already began to dread in anticipation as a prison-house. Our Tawarah could not take us to Wady Mûsa without invading the rights of another tribe, and exposing themselves to reprisals ; but both they and the governor said they could carry us across the western desert to Gaza or the vicinity, without danger of being interfered with by any one. On further inquiry, we found also that the same route would lead us to Gaza or Hebron, as we pleased ; and we need not decide for either until we should approach the confines of Palestine. The journey, it was said, would occupy five or six days. As this was a route for the most part hitherto untrodden by any modern traveller, and we should thus avoid delay and all necessity of intercourse with the 'Alawin, we determined (if possible) to make a new contract with our faithful Tawarah, and proceed in this direction ; leaving a visit to Wady Mûsa to be afterwards connected with our contemplated excursion to the south end of the Dead Sea. On inquiring of the Tawarah, they expressed a willingness to go with us ; but, taking their tone from the atmosphere of the castle, or from what they had heard of the 'Alawin, they demanded for each camel two hundred piastres for the journey ; a larger sum than we had paid them for the whole distance from Cairo to this place. So the matter rested for the night.

Thursday, April 5th. Forenoon. This morning the negotiation was resumed with an offer of one hundred and twenty piastres on our part, and a demand from the Arabs of one hundred and seventy, which they afterwards abated to one hundred and fifty. As they were sitting with us to talk the matter over, the governor came in with his attendants and cushions ; and seating himself, ordered coffee to be made and served round. Our own breakfast was now brought ; and our own Arabs had the tact to go away. The governor and his attendants remained ; but declined partaking of the meal to which we invited them, except so far as to drink a cup of tea. They afterwards withdrew ; and our Arabs again took up the negotiation. After long and grave discussion, the result was, that the intermediate sum of one hundred and thirty-five piastres was agreed to by both parties. In the place of the dead camel, one of Tuweileb's was to carry a load ; and we undertook to furnish provisions for the men upon the way. This was no great matter, for their wants are few and their palates not difficult. Bread and rice are luxuries which they seldom enjoy ; and of these we had an ample supply. The commissary in the castle had also a few stores for sale, at enormous prices ; but we bought little ex-

i. 245, 246

cept a supply of lentiles or small beans, which are common in
Egypt and Syria under the name of *'Adas ;* the same from
which the pottage was made for which Esau sold his birthright.
We found them very palatable, and could well conceive, that
to a weary hunter, faint with hunger, they might be quite a
dainty.[1]

While these negotiations were going on, I took a stroll alone
without the walls along the shore. The castle is situated quite
at the eastern part of Wady el-'Arabah, on the gravel slope
which here rises from the water towards the eastern mountain.
Directly back of the castle the mountain is high, and bears the
name of Jebel el-Ashhab ; but further south the hills near the
coast become much lower. The slope back of the castle is cut
up with gullies from mountain torrents ; without however presenting any large and distinct water-course. Wady el-Ithm
enters the 'Arabah further north on the same side ; and I was
disappointed in not finding, anywhere in the latter valley, more
traces of the waters which must rush into it during the rainy
season. Indeed very little water would seem to flow along it
into the gulf ; the greater part being probably absorbed by the
sand.

On the shore I tried the experiment which both Rüppell
and Laborde mention, of obtaining fresh water by digging holes
in the sand when the tide is out. It was in part successful ;
though less so than I had been led to expect from their accounts.
On digging a hole with the hands, it gradually filled with water,
which at first was salt ; but when this was removed, the hole
again became slowly filled with fresh water. The Arabs had
dug several larger holes just by, in which fresh water was standing. The language of Laborde seems to imply, that the chief
supply of water for the fortress is obtained in this way ; but this
is not the case ; as there is a large well within the walls, only
fifteen or twenty feet deep, which furnishes an abundance of
good water. There are also other like wells in the vicinity of
the fortress. Indeed the fresh water on the shore is apparently
on about the same level with the bottom of these wells ; and the
supply of both probably comes from water, that filters its way
down from the eastern mountain under the gravel which here
forms a slope quite to the sea. This appearance of water is confined to the shore near the castle ; for I repeated the same experiment afterwards in several places towards the middle of
Wady el-'Arabah without the slightest success.

Immediately around the fortress, several families of the
Arabs 'Amrân have taken up their abode, and built themselves

---

[1] Gen. 25, 34. The name in Hebrew and Arabic is the same.

i. 246-248

huts of stone ; long low rude hovels, roofed only with the stalks
of palm leaves. The proper territory of the tribe commences
here, and includes the mountains further south and southeast ;
but these appeared to be a sort of dependants on the castle,
employed in its service as menials. The number would seem to
have been formerly much greater ; as dwellings of the same kind
in ruins extend northwest nearly to the mounds of Ailah. Half
an hour south of the fortress, in the mouth of the Wady Elteit,
is the ruin of a small Arab fort or castle, called Kûsr el-Bedawy ; which may perhaps have served for the protection of the
Haj or caravan of pilgrims before the present larger one was
built.—According to Rüppell's observations, the castle of 'Akabah lies in Lat. 29° 30' 58" N. and Long. 32° 40' 30' E. from
Paris, or 35° 0' 54" E. from Greenwich.[1] From it the little
island of Kureiyeh with its ruins bears W. S. W. at the distance
of eight or ten miles.

On returning into the fortress at 10 o'clock, I found all our
own preparations completed ; and we wished to set off without
delay. But as we were about to take a route which our Tawarah
had never travelled, it was necessary to have with us a guide acquainted with the country. With such an one the governor undertook to furnish us ; and besides, he went very methodically
to work, and gave and took papers to secure both himself and us.
These were : *First*, an acknowledgment from us, that he had
fulfilled to our satisfaction the requisitions contained in the letter
of Habib Effendi. *Second*, a *Tezkirah* or protection for us,
stating all the circumstances of the case, and that no one had a
right to interfere with our journey, and forbidding all interference.[2] *Third*, a pledge from our Tawarah Arabs for our safe
conduct to Gaza, etc. The preparation of these papers, the instructions to the guide, the loading of the camels, and the like,
occupied the whole time till 1 o'clock P. M.

As we were leaving the castle, we tendered as a matter of
course to the governor a present, such as experience had shown
us to be about "the thing." He declined it however for himself, with the remark, that the other three officers were also accustomed to receive presents. My companion replied, that we

[1] See Berghaus' Memoir zu seiner Karte
von Syrien, pp. 28, 30.—This gives the
difference of longitude between 'Akabah
and Suez at 2° 29' 21". The longitude
of 'Akabah given by Moresby on his Chart
of the Red Sea is 35° 6' E. from Greenwich, equal to 32° 45' 36" E. from Paris;
and differing from the specification of
Rüppell by more than 5 minutes. But
the distance between 'Akabah and Suez
on the same chart is in like manner only
i. 248, 249

2° 29'; so that a like variation is found
at both places. Hence, as the longitude
of Suez has been several times determined,
Rüppell's specification at 'Akabah is to be
preferred; especially as that of Moresby
was reckoned by chronometer from Bombay.

[2] This paper is so curious in its details,
that I give a translation of it in Note XXI,
at the end of the volume.

had had nothing to do with them, and had not even seen them all; yet if he chose to divide the money among them, we had no objection; or if he would tell us how much more was necessary, and would give us a receipt to be shown to the consul in Cairo, they should have it.   But this he did not seem much to relish, and ran shuffling after us in his slippers to return the money; probably thinking it was not enough to satisfy all his brother spies.   Indeed we found the whole establishment to be a nest of harpies; and were heartily glad to quit the castle. Yet, for a traveller who has a bargain to make with the 'Alawin, it might be well to propitiate all these dignitaries by presents of small articles of dress, such as a cap, handkerchief, or the like, rather than money; for they can be of great assistance to him in dealing with these most faithless of the Bedawin.

Just before setting off, we saw in one corner the process of manufacturing the goats' hair cloth of which the common Arab cloaks are made.   A woman had laid her warp along the ground for the length of several yards, and sat at one end of it under a small shed, with a curtain before her to ward off the eyes of passers-by.   She wove by passing the woof through with her hand, and then driving it up with a flat piece of board having a thin edge.

In very ancient times there lay at this extremity of the eastern gulf of the Red Sea, two towns of note in Scripture history, Ezion-geber and Elath.   The former is mentioned first, as a station of the Israelites, from which they returned to Kadesh probably a second time; and both towns are again named after that people had left Mount Hor, as the point where they turned eastward from the Red Sea in order to pass around on the eastern side of the land of Edom.[1]   That they were near each other is also said expressly in another place.[2]

Ezion-geber became famous as the port where Solomon, and after him Jehoshaphat, built fleets to carry on a commerce with Ophir.[3]   Josephus says it lay near Ælana, and was afterwards called Berenice.[4]   But it is mentioned no more; and no trace of it seems now to remain; unless it be in the name of a small Wady with brackish water, el-Ghûdyân, opening into el-'Arabah from the western mountain some distance north of 'Akabah.[5]

[1] Num. 33, 35. 21, 4. Deut. 2, 8, "by way of the plain [which extends] from Elath and Ezion-geber." The Hebrew word here translated 'plain' is 'Arabah, the same as the present Arabic name of the great valley.

[2] 1 Kings 9, 26. "Ezion-geber which is beside [or at] Elath, on the shore of the Red Sea." Compare 2 Chron. 8, 17. 18.

[3] See the preceding Note; also 1 Kings 22, 49. [48.]

[4] Antiq. 8. 6. 4.

[5] However different the names el-Ghûdyân and Ezion may be 'in appearance,

May it not be, perhaps, that the northern shallow portion of the gulf anciently extended up to this fountain? In that case, Elath was situated on a projecting point south of the northern extremity of the gulf, just where the great road from Petra on the east of the mountains, descended through Wady el-Ithm to the shore.[1]

Elath, called by the Greeks and Romans Ailah and Ælana, appears to have supplanted by degrees its less fortunate neighbour; perhaps after having been rebuilt by Azariah (Uzziah) about 800 B. C. Some fifty years later it was taken from the Jews by Rezin king of Syria, and never came again into their possession.[2] The notices of this city found in Greek and Roman writers, are fully collected in the great works of Cellarius and Reland.[3] In the days of Jerome it was still a place of trade to India; and a Roman legion was stationed here. Theodoret a little later remarks, that it had formerly been a great emporium, and that ships in his time sailed from thence to India.[4] Ailah became early the seat of a Christian church; and the names of four bishops of Ailah are found in various councils from A. D. 320 to A. D. 536.[5] In the sixth century also, Procopius speaks of its being inhabited by Jews under the Roman dominion.[6] A few *Notitiæ* of ecclesiastical and other writers, which mention Ailah, refer also to this period.[7] But when in A. D. 630, Muhammed had carried his victorious arms northward as far as to Tebûk, it was the signal for the Christian communities of Arabia Petræa to submit voluntarily to the conqueror, and obtain peace by the payment of tribute. Among these was John, the Christian ruler of Ailah, who became bound to pay an annual tribute of three hundred gold pieces.[8]

From this time onward, Ailah became lost under the shroud of Muhammedan darkness; from which it has fully emerged only during the present century. It is simply mentioned by the supposed Ibn Haukal perhaps in the eleventh century; and after the middle of the twelfth, Edrîsi describes it as a small town frequented by the Arabs, who were now its masters, and forming an important point in the route between Cairo and Me-

yet the letters in Arabic and Hebrew all correspond. The name *'Asyân* mentioned by Makrizi, (as quoted by Burckhardt, p. 511,) seems merely to refer to the ancient city, of which he had heard or read.—Schubert suggests that the little island Kureiyeh may have been the site of Eziongeber; but this, as we have seen, is merely a small rock in the sea, 300 yards long. Reise, etc. II. p. 379.

[1] I owe this suggestion (1855) to Dr. Kiepert.

[2] 2 Kings 14, 22. 16, 6.

i. 251, 252

[2] Cellarius Notit. Orb. II. p. 582 sq. Reland Palæstina, p. 554 sq.

[4] Hieron. Onomast. art. *Ailath.* Theodoret Quæst. in Jer. c. 49.

[5] Le Quien Oriens Christ. III. p. 759. Reland Pal. p. 556.

[6] Procop. de Bell. Pers. 1. 19.

[7] See these collected in Reland's Palæst. pp. 215-230.

[8] Abulfedæ Annales Muslemici, ed. Adler, 1789. Tom. I. p. 171. Ritter Erdk. XII. p. 71.

dîneh.[1] In A. D. 1116 King Baldwin I. of Jerusalem with two hundred followers made an excursion to the Red Sea; took possession of Ailah which he found deserted; and was restrained from advancing to Sinai only by the entreaties of the monks.[2] It was again wrested from the hands of the Christians by Saladin in A. D. 1167, and never again fully recovered by them; although the reckless Rainald of Chatillon in A. D. 1182 seized upon the town for a time, and laid siege unsuccessfully to the fortress in the sea.[3] In Abulfeda's day, and before A. D. 1300, it was already deserted; for this writer expressly says of Ailah: "In our day it is a fortress, to which a governor is sent from Egypt. It had a small castle in the sea; but this is now abandoned, and the governor removed to the fortress on the shore."[4] Such as Ailah was in the days of Abulfeda, is 'Akabah now. Mounds of rubbish alone mark the site of the town; while a fortress, as we have seen, occupied by a governor and a small garrison under the Pasha of Egypt, serves to keep the neighbouring tribes of the desert in awe, and to minister to the wants and protection of the annual Egyptian Haj. Shaw and Niebuhr only heard of 'Akabah; Seetzen and Burckhardt attempted in vain to reach it; and the first Frank who has visited it personally in modern times, was Rüppell in A. D. 1822.[5] For the last ten years, there has been no lack of European visitors.

The modern name 'Akabah, signifying a descent or steep declivity, is derived from the long and difficult descent of the Haj route from the western mountain. This pass is called by Edrisi *'Akabat Ailah.*[6] It is sometimes also termed el-'Akabah el-Musriyeh, the Egyptian 'Akabah, in distinction from el-'Akabah esh-Shâmiyeh or the Syrian 'Akabah, a similar pass on the route of the Syrian Haj, about a day's journey eastward from this end of the Red Sea.[7]

Ailah or 'Akabah has always been an important station upon the route of the Egyptian Haj; the great caravan of pilgrims which annually leaves Cairo for Mecca. Such indeed is the importance of this caravan both in a religious and political respect, that the rulers of Egypt from the earliest period have given it

[1] Ouseley's translation of Ebn Haukal, pp. 37, 41. Edrisi, ed. Jaubert, Tom. I. pp. 328, 332.

[2] Fulcher. Carnot. 43. Gesta Dei, p. 611. Will. Tyr. XI. 29. Comp. Wilken Gesch. der Kreuzz. II. p. 403. See also p. 127 above.—The historians of the crusades call the place *Helim,* and mistook it for the Elim of Scripture.

[3] Wilken Gesch. der Kreuzz. III. ii. pp. 139, 222.

[4] Abulfedæ Arabia, in Geogr. vet. Scriptores min. ed. Hudson, Oxon. 1712, Tom.

III. p. 41. Schultens Index Geogr. in Vit. Saladini, art. *Ailah.*

[5] Shaw's Travels, 4to. p. 321. Niebuhr's Beschr. von Arab. p. 400. Seetzen in Zach's Monatl. Corresp. XXVII. p. 65. Burckhardt's Travels, etc. p. 508. Rüppell's Reisen in Nubien, etc. p. 248.

[6] Edrisi Geogr. I. p. 332, ed. Jaubert. The assertion of Niebuhr, that 'Akabah is also called *Hâle* by the Bedawin, I must regard as doubtful; Beschr. von Arab. p. 400.

[7] Burckhardt's Travels, etc. p. 658.

i. 252, 253

convoy and protection. For this purpose, a line of fortresses similar to that of 'Akabah has been established at intervals along the route; with wells of water, and supplies of provisions for the pilgrims of the Haj. At these castles the caravan regularly stops, usually for two days. The first fortress on the route is 'Ajrûd; the second Nûkhl on the high desert north of Jebel et-Tih; the third 'Akabah; and a fourth at Muweilih or Mawâlih, on the coast of the Red Sea outside of the entrance to the gulf of 'Akabah. From 'Akabah the route follows the eastern shore of the gulf a long day's journey to Hakl. In this part the road leads around a promontory, where the space between the mountain and the sea is so narrow, that only one camel can pass at a time. It is considered very dangerous. Before reaching Hakl there is also a place with palm trees called Daher el-Humr. At Hakl the route leaves the shore, and passing through the mountains that here skirt the gulf, continues along the eastern side of them to Muweilih. Further than this, none of the Arabs we met with were acquainted with the road.

In the intervals between these fortresses, there are certain regular stations or halting-places, often without water, where the caravan stops for a shorter time for rest and refreshment. The various tribes of Bedawin through whose territory the route passes, are held responsible for its safety between certain fixed points. They have the prescriptive right of furnishing a convoy or escort for the Haj during its march between those points; and most of them receive for this service a certain amount of toll from the caravan.[1]

---

[1] A list of the fourteen stations of the Haj, as far as to Muweilih, as also the parts of the route allotted for convoy to i. 253, 254 the different Arab tribes, is given in Note XXII, at the end of the volume.

SECTION V.

Thursday, April 5th, 1838. *Afternoon.* Having at last made all our arrangements, we left the castle of 'Akabah at a quarter past 1 o'clock, P. M., and were as happy as any Bedawin to be in the desert again. From 'Akabah two roads lead across the western desert towards Gaza or Hebron; one said to be difficult, passing along the 'Arabah for some distance, and ascending the western mountain further north; the other following the Haj route to the top of the western ascent, and then striking off across the desert to the right. We took the latter as the easiest. Instead of one guide, we now found we had two; both of them 'Amrân, dependants on the castle, and born in its vicinity. They were instructed by the governor in our presence to conduct us in safety as far as to Wady el-Abyad, near the fork of the roads to Gaza and Hebron. The eldest was called Sâlim; both were tolerably intelligent; but they were dark thievish looking fellows, not to be compared with our Tawarah.

Our course lay along the head of the gulf on the Haj road by which we had come yesterday. At 2.40 we reached the foot of the western ascent, where the hills of conglomerate, which we had passed yesterday further south, sink down into a steep slope of gravel, extending far to the north. This we ascended about W. N. W. and at 3.25 crossed the shallow Wady Khurmet el-Jurf, which runs down towards the right; and then came among low hills of crumbled granite. Beyond these there is again an open gravel slope in some parts, before reaching the higher granite cliffs. At 4 o'clock we encamped on the side of the mountain, in a narrow branch of the same water-course, called Wady edh-Dhaiyikah.

From this elevated spot we had a commanding view out over the gulf, the plain of el-'Arabah, and the mountains beyond.

The castle bore from this point S. E. by E. Behind it rose the
high mountain el-Ashhab ; and back of this, out of sight, is el-
Hismeh, a sandy tract surrounded by mountains. But no one
of our guides knew this latter name as a general appellation for
these mountains.[1] At the south end of the Ashhab, the small
Wady Elteit comes down to the sea, having in it the ruin Küsr
el-Bedawy, bearing from here S. 40° E. More to the south, the
hills along the eastern coast are lower, having the appearance of
table land ; while further back are high mountains, and among
them the long ridge en-Nukeirah. These extend far to the south,
and there take the place of the lower hills along the coast. North
of the castle the large Wady el-Ithm comes down steeply from
the northeast through the mountains ; forming the main passage
from 'Akabah to the eastern desert. By this way doubtless the
Israelites ascended from the Red Sea in order to " compass Edom,"
and pass on to Moab and the Jordan. Wady el-Ithm now bore
E. 1° S. while a mountain further north called Jebel el-Ithm
bore E. 1° N. Then a smaller Wady comes down named es-
Sidr. To the northward of this was Jebel esh-Sha'feh, N. 70°
E. ; and still further north our guides professed to point out
Jebel esh-Sherâh, bearing N. 50° E. and separated from esh-
Sha'feh by Wady Ghŭrŭndel. On this point, however, we had
doubts.

   Friday, April 6th. The bright morning presented a beautiful view of the sea, shut in among mountains like a lake of
Switzerland. The eastern mountains too glittered in the sun ;
fine, lofty, jagged peaks, much higher than those we were to
climb. We set off at 6 o'clock, ascending W. N. W. We soon
reached the granite hills, and entering among them over a low
ridge, descended a little to the small Wady er-Rizkah at 6.25.
It flows to the left into the Musry, within sight a little below.
Passing another slight ridge, we reached Wady el-Musry at 6¾
o'clock. This is a large Wady coming down from the north obliquely along the slope of the mountain, and running down by
itself to the sea, which it was said to enter just north of Râs el-
Musry. Our route now lay up along this valley, winding considerably, but on a general course about northwest. The ridge
upon the left was of yellow sandstone resting on granite ; while
on the right was granite and porphyry. The scenery around was
wild, desolate and gloomy ; though less grand than we had seen
already. At 7 o'clock, limestone appeared on the left ; and we
turned short from the Musry towards the left, into a narrow
chasm between walls of chalk with layers of flint. Ten minutes

---

See Burckhardt, pp. 433, 440. Yet   Tûr Hismeh ; as appears also from Burck-
the mountains adjacent to this tract may   hardt, p. 444. Laborde, p. 63. [218.]
not improbably have been spoken of as
     i. 256, 257

now brought us to the foot of the steep and difficult ascent; so
that this last ravine might well be termed the gate of the pass.
The ascent is called simply en-Nŭkb, or el-'Arkûb, both signifying "the pass" up a mountain; and our guides knew no other
name.   The road rises by zigzags along the projecting point of a
steep ridge, between two deep ravines.   It is in part artificial;
and in some places the thin layer of sandstone has been cut away
twenty or thirty feet in width down to the limestone rock.   Portions of this work have probably been done at the expense of
pious Mussulmans, to facilitate the passage of the Haj.   Two
Arabic inscriptions on the rock, one of them at the top of the ascent, apparently record the author of the work.   Near the top is
something like a modern improvement; a new road having been
cut lower down on the side of the ridge, rising by a more gradual
ascent.   The whole road is said by Makrizi to have been first
made by Ibn Ahmed Ibn Tulûn, Sultan of Egypt in A. D. 868-84.[1]

We reached the top of the steep ascent at 8 o'clock; but
continued to rise gradually for half an hour longer, when we came
to Râs en-Nŭkb, the proper "Head of the Pass."   Here however we had immediately to descend again by a short but steep
declivity, and cross the head of Wady el-Kureikireh running off
south to Wady Tâba', of which it would seem to be a main
branch.   Ascending again along a ridge at the head of this valley, still on a course W. N. W., we had on our right a deep
ravine called Wady er-Riddâdeh, running eastward, a tributary
of the Musry.   At 9 o'clock we finally reached the top of the
whole ascent, and found ourselves on the high level of the desert
above.   During the whole way, we had many commanding views
of the gulf and of el-'Arabah; which latter, as seen from this distance, seemed covered in parts with a luxuriant vegetation.   But
we had viewed it too closely to be thus deceived.   The point where
we now were, afforded the last, and one of the finest of these
views.   The castle of 'Akabah still bore S. E. by E., and the
mouth of Wady el-Ithm E. by S.   At 9.25 we came to the fork
of the roads, called Mufârik et-Turk, where the Haj route keeps
straight forward, while the road to Gaza turns more to the right.
The former, so far as we had now followed it, bears every mark
of a great public route.   This pass is especially famous for its
difficulty, and for the destruction which it causes to animals of
burden.   Indeed the path is here almost literally strewed with
camels' bones, and skirted with the graves of pilgrims.

Having thus reached the level of the great western desert,
we left the Haj road, and setting our faces towards Gaza and
Hebron, on a course northwest, we launched forth into the "great
and terrible wilderness."   We entered immediately upon an im-

---

[1] Makrizi, as cited by Burckhardt, p. 511.

mense plain, called Kâ'a en-Nŭkb, extending far to the west, and apparently on so dead a level, that water would hardly flow along its surface. It has, however, as we found, a slight declivity towards the W. and N. W.; for on our left was the commencement of a shallow Wady called el-Khureity, running off in that direction. The plain, where we entered upon it, was covered with black pebbles of flint; then came a tract of indurated earth; and afterwards again similar pebbles. The whole plain was utterly naked of vegetation. The desert however could not be said to be pathless; for the many camel tracks showed that we were on a great road. One of the first objects which here struck our view, was the *mirage,* presenting the appearance of a beautiful lake on our left. We had not seen this phenomenon in the whole peninsula, nor since the day we left Suez; and I do not remember that we ever again had an instance of it.

On this high plain, we now found ourselves above all the peaks and hills through which we had just before ascended. We could overlook them all, and saw beyond them the summits of the eastern mountains; which the level of the plain, on which we were, seemed to strike at about two thirds of their altitude. From this and other circumstances, we judged the elevation of this plain to be about fifteen hundred feet above the level of the gulf and el-'Arabah.[1] Far in the south, ridges of high land were visible; and nearer at hand, at the distance of three or four hours, a range of high hills called Tawârif el-Belâd, running from E. S. E. to W. N. W. the middle of which at 9½ o'clock bore S. W. Further to the right lay a similar ridge, called Tûrf er-Rukn, running in a direction about from S. S. E. to N. N. W. and highest towards the northern end, which bore at the same time N. 70° W. The Haj route passes along at the northern base of this range; and southwest of it is the well eth-Themed, from which water is obtained for the caravan.[2]

The plain we were crossing was terminated in this part towards the north by a ridge of low dark-coloured granite hills, running off W. S. W. which we reached at 11 o'clock. This ridge, a similar one beyond, and the tract between, all bear the

---

[1] According to the barometrical measurements of Russegger, who crossed the desert from the convent to Hebron a few months after us, the elevation of the castle Nŭkhl above the sea is 1496 Paris feet. This point is probably somewhat lower than the plain in question. See Berghaus' Annalen der Erdkunde, etc. Feb. und März, 1839. p. 429.
i. 259, 260

[2] Burckhardt's Travels in Syria, etc. p. 448. This mountain is the Dharf el-Rokob of that traveller; but although we inquired much after this name, we could not make it out in this form. His guides were from the desert east of the 'Arabah, and had perhaps another name or a different pronunciation. Rüppell gives it very corruptly the form Darfurock.

name of el-Humeirâwât. Passing through these hills, our course became N. N. W. for the remainder of the day. We now crossed another open plain, having at some distance on our left Wady el-Khureity. In some of the smaller water-courses were a few herbs and some Seyâl trees. We passed the next range of hills before noon; and from it descended to Wady el-Khûmîleh at 12.10, a broad shallow depression, coming from the right from near the brow of el-'Arabah, and full of herbs and shrubs. Towards the left a wide open tract of the desert extended beyond the northern extremity of Tûrf er-Rukn; and through this plain runs Wady Mukûtta' et-Tawârik after having received the Khureity and other Wadys. The Mukûtta' runs on northwesterly to join the Jerâfeh, which was continually spoken of as the great drain of all this part of the desert. The Khûmîleh continued for a time parallel to our route. The smaller Wadys were now full of herbs, and gave to the plain the appearance of a tolerable vegetation, indicating that more rain had fallen here than further south in the peninsula. Far in the W. N. W. ridges apparently of limestone hills were visible, running from south to north. At 12½ o'clock a small Wady called el-Erta crossed our path from the right and joined the Khûmîleh. A low limestone ridge now lay before us, which we crossed through a gap at half past one; and came upon the broad sandy Wady or rather plain el-'Adhbeh, descending towards the left. On the northern side of this latter we encamped at 3 o'clock, not far from the foot of another similar ridge. From this point the high northern end of Tûrf er-Rukn bore S. 60° W.

The weather had been all day cold, with a strong north wind; it was indeed the most wintry day I had experienced since entering Egypt. Our Arabs were shivering with the cold, and this induced us to encamp so early. They kindled large blazing fires; and at night, as they sat around them, the light flashing upon their swarthy features and wild attire, the scene was striking and romantic. The camels, like their masters, crouched and crowded around the fires, and added to the picturesque effect of the scene.

The general character of the desert on which we had now entered, is similar to that between Cairo and Suez; vast and almost unbounded plains, a hard gravelly soil, irregular ridges of limestone hills in various directions, the *mirage*, and especially the Wadys or water-courses. On reaching this high plateau, we were somewhat surprised to find all these Wadys running towards the northwest and not towards the east into the 'Arabah, as we had expected from its near vicinity. To all this desert our Arabs gave the general name of et-Tih, "Wandering;"

and said that the mountain ridge which skirts it on the south, takes the same name from the desert.[1]

This whole region, up to the present time, has been a complete *terra incognita* to geographers. Not that travellers had not already crossed it in various directions; for Seetzen in 1807 had gone from Hebron to the convent of Sinai; and Henniker in 1821, and Bonomi and Catherwood and their party in 1833, had passed from the convent to Gaza. Yet there exists only a meager record of all these journeys, so meager indeed, that the respective routes can with difficulty be traced.[2] M. Linant was said also to have visited some parts of this desert; but has given no report. Burckhardt likewise crossed in 1812 from Wady Ghúrúndel and the 'Arabah to Núkhl and 'Ajrûd; but his notes are here less full than usual. Rüppell in 1822 explored the Haj route to 'Akabah.[3] Of the road, therefore, which we were now to travel, there was no report extant; nor was I aware until after my return to Europe, that any portion of it had been followed by M. Callier in 1834.[4] We felt, consequently, that we were in part treading on new ground; and although we expected to make no discoveries, (which indeed the very nature of the country in a measure forbade,) yet we felt it to be due to the interests of science, to take note of all that offered itself to our observation. On similar grounds, I hope to be pardoned by the reader, if the account of this journey should appear perhaps unnecessarily minute and tedious.

To us the journey was one of deep interest. It was a region into which the eye of geographical science had never yet penetrated; and which, as its name implies, was supposed to be the scene of the wanderings of the Israelites of old. Our feelings were strongly excited at this idea of novelty, and with the desire of exploring this "great wilderness;" so as to ascertain, if possible, whether there was any thing here to throw light on the darkness, which hitherto has rested on this portion of Scriptural history. How far we were successful, the reader will learn, not from the account of this journey alone; but from this in connection with our subsequent excursion from Hebron to Wady Mûsa.

Saturday, April 7th. We set off at 6.10, and continuing N. N. W. came in forty-five minutes to the top of the low lime-

---

[1] The name et-Tíh as applied to this desert, is found in both Edrísi and Abulfeda; who refer it to the wanderings of the children of Israel. Edrisi par Jaubert, I. p. 360. Abulfed. Tab. Syr. ed. Köhler, p. 4, et Addenda. So too Ibn el-Wardi, ibid. p. 170.

[2] Seetzen in Zach's Monatl. Corresp. XVII. p. 143 sq. Henniker's Notes, etc. i. 262, 263.

p. 256 sq. Arundale's Tour to Jerusalem and Mount Sinai, 4to.—Arundale travelled in company with Bonomi and Catherwood.

[3] Burckhardt's Travels, etc. p. 444 sq. Rüppell's Reisen in Nubien, p. 241.

[4] See his Letter to Letronne, Journal des Savans, Jan. 1836. I am not aware that anything further has yet appeared.

stone ridge before mentioned. Here another similar prospect opened on our view. Before us lay an almost level plain, covered with pebbles and black flints; beyond which, at a great distance, a lone conical mountain appeared directly ahead, at the base of which, it was said, our road would pass. This mountain is called Jebel 'Aráif en-Nákah; and standing almost isolated in the midst of the desert, it forms a conspicuous landmark for the traveller. It here bore N. by W., and our course was directed towards it for the remainder of the day with little deviation. We could see low ridges extending from it both on the eastern and western sides. That towards the east, at first low, becomes afterwards higher, and terminates at the eastern end in a bluff called el-Múkráh. This latter is not very far from Wady el-'Arabah, as we saw at a later period. At the foot of this bluff, our Arabs said, is a spring of good living water, called esh-Shehábeh or Shehábíyeh.

In crossing the plain above mentioned, we had on our right a range of low hills running from south to north, terminating in a low round mountain called es-Suweikeh, which at 8 o'clock bore N. E. ½ E., and again at 10 o'clock E. S. E. These hills, and the ascending slope towards the brow of el-'Arabah, prevented our seeing the mountains east of the great valley, either now or afterwards, except occasionally, and then very indistinctly.[1] On our left the plain extended almost to the horizon, where a low range of mountains (already mentioned) run northward from near Túrf er-Rukn, at the distance of six or eight hours from our path. For these our Arabs knew no other name than et-Tíh.[2] They said, this range formed the dividing line between the desert on the east, drained by the Jeráfeh, which runs to the 'Arabah; and the more western desert, drained by the great Wady el-'Arísh running down to the Mediterranean.

At 9.10 we were opposite Suweikeh, bearing east, and twenty minutes later crossed Wady el-Ghaidherah, here coming from the southwest, but afterwards sweeping round to the northwest and again crossing our path to join the Jeráfeh. We passed it the second time at 10.40 running northwest, where it continued for some distance on the left parallel to our road. At 11¼ o'clock we found in it, near our path, a small pool of rain water in a deep gully. It is one of the chief watering places of the Arabs in these parts; and from the number of camels and flocks, which come here to drink, the water had acquired a strong smell, and was anything but inviting. Yet as we had found

---

[1] According to Burckhardt, who crossed this desert in 1812, Jebel es-Suweikeh lies eight hours or more distant from the brow of the 'Arabah. He passed at the distance of two hours north of this mountain, on a course towards Túrf er-Rukn. Travels in Syria, etc. pp. 444-48.

[2] They would seem to be the continuation of the ridge which further south Burckhardt calls el-Ojmeh; p. 449.

i. 263±265

no water on the way, nor were likely to meet with any for two
or three days to come, the water skins were filled amid the
drinking of camels, goats, and dogs. We were thus detained
three quarters of an hour. This kind of puddle is called Ghŭ-
dhîr. A few tufts of grass were growing on the sides of the pool,
the second time we had seen grass since leaving the region of the
Nile. Several very old Tŭlh trees were also scattered around.
We found here a few Arabs of the Haweitât, stragglers from the
party which had passed 'Akabah a few days before. They had
charge of several milch camels with their young; and seemed to
have lingered behind their party on account of these. We were
amused at the staid and sober demeanour of the young camels.
Instead of the frisky playfulness and grace of other young animals, they had all the cold gravity and awkwardness of their
dams.—From this point the cliff el-Mŭkrâh bore N. N. E.

Leaving the pool at noon, we soon saw Wady el-Jerâfeh
upon the left, with many low trees, running for a time nearly
parallel to the Ghaidherah. The two unite not far below, in
sight of the road. At half past one, we reached the Jerâfeh,
here coming from the S. S. W. and flowing off nearly northeast
towards el-'Arabah, which it enters a little to the right of the bluff
el-Mŭkrâh. It was said to rise far to the south, near the northern ridge of Jebel et-Tîh, and passes along on the eastern side
of the ridge Tŭrf er-Rukn, apparently between that mountain
and the ridge Tawârif el-Belâd; receiving on the east all the
Wadys we had crossed, and others in like manner from the
west.[1] Indeed it is the great drain of all the long basin between
the 'Arabah and the ridges west of Tŭrf er-Rukn, extending
from Jebel et-Tîh on the south to the ridge between Jebel 'Arâif
and el-Mŭkrâh on the north. The Jerâfeh exhibits traces of a
large volume of water in the rainy season; and is full of herbs
and shrubs, with many Seyâl and Tŭrfa trees. At some distance
from our path on the right, rain water is found in holes dug in
the ground, which are called Emshâsh.[2] We were greatly struck
at the time with the singular conformation of this region, on
the supposition that all the waters of this basin should be carried
so far to the north, in order again to flow through the 'Arabah
southwards to the Red Sea. We were at a loss to conceive how

<hr/>

[1] According to Lord Prudhoe's notes,
the Jerâfeh is five and a half hours from
Wady Ghureir on a southeast course.
From Burckhardt it appears that the
north end of Tŭrf er-Rukn is three and a
half hours eastward of the same Wady
Ghureir; pp. 448, 449. Our map was
constructed according to these data; but
exhibits the Jerâfeh as thus making a
very large bend towards the east. There
i. 265, 266

may be doubts, after all, whether it does
not pass west of Tŭrf er-Rukn.
[2] This seems to be the place visited by
Burckhardt; p. 447. The Wady Leh-
yâneh which he mentions, is a tributary of
the Jerâfeh, entering it from the south,
and lying wholly to the right of our road.
The other route from 'Akabah passes along
it for some distance.

this could well take place, without leaving more traces of a water-course in the latter valley near 'Akabah. It was not until after several weeks, and upon a different journey, that we ascertained the real circumstances of the case.

The country continued still of the same character. At 3 o'clock we passed Wady el-Ghubey, running E. N. E. to the Jerâfeh. Another tributary of the same, Wady Bûtlihât, followed half an hour beyond. In this latter on the right of the road, is rain water collected in pits called Themileh. Another half hour brought us to the top of a gravelly ascent, from which we had a view of a more broken tract of country before us. Hitherto the desert had consisted of wide plains, often covered with pebbles and flints, with low ridges and few undulations, and the Wadys slightly depressed below the general level. The whole region thus far was the very picture of barrenness ; for not a particle of vegetation exists upon it, except in the Wadys ; and in these we had found the herbage and the few trees increasing as we advanced, indicating a better supply of rain. The tract now before us was more uneven and hilly ; and the valleys deeper, with much loose sand. A somewhat steep descent brought us to the broad sandy Wady el-Ghûdhâghidh, which drains the remainder of this region between the Jerâfeh and el Mûkrâh, and carries its waters eastward to the Jerâfeh. We encamped in this Wady at 4¾ o'clock, near its northern side.

The weather this day was again cold and cheerless. During the afternoon several showers of rain rose from the southwest and west, and passed along the horizon towards Syria. At 2½ o'clock we too had a considerable shower, and several slighter ones afterwards. This was the first rain of any consequence that I had seen since leaving Alexandria. It was grateful to us in itself ; and also as showing that we were approaching Palestine, where the latter rains sometimes continue till this season, and usually come from the southwest.

Our guides of the 'Amrân proved to be a very different sort of men from our Tawarah. They were lazy good-for-nothing fellows ; and we soon learned to place no confidence in them, nor in their word, except so far as their assertions tallied with other evidence. According to them, none of the 'Amrân, not even the Sheikhs, can read ; it being considered disgraceful for a Bedawy to learn to read ; very few also know how to pray. The 'Amrân, they said, are divided into five clans, viz. el-Ûsbâny, el-Humeidy, er-Rûbi'y, el-Humâdy, and el-Fûdhly. The present head Sheikh over the whole is named el-Makbûl. None of the tribe have horses, except the Sheikh ; and he only four or five. This fact shows that their country is a desert.[1] The

---

[1] Horses and neat cattle require a supply of water and fresh pasturage. Hence

'Amrân and Haweitât are leagued tribes. The right of pasturage in a given region does not belong exclusively to the tribe
inhabiting the tract : but any foreign tribe that chooses, may
come in and pasture, and go away again, without asking permission. In this way bands of the Haweitât (as we had seen)
were now migrating, for the season, to the southern borders of
Palestine.—If any one steals, the loser takes from the thief an
article of equal or greater value, and deposits it with a third
person. The thief is then summoned to trial ; and if he refuses,
he forfeits the thing thus taken from him. The judges are not
always the Sheikhs ; other persons may exercise this office. If
a person slays another, the nearest relative of the deceased is
entitled to a certain number of camels, or to the life of one equal
to the deceased.[1]

The following are the Wadys and springs known to our
guides, running down into el-'Arabah from the western mountain. They are all small, except the Jerâfeh ; and all the fountains are living water. Beginning from the south, the first is
el-Hendis with sweet water ; then el-Ghŭdyân (Ezion?) with
brackish water ; esh-Sha'ib with a road ascending through it ;
el-Beyâneh with the most direct road from 'Akabah to Gaza ;
el-Jerâfeh nearly opposite mount Hor ; el-Weibeh ; el-Khŭrâr.
With the last three we became better acquainted at a later
period ; of the others we learned nothing more.

Sunday, April 8th. We remained all day encamped. The
morning was clear and cold ; the coldest indeed which we at any
time experienced ; the thermometer having fallen at sunrise to
35° F. The day became also windy ; so that we were somewhat
incommoded in our tent by the drifting sand. Our Arabs had a
visit from some of the Haiwât, who are the possessors of all this
eastern part of the desert ; and afterwards from several of the
party of the Haweitât whom we had seen the day before. We
obtained from them camel's milk for our tea, and found it richer
and better than that of goats.

Our Arabs bought of their visitors a kid, which they killed
as a " redemption " (Arabic Fedu), in order, as they said, that
its death might redeem their camels from death ; and also as a
sacrifice for the prosperity of our journey. With the blood they
smeared crosses on the necks of their camels, and on other parts
of their bodies. Such sacrifices are frequent among them. This
mark of the cross we supposed they had probably imitated from
their neighbours, the monks of Sinai ; or perhaps they only made
it as being one of the simplest marks.

by inquiring after the animals which a   [1] Compare the similar traits of law
tribe possessed, we were always able to   among the Tawarah, p. 140–142 above.
ascertain the nature of their country.

i. 268, 269

Monday, April 9th. Soon after retiring to rest last night, we had quite a little alarm. For two or three days a lean half starved Arab dog, probably from the Haiwât or Haweitât, had attached himself to our caravan, and like his masters was particularly attentive to Komeh and his kitchen. About 11 o'clock, when I was already sound asleep, this dog, himself half wolf, began to bark. This was an indication that some strange person or animal was near us ; and we remembered the barking of old 'Aid's dog, the night before Burckhardt and his party were attacked by robbers. In the present case it might be some prowling hyæna ; or some of our visitors of yesterday, looking around for an opportunity of thieving ; or it might be also a party of armed robbers from beyond the 'Arabah. We had heard indeed at 'Akabah, that two tribes of that region, the Beni Sûkhr and the Hejâya, were at war with the Arabs of the desert et-Tih, often committing robberies in the 'Arabah itself, and sometimes extending their marauding expeditions into the western desert ; and it was not impossible, that we might now be threatened with a visit of this nature. Our Arabs were evidently alarmed. They said, if thieves, they would steal upon us at midnight ; if robbers, they would come down upon us towards morning. All proposed and promised to watch during the whole night ; and we also thought it best to sit up in turn. But we heard nothing further ; and the morning found us undisturbed. One of our 'Amrân guides professed afterwards to have found the tracks of a hyæna not far from the tent ; or the alarm may very probably have proceeded from a thief, who withdrew at the barking of the dog. We now took the poor dog into more favour ; he proved a faithful guard, and continued with us all the way to Jerusalem. But his Bedawy habits were too strong to be overcome ; and he vanished as we entered the city.

We were again upon our way at 5¾ o'clock, ascending by a small branch Wady, called Raudh el-Hûmârah, through a tract of undulating country, of limestone formation like all this desert, and covered with black flints and pebbles. At 7 o'clock we came out of this Wady and up a low ascent to a small plain, crossing the heads of several more *Ridhân* or dry brooks of the same name. At this place, two or three years before, a robbery had been committed by a party of the Hejâya, one of the tribes "from the rising sun," on a caravan of the 'Amrân. They fell upon the caravan as it was encamped at night, seizing the plunder and taking the lives of one or two.

Our road now led over a most desert tract of swelling hills, covered in like manner with black flints ; our course being still N. by W. towards Jebel 'Aráif. At 7.20 the cliff el-Mûkrâh bore N. E. while the western end of its high ridge bore north.

i. 269–271

Ten minutes farther on, the road from 'Akabah through Wady
Beyâneh fell into ours from the right. At 7.40 we crossed a
Wady running off to the right to Wady el-Ghûdhâghidh and
so to el-'Arabah. Ascending again slightly to a small plateau,
we came immediately upon the water-shed, or dividing line between the waters of el-'Arabah and those of the Mediterranean;
the former drained off by the Jerâfeh, and the latter by the great
Wady el-'Arîsh. At no great distance on our left were low
chalky cliffs of singular form, apparently spurs from the ridges
we had before seen in that direction. Descending a little, we
immediately struck and crossed Wady el-Haikibeh at 8 o'clock,
here running towards the northeast, but sweeping round again
afterwards to the northwest, so that our path crossed it a second
time after three quarters of an hour. It is full of shrubs. We
now continued along its side N. N. W. until a quarter past nine
o'clock, and then left it running to join the Kureiyeh, a tributary of Wady el-'Arish. Just beyond this Wady were the
chalky cliffs above mentioned; and as we left them behind, other
low ridges appeared on our left at different distances of five, ten,
or fifteen miles. We now rode over another barren flinty tract,
with a few small Rîdhân running towards the Haikibeh. In
some spots we found very small tufts of grass springing up
among the pebbles, the effect of recent rains. Our guides said,
that in those years when there is plenty of rain, grass springs up
in this way all over the face of the desert. In such seasons,
they said, the Arabs are kings. At 10 o'clock a path went off
to the right leading to some wells of sweet water called el-
Mâyein, lying in a direction N. by E. in the mountains beyond
Jebel 'Arâif. This path passes to the right of 'Arâif, over the
low part of the ridge extending east from that mountain; and
falls again into our road further on.

We reached Wady el-Kureiyeh at 10.10, coming down from
near the ridge of el-Mûkrâh, which was now not far off. Here a
round mountain on our left called Jebel Ikhrimm bore W. by N.
The Kureiyeh bends around and passes at the northern base of
this hill; and further west, about half a day's journey from
the point where we crossed, there are in it pits of rain water,
Emshâsh, forming a station on the great road from the convent
to Gaza.—Another similar flinty tract now succeeded, called
Hemâdet et-'Anaz, over which our course was N. N. W. A
clayey Wady called Abu Tîn followed at 12.50; and another,
the deep bed of a torrent, el-Khŭrâizeh, at half past one; both
running southwest into the Kureiyeh. The country now became
open quite to the base of Jebel 'Arâif en-Nâkah, which had so
long been our landmark. The mountain is of a conical form,
five or six hundred feet high, consisting of limestone thickly

i. 271. 272

strewed with flints. At a distance it seems wholly isolated; the low ridges, which extend from it east and west, being there over-looked. That on the east, as has been said already, connects with higher ridges further on, and terminates in the bluff el-Mŭkrâh; while that on the west continues lower and more broken. The 'Arâif forms a striking object, as thus seen in the middle of the mighty waste. It is indeed a huge bulwark, ter-minating the open desert on this part, and forming the outwork or bastion of a more mountainous tract beyond.—At $2\frac{1}{2}$ o'clock a Wady came down directly from the mountain, (here half an hour or more distant,) bearing the same name, 'Arâif, and pass-ing on W. S. W. to the Kureiyeh. Under one of its low banks the corpse of a man had been recently half buried, and a few stones placed around; some of the toes and a few rags were vis-ible; and our Arabs said the hyænas would soon devour the body.

Proceeding on the same course N. N. W. we came at 3 o'clock to the top of the low ridge, running out west from Jebel 'Arâif. Here we could look back over the desert tract we had just crossed, bounded on the south by low hills at a great dis-tance, the whole of it drained by the Kureiyeh into Wady el-'Arîsh. Before us was another plain, extending into the mountains towards the right, and bounded on the north by a line of higher hills about two hours distant. From this point in our road, Jebel 'Arâif bore N. 70° E. about a mile distant. Jebel Ikhrimm bore west, being separated from the ridge on which we stood only by Wady el-Kureiyeh. At a much greater distance in the W. N. W. appeared a high and longer mountain called Yelek; and more to the right, about N. N. W. another called el-Helâl. Both these last were said to be beyond Wady el-'Arîsh.

A short and steep descent now brought us in ten minutes to the bed of Wady el-Mâyein or el Ma'ein, which flowing along the northern base of Jebel 'Arâif and the ridge further west goes to unite with the Kureiyeh. It has its head far up among the mountains on the right; and in it are the wells of the same name already mentioned. Its bed bears evident traces of a large volume of water; and the flat plain beyond is much cut up by its torrents. The bed of the Wady and the adjacent part of the plain are covered with stones, some quite large, apparently brought down by the waters from the mountains. Crossing the plain on a course north, we encamped at half past 4 o'clock at the foot of the line of hills which bound it on this side; Jebel 'Arâif bearing from our tent S. 55° E. in full view, about three miles distant. On this plain comes in the road from the con-vent to Gaza, which passes by 'Ain and eth-Themed.—Our tent

was pitched near a shallow water-course running off to Wady
el-Mâyein, full of herbs and shrubs like most of the Wadys we
had passed, and affording fine pasture for the camels. Among
the shrubs of the desert, the Retem or broom was particularly
abundant, and of a larger size than we had before seen it.

We had now left the country of the Haiwât, and entered
that of the southern Tiyâhah. Here too ends the region or
desert of the Tîh, through which we had been travelling ever
since we left the 'Arabah. The territory of the Haiwât commences, as we have seen, at the northern ridge of Jebel et-Tîh;
and extends northwards along and adjacent to the 'Arabah as
far as to the mountains 'Arâif and el-Mŭkrâh; where the high
ridge between rises like a wall and forms a boundary on this side.
On the west of this tribe lies the country of the Tiyâhah, also
extending from Jebel et-Tîh through the middle of the desert
northwards beyond that of the Haiwât, to the vicinity of Gaza
and Beersheba. The Tiyâhah are divided into the Benciyât
and the Sukeirât. Still further west are the Terâbîn, dwelling
from the mountains near Suez to the region of Gaza; their
main body being found not far distant from the latter place.
This tribe is the strongest of all, and is closely leagued with the
Tiyâhah.

The mountainous district north of Jebel 'Arâif and el-Mŭkrâh, and between el-'Arabah and the Tiyâhah, is inhabited by
the 'Azâzimeh, who are in close alliance with the former tribe,
and sometimes pasture within their territory. Still further north
along the Ghôr, are the Sa'idîn or Sa'idîyeh, the Dhŭllâm, and
the Jehâlîn; the latter dwelling between Hebron and the Dead
Sea. Our guides mentioned also the names of the Sawârikeh,
the Jebârât, and the Henâjireh, as living in the same region;
respecting whom we learned nothing further, and heard of them
no more.—The above, so far as we could ascertain, are all the
Arab tribes inhabiting the great western desert.

We had now become so far acquainted with the general features of this region, as to perceive the reason, why all the roads
leading across it from 'Akabah and from the convent to Hebron
and Gaza, should meet together in one main trunk in the middle
of the desert. The whole district adjacent to the 'Arabah, north
of Jebel 'Arâif and el-Mŭkrâh, as has been said, is mountainous;
and is composed, as we afterwards found, of steep ridges running
mostly from east to west, and presenting almost insuperable obstacles to the passage of a road parallel to the 'Arabah. In consequence, no great route now leads, or ever has led, through this
district; but the roads from 'Akabah, which ascend from Wady
el-'Arabah and in any degree touch the high plateau of the desert
south of el-Mŭkrâh, must necessarily curve to the west, and

i. 274. 275

passing around the base of Jebel 'Aráif el-Nákah, continue along
the western side of this mountainous tract.

We felt assured, therefore, that we were now upon the ancient
Roman road, as marked upon the Peutinger Tables, leading
across this desert from 'Akabah to Jerusalem ; whether it ascended from the 'Arabah by the route we had followed ; or, as
is more probable, kept along the 'Arabah for a time and then
ascended through Wady Beyâneh. We inquired very minutely
after the names of Rasa (Gerasa) and Gypsaria, the first stations
marked on the ancient road, and also mentioned by Ptolemy ;
but could find no trace of anything corresponding to them.   Of
the other stations, still north of us, Lysa, Eboda, and Elusa, as
also Beersheba, we hoped to be able to give a better account ;
for our guides had already spoken of a Wady Lussân, of ruins
called 'Abdeh and Khûlasah, and of wells at Bir es-Seba'.

In respect to the route of the Israelites in approaching Palestine, we here obtained only the conviction, that they could not
have passed to the westward of Jebel 'Aráif ; since such a course
would have brought them directly to Beersheba, and not to
Kadesh, which latter city lay near to the border of Edom.[1]

Tuesday, April 10th.   Mounting at 5¾ o'clock, we ascended
the line of hills immediately before us, by a very stony path,
reaching the top in twenty-five minutes.   We found the ridge to
be broad ; though we began soon to descend gradually through
a small Wady.   On our right and towards the northeast was
now a mountainous tract ; consisting of steep limestone ridges
running parallel to each other from east to west three or four
hundred feet in height, and terminating towards the west in steep
bluffs.   Our course was still N. by W. parallel to the end of
these bluffs, and at no great distance from them, through a lower and more open region.   Before us was another large Wady
running west, and then another line of hills lower than the bluffs ;
and such continued to be the make of the land for the greater
part of the day.   At 6.35 we came down upon Wady Lussân, a
broad plain swept over by torrents descending from the mountains on the right, and flowing to Wady el-'Arîsh.   Our guides
knew of no fountain or water in this valley ; nor of any ruins.
The name, however, and perhaps the position, corresponds to
Lysa, a station on the Roman road, lying according to Rennell
about fifty-five geographical miles from Ailah ;[2] from which place
we had now travelled about thirty hours by a longer route.   The
ancient road could only have been, like ours, a caravan path ;

---

[1] Num. 20, 16.
[2] Comparat. Geogr. of Western Asia, I.
p. 92.—It is marked in the Peutinger Tables at 48 R. M. south of Eboda, equiva-

lent to about 18 hours with camels. From
Wady Lussân, however, to Eboda, we
found only 14 hours.

and Lysa and the other places marked upon it further south, were very probably mere stations, with a guard and a few tents or huts, and without water except as supplied from cisterns or from a distance. On our left, just as we reached the plain, were a few remains of rude walls and foundations, which we regarded at the time as marking only the site of a former Arab encampment. But from the many similar remains which we afterwards saw along the road, I am now inclined to suppose, that they may have belonged to the substructions of Lysa.

We were fifteen minutes in crossing this plain, and at 6.50 entered upon another tract of undulating hilly country, which indeed might almost be called mountainous. A path went off on the right, leading to some rain water in the rocks at the head of Wady Jerûr ; falling into our road again further on. In a few minutes more, the path from the fountain Mâyein, which left ours yesterday, came in from the right. We here entered a large plain, or basin, drained by a water-course near the middle, with its branches, called Wady el-Muzeiri'ah, running southwest to the Lussân. This we reached at a quarter past seven. This whole basin was full of shrubs and vegetation, and seemed capable of tillage. Indeed, in several spots we saw traces of rude ploughing ; and were told, that in years of rain the Arabs are accustomed to plough and sow here. A thin meager grass was springing up in various places. Such spots as these we had not seen or heard of, since passing Wady Ghŭrŭndel on the gulf of Suez. In all the region of the Tawarah, the 'Amrân, and the Haiwât, there are none.

We now ascended along a narrow Wady to the top of another sloping parallel ridge, on which we came out at 8 o'clock. Vegetation continued quite to the summit, consisting of shrubs and thin tufts of slender grass. This point commands a wide view over a broad open tract of country on the left and towards the northwest, extending apparently to the mountains Yelek and el-Helâl, broken in some parts by low limestone ridges and hills of chalk ; while on our right the precipitous chalky cliffs of the mountainous district continued. Through the plain before us, passed down Wady Jerûr. But the weather was now so hazy, that we were unable to see the country so distinctly as we wished ; especially the distant mountains. Around us vegetation seemed more abundant ; and camels were at pasture on our left, belonging to the Haweitât who had passed on a few days before. Here Sâlim, one of our 'Amrân guides, went on ahead of our caravan, and lay down to sleep. On our coming up, we found him with a large scratch on his face and a slight cut on his shoulder, which he said had been given him by two Arabs, who fell upon him while asleep, and tried to rob him of his dagger and cloak. We

i. 277, 278

doubted the truth of this part of his story ; for he was an impudent blackguard, and very likely to get into a quarrel.

We reached the bed of Wady Jerûr at 9 o'clock, coming from the mountains on our right and running west to the 'Arîsh. Our guides knew of no water in it above or below, (except the rain water among the rocks near its head, as already mentioned,) nor of any cultivation ; though Tuweileb and others had crossed it further down near its mouth.[1] Our path now ascended very gradually, and at 9.55 again descended through a narrow Wady, where we found a little rain water standing in the rocks at the bottom, of which the guide and dog drank together. Indeed, in several Wadys both yesterday and to-day, we had seen traces of running water from the late rains. At 10½ o'clock, we passed a limestone ridge of some height by a gap. Here we had our last view of Jebel 'Arâif, bearing S. by E. From this point our course became N. N. E. for the remainder of the day. Half an hour later we came upon three broad and shallow water-courses, full of the shrub Retem, uniting below and called Wady es-Sa'idât, which runs down to join the Jâifeh before us. This latter valley followed at 11.50, very broad and full of pasture ; coming from the E. S. E. where are many spots in it tilled and sown by the Tiyâhah. It passes on to the 'Arîsh ; having no water known to our guides. In it, on our left, many camels were browsing, belonging to the main body of our new friends the Haweitât, who had passed us near 'Akabah.

After another hour a slight ascent brought us out upon a high stony plain ; while our course was bringing us nearer and nearer to the mountains on our right. At 1.10 we came upon Wady Abu Retemât, a wide plain with shrubs and Retem ; beyond which a limestone ridge of some height stretched from the eastern mountains far to the west, having in it several gaps and passes. We soon came close to the mountain on our right, and began to ascend gradually through a Wady with many herbs, coming down from the northeast into Abu Retemât, and forming a wide pass between the mountain and the beginning of the ridge just mentioned. Beyond the eastern mountain at some distance is a large fountain with sweet running water, named 'Ain el-Kudeirât, but more usually called simply el-'Ain.[2] From it a Wady, also called el-'Ain, runs off towards the north,

---

[1] The name *Jerûr* in Arabic corresponds to the Hebrew *Gerar ;* but neither the position nor the character of this Wady admits the supposition of its being the same with the Gerar of Scripture. This lay much nearer to Gaza, in the country of the Philistines, and was very fertile. Gen. 20, 1.   26, 6. 8.

[2] This is the spot called by Mr. Row-lande, *Kûdês,* and visited by him as Kadesh Barnea. He obviously made out the name *Kûdês* by misunderstanding *el-Kudeirât,* the name of the tribe who water at this fountain. There is no other foundation for supposing a Kadesh here ; as we shall see further on. See Williams' Holy City, edit. 2, I. p. 466.

and sweeping round northwest through a tract of open country, goes to join the 'Arish. A path went off from our road at 1¾ o'clock, leading to the wells el-Bircin, lying a little to the right of our way, half a day's journey from this spot. We reached the top of the pass, which is everywhere sprinkled with herbage, at 2 o'clock. It opens out upon a large gravelly plain or basin, thickly covered in many parts with shrubs and coarse herbage, and having in other parts tracts of naked sand. Here the line of the eastern mountains abruptly retires; the plain extends up far to the right; and is shut in on the east, south, and west, by limestone hills.

Crossing the plain for twenty minutes, we came to several pits of bluish, brackish water, dug a few feet deep in a bed of blue clay, surrounded by an abundance of coarse bulrushes and rank vegetation. Only one pit had water in it at the time. Here we stopped for half an hour; watered the camels, which seemed thirsty; and filled some of the water-skins. To do this the more quickly, Tuweileb's boy went down naked into the water, and handed it up in our leathern bucket. These wells lie in a shallow Wady called el-Kusâimeh, which rises in the plain and runs off W. N. W. among the western hills.— From this spot the northern end of Jebel el-Helâl beyond Wady el-'Arish bore N. 80° W. The same seen from Wady el-Jâifeh at 11.50 bore N. 55° W. The opening by which Wady el-'Ain leaves the mountains, bore from here southeast. The bed of this Wady passes across the plain to the eastward of the wells, and then sweeps around to the northwest.

Leaving the wells at 2.50 we ascended gently among low chalky hills for half an hour; when we again descended gradually, and passing two or three small Wadys, came upon Wady el-'Ain, here running to the left through a wide gravelly plain with occasional tracts of sand, thinly covered in this part with shrubs and herbage. We reached the deep gully which forms its water-course, at 4 o'clock; and found it bordered with grass, daisies, and other small flowers, most refreshing to the eye after so long an abstinence. Indeed, we had found to-day more vegetation in the desert, than before in all the way from Egypt. This Wady, as we have seen, comes from el-'Ain, the fountain above mentioned, by a circuitous course; and continues on to join Wady el-'Arish. Further down, a Wady enters it from the left, having in it brackish water called el-Muweilih, forming a station on the western road from the convent to Gaza.

After crossing the water-course, we came upon a broad tract of tolerably fertile soil, capable of tillage, and apparently once tilled. Across the whole tract the remains of long ranges of low stone walls were visible, which probably once served as the divi-

i. 280, 281

sions of cultivated fields. The Arabs call them el-Muzeiri'àt, "little plantations." We afterwards saw many such walls, which obviously were not constructed by the present race of Arab inhabitants ; but must be referred back to an earlier period. We neither saw nor heard of any site of ruins in this valley ; it may have been tilled by the inhabitants of some place not far remote. We encamped at 4.25 upon the plain. On its northern side rose a swelling ridge of considerable elevation, with several sharp chalky peaks ; the most prominent of which was called Ràs es-Seràm. Towards the east, mountains were visible only at a distance.

The country through which we had passed to-day, though in itself barren and desolate in the extreme, yet in consequence of the recent rains presented the appearance of a less frightful desert. Some grass, a few flowers, more frequent herbs and shrubs, and a few faint traces of tillage, were to us agreeable novelties ; the more grateful, as they gave promise of better things to come.

Wednesday, April 11th. The morning was bright and beautiful ; and we set off at 5¾ o'clock in high spirits, in the hope of finding to-day, not indeed Arab habitations, but the more interesting remains of the dwellings of former generations. Our guides had promised to take us to a place with ruins, not far from our path, which they knew only by the name of 'Aujeh ; but which Tuweileb said was also called 'Abdeh. Our course lay first across the plain N. E. by N. and our main route continued in this direction all day. On both sides of the way patches of wheat and barley were seen ; their deep green contrasting strongly with the nakedness around. We saw many such patches in the course of the day ; but they were mostly stunted and poor, in consequence of the little rain. The plain now became a gradual acclivity ; and following up a broad Wady, or tract covered with herbs, we came out at 6.40 on a smaller high circular plain, surrounded by chalky hills, which from a distance appear like mountain peaks. This plain is about a mile in diameter, and covered with shrubs. One of the hills, a chalky cone on the southwest, is the Ràs es-Seràm seen yesterday. It is so called from Wady es-Seràm of which this plain is the head, and which issues from it on the opposite or northeast part. On this plain comes in the great western road from the convent of Sinai to Gaza ; the different routes over Jebel et-Tih, by the two passes er-Ràkineh and el-Murcikhy, having united long before reaching this point. Thus all the roads across the desert were now combined into one main trunk, and continued so for the remainder of the day.

We crossed the plain ; and at a quarter past 7 o'clock en-

tered and descended Wady es-Serâm. The desert began to assume a gentler aspect. The Serâm spread out further down into
a wide plain, with shrubs and grass and patches of wheat and
barley, looking almost like a meadow. A few Arabs of the
'Azâzimeh were pasturing their camels and flocks. The country
around became gradually still more open, with broad arable valleys separated by low swelling hills. Grass increased in the
valleys, and herbs were sprinkled over the hills. We heard this
morning, for the first time, the songs of many birds, and among
them the lark. I watched the little warbler rising and soaring
in his song ; and was inexpressibly delighted. On reaching the
plain, we sent two Arabs with a camel over the hills on the
right to the wells Bîrein for water, with directions to overtake
the party again in the course of the day. At 8 o'clock, leaving
our servants and camels to continue in the direct route to Ruhaibeh, where we were to encamp, we ourselves with the dromedaries and three Arabs turned off the road towards the left of a
low range of hills, in order to visit the ruins of 'Aujeh or 'Abdeh.
In half an hour, travelling about north, we came upon a low
ridge, commanding a view out over a boundless plain or slightly
undulating tract towards the east, often sandy, but everywhere
sprinkled with shrubs and herbs like a Wady. The Serâm ex-
pands into this plain, as do also Wady el-Bîrein from the south,
and Wady el-Hûfir from the southeast. The water-course of the
Serâm keeps along on the western side of the plain beneath the
hills on which we now were. We here struck a track coming
from Wady es-Serâm on the right and going off to Gaza ; but it
was not the usual Gaza road. We soon left it, and turning
more to the right, saw, at three quarters past 8, the ruins on a
hill north.

Descending along a little Wady, we struck the water-course
of the Serâm at 9 o'clock, still running north along the base of the
low hills which continue to skirt the plain on this side. Here we
came upon the remains of walls similar to those we had seen near
Wady el-'Ain, apparently once enclosing fields or gardens, along
the tract overflowed by the torrent during the rainy season. At
first these walls were slight, but became thicker and more solid
as we advanced. Most of them are two or three feet thick, and
double ; the faces being laid up very neatly with round stones
from the torrent, and the middle filled in with gravel. Some,
built across the water-course, are six or eight feet thick, forming
a solid dam ; and were doubtless intended to regulate the flowing and distribution of the water. In some of the walls, the
sides are perpendicular ; in others sloping ; and occasionally the
round stones are broken to a face. At 9.10 the water-bed of
Wady el-Bîrein came in across the plain, and gave its name to
i. 283, 284

the whole. Five minutes further on was a *Ghŭdir* or pool of
rain water in its bed, and another just below. This point was
about a quarter of an hour distant from the hill with ruins.
Here we dismounted, and turned up a little Wady coming in
from the west, to visit the ruin of a square tower of hewn stone
on its southern bank. Near by it the foundations of houses
were visible ; and many hewn stones and fragments of pottery
were strewn around. On the north side of the little Wady, opposite the tower, is a deep cavern in the limestone hill, apparently once a quarry, with pillars left to support the roof. From
it the materials for the neighbouring buildings were probably
taken. It is more than a hundred feet in length ; and has been
apparently inhabited, perhaps by the Arabs ; as fragments of
pottery were scattered in it. It is now the resort of multitudes
of pigeons, which flew out in a cloud as we entered.

The principal ruins are situated on a hill or rocky ridge,
from sixty to one hundred feet high, running out like a promontory towards the east from the elevated land on our left, and
overlooking the broad plain in front ; while the bed of the torrent sweeps in a deep channel close around its end. On this hill
two ruins were conspicuous, resembling the fortresses of an acropolis. As we approached, there was on our left apparently an
ancient reservoir, which received its water from the hills above.
Here we found Arabs with their camels and goats at pasture ;
they proved to be a family of the Tawarah, who had wandered
off thus far from their home. Arriving at the foot of the hill,
we found the southern base and slope covered with the ruins of
buildings of hewn stone, thrown together in utter confusion, and
showing this to have been the main site of the ancient town.
Among these we noticed several columns and entablatures. On
the top of the hill, the westernmost building, near the middle
of the ridge, proved to be a Greek church, fronting towards the
east, about one hundred and twenty feet in length, and of pro-
portional breadth. The walls are still in great part standing,
built of hewn stone apparently from the neighbouring quarry,
and of good workmanship. The arched recess or place of the
altar was yet visible, with a similar smaller recess on each side
quite entire. In the western part was a side chapel with two
or three smaller rooms. The space within the walls was strewn
with broken columns and entablatures.

About one hundred and fifty paces further east, near the extremity of the ridge, are the ruins of a fortress or castle ; a large
parallelogram likewise built of hewn stone from the quarry.
The length of the enclosure, of which the walls are still standing, is more than three hundred feet from east to west. On
the eastern end there would seem to have been another and per-

haps stronger part of the fortress, extending a hundred feet further quite to the brow of the precipice. This part is now wholly
destroyed ; and of the larger enclosure no portion is covered
over. The entrance was from the west, by a fine arched portal
now broken at the top. We looked here, as well as in the church,
for inscriptions ; but without success. At the eastern end, beyond the present wall, but within the circuit of the smaller fortress, is a very deep cistern, capable of holding several hundred
hogsheads ; and further on, near the extreme point of the rock,
a well about one hundred feet deep, now dry. The bottom of
this well for some sixty feet is wholly sunk in the solid rock ;
while the top, for about forty feet, is walled up eight feet square
with hewn stones in an uncommonly good style of masonry. An
arch was formerly thrown over the top, which is now broken
down. The walls of the smaller part of the fortress included
both the cistern and well. At the bottom of the hill immediately below this point, is another well about forty feet deep,
walled up in the same manner.—On the east of the water-course
of Wady el-Birein are also ruins of buildings ; and the walls of
fields, similar to those we saw at first, extend far out into the
plain.

From the castle the direction of the wells Birein was pointed
out about S. by E. Further to the east the water-course
of Wady el-Hŭfir comes down across the plain ; and uniting
with that of Wady el-Birein just north of the castle, gives its
name to the whole. It then runs off northwest to join Wady
el-Abyad.

We had no doubt at the time, nor have I any now, that
these were the ruins of the ancient *Eboda* or Oboda, a city mentioned only by Ptolemy, and marked on the Peutinger Tables as
lying on the Roman road twenty-three Roman miles to the
southward of Elusa ; equivalent to nine hours with camels at
the usual rate of travel. We were afterwards eight hours in
passing from these ruins to the site of Elusa, at a rate more
rapid than usual ; so that the correspondence is here sufficiently
exact ; and the name of 'Abdeh, which the spot still bears, is
decisive. It must have been a place of importance and of great
strength. The large church marks a numerous Christian population ; though Eboda is nowhere mentioned among the episcopal cities. It is rare also to find in the desert a fortress of such
extent, and built with so much care. But the desert has reassumed its rights ; the intrusive hand of cultivation has been
driven back ; the race that dwelt here have perished ; and their
works now look abroad in loneliness and silence over the mighty
waste.[1]

[1] See note XXIII, at the end of the volume.

i. 286, 287

We left the ruins at 10¾ o'clock. Just as we were mounting our camels, one of the 'Azâzimeh, who was pasturing in the vicinity, came up and scolded our guides most violently for bringing Christians to view his country. Our course lay N. E. by E. across the plain to regain our former road. The character of the desert began to change, and became more and more sandy as we advanced. We struck the route at a quarter past noon ; and fell in again with our acquaintances, the Haweitât, who were now going the same road. We soon passed by their caravan, and saw them no more.

During this time we were exposed to a violent sirocco, which continued till towards evening, resembling the Khamsîn of Egypt. The wind had been all the morning northeast, but at 11 o'clock it suddenly changed to the south, and came upon us with violence and intense heat, until it blew a perfect tempest. The atmosphere was filled with fine particles of sand, forming a bluish haze ; the sun was scarcely visible, his disk exhibiting only a dun and sickly hue ; and the glow of the wind came upon our faces as from a burning oven. Often we could not see ten rods around us ; and our eyes, ears, mouths, and clothes, were filled with sand. The thermometer at 12 o'clock stood at 88° F. and had apparently been higher ; at 2 o'clock it had fallen to 76°, although the wind still continued.

We kept on our way, proceeding among sand-drifts, the ground in spots being white with broken snail-shells ; and began to descend very gradually towards Wady el-Abyad. At 12.50 there were again walls of fields, marking an extensive enclosure. At 1 o'clock we came to an Arab cemetery, with a rude heap of stones, called the tomb of Sheikh el-'Amry, whom the Arabs never mention without a curse. A ridiculous story of Arab superstition is attached to this tomb. There seemed also to be the foundations of a village or the like, connected with the said fields. Close by is the bed of Wady el-Abyad, running to the left into the 'Arish ; it was said to be the last Wady on our route, that joins the latter valley. The region is here all sand ; and we now passed among swelling hills, which, though of sand, were yet covered to the top with tufts of herbs and shrubs, like the valleys and plains ; all greener than before, and indicating our approach to a land of rain. Among these hills we passed at half past two through a large basin, the head of a Wady called Nehiyeh, running off west to Wady el-Abyad. Here we overtook our two men with a load of good water from el-Birein. They reported that the wells were *four* instead of two ; all twenty-five or thirty feet deep, walled up with hewn stone, and containing living water. The plain beyond the wells, they said, was extensively cultivated by the Arabs.

We overtook the rest of our party not long after, and soon began to descend gradually towards the head of Wady er-Ruhaibeh. The tempest continued unabated, although the burning glow had in part passed away. As we crossed a plain slightly descending towards the northeast, there were, at 3.20, traces of walls and former fields. Ten minutes further brought us to the entrance of Wady er-Ruhaibeh, which runs from the plain towards the northeast. Here is the fork of the two main roads leading to Gaza and Hebron. We encamped at 3¾ o'clock in the Wady, which is at first narrow, lying between hills of gentle acclivity.

The tempest now seemed to have reached its greatest fury, and had become a tornado. It was with the utmost difficulty that we could pitch our tent, or keep it upright after it was pitched. For a time the prospect was dreadful; and the storm in itself was probably as terrific, as most of those which have given rise to the exaggerated accounts of travellers. Yet here was no danger of life; though I can well conceive that in certain circumstances, as where a traveller is without water and is previously feeble and exhausted, such a "horrible tempest" may well prove fatal. Most of our Arabs covered their faces with a handkerchief, although we were travelling before the wind. After 5 o'clock the wind fell; the air became less obscure; a breeze sprung up from the northwest, which soon purified the atmosphere, restored the sun to his splendour, and brought us a clear and pleasant evening, with a temperature of 66° F. It was no little labour to free ourselves from the casing of sand in which we were enveloped.

We had not been told of ruins at this place, or only in general terms; and were therefore the more surprised to find here also traces of antiquity. In the valley itself, just at the left of the path, is the ruin of a small rough building with a dome, built in the manner of a mosk; it was obviously once a *Wely* or tomb of a Muhammedan saint. On the right of the path is a confused heap of hewn stones, the remains of a square building of some size, perhaps a tower. On the acclivity of the eastern hill we found traces of wells; a deep cistern, or rather cavern, which seemed to have been used as such; and a fine circular threshing floor, evidently antique. But on ascending the hill on the left of the valley, we were astonished to find ourselves amid the ruins of an ancient city. Here is a level tract of ten or twelve acres in extent, entirely and thickly covered over with confused heaps of stones, with just enough of their former order remaining, to show the foundations and form of the houses, and the course of some of the streets. The houses were mostly small, all solidly built of bluish limestone, squared and often

i. 289, 290

hewn on the exterior surface. Many of the dwellings had each
its cistern, cut in the solid rock; and these still remained quite
entire. One mass of stones larger than the rest, appeared to be
the remains of a church, from the fragments of columns and entablatures strewed around. Another large mass lay further to
the north, which we did not visit. There seemed to have been
no public square, and no important or large public buildings;
nor could we trace with certainty any city walls. We sought
also in vain for inscriptions. Once, as we judged upon the spot,
this must have been a city of not less than twelve or fifteen
thousand inhabitants. Now, it is a perfect field of ruins, a
scene of unutterable desolation; across which the passing stranger can with difficulty find his way. Multitudes of lizards were
briskly and silently gliding among the stones; and at evening,
as we sat writing, the screechings of an owl were the only sound
to break in upon the death-like stillness.

These ruins have apparently been seen by no former traveller; and it was only by accident that we stumbled upon them.
The place must anciently have been one of some note and importance; but what city could it have been? This is a question, which after long inquiry, and with the best aid from the
light of European science, I am as yet unable to answer. The
name er-Ruhaibeh naturally suggests the Hebrew *Rehoboth*, one
of Isaac's wells in the vicinity of Gerar;[1] but this appears to
have been nothing but a well, and there is no mention in Scripture or elsewhere of any city connected with it. Here, on the
other hand, was a city, but, it would seem, no well; the inhabitants having been apparently supplied with rain water by
means of cisterns. The position of Isaac's well, too, appears to
have been much further north, and between Gerar and Beersheba, where he was residing. But these ruins are a large eight
hours distant from Beersheba; and not in the direction of Gerar.
No town of this name is spoken of in all this region; and I am
still, after many years, unable to solve the mystery.[2]

The ruined Wely above mentioned seems to indicate, that
the place was inhabited, or at least frequented, down to a period
considerably later than the Muhammedan conquest.

As Ruhaibeh is the great point from which the roads across
the desert, after having been all united, again diverge towards

[1] Gen. 26, 22.

[2] In the *Notitia Dignitatum* (c. 29), a
place *Robotha* is named in the rude drawing at the head of the chapter; but is
omitted in the list. This name might answer to *Rehoboth* (Ruhaibeh); but as the
place is mentioned along with *Moahila*,

Aila, Haaara, and *Zadacatha,* all of which
are on the east of the 'Arabah, it more
probably represents the 'Ρωβᾶs or *Robooth*
of Eusebius and Jerome, which they place
in Gabalene, meaning Idumæa. See Notit. Dign. p. 78, 346. ed. Böcking; p. 215,
216, ed. Pancerol; Reland. Palæst. p. 231.

i. 290, 291

Gaza and Hebron, the present is a fit occasion for bringing together all that remains to be said of these routes and of the region further south. We travelled the road from this point to Hebron, a journey of two days, which is described in the following pages. Gaza (Arabic Ghüzzeh) was said to be only one day distant from Ruhaibeh, though it must be a very long day's journey. Our guides knew of no ruins on the way; and only of one place of any note, called Nŭttâr Abu Sŭmâr, where the Arabs have magazines of grain.

From 'Akabah to Hebron and Gaza, one road passes along nearly the whole length of the great Wady el-'Arabah, and ascends from it to the high western plateau by several passes, not far from the south end of the Dead Sea. These we shall have occasion to describe at a later period. From 'Akabah to Ruhaibeh there are two roads for a part of the way; one, the route we travelled; and the other, keeping for some time along the 'Arabah, as has been already mentioned, and then ascending through Wady el-Beyâneh to join our road before reaching Jebel 'Arâif.

From the convent of Sinai, (and consequently also from Tûr,) three roads cross by the three great passes of Jebel et-Tih, and unite before reaching Ruhaibeh. The easternmost is the road passing by el-'Ain and also by the well eth-Themed, west of the mountain Tŭrf er-Rukn; and falling into our route at Wady el-Mâyein near Jebel 'Arâif. The middle road crosses the Tih by the pass el-Mureikhy; and the western one by the pass er-Râkineh. These unite before reaching the Haj route; and fall into our road on the circular plain at the head of Wady es-Serâm, about one day's journey from Ruhaibeh. This united route passes some distance to the eastward of the fortress Nŭkhl on the Haj road; six hours, according to Seetzen's information.[1] A branch route, however, from both the passes, goes off by way of Nŭkhl, and falls in again further north; but this increases the distance one day's journey. From the convent to Ruhaibeh is reckoned nine days' journey on all the direct roads; and by way of Nŭkhl, ten days. The middle route, across the pass el-Mureikhy, is the one most commonly travelled by the Tawarah; though Tuweileb was acquainted with them all.

These roads, it will be seen, all lie to the eastward of Wady el-'Arish; the westernmost crossing that Wady from west to east, not far above Jebel Ikhrimm. But another branch keeps on from that point to Gaza, along the western side of the 'Arish, crossing it much further down, and leaving Ruhaibeh at some distance on the right. This would seem to be the

---

[1] Zach's Monatl. Corresp. XVII. p. 147.

route taken by the pilgrims, who travelled in the fifteenth and sixteenth centuries from Gaza to Mount Sinai.

The above are all the roads we heard of, across the desert, from south to north. But an important road leads from Cairo by way of 'Ajrûd to Hebron, and falls into our route at the head of Wady es-Scrâm, before reaching Ruhaibeh.—A few days before we passed, Lord Prudhoe had also travelled directly from Nŭkhl to Wady Mûsa, and kindly furnished us with the notes of his route.

The notices thus collected by us for the first time from the Arabs, together with our own observations and Burckhardt's route in 1812, furnished, so far as I know, the only topographical details as yet given to the public, respecting the great desert north of Jebel et-Tih and the Haj route; excepting a very brief account by Russegger of his journey from the convent to Hebron a few months after we had passed. The details are embodied in a note at the end of the volume.[1]

From a comparison of all these notices, it appears, that the middle of this desert is occupied by a long central basin, extending from Jebel et-Tih to the shores of the Mediterranean, descending towards the north with a rapid slope, and drained through all its length by Wady el-'Arish, which enters the sea near the place of the same name. West of this basin, other Wadys run by themselves down to the sea. On the east of the same central basin is another similar and parallel one, between it and the 'Arabah, (the two being separated by the chain el-'Ŏjmeh and its continuation,) extending from the Tih nearly to Jebel 'Arâif and el-Mŭkrâh, and drained throughout by the Wady el-Jerâfeh; which having its head in or near the Tih, empties into the 'Arabah not far from el-Mŭkrâh. North of this last basin, the tract between the 'Arabah and the basin of the 'Arish, is filled up by ranges or clusters of mountains; from which on the east short Wadys run to the 'Arabah, and on the west longer ones to Wady el-'Arish; until further north, these latter continue by themselves to the sea nearer Gaza.

Comparing now this formation of the northern desert with the notices already given respecting the peninsula of Sinai, we obtain a more distinct view of the general features of the latter. If the parallel of the northern coast of Egypt be extended eastward to the great Wady el-'Arabah, it appears that the desert, south of this parallel, rises gradually towards the south, until on the summit of the ridge et-Tih, between the gulfs of Suez and 'Akabah, it attains the elevation of 4322 feet, according to Russegger. The waters of all this great tract flow off north-

[1] See Note XXIV, end of the volume. For the routes of the few travellers since 1840, see Ritter Erdk. XIV. p. 866 sq.

wards either to the Mediterranean or the Dead Sea. The Tîh forms a sort of offset; and along its southern base the surface sinks at once to the height of only about 3000 feet, forming the sandy plain which extends nearly across the peninsula. After this the mountains of the peninsula proper commence, and rise rapidly through the formations of sandstone, grünstein, porphyry, and granite, into the lofty masses of St. Catharine and Um Shaumer; the former of which has an elevation of more than 8000 Paris feet, or nearly double that of the Tîh. Here the waters all run eastward or westward to the gulfs of 'Akabah and Suez.

Thursday, April 12th. Our 'Amrân guides had been engaged only as far as to Sheikh el-'Amry, which we passed yesterday; but as they professed to be going to Gaza, they continued with us to Ruhaibeh, and left us at evening. We ourselves had been long undecided which route to take from this point. But as we learned that there were no places of importance on the Gaza road; and by taking it we should probably arrive a day later at Jerusalem; while the way by Hebron was more direct and apparently passed the sites of important ancient cities; we determined to follow the latter. The journey of yesterday had been one of deep interest to us; nor did that of to-day afford results less unexpected or gratifying.

Starting at 5½ o'clock, we proceeded on a general course northeast down Wady er-Ruhaibeh, which becomes broad and arable, with rounded hills on either side. After three quarters of an hour there was a ruin on the hill on our right, a square tower of hewn stones, with a large heap of stones adjoining. A small Wady called esh-Shutein comes in at this point from the same side; and on the hills further north we saw other heaps of squared stones. As we advanced, the valley became quite green with grass; and in a season of ordinary rain would be verdant and full of luxuriant herbage. The birds were now more frequent, warbling forth their carols and filling the air with melody. We noticed the quail with his whistle, and the lark with her song; besides many smaller warblers. In the course of the day, we heard also the notes of the nightingale. At half past six a ruined village was on the left-hand hill. Five minutes later we left Wady er-Ruhaibeh running northwest to join Wady el-Kŭrn; and passed up a small side valley, Wady el-Futeis. We had overtaken a straggling family of the Hawcitât, with three or four camels, travelling on our route; and as the man seemed acquainted with the country, having

i. 294, 296

often been here, (as he said,) we engaged him as a guide as far as to the vicinity of Hebron.

Our path now led over a hill and down another small valley, running nearly E. N. E. towards a wide open country, which spread itself out on every side with swelling hills, but no mountains, almost as far as the eye could reach. Herbs were abundant; but the scanty grass was withered and parched. Crossing a tract of low hills extending along from the left, we came at 8.20 to the bed of Wady el-Kŭrn. This is a valley or plain of some width, with a water-course in the middle, running here west, and then northwest and joining the Ruhaibeh. As we approached its bed from the south, we perceived a wall of hewn stone, extending for some distance obliquely from the bed; and many small fragments of pottery were strewed over the soil. We halted on the northern bank at a fine well, surrounded with several drinking-troughs of stone for watering camels and flocks. The well is circular, eight or ten feet in diameter; and measured twenty-seven feet in depth to the surface of the water. It is very neatly stoned up with good masonry; but the bottom seemed to have been partly filled with rubbish. The water was slightly brackish, and was said never to fail. Adjacent to this well the ground was strewed with ruins, which our Arabs called el-Khŭlasah; in which name we could not but recognise the ancient *Elusa*.

These ruins cover an area of fifteen or twenty acres, throughout which the foundations and enclosures of houses are distinctly to be traced; and squared stones are everywhere thinly scattered. Toward the western side are two open places, perhaps open squares of the ancient city. Several large heaps of hewn stones in various parts probably mark the sites of public buildings; but they are thrown together in too much confusion to be easily made out. Occasional fragments of columns and entablatures were visible. We found no cisterns; the city having been apparently supplied with water from the public well. The space covered by the ruins is at least one third greater than that at Ruhaibeh; but the city was apparently less compactly built; and the masses of ruins are much less considerable. The limestone is here softer, and is much decayed from the influence of the weather; many of the blocks being eaten through and through like a honeycomb. In this way probably a large portion of the materials has perished. We judged that here must have been a city with room enough for a population of fifteen or twenty thousand souls.

The city of Elusa lay without the borders of Palestine; and its name is not found in the Bible. It is first mentioned by Ptolemy in the first half of the second century, among the cities

i. 296, 297

of Idumea, west of the Dead Sea ; and is marked in the Peutinger Tables as lying on the Roman road, seventy-one Roman
miles southward from Jerusalem. This distance we afterwards
travelled in twenty-six hours and a quarter, at a pace somewhat more rapid than our average rate ; affording a coincidence
near enough to determine the site, even if the name were not
decisive.[1]

Profane history makes no further mention of Elusa ; but from
ecclesiastical writers we learn, that although there was here a
Christian church with a bishop, yet the city was chiefly inhabited by heathen, connected with the Saracens of the adjacent
deserts. Jerome relates of St. Hilarion, that travelling with a
company of monks into the desert of Kadesh, he came to Elusa
just as an annual festival had collected all the people in the
temple of Venus ; whom they worshipped, like the Saracens, in
conjunction with the morning star. The town itself, he says,
was for the most part semi-barbarous. As an episcopal city,
Elusa was reckoned to the third Palestine. About A. D. 400,
the son of Nilus was brought here as a prisoner from Mount
Sinai, and redeemed by the bishop ; as has been already related
in speaking of the convent.[2] The names of four other bishops
are found in the records of councils, as late as to A. D. 536.
About A. D. 600, Antoninus Martyr appears to have passed
from Palestine to Sinai by Elusa, which he calls Eulatia. The
Notitiæ of ecclesiastical writers, collected by Reland, refer to
nearly the same period. From that time onward until now, an
interval of more than eleven centuries, Elusa has remained un-
mentioned, and its place unknown ; until we were thus permitted
to rescue it again from this long oblivion.[3]

Leaving the well at a quarter past 9 o'clock, we proceeded
on our way, on a course N. N. E. Of Wady el-Kŭrn, (sometimes called also Wady el-Khŭlasah,) we had two accounts.
Tuweileb thought that after the junction of the Ruhaibeh with
it, the two form Wady Khŭbarah, which enters the 'Arîsh. This
Wady, the Khŭbarah, though without living water, is very fertile, and yields good crops of grain and also of melons. On the

---

[1] From a remark of Jerome, (Comm.
in Esa. 15, 4,) it would appear, that the
Aramæan name of this city was חֲלוּצָה
which was softened in Greek to Ἔλουσα.
The Arabic version in Gen. 20, 1. 2, and
26, 1, instead of Gerar, reads el-Khŭlŭs,
as if referring it to Elusa. See Reland
Palæst. pp. 755, 805. Bochart Phaleg,
p. 309.—The length of the Roman mile is
commonly assumed at 75 to the degree ;
or 5 Roman miles equal to 4 geographical
miles. Our rate of travel was here somewhat more than 2 G. M. or 2½ R. M. the
i. 207, 208

hour. See in Note VII, at the end of the
volume.
[2] See above, p. 124.
[3] See in general, Reland Palæst. pp.
213, 218, 223 ; also p. 755 sq. Le Quien
Oriens Christ. III. p. 735. Itin. Antonini
Mart. xxxv.—M. Callier passed from Hebron to Dhoheriyeh, and thence to Wady
Khŭlasah ; but he appears to have struck
the valley at a point further east. Journal des Savans, Jan. 1836. p. 47. Nouv.
Annales des Voyages, 1839. Tom. III. p.
274.

other hand, our 'Amràn and Haweitât guides affirmed, that the
united Wady receives the Mûrtûbeh further down, and thus
forms Wady es-Sûny, which joins the Sherî'ah near the sea not
far south of Gaza. Of these accounts the former, from the construction of the map, seems the most probable.—Our path led
for a time over sandy hills, called Rumeilet Hâmid, sprinkled
with herbs and shrubs, but with little grass. The shrubs which
we had met with throughout the desert still continued. One of
the principal of these is the *Retem* already mentioned, a species
of the broom plant, *Genista rœtam* of Forskal. This is the
largest and most conspicuous shrub of these deserts, growing
thickly in the water-courses and valleys. Our Arabs always
selected the place of encampment (if possible) in a spot where
it grew, in order to be sheltered by it at night from the wind ;
and during the day, when they often went on in advance of the
camels, we found them not unfrequently sitting or sleeping under
a bush of Retem to protect them from the sun. It was in this
very desert, a day's journey from Beersheba, that the prophet
Elijah lay down and slept beneath the same shrub.[1]

We came at $10\frac{3}{4}$ o'clock to a broad Wady, with a large
tract of grass, called el-Khûza'y. As we advanced, the loose
sand ceased, and the country exhibited more grass mingled with
the herbs. At 11.55 we crossed the bed of Wady el-Mûrtûbeh,
a wide tract bearing marks of much water. Just before reaching
it a path had crossed ours, leading to water in the same Wady
not far to the left, in pits called *Themâil.* Lower down, this
Wady receives the Khûza'y, and afterwards unites with the
Kûrn, as above described.

Our road thus far had been among swelling hills of moderate
height. We now began gradually to ascend others higher, but
of the same general character. The herbs of the desert began to
disappear, and the hills were thinly covered with grass, now dry
and parched. The ascent was long and gradual. We reached
the top at a quarter past 1 o'clock, and looked out before us
over a broad lower tract ; beyond which our eyes were greeted
with the first sight of the mountains of Judah, south of Hebron,
which skirted the open country and bounded the horizon in the
east and northeast. We now felt that the desert was at an end.
Descending gradually, we came out at 2 o'clock upon an open
undulating country ; the shrubs ceased, or nearly so ; green
grass was seen along the lesser water-courses, and almost green
sward ; while the gentle hills, covered in ordinary seasons with

[1] 1 Kings 19, 4. 5. The Hebrew name
רֹתֶם *rothem* is the same as the present
Arabic name. The Vulgate, Luther, English version, and others, translate it
wrongly by *juniper.* The roots are very
bitter ; and are regarded by the Arabs as
yielding the best charcoal. This illustrates
Job 30, 4, and Ps. 120, 4. Comp. Burckhardt, p. 483.

grass and rich pasture, were now burnt over with drought. Arabs were pasturing their camels in various parts ; but no trace of dwellings was any where visible. At 2¾ o'clock we reached Wady es-Seba', a wide water-course, or bed of a torrent, running here W. S. W. towards Wady es-Sûny. Upon its northern side, close upon the bank, are two deep wells, still called Bir es-Seba', the ancient *Beersheba*. We had entered the borders of Palestine !

These wells are some distance apart; they are circular, and stoned up very neatly with solid masonry, apparently much more ancient than that of the wells at 'Abdeh. The larger one is twelve and a half feet in diameter, and forty-four and a half feet deep to the surface of the water; sixteen feet of which at the bottom is excavated in the solid rock. The other well lies fifty-five rods W. S. W., and is five feet in diameter and forty-two feet deep. The water in both is pure and sweet, and in great abundance ; the finest indeed we had found since leaving Sinai. Both wells are surrounded with drinking-troughs of stone for camels and flocks; such as were doubtless used of old for the flocks which then fed on the adjacent hills. The curb-stones were deeply worn by the friction of the ropes in drawing up water by hand.[1]

We had heard of no ruins here, and hardly expected to find any ; for none were visible from the wells ; yet we did not wish to leave so important a spot without due examination. Ascending the low hills north of the wells, we found them covered with the ruins of former habitations, the foundations of which are still distinctly to be traced, although scarcely one stone remains upon another. The houses appear not to have stood compactly, but scattered over several little hills and in the hollows between. They seem to have been built chiefly of round stones ; though some of the stones are squared and some hewn. It was probably only a small straggling city. This very expression I wrote in pencil on the spot ; and was afterwards gratified to find, that Eusebius and Jerome both describe it only as a "large village" with a Roman garrison.[2] We could find no special traces of churches or other public buildings ; although one or two larger heaps of stones may probably have been such edifices. These ruins are spread over a space half a mile in length along the

[1] The Hebrew name Beersheba signifies "Well of the Oath;" or as some suppose, "Well of the Seven," referring to the seven lambs which Abraham gave to Abimelech in token of the oath between them. See Gen. 21, 28–32. The Arabic name Bir es-Seba' signifies "Well of the Seven," and also "Well of the Lion."— Some writers have regarded the name as

i. 300, 301

implying *seven wells;* but without the slightest historical or other ground. On the map of our route across the desert, published in the Journal of the Royal Geographical Society of London for 1839, a similar explanation was inserted without my knowledge.

[2] Onomast. art. *Bersabee.* Euseb. κώμη μεγίστη. Jerome, "vicus grandis."

northern side of the water-course and extending back about a
quarter of a mile. Fragments of pottery are scattered over the
whole. —On the south side of the water-course is a long wall of
hewn stone under the bank, extending for several hundred feet,
apparently intended to protect the bank from being washed away
by the torrent. Probably gardens or some important building
may have been situated on the bank above ; of which however
there is now no trace. On the same side are several heaps of
stones ; and the ground is also strewed with small fragments of
pottery.

Here then is the place where the patriarchs Abraham, Isaac,
and Jacob often dwelt! Here Abraham dug perhaps this very
well ; and journeyed from hence with Isaac to Mount Moriah, to
offer him up there in sacrifice. From this place Jacob fled to
Padan-Aram, after acquiring the birthright and blessing belonging to his brother ; and here too he sacrificed to the Lord on
setting off to meet his son Joseph in Egypt. Here Samuel made
his sons judges ; and from here Elijah wandered out into the
southern desert, and sat down under a shrub of Retem, just as
our Arabs sat down under it every day and every night. Here
was the border of Palestine proper, which extended from Dan to
Beersheba.[1] Over these swelling hills the flocks of the patriarchs
once roved by thousands ; where now we found only a few camels,
asses, and goats!

Beersheba is last mentioned in the Old Testament, as one of
the places to which the Jews returned after the exile.[2] The
name does not occur in the New Testament ; nor is it referred to
as then existing by any writer earlier than Eusebius and Jerome
in the fourth century. They describe it as a large village with a
Roman garrison.[3] It is found as an episcopal city in the early
ecclesiastical and other *Notitiæ* referring to the centuries before
and after the Muhammedan conquests ;[4] but none of its bishops
are anywhere mentioned. Its site was in like manner long forgotten ; and the crusaders assigned this name to the place now
called Beit Jibrin, lying between Hebron and Askelon.[5] About
the middle of the fourteenth century, Sir John Maundeville and
also Ludolf de Suchem and William de Baldensel passed on this
route from Sinai to Hebron and Jerusalem ; and all of them
mention here Beersheba. The two latter say it was then unin-
habited ; but some of the churches were still standing. From
this time onward for five centuries, it has again remained until

[1] See Gen. 21, 31 sq. 22, 19. 26, 23.
28, 10. 46, 1. 1 Sam. 8, 2. 1 Kings
19, 3. 2 Sam. 17, 11. Compare in general, Reland's Palest. p. 620.
[2] Neh. 11, 27. 30.
[3] Onomast. art. *Bersabee.*—Josephus

indeed mentions a Bersabee among the
towns which he fortified ; but this was
in Galilee. B. J. 2. 20. 6. Vit. 37.
[4] Reland's Pal. pp. 215, 217, 222, 229.
[5] Will. Tyr. 14. 22.

this day apparently unvisited and unknown ; except the slight notice which Seetzen obtained respecting it from the Arabs.[1]

We remained nearly an hour upon this interesting spot ; where all that is now to be seen, lies within a very narrow compass. Meantime several flocks of goats came up for water ; or perhaps because their keepers wished to get a nearer view of the strangers. After some chaffering, we bought a kid for our Arabs ; intending to give them a good supper, inasmuch as we were approaching the end of our journey. We set off again at 3.35, on a course northeast, the path gradually ascending over an open tract, which in ordinary seasons must be a fine grazing country. Not a precipice, not a tree, was to be seen ; nothing but grassy hills. At 4.25 we passed the site of a village, the stone houses of which had been thrown down to the very foundation. We could learn no name. Ten minutes later we encamped in this open tract, for the first time on grass, or rather what had once been grass ; for it was now parched and brown. Yet it was something better than the desert ; where hitherto the floor of our tent had always been the naked sand or gravel.

Our Arabs quickly slaughtered the poor goat ; and the different portions were speedily in the process of cooking at different fires. This time they had no guests, bidden or unbidden, to interrupt the full enjoyment of their savoury repast. Such probably in kind was the " savoury meat " which Isaac loved ; and with which, in this very neighbourhood, Jacob enticed from him the blessing intended for his elder brother.[2] Our Haweity guide had brought along his family, with two or three camels ; and to them the offals of the kid were abandoned. I looked in upon this feast ; and found the women boiling the stomach and entrails, which they had merely cleaned by stripping them with the hand, without washing ; while the head unskinned and unopened, was roasting underneath in the embers of a fire made chiefly of camels' dung. With such a meal our Tawarah would hardly have been content. Indeed all the Bedawin we had yet met with out of the peninsula, the 'Amrân, the Haiwât, the Haweitât, and the Tiyâhah, were obviously upon a lower scale of civilization than the Tawarah ; and seemed little if any further removed from savage life, than the red man of the American wilds.

---

[1] Zach's Monatl. Corresp. XVII. 143. At the time of our visit I was under the impression, that Seetzen had himself been at Beersheba. But he went from Hebron first to the vicinity of Gaza ; and thence direct to Sinai ; and only speaks of the wells of Bir es-Seba' as being several hours E. N. E. of the spot where he then was.—Eusebius and Jerome place Beersheba at *twenty* Roman miles from Hebron towards the south. This is a striking instance of their loose and vague manner of specifying distances and bearings not definitely known to them. We found the distance from Beersheba to Hebron to be a good 12 hours with camels ; equivalent to nearly 25 G. M. or more than 30 Roman miles, on a general course N. E. by E. Compare Reland's Pal. p. 474 sq.

[2] Gen. 27, 9 sq.

i. 303, 304

Our guide of the Haweitât was from the country east of the
gulf of 'Akabah and north of the Haj route. Like so many
others of his tribe, he had been driven out by the drought; and
had wandered off hither to the south of Syria in search of pasture. We afterwards found similar wanderers in the district
around Wady Mûsa. He said that in his country there were
many ruined towns, which had never yet been "written down."
His tribe have no horses; not one of them, not even the Sheikh,
can read; nor did he know of any Bedawy who could. When
the Haweitât of that region receive letters, they apply to the
Arabs *Hâdhr*, "townsmen," of Muweilih to have them read.
These Haweitât are at enmity with the Arabs of Khaibar.—
This guide, as well as our other Arabs, called the wind we had
yesterday *Shŭrkiyeh*, an east wind, although it blew from the
south.[1] The Simoom, they said, differs from it only in its greater
heat; the haze and sand and discoloration of the air being alike
in both. Should it overtake a traveller without water, it may
in certain circumstances prove fatal to him. He needs water
not only to drink; but it is well to wash the skin. The Simoom,
they said, prevails only during the season when the Khamsin
blows in Egypt. This is during the months of April and May.[2]

Friday, April 13th. We started at 5.25, and in five minutes
crossed a track leading off N. by W. to the well of Khuweilifeh, situated in a Wady of the same name on the road from
Hebron by Dhoheriyeh to Gaza. It was described to us as
similar to the smaller well at Bir es-Seba'.[3] Fifteen minutes
more brought us out upon a wide open grassy plain, suffering
greatly indeed from drought, but in which many fields of wheat
were scattered, looking beautifully in their vesture of bright
green. The ground too was in many places decked with flowers;
among them were an abundance of low scarlet poppies. The
morning was lovely; the sky perfectly serene, with a refreshing
breeze from the southwest; the air full of the sweet carols of
birds. Thus we spent our first morning in Palestine. It was a
delightful entrance to the Promised Land.

The plain over which we now travelled on a course N. E.
by E. has an undulating surface, and extends very far towards
the southeast. No shrubs nor trees were visible; nothing but
grass and flowers and green fields. It reminded me of the vast
plains of northern Germany. On the east and north were hills
and ridges, the beginning of the mountains of Judah, forming an
angle in the northeast towards which our course led. The plain
was much cut up by deep gullies with precipitous banks, mostly

---

[1] This name Shŭrkiyeh suggests an obvious etymology of the Italian word *Sirocco*.

[2] Lane's Mod. Egypt. I. pp. 2, 3.

[3] See more respecting this well under
date of June 7th.

; 305. 306

running towards the left, worn by the wintry torrents. At 6.10 a track went off to the left towards the north to a place, where the Bedawin have their magazines of grain, called Nüttâr el-Lükiyeh. About 7 o'clock we crossed a Wady running northwesterly through the plain ; it was said to be the Khuweilifeh, which after passing the well of that name, bends round to join the Wady Seba'. We had however some doubt as to the correctness of this information.

Ten minutes later we crossed the road leading from Gaza to Wady Mûsa and Ma'ân. According to our Haweity guide, it unites with the road from Hebron at or near a well called el-Milh, and then divides and descends to the 'Arabah by two passes called el-Ghârib and er-Râkib. We learned more of this road at a later period ; but heard nothing further of this latter pass.[1] As we advanced, the hills from the northwest approached more and more to meet those upon the east ; and a small Wady was visible descending from the angle. At 8.20 a path went off to the right, which was said to lead to a village in the mountains. At three quarters past eight, the plain terminated ; we began to get among the hills, and entered the Wady above mentioned, which our Arabs chose to call Wady el-Khûlil ; but whether for any other reason than because it was leading us towards el-Khûlil or Hebron, is doubtful. In this valley were fields of grain ; and half an hour after entering it, we found a man ploughing with two heifers in order to sow millet. His plough was very simple, and by English and American farmers would be called rude. Yet it did its work well, and was of a much lighter and better construction than the coarse plough of Egypt. The ancient form is not improbably still preserved.

We now began to ascend more rapidly ; the limestone hills on each side became rocky and higher, and were green with grass ; while low trees were occasionally scattered over them. Among these the Butm, *Pistacia Terebinthus* of Linnæus, the Terebinth of the Old Testament, was the most frequent. We noticed here red clover growing wild along our path. At 9¾ o'clock we reached the head of the valley, and came out upon a ridge, from which a very steep descent brought us to the bottom of another deep and narrow Wady coming down from the northeast. This latter here turned short towards the southeast. We could learn neither its name, nor in what direction its waters were ultimately carried off ; but we afterwards found, that it joins the great valley which passes down further east from near Hebron to Wady es-Seba'. Our path now followed up this Wady, still on a general course N. E. by E. It is quite narrow and winds much among the hills ; so that it seemed to be almost inter-

---

[1] See under date of June 2d and 3d.

minable. The sides were rocky, but clothed with grass and the shrub Bellân, a sort of furze. Here we met several wild savage-looking Arabs ; and further on, a man on horseback, the first we had seen since leaving Egypt. He was on a sleek mare, which brought him rapidly down the steep rocky side of one of the hills. The bottom of the valley in its steeper parts was formerly laid off into terraces, of which the massive walls still remain ; but nothing more. After some time flocks of sheep and goats mingled together were seen feeding on the hills ; and we fell in with other flocks consisting of young kids alone. Not long after, we came upon herds of neat cattle and donkeys grazing; and at length, at a quarter past 11 o'clock, got sight of the village of edh-Dhoheriyeh on the summit of a hill terminating the Wady, the head of which here opens out into a green basin. This and the hills around were covered with flocks and neat cattle in the an-cient patriarchal style, with many horses, asses, and camels, all in fine order ; and affording to us a most pleasing prospect, after having been for thirty days confined to the dreary nakedness of the desert. We reached Dhoheriyeh at 11.35.

Our Tawarah Arabs had always said, that they could take us only as far as to this village, the first on this road within the borders of Syria. They had represented it too as being very near to Hebron. The Bedawin never bring travellers or loads further than this point ; as the inhabitants, living on the great road from Hebron to Gaza and Egypt, have the monopoly of trans-porting all goods and passengers that come by way of the desert. Our first object therefore was to obtain the means of proceeding without delay to Hebron ; the day being not yet half spent. We sought for the Sheikh of the village, but he was absent. The person who acted for him, we found sitting with a number of the inhabitants. He informed us that we could obtain no animals until the next day ; when they would engage to take us through to Jerusalem. To all our pressing solicitations to be sent forward immediately, they turned a deaf ear ; probably be-cause they did not wish to stop for the night with us at Hebron ; but they said our Arabs might go on with us, if they would. This we then proposed ; but the Tawarah said they were strangers here, and feared that if they went to Hebron their camels would be pressed for the service of the government ; a thing not at all unusual, as we knew. We now tried to ascertain the distance to Hebron ; thinking we could perhaps send one of our servants thither and obtain animals. Some said it was three, some four, and some five hours distant ; nor was it till we had actually travelled over the ground ourselves, that we arrived at any certainty ; and then we found the largest estimate correct.— Under all the circumstances, much as we wished to get on, we felt compelled to have the camels unloaded, and the tent pitched. This was done for the first time on *green* grass, and among olive trees, in the basin just below the village on the southeast. Our intention was to pay off and dismiss our Tawarah ; and then, if possible, obtain animals from Hebron.

We found no difficulty in satisfying all our Arabs, whose camels had brought loads from the convent ; but an unexpected question arose in the case of Tuweileb. We had regarded him merely as taking the place of Beshârah, as head of the party and guide ; which, according to the express stipulation of our contract, he was to do without additional expense to us, except such slight presents as we might choose to give him. I have already mentioned, that he had brought with him two extra camels, apparently for himself and children ; one of which had been taken into our service at 'Akabah, instead of a camel which had died by the way. But his views, it seems, in entering upon the journey, had been different from ours ; and Beshârah had told him, that we would take him as Sheikh of the party, and pay him the hire of a dromedary for himself ; or rather, would make him an equivalent and generous present. Thus the animal, which all along upon the journey had been nothing more than a broken down camel, was now suddenly transformed into the dromedary of a Sheikh. We had already paid him enough, as we supposed ; but this was a higher claim, touching his honour as a Sheikh and as a Bedawy. He had been understood to come as the Sheikh of our party ; he had consented that his dromedary should bear a burden for our accommodation ; and now both he and his dromedary would be forever degraded in the eyes of his tribe, unless we made him a fitting present for a Sheikh. To all this we had nothing to reply, except the words of our contract, which he could not read. We cut the matter short at last, by giving him our old pistols, which he had usually paraded in his girdle on the way, and which we had bought for a trifle in Cairo. With this present he seemed highly gratified. But we were not sure, that he did not immediately sell the pistols in the village ; where fire-arms were sought with avidity, in consequence of the disarming of the people by the Egyptian government.

We had on the whole been much pleased with Tuweileb ; although, as I have already remarked, he had seen his best days, and for much of the time had been quite unwell. He was uniformly kind, patient, accommodating, and faithful ; and until now had shown himself less a beggar than his companions. He gave us his adieu by repeatedly kissing each on both cheeks, in addition to the usual kiss of the hand. We parted with our Tawarah Arabs with regret and with the kindest feelings. For thirty days they had now been our companions and guides through the desert; and not the slightest difficulty had arisen between us. On the contrary, they had done all in their power to lighten the toils of our journey, and protect us from discomforts by the way. In all our subsequent journeyings, we found no guides so faithful and devoted.

By this time it was too late to think of reaching Hebron. We therefore sent and engaged camels for Jerusalem, to take us and our luggage at midnight, and reach the Holy City before the next evening. The journey through the desert had made such inroads upon our stores, that the Sheikh of the camels required us to take only six, instead of the nine which had brought us thus far. They were however much larger and stouter than those of the Bedawîn.

The village of Dhoherîyeh lies high, and is visible from a great distance in every direction. It is a rude assemblage of stone hovels; many of which are half under ground, and others broken down. A castle or fortress apparently once stood here; the remains of a square tower are still to be seen, now used as a dwelling; and the doorways of many hovels are of hewn stone with arches. It would seem to have been one of the line of small fortresses, which apparently once existed all along the southern border of Palestine. The village contains, according to the government census, one hundred full grown men; of whom thirty-eight had been taken at three separate times for the Egyptian army. Though half in ruins, it is yet rich in flocks and herds, and has at least a hundred camels. The inhabitants are Hûdhr, or townsmen; and belong to the party called Keis. Most of the villagers in this quarter are of this party; as well as some of the Bedawîn.

The country around looks barren; the limestone rocks come out in large blocks and masses upon the sides and tops of the hills; and give a whitish cast to the whole landscape. No trees were visible; nor any fields of grain, except in the bottoms of the narrow valleys. Indeed the aspect of the whole region was stern and dreary. Yet it must be a fine grazing country; as is proved by the fat and sleek condition of the herds and flocks; and by its having been, from the days of Abraham onward, a place of resort for nomadic herdsmen.

Towards evening we went to the top of a hill just east of our tent; but could see nothing all around save rocky hills and swells. On one of these in the direction E. by S. was a ruined castle; which proved to be Semû'a, on the road from Wady Mûsa to Hebron. In its immediate vicinity, the Arabs said there were two other like ruins; one called 'Attîr, and the other Husn el-Ghûrâb. Of the latter we heard no more; but saw the former place as we afterwards returned from Wady Mûsa through Semû'a.

During the evening we lay down and slept. At the rising of the moon, about 10 o'clock, the camels came, and we fixed the time for loading at half past twelve; not wishing to reach Hebron before day. They all, camels and men, lay down upon the ground, and were soon in deep sleep. My companions also lay down; while I sat up alone to watch during the few hours that yet remained.

Saturday, April 14th. Half an hour after midnight we mustered again, and set to work on the luggage; but such was the inefficiency and stupidity of our new camel drivers, that nearly two hours elapsed, before we could mount. One camel proved refractory and refused its load; and another had to be brought from the village in its stead. We started at length at 2¼ o'clock; but in descending the long and steep hill from the village, we were delayed nearly three quarters of an hour by the necessity of repacking one of the loads; and this with various other hindrances, caused us to lose not less than an hour upon the way. The course from Dhoheriyeh to Hebron, as we afterwards found by observation, is N. 54° E. The hill we first descended is very steep and rocky; and the path winds down among the stones. It brought us to the bottom of a deep valley, running towards the right, probably to the great Wady which drains the region around Hebron. The road continued to wind among valleys and over hills; but the darkness prevented us from observing much of the country. The hills, we could see, began to be covered with shrubs; and these increased as we advanced, and were intermingled with evergreen or prickly oaks, arbutus, and other dwarf trees and bushes. At half past five there was a spring of living water; the first we had seen.

As the sun rose we heard upon the left the bleating of flocks and the crowing of cocks, as if from a village. On inquiring, we were told that there was none; but a company of peasants were living there in caves, pasturing their flocks. In summer, it was said, a large portion of the peasantry leave their villages, and dwell in caves or ruins, in order to be nearer to their flocks and fields. At 6.10 there was another fountain with a square reservoir below it on the right; and ten minutes further on, a running brook, the first we had seen since leaving the Nile. This was in a Wady called ed-Dilbeh, running off to the right, and partially cultivated. Near by was the site of a ruined village, called ed-Daumeh.

The camels we now had, were huge, fat, and powerful, each stronger than any two of our former Bedawin animals. At the same time they were harder in their gait, treading more firmly,

i. 312-314

from being accustomed to carry only burdens and not to travel as dromedaries. Two of the owners had started with us; but soon abandoned us under the pretext of speedily returning, leaving us and their animals to the care of two ordinary camel drivers and a young Nubian slave, who all knew nothing of the country except what lay just upon the road. As we advanced, the hills were more thickly clothed with bushes, and covered with great quantities of the Za'ter, a species of thyme, scented almost like balm, and used in cooking. At 7.20 we left the direct road to Jerusalem, which passes on the left of Hebron, and turned somewhat more to the right. Crossing a ridge we came at a quarter before 8 o'clock to a little valley with many olive trees and enclosed vineyards, indicating our approach to a land of higher cultivation. The region around Hebron abounds with vineyards, and the grapes are the finest in Palestine. Each vineyard has a small house or tower of stone, which serves for a keeper's lodge ; and, during the vintage, we were told that the inhabitants of Hebron go out and dwell in these houses, and the town is almost deserted. In this little valley every thing looked thrifty ; and round about were large flocks of sheep and goats, all in good condition.

Ascending gradually another ridge, we at length from its top saw Hebron, now called el-Khŭlil, below us in a deep narrow valley running from N. N. W. to S. S. E. into the great Wady which flows off to Wady es-Seba'. The spot where we were, affords one of the best views of the place. The town lies low down on the sloping sides of this valley, chiefly on the eastern ; but in the southern part extends across also to the western side. The houses are all of stone, high and well built, with windows and flat roofs ; and on these roofs small domes, sometimes two or three to each house ; a mode of building apparently peculiar to Judea, for I do not remember to have seen it further north than Nâbulus. This gave to the city in our eyes a new and rather striking aspect ; and the whole appearance was much better than I had anticipated. We descended from the west into the valley by a very rocky path ; and halted at 8¼ o'clock on the green slope overagainst the northern part of the town; which is partly occupied as a cemetery. We had thus found the distance from Dhoheriyeh to Hebron to be five hours of travel.

We had now reached a most interesting point in our journey. The town before us was one of the most ancient still existing cities mentioned in the Scriptures, or perhaps in the records of the world.[1] Here Abraham and the other patriarchs dwelt and communed with God ; and in this vicinity they and their wives

[1] Gen. 13, 18.

were buried. Here too had been for seven years the royal residence of David; and before us was the pool in Hebron, over
which he hanged up the murderers of his rival Ishbosheth.[1] In
Hebron too he probably composed many of his Psalms, which
yet thrill through the soul and lift it up to God. Our minds
were deeply affected by all these associations, and we would fain
have devoted the day to a closer examination of the place. But
the strong desire we felt of reaching Jerusalem before night,
and thus closing our long and wearisome journey; together with
the expectation we cherished of revisiting Hebron at a later
time; induced us to forego all other considerations, and press
forward as soon as possible to Jerusalem. Nearly six weeks
afterwards we spent several days in Hebron; and I therefore
defer a fuller account of the city and its neighbourhood until that
time.[2]

Taking a hasty ramble through the streets of Hebron, we
were again upon our way at 9¼ o'clock, after a stop of a single
hour. The road to Jerusalem is rough and mountainous, but
very direct; the general course being between N. E. by N. and
N. N. E. As we issued from the town, the path for a short distance was full of mud and puddles from a spring near by; and
to us, coming out of the desert, this was quite a refreshing sight.
The road leads up the valley for a short time; and then up a
branch coming from the northeast. The path is here paved; or
rather laid unevenly with large stones, in the manner of a Swiss
mountain road. It passes between the walls of vineyards and
olive yards; the former chiefly in the valley, and the latter on
the slopes of the hills, which are in many parts built up in terraces. These vineyards are very fine, and produce the largest
and best grapes in all the country. This valley is generally
assumed to be the Eshcol of the Old Testament, whence the
spies brought back the cluster of grapes to Kadesh; and apparently not without reason. The character of its fruit still
corresponds to its ancient celebrity; and pomegranates and
figs, as well as apricots, quinces, and the like, still grow there in
abundance.[3]

This road bears every mark of having always been a great
highway between Hebron and Jerusalem. It is direct; and in
many parts artificially made, evidently in times of old. But
wheels probably never passed here; the hills are too sharp and

---

[1] 2 Sam. 4, 12.
[2] See under May 24 and 25.
[3] Num. 13, 23. The situation of Eshcol is not specified in this passage. But
in Gen. 14, 24 we are told that Abraham
in his pursuit of the four kings from Hebron, was accompanied by his friends
i. 315-317

Aner, Eshcol, and Mamre. Now Mamre
gave his name to the terebinth near Hebron, by which Abraham dwelt (Gen. 13,
18); and in like manner, the name of the
valley was not improbably derived from
that of his companion Eshcol.

steep, and the surface of the ground too thickly strewn with rocks, to admit of the possibility of vehicles being used in this mountainous region, without the toilsome construction of artificial roads, such as never yet existed here. Indeed we nowhere read of wheeled carriages in connection with the country south of Jerusalem; except where Joseph is said to have sent waggons to bring down his father Jacob into Egypt. These came to Hebron; and Jacob travelled with them thence to Beersheba.[1] We had this circumstance in mind on our journey from Beersheba to Hebron; and long before reaching Dhoheriyeh, we were convinced, that waggons for the patriarch could not have passed by that route. Still, by taking a more circuitous course up the great Wady el-Khûlil, more to the right, they might probably reach Hebron through the valleys without great difficulty.

In about three quarters of an hour we came to the head of the valley; the vineyards ceased; we came out upon an open tract, having on our left at 10 o'clock the ruins of a village once inhabited by Christians, now called Khurbet el-Nûsârah. The inhabitants, it was said, were massacred by the Muslims; and now there are no Christians in all the province of Hebron.

At one hour from Hebron a blind path went off to the right at right angles, leading to Tekû'a; and on it, about five minutes' walk from our road, are the foundations of an immense building, which excited our curiosity. We ran thither on foot, leaving our beasts to proceed slowly; and found the substructions of an edifice, which would seem to have been commenced on a large scale, but never completed. They consist of two walls apparently of a large enclosure; one facing towards the southwest, two hundred feet long; and the other at right angles facing northwest one hundred and sixty feet long, with a space left in the middle of it as if for a portal. There are only two courses of hewn stones above ground, each three feet four inches high; one of the stones measured fifteen and a half feet long by three and one third feet thick. In the northwest angle is a well or cistern arched over, but not deep. There are no stones nor ruins of any kind lying around, to mark that these walls were ever carried higher. It is difficult to say, judging merely from the remains themselves, what could have been the object for which the building was intended. It may have been a church; though it does not lie, like most ancient churches, in the direction from west to east. Or it might possibly have been begun as a fortress; though there would seem to be nothing in the vicinity to guard. At any rate, these walls cannot have been constructed later than the first centuries after the Christian era,

[1] Gen. 45, 19. 21. 27.   46, 1.

i. 317, 318

and the size of the stones points rather to an earlier age. The spot is called by the Arabs Râmet el-Khûlil. The Jews of Hebron call it the House of Abraham ; and regard this as the place of Abraham's tent and terebinth at Mamre. May we not perhaps suppose, that these massive walls are indeed the work of Jewish hands, erected here in ancient days around the spot where the founder of their race had dwelt ? On such a supposition, the structure would have corresponded to that around his sepulchre in Hebron.[1]

The country was still rocky and uneven, though somewhat cultivated. At 10¾ o'clock a ruined mosk, called Neby Yûnas (Prophet Jonah), was upon a long hill parallel to our road on the right, at the distance of half an hour or more, looking much like the church of a New England village. Around this mosk, as we afterwards learned, are the remains of walls and foundations, marking an ancient site. The place is called by the Arabs Hûlhûl ; doubtless the ancient Halhul, a city in the mountains of Judah, which Jerome places near to Hebron.[2] Another road from Hebron to Jerusalem, which some of our friends took a few weeks later, leads by this place. We saw it again from the east on a subsequent excursion from Jerusalem ; but did not visit it.[3] At some distance beyond the same hill, runs the great valley, which passing down southwest to Wady es-Seba', drains the whole region around Hebron and Dhoheriyeh.

A large village was now visible in the N. N. E. at the distance of an hour or more, called Beit Ummar ; but we did not observe it afterwards. At 11.10 there was on our left a ruined tower, perhaps of the time of the crusades ; and in five minutes more we came to a fountain on the right with a stone trough, and with ruins around as of a former church. The stones are

[1] See the Haram under May 24th.— This Jewish tradition and name is at least as old as the crusades: Benj. of Tud. by Asher, I. p. 77. Von Troilo also speaks of the spot and wells as Mamre ; Reisebeschr. p. 319, Dresd. 1676. If the supposition in the text be not admissible, these remains may perhaps be regarded as belonging to the church erected by order of Constantine, near the supposed place of Abraham's terebinth ; see Euseb. Vit. Const. III. 51–53, and Valesius' Notes on c. 53. Hieron. Onomast. art. Arboch and Drys. The Itin. Hieros. in A. D. 333, speaks of this church as two Roman miles from Hebron towards Jerusalem. According to Sozomen it was 15 stadia in the same direction ; Hist. Ecc. II. 4. Adamnanus mentions here these walls as of a church ; lib. II. 11. See generally Reland Palæst. p. 711 sq. Josephus on the
i. 318, 319

other hand places the terebinth of Mamre at only six stadia from Hebron ; B. J. 4. 9. 7.—The English version has less correctly *plain* of Mamre ; Gen. 13, 18. etc. —We again visited this spot in 1852 ; see Vol. III. Sect. VI, under May 7, 1852.

[2] Josh. 15, 58. Hieron. Onomast. art. *Elul.*

[3] It is also mentioned by Ibn Batûta in the fourteenth century as the tomb of Jonah ; see his Travels translated by Prof. Lee, Lond. 1829. p. 20. Niebuhr seems first to have heard the name Hûlhûl, as a village where the Jews venerate the tomb of the prophet Nathan ; Reisebeschr. III. p. 69. Schubert visited the place in 1837, and makes a similar report of the tomb of Nathan and of ancient walls ; but seems not to have heard the name Hûlhûl. Reise II. p. 487.

very large, and the adjacent rocks hewn away to a perpendicular face. The place is called ed-Dirweh.[1] The country now became more open. The valleys were wider and apparently fertile; and the hills were covered with bushes, arbutus, and dwarf oaks, exhibiting also in their terraced sides the traces of ancient cultivation. This tract seemed to be full of partridges; whose calling and clucking we heard on every side. Crossing a valley obliquely, we came at a quarter past noon to the ruins of another village called Kúfin,[2] with olive trees and tillage around, and a reservoir of rain water. Here we could see the road at some distance before us, ascending the side of a long ridge. Half an hour further on, there was another ruined tower upon our left. The road up the ascent just mentioned, is artificial; half way up is a cistern of rain water, and an open place of prayer for the Muhammedan traveller. From the top, the path descends into a long straight valley, which it follows for an hour, called Wady et-Tuheishimeh. At 2¼ o'clock the hills became higher and more rocky; the valley narrower and winding; while the road ascends obliquely on the left, and bends around the eastern point of a high hill, leaving the valley very deep below on the right. In this part of it are the ruins of a large square building, perhaps once a convent; and here too was the scene of one of the battles between Ibrahim Pasha and the rebel Felláhs in A. D. 1834. The valley passes on towards the right, and further down (as I suppose) receives that which descends from Solomon's Pools, and so runs to the Dead Sea.

Our road now crossed the ridge obliquely towards the left; and brought us at half past two to a narrow valley descending towards the east. Along the side of the northern hill was an aqueduct, which, as we afterwards found, passes around the eastern end of the same hill and enters the lower pool. Crossing this ridge we came upon the more open valley in which are the pools. This also descends towards the east; receives the Wady we had just crossed; and further on unites with Wady et-Tuheishimeh. From the hill we could see before us, at a distance across the valley, the little village and small church of St. George, called by the Arabs el-Khúdr.[3] Our path led us along the upper end

---

[1] In afterwards searching for the site of the ancient Beth-zur, this place recurred to our minds. That city was probably not far from Halhul (Josh. 15, 58), on the way from Jerusalem to Hebron, near a fountain; Euseb. et Hieron. Onomast. art. *Bethsur*. But Euseb. and Jerome both place Beth-zur at 20 miles from Jerusalem, and of course only two miles from Hebron; while this spot is two hours with camels, or some five Roman miles from the latter place. The *Itin. Hieros.* makes it eleven miles from Hebron. Yet this spot is the true Beth-zur; see under May 7, 1852.—This certainly cannot have been the water at which the eunuch was baptized; for he was driving in his chariot towards Gaza, and never could have passed on this route. Acts 8, 26 sq. Comp. Schubert's Reise, II. p. 488. See more under June 7th.

[2] Not Abu Fid, as in the former edition.

[3] See under May 17th.

of the upper pool, which we reached at 2¾ o'clock. There are three of these immense reservoirs, lying one above another in the sloping valley, and bearing every mark of high antiquity. A small aqueduct is carried from them along the sides of the hills to Bethlehem and Jerusalem. Their name in Arabic is el-Burak. Close by is a large square Saracenic fortress, called Kŭl'at el-Burak; which seemed now to be inhabited only by the keeper of the pools.[1]

We stopped for half an hour, and took a hasty survey of the reservoirs; but as we afterwards visited them again and examined them more at leisure, I defer the description of them for the present.[2] A road passes from hence to Bethlehem along the aqueduct; but as we wished to press forward, we took one more direct, which leads obliquely up the gentle ascent north of the pools; setting off at a quarter past three o'clock. The path passes afterwards over a level, but exceedingly rocky tract, and was difficult for the camels. Our road lay nearly half a mile to the left of Bethlehem, which we saw from a distance; but it was afterwards hidden from us by the intervening hill. The Arab name is Beit Lahm. On our left was the head of a valley, running at first parallel to our course, and then bending to the northwest around a hill on the left, towards the Mediterranean. It is here called Wady Ahmed. On the eastern slope of this hill, over against Bethlehem, lies the large village of Beit Jâla, inhabited like Bethlehem by Christians, and surrounded by olive groves extending into the valley. At 4.10 we were opposite Bethlehem, between it and Beit Jâla. The road then passes along a low swell or ridge between Wady Ahmed on the left, and the head of a Wady on the right, which flows off north of Bethlehem to the Dead Sea.

Someways up the gentle acclivity, which here rises towards the northeast from Wady Ahmed, stands the Kubbet Râhil, or Rachel's Tomb, which we reached at 4.25. This is merely an ordinary Muslim Wely, or tomb of a holy person; a small square building of stone with a dome, and within it a tomb in the ordinary Muhammedan form; the whole plastered over with mortar. Of course the building is not ancient; in the seventh century there was here only a pyramid of stones.[3] It is now neglected, and falling to decay; though pilgrimages are still made to it by the Jews. The naked walls are covered with names in several languages; many of them in Hebrew. The general correctness

[1] In 1852 we again passed over this same road from the pools to Râmet el-Khŭlil; see under May 7, 1852.

[2] See under May 8th.

[3] Adamnanus ex Arculfo, II. 7.—The present building had formerly open arches i. 321, 322.

on the four sides, which were walled up about a century ago. It seems to have been built before Edrisi's day; see Edrisi, p. 345, ed. Jaub. Comp. Cotov. Itin. p. 245. Pococke II. i. p. 39.

of the tradition which has fixed upon this spot for the tomb of Rachel, cannot well be drawn in question; since it is fully supported by the circumstances of the Scriptural narrative. It is also mentioned by the *Itin. Hieros.* A. D. 333, and by Jerome in the same century.[1]

Still ascending the hill towards the Greek convent of Mâr Elyâs, the road passes to the left around the head of a deep valley running off eastward to the Dead Sea; and affords a wide view out over the mountainous regions towards and beyond that sea, including Bethlehem and the Frank mountain. The deep basin of the sea could also be in part made out; but its waters were not visible. Here we began to see traces of the pilgrims now collected in Jerusalem at the festival of Easter. A large number of their horses were feeding on this spot, guarded at the moment only by a single man. The animals were sleek and in good case; and had no appearance of having made a long journey. The same night, as we afterwards learned, the keepers were attacked by robbers; one man was killed; another wounded; and some of the horses driven off.

At 4.55 we came opposite the convent of Mâr Elyâs, which lies on the brow of the high ridge, overlooking Bethlehem and the deep valley around which we had just passed; while towards the north the descent is small, and the waters run again towards the Mediterranean. Here we got our first view of a portion of the Holy City,—the mosk and other high buildings standing on Mount Zion without the walls. As we advanced we had on the right low hills; and on the left the cultivated valley or plain of Rephaim or the Giants, with gentle hills beyond. This plain is broad, and descends gradually towards the southwest until it contracts in that direction into a deeper and narrower valley, called lower down Wady el-Werd, which unites further on with Wady Ahmed, and finds its way to the western plain.[2] Along this plain we met many people, mostly Christians, men, women and children, returning from Jerusalem. It was now the eve of Easter Sunday; and the miracle of the Greek holy fire had just been performed. They were dressed in their best attire, and seemed light-hearted and gay.

The plain of Rephaim extends nearly to the city; which, as seen from it, appears to be almost on the same level. As we advanced, the plain was terminated by a slight rocky ridge, forming the brow of the valley of Hinnom. This deep and narrow dell, with steep rocky sides, often precipitous, here comes down from

[1] Gen. 35, 16–20. Hieron. Epist. lxxxvi. ad Eustoch. Epitaph. Paulæ, Opp. Tom. IV. ii. p. 674. ed. Mart.—See more in Biblioth. Sacra, 1844, p. 602 sq.

[2] Josephus says expressly, that the val-ley of the Giants (Rephaim) was near Jerusalem, and extended towards Bethlehem; Antiq. 7. 4. 1. ib. 7. 12. 4. See also Josh. 15, 8. 18, 16. 2 Sam. 5, 18. 22. 23, 13. 14.

i. 323, 324

the north from as far as the Yâfa gate; and sweeping around
Mount Zion at almost a right angle, descends with great rapidity
into the very deep valley of Jehoshaphat. The southern side of
Zion is very steep, though not precipitous; while the great depth
of the valley of Jehoshaphat struck me with surprise. We
crossed the valley of Hinnom opposite the southwest corner of
Zion; and passed up along the eastern side of the valley to the
Hebron or Yâfa gate. On our left was the lower pool, an immense reservoir now broken down and dry. Above this the
aqueduct from Solomon's pools curves across the valley on very
low arches. At length, at 6 o'clock, we entered the Holy City,
el-Kuds, just at the closing of the gates on the evening before
Easter Sunday; and found a welcome home in the houses of our
missionary friends and countrymen.

This was the most fatiguing day of our whole journey. We
had been for sixteen hours almost constantly upon our camels;
yet the exhaustion arose more from want of rest and sleep, than
from any great exertion.—The distance between Hebron and
Jerusalem is definitely given by Eusebius and Jerome at twenty-
two Roman miles; equivalent to about seventeen and a half
geographical miles. Our time between the two cities was eight
and a quarter hours with camels; affording a coincidence sufficiently exact.

i. 324, 325

SECTION VI.

JERUSALEM.

INCIDENTS AND FIRST IMPRESSIONS.

THE feelings of a Christian traveller on approaching Jerusalem, can be better conceived than described. Mine were strongly excited. Before us, as we drew near, lay Zion, the mount of Olives, the vales of Hinnom and Jehoshaphat, and other objects of the deepest interest ; while, crowning the summits of the same ancient hills, was spread out the city where God of old had dwelt, and where the Saviour of the world had lived and taught and died. From the earliest childhood I had read of and studied the localities of this sacred spot ; now I beheld them with my own eyes ; and they all seemed familiar to me, as if the realization of a former dream. I seemed to be again among cherished scenes of childhood, long unvisited, indeed, but distinctly recollected ; and it was almost a painful interruption, when my companion (who had been here before) began to point out and name the various objects in view.

At length " our feet stand within thy gates, O Jerusalem ! —Peace be within thy walls and prosperity within thy palaces !" We entered the Yâfa gate, passed the small open place within, and descended the steep and narrow way along the head of the ancient Tyropœon, or valley of the Cheesemakers, until we came to the first street leading north below the pool of Hezekiah. In this street, nearly against the middle of the pool, was the residence of the Rev. Mr Whiting, where we stopped for a few moments, while our camels were unloaded and dismissed. Thence proceeding a little further north, we crossed down through the court of the church of the Holy Sepulchre to the next parallel street ; and turning to the left a few steps we en-

tered the first right-hand lane, and found ourselves after two or
three doors at the dwelling of the Rev. Mr Lanneau. Here a
home was already prepared for us ; where we remained during
our sojourn in the city. Both these gentlemen were our countrymen ; and had already been established in the Holy City as
missionaries for several years. The house of the latter was one
of the better class ; it was large, with marble floors, and had on
one side an extensive and pleasant garden, with orange and other
fruit trees and many flowers. It furnished indeed one of the
most desirable and healthful residences in the city. Yet the
rent was less than fifty Spanish dollars a year.

In the houses of our friends, we found collected all the members of the Syrian mission, with a single exception, from the
stations at Beirût and in Cyprus ; and one also from the mission
at Constantinople.[1] They had come up with their families, like
the Hebrews of old, at the time of the Passover, to worship in
this place, and to consult together on the best measures for promoting the great work in which they were engaged. Among the
eight missionaries thus assembled, it was with feelings of no ordinary gratification, that I could welcome five as former friends
and pupils. In those days of former intercourse, we had never
thought thus to see each other on earth upon Mount Zion ; and
so much the more deeply did we all now feel and prize the high
privilege of meeting on this sacred spot, where we might again
" take sweet counsel together, and walk unto the house of God
in company."

I have already remarked, that as we crossed the valley of
Hinnom, I was particularly struck with its rapid descent, and
the great depth of the vale of Jehoshaphat or the Kidron, into
which it opens. In the city itself, the steepness of the streets
which descend towards the east was greater than I had anticipated. But on entering the gates of Jerusalem, apart from the
overpowering recollections which naturally rush upon the mind,
I was in many respects agreeably disappointed. From the descriptions of Chateaubriand and other travellers, I had expected
to find the houses of the city miserable, the streets filthy, and
the population squalid. Yet the first impression made upon my
mind was of a different character ; nor did I afterwards see any
reason to doubt the correctness of this first impression. The
houses are in general better built, and the streets cleaner, than
those of Alexandria, Smyrna, or even Constantinople. Indeed,
of all the oriental cities which it was my lot to visit, Jerusalem,
after Cairo, is the cleanest and most solidly built. The streets
indeed are narrow, and very rudely paved ; like those of all cities

---

[1] I speak here of course only of mis- of Commissioners for Foreign Missions,
sionaries sent out by the American Board which has its central offices in Boston.
    i. 327, 328

in the east. The houses are of hewn stone, often large, and furnished with the small domes upon the roofs, which have been already mentioned at Hebron, as perhaps peculiar to the district of Judea. These domes seem to be not merely for ornament; but are intended, on account of the scarcity of timber, to aid in supporting and strengthening the otherwise flat roofs. There is usually one or more over each room in a house; and they serve also to give a greater elevation and an architectural effect to the ceiling of the room, which rises within them. The streets and the population that throngs them, may also well bear comparison with those of any other oriental city; although if one seeks here, or elsewhere in the east, for the general cleanliness and thrift which characterize many cities of Europe and America, he will of course seek in vain.

Sunday, April 15th. This was the Christian Sabbath, and it was also Easter Sunday. It was in a special manner a "great day" in Jerusalem, inasmuch as the Easter of the Romish and that of the Oriental churches, which usually occur on different days, fell together for the present year. During Easter week, the city had been thronged, though not very fully, with pilgrims. These were mostly Greeks and Armenians; very few Latins were seen; and only now and then a straggling Copt. The whole number had been less than usual. The annual excursion to the Jordan had been made, in which some of our friends had joined; and the annual mockery of the Greek holy fire had taken place just before we entered the city. The Latins too had enacted their mummery, representing the scenes of the crucifixion. In consequence of our late arrival, we thus missed all the incidents of the holy week. This however we counted as no loss, but rather a gain; for the object of our visit was the city itself, in relation to its ancient renown and religious associations; not as seen in its present state of decay and superstitions or fraudful degradation. The Jews were celebrating their passover; and our friends had received a present of some of their unleavened bread. It was spread out into very thin sheets, almost like paper, very white, and also very delicate and palatable. Thus to all the inhabitants, except to the Muhammedans; and to all the strangers who were present, save the few Protestants; this was the greatest festival of the year.

The different sects of Christians who have possession of the church of the Holy Sepulchre, had of course been compelled to alternate in their occupancy of it, and in the performance of their religious ceremonies. On this last "high day" of the festival, the Greeks held their grand mass at the sepulchre before break of day; and the Latins followed at 9 o'clock. I looked in for a few moments, with a friend, upon this latter

i. 328–330

ceremonial. Few persons were present, except those engaged in the service. These few were all below in the body of the church; in the galleries there were no spectators. The reputed sepulchre, as is well known, stands in the middle of the spacious rotunda, directly beneath the centre of the great dome, which is open to the sky. The high altar was placed directly before the door of the sepulchre; so that we could not enter the latter. The ceremonies we saw consisted only in a procession of the monks and others marching around the sepulchre; stopping occasionally to read a portion of the Gospel; and then again advancing with chanting and singing. I was struck with the splendour of their robes, stiff with embroidery of silver and gold, the well meant offerings probably of Roman Catholics out of every country of Europe; but I was not less struck with the vulgar and unmeaning visages that peered out from these costly vestments. The wearers looked more like ordinary ruffians, than like ministers of the cross of Christ. Indeed there is reason to believe, that the Latin monks in Palestine are actually for the most part ignorant and often illiterate men, chiefly from Spain, the refuse of her monks and clergy, who come or are sent hither as into a sort of exile, where they serve to excite the sympathies and the misplaced charities of the Romanists of Europe. There was hardly a face among all those before us, that could be called intelligent. A few fine looking French naval officers, and one or two Irish Catholics, had joined the procession; but seemed quite out of place, and as if ashamed of their companions.

I make these remarks merely as relating a matter of fact; and not, I trust, out of any spirit of prejudice against the Romish church or her clergy. I had once spent the holy week in Rome itself; and there admired the intelligent and noble countenances of many of the clergy and monks congregated in that city. For this very reason the present contrast struck me the more forcibly and disagreeably. The whole scene indeed was to a Protestant painful and revolting. It might perhaps have been less so, had there been manifested the slightest degree of faith in the genuineness of the surrounding objects; but even the monks themselves do not pretend, that the present sepulchre is any thing more than an imitation of the original. But to be in the ancient city of the Most High, and to see these venerated places and the very name of our holy religion profaned by idle and lying mummeries; while the proud Mussulman looks on with haughty scorn; all this excited in my mind a feeling too painful to be borne; and I never visited the place again.

We now repaired to the house of Mr Whiting; where in a large upper room our friends had long established regular divine

i. 330, 331

service in English every Sunday; in which they were assisted by Mr Nicolayson, the able missionary of the English church, sent out hither by the London Missionary Society for the Jews. We found a very respectable congregation, composed of all the missionary families, besides several European travellers of rank and name.   It was, I presume, the largest Protestant congregation ever collected within the walls of the Holy City; and it was gratifying to see Protestants of various names here laying aside all distinctions, and uniting with one heart to declare by their example in Jerusalem itself, that "God is a Spirit; and they that worship him, must worship him in spirit and in truth." [1] The simplicity and spirituality of the Protestant worship was to me affecting and doubly pleasing, in contrast with the pageant of which we had just been spectators.

Early in the afternoon we were also present at the service in Arabic, which the same missionaries had established in the house of Mr Lanneau, and which was then regularly attended by some twenty or thirty Arab Christians of the Greek rite. [2] These were men of respectable appearance, merchants and others; and seemed to yield attention to the things which they heard.

It may not be out of place here to remark, that the object of the American missions to Syria and other parts of the Levant, was not to draw off members of the Oriental churches to Protestantism; but to awaken them to a knowledge and belief of the Gospel truth, in the purity and simplicity of its original scriptural form.   To this end all the efforts of the missionaries were directed; in the hope, that individuals thus enlightened, and remaining, if they chose, within the pale of their own churches, might by degrees become instrumental in infusing into the latter life and vigour and a love of the truth, before which the various forms of error and superstition would of themselves vanish away.   The missionaries would seem thus to have taken the proper course, in going forward simply as preachers of the Gospel, and not as the direct assailants of specific errors; striving to overcome darkness by diffusing light, and not by denouncing it as gross darkness.   True, in this way they would make less noise; for the mere presentation of truth excites less opposition than the calling in question of long cherished error; but, with the blessing of God, they would be likely to reap a more abundant harvest, and exert a larger and more lasting influence in the moral regeneration of the east.   At this time the Protestant movement which has since spread so widely had not yet begun.

[1] John 4, 24.

[2] The great body of the Christians in Palestine are of the Greek church; but they are all native Arabs, and employ only the Arabic language in their worship.

i. 331–333

Towards evening, the families again came together in a less formal manner for an hour of prayer and religious exhortation. These various exercises, with others occasionally upon other days, were regularly kept up by the missionaries whenever circumstances permitted. So long as we remained in the city, they were continued without interruption; but subsequently, the occurrence of the plague broke up all regularity; and other circumstances conspired to suspend wholly, for a time, the labours of the American mission in Jerusalem.[1]

Monday, April 16th. After our long banishment in the desert, I had now of course many letters to write, in order to inform my family and distant friends of our general welfare and safe arrival in the Holy City. Up to the time of our leaving Cairo, there had been no difficulty in despatching letters when we pleased; as the various lines of French and Austrian steamers had already rendered intercourse with the west as direct and frequent, as between different parts of Europe itself. But these facilities had not yet been extended to Syria. The English steamer from Malta to Alexandria came indeed once a month from the latter place to Beirût for a few hours; and this was the only regular mode of sending off letters from Jerusalem to Europe, in connection with a weekly private post, which had just been established to Beirût. The Pasha's line of posts from Cairo to Damascus and Aleppo passed through Gaza and Yâfa, without communicating with Jerusalem. Of this we were able to avail ourselves by transmitting letters to our consular agent at Yâfa, who could thence forward them under cover to the consuls in Cairo and Alexandria. I did this also once in Gaza; and once an opportunity occurred, of sending by a government express direct from Jerusalem to Alexandria.

The general meeting of the missionaries was to be one of business, in which several important questions were to be considered and decided. They met this day for the first time; and continued their sessions, morning and afternoon, for about ten days. The time of my companion was necessarily chiefly occupied in these meetings. For myself, I had enough to do at first in the writing of letters and the arrangement of my journals; to say nothing of the reading necessary to prepare upon the spot for a close examination of Jerusalem itself, and for our future excursions into the country round about. I took great pleasure also in attending the meetings of the missionaries, so far as time and circumstances permitted. It was truly gratifying to observe the

---

[1] Mr and Mrs Whiting were compelled a few months later to return for a time to the United States, in consequence of her declining health. Mr Lanneau was driven by a severe affection of the eyes to Beirût for medical advice, where he remained during the subsequent winter. The mission was afterwards re-established, but has since been wholly withdrawn. Mr Lanneau has returned to the United States.

i. 333, 334

spirit of love and harmony by which they were all actuated. On many points, it was hardly to be expected that there should not at first be diversity of opinion; but there was manifestly a strong desire and endeavour, by ripe deliberation and mutual concession, to arrive in every case at some conclusion in which all might cordially unite. The results to which they came, were I believe in every instance unanimous; and the influence of this meeting and of these deliberations, in strengthening among them the bonds of mutual affection and respect, (if I may judge from my own feelings,) will not soon pass away.

Under the influence of such feelings and impressions, the evening of the following Christian Sabbath was devoted to the celebration of the holy sacrament of the Lord's Supper. In the "large upper room" of Mr Whiting's house, where "prayer was wont to be made," eleven sojourners in the Holy City, all Protestant ministers of the Gospel, and ten of them from the new world, sat down in company with several female friends and others, to celebrate the dying love of the Redeemer, near the spot where the ordinance was first instituted. The occasion, the thrilling recollections which it called up in connection with the city and the mount of Olives which lay before us; the unexpected coincidences of time, place, and number; all these were deeply impressive, and stamped upon this hour a character of sacredness and profound emotion, that can never be forgotten. In my own case, the thought that this was the one only time of my life, that I could hope to enjoy this high privilege, was inexpressibly solemn.

_____

In occupations and enjoyments like these, there was enough to fill up usefully and agreeably all my time, had I been so disposed. But I had other duties. The object of my journey to Jerusalem was not to visit friends, nor to inquire into the character of the present population, nor to investigate their political or moral state, except as incidental points. My one great object was the city itself, in its topographical and historical relations, its site, its hills, its dales, its remains of antiquity, the traces of its ancient population; in short, every thing connected with it that could have a bearing upon the illustration of the Scriptures. In all these respects, our friends, who had been long upon the ground, were ready and desirous to lend a helping hand; and although they were much occupied with the business before them, yet we often found time at morning or evening, and occasionally during the day, to take frequent and sometimes long walks through the more interesting portions of the city and its environs. Time and again we visited the more important spots, and repeated our observations; comparing meanwhile what we

i. 334–336

had seen ourselves with the accounts of ancient writers and former travellers, until at length conjectures or opinions were ripened into conviction or gradually abandoned. Our motto was in the words, though not exactly in the sense of the apostle: "Prove all things; hold fast that which is good." During the same interval, I also took many measurements both within and around the city.

These repeated examinations of the same objects gave henceforth to our researches in Jerusalem a more desultory character; which renders it difficult, or at least not advisable, to record them any further in the form of a journal. It will therefore be my endeavour, after describing a few of our most interesting walks in and around Jerusalem, and some of the incidents of our residence there, to bring together in another Section the results of our researches relative to the topography and antiquities of the city, interweaving so far as may be necessary the slighter incidents personal to ourselves; thus presenting a general description of the place and its environs. In this way, and with the aid of the accompanying Plan, the reader will be best able to follow out our researches; and judge for himself of the grounds on which our conclusions rest.

In these walks, our main object was, not so much to investigate, as to obtain a general impression of the city and its environs, in order to prepare the way for more particular examination at another time. I describe them here with the same intent, and in order to impart the same general impression to the reader; reserving a more detailed account of the various objects, and the questions as to their identity, to the subsequent pages.

ZION, SILOAM, ETC.

Our first walk was on Tuesday, April 17th, after having dined with our friend Mr Nicolayson, at his house near the Jews' quarter on the northern part of Zion. Towards evening, our host, Mr Smith, and myself, went out of the city by the Yâfa gate, and turning to the left descended the slope along the side of the deep trench which here skirts the castle. This brought us to the bottom of the valley of Hinnom, along which leads for a time the road to Bethlehem by which we had approached on Saturday. Another path quits this almost immediately towards the left, and begins to ascend obliquely the slope of Zion towards the southwest corner of the city wall, which lies high above the valley. Reaching this latter point, we came out upon the high level part of Zion, not included in the modern city. It is mostly an open tract, in some parts tilled, with a few scattered buildings. The chief of these are the

i. 336, 337

House of Caiphas, so called, now an Armenian convent; and the Muslim tomb of David with a mosk. A few enclosures of stone walls are seen round about these buildings and in other parts. But what chiefly attracted our attention now, was the Christian cemeteries, all of which lie upon this open place; first that of the Armenians, nearest to their great convent in the southwest corner of the city; south of this, that of the Greeks; and more to the eastward that of the Latins. The graves in these cemeteries are simply marked (if marked at all) by a flat stone laid upon them with an inscription.

In the Latin quarter one inscription struck my eye particularly; it contained the name of my own country, and marked the grave of a young American. Ten years ago I had known him in Paris in the flower of his youth, a favourite in the family of Lafayette, and moving in the gay circles of that gay metropolis. He had soon after wandered off to Egypt and the east; and in 1830 died here alone and friendless in the Latin convent. The epitaph with which the monks have honoured him, declares, that "of his own accord he abjured the errors of Luther and Calvin, and professed the Catholic religion." Poor youth! he knew too little of the doctrines of the Reformers, and still less of those of the Romish church. No friend was near to watch over his last moments; and the strongest inference that can be drawn from the above language is, that in order to be left in quiet he gave assent to all their questions. Or, not improbably, the assertion may rest merely on the fact, that in his dying hour, when consciousness perhaps was gone, they administered to him extreme unction. The stone purports to have been placed by "weeping friends,"—rejoicing Catholics of course; for no others could have put an inscription like the following over his grave:

D. O. M.

HIC JACET

C. B. EX AMERICÆ REGIONIBUS,

Lugduni Galliæ Consul, Hierosolymis tactus intrinsecus sponte

Erroribus Lutheri et Calvini abjectis

Catholicam religionem professus, synanche correptus,

E vita decessit IV nonas Augusti MDCCCXXX,

Ætatis suæ

XXV.

Amici mœrentes posuere.

Orate pro eo.

Near by is the grave of another Frank, whose death took place under circumstances of peculiar interest. I mean that of Costigan, the Irish traveller, who died in 1835 in consequence of his romantic though rash attempt to explore the Dead Sea in an open boat in the middle of July. He had contrived to have a small boat carried over on camels from the shore of the Mediterranean to the lake of Tiberias ; and thence followed the Jordan down to the Dead Sea. Here he launched forth alone with his Maltese servant upon these waters, and succeeded in reaching the southern extremity ; but by some mismanagement they were left for two or three days without fresh water, exposed to the fierce rays of a cloudless sun, and compelled to row hard to get back to the northern end. After reaching the shore they lay for a whole day, too weak to move, and trying to regain strength by laving each other with the heavy waters of the lake. At length the servant made shift to crawl up to Jericho, where Costigan had left his horse ; which was immediately sent to him with a supply of water. He was brought to the village ; and the next morning despatched a messenger on his own horse to Mr Nicolayson, requesting medicine and expressing fears of his case. This gentleman immediately set off to visit him ; and reached him at 2 o'clock on Thursday morning. He found him very ill, with a high intermittent fever. As there could be no hope of his recovery at Jericho, Mr N. tried every means to get persons to carry him to Jerusalem in a litter ; but without success. The only way of removing him, was to sling a large sack of straw on each side of a horse, and then place his bed upon the horse's back. In this way the sufferer was brought to the city with great difficulty ; leaving Jericho on Friday evening, and reaching Jerusalem at 8 o'clock the next morning. The journey exhausted him much ; no medicine could be brought to operate ; and he died on Monday morning in the Latin convent, where he had a room. No notes, nor any account of his voyage, were found among his papers. These circumstances were related to us by Mr Nicolayson, as we stood around his grave.[1]

A little to the southward of the Latin cemetery, and adjacent to the northwestern enclosures connected with the mosk and tomb of David, is a small plat of ground, which has been purchased by the American missionaries as a place of burial for their dead. To this measure they were driven almost by necessity. Two of their members, Mrs Thomson and Dr Dodge, had already died in Jerusalem. For the former a grave was sought and obtained without difficulty in the cemetery of the Greeks. In the case of the latter, the same permission was granted, and a grave dug ; but as they were about to proceed to the burial, word was brought, that the permission had been recalled and the grave filled up. On a strong representation of the case to the heads of the Greek convent, the burial was allowed to take place, with

---

[1] Mr Stephens saw the servant of Costigan at Beirût, and endeavoured to extract from him information as to the voyage ; but all that he obtained is confused and of little value. The sketch of the Dead i. 339, 340 Sea which Mr S. added from this report, lies before me as I write ; it has little resemblance to that sea, except in being longer than it is broad. Incidents of Travel, Vol. II.

the express understanding, that a like permission would never more be given. In consequence, the missionaries purchased this little spot upon Mount Zion, and enclosed it with a common wall of stone. The plat contains two or three olive trees, and looked green and peaceful; but it was yet untenanted. After the purchase had been made and possession delivered, the authorities of the city hesitated to give it the last legal sanction. They did not object to the transaction itself; but as they wanted a bribe of some fifty dollars in their own pockets, they professed to entertain scruples, whether it was fitting that Christian corpses should be buried so near the sacred tomb of David. The matter had not at that time been brought to a close; and until this was done, the missionaries did not choose to transfer thither the relics of their friends. I have since learned, that during the last year (1840) the Mission caused a permanent wall to be erected around the plat, with a door under lock and key; and shortly afterwards, on the death of a child of Mr Nicolayson, the body was interred with all due formalities within the precincts. All this was done without opposition on the part of the authorities; and as such matters are here usually settled by full possession and prescription, no further difficulty was apprehended.

From the cemeteries we proceeded eastward along the southern wall of the city; passing by the Zion gate, and then descending along the slope towards the valley of the Tyropœon or Cheesemakers. A path soon leaves the wall and leads obliquely down the slope southeast in the direction of Siloam. In this part it becomes steep; and the Tyropœon, as it comes down from the wall near the great mosk, is also steep, and forms a deep ravine with banks almost precipitous. At its lower end it turns east and issues into the vale of the Kidron.

Here, still within the Tyropœon, is the pool of Siloam, a small deep reservoir in the form of a parallelogram, into which the water flows from under the rocks, out of a smaller basin hewn in the solid rock a few feet further up; to which is a descent by a few steps. This is wholly an artificial work; and the water comes to it through a subterraneous channel from the fountain of Mary, so called, higher up in the valley of Jehoshaphat. The hill or ridge Ophel lying between the Tyropœon and the valley of Jehoshaphat, ends here, just over the pool of Siloam, in a steep point of rock forty or fifty feet high. Along the base of this the water is conducted from the pool in a small channel hewn in the rocky bottom; and is then led off to irrigate gardens of fig and other fruit trees and plants, lying in terraces quite down to the bottom of the valley of Jehoshaphat; a descent still of some forty or fifty feet. The waters of Siloam, as we saw them, were lost in these gardens. On the right, just

i. 340–342

below the pool, and opposite the point of Ophel, is a large mulberry tree, with a terrace of stones surrounding its trunk, where they say Isaiah was sawn asunder. Here are also traces of a former larger reservoir.

We now passed along up the valley of Jehoshaphat, which is here narrow and the sides high and steep. On our right, clinging to the rocky side of the mount of Offence, so called, are the stone hovels of the straggling village of Siloam, Kefr Selwân, many of which are built before caves or rather excavated sepulchres; while in various places the sepulchres themselves, without addition, are used as dwellings. A little further up the valley, under the western hill, is the fountain of the Virgin,[1] a deep excavation in the solid rock, evidently artificial, into which one descends by two successive flights of steps. The water is apparently brought hither by some unknown and perhaps artificial channel; and flows off through a subterraneous passage under the hill Ophel to the pool of Siloam. At a later period we crawled through the whole length of this passage. We drank of the water, and remarked a peculiar though not unpleasant taste. We had been told that the people did not use it for drinking; but we found here, as at Siloam, women filling their water skins, which like Hagar they bore off on their shoulders. They said they used it now for drinking; but when in summer the water becomes lower, it is then not good and has a brackish taste.

Above this fountain the valley becomes very narrow. It is everywhere only a water-course between high hills; and the brook Kidron now never flows, and probably never flowed along its bottom, except after heavy rains.

From the fountain a path ascends obliquely, but steeply, to the southeast corner of the area of the great mosk. This forms at the same time the extreme southeast corner of the city wall, and stands directly on the brow of the almost precipitous side of the valley, here about one hundred and fifty feet deep. Further north the brow juts out a little more, leaving a narrow strip of level ground outside of the wall, which is occupied as a Muhammedan cemetery. The tombs are here thickly crowded together; and frequently, as we passed this way afterwards, there was a stench arising apparently from corpses mouldering in their shallow graves. The Muhammedans prefer this cemetery to all the others, as being very near to the great mosk.[2]

The lower part of this wall in several places is composed of very large hewn stones, which at once strike the eye of the be-

---

[1] Called by some travellers the *fountain* of Siloam in distinction from the *pool* of Siloam below; but without any good reason. i. 342, 343

[2] Hist. of Jerus. in Fundgr. des Or. II. p. 134.

holder as ancient, as being at least as old as the time of Herod, if not of Solomon. The upper part of the wall is everywhere obviously modern; as is the whole wall in many places. The Golden gate, which once led out from the area of the mosk upon this side, is now walled up. Near the northeast corner of this area, towards St. Stephen's gate, we measured one of the large stones in the wall, and found it twenty-four feet long, by six feet broad and three feet high. Just north of the same gate is a small tank or reservoir on the outside; and within the gate, on the left hand, is the very large and deep reservoir, to which the name of Bethesda is commonly given, though probably without good reason. It is entirely dry; and large trees grow at the bottom, the tops of which do not reach the level of the street. North of this, a little to the right of the street, is the dilapidated church of St. Anne, over the grotto which is shown as the birthplace of the Virgin. The church has pointed arches; and was obviously the work of the crusaders.[1]

We now returned home along the *Via dolorosa;* in which monkish tradition has brought together the scenes of all the events, historical or legendary, connected with the crucifixion.[2] Along this way, they say, our Saviour bore his cross. Here one may see, if he pleases, the place where the Saviour, fainting under his burden, leaned against the wall of a house; and the impression of his shoulder remains unto this day. Near by are also pointed out the houses of the rich man and Lazarus in the parable. To judge from present appearances the beggar was quite as well lodged as his opulent neighbour. But enough of these absurdities!

GETHSEMANE, THE MOUNT OF OLIVES, ETC.

The forenoon of the next day, Wednesday, April 18th, taking our servant Ibrahim, I went alone with him out of the Yâfa gate, and keeping to the right passed around the northwest corner of the city wall, where stands a terebinth or Butm tree of considerable size; and then descended to the Damascus gate. Here I struck out to the left through the open field to the grotto of Jeremiah, so called by the monks. It lies under a round isolated

---

[1] William of Tyre mentions on this spot the house of Anna, as a place where three or four poor women had consecrated themselves to a monastic life. About A. D. 1113, King Baldwin I. compelled his Armenian wife to take the veil in this convent; which at the same time he richly endowed. Will. Tyr. 11. 1. Wilken Gesch. der Kreuzz. II. p. 397. According to Jac. de Vitriaco, this was called the Abbey of St. Anne, and was inhabited by an Abbess and Black nuns, i. e. of the Benedictine order; Hist. Hieros. 58. p. 1078.—Sæwulf in 1102-3 already speaks of a church here; p. 264. Wright's Early Travels in Palest. p. 41.

[2] The earliest allusion I have been able to find to the *Via dolorosa*, is in Marinus Sanutus in the fourteenth century; de Secret. fid. Cruc. 3. 14. 10.

rocky hill, the south side of which has apparently been cut away to an irregular face, under which is the entrance to the grotto. In front is a small garden walled in; but the door was closed, so that I could not gain access to the cavern itself; nor were we more successful at a subsequent visit. The top of the hill is occupied as a Muslim cemetery.[1] The southern front of this hill stands overagainst the precipitous northern side of Bezetha, crowned by the city wall; and one might almost imagine that the two hills once formed one ridge, of which the intervening portion had been cut away by art.

Returning to the path, I kept along the city wall towards the east. Before reaching the northeast corner of the city, there is near the wall, or indeed in the trench, a small reservoir for water, still in use. Passing down the steep hill from St. Stephen's gate into the valley of the Kidron, and crossing the bridge over the dry water-course, one has on the left the half subterranean church of the Virgin Mary, with an excavated grotto or chapel called her tomb. Before the low building is a small sunken court; from which there is a descent by many steps into the church. The earliest notice of this tomb and church is in the seventh century; and it is also mentioned by the historians of the crusades.[2]

Near the same bridge and church, on the right, is the place fixed on by early tradition as the site of the garden of Gethsemane. It is a plat of ground nearly square, enclosed by an ordinary stone wall. The northwest corner is one hundred and forty-five feet distant from the bridge. The west side measures one hundred and sixty feet in length; and the north side one hundred and fifty feet. Within this enclosure are eight very old olive trees, with stones thrown together around their trunks.[3] There is nothing peculiar in this plat to mark it as Gethsemane; for adjacent to it are other similar enclosures, and many olive trees equally old. The spot was not improbably fixed upon dur-

---

[1] Prokesch describes the interior of this grotto as nearly round, some forty paces in diameter, perhaps 30 feet high in the middle, and supported by two massive pillars. It is inhabited by a Muslim saint, who sells places for graves in the grotto and in the garden before it, while above are also graves; Reise ins heil. Land, p. 95. The place was in much the same state early in the sixteenth century; see Hist. of Jerusalem in Fundgr. des Orients, II. p. 133.

[2] First by Adamnanus ex Arculfo (I. 13) about A. D. 697; then by St. Willibald about A. D. 765. Also by Will. Tyr. 8. 2. Brocardus. c. 8. Mar. Sanut. 3. 14. 9.—Monkish tradition almost as a matter
i. 345, 346

of course now refers the building of this church to Helena; though Marinus Sanutus (and apparently Brocardus) gravely supposes it to have existed before the destruction of the city by Adrian, and to have been thus deeply covered over by the ruins then thrown down into the valley; de Secret. fid. l. c. But Nicephorus Callistus in the same (fourteenth) century, already ascribes it to Helena; lib. VIII. c. 30.—Arabian writers call this church el-Jesmâniyeh, i. e. Gethsemane; and so the natives at the present day. Edrisi par Jaubert, p. 344. Hist. of Jerus. in Fundgr. des Orient. II. p. 132.

[3] In 1852 we found this plot enclosed by a high wall.

ing the visit of Helena to Jerusalem, A. D. 326 ; when the places of the crucifixion and resurrection were supposed to be identified. Before that time no such tradition is alluded to. Eusebius, writing apparently a few years afterwards, says Gethsemane was *at* the Mount of Olives, and was then a place of prayer for the faithful.[1] Sixty years or more afterwards, Jerome places it at the foot of the mountain, and says a church had been built over it ; which is also mentioned by Theophanes as existing near the end of the seventh century.[2] The garden is likewise spoken of by Antoninus Martyr at the end of the sixth century, by Adamnanus, and by writers of the times of the crusades.[3] There would seem therefore little reason to doubt, that the present site is the same to which Eusebius alludes. Whether it is the true site, is perhaps a matter of more question.[4]

Giving myself up to the impressions of the moment, I sat down here for a time alone beneath one of the aged trees. All was silent and solitary around ; only a herd of goats were feeding not far off, and a few flocks of sheep grazing on the side of the mountain. High above towered the dead walls of the city ; through which there penetrated no sound of human life. It was almost like the stillness and loneliness of the desert. Here, or at least not far off, the Saviour endured that "agony and bloody sweat," which was connected with the redemption of the world ; and here in deep submission he prayed : "O my father, if this cup may not pass away from me except I drink it, thy will be done !"[5]

From the bridge three paths lead up to the summit of the mount of Olives. One, a mere footpath, strikes up in a direct course along a steep projecting part of the hill ; a second passes up more circuitously to the left, where the hill retires a little and has a more gradual slope ; and the third winds up along the face further south. The sides of the mountain are still sprinkled with olive trees, though not thickly, as was probably the case of old ; and a few other trees are occasionally seen. I took the middle path, which brought me out at the church of the Ascension and the mosk, situated on the summit.[6] Around them are a few

[1] The *Itin. Hieros.* A. D. 333, mentions the "rock where Judas betrayed Christ" as being in the valley of Jehoshaphat.

[2] Eusebius et Hieron. Onomast. art. *Gethsemani.* Theophan. Chron. A. D. 683. Comp. Reland Pal. p. 857.—Cyrill of Jerus. also speaks of Gethsemane ; Catech. XIII. p. 140. ed. Oxon.

[3] Antonin. Mart. 17. Adamnanus ex Arculf. I. 13. Jac. de Vitr. Hist. Hierosol. 63. Brocardus, c. 8.

[4] According to the Evangelist John, Jesus "went forth over the brook Cedron,

where was a garden," 18, 1. 2. But Luke says he "went out *as he was wont* to the mount of Olives," 22, 39. This last passage, taken in connection with Luke 21, 37, where it is said that he taught in the day time in the temple, and at night went out and abode in the mount of Olives, may suggest a doubt, whether Gethsemane was not perhaps situated higher up on the mount of Olives.

[5] Matt. 26, 42.

[6] The various supposed sites of scriptural events, which the monks have fixed

huts, forming a miserable village. Here one is able to look down upon the city and survey at least the roofs of the houses. The view may be said indeed to be a very full one; but it is not particularly interesting. It presents a dull mixed mass of roofs and domes; but the distance is too great to be able to distinguish the buildings or the topography of the city in any good degree. A more pleasing view is obtained from various points lower down the side of the mountain.

From the church on the summit, only the city and the western prospect are visible; the eastern view being cut off by a higher part or ridge of the hill some twenty or thirty rods further east, with a Wely or tomb of a Muslim saint upon it. From this Wely one obtains a commanding view of the northern end and portion of the Dead Sea, and also of the adjacent country, including a large part of the valley of the Jordan, as well as the naked dreary region lying between Jerusalem and Jericho, and between Bethlehem and the Dead Sea. The course of the river Jordan could be traced by the narrow strip of verdure which clothes its banks. Beyond its valley, the eastern mountains stretch off northward and southward in a long even ridge, apparently unbroken. They present to the view, as here seen, no single peak or separate summit, which could be taken for the Nebo of the Scriptures. At a considerable distance north of Jericho, indeed, a loftier summit is seen, forming the highest point of the mountains of Gilead, just north of es-Salt; but this could not have been Nebo.

The atmosphere was at the time perfectly clear, and the waters of the Dead Sea lay bright and sparkling in the sunbeams, seemingly not more than eight or ten miles distant, though actually much further off. I unfortunately neglected to look for Kerak, which would doubtless have been visible in so clear a day. When we sought for it in a later visit, the haziness of the atmosphere prevented us from distinguishing it. Towards the west and northwest the view extends to the Terebinth valley so called, and the high point and mosk of Neby Samwil.

I returned down the mount by the more southern path; from which a branch led me across the Jewish cemetery to the tombs of Absalom and Zechariah so called, at the bottom of the valley, just under the southeast corner of the wall of the mosk and city. Here is the narrowest path of the valley. Close by the tombs is a well, which then had water, though it seemed not to be used; and here is also another bridge of stone over the

upon the side of the mount of Olives, may be seen in Maundrell, Prokesch (p. 80), and other travellers.—Edrisi speaks of a large church on the acclivity, called Pater Noster; p. 344, ed. Jaubert. This is probably the same mentioned by Sir J. Maundeville, as on or near the spot where Jesus taught his disciples the Lord's prayer; p. 96. Lond. 1839.

i. 348, 349

torrent bed with a fine arch. From this point a rugged footpath ascends towards St. Stephen's gate; entering which, I returned home by the *Via dolorosa*.

JEWS' PLACE OF WAILING, ETC.

In the afternoon of the same day, I went with Mr Lanneau to the place where the Jews are permitted to purchase the right of approaching the site of their temple, and of praying and wailing over its ruins and the downfall of their nation. The spot is on the western exterior of the area of the great mosk, considerably south of the middle; and is approached only by a narrow crooked lane, which there terminates at the wall in a very small open place. The lower part of the wall is here composed of the same kind of ancient stones, which we had before seen on the eastern side. Two old men, Jews, sat there upon the ground, reading together in a book of Hebrew prayers. On Fridays they assemble here in greater numbers. It is the nearest point in which they can venture to approach their ancient temple; and fortunately for them, it is sheltered from observation by the narrowness of the lane and the dead walls around. Here, bowed in the dust, they may at least weep undisturbed over the fallen glory of their race; and bedew with their tears the soil, which so many thousands of their forefathers once moistened with their blood.

This touching custom of the Jews is not of modern origin. Benjamin of Tudela mentions it, as connected apparently with the same spot, in the twelfth century; and very probably the custom has come down from still earlier ages.[1] After the capture of Jerusalem under Adrian, the Jews were excluded from the city; and it was not till the age of Constantine that they were permitted to approach, so as to behold Jerusalem from the neighbouring hills.[2] At length they were allowed to enter the city once a year, on the day on which it was taken by Titus, in order to wail over the ruins of the temple. But this privilege they were obliged to purchase of the Roman soldiers.[3]—According to Benjamin, as above cited, the Jews in his day regarded this portion of the wall as having belonged to the court of the ancient temple.

---

[1] Benj. of Tud. by Asher, I. p. 70.

[2] Sulpic. Sev. Hist. Sacr. II. 45. Euseb. Chron.—Also Euseb. in Psalm. ed. Montfauc. p. 267, 382. Hilar. in Psalm. 58. No. 12. See Münter, der Jüdische Krieg unter Trajan und Hadrian, p. 97.

[3] Münter l. c. Hieron. in Zephan. c. i. 15, " Et, ut ruinam suæ eis flere liceat civitatis, pretio redimunt; ut qui quondam emerant sanguinem Christi, emant lacrymas suas. Et ne fletus quidem eis gratuitus sit; videas in die quo capta est a Romanis et diruta Jerusalem, venire populum lugubrem . . . . . plangere ruinas templi sui; et miles mercedem postulat, ut illis flere plus liceat."—See also Gregor. Nazianz. Orat. XII. Valesii Annot. in Euseb. Hist. Ecc. IV. 6.

i. 349–351

Turning back somewhat from this spot, and threading our way through other narrow lanes with sharp corners, and then through a tract planted with the prickly pear, we came to the southwest corner of the area of the great mosk, where the wall is quite high. Around this corner is an open level plat of ground, which was now ploughed, extending to the city wall on the south. This latter, which here runs from west to east, is low on the inside, but high on the outside; forming a high offset between the level plat above and the open fields further south. Further east this wall turns north at a right angle and unites with the southern wall of the area of the mosk, about one third of the way between the southwest and the southeast corner. The stones in the lower part of the wall of the area at the southwest corner, are of immense size; and on the western side, at first view, some of them seem to have been started from their places, as if the wall had burst and was about to fall down. We paid little attention to this appearance at the time; but subsequent examination led here to one of our most interesting discoveries. South from this corner, in the city wall, and near the bed or channel of the Tyropœon, is a small gate now closed up. This the monks in their zeal to find an application for all scriptural names, have honoured (or dishonoured) with the name of the Dung gate; although neither the ancient gate of that name, nor the ancient wall, could have been anywhere in this vicinity.

The present city wall is built for the most part with a breastwork; that is, the exterior face is carried up several feet higher than the interior part of the wall, leaving a broad and convenient walk along the top of the latter for the accommodation of the defenders. This is protected by the parapet or breastwork, which has battlements and loopholes. There are also flights of steps to ascend or descend at convenient distances on the inside. Mounting upon the city wall in this manner near the area of the mosk, we kept along over the Dung gate so called, and up Mount Zion, passing a well with water on the way; and then descending from the wall near the gate of Zion, we returned home through the Jews' quarter on the northeast slope of the same hill.

UPPER POOL, GIHON, ETC.

In the afternoon of the following day, (Thursday, April 19th,) Messrs Smith and Nicolayson and myself took a short walk to look at the ground and objects west and northwest of the Yâfa gate, and along the road to Yâfa. We went first to the large tank lying in the basin which forms the head of the valley of Hinnom, or more properly perhaps of the valley of

i. 351, 352

Gihon; since this would seem to be the quarter to which that name of old belonged. The tank was now dry; but in the rainy season it becomes full; and its waters are then conducted by a small rude aqueduct or channel to the vicinity of the Yâfa gate, and so to the pool of Hezekiah within the city. The tract around this tank, especially towards the northeast, is occupied as a Muslim cemetery, the largest around the city. The tombs are scattered and old; some of the larger ones indeed have the appearance of great antiquity.

We returned across the higher ground on the north of this basin, towards the Damascus gate, in order to examine whether perhaps the valley of the Tyropœon extended up at all beyond the city in that direction. There is however no trace of any valley or of any depression in this quarter, before reaching the declivity stretching down to the Damascus gate. The whole interval between this gate and Gihon is occupied by a broad swell of land, rising somewhat higher than the northwest part of the city itself. The ground on the west, as well as on the north of the present city, would seem to have once been built over; or at least occasional buildings once stood upon it. Fragments of polished marble are often picked up here; and especially the small cubes of marble of different colours, not much larger than dice, which were employed in the construction of the ancient tesselated pavements.

We entered the city again by the gate of Yâfa or Hebron; and threading our way towards the left through several lanes, passed the Coptic convent, then rebuilding, at the northern end of the pool of Hezekiah. This latter still had water covering its bottom, though apparently not deep.

VALLEY OF HINNOM, WELL OF JOB, ETC.

Walking out alone one day, I passed over Mount Zion to its southern brow, and then descended its steep side without a path and with some difficulty, to the valley of Hinnom. The bottom of the valley has here more width and descends rapidly towards the east; further down it is narrower and has a still steeper descent. On the south the hill in many parts rises at first in rocky precipices, with other ledges of rocks higher up on the steep side; and these rocks and the whole face of the hill are full of excavated tombs. On the same hill-side, further east along the valley, is the Aceldama or Potter's Field, so called. The tombs continue quite down to the corner of the mountain, where it bends off southwards along the valley of Jehoshaphat.

My course was along the side of the hill among the tombs; and then descending near the junction of the two valleys, I came

i. 352–354

to the well of Nehemiah as the Franks call it, or the well of Job according to the natives. Neither name has apparently any good foundation. We shall afterwards see that this is without much doubt the En-Rogel of Scripture. It is a deep well of living water ; but in the rainy season overflows.

Passing from hence up the valley of Jehoshaphat and visiting again Siloam and the tomb of Absalom, I returned home by St. Stephen's gate. This walk gave me a stronger impression of the height and steepness of Zion, than I had before received.

TOMBS OF THE KINGS AND JUDGES, MOUNT ZION, ETC.

We visited several times the tombs of the Kings, so called, (probably the tomb of Helena,) and took the measurement of them, as will be described in the proper place. They lie directly north of the Damascus gate, just on the eastern side of the great road to Nâbulus. The way leads to them through the olive grove which now covers the level tract on this side of the city. A considerable portion of this plain was once apparently occupied by buildings. Fragments of marble and mosaic tesseræ are often found here ; and many ancient cisterns, now partly fallen in, furnish unequivocal evidence of former habitations. The stones with which the soil was thickly strewed, have been gathered into heaps or laid up in terraces ; and the fields thus cleared have now been tilled for centuries.

One forenoon, (Friday, April 27th,) Messrs Smith and Lanneau and myself went out to the tombs of the Kings, to look at them again, and to inspect the progress of some excavations which we had set on foot. We remained here but a short time ; and then proceeded further. Just beyond these tombs the valley of the Kidron, which thus far extends up north from the city, turns to the west at a right angle, and then shortly again resumes its former direction, running up north nearly to the tombs of the Judges. The great Nâbulus road crosses the valley here, where it runs from west to east. On the right side of this road, five minutes from the tombs of the Kings, and just as it descends into the valley, is a Wely, or tomb of a Muslim saint, with which is connected a small Khân now half in ruins. Here a deformed Sheikh resides as keeper, with a jug of water and a coffee pot for the refreshment of travellers ; expecting from them presents in return, by which to live. As Mr L. was acquainted with the Sheikh, we stopped for a few moments, took coffee, and looked in upon his Khân. The arched stalls for the animals around the small court remain ; but the chambers above for the guests are gone. The name of the saint was Husein Ibn 'Isa el-Jerrâhy.

i. 354, 355

According to the tradition of the Sheikh, he was one of the companions of the Khalif Omar when he took Jerusalem.

Passing along up the valley of Jehoshaphat, the sides of which are everywhere studded with sepulchres excavated in the rocks, we came to the tombs of the Judges so called. These lie near the head of the valley, on the right hand of the path, just beyond the water-summit between the waters of the Dead Sea and Mediterranean. Here the ground begins to descend north-west towards the great valley usually (though falsely) called by Franks the valley of the Terebinth ; but for which the natives have here no other name than Wady Beit Hanîna. At this point we were in full view of Neby Samwîl, bearing N. 40° W. on the high hill beyond that valley ; and could also see Kûstûl bearing W.

After examining the sepulchres, we returned over the eastern hill, striking the great northern road near the brow of the ascent by which it rises after crossing the valley. This is doubtless the Scopus of the ancients ; it affords one of the most pleasing views of the city ; though less distinct than one from a point further southeast. Passing again the tombs of the Kings, we directed our course towards the northwest corner of Jerusalem, in order to trace out, if possible, some foundations we had before seen, apparently belonging to the third wall of the ancient city, as described by Josephus. In this we were partially successful.

We came at length to the Yâfa gate, shortly after 12 o'clock, and found it shut. It was Friday, the Muhammedan Sabbath ; on which day the gates of Jerusalem are closed for an hour at noon, as the principal season of Muhammedan prayer. Passing around the city on the west, we spent the hour in wandering over Mount Zion. We looked here also for traces of the ancient wall along the western and southern brow ; followed out for some distance the aqueduct from Solomon's pools, which winds around the southeast slope ; and then returned up towards the Zion gate. It was not yet opened, and we went to call on the Sheikh of the Muslim tomb of David, with whom Mr Lanneau was acquainted. He was out ; but we visited the room over the tomb, where legendary tradition relates that the Lord's Supper was instituted. It is a large dreary "upper room" of stone, fifty or sixty feet long by some thirty feet in width. At the east end is a small niche in the wall, which the Christians use at certain seasons as an altar to celebrate mass. On the south side is a similar but larger recess, which serves the Muhammedans as a Mihrâb towards which to direct their prayers.[1] Thus the two superstitions stand here

[1] As the Muhammedans always turn their faces towards Mecca during their prayers and prostrations, every mosk has a niche in the wall to show the proper direction. This niche is the *Mihrâb ;* and the place or direction towards which the face is turned, is the *Kibleh.* Mecca lies nearly south of Syria ; and hence the word *Kibleh* is also in common use among the Syrian Arabs to denote the south.

side by side in singular juxtaposition. The pretended tomb itself no one is permitted to enter.

This building was formerly a Christian church ; and as such
the site at least is of high antiquity. It is apparently the same
spot, and perhaps the same building, referred to by Cyrill in the
fourth century, as the church of the Apostles, where they were
said to be assembled on the day of pentecost. This implies that
it was then regarded as at least older than the age of Constantine.
About the same time Epiphanius speaks of it distinctly under
the same name ; and about A. D. 697, Adamnanus mentions it
in like manner. It was then held to be the Cœnaculum, and to
contain also the column to which Christ was bound in order to
be scourged.[1] The same column is mentioned in the Jerusalem
Itinerary (A. D. 333), and by Jerome near the close of the same
century. The latter writer describes this column in his day as
sustaining the portico of a church on Mount Zion, and as still
stained with the Saviour's blood ; but neither he nor any of the
earlier writers speak of any tradition relating to the Lord's Supper.[2] Writers of the times of the crusades often allude to this
church as the church of Zion ; and regard it as the place where
the protomartyr Stephen was buried for a time.[3] According to
Sir J. Maundeville and also L. de Suchem, it would seem to
have been still in the hands of the Latins so late as about A. D.
1350 ; and at that time it was one of the many churches which
tradition began to ascribe to the empress Helena.[4] More than a
century later, A. D. 1479, Tucher of Nürnberg found the building converted into a mosk, or at least the lower part of it, and
already containing the tombs of David, Solomon, and other kings.
—The adjacent buildings were formerly a convent of the Minorites or Franciscans, who retained possession of them for a century
or more after the church had been partially at least wrested from
their hands.[5] In these buildings Ibrahim Pasha was accustomed
to reside when he visited Jerusalem.

[1] Cyrill. Cat. XVI. 2, p. 225. Oxon.
1703. Epiphan. de Mensur. et Pond. no.
14. Comp. le Quien Oriens Christ. III. p.
105.—Adamnan. ex Arculfo, I. 13. St.
Willibald, A. D. 765, calls it the church
of Zion ; Hodœpor. 18.

[2] Epitaph. Paulæ, ad Eustoch.

[3] Will. Tyr. 8. 5. Jac. de Vitr. Hist.
Hieros. 61. Phocas de Locis Sanct. 14.

[4] First mentioned as one of Helena's
churches by Nicephorus Callistus, 8. 30 ;
a writer of the fourteenth century.

[5] Adrichomius Theatr. Terræ Sanct. p.
150. Quaresmius Terræ Sanct. Elucid.
II. pp. 51, 122. It appears that the Franciscans or Minorites had their chief seat
here from A. D. 1313 to A. D. 1561.
        i. 357, 358

They were then driven out by the Muhammedans ; and having purchased the
present Latin convent of St. Salvator in
the city, which had formerly belonged to
the Georgian Greeks, they removed to it.
Quaresmius, l. c. Comp. Wadding Annal.
Minor. Ed. 2. III. p. 485 sq. Belon about
1547 lodged in their convent on Zion, and
speaks of it as the only Latin convent ;
Observations, etc. Paris 1588. p. 313 ;
also in Paulus' Sammlung, Th. 1. p. 259.
So Baumgarten in 1512, lib. II. 5 ; and
other travellers. Belon likewise remarks,
that the monks had in his day regained
possession of the Cœnaculum ; l. c. p.
315.—This convent was erected for the
Franciscans by Sancia, queen of Robert

Further north, nearer to the gate, stands an Armenian convent, enclosing a small church, which according to a similar tradition marks the spot where once stood the house of Caiphas. We entered and were conducted through it. Here the Armenian patriarchs of Jerusalem lie buried ; their monuments are in the small court. Under the altar of the church they still profess to show the stone which closed the Holy Sepulchre. They point out also what they call the prison of our Lord ; as well as the spot where Peter denied his Master, and the court where the cock crew. This church cannot well be very ancient ;[1] nor have I been able to find any mention of it before the fourteenth century. It was then called, as now, the church of St. Salvator, and was already ascribed to Helena.[2] The Armenians appear to have had it in possession very early after the crusades.[3]

We reached the Zion gate just as it was opened at one o'clock. Within the gate, a little towards the right, are some miserable hovels, inhabited by persons called leprous. Whether their disease is or is not the leprosy of Scripture, I am unable to affirm ; the symptoms described to us were similar to those of elephantiasis. At any rate they are pitiable objects, and miserable outcasts from society. They all live here together, and intermarry only with each other. The children are said to be healthy until the age of puberty or later ; when the disease makes its appearance in a finger, on the nose, or in some like part of the body, and gradually increases so long as the victim survives. They were said often to live to the age of forty or fifty years.

Our way home led us through the Jews' quarter ; and we looked in for a moment upon their preparations for building a new synagogue. In digging for its foundations they had uncovered several small houses and rooms, which had before been completely buried beneath the accumulated rubbish. These presented nothing of interest. It was also reported, that they had found pieces of marble, and even columns ; but we were able to learn nothing definite on the subject.

of Sicily ; who also repaired or rebuilt the Cœnaculum ; see Quaresmius, l. c. p. 122, and Tom. I. p. 176. Wadding, l. c.

[1] Benjamin of Tudela says, that in his day, soon after A. D. 1160, there was no building on Zion save one Christian church, doubtless the Cœnaculum ; I. p. 72, ed. Asher.

[2] Marin. Sanut. Secr. fidel. Crucis, 3. 14. 8.   L. de Suchem Itin. p. 78. Reissb. p.

844. Niceph. Call. 8. 30.—The Jerusalem Itinerary, (A. D. 333,) speaks of the house of Caiphas as having stood on Mount Zion, "ubi *fuit* domus Caiphæ ;" but says nothing of any building then existing. Comp. Cyrill. Cat. XIII. 19.

[3] Tucher of Nürnberg found it in their hands in A. D. 1479. See Reissb. des heil. Landes, p. 659.

EL-HARAM.   TOWER OF DAVID.

We made no attempt to obtain admission to the Haram esh-Sherif, or great mosk.   This has been visited and described by others, and did not form in itself any part of the object of our journey.   Could there have been a hope of penetrating into the vaults and subterranean passages which are known to exist beneath its area, so as to explore them, we would have spared no effort to have obtained the requisite permission.   But as it was, we thought it more prudent to pursue our researches in silence, rather than by ill timed or ill advised application to the authorities, to run the risk of exciting on their part suspicion or jealousy. We found no difficulty at any time in approaching the entrances, and looking in upon the area, as long as we pleased.

Wishing however to obtain a better view of the Haram, and also to visit the citadel near the Yâfa gate, Mr Smith with our friends waited on the Kâim Makâm, the military commander of the city, to obtain an order for this purpose.   This officer received them with great courtesy ; immediately granted their request ; and even sent his secretary to accompany them and introduce them at each place.   They now came back for me ; and we went first to the building on the northwest corner of the area of the Haram.   This was formerly the residence of the governor ; and stands near the site of the ancient fortress Antonia.   It is now used as a barrack.   From the flat roof there is a full view of the mosk and its court, a large and beautiful area, with trees scattered over it, and several fountains ; the whole forming a fine promenade.   We saw there quite a number of females, and many children playing.

The great mosk itself, *Kubbet es-Sŭkhrah,* "Dome of the Rock," is an octagonal building with a noble dome, standing upon a platform near the middle of the court, elevated by several steps above the general level.   Quite on the southern side of the area, stands another large mosk, *el-Jâmi'a el-Aksa ;* and there are other smaller mosks and buildings adjacent to the walls in other parts.   The whole enclosure, with all its sacred buildings and appurtenances, is called *el-Haram,* "the Holy," and also *el-Haram esh-Sherif,* "the noble Sanctuary."   In the northern part of the area, the rocky surface is visible, which has evidently been levelled off by art.   The height of the wall around the court on the inside we judged to be from twelve to sixteen feet.—Towards the west the houses of the city rise steeply one above another, and the two hills of Zion and Akra are distinctly marked.[1]

[1] The spot where we stood is the same   for the noble Panorama of Jerusalem by from which the drawings were taken   Catherwood, since destroyed by fire.
{ 860 861

We now repaired to the castle or citadel, and were taken through its various parts; but our attention was confined chiefly to the one old tower, apparently ancient, which is usually called by the Franks the tower of David. This we measured; and it will be described in another place. From its top there is an extensive view, especially towards the southeast, where a small portion of the Dead Sea is visible, and beyond it the mountains of Arabia. As we looked down upon and over the city itself, it seemed almost like a plain; the appearance of descent being in a great measure lost.[1]

Both here and at the barracks, the deportment of the officers and soldiers we encountered, was extremely civil. The secretary who attended us was an intelligent man; and when we parted, he politely declined the *bakhshish* we proffered him. This was, I think, the only instance of the kind in all our journey.

In our walks through the city and its environs, we were struck with the comparatively few people we met, and the indifference with which they seemed to regard us and our movements. In the city itself, the bazars were usually thronged; so that it was sometimes difficult to make one's way through them. In the larger streets also, such as that leading down from the Yâfa gate to the great mosk, and those between the bazars and the Damascus gate, there were commonly many persons passing to and fro; but all the other streets were comparatively solitary. Outside of the city, a few peasants with their asses wending their way to or from the gates; a few shepherds watching their flocks on the side of Mount Olivet; a few women with their waterskins around the fountains in the valley of Jehoshaphat; and occasionally Muslim females veiled in white sitting or strolling among the tombs of their people; these were ordinarily the only signs of life and activity which the stranger could perceive, as he wandered around this former "city of the great King." Yet sometimes we lighted upon more stirring scenes. One day as we were standing near the large terebinth at the northwest corner of the city wall, the Mutesellim or governor with a party of ten or twelve horsemen passed by, on their return from a ride and from practising the *Jerid*. They were all gaily caparisoned, and rode in fine style; their horses prancing and now and then darting off at full speed along the rocky road. At another time the dead monotony was broken in upon, by the departure of a large body of troops for Ramleh.

[1] We were not so fortunate as Stephan Schulz; who professes to have seen from this tower Mount Horeb in the south, and Mount Tabor in the north! Leitungen des Höchsten, etc. Th. V. p. 161.

We took measurements within and without the city in all directions, without interruption, and without being subjected to the slightest inquiry or token of suspicion. Indeed, the indifference with which these operations were apparently regarded, was rather a matter of surprise. A few persons only occasionally stopped to look at us, and then passed on; and I am persuaded that neither in London nor New York could any thing similar be undertaken, without exciting far more attention, and probably drawing together a crowd of idlers. We just pursued our own course; went where we would, and undertook what we pleased; asked no leave of the government or others, whenever it could be avoided; and thus encountered no opposition. In the one instance where we had occasion to ask a favour of the Kâim Makâm or military commander, it was courteously granted; in another instance, the Mufti declined to concede what he previously had expressed a willingness to have take place.

With the native population of the city, we had, through our friends, the opportunity of frequent intercourse, to any extent we might desire. The house of Mr Lanneau, in which we resided, was situated in the Muhammedan quarter, next door to that of the Mufti of Jerusalem; and the circumstance of his having taken a house in their quarter and among them, was looked upon with favour by the Muslims. His neighbours, some of the chief men of the city, were in the habit of making frequent calls; and an interchange of friendly courtesies was sedulously maintained. A native Greek merchant, Abu Selâmeh, who was seeking the appointment of agent from the American consul at Beirût, was very attentive; and through him and the chief physician or apothecary of the garrison, we received all the intelligence and current reports of the day.

The Mutesellim or governor of the city at this time, was Sheikh Mustafa, a young man of a fine figure and prepossessing countenance, the son of Sheikh Sa'id, governor of Gaza. He was said however to be prejudiced against the Franks; and to be in the habit of turning an ungracious ear to all their applications. We had no occasion to apply to him while in Jerusalem; except once, as a matter of policy, to send our Firmân for his inspection before setting off for the Dead Sea; but we afterwards met him in Hebron and were struck with his graceful deportment. The Kâim Makâm, or military governor, was regarded as more frank and courteous; and our friends were in the habit of applying to him, when necessary, rather than to Sheikh Mustafa.

Our neighbour the Mufti called one morning soon after breakfast, and sat with us for an hour. This dignitary is in high repute among the Mussulmans; being subordinate in rank only to

i. 303. 364

the Muftis of Mecca and Constantinople. He was a fine looking man between sixty and seventy years of age, with a long white beard neatly trimmed, intelligent eyes, and great vivacity for a Muhammedan. He declined the proffered pipe, assuring us that he never smoked. He was near sighted, and had an ordinary eyeglass; but my spectacles, and especially those of one of the missionaries, delighted him greatly. He was prompt in offering us all the facilities we might need in prosecuting our researches; and so far as his own personal feelings were concerned, this offer was perhaps sincere. The flat roof of Mr Lanneau's house was separated from his premises only by a low parapet; and some of our friends having casually looked over it into his court, he had sent a civil message to request that this might not be done any more. One object of his present visit was to apologize, or rather to explain the reason, for sending such a message.

Another day we had a similar call from Abu Ghaush, the former governor of Jerusalem, noted as one of the Sheikhs of the village of Kuryet el-'Enab on the way to Yâfa, where some years ago travellers were often robbed. He is now old, with a keen robber's eye, and an intelligent face. This is a family name; and there are several brothers Abu Ghaush. An older one, Ibrahîm, was the most notorious as a robber; but he was said not now to be acknowledged as the head of the family.

Before we left Cairo, intelligence had been received there of the insurrection of the Druzes in Haurân; and as they were known to be a brave and injured people, fears were entertained (and not unjustly) that a protracted war might follow, the end of which no one could foresee. The occasion of the insurrection was understood to be, the attempts of the Egyptian government to introduce the conscription, and to seize upon their young men by force as recruits for the army. This kind of oppression had been already introduced into other parts of Syria, although not with the same success as in Egypt; but the comparatively free and high spirited Druzes could not brook it. War ensued. The Druzes fought with desperation; and were killed outright whenever taken. Their country was overrun and wasted; their villages burned with fire; their wives and children sold as slaves in the markets of Damascus. The survivors withdrew to the rocks and fastnesses of el-Lejah; for a time there would be a calm, and then the war burst forth again with redoubled fury. After continuing for more than a year, the war appears to have been finally terminated by the concession, on the part of the government, of all that for which the Druzes had at first taken up arms; a concession extorted perhaps by the indications of an approaching war with Turkey.

During our journey through the deserts south of Palestine,

i. 364–366

we of course heard little of this war. The Bedawîn knew that it
had broken out ; but they had no definite information respecting
it ; and the scene of conflict was too remote to affect them directly, or awaken an interest in their bosoms. When we arrived at Jerusalem, the first throes of the struggle were not yet
over ; and the minds of men were in uncertainty. For some
time no definite intelligence had been received from the seat of
war ; and the city was full of rumours. No one knew where
Ibrahim Pasha was ; and it was even said, that a large body of
his troops had been defeated, and another party of several hundreds wholly cut off. In this state of things, the unquiet spirits
of the land, who under the strong arm of Egyptian rule had become quiet and peaceable citizens, began to rouse themselves,
and desired again to taste the sweets of anarchy and lawless de-
predation. Several robberies and murders were committed in
the vicinity of Jerusalem ; one of which has been already alluded
to.[1] In another instance a pilgrim was shot, robbed, and left
wounded on the road to Yâfa. He was brought to the city, and
some of our friends saw him lying helpless and apparently dying,
in the open court of the Greek convent, waiting until the authorities of the city or the convent should make some provision
for his need. Reports of other robberies were very frequent ; but
were evidently much exaggerated, if not wholly groundless.

Under these circumstances, the prospect before us was dreary;
and it was for a time doubtful, whether we should be able to
travel at all in the country, without (or even with) an armed
guard. Were the Druzes able to maintain themselves and make
head against the Pasha's troops, then all the roads in Palestine
would become unsafe ; for however well affected the better portion of the people might be, still this would not keep in check
the bands of lawless adventurers, who were only waiting for an
opportunity to prowl over the country. Many days however had
not elapsed, before the certain news arrived, that Ibrahim was at
Damascus, where he had concentrated his troops ; and that he
had totally defeated the Druzes. After this all was again quiet ;
the reports of robbery and murder were no longer heard ; and we
subsequently travelled through the length and breadth of the
land without fear or interruption ; indeed, with the same feeling
of security as in England or our native country. It was not until two months later, that a fresh outbreak of the insurrection in
the region of Jebel esh-Sheikh, hindered us from approaching
Damascus.

As if we were to have a specimen of all the evils to which the
oriental world is exposed, a few days after our arrival in the Holy
City, rumours of the plague began to be circulated. It had

[1] See above, p. 219.

i. 366 367

broken out with violence in Alexandria ; and in consequence a strict quarantine had been established at Yâfa. Yet on Sunday, April 22d, the report came that the plague had made its appearance in Yâfa also; supposed to have been introduced by pilgrims from the southern coast of Asia Minor. Some of these pilgrims were known to have come up to Jerusalem ; and now the inhabitants were tormented day by day, with various rumours of its existence both at Yâfa and among themselves. At first many doubted ; but several fearful cases at Yâfa, in the families of some of the Frank consuls, speedily put the question beyond doubt in respect to that place. In Jerusalem there were for some days no very decided cases. Deaths indeed occurred, which were ascribed to the plague ; but no one pronounced authoritatively upon them. Yet all were in fear and upon their guard ; several houses were barricadoed by the police ; many families and some of the convents put themselves in quarantine ; and all took care, in passing to and fro along the streets, not to come in contact with any other person. At length, after a few days, the plague developed itself decidedly ; all doubt was at an end ; and the disease continued to extend its ravages on every side continually, though mildly.

This was a state of things such as I had never anticipated, and which I shall never forget. Men's lives seemed to hang in doubt before them. No one knew what to do or whither to turn himself. All who could, hurried away from the city ; for they feared that, according to despotic custom, Jerusalem would be shut up and a cordon of troops drawn around it, in order to prevent the plague from spreading among the villages of the country. Nor was this fear groundless. All business was at a stand. The merchants from Damascus and other places left the city. The missionaries broke off their sittings, and those from abroad hastened to depart with their families. · They left on the 30th of April. Several Frank travellers also hurried away ; and some who were upon the road from Beirût to Jerusalem, turned back at Nâbulus.

Meanwhile we continued our investigations without interruption, taking care to come in contact with no one as we passed along the streets ; and a kind Providence preserved us from the dangers by which we were surrounded. On the 18th of May the city was actually shut up, and no one permitted to go out. We had left it the day before on a long excursion to Gaza, Hebron, and Wady Mûsa ; and although we afterwards returned to its gates, yet we did not enter them again. The city remained shut up until the beginning of July.

Indeed, during our whole journey in the east, although surrounded by war, pestilence, and quarantines, we were enabled to

i. 367–369

pass through them all without harm or hindrance ; without being detained from these causes even for an hour.

Not all travellers, however, were thus favoured. On the 2d of May, I met at the house of Mr Nicolayson an English gentleman, the chaplain of a ship of war, who left Cairo just one week after ourselves, and had come by the most direct route to Jerusalem. He had descended the Nile to Damietta, where he was detained seventeen days waiting for a vessel for Yâfa. In this latter place he had performed a quarantine of fifteen days ; and then five more on his arrival in Jerusalem. These last had ended only on the preceding day. Thus of the forty-three days which had elapsed since his departure from Cairo, six had been spent in travelling, and thirty-seven in quarantines and delay ! Yet he was not disheartened ; and actually left Jerusalem the very next day for Beirût. It may also be mentioned, as showing the security of the roads at the time, that without knowing a word of Arabic, he set off alone with a single muleteer on this long journey ; and reached Beirût without any other difficulties, than those which are of course incident to such a mode of travel.

Not long afterwards, duke Maximilian of Bavaria arrived at Jerusalem with a somewhat numerous suite ; and left it again, as we understood, about the same time we did, just before the city was shut up. He was less fortunate or less cautious than we were, in respect to the plague ; for after he had left the city this terrible scourge broke out among his attendants. His physician died of it at Nazareth ; and another attendant, a mulatto, was left ill in the lazaretto at Sidon, where he lingered for several weeks and died.

Among other travellers who left the Holy City, was M de Bertou, a Frenchman, who had just returned from an excursion to Wady Mûsa and 'Akabah by way of the Dead Sea and Wady el-'Arabah. We had hoped to have been the first to explore the northern part of this great Wady ; but were not the less gratified to learn from him the results of his journey. He spent the evening of April 30th with us ; and thought he had found the name of *Kadesh*, at a place not far from the junction of the roads from Hebron and Gaza to Wady Mûsa ; and also that of *Zoar* on the western side of the Dead Sea. Both of these suppositions we afterwards found, by inquiry on the spot, to be erroneous

i. 369. 370.

SECTION VII.

JERUSALEM.

TOPOGRAPHY AND ANTIQUITIES.[1]

WE enter here upon a more detailed description of the Holy City, and its remains of antiquity. In doing this, I must request the reader to bear in mind, that for the lapse of more than fifteen centuries, Jerusalem has been the abode not only of mistaken piety, but also of credulous superstition, not unmingled with pious fraud. During the second and third centuries after the Christian era, the city remained under heathen sway; and the Christian church existed there, if at all, only by sufferance. But when, in the beginning of the fourth century, Christianity became triumphant in the person of Constantine; and at his instigation, aided by the presence and zeal of his mother Helena, the first great attempt was made in A. D. 326, to fix and beautify the places connected with the crucifixion and resurrection of the Saviour; it then, almost as a matter of course, became a passion among the multitudes of priests and monks, who afterwards resorted to the Holy City, to trace out and assign the site of every event, however trivial or legendary, which could be brought into connection with the Scriptures or with pious tradition. The fourth century appears to have been particularly fruitful in the fixing of these localities, and in the dressing out of the traditions or rather legends, which were attached to them.[2] But the inven-

[1] This section remains as it was in the first edition, excepting a few slight corrections. The results of our second visit, in 1852, are given in Vol. III. Sec. IV and V.
[2] The *Itin. Hierosol.* A. D. 333, mentions the palm tree as still standing on the side of Mount Olivet, from which the people broke off branches to strew before Je-

sus. Cyrill also speaks of it in the same century; Cat. X. 19. The column to which Christ was bound and scourged, was already found; but the blood upon it is first mentioned by Jerome nearly a century afterwards. The *Cœnaculum* connected with it was the work of a still later age; as we have already had occasion to remark. See p. 242, above.

tion of succeeding ages continued to build upon these foundations,[1] until, in the seventh century, the Muhammedan conquest
and subsequent oppressions confined the attention of the church
more exclusively to the circumstances of her present distress ;
and drew off in part the minds of the clergy and monks from the
contemplation and embellishment of Scriptural history. Thus
the fabric of tradition was left to become fixed and stationary as to
its main points ; in much the same condition, indeed, in which it
has come down to our day. The more fervid zeal of the ages of
the crusades, only filled out and completed the fabric in minor
particulars.[2]

It must be further borne in mind, that as these localities were
assigned, and the traditions respecting them for the most part
brought forward, by a credulous and unenlightened zeal, well meant,
indeed, but not uninterested ; so all the reports and accounts we
have of the Holy City and its sacred places, have come to us from
the same impure source. The fathers of the church in Palestine,
and their imitators the monks, were themselves for the most part
not natives of the country. With few exceptions they knew
little of its topography ; and were mostly unacquainted with the
Aramæan, the vernacular language of the common people.[3] They
have related only what was transmitted to them by their predecessors, also foreigners ; or have given opinions of their own,
adopted without critical inquiry and usually without much knowledge. The visitors of the Holy Land in the earlier centuries,
as well as the crusaders, all went thither in the character of pilgrims ; and looked upon Jerusalem and its environs, and upon
the land, only through the medium of the traditions of the church.

[1] Thus the traditions respecting the house of Caiaphas, Gethsemane, and various other sites, although slight traces of them are found quite early, appear to have been decked out with new circumstances, as centuries rolled on. In A. D. 870 the monk Bernard speaks of a church on the side of the mount of Olives, on the spot where the Pharisees brought to Jesus the woman taken in adultery. In the church was preserved a marble tablet, with the writing which our Lord there wrote upon the ground ! Itinerar. 13, in Acta Sanctor. Ord. Benedict. Sæc. III. Pars II. p. 525.

[2] A multitude of the minor legends, such as those relating to the place where Peter's cock crew, the houses of the rich man and Lazarus, and the like, were probably the work of more modern times. Even the Via dolorosa seems to have been first got up during or after the times of the crusades ; see above, p. 233.

[3] Though the Greek language was universally understood and spoken by the inhabitants in general, yet there is reason to believe that the real mother tongue of the common people was still the Aramæan. Origen and Jerome appear to have been the only fathers in Palestine who understood Hebrew. The latter, who died in Palestine A. D. 420, made it a particular study, in order to translate the Bible. He mentions the Punic dialect, by which he probably means the Phœnician, as a spoken language ; Quæst. ad Gen. 36, 24. ad voc. םימר. See Gesenius Script. et Linguæ Phœnic. Monumenta, pp. 331, 337. In his Comm. in Esa. 19, 18, Jerome also speaks expressly of a " lingua Canaanitide, quæ inter Ægyptiam et Hebræam media est et Hebrææ magna ex parte confinis." Various other circumstances go also to show the long continuance of the Aramæan among the common people. The subject is worthy of a more particular investigation than has yet been bestowed upon it.

i. 372, 373

And since the time of the crusades, from the fourteenth century onwards to the present day, all travellers, whether pilgrims or visitors, have usually taken up their abode in Jerusalem in the convents ; and have beheld the city only through the eyes of their monastic entertainers. European visitors, in particular, have ever lodged, and still lodge, almost exclusively, in the Latin convent ; and the Latin monks have in general been their sole guides.

In this way and from all these causes, there has been grafted upon Jerusalem and the Holy Land a vast mass of tradition, foreign in its source and doubtful in its character ; which has flourished luxuriantly and spread itself out widely over the western world. Palestine, the Holy City, and its sacred places, have been again and again portrayed according to the topography of the monks ; and according to them alone. Whether travellers were Catholics or Protestants, has made little difference. All have drawn their information from the great storehouse of the convents ; and, with few exceptions, all report it apparently with like faith, though with various fidelity. In looking through the long series of descriptions, which have been given of Jerusalem by the many travellers since the fourteenth century, it is curious to observe, how very slightly the accounts differ in their topographical and traditional details. There are indeed occasional discrepancies in minor points ; though very few of the travellers have ventured to depart from the general authority of their monastic guides. Or even if they sometimes venture to call in question the value of this whole mass of tradition ; yet they nevertheless repeat in like manner the stories of the convents ; or at least give nothing better in their place.[1]

Whoever has had occasion to look into these matters for himself, will not be slow to admit, that the views here expressed are in no degree overcharged. It follows from them,—and this is the point to which I would particularly direct the reader's attention,—that *all ecclesiastical tradition respecting the ancient places in and around Jerusalem and throughout Palestine,* IS OF NO VALUE, *except so far as it is supported by circumstances known to us from the Scriptures, or from other cotemporary testimony.* Thus one of the very earliest traditions on record, that which points out the place of our Lord's ascension on the summit of the mount of Olives, and which certainly existed in the third century, long before the visit of Helena, is obviously, false ; because it stands in contradiction to the Scriptural ac-

---

[1] Even Maundrell, shrewd and accurate as he is elsewhere, gives in Jerusalem little more than what he heard from the monks. Of other travellers, Rauwolf was one of the most independent ; and the accounts of Cotovicus (Kootwyk) sometimes vary from the usual form. The independence of Dr. Clarke is sufficiently manifest ; but it led him over into an opposite extreme of extravagant hypothesis

count, which relates that Christ led out his disciples "as far as
to Bethany," and there ascended from them into heaven.[1]   On
the other hand, I would not venture to disturb the traditional
location of Rachel's grave on the way towards Bethlehem; for
although this is first mentioned by the *Itin. Hieros.* and by
Jerome in the fourth century, yet the Scriptural narrative necessarily limits the spot to that vicinity.[2]

On the same general principle, that important work the
Onomasticon, the production of the successive labours of Eusebius and Jerome, which gives the names and describes the situation of places in the Holy Land, can be regarded in an historical
respect, only as a record of the traditions current in their day,
sanctioned indeed by the judgment of those fathers.   The
names thus preserved are of the highest importance; but the
value of the traditions connected with them, must be proved in
the same manner as all others; although in general they were
then far less corrupted than in the lapse of subsequent centuries.

In the history of this foreign tradition, three ages or periods
are distinctly marked by documents, which show us, with tolerable completeness, its state and character at the time.   The
first falls in the fourth century, about A. D. 333, when foreign
influence had just acquired a firm and permanent footing, and
had not as yet very greatly swerved from the tide of native tradition.   Of this period we have a record in the Onomasticon of
Eusebius, and the Jerusalem Itinerary.   The *second* is the age
of the crusades, in the twelfth and thirteenth centuries; the
traditions of which are best registered in the tract of Brocardus,
about A. D. 1283.   The *third* period occurs at the beginning
of the seventeenth century; when the volumes of Quaresmius
exhibit, in full, the state of the tradition then current in the
convents, the great source from which most European travellers
have drawn their information.—In comparing these three periods,
it is interesting, though painful, to perceive, how the light of
truth has gradually become dim, and at length often been
quenched in darkness.   The Onomasticon, with all its defects
and wrong hypotheses, has yet preserved to us much of the tradition of the common people; and contains many names of
places never since discovered, though still existing; while the
few pages of Brocardus are worth more, in a topographical respect, than the unwieldy folios of Quaresmius.   It is certain,
that in the long interval between Eusebius and the crusades,

---

[1] Luke 24, 50. 51. Compare Acts 1,
12, where it is only said, that the disciples
returned from Mount Olivet; not that
Christ ascended from it.—The tradition
alluded to in the text is mentioned by Eusebius, Demonstr. Evang. VI. 18. p. 288.
i. 375

Col. Agr. This work, according to Valesius, was written about A. D. 315, ten
years or more before the visit of Helena
to Palestine. De Vit. et Script. Euseb.
[2] Gen. 35, 16–20. See above, pp. 218,
219.

very much was forgotten by the church which still existed among the people ; and in the subsequent period, the progress of oblivion was perhaps not less rapid.   Even within the last two centuries, so far as the convents and travellers in Palestine are concerned, I fear the cause of Biblical Geography can hardly be said to have greatly advanced.

The preceding remarks apply more particularly to Jerusalem, and to those parts of Palestine with which the fathers of the church and the hosts of monks have chiefly occupied themselves. But there is in Palestine another kind of tradition, with which the monasteries have had nothing to do; and of which they have apparently in every age known little or nothing.   I mean, *the preservation of the ancient names of places among the common people.*   This is a truly national and native tradition ; not derived in any degree from the influence of foreign convents or masters ; but drawn in by the peasant with his mother's milk, and deeply seated in the genius of the Semitic languages.   The Hebrew names of places continued current in their Aramæan form long after the times of the New Testament ; and maintained themselves in the mouths of the common people, in spite of the efforts made by Greeks and Romans to supplant them by others derived from their own tongues.[1]   After the Muhammedan conquest, when the Aramæan language gradually gave place to the kindred Arabic, the proper names of places, which the Greeks could never bend to their orthography, found here a ready entrance ; and have thus lived on upon the lips of the Arabs, whether Christian or Muslim, townsmen or Bedawin, even unto our own day, almost in the same form in which they have also been transmitted to us in the Hebrew Scriptures.[2]

The nature of the long series of foreign tradition has sometimes been recognised and lamented by travellers and others ; while that of the native Arab population has been for the most part overlooked, and its existence almost unknown.[3]   Travellers have in general been unacquainted with the Arabic language, and

[1] It is sufficient to mention here the sounding names Diospolis, Nicopolis, Ptolemais, and Antipatris, which have perished for centuries ; while the more ancient ones which they were intended to supplant, are still current among the people, Ludd (Lydda), 'Amwâs (Emmaus), 'Akka, and Kefr Sâba.   Yet a few Greek names thus imposed have maintained themselves instead of the ancient ones ; as Nâbulus (Neapolis) for Shechem, and Sebûstieh (Sebaste) for Samaria.

[2] The Semitic letter *'Ain* in particular, so unpronounceable by other nations, has a remarkable tenacity.   Of the very many Hebrew names containing this letter, that

still survive in Arabic, our lists exhibit only two or three in which it has been dropped ; and perhaps none in which it has been exchanged for another letter.

[3] It may perhaps be asked, whether there does not exist a Jewish tradition, which would also be trustworthy ?   Not in respect to Jerusalem itself ; for the Jews for centuries could approach the Holy City only to weep over it ; see p. 237, above.   In other parts of Palestine, a regular Jewish tradition could not well be different from that handed down among the common people.   Their early written accounts, as is well known, are not less legendary than those of the Christians.

i. 375, 376

unable to communicate with the common people except through the medium of illiterate interpreters; they have mostly followed only beaten paths, where monkish tradition had already marked out all the localities they sought; and in this way few have ever thought of seeking for information among the Arab peasantry. Yet the example of Seetzen and Burckhardt in the countries east of the Jordan might have pointed out a better course; and the multitude of ancient names which they found still current in those regions, where monastic influence had more rarely penetrated, might have stimulated to like researches in western Palestine. Yet this had never been done; and in consequence of this neglect, and of the circumstances alluded to above, it had become a singular, though notorious fact, that notwithstanding the multitude of travellers who have swarmed through Palestine, the countries east of the Jordan were in many respects more accurately and distinctly known, than those upon the west.

In view of this state of things, we early adopted two general principles, by which to govern ourselves in our examination of the Holy Land. The *first* was, to avoid as far as possible all contact with the convents and the authority of the monks; to examine everywhere for ourselves with the Scriptures in our hands; and to apply for information solely to the native Arab population. The *second* was, to leave as much as possible the beaten track, and direct our journeys and researches to those portions of the country which had been least visited. By acting upon these two principles, we were able to arrive at many results, that to us were new and unexpected; and it is these results alone, which give a value (if any it have) to the present work.

In Jerusalem itself, circumstances favoured our determination. The presence of our countrymen and friends enabled us to live aloof from the convents, and pursue our inquiries with entire independence; a privilege which all travellers cannot command.[1] During the whole time of our sojourn in the Holy City, it so happened that I never entered the Latin convent, nor spoke with a monk. This neglect was not however intentional; for I several times made an appointment to visit the convent, and my companion was there repeatedly. Once only we visited together the great convent of the Armenians, to call upon an English friend who was residing there; and we took this opportunity to look at the richly decorated, but tawdry church of St. James connected with it, which former travellers have sufficiently described.

---

[1] The Latin convent has in former years erected a building, the *Casa nuova*, expressly for the entertainment of travellers and strangers. This was a great convenience in such a city, where inns were unknown; and most travellers were compelled to avail themselves of it. Since then several hotels have been established.

377, 378

Among the Arab population our inquiries were frequent and minute ; and they were answered with kindness and often with good fruit. Yet, as might have been expected, we found less of new information among the Arabs in the Holy City itself, than in other parts of the country. The names of the chief natural features in and around Jerusalem, have been so long and in general so correctly fixed, and have become so familiar to the Christian ear, that whether adopted by the Arabs or not, the Christian traveller involuntarily employs them. Especially is this the case, where the ancient appellation has been dropped by the common people. Thus, who would abandon the hallowed name of the mount of Olives, for that of Jebel et-Tûr ? or Bethany, for el-'Azarîyeh ? In like manner the names of the valleys of Jehoshaphat or the Kidron and of Hinnom, have become so fixed in Christian usage, that we even forgot at the time to inquire, whether the Arabs now give them a different appellation.[1]

After these preliminary observations, the reader will be prepared to judge for himself of the following description and details of the Holy City and its antiquities. This account contains nothing but what we ourselves saw, or what we learned on native authority; and is wholly drawn out from our notes written down upon the spot;[2] together with such historical notices as I have been able to collect. The convents and churches and mosks have been described time and again by other travellers; and the traditions of the church and of the monks lie before the Christian world in hundreds of tomes of every size, from the ponderous folios of Quaresmius down to the spruce duodecimos of the Modern Traveller. We did not particularly examine these objects; and therefore I do not describe them.

In respect to those points in which the following account may seem to be at variance with those of former travellers, I have only to say, that we always aimed at the truth according to the best of our ability; and the public must judge of the degree of credit due to our assertions. To point out discrepancies and refute the errors of others, would be a thankless task; and therefore, except in a few special cases, I leave these matters to the consideration and judgment of those who are interested in such researches.

[1] Since the above remark was written, I have ascertained that the Arabs employ the same names, viz. Wady Kidrón or Ye-hôshàfàt, and Wady Jehennam.

[2] I must here except the notices kindly communicated to me after my return by Mr Catherwood.

i. 378, 379

I. GENERAL TOPOGRAPHY.

Jerusalem, now called by the Arabs *el-Kuds*, "the Holy," and also by Arabian writers *Beit el-Mûkdis* or *Beit el-Mukaddas,* "the Sanctuary,"[1] lies near the summit of a broad mountain ridge. This ridge or mountainous tract extends without interruption, from the plain of Esdraelon to a line drawn between the south end of the Dead Sea and the southeast corner of the Mediterranean; or more properly, perhaps, it may be regarded as extending as far south as to Jebel 'Arâif in the desert; where it sinks down at once to the level of the great western plateau. This tract, which is everywhere not less than from twenty to twenty-five geographical miles in breadth, is in fact high uneven table land. It everywhere forms the precipitous western wall of the great valley of the Jordan and the Dead Sea; while towards the west it sinks down in some parts by an offset into a range of lower hills, which lie between it and the great plain along the coast of the Mediterranean. The surface of this upper region is everywhere rocky, uneven, and mountainous; and is moreover cut up by deep valleys, which run east or west on either side towards the Jordan or the Mediterranean. The line of division, or water-shed, between the waters of these valleys, a term which here applies almost exclusively to the waters of the rainy season, follows for the most part the height of land along the ridge; yet not so but that the heads of the valleys which run off in different directions, often interlap for a considerable distance. Thus, for example, a valley which descends to the Jordan often has its head a mile or two westward of the commencement of other valleys, which run to the western sea.

From the great plain of Esdraelon onwards towards the south, the mountainous country rises gradually, forming the tract anciently known as the mountains of Ephraim and Judah; until in the vicinity of Hebron it attains an elevation of nearly 3000 Paris feet above the level of the Mediterranean Sea. Further north, on a line drawn from the north end of the Dead Sea towards the true west, the mountainous tract has an elevation of only about 2500 Paris feet; and here, close upon the water-shed between the Dead Sea and the Mediterranean, lies the city of Jerusalem.[2]

---

[1] Abulfed. Syr. ed. Köhler, p. 9. Edrisi ed. Jaubert I. p. 341. Freytag Lex. Arab. III. p. 408.—Edrisi also once gives it the name *Aurashlim*, which is said to be sometimes used by the native Christians; l. c. p. 345.

[2] According to Schubert's measurements, i. 380. 381

the town of Hebron, which lies in a valley, has an elevation of 2664 feet. Russegger gives the same at 2842 feet. The adjacent hills are two or three hundred feet higher. —The height of the mount of Olives, overagainst Jerusalem, according to Schubert, is 2555 Paris feet.

The mean geographical position of the Holy City is in Lat. 31° 46' 43" N. and Long. 35° 13' E. from Greenwich.[1]

Six or seven miles north and northwest of the city is spread out the open plain or basin round about el-Jîb (Gibeon), extending also towards el-Bireh (Beeroth); the waters of which flow off at its southeast part through the deep valley here called by the Arabs Wady Beit Hanina ; but to which the monks and travellers have usually given the name of the valley of the Terebinth, on the mistaken supposition that it is the ancient valley of Elah.[2] This great valley passes along in a southwest direction an hour or more west of Jerusalem ; and finally opens out from the mountains into the western plain, at the distance of six or eight hours southwest from the city, under the name of Wady es-Sŭrâr. The traveller on his way from Ramleh to Jerusalem, descends into and crosses this deep valley at the village of Kŭlônieh on its western side, an hour and a half from the latter city. On again reaching the high ground on its eastern side, he enters upon an open tract sloping gradually downwards towards the south and east; and sees before him, at the distance of a mile and a half, the walls and domes of the Holy City, and beyond them the higher ridge or summit of the mount of Olives.

The traveller now descends gradually towards the city along a broad swell of ground, having at some distance on his left the shallow northern part of the valley of Jehoshaphat; and close at hand on his right the basin which forms the beginning of the valley of Hinnom. Further down, both these valleys become deep, narrow, and precipitous ; that of Hinnom bends south and again east nearly at right angles, and unites with the other; which then continues its course to the Dead Sea. Upon the broad and elevated promontory within the fork of these two valleys, lies the Holy City. All around are higher hills ; on the east, the mount of Olives ; on the south, the hill of Evil Counsel, so called, rising directly from the vale of Hinnom; on the west, the ground rises gently, as above described, to the borders of the

---

[1] The latitude here given is the mean of four observations, viz.

Niebuhr	31°	46' 34"	Reisebeschr. Bd. III. Anh. p. 116.
Seetzen	31	47 47	Zach's Monatl. Corr. XVIII. p. 542.
Capt. Corry	31	46 46	Comm. by Sec. of R. Geogr. Soc. Lond.
Moore and Beke	31	45 45	Journ. of R. Geogr. Soc. Lond. Vol. VII. 1837. p. 456.

Mean 31° 46' 43" differing only 3" from Corry, and 9" from Niebuhr.

The longitude is that found by Capt. Corry from a lunar observation in 1818, kindly communicated by the Sec. of the R. Geogr. Soc. London. This is the only tolerable observation yet made for the longitude. Seetzen indeed observed imperfectly at three different times ; but his results vary more than a degree from each other. See Zach's Monatl. Corr. XVIII.

p. 544. Berghaus has 35° 13' 33" E. Greenwich ; a casual approximation deduced from a comparison of Itineraries from Yâfa. Memoir zu seiner Karte von Syrien, pp. 28, 29.—The latest result is given in Vol. III. Sect. IV, under Apr. 30th, end.

[2] 1 Sam. 17, 2. 19.

great Wady; while on the north, a bend of the ridge connected with the mount of Olives, bounds the prospect at the distance of more than a mile. Towards the southwest the view is somewhat more open; for here lies the plain of Rephaim, already described,[1] commencing just at the southern brink of the valley of Hinnom, and stretching off southwest, where it is drained to the western plain. In the northwest too the eye reaches up along the upper part of the valley of Jehoshaphat; and, from many points, can discern the mosk of Neby Samwil, situated on a lofty ridge beyond the great Wady, at the distance of two hours.

The surface of the elevated promontory itself, on which the city stands, slopes somewhat steeply towards the east, terminating on the brink of the valley of Jehoshaphat. From the northern part, near the present Damascus gate, a depression or shallow Wady runs in a southern direction, having on the west the ancient hills of Akra and Zion, and on the east the lower ones of Bezetha and Moriah. Between the hills of Akra and Zion another depression or shallow Wady (still easy to be traced) comes down from near the Yâfa gate, and joins the former. It then continues obliquely down the slope, but with a deeper bed, in a southern direction quite to the pool of Siloam and the valley of Jehoshaphat. This is the ancient Tyropœon. West of its lower part, Zion rises loftily, lying mostly without the modern city; while on the east of the Tyropœon and the valley first mentioned, lie Bezetha, Moriah, and Ophel, the last a long and comparatively narrow ridge also outside of the modern city, and terminating in a rocky bluff over the pool of Siloam. These last three hills may strictly be taken as only parts of one and the same ridge. The breadth of the whole site of Jerusalem, from the brow of the valley of Hinnom near the Yâfa gate to the brink of the valley of Jehoshaphat, is about 1020 yards, or nearest half a geographical mile; of which distance 318 yards is occupied by the area of the great mosk, el-Haram esh-Sherif. North of the Yâfa gate the city wall sweeps round more to the west, and increases the breadth of the city in that part.

The country around Jerusalem is all of limestone formation; and not particularly fertile. The rocks everywhere come out above the surface, which in many parts is also thickly strewed with loose stones; and the aspect of the whole region is barren and dreary. Yet the olive thrives here abundantly; and fields of grain are seen in the valleys and level places; but they are less productive than in the region of Hebron and Nâbulus. Neither vineyards nor fig trees flourish on the high ground around the city; though the latter are found in the gardens below Siloam, and are very frequent in the vicinity of Bethlehem.

[1] See above, p. 219.

i. 383, 384

II. THE CITY, ITS INTERIOR, ETC.

The Walls. An inscription in Arabic over the Yâfa gate, as well as others in various places, records that the present walls of Jerusalem were rebuilt by order of Sultan Suleimân in A. H. 948, corresponding to A. D. 1542.[1] They appear to occupy very nearly the site of the former walls of the middle ages, which were several times thrown down and rebuilt during the crusades ;[2] a slight deviation only being visible around the northwest corner, on both the western and northern sides. The materials were probably those of the former walls ; and are in great part apparently ancient. They consist wholly of hewn stones, in general not very large, laid in mortar.[3] Many of them are bevelled in the manner which will be described hereafter, evincing an antiquity not later than the times of the Romans ; and these are intermingled with others plainly hewn, especially in the upper part of the walls. On the eastern side, the wall of the area of the Haram esh-Sherif, constitutes also the wall of the city for about half the extent upon this side. The same is true of the southern wall of this area for about two hundred yards from its southeast corner ; at which point the city wall comes up at right angles from the south and unites with the former. The parts of the wall thus connected with the mosk, would seem not to have been rebuilt at the same time with the rest ; they are apparently older and more dilapidated ; although they exhibit an abundance of patchwork.

The walls of the city have quite a stately and imposing appearance ; all of hewn stone, with towers and battlements ; the latter crowning a breastwork with loopholes. This has already been described, as protecting the broad walk along the top of the wall within, to which flights of steps lead up at convenient intervals.[4] The height of the walls on the outside varies much with the inequalities of the ground in different parts, from some twenty to fifty feet. At the northeast corner and along a portion of the northern side, a trench has been cut in the rock outside, along the wall, apparently as a further defence ; but in other places equally exposed, there is no trace of any trench. Indeed the walls of Jerusalem, notwithstanding their elevation

---

[1] Or as usually given, A. D. 1543.—Quaresmius assigns the building of the walls to Selim in A. D. 1517; he doubtless could not read the inscriptions. Elucid. II. p. 41.—Belon, who was here about A. D. 1547, mentions that the walls had been recently built up; Observations, etc. p. 143. Paulus' Samml. I. p. 162.—Schweigger in 1576 also ascribes them to Selim, and tells a fabulous story of his causing the lions to be carved over St. Stephen's gate; Reissbuch des h. Landes, II. p. 122.

[2] See further on under "Walls of the Middle Ages."

[3] Notwithstanding the mortar, the walls are full of crevices; furnishing a retreat to multitudes of lizards, which are seen gliding over them in all directions.

[4] See above, p. 238.

i. 384, 385

and imposing aspect, would probably present no great obstacle to the entrance of a regular besieging army.

Gates. Jerusalem at present has only four open gates, one on each of the four sides of the city, looking towards the north, south, east, and west. Besides these there were formerly four other mostly smaller gates, now closed up with walls. All these gates appear to occupy the same places as those which existed before the present city wall was rebuilt ; and some of them are evidently themselves earlier structures, which were retained at that time. In this respect we shall recur to them again hereafter, confining ourselves here to their present state and names.

On the west side of the city is the gate called by the natives *Bâb el-Khûlil,* or Hebron gate ; but which the Franks call also the gate of Bethlehem, or of Yâfa, and sometimes gate of the Pilgrims. From it lead the roads to all these three towns. It consists of a massive square tower ; and in going out of the city one enters it from the east and passes out through its northern side. The breadth of the city from this gate to the western entrance of the Haram esh-Sherîf, is about 2100 feet or 700 yards, as near as we could determine it by paces.

On the north is the Damascus gate of the Franks ; called by the natives *Bâb el-'Amûd,* " Gate of the Pillar." It is more ornamented than the rest. The great road to Nâbulus, Damascus, and the north, leads from it.

St. Stephen's gate, so called by the Franks, is on the east side of the city, a little north of the area of the great mosk. The Muslims call it *Bâb es-Sûbât,* " Gate of the Tribes ; " while the native Christians give it the name *Bâb Sitty Meryam,* " Gate of my Lady Mary," probably in reference to the church and tomb of the Virgin Mary in the valley of Jehoshaphat below. From it lead the roads to the mount of Olives, Bethany, 'Anâta, etc. Over this gate on the outside are sculptured four lions ; which shows at least that it was not originally the work of Muhammedans.

The southern gate, called by the Franks that of Zion, and by the natives *Bâb en-Neby Dâûd,* " Gate of the Prophet David," opens out only upon the exterior part of Zion, towards the Muslim tomb of David, etc. Several paths indeed wind down from it to the valleys of Hinnom and Jehoshaphat ; but no important road leads from it.

Of the gates now closed up, one is on the north side, about half way between the Damascus gate and the northeast corner of the city. It is only a small portal in one of the towers. This is called by Franks the Gate of Herod, and by the natives *Bâb ez-Zahary,* " the flowery."—Another small portal, the Dung gate of the Franks, is on the south side of the city, a little west of south

i. 386, 387

from the southwest corner of the area of the mosk, and near the
bed of the Tyropœon.   The native name is *Bâb el-Mughâribeh*,
" Gate of the Western Africans."[1]—A third is the large double
gateway on the eastern side of the area of the great mosk, now
called by the natives *Bâb ed-Dahariyeh*, " the Eternal gate ;" but
which Franks are wont to speak of as the Golden gate, *Porta
aurea*.[2]   This is evidently a structure of antiquity, and will be
more fully described hereafter.—The fourth of these gates is adjacent to the south wall of the area of the mosk, just in the corner
where the city wall comes up and joins it.   It is a low square
structure ; and if seen only from the outside, looks as if it had once
led up into the area of the mosk.   We examined it, and entered
it afterwards from the inside, and found that it led only into the
city.   The workmanship of it is quite modern.   Of this gate I
have been able to find no mention, either in Arabian or early
Christian writers.   Quaresmius is silent as to it ; and no Frank
traveller appears to have observed it, until within a few years.
Richardson saw it only from the outside, and speaks of it under a
wrong name, as leading up into the mosk el-Aksa.[3]

The Golden gate has been walled up for centuries ; and the
one last mentioned, adjacent to the south side of the same area,
would seem also to have been very long disused.   There is no
trace of any former path connected with it, either within or without the city.   The other two gates, or rather portals,—the Dung
gate and that of Herod, so called,—have been apparently more
recently closed.   They seem to have been open in Niebuhr's day;[4]
and several travellers of the present century mention their names,
without specifying whether they were still open or not.[5]   At present they are firmly walled up ; although a lane which even now
leads down through fields of prickly pear towards the Dung gate,
would seem to indicate that the latter had not long been closed.[6]

Mount Zion.   Of the hills by which the surface of the city
was and is divided into various quarters, that of Zion is the most
extensive and important.   Its northern part or brow is just south
of the street which leads down directly east from the Yâfa gate,
along the bed of the ancient Tyropœon. In going from this street

---

[1] The adjacent quarter of the city, near
the southwest part of the court of the
great mosk, appears at one time to have
been inhabited by a colony of these people. See the History of Jerusalem by
Mejr ed-Din in A. D. 1495, translated by
von Hammer, Fundgruben des Orients, II.
pp. 98, 125.

[2] The name *Porta aurea* goes back at
least to the times of the crusades ; Will.
Tyr. 8. 3.

[3] Richardson's Travels, etc. II. pp. 255,
292. Prokesch Reise ins h. Land. p. 85.

[4] Niebuhr's Reisebeschr. III. p. 52.
Comp. Kortens Reise, p. 112.

[5] Travels of Ali Bey II. p. 244. Chateaubriand Itin. II. pp. 67, 68. Par. 1837.
Richardson II. pp. 254, 255. Prokesch,
pp. 85, 86.

[6] According to Schubert, both these
gates have been closed up only since the
rebellion of 1834 ; Reise etc. II. pp. 542,
544.—A door still leads into the interior
of the Dung gate ; which is sometimes
found open. See under Apr. 28, 1852.

i. 387, 388

southwards near the bazars, one comes almost immediately to a sharp though short ascent; and turning to the right along its brow, finds himself higher than the roofs of the small houses which line the street below. The ascent towards the south along the street near by the citadel is more gradual.

On the west and south, Zion rises abruptly from the valley of Hinnom, which sweeps around its southwest corner almost at a right angle, descending very rapidly first towards the south and then towards the east to the valley of Jehoshaphat. This circumstance renders the southwest brow of Zion apparently more lofty than any other point connected with the city now or anciently. This we measured approximately. Beginning at the first tower from the southwest corner of the city wall, we measured 865 feet on a course due south to the brow of Zion. Hence the well of Job or Nehemiah bore S. 58° E. at an angle of depression of 12°. Descending now very steeply, still due south, we measured 140 feet at an angle of 11° depression, and 530 feet at an angle of 23¼°; and came thus to the bottom of the valley of Hinnom just east of the road which there crosses it. This gives an elevation above the valley at this point of 154 English feet; which is probably not very far from the truth. The height of Zion above the valley at the southwest corner of the wall of the city, obtained in the same way, is 104 feet; and that of the ground at the Yâfa gate, 44 feet. But these differences arise at least as much from the rapid sinking of the valley, as from the increased height of Zion towards the south. The elevation of the southern brow of Zion above the well of Nehemiah, we were unable to obtain; but from the very rapid descent of the valley of Hinnom in that part, I should be inclined to estimate it at not less than 300 feet.[1]

The summit of Zion presents a level tract of considerable extent along its western brow. The eastern side of the hill slopes down steeply, but not in general abruptly, to the Tyropœon, which separates it from the narrow ridge south of the Haram; while at the extreme southeast part, below Siloam, it extends quite down to the valley of Jehoshaphat. Only the northern portion of Zion is included in the modern walls; and this is occupied chiefly by the Jewish quarter, and by the great Armenian convent. Here the eastern side of Zion within the city, adjacent to the Tyropœon after the latter bends south, is an abrupt precipice

[1] According to Schubert's barometrical measurements, Zion is 241 Paris feet higher than the valley of Jehoshaphat. But it is not said at what point in that valley the observation was taken; though various reasons render it probable, that it was not lower down than opposite the great mosk. If so, the estimate in the text accords well with that result; for the descent of the valley of Jehoshaphat from that point to the well of Job, is certainly not less than 60 feet. Schubert's Reise, II. p. 521.

i. 389, 390

of rock from twenty to thirty feet high, lying overagainst the south-west part of the area of the Haram esh-Sherîf. This rock is still in its natural state ; and probably presents the same appearance as it did in the days of Josephus ; though the adjacent valley has doubtless been greatly filled up with rubbish.

Without the walls, the level part of Zion, as we have seen, is occupied by the Christian cemeteries, the house of Caiaphas now an Armenian convent, the Cœnaculum or Muslim tomb of David, and the adjacent buildings, formerly a Latin convent. The rest of the surface is now tilled ; and the city of David has become a ploughed field ! The eastern slope is likewise in part cultivated ; and paths wind down along the declivity to Siloam, and also more to the right to the bottom of the valley of Hinnom. The aqueduct from Solomon's pools, which crosses the valley of Hinnom at a point north of the southwest corner of the city wall, is then carried along and around the southwest part of Zion above the valley, till it comes out again high up along the eastern slope and enters the city.

Below the aqueduct, and indeed near the bed of the Tyro-pœon, a few rods south of the Dung gate, is a low arch, forming the outlet of a large sewer from the city. We could not ascertain from what point within the walls the sewer comes, but it is not improbably brought along beneath the eastern brow of Zion. It was now entirely dry. During the rebellion of the Fellâhs and their siege of Jerusalem in 1834, some of the leaders are said to have passed up through this sewer, and thus got possession of the city.

Akra. North of Zion is the hill of Akra. It is the continuation or rather the termination of the broad ridge or swell of land, which lies north of the basin at the head of the valley of Hinnom, and extends down into the city, forming its northwest part. Indeed the northwest corner of the city wall is directly on this ridge ; from which spot the wall descends immediately towards the northeast and also though less rapidly towards the southeast. To the whole ridge, both without and within the city, a comparatively modern tradition has given the name of Mount Gihon ; though there is no trace of any hill so named in Scripture or other ancient history.[1]   Within the walls, this hill or ridge is separated from Zion, as we have seen, by the upper part of the Tyropœon ; which commences as a shallow depression near the Yâfa gate.

When one enters the Yâfa gate and takes the first street leading north immediately from the adjacent open place, he has before him at first a considerable ascent ; though afterwards the

[1] The name of Gihon, as applied to this ridge, seems to be first mentioned by Brocardus about A. D. 1283 ; cap. 9.

way is more level quite to the Latin convent in the northwest part of the city. In the street leading north below the pool of Hezekiah, and also in that along the bazars, this ascent is less perceptible. The church of the Holy Sepulchre stands directly on the ridge of Akra; and from it and from that neighbourhood, there is everywhere a considerable declivity towards the Damascus gate. The ground also descends eastward from the Latin convent to the same church; and then again by a still deeper declivity, from the church to the street along the valley lying between Akra and the area of the great mosk.

Bezetha. Eastward from the Damascus gate, and northeasterly from Akra, lies the hill of Bezetha. It is separated from Akra by the rather broad valley which has its commencement in the plain just around and outside of the Damascus gate, and runs in a southerly direction till it unites with the Tyropœon below the point of Akra. The western side of Bezetha is nearly or quite as high as Akra;[1] while towards the east it slopes gradually down, but with another lower ridge or wave between it and the brow of the valley of Jehoshaphat. The western side, near the gate of Damascus, is very steep; as are also the northern and southern sides in this quarter. Indeed the north wall of the city runs along its northern brow; and the rock on the outside is there precipitous; with a wide and deep trench at its base cut through the solid rock.

The summit of Bezetha is now mostly covered with low buildings, or rather hovels; and on the southeast part are also dwellings and the ruined church connected with the former nunnery of the house of Anna.[2] But in the northeast the whole slope within the city walls is occupied by gardens, fields, and olive yards, with comparatively few houses or ruined dwellings; the whole having more the aspect of a village in the country, than of a quarter in a city. The top of the hill presents a fine view of the other parts of Jerusalem. We saw here no traces of ancient ruins; although the monks have chosen to assign this location to a palace of the younger (Herod) Agrippa.[3]

Moriah. I have already remarked, that the part of Jerusalem lying between the valley of Jehoshaphat and the valley run-

---

[1] Josephus says Bezetha was higher than any of the other hills; B. J. 5. 5. 8. This is probably meant of the hills of the lower city, Moriah and Akra; and is true as to the part of Akra which lay within the second wall. But the language could not well be true in respect to Zion.

[2] See above, p. 233.

[3] This hypothesis is mentioned by Marinus Sanutus, A. D. 1321, (3. 14. 10,) but appears to be wholly groundless. The main passage which Quaresmius cites

from Josephus in support of it, (Ant. 20. 8, 11,) contradicts it expressly. Josephus there relates, that Agrippa built a house or palace near the Xystus, whence he could see from his couch whatever was going on in the temple; and to prevent this the Jews raised a high wall on the *west* side of the temple. All this of course fixes the site of the palace upon the northeast part of Zion. See Quaresm. Elucid. Terræ Sanct. II. p. 204.

i. 391–393

ning down from the Damascus gate to the pool of Siloam, may
be regarded as one ridge, having on it the separate summits or
hills Bezetha and Moriah; and corresponding further down perhaps to the ancient quarter Ophel.   Moriah was apparently at
first an elevated mound of rock, rising by itself upon this ridge,
overagainst the eastern point of Akra.   The temple was placed
upon the levelled summit of this rock ; and then immense walls
were erected from its base on the four sides ; and the interval between them and the sides filled in with earth, or built up with
vaults ; so as to form on the top a large area on a level with the
temple.[1]   This area or court of the ancient temple, as we shall
see hereafter, was probably not very different from the present enclosure of the Haram esh-Sherif.   This is now separated from
the rocky brow of Zion by the Tyropœon ; and from Akra by the
valley which comes from the Damascus gate.

In passing along this latter valley through the present street,
towards the south, apparently just before coming to the Tyropœon, one crosses over a mound or low ridge of ground.   This
mound serves to carry the aqueduct from Solomon's pools into
the area of the mosk ; which is everywhere higher than the bottom of this valley.   Indeed all the western entrances of the mosk
are reached by an ascent ; and some of them at least by steps.

On the north side, Moriah is not now separated from Bezetha
by any valley or trench ; except in part by the large reservoir
commonly called Bethesda.   The street which leads to the eastern gate of the city passes here ; ascending somewhat from the
valley near the northwest corner of the area, having the steep
part of Bezetha on the left ; and then descending gradually to
St. Stephen's gate.

Ophel.   This is the remainder of the ridge extending south
from Moriah to Siloam, between the deep valley of Jehoshaphat
on the east and the steep but shallower Tyropœon on the west.
The top of the ridge is flat, descending rapidly towards the south
sometimes by offsets of rock ; and the ground is tilled and planted with olive and other fruit trees.   At the northern end, just at
the southeast corner of the *city* wall, (not that of the mosk,) the
surface is already 100 feet lower than the top of the wall of the
area of the mosk.   From this point I measured 1550 feet or
about 516 yards on a course S. 20° W. to the end of the ridge,
a rocky bluff forty or fifty feet above the pool of Siloam in the
mouth of the Tyropœon.   The breadth of the ridge, as measured
about the middle, I found to be 290 feet, or about 96 yards, from
brow to brow.

Chief Streets.   The principal streets in Jerusalem run nearly
at right angles to each other.   Very few if any of them bear

---

[1] Joseph. B. J. 5. 5. 1.

names among the native population.[1] They are narrow and
badly paved, being merely laid irregularly with large stones, with
a deep square channel in the middle ; but the steepness of the
ground contributes to keep them cleaner than in most oriental
cities. Of those running down eastwards from the upper to the
lower part of the city, the chief are, the one leading from the
Yâfa gate directly to the Haram esh-Sherif, and that from the
Latin convent to St. Stephen's gate. This last includes the *Via
dolorosa.* The principal streets running from south to north are,
that just below the pool of Hezekiah, those of the Bazar, and
that along the hollow parallel to the Haram. Those on Zion
seem in general to be less frequented.

Circumference of the Holy City. One of the first measurements which I took in Jerusalem, was that of the circumference
of the walls. This was done with a measuring tape of one
hundred English feet, carried by our two servants, while I noted
down the results. We measured as closely as possible to the
walls, yet without regarding the short angles and smaller zigzags. We started from the Yâfa gate and proceeded first southwards and so around the city.

		Eng. Feet.	Gen. Course.
1.	From the Yâfa gate to the southwest corner of the city, first descending and then ascending . .	1400	S.
2.	Zion gate, level	600	Easterly.
3.	Dung gate (closed), descending . . .	1700	N. Easterly
4.	Southeast corner of *city* wall, nearly level .	500	E.
5.	Wall of area of great mosk, south side, ascending	290	N.
6.	Southeast corner of wall of mosk, level . .	630	E.
7.	Golden gate (closed), slightly ascending . .	1045	N.
8.	Northeast corner of area of mosk, level . .	483	N.
9.	St. Stephen's gate, level	200	N.
10.	Northeast corner of city, level . . .	1062	N.
11.	Herod's gate (closed), along the trench, level .	1000	Westerly
12.	Damascus gate, uneven	1200	Westerly
13.	Northwest corner of city, ascending . .	1990	S. Westerly
14.	Yâfa gate, descending gradually . . .	878	S. 40° E.

12,978 Feet,
or 4,326 Yards.

This gives for the whole circumference a distance of 2½ English miles less 74 yards ; or very nearly 2⅛ geographical miles.

III. ADJACENT VALLEYS AND HILLS.

Valley of Jehoshaphat. . Brook Kidron. The deep valley
on the east of Jerusalem appears to be mentioned both in the

[1] Chateaubriand in his *Itineraire* professes to give the names of all the chief
streets ; but our friends, who had resided
i. 394–396
several years in the city, and made frequent inquiries, had never been able to
hear of any, except in a few instances.

Old and New Testament only under the name of the brook or torrent Kidron. Josephus also gives it only the same name.[1] The prophet Joel speaks indeed of a valley of Jehoshaphat, in which God will judge the heathen for their oppression of the Jews; but this seems to be merely a metaphorical allusion to the signification of the name.[2] There is not the slightest historical ground, either in the Scriptures or in Josephus, for connecting it with the valley of the Kidron.[3] Yet on this slender foundation appears to rest the present name of the valley; and also the belief current among the Catholics, Jews, and Muhammedans, that the last judgment will be held in it.[4] The name Jehoshaphat, however, was already applied to it in the earliest ages of the Christian era; for it is found in Eusebius and other writers of the fourth century.[5] There is therefore no good reason, why we should not employ this name at the present day. The Arabs too have adopted it, under the form of Wady Yehôshâfât.

It is remarkable that no writer (at least so far as I have been able to discover) has given the topography of the upper part of this valley; nor correctly described either the place of its beginning, nor its course below the well of Nehemiah. One of the latest and most exact travellers has even said, that it commences near the northeast corner of the city.[6] For this reason, the following details are here given.

In approaching Jerusalem from the high mosk of Neby Samwil in the northwest, the traveller first descends and crosses the bed of the great Wady Beit Hanîna already described. He then ascends again towards the southeast by a small side Wady and along a rocky slope for twenty-five minutes, when he reaches the tombs of the Judges, lying in a small gap or depression of the ridge, still half an hour distant from the northern

---

[1] 2 Sam. 15, 23. 1 Kings 2, 38. etc. The Hebrew word is נַחַל, which may be taken as nearly equivalent to the Arabic *Wady*. The Seventy, the New Testament, and also Josephus, have χείμαρρος, a storm brook, winter torrent; see as above, and John 18, 1. Joseph. Antiq. 8. 1. 5. Josephus has also φάραγξ Κεδρών, B. J. 5. 2. 3. ib. 5. 4. 2.

[2] Joel 3, [4,] 2. 12. Jehoshaphat, Heb. יְהוֹשָׁפָט i. e. *Jehovah judgeth*. The reference sometimes made to 2 Chr. c. 20, has no bearing upon the illustration of Joel l. c.

[3] It is hardly necessary to remark, that there is likewise no historical ground for connecting this valley in any way with the valley of Shaveh or the King's dale, Gen. 14, 17. 2 Sam. 18, 18.

[4] Doubdan Voyage, etc. p. 262. Quaresmius Elucid. Terr. Sanct. II. p. 156. Reland Pal. p. 355. Travels of Ali Bey, II. p. 224. Hist. of Jerus. by Mejr ed-Dîn, Fundgruben des Orients, II. p. 381. —This latter writer calls the valley, or at least the part north of the city, in allusion to the same belief, *es-Sâherah*; p. 133. But both he and also Bohaeddin in the twelfth century, give to the part along and below the city, the name of *Jehennam* (Gehinnom); ibid. p. 133. Bohaed. Vit. Saladin, p. 73. ed. Schult.

[5] Euseb. Onomast. art. Κοιλάς, *Coelas*. Cyrill in Joel 3, [4,] 2. 12. Itinerar. Hierosol. p. 594, ed. Wesseling.

[6] Prokesch, p. 86. So also, by implication, Quaresmius, Tom. II. pp. 151, 155.

gate of the city. A few steps further he reaches the water-shed between the great Wady behind him and the tract before him; and here is the head of the valley of Jehoshaphat. From this point the dome of the Holy Sepulchre bears S. by E. The tract around this spot is very rocky; and the rocks have been much cut away, partly in quarrying building-stone, and partly in the formation of sepulchres. The region is full of excavated tombs; and these continue with more or less frequency on both sides of the valley, all the way down to Jerusalem. The valley runs for fifteen minutes directly towards the city; it is here shallow and broad, and in some parts tilled, though very stony. The road follows along its bottom to the same point. The valley now turns nearly east, almost at a right angle, and passes to the northward of the tombs of the Kings and the Muslim Wely before mentioned.[1] Here it is about two hundred rods distant from the city; and the tract between is tolerably level ground, planted with olive trees. The Nâbulus road crosses it in this part, and ascends the hill on the north. The valley is here still shallow, and runs in the same easterly direction for about ten minutes. It then bends again to the south, and following this general course, passes between the city and the mount of Olives.

Before reaching the city, and also opposite its northern part, the valley spreads out into a basin of some breadth, which is tilled, and contains plantations of olive and other fruit trees. In this part it is crossed obliquely by a road leading from the northeast corner of Jerusalem across the northern part of the mount of Olives to 'Anâta. Its sides are still full of excavated tombs. As the valley descends, the steep side upon the right becomes more and more elevated above it; until at the gate of St. Stephen, the height of this brow is about 100 feet. Here a path winds down from the gate on a course S. E. by E. and crosses the water-bed of the valley by a bridge; beyond which are the church with the tomb of the Virgin, Gethsemane, and other plantations of olive trees, already described.[2] The path and bridge are on a causeway, or rather terrace, built up across the valley, perpendicular on the south side; the earth being filled in on the northern side up to the level of the bridge. The bridge itself consists of an arch, open on the south side, and 17 feet high from the bed of the channel below; but the north side is built up, with two subterranean drains entering it from above; one of which comes from the sunken court of the Virgin's tomb, and the other from the fields further in the northwest.[3] The breadth of the valley at this point, will appear from the meas-

[1] Page 240.
[2] See pages 234, 235.
[3] This bridge too has been ascribed to i. 397–399

Helena; Breydenbach in Reissbuch des heil. Landes, p. 111. Adrichom. Theatrum Terræ Sanct. page 171.

urements which I took from St. Stephen's gate to Gethsemane, along the path, viz.

		Eng. Feet.
1. From St. Stephen's gate to the brow of the descent, level	.	135
2. Bottom of the slope, the angle of the descent being 16½°	.	415
3. Bridge, level	.	140
4. Northwest corner of Gethsemane, slight rise . . .	.	145
5. Northeast corner of do. do.	.	150

The last three numbers give the breadth of the proper bottom of the valley at this spot, viz. 435 feet, or 145 yards. Further north it is somewhat broader.

Below the bridge the valley contracts gradually, and sinks more rapidly. The first continuous traces of a water-course or torrent bed commence at the bridge; though they occur likewise at intervals higher up. The western hill becomes steeper and more elevated; while on the east the mount of Olives rises much higher, but is not so steep. At the distance of 1000 feet from the bridge on a course S. 10° W. the bottom of the valley has become merely a deep gully, the narrow bed of a torrent, from which the hills rise directly on each side. Here another bridge is thrown across it on an arch; and just by on the left are the alleged tombs of Jehoshaphat, Absalom, and others; as also the Jewish cemetery. The valley now continues of the same character, and follows the same course (S. 10° W.) for 550 feet further; where it makes a sharp turn for a moment towards the right. This portion is the narrowest of all; it is here a mere ravine between high mountains. The southeast corner of the area of the mosk overhangs this part, the corner of the wall standing upon the very brink of the declivity. From it to the bottom, on a course southeast, the angle of depression is 27°, and the distance 450 feet; giving an elevation of 128 feet at that point; to which may be added 20 feet or more for the rise of ground just north along the wall; making in all an elevation of about 150 feet.[1] This however is the highest point above the valley; for further south, the narrow ridge of Ophel slopes down as rapidly as the valley itself. In this part of the valley one would expect to find, if anywhere, traces of ruins thrown down from above, and the ground raised by the rubbish thus accumulated. Occasional blocks of stone are indeed seen; but neither the surface of the ground, nor the bed of the torrent, exhibits

[1] The first time we passed along the western brow of the valley of Jehoshaphat in this part, in company with Mr Nicolayson, and looked down upon it from above at the southeast corner of the area of the mosk, we all judged the depth to be 200 feet. By an error, which is very remarkable in him, Niebuhr estimates the general depth of the valley here at only 40 or 50 feet; Reisebeschr. III. p. 54; Anhang p. 143. Olshausen's Topogr. des alt. Jerus. pp. 72, 73.—The measurement given in the text, although only an approximation, is yet near enough to the truth to correct both these estimates.

any special appearance of having been raised or interrupted by masses of ruins.

Below the short turn above mentioned, a line of 1025 feet on a course southwest brings us to the fountain of the Virgin, lying deep under the western hill. The valley has now opened a little ; but its bottom is still occupied only by the bed of the torrent. From here a course S. 20° W. carried us along the village of Siloam (Kefr Selwân) on the eastern side, and at 1170 feet we were opposite the mouth of the Tyropœon and the pool of Siloam, which lies 255 feet within it. The mouth of this valley is still 40 or 50 feet higher than the bed of the Kidron. The steep descent between the two has been already described as built up in terraces; which, as well as the strip of level ground below, are occupied with gardens belonging to the village of Siloam. These are irrigated by the waters of the pool of Siloam, which at this time were lost in them. In these gardens the stones have been removed, and the soil is a fine mould. They are planted with fig and other fruit trees, and furnish also vegetables for the city. Elsewhere the bottom of the valley is thickly strewed with small stones.

Further down, the valley opens more, and is tilled. A line of 685 feet on the same course (S. 20° W.) brought us to a rocky point of the eastern hill, here called the mount of Offence, over-against the entrance of the valley of Hinnom. Thence to the well of Job or Nehemiah, is 275 feet due south. At the junction of the two valleys, the bottom forms an oblong plat, extending from the gardens above mentioned nearly to the well of Job, and being 150 yards or more in breadth. The western and northwestern parts of this plat are in like manner occupied by gardens ; many of which are also on terraces, and receive a portion of the waters of Siloam.

Below the well of Nehemiah, the valley of Jehoshaphat continues to run S. S. W. between the mount of Offence and the hill of Evil Counsel, so called. At 130 feet is a small cavity or outlet by which the water of the well sometimes runs off. At about 1200 feet or 400 yards from the well, is a place under the western hill, where in the rainy season water flows out as from a fountain. At about 1500 feet or 500 yards below the well, the valley bends off S. 75° E. for half a mile or more ; and then turns again more to the south and pursues its way to the Dead Sea. At the angle where it thus bends eastward, a small Wady comes in from the west, from behind the hill of Evil Counsel. The width of the main valley below the well as far as to the turn, varies from 50 to 100 yards ; it is full of olive and fig trees, and is in most parts ploughed and sown with grain.—Further down, it takes the name among the Arabs of Wady er-

i. 400–402

Râhib, 'Monks' Valley,' from the convent of St. Saba situated on it; and still nearer to the Dead Sea it is also called Wady en-Nâr, 'Fire Valley.'

The channel of the valley of Jehoshaphat, the brook Kidron of the Scriptures, is. nothing more than the dry bed of a wintry torrent, bearing marks of being occasionally swept over by a large volume of water. No stream flows here now except during the heavy rains of winter, when the waters descend into it from the neighbouring hills. Yet even in winter there is no constant flow; and our friends, who had resided several years in the city, had never seen a stream running through the valley. Nor is there any evidence, that there was anciently more water in it than at present. Like the Wadys of the desert, the valley probably served of old, as now, only to drain off the waters of the rainy season.

Valley of Hinnom. This valley is so called in the Old Testament; though more commonly in the fuller form, valley of the Son of Hinnom.[1] The Arabian writer Edrisi in the twelfth century apparently includes the lower part of it under the name Wady Jehennam; and this is the usual name for the whole Wady among the Arabs at the present day.[2] Its commencement, as we have seen, is in the broad sloping basin on the west of the city, south of the Yâfa road, extending up nearly to the brow of the next Wady on the west. The large reservoir, commonly called the Upper Pool, or Gihon, may be regarded as a sort of central point in this basin; from which the land slopes upwards by a gentle acclivity on every side except the east. On this side the ground descends towards the Yâfa gate, forming a broad hollow or valley between the two swells on the north and south. This part might perhaps not improperly be termed the valley of Gihon; though the name Gihon in Scripture is applied only to a fountain.

From the eastern side of the said upper pool the course of the valley is S. 51° E. for the distance of 1900 feet to the bend opposite the Yâfa gate. The valley is here from 50 to 100 yards in width. The bottom is everywhere thickly covered with small stones; but is nevertheless sown, and a crop of lentiles was now growing upon it. From this point up to the Yâfa gate was a distance of 400 feet, viz. 100 in the valley, 200 on the steep slope at an angle of 20°, and 100 on the level of the gate above. Hence the depth of the valley is here 44 feet below the gate.—The valley now descends on a course S. 10° W. for 2107 feet, to the bend at the southwest corner of Zion. In this dis-

---

[1] גֵּיא הִנֹּם Josh. 15, 8. גֵּי בֶן הִנֹּם Jer. 19, 2. 6. Hence are derived the Greek Γέεννα, and the corresponding English forms *Gehinnom, Gehenna.*

[2] Edrisi, p. 345. ed. Jaubert. Other Arabic writers, as we have seen, apply this name to the valley of Jehoshaphat. See above, p. 269, Note 4.

i. 402, 403

tance, 875 feet brings us to the aqueduct as it crosses the valley ; at 220 feet further is the upper end of the lower pool, the length of which in the middle is 592 feet ; and the remaining 420 feet lie between the pool and the angle of the valley. In this part the valley continues about of the same breadth, grows deeper, is planted with olive and other fruit trees, and is in some places tilled.—A new course of S. 40° E. strikes the south side at the distance of 700 feet ; and then another of S. 75° E. carries us 625 feet further. In this last, at 130 feet, a path crosses the valley leading up over the hills towards Bethlehem ; and 75 feet below this road is the point to which we measured in order to determine the height of Zion ; which last is here 154 feet.[1] From the end of this course, the valley runs due east, for the space of 1440 feet. For about 400 feet of this distance, the breadth remains the same as above ; and the fruit trees and tillage continue. The southern hill is steep, rocky, and full of tombs. At 440 feet the valley contracts, becomes quite narrow and stony, and descends with much greater rapidity. Towards the end of the course it opens again, and meets the gardens in the oblong plat where it forms a junction with the valley of Jehoshaphat. The southeast corner of Zion here runs down and out in a low point. From the end of the last course to the well of Nehemiah, is a distance of 480 feet, measured on a course S. 30° E.

In these gardens, lying partly within the mouth of Hinnom and partly in the valley of Jehoshaphat, and irrigated by the waters of Siloam, Jerome assigns the place of Tophet ; where the Jews practised the horrid rites of Baal and Moloch, and " burned their sons and their daughters in the fire."[2] It was probably in allusion to this detested and abominable fire, that the later Jews applied the name of this valley (Gehenna), to denote the place of future punishment or the fires of hell. At least there is no evidence of any other fires having been kept up in this valley ; as has sometimes been supposed.[3]

Mount of Olives. This mountain, so celebrated both in the Old and New Testament, is called by the Arabs, Jebel et-Tûr ;[4] and lies on the east of Jerusalem, from which it is separated only by the narrow valley of Jehoshaphat, as above described. It is usually said to have three summits ; the middle and ap-

---

[1] See above, p. 264.
[2] 2 Kings 23, 10. Jer. 7, 32. Hieron. Comm, in Jer. 7, 31. Ejusd. Comm. in Matth. 10, 28. The description in the text explains an apparent inconsistency in the language of Jerome in the passages here cited. In the first he speaks of Tophet as a pleasant spot in the valley of Hinnom, with trees and gardens watered from Siloam. In the other, he describes it in like manner, but as lying at the foot of Moriah, near Siloam. He evidently regarded Ophel as belonging to Moriah.
[3] See Rosenmüller Biblische Geogr. II. i. pp. 156, 164.
[4] Edrisi writes also Jebel Zeitûn, i. e. Mount of Olives; p. 344. ed. Jaubert.

i. 403–405

parently the highest of which, directly opposite the city, has been falsely assumed by a very early tradition, as the place of our Lord's ascension.[1]   Towards the south it sinks down into a lower ridge overagainst the well of Nehemiah, called now by Franks the mount of Offence, in allusion to the idolatrous worship established by Solomon " in the hill that is before [eastward of] Jerusalem."[2]   Across this part leads the usual road to Bethany. Towards the north, at the distance of just about an English mile, is another summit, nearly or quite as high as the middle one. The ridge between the two, curves somewhat eastwards, leaving room for the valley below to expand a little in this part.   The view of Jerusalem and of the Dead Sea from the middle summit has already been described.   That from the northern one is similar.[3]

The elevation of the central summit of the mount of Olives above the sea is given by Schubert at 2556 Paris feet, or 416 Paris feet above the valley of Jehoshaphat.   Hence it appears to be 175 Paris feet higher than the highest point of Zion.[4] From the Wely on the eastern point of this summit, I took the following bearings among others :

Neby Samwil	N. 40° W.
Eastern dome of church of the Holy Sepulchre . . .	N. 86½° W.
Frank mountain	S. 9½° W.
N. W. corner or bay of Dead Sea	S. 81° E.

Bethlehem is not seen from the Wely ; nor was Kerak visible at the time, to my great regret, in consequence of the hazy atmosphere.

Beyond the northern summit, the ridge of the mount of Olives sweeps round towards the west, and spreads out into the high level tract north of the city, which is skirted on the west and south by the upper part of the valley of Jehoshaphat.   The road to Nâbulus, passing near the tombs of the Kings, crosses the valley and rises by a somewhat long but not steep ascent to this high tract, on which lies the village of Sha'fât on the west of the road, about fifty minutes distant from the Damascus gate. The brow of the main ascent, distant about twenty-five minutes from the same gate, presents the interesting northern prospect of the city, which has been so celebrated by travellers.   It is indeed fine ; but a still better point of view is that upon the

[1] For the date and character of this tradition, see above, p. 253.   The chapel founded originally by Helena, is now in the possession of the Armenians, who have recently erected here a new building. See Euseb. de Vit. Const. 3. 43.

[2] 1 Kings 11, 7. 8.   I have been able to find neither the name *Mons Offensionis*,

nor any allusion to this spot as the place of Solomon's idolatry, earlier than the time of Brocardus, A. D. 1283; cap. 9.

[3] See Note XXV, at the end of the volume.—Maundrell regards the northern summit as the highest point of all ; which indeed may very possibly be the fact.

[4] Schubert's Reise, II. p. 521.

other road more to the right, leading over to 'Anâta.—This high level tract and brow upon the Nâbulus road, is without much doubt the Scopus of Josephus, where Cestus coming from Gabaon (el-Jib), and afterwards Titus coming from Gophna, both encamp, at the distance of seven stadia from Jerusalem ; and the latter obtains his first view of the splendid city and its magnificent temple.[1]

Hill of Evil Counsel. South of Zion, beyond the valley of Hinnom, rises the hill of Evil Counsel so called ; forming the steep southern side or wall of that valley. From the bottom, it rises in most parts very steeply for twenty or thirty feet, with precipitous ledges of rock, in which are many excavated sepulchres. Higher up, the acclivity is more gradual. The highest point is on the west, nearly south of the southwest part of Zion, and a little to the east of the Bethlehem road. This is nearly or quite as high as Zion itself, but not so steep ; and from it the ridge slopes down towards the east to the valley of Jehoshaphat, in the same manner as Zion, though not so rapidly. South of this ridge, a small Wady has its head, which runs down eastwards, and enters the valley of Jehoshaphat, as we have seen, 500 yards below the well of Nehemiah, just where the latter valley turns to the east. This Wady is of course parallel to that of Hinnom ; but is not half so deep. Still further south, beyond the Wady, is another higher hill or mountain, which continues towards the east without sinking from its high level, and skirts the valley of Jehoshaphat on the south after the latter has turned eastward on its course towards the Dead Sea.

The summit of the hill overagainst Zion affords a pleasing view towards the southwest down the broad valley of Rephaim, which was now almost covered with green fields of wheat. Here are also remains of buildings apparently of no antiquity. One in particular seemed once to have been a small church, or perhaps a Muslim Wely, or other tomb. The general appearance is that of the ruins of an Arab village ; and such an one stood here two centuries ago.[2] We suppose this to be the site named by the Arabs Deir el-Kaddis Môdistûs, called also Deir Abu Tôr. These ruins the monks dignify with the name of the villa or country house of Caiaphas ; in which, according to them, the Jews took counsel to destroy Jesus. Hence the present appellation of the hill ; of which name however there is no trace extant, so far as I can find, earlier than the latter part of the fifteenth century.[3] Nor does the name

---

[1] Joseph. B. J. 2. 19. 4. ib. 5. 2. 3.
[2] So Cotovicus in A. D. 1598 ; p. 223. Doubdan in A. D. 1652 ; p. 139.
[3] Matt. 26, 3. 4. John 11, 47–53. This legend is apparently first mentioned by Felix Fabri in A. D. 1483 ; but he i. 407, 408

calls the hill Gyon (Gihon), contrary to Brocardus and others ; Reissbuch des h. Landes, Ed. 2. p. 257. De Salignac in 1522 has *Castrum Mali Consilii ;* Tom. X. c. 2. Cotovicus mentions both names, as applying only to the village which he seem to have become very well settled; for travellers vary considerably in respect to the application of it.[1] I have here retained it for want of a better; and because we did not learn the Arabic name.

IV.   TOPOGRAPHY OF JOSEPHUS.

Having thus gone through with the topographical details of the present city and its environs, let us now cast a glance back upon the earliest historical accounts, and see how far the notices they contain of the topography of the city as it then was, correspond to its present state; and whether they serve to identify, in any degree, the site of ancient Jerusalem with that of the modern city, upon which its name and history have descended as by inheritance. The Scriptures furnish us, in this respect, with only scattered notices; which although strongly illustrating occasional facts, cannot be combined into a uniform whole. But in Josephus, the historian of his nation, who brings down his account to the terrible destruction of Jerusalem under Titus, we have a tolerably full description of the city, as it was in his day. Having sketched the progress of the Roman conqueror in his advance to the very gates, and recounted his dispositions for the siege, this writer stops short in his narrative, in order to lay before his readers a topographical sketch of the city and temple, as they then existed, before the tremendous overthrow to which they were so soon subjected. This account is to us invaluable; and could not be supplied from any or all other sources.

The account which Josephus has thus left us of the city and of the temple, with its courts and walls, as they existed in his day, is in some particulars confused, and in others undoubtedly exaggerated. He wrote at Rome, far from his native land, and long after the destruction of Jerusalem; nor is there any evidence or probability, that he had collected specific materials for his works in his own country, previously to that event. Hence, when he enters into minute descriptions, and professes to give the exact details and measurements of heights and magnitudes, there is every reason to distrust the accuracy of his assertions; except perhaps in things of public notoriety, such, for example, as the distances between places situated on the great roads. But in cases where he describes in specific terms the length and breadth and height of buildings or the like,—measures which he himself had certainly never taken, and which were not likely to be publicly known,—we can regard these only as matters of estimate or conjecture, on the part of an author writing far remote from the

saw on the summit, viz. *Villa Caiphœ*, and *Vicus Mali Consilii;* p' 223. Quaresmius has *Mons Mali Consilii;* Elucid. II. p. 177.

[1] Zuallart, A. D. 1586, makes this the mount of Offence; Voyage, Anvers 1626, liv. 3. p. 58.

objects described, and prone, from national vanity as well as from
his peculiar position, to amplify and embellish all those particulars, which might in any way contribute to the honour of his people, or to the glory of his subsequent protectors.

According to Josephus,[1] Jerusalem was enclosed by a triple
wall, wherever it was not encircled by impassable valleys; for
here it had but a single wall.   The ancient city lay upon two
hills overagainst each other, separated by an intervening valley,
at which the houses terminated.   Of these hills, that which bore
the upper city, was the highest, and was straighter in extent.   On
account of its fortifications, it was called by king David the fortress or citadel;[2] Josephus calls it the Upper Market.   The other
hill, sustaining the lower city, and called Akra, had the form of
the gibbous moon.[3]   Overagainst this was a third hill, naturally
lower than Akra, and separated from it by another broad valley.
But in the time when the Asmoneans had rule, they threw earth
into this valley, intending to connect the city with the temple;
and working upon Akra, they lowered the height of it, so that
the temple rose conspicuously above it.[4]   The valley of the Tyropœon or Cheesemakers, as it was called, which has already been
mentioned as separating the hills of the upper and lower city,
extended quite down to Siloam; a fountain so named, whose
waters were sweet and abundant.   From without, the two hills
of the city were enclosed by deep valleys; and there was here no
approach because of the precipices on every side.

Of the walls of the ancient city, as described by Josephus, it
will be sufficient for our present purpose to give here merely an
outline; reserving a more exact examination to another place.
The single wall, which enclosed that part of the city skirted by
precipitous valleys, began at the tower of Hippicus.[5]   On the
west it extended (southwards) to a place called Bethso and the

---

[1] De Bell. Jud. 5. c. 4.   The description of the temple follows in c. 5.—The
works of this writer are too common, both
in the original and in translations, to render anything more than an abstract necessary in the text.
[2] This serves to identify it with the hill
of Zion; comp. 2 Sam. 5, 7-9.—Josephus
seems studiously to avoid using the name
Zion, which I have not been able to find
in his works.   The writer of the first book
of Maccabees, on the other hand, applies
it to the site of the temple; i. e. he makes
it include Moriah.   1 Macc. 4, 37. 60. etc.
[3] In Greek, ἀμφίκυρτος.   See Reland
Palœst. p. 852.   But this word may also
mean nothing more than that Akra was
"sloping on both sides," i. e. was a ridge
running down into the city.
i. 409, 410

[4] There is some doubt as to the correctness of this account.   Josephus elsewhere
connects this lowering of the hill Akra
with the demolition of a fortress built
upon it by Antiochus and the Syrians;
Ant. 13. 6. 6.   Comp. 12. 5. 4.   But the
writer of the first book of Maccabees, an
earlier authority, describes this fortress as
having been in the city of David; and instead of its having been destroyed, Simon
Maccabeus strengthened it, and made it his
residence; 1 Macc. 1, 33. [35.] 13, 50 sq.
14, 36. 37.   See Crome, art. Jerusalem,
p. 291 sq. in Ersch and Gruber's Encyclo-
pädie.   But the two accounts are not necessarily inconsistent with each other; see
Biblioth. Sacra, 1846, p. 629 sq.
[5] Joseph. B. J. 5. 4. 2.

gate of the Essenes ; thence it kept along on the south to a point over Siloam ; and thence on the east was carried along by Solomon's pool and Ophla (Ophel), till it terminated at the eastern portico of the temple.[1]—Of the triple walls, the following account is given. The first and oldest of these began at the tower of Hippicus, on the northern part, and extending (along the northern brow of Zion[2]) to the Xystus, afterwards terminated at the western portico of the temple. The second wall began at the gate of Gennath, (apparently near Hippicus,) and encircling only the northern part of the city, extended to the castle of Antonia, probably at the northwest corner of the area of the temple.[3] The third wall was built by Agrippa at a later period ; it also had its beginning at the tower of Hippicus, ran northwards as far as to the tower Psephinos ; and then sweeping round towards the northeast and east it turned afterwards towards the south, and was joined to the ancient wall at or in the valley of the Kidron. This wall first enclosed the hill Bezetha.

Let us now for a moment search further for some notices, which may determine the relative position of the parts of the ancient city in respect to each other. We have seen that the upper city or citadel (Zion) was separated from the lower city or Akra by the Tyropœon ; that the temple was situated "over-against" Akra, and separated from it by another valley distinct from the Tyropœon ; and that the first of the three walls on the north commenced at Hippicus, and extending along the brow of Zion to the Xystus, ended at the western portico connected with the temple. From other passages we learn, that the Xystus, so called, was an open place in the extreme part of the upper city, where the people sometimes assembled ; and that a bridge connected it with the temple.[4] During the siege of the city also, we are told,[5] that Titus having become master of the temple, held a colloquy with the leaders of the Jews, who still had possession of the upper city. For this purpose he placed himself upon the western side of the exterior temple or court, where the bridge joined the temple to the upper city at the Xystus ; and this bridge alone was interposed between him and the Jews with whom he spoke.—Further we are informed,[6] that on the western

---

[1] Josephus, B. J. 5. 4. 2. The phrases πρὸς δύσιν, πρὸς νότον, πρὸς ἀνατολήν, in this passage, as applied to the wall, can only mean, *towards* or *on the west, south, east,* etc. equivalent to *the western, south-ern, eastern, wall.* This is shown both by the nature of the case, and by the similar phrase τᾶ πρὸς ἀνατολὴν στοᾷ τοῦ ἱεροῦ in the same sentence, which no one ever thought of rendering otherwise than *the eastern portico of the temple.* Had this form of expression been always so under-

stood, it would have saved great confusion among commentators, both as to the course of the wall and the position of Siloam. See Reland Palæst. p. 858, and his plan in Havercamp's Josephus, Vol. II. p. 327.

[2] Ibid. 5. 4. 4.
[3] Ibid. 5. 5. 8.
[4] Joseph. B. J. 2. 16. 3. ib. 6. 6. 2. ib. 6. 8. 1. Comp. Antiq. 14. 4. 2.
[5] Ibid. 6. 6. 2.
[6] Joseph. Ant. 15. 11. 5.

i. 411, 412

side of the temple area were four gates ; one leading over the valley to the royal palace (on Zion) adjacent to the Xystus,[1] probably by the bridge just mentioned ; two conducting to the suburb (or new city) on the north ; and the remaining one leading to the "other city," first by steps down into the intervening valley, and then by an ascent. By this "other city" can be meant only the lower city or Akra.—The hill Bezetha lay quite near on the north of the temple.[2]

During the siege by the Romans, Titus made all his approaches from the north ; took first the external and second wall upon that part ; and then assaulted the fortress Antonia and the temple, which he captured and destroyed.[3] All this time the Jews still held possession of the upper city ; of which the northern wall ran in part along a precipice, so that the Romans could not assail it with their machines and towers.[4] To work upon the fears of the Jews and overcome their obstinacy, the Romans now set fire to Akra, Ophla, and other parts of the city, quite down to Siloam.[5]—Hence it follows, that the interior and most ancient of the three walls on the north, lay between Akra and the upper city ; forming the defence of the latter on this part. It was, no doubt, the same wall which ran along the northern brow of Zion.

The main results to be derived from the preceding historical notices, so far as they are necessary to our present purpose, are chiefly the following. The hill Moriah, on which the temple stood, was on the eastern part of the city, overlooking the valley of the Kidron.[6] Directly " overgainst " the temple on the west, was the hill Akra, with the lower city, to which a gate led from the western side of the temple area. This hill was separated from the temple by a broad valley, which had been partly filled up by the Asmonean princes ; who also had lowered the point of Akra. West of the southwest part of the temple area, lay the northern portion of the upper city or Zion, with the Xystus, connected with the temple by a bridge, which led out from the western side of the court of the latter over the intervening valley. Zion therefore lay south of Akra ; and was separated from it by the Tyropœon, which extended also down to Siloam ; and likewise by the wall which ran from Hippicus along its brow, on the north of the Xystus and the bridge, to the western portico of the temple. The tower of Hippicus therefore must be sought at the northwest corner of Zion.—On those parts where the city had but a single wall, it was skirted by valleys impassable by a hostile force. But this single wall existed only on the western and southern sides of Zion, and on the east along by Siloam and

[1] Joseph. Ant. 20. 8. 11.
[2] Joseph. B. J. 5. 5. 8.
[3] Ibid. 5. 7. 2. ib. 5. 8. 1, 2. ib. 6. 1.
7. ib. 6. c. 4.
    i. 412, 413

[4] Joseph. B. J. 5. 4. 4. ib. 6. 8. 4.
[5] Ibid. 6, 6. 3. ib. 6. 7. 2.
[6] See also Antiq. 15. 11. 3.

Ophel and the temple ; and here therefore were the deep valleys. The triple wall was towards the north and northwest.

If now we compare these results with the description which has been given above of the hills and valleys connected with the modern city,—a description which, I am happy to say, was written before the preceding notices from Josephus were collected or compared,—I am unable to perceive any other than a striking and almost exact coincidence. True, the valley of the Tyropœon, and that between Akra and Moriah, have been greatly filled up with the rubbish accumulated from the repeated desolations of nearly eighteen centuries. Yet they are still distinctly to be traced ; the hills of Zion, Akra, Moriah, and Bezetha, are not to be mistaken ; while the deep valleys of the Kidron and of Hinnom, and the mount of Olives, are permanent natural features, too prominent and gigantic indeed to be forgotten, or to undergo any perceptible change. The only topographical notice of Josephus as to which I have doubts, is the remark quoted above, that "from without, the *two* hills of the city were enclosed by deep valleys."[1] If he here means the two particular hills of Zion and Akra, (as the insertion of the Greek article might seem to imply,) the language is not literally exact ; but if, as is more probable, this is a mere form of expression intended to embrace the whole site of the city, then it presents no difficulty. Indeed, after having looked through the whole subject and studied the topography of modern Jerusalem upon the spot, with the volumes of Josephus in my hands, I am not aware of any particulars, which can excite a doubt as to the identity of the site of the ancient and modern cities. Certainly there is here no more room for question, than in the parallel cases of Athens and Rome.[2]

Thus far we have had regard to the general topography of the Holy City, and the correspondence of its present features with the descriptions of it in ancient times. We are now further to inquire, whether in particular parts of the city, there remain any such vestiges of antiquity, as may serve to add strength to our general conclusion.

V. AREA OF THE ANCIENT TEMPLE.

Of the temple and its appendages, Josephus has left us two descriptions ; one in his Antiquities, where he narrates the reconstruction of the *Naos* or body of the temple by Herod the Great ; and the other in his Jewish Wars, just before the account of its destruction by Titus.[3] The latter is the most minute and con-

[1] See above, p. 278.
[2] For the theories of Clarke and Olshausen respecting Zion and Akra, see Note XXVI, at the end of the volume.

[3] Antiq. 15. 11. 3 sq. B. J. 5. 5. 1–6. Comp. Antiq. 8. 3. 9.—The *ναός* was the temple or fane ; the *ἱερόν* comprised the *ναός* and all its courts and appurtenances.

sistent ; and I therefore follow it here, introducing only occasional circumstances from the other.

The temple, according to this account, stood upon a rocky eminence in the eastern part of the city, on which at first there was scarcely level space enough for the fane and altar; the sides being everywhere steep and precipitous. Solomon built first a wall around the summit ; (probably in order to gain space for the body of the temple ;) and built up also a wall on the east, filled in on the inside apparently with earth, on which he erected a portico or covered colonnade. The temple itself was thus left naked on three sides. In process of time, however, the whole enclosure was built up and filled in, quite to a level with the hill, which in this way was enlarged ; a threefold wall being carried up from the bottom, and thus both the upper enclosure and the lower [parts of the] temple constructed.[1]   Where these last were the lowest, they built up three hundred cubits ; and in some places more.[2]   Nor yet was the whole depth of the foundations visible ; for to a great extent they filled in the valleys with earth, desiring to level off the abrupt places of the city. In the construction of this work, they used stones of the size of forty cubits. These stones, (according to the other account,) were bound together with lead and iron into a compact mass, immovable for all time. The enclosure thus constructed was a quadrangle, measuring one stadium on each side, or four stadia in circumference. In another place the circumference, including the fortress Antonia, is given at six stadia.[3]

The interior of this enclosure was surrounded by porticos or covered colonnades along the walls; and the open part was laid or paved with variegated stones.[4]   This was a great place of resort for Jews and strangers ; and became at length also a place of trade and business, so far as related to the sale of animals for sacrifice, and the exchange of money for the yearly offering.[5]   It is sometimes called by Christian writers the court of the Gentiles.[6]—— Near the middle of this court, an ornamented wall or balustrade of stone, three cubits high, formed the boundary of a smaller enclosure ; which neither foreigners nor the unclean might pass.

---

[1] The word τριχῆ, threefold, used here in connection with walls built up from the bottom of the hill, cannot well refer to anything else than the three walls built up on the three sides of the hill, which are said to have been left open by Solomon. If this form of expression is not very exact, neither is that which is indicated by κύκλῳ (circle) in the same connection ; for there is abundant evidence, that the enclosure was not a circle, but a quadrangle.

[2] So I must venture to understand the τούτου τὸ ταπεινότατον of the original, in

connection with the τὸ κάτω ἱερόν before it, meaning, not the part where the top of these walls was lowest, but the part where the foundations, or the ground on which they stood, was lowest. Taken in this sense, the expression is not unnatural; though still greatly exaggerated. In the other sense, it is perfectly unintelligible.

[3] Joseph. B. J. 5. 5. 2.
[4] Ibid. 5. 5. 2.
[5] Matt. 21, 12. Luke 19, 45.
[6] Lightfoot Opera, Tom. 1. pp. 415, 590.

i. 416, 417

Within this an inner wall, forty cubits high from its foundation, surrounded the second or inner court ; but it was encompassed on the outside by fourteen steps, leading up to a level area around it of ten cubits wide ; from which again five other steps led up to the interior.   This wall on the inside was twenty cubits high.   The principal gate of this second court was on the east ; and there were also three gates upon the northern side, and three upon the south.   To these were afterwards added three others for the women, one upon the north, south, and east.   On the west there was no gate.[1]

Within this second court, was still the third or most sacred enclosure, which none but the priests might enter ; consisting of the *Naos* or temple itself, and the small court before it, where stood the great altar.   To this there was an ascent from the second court by twelve steps.[2]   It was this *Naos*, or the body of the temple alone, which was rebuilt by Herod ; who also built over again some of the magnificent porticos around the area. But no mention is made of his having had any thing to do with the massive walls of the exterior enclosure.[3]   We have already seen, that on the west side of this great outer court, four gates led out into the city ; the southernmost of which opened upon the bridge connecting the area of the temple with the Xystus on Mount Zion.[4]   Josephus relates also, that there was a gate in the middle of the southern side of the same enclosure.

Further than this, our present object does not require us to enter into a description of the temple or its appurtenances.

If now, with these accounts before us, we turn our eyes upon the present similar area of the grand mosk of Omar, it would seem to be hardly a matter of question, that the latter occupies in part or in whole the same general location.   But how far there exist traces which may serve to mark a connection between the ancient and modern precincts, or perhaps establish their identity, is a point which, so far as I know, has never been discussed.   It is to this point mainly, that our inquiries will now be directed.

The area of the great mosk is an elevated plateau or terrace, nearly in the form of a parallelogram, supported by and within massive walls built up from the valleys or lower ground on all sides ; the external height varying of course in various parts according to the nature of the ground, but being in general greatest towards the south.   The area or court within these walls is level ; exhibiting on the north of the mosk, as we have seen, and perhaps around the same, the surface of the native rock levelled

<hr>

[1] Antiq. 15. 11. 5.   B. J. 5. 5. 2.
[2] Antiq. 15. 11. 5, ult.   B. J. 5. 5. 4.
[3] Antiq. 15. 11. 3. B. J. 1. 21. 1.   When Josephus here says that Herod enlarged the area around the temple to double its

former size, he probably refers to the adjacent fortress Antonia, as mentioned above at the close of the second preceding paragraph.
[4] See above, p. 280.   Jos. Ant. 15. 11. 5.

i. 417–419

off by art.[1]   The general construction therefore of this area, does
not differ from that of the ancient temple.

The length of this enclosure on the east side, measured externally along the wall, is 1528 English feet or nearly 510 yards ;[2]
the breadth at the south end is 955 feet or about 318 yards.[3]
Neither the western side nor the northern end is accessible externally ; yet the latter may be measured approximately along the
parallel street.   Its length is thus found to be not far from 1066
feet, or perhaps 350 yards ; the breadth of the area being here
some yards greater than on the south.   The direction of the eastern side, taken from the southeast corner, is at first due north by
compass ; and that of the southern side, due west.   The course
of the western wall at its south end is likewise due north.   Beyond the area towards the north, the eastern wall of the city de-
viates slightly from the magnetic meridian towards the east.—
From these measurements it is apparent, that the extent of the
present area is much greater than that assigned by Josephus to
the ancient temple.

The southeast corner of the enclosure stands directly on the
very brink of the steep descent, and impends over the valley of
Jehoshaphat ; which, as we have seen, is at this point about 130
feet deep ; while just north the ground rises some 20 feet more.
The height of the wall at this angle we judged to be at least 60
English feet.[4]   Further north as the ground ascends, the wall is
less elevated above it.   The brow of the valley also advances a
little, leaving a narrow strip of level ground along the wall, which
is occupied by the Muslim cemetery already mentioned.[5]   Towards the gate of St. Stephen, this level brow widens to about
100 feet, and continues of this breadth along the city wall northwards.   The Golden gate on this side is not opposite the middle of the area ; but at some distance further north.

On the northern side, the area is skirted for nearly half its
breadth by the deep pool or trench usually called Bethesda, and
vaults connected with it.   At the northeast corner is a place of
entrance, and a way leading to it from St. Stephen's gate along
the inside of the city wall.   Further west and near the middle,
are two other entrances from the *Via dolorosa*.   At the northwest corner stands what was formerly the governor's house, now
converted into a barrack, and probably occupying in part the site

---

[1] See above, p. 244.

[2] Ali Bey gives the interior length of
the enclosure at 1369 Paris feet ; and the
interior breadth at 845 Paris feet.   Travels II. p. 215.

[3] This last measurement is too large by
some 50 feet ; see the correction in Vol. III.
Sec. IV, April 29th, 1852.

[4] There are here fifteen courses of very
i. 419, 420

large stones, having an average thickness of
more than three feet.   Above these to the
top is at least fifteen feet more.—The wall,
I since learn, was measured at this point
by Mr. Catherwood.   The actual height is
sixty feet to the level of the area within,
and sixteen feet more to the top of the
battlements ; in all 76 feet.

[5] See above, p. 232.

of the ancient fortress Antonia. From the roof of this building
is obtained a commanding view of the interior and the edifices of
the court.[1]

The western wall is mostly hidden by the houses of the city,
except near its southern end. There are on this side four entrances, to which streets lead down from the city. These streets,
after crossing the hollow or valley which here runs parallel to the
wall, lead up an ascent to the places of entrance ; some of which
are reached by steps. Near the northwest corner, this ascent is
of course smaller than it is further south. The street leading
down from the Yâfa gate crosses the valley upon the mound already mentioned. Near the southwest corner, the wall is again
exposed, and is not less than about sixty feet in height.

The wall on the south is the highest of all ; for here the
ground appears originally to have sloped down more rapidly from
the top of Moriah than in any other part. This wall was apparently built, not on the brow of a valley, but on the side of
a declivity, which descended steeply for a time, and then ran off
in a more gradual slope, forming the ridge of Ophel. Here we
judged the wall of the enclosure to be in general about sixty feet
in height.[2] At the distance of 290 feet south of this wall, the
city wall runs for a time parallel to it ; then turning at a right
angle, the city wall rises by a considerable ascent, and joins the
high wall of the area, in the manner already described, at a
point 325 feet[3] distant from the southwest corner. This leaves
here a tolerably level plat of ground between the two walls, nearly square, said to belong to the mosk el-Aksa. It was now a
ploughed field.[4] Here however the earth has evidently been filled
in, in order to render the plat level ; for the city wall on the
south, which within is very low, measures on the outside fifty feet
in height. This gives 110 feet for the proximate elevation of the
southern wall of the area of the mosk above the exterior base of
the parallel city wall.—On this side, viewed externally, there
would seem never to have been a place of entrance or access to
the court above. Yet Josephus makes mention here of a gate in
the middle of the southern side of the area ; and we shall hereafter
see, that an ancient subterranean gateway still exists under the
mosk el-Aksa, with a passage to it from above, but walled up on
the outside.[5]

Allusion has already been made to the immense size of the
stones, which compose in part the external walls of the enclosure

---

[1] See above, p. 244.
[2] There are here eight courses of stones
having an average thickness of at least
3 feet ; and above these are 24 smaller
courses, each apparently from 1 foot to 1½

feet thick. This gives very nearly the estimate of the text.
[3] See note 3, p. 284.
[4] See above, p. 238.
[5] Joseph, Antiq. 15. 11. 5.

i. 420–422 -

of the mosk.[1] The upper part of these walls is obviously of modern origin; but to the most casual observer it cannot be less obvious, that these huge blocks which appear only in portions of the lower part, are to be referred to an earlier date.[2] The appearance of the walls in almost every part, seems to indicate that they have been built upon ancient foundations ; as if an ancient and far more massive wall had been thrown down, and in later times a new one erected upon its remains. Hence the line between these lower antique portions and the modern ones above them, is very irregular ; though it is also very distinct. The former, in some parts, are much higher than in others; and occasionally the breaches in them are filled out with later patch-work. Sometimes too the whole wall is modern.

We first noticed these large stones at the southeast corner of the enclosure ; where perhaps they are as conspicuous, and form as great a portion of the wall, as in any part. Here are several courses, both on the east and south sides, alternating with each other, in which the stones measure from 17 to 19 feet in length, by 3 or 4 feet in height ; while one block at the corner is 7½ feet thick. Here also, on the east side, the lower part is patched in spots. Further to the north, the wall is mostly new until towards the northeast corner of the area, where the ancient stones again appear ; one of them measuring 24 feet in length, by 3 feet in height and 6 feet in breadth.—On the northern and western sides, the walls are less accessible, until we reach the Jewish place of wailing, considerably south of the middle of the latter. Here the stones are of the same dimensions, and the wall of the same character, as in the parts already described.[3]—At the southwest corner, huge blocks become again conspicuous for some distance on each side, and of a still greater size. The corner stone on the west side now next above the surface of the ground, measures 30 feet 10 inches in length by 6½ feet broad ; and several others vary from 20½ to 24½ feet long, by 5 feet in thickness.

It is not however the great size of these stones alone which arrests the attention of the beholder ; but the manner in which they are hewn, gives them also a peculiar character. In common parlance they are said to be *bevelled;* which here means, that after the whole face has first been hewn and squared, a narrow strip along the edge is cut down a quarter or half an inch lower than the rest of the surface. When these bevelled stones are laid

---

[1] See above, pp. 232, 233, 238.

[2] Such has been the conviction of many travellers, judging merely from the aspect of the stones. See Raumer's Palästina, p. 261, 262, ed. 3.

[3] I learn from Mr Catherwood, who examined and measured the area and buildings of the Haram, both within and without, very minutely in 1833, that the western wall, as seen from the courts in the rear of the houses north of the Jews' place of wailing, consists of large ancient stones of the same character as those above described, to the height of thirty feet or more.

up in a wall, the face of it of course exhibits lines or grooves formed by these depressed edges at their junction, marking more distinctly the elevation of the different courses, as well as the length of the stones of which they are composed. The face of the wall has then the appearance of many pannels. The smaller stones in other parts of the walls are frequently bevelled in like manner; except that in these, only the bevel or strip along the edge is cut smooth, while the remainder of the surface is merely broken off or rough-hewn. In the upper parts of the wall, which are obviously the most modern, the stones are small and are not bevelled.

At the first view of these walls, I was led to the persuasion, that the lower portions had belonged to the ancient temple; and every subsequent visit only served to strengthen this conviction. The size of the stones and the heterogeneous character of the walls, render it a matter beyond all doubt, that the former were never laid in their present places by the Muhammedans; and the peculiar form in which they are hewn, does not properly belong, so far as I know, either to Saracenic or to Roman architecture.[1] Indeed, everything seems to point to a Jewish origin; and a discovery which we made in the course of our examination, reduces this hypothesis to an absolute certainty.

I have already related in the preceding section, that during our first visit to the southwest corner of the area of the mosk, we observed several of the large stones jutting out from the western wall, which at first sight seemed to be the effect of a bursting of the wall from some mighty shock or earthquake.[2] We paid little regard to this at the moment, our attention being engrossed by other objects; but on mentioning the fact the same evening, in a circle of our friends, we found that they also had noticed it; and the remark was incidentally dropped by Mr Whiting, that the stones had the appearance of having once belonged to a large arch. At this remark a train of thought flashed upon my mind, which I hardly dared to follow out, until I had again repaired to the spot, in order to satisfy myself with my own eyes, as to the truth or falsehood of the suggestion. I found it even so! The courses of these immense stones, which seemed at first to have sprung out from their places in the wall in consequence of some enormous violence, occupy nevertheless their original position; their external surface is hewn to a regular curve; and being fitted one upon another, they form the commencement or foot of an immense arch, which once sprung out fromt his western wall in

---

[1] Something of a similar kind is indeed found in the later Roman architecture, under the later emperors. But the edges of the stones are there usually merely slanted off, or else the surface is left rough; giving to the whole a different and more *rustic* character.   See Hirt's Baukunst nach den Grundsätzen der Alten, Berl. 1809. fol. p. 152, und Pl. XXXI.

[2] See above, p. 238.

a direction towards Mount Zion, across the valley of the Tyropœon. This arch could only have belonged to THE BRIDGE, which according to Josephus led from this part of the temple to the Xystus on Zion ; and it proves incontestably the antiquity of that portion of the wall from which it springs.

The traces of this arch are too distinct and definite to be mistaken. Its southern side is thirty-nine English feet distant from the southwest corner of the area, and the arch itself measures fifty-one feet along the wall. *Three* courses of its stones still remain ; of which one is five feet four inches thick, and the others not much less. One of the stones is 20½ feet long ; another 24½ feet ; and the rest in like proportion. The part of the curve or arc, which remains, is of course but a fragment ; but of this fragment the chord measures twelve feet six inches ; the sine eleven feet ten inches ; and the versed sine three feet ten inches.—The distance from this point across the valley to the precipitous natural rock of Zion, we measured as exactly as the intervening field of prickly pear would permit ; and found it to be 350 feet or about 116 yards. This gives the proximate length of the ancient bridge. We sought carefully along the brow of Zion for traces of its western termination ; but without success. That quarter is now covered with mean houses and filth ; and an examination can be carried on only in the midst of disgusting sights and smells.

The existence of these remains of the ancient bridge, seems to remove all doubt as to the identity of this part of the enclosure of the mosk with that of the ancient temple. How they can have remained for so many ages unseen or unnoticed by any writer or traveller, is a problem, which I would not undertake fully to solve. One cause has probably been the general oblivion, or want of knowledge, that any such bridge ever existed. It is mentioned by no writer but Josephus ; and even by him only incidentally, though in five different places.[1] The bridge was doubtless broken down in the general destruction of the city ; and was in later ages forgotten by the Christian population, among whom the writings of Josephus were little known. For a like reason, we may suppose its remains to have escaped the notice of the crusaders and the pilgrims of the following centuries. Another cause which has operated in the case of later travellers, is probably the fact, that the spot is approached only through narrow and crooked lanes, in a part of the city whither their monastic guides did not care to accompany them ; and which they

[1] Antiq. 14. 4. 2. B. J. 1. 7. 2. ib. 2. 16. 3. ib. 6. 6. 2. ib. 6. 8. 1. Comp. Antiq. 15. 11. 5.—There is no mention of the time when, nor of the person by whom, the bridge was built. As however it ex-
i. 425, 426
isted in the time of Pompey about 63 B. C. (Antiq. l. c.) it was probably then ancient. At any rate it could not have been the work of Herod.

themselves could not well, nor perhaps safely, explore alone. Or if any have penetrated to the place, and perhaps noticed these large stones springing from the wall, they have probably (as I did at first) regarded their appearance as accidental; and have passed on without further examination.[1]

Here then we have indisputable remains of Jewish antiquity, consisting of an important portion of the western wall of the ancient temple area. They are probably to be referred to a period long antecedent to the days of Herod; for the labours of this splendour-loving tyrant appear to have been confined to the body of the temple and the porticos around the court.[2] The magnitude of the stones also, and the workmanship as compared with other remaining monuments of Herod, seem to point to an earlier origin. In the accounts we have of the destruction of the temple by the Chaldeans, and its rebuilding by Zerubbabel under Darius, no mention is made of these exterior walls. The former temple was destroyed by fire, which would not affect these foundations; nor is it probable that a feeble colony of returning exiles could have accomplished works like these.[3] There seems therefore little room for hesitation in referring them back to the days of Solomon, or rather of his successors; who, according to Josephus, built up here immense walls, "immovable for all time."[4] Ages upon ages have since rolled away; yet these foundations still endure, and are immovable as at the beginning. Nor is there aught in the present physical condition of these remains, to prevent them from continuing as long as the world shall last. It was the temple of the living God; and, like the everlasting hills on which it stood, its foundations were laid "for all time."

Thus then we have here the western wall of the ancient temple area; on which is built up the same wall of the modern enclosure, though with far inferior materials and workmanship. The ancient southern wall is at the same time determined in like manner; for at the southwest corner the lower stones towards the south have precisely the same character as those on the west; they are laid in alternate courses with the latter; and the whole corner is evidently one and the same original substruc-

---

[1] Maundrell must have passed near this spot, when he saw the large vaults with columns which he describes as running in on the south side of Moriah. Pococke was also apparently here, and speaks of the large stones; Vol. II. i. p. 15.—Since the above was written, I have been informed by both Messrs Bonomi and Catherwood, the well known artists, that they likewise remarked these large stones in 1833, and recognised in them the beginning of an immense arch. They regarded them too as probably among the most ancient remains in or around Jerusalem; but had no suspicion of their historical import. See more in Note XXVII, end of the volume.

[2] See above, p. 283.

[3] Ezra c. 1. c. 3, 8 sq. c. 6. Joseph. Antiq. 10. 8, 5. ib. 11. 3. 7. ib. 11. 4. 2. Here also it is the ναός, not the ἱερόν, which was destroyed and afterwards rebuilt by Zerubbabel.

[4] Antiq. 15. 11. 3, ἀκινήτους τῷ παντὶ χρόνῳ. B. J. 5. 5. 1.

i. 426-428

tion. Proceeding to the southeast corner, we find its character to be precisely similar; the same immense stones as already described,[1] both towards the east and south, on the brink of the valley of Jehoshaphat; and the line of the southern wall at this point corresponding with that at the southwest corner. We have, then, the two extremities of the ancient southern wall; which, as Josephus informs us, extended from the eastern to the western valley, and could not be prolonged further.[2] Thus we are led irresistibly to the conclusion, that the area of the Jewish temple was identical on its western, eastern, and southern sides, with the present enclosure of the Haram.

The specifications of Josephus in respect to the immense height of these ancient walls and of the porticos which rose above them, have occasioned great difficulty and perplexity to commentators; partly because of the undoubted exaggerations of the writer; and partly from want of an acquaintance with the nature of the ground. At the southwest corner, there can be little doubt that the ground has been raised very considerably; and not improbably future excavations may yet lay bare stones of a larger size than any which are now visible. But at the southeast corner, and along the eastern and southern sides in general, there is little appearance of any considerable accumulation of earth or rubbish.

Upon the interior southern part of the high enclosure or platform, according to Josephus, " a broad portico ran along the wall, supported by four rows of columns, which divided it into three parts, thus forming a triple colonnade or portico. Of these the two external parts were each thirty feet wide, and the middle one forty-five feet. The height of the two external porticos was more than fifty feet, while that of the middle one was double, or more than a hundred feet. The length was a stadium, extending from valley to valley. Such was the elevation of the middle portico above the adjacent valley, that if from its roof one attempted to look down into the gulf below, his eyes became dark and dizzy before they could penetrate to the immense depth."[3] The valley thus meant, can well be no other than that of the Kidron, which here actually bends southwest around the corner, so that the eastern end of this high southern portico impended over it. The depth of the valley at this point, as we have seen, is about one hundred and fifty feet; which with the elevation of the wall and portico gives a total height of about 310 feet above the bottom of the valley; an elevation sufficient to excuse the somewhat hyperbolical language of the Jewish historian.[4] The portico along the

[1] See above, p. 286.
[2] Antiq. 15. 11. 5.
[3] Joseph. Antiq. 15. 11. 5.
[4] J. D. Michaelis understood this language as referring to the elevation of the i. 428, 429

wall and portico above a valley along the south side of the temple area; see his *Zerstreute Kleine Schriften*, p. 394 sq. But Josephus here and elsewhere speaks only of valleys on the east and west

eastern wall is described by Josephus in like manner as rising above the same valley to the enormous height of 400 cubits, or more than 500 feet ; which doubtless is merely an exaggerated estimate.[1] At the northeast corner too, the same portico was near the valley of the Kidron ; which is said to have had here " a fearful depth."[2]

A greater difficulty arises, when we undertake to reconcile the length and breadth of the temple area, as it now appears, with the accounts which have come down to us from antiquity. We have seen that the length of the present southern wall, which is identical with the ancient one, is 955 English feet, or about 318 yards.[3] But both Josephus and the Talmud describe the upper area as a square, of which each of the sides measured, according to the former one stadium, and according to the latter 500 cubits.[4] In the uncertainty which exists as to the length of the Jewish cubit, these two specifications throw little light upon each other. But the length of a stadium of 600 Greek feet, which is usually regarded as equal to the tenth part of a geographical mile or a fraction less than 204 yards,[5] makes the southern side of the enclosure to be only two thirds as long, as we now find it to be by actual measurement ; presenting a difference of 114 yards. This may in part be accounted for, by supposing the ancient specifications to refer only to the interior open space surrounded by the broad porticos within the walls ; while our measurements were taken along the outside of the walls. But even this supposition cannot well cover the whole difference ; and we must here again admit, that Josephus probably had no definite measurements, but assumed one stadium as a convenient estimate.—If, on the other hand, the Jewish cubit may be taken at $1\frac{3}{4}$ feet, (as is often done,) then the Rabbinic specification of 500 cubits, or 875 feet, if reckoned only from portico to portico, would not vary very materially from the results of our measurement.

According to both Josephus and the Talmud, the area o the temple was a square ; the length and the breadth being equal. But we now find the length to be 1528 feet, while the breadth is only 955 feet ; the former exceeding the latter by 573 feet or more than one half. Although in this case also, we are not bound to attribute any special exactness to these writers ; yet the discrepancy is here too great to be accounted for in any other way, than by supposing that the present enclosure has been enlarged

sides. See also Niebuhr's remarks on this hypothesis of Michaelis ; Reisebeschr. Bd. III. Anhang, p. 140 ; printed also in Olshausen's Topographie des alten Jerus. p. 70 sq.

[1] Antiq. 20. 9. 7. See above on Josephus, p. 277.

[2] B. J. 6. 3. 2.

[3] Here is an error ; see above, p. 284. note 3.

[4] Joseph. Antiq. 15. 11. 3. Lightfoot Opera I. p. 554.

[5] The more exact specification is 604 Olympic stadia to a degree.

towards the north. This has not improbably been done by in-cluding within its walls the area of the ancient fortress Antonia.

This fortress, according to Josephus, stood on the north side of the area of the temple.[1] It was a quadrangle, erected first by the Maccabees under the name of Baris ; and then rebuilt by the first Herod with great strength and splendour. A more particu-lar description [2] places it, or at least its main citadel, upon a rock or hill at the northwest corner of the temple area, fifty cubits high ; above which its walls rose to the height of forty cubits. Within, it had all the extent and appearance of a palace ; being divided into apartments of every kind, with galleries and baths, and also broad halls or barracks for soldiers ; so that, as having every thing necessary within itself, it seemed a city, while in its magnificence it was a palace. At each of the four corners was a tower ; three of these were fifty cubits high ; while the fourth, at the southeast corner, was seventy cubits high, and overlooked the whole temple with its courts. The fortress communicated with the northern and western porticos of the temple area ; and had flights of stairs descending into both ; by which the garrison could at any time enter the court of the temple and prevent tu-mults.[3] The fortress was separated from the hill Bezetha, on the north, by a deep artificial trench, lest it should be approachable from that hill ; and the depth of the trench added greatly to the elevation of the towers.[4]

The extent of the fortress, or the area covered by it, is no-where specified ; except where the same writer says that the cir-cumference of the temple, including Antonia, was six stadia.[5] Now as we are elsewhere told that the temple area by itself was a square of one stadium on each side ; [6] it follows that the length of each side of the fortress must also have been one stadium, and its area equal to that of the temple. And although this again is probably a mere estimate on the part of the writer, yet the con-clusion would seem to be a fair one, that the area covered by Antonia was probably much greater than has usually been sup-posed.

In view of all these circumstances I venture to propose the following conjecture ; which indeed is supported by various facts ; while it is, so far as I know, contradicted by none. In looking at the nature of the ground, it seems probable that the rock, on which the fortress stood, was a prolongation of the hill Bezetha

---

[1] Ant. 15. 11. 4, κατὰ τὴν βόρειον πλευ-ράν. See B. J. 1. 5. 4. ib. 1. 21. 1.

[2] Joseph. B. J. 5. 5. 8.

[3] It was this " castle " into which Paul was carried by the soldiers, after being dragged out of the temple ; and from its stairs he addressed the people collected be-low ; Acts 21, 30–40. In the New Testa-ment the fortress is called ἡ παρεμβολή, Acts 21, 34. 37.

[4] Joseph. B. J. 5. 4. 2.

[5] Ibid. 5. 5. 2.

[6] Antiq. 15. 11. 3.

i. 431, 432

towards the south, which was cut through and separated from
that hill by the trench above mentioned.[1] This rock, or ridge,
must have lain partly at least within the present enclosure, at its
northwest corner; for between the enclosure and the precipitous
part of Bezetha, there now intervenes only a house or barrack
and the narrow street, presenting a space wholly insufficient for
the fortress and its deep trench. On this rock or ridge, I conjecture, lay the main fortress or "acropolis"[2] of Antonia; while
the remaining part, comprising the halls and palace-like apartments and barracks, extended probably along the northern wall
of the temple quite to its northeast corner, adjacent to the brow
of the valley of the Kidron. On the north it was doubtless protected by the trench; and of this trench the greater part still
remains, as I apprehend, in the deep reservoir commonly called
the pool of Bethesda.

The supposition therefore is, that the fortress Antonia occupied the whole breadth of the northern part of the present enclosure; between the ancient northern wall and the present Bethesda. This would make its length from west to east the same
as that of the area of the temple; while its breadth from north
to south might have been nearly two thirds as great, or some 600
feet, and yet leave to the temple area its square form. The peculiar character and great depth of the pool Bethesda, so called,
have been a stone of stumbling to many travellers; but by thus
bringing it into connection with the fortress, its peculiarities are
at once accounted for. Indeed, the fortress and the trench serve
to illustrate and mark the limits of each other; and it is on this
ground chiefly, that I venture to extend the fortress thus far towards the east.

This reservoir lies along the outside of the present northern
wall of the enclosure; of which wall its southern side may be
said to form a part. Its eastern end is near the wall of the city;
so near indeed, that only a narrow way passes between them
leading from St. Stephen's gate to the great mosk. The pool
measures 360 English feet in length, 130 feet in breadth, and 75
feet in depth to the bottom, besides the rubbish which has been
accumulating in it for ages. It was once evidently used as a reservoir; for the sides internally have been cased over with small
stones, and these again covered with plaster; but the workmanship of these additions is coarse, and bears no special marks
of antiquity. The western end is built up like the rest, except
at the southwest corner; where two lofty arched vaults extend
in westward side by side under the houses which now cover that

---

[1] The rock on which the fortress stood,
could not have been further west than the
western line of the temple area; for here

ran and runs the valley, which separated
Bezetha and Moriah from Akra.
[2] Antiq. 15. 11. 4.

part. The southernmost of these arches is 12 feet in breadth, and the other 19 feet; they are both filled up with earth and rubbish, and a vast quantity of the same lies before them. Yet I was able to measure 100 feet within the northern one, and it seemed to extend much further. This gives to the whole work a length of at least 460 feet, equal to nearly one half of the whole breadth of the enclosure of the mosk; and how much more, we do not know.[1] It would seem as if the deep reservoir formerly extended further westward in this part; and that these vaults were built up in and over it to support the buildings above. Whether this deep excavation was anciently carried through the ridge of Bezetha along the northern side of Antonia to its northwest corner, may be doubtful.

Although the fortress, as we have seen, was connected with the porticos at the northwest corner of the temple area; yet these entrances might be closed; and a strong wall would seem to have existed between the temple and the fortress. After Titus was in full possession of Antonia, he had yet to make regular approaches with mounds against this wall and its portico, which was still defended by the Jews. For seven days the Romans were employed in levelling the very foundations of Antonia, in order to form a broad place by which to approach the temple walls. They then built up four mounds against these walls; one overagainst the northwest corner of the inner temple (which would seem to have been near); another opposite the northern gallery between the two gates; a third against the western portico of the exterior temple; and the fourth against the outside of the northern portico.[2] This description is not very clear; but it serves to show, that the possession of Antonia did not make the Romans masters of the temple.[3] It seems further, that after thus labouring for seven days to subvert the foundations of Antonia, the Romans still did not destroy the whole fortress; for during the subsequent siege and assaults upon the temple, Titus continued to have his headquarters in Antonia, and beheld the daily conflicts probably from one of its towers.[4] The grand attack was evidently made upon the northwest part of the area; and here it would almost seem, the Romans had levelled the "acropolis" and its rock to the ground; filled up a portion of the deep trench; and formed a broad approach on which they could erect their works; while further east the halls and apartments, and

---

[1] Mr Wolcott found, a few years later, that "the southern vault extends 130 feet; and the other apparently the same. At the extremity of the former was an opening for drawing up water." Biblioth. Sacra. 1843, p. 33.

[2] Joseph. B. J. 6. 2. 7.

i. 434 435

[3] Pompey found also a strong wall and towers on the north of the temple, before the time of Herod; as also a deep trench, which he filled up. Joseph. Antiq. 14. 4. 2. B. J. 1. 7. 3.

[4] Joseph. B. J. 6. 2. 5. ib. 6. 4. 4, 5.

probably the southeast tower of Antonia, were left as a shelter for the troops and the headquarters of their commander.   It was not until after many days, when the various porticos had been successively carried with fire and sword, that an assault was made upon the temple or *Naos* itself ; and this at last yielded only to the horrible conflagration by which it was destroyed.[1]

In this way, as it appears to me, we may clearly account for all the facts and circumstances, which have come down to us respecting the fortress Antonia and its connection with the ancient temple.   At the same time, we remove the difficulty arising from the greater length of the modern enclosure, as compared with the ancient one ; and obtain also a satisfactory explanation, as to the original purpose of the deep and otherwise inexplicable excavation now called Bethesda.[2]

A few remarks upon the subsequent history of this area and the buildings erected upon it, may conclude this part of our subject.

It is related of our Saviour near the close of his life, that as he went out of the temple, apparently for the last time, his disciples came to him, " to show him the buildings of the temple. And Jesus said unto them, See ye not all these things ?   Verily I say unto you, There shall not be left here one stone upon another, that shall not be thrown down." [3]   This language was spoken of the " buildings of the temple," the splendid fane itself and its magnificent porticos ; and in this sense the prophecy has been terribly fulfilled, even to the utmost letter.   Or, if we give to the words a wider sense, and include the outer works of the temple and even the whole city, still the spirit of the prophecy has received its full and fearful accomplishment ; for the few substructions which remain, serve only to show where once the temple and the city stood.   In the case of the temple, the remaining substructions of its exterior walls are easily accounted for ; even on the supposition that the Romans were bent upon their utter subversion.   The conquerors doubtless commenced the work of destruction by casting down the stones outwards from above ; these of course accumulated at the foot of the walls ; covered the lower parts ; and thus naturally protected them from further demolition.

For half a century after the destruction of Jerusalem, there is no mention of the temple.   The Jews had again tried the fortune of war under Trajan and Adrian ; they had been defeated, and Jerusalem again taken by the latter emperor ; when in A. D.

---

[1] Joseph. B. J. 6. 2. 8, 10.   ib. 6. 3. 1–3.   ib. 6. 4. 2–5.

[2] Pococke also regarded the reservoir as the remains of an ancient fosse, which perhaps " was carried all along to the north of Mount Moriah ;" Descr. of the East, II. i. p. 15.

[3] Matt. 24, 1. 2.   So Mark 13, 1. 2. which is more explicit.

i. 436, 437

136 he consecrated here a new city, called after one of his own names, Ælia.[1] At the same time he erected a temple of Jupiter on the site of the Jewish temple ;[2] and decorated it with two statues of himself, one of which at least was equestrian.[3] It seems probable, that the walls of the area were at this time also rebuilt, at least in part ; for the architecture of the Golden gateway in the eastern wall seems to be of this era. This is a massive structure forming a double gateway, projecting from the wall into the area of the Haram ; its floor being several feet below the level of the area. The whole is now used as a Muslim place of prayer. The external front and arches of this gateway, which we saw, are evidently of Roman origin ; and of the interior Mr Bonomi remarks, " that a central row of noble Corinthian columns, and a groined roof, had once formed a stately portico of Roman workmanship."[4] This gate is situated nearly 300 feet north of the middle of the present enclosure. In erecting these walls, the former area of the fortress Antonia might have been included, quite to the deep fosse, as it exists at present ;[5] while perhaps a portion of the southern part of the ancient area was left out. Of the demolition of Adrian's temple we have no account. The *Itiner. Hieros.* speaks of the statues as still standing in the days of Constantine, A. D. 333, and seems also to imply that other lofty buildings existed there. Nor does this emperor nor his mother Helena appear to have included this enclosure in their projects of embellishment; for in the days of Jerome, about the close of the same century, the equestrian statue of Adrian yet stood upon the supposed place of the Holy of Holies.[6] Before this time, about A. D. 362, had occurred the abortive attempt of the Jews, under Julian, to rebuild their temple.[7]

Not long before the middle of the sixth century, the emperor Justinian erected a magnificent church in Jerusalem, in honour of the Virgin. The description which the historian Procopius gives of the site and construction of this edifice, is not very clear ; and borders somewhat on the fabulous.[8] He represents it as

---

[1] See Münter's Jüd. Krieg unter Trajan und Hadrian, 1821, p. 87, etc. See further in Sect. VIII.

[2] Dio Cass. 69. 12, καὶ ἐς τὸν τοῦ ναοῦ τοῦ θεοῦ τόπον, ναὸν τῷ Διὶ ἕτερον ἀντεγείραντος.

[3] Itiner. Hieros.—Jerome, as quoted in note 6, below.

[4] So Mr Bonomi orally, and in Hogg's Visit to Alexandria, etc. II. p. 283. Mr Catherwood confirms this description. A view of the interior of this gateway by the latter, is found in Catherwood's large map of Jerusalem.

[5] Pococke speaks also of large hewn i. 437, 438

stones and an entablature in good taste at the northeast entrance, near the wall ; and supposes this entrance may have been made by Adrian. Vol. II. i. p. 15.

[6] Hieron. Comm. in Esaiam 2, 8, "Ubi quondam erat templum et religio Dei, ibi Hadriani statua et Jovis idolum collocatum est." Comm. in Matt. 24, 15, " de Hadriani equestri statua, quæ in ipso Sancto Sanctorum loco usque in presentem diem stetit."

[7] Socrates Hist. Ecc. 3. 20. Sozom. 5. 22. Ammian. Marcell. 23. 1.

[8] Procop. de Ædificiis Justiniani, 5. 6.

placed upon the loftiest hill of the city, where there was not space enough to allow of the prescribed dimensions, so that they were obliged to lay the foundation on the southeast side at the bottom of the hill, and build up a wall with arched vaults in order to support that part of the building.   There is nothing in the subsequent history nor in the modern topography of Jerusalem, which in the least degree corresponds to this description, except the present mosk el-Aksa at the southern extremity of the enclosure of the Haram.   This stands adjacent to the southern wall, where, as we have seen, the latter is in itself about 60 feet high, or 100 feet above the foundation of the parallel city wall; indicating here a steep declivity towards the south.[1]   The present structure is about 280 feet in length from north to south by 190 feet broad.[2] This mosk is universally regarded by oriental Christians, and also by the Frank Catholics, as an ancient Christian church, once dedicated to the Virgin ; and the latter now give it the name of the church of the Presentation.[3] The earlier travellers speak of it also as a church ; and of late years Richardson, and also Bonomi and Catherwood, all of whom entered and examined it, describe it in the same manner.[4]   Mr Bonomi, whose judgment as an artist cannot well be drawn in question, remarks expressly, that " the structure is similar in appearance to those raised in the early ages of Christianity.'[5]   If now we may suppose, that the enclosure of Adrian's temple did not include the whole of the southern part of the ancient temple area ; perhaps because the southern wall of the latter, having been thrown down by the Romans, had never again been built up;[6] then the site and architecture and other circumstances of this mosk or ancient church, correspond very nearly to the above description of the church erected by Justinian.   Indeed, there is no other site nor edifice which at all accords with this description ; nor any other description or historical notice which applies to this edifice.[7]

A century later, in A. D. 636, the followers of Muhammed,

---

[1] See above, p. 285.

[2] According to the measurements and manuscript plan of Mr Catherwood.

[3] I have not been able to trace this name further back than to Quaresmius, Vol. II. p. 77 sq. It is likewise sometimes called the church of the Purification; which name Quaresmius rejects.

[4] Breydenbach and F. Fabri in A. D. 1483; Reissbuch des heil. Landes, pp. 111, 251. Baumgarten in A. D. 1507, p. 86. Richardson's Travels, II. p. 304. Lond. 1822. See Bonomi's account in Hogg's Visit to Alexandria, Jerusalem, etc. Lond. 1835. Vol. II. p. 280.

[5] Mr Bonomi in a subsequent personal interview remarked to me, that the interior of el-Aksa has entirely the appearance of an ancient Basilica. The same has since been confirmed to me by Mr Catherwood; who has plans and measurements of the whole edifice of el-Aksa, as well as of the adjacent buildings.

[6] See above, p. 296. Such an hypothesis may perhaps have further a slight support in the fact, that the Golden gate, which would naturally have been placed opposite to the middle of Adrian's enclosure, is actually situated some 300 feet north of the middle of the present area.

[7] Quaresmius also ascribes this church to Justinian; Tom. II. p. 79.

under Omar, took possession of the Holy City ; and the Khalif determined to erect a mosk upon the site of the ancient Jewish temple.   Inquiring of the patriarch Sophronius and others after the spot, he was led after some evasion to a large church, to the area of which there was an ascent by a flight of steps.   Near this, according to William of Tyre, he was shown some vestiges of ancient works ; or according to Arabian writers, he here found or was led to the celebrated rock es-Sûkhrah, then covered over with filth in scorn of the Jews.[1]   This rock he himself aided to cleanse ; and erected over it a mosk, which is usually regarded as that at present existing.[2]   But the Arabian historians relate, that the Khalif Abd el-Melek caused this mosk to be rebuilt, he himself prescribing the form ; and that it was commenced in A. H. 66 (A. D. 686) and completed in seven years.[3]   This was the present splendid edifice, Kubbet es-Sûkhrah, ' Dome of the Rock.'   The church above mentioned was probably that which we have attributed to Justinian, the present mosk el-Aksa.   To this, which must early have been converted into a mosk, the successors of Omar would seem also to have made additions ; a nave or vault upon the eastern part is even said to have been erected by Omar himself, and still bears the name of the mosk of Omar.   In another part of this mosk he is said also to have prayed, and his altar is still shown.[4]   The exterior walls of the great area appear at the same time to have been built up and strengthened ; the place beautified ; the buildings richly decorated with gold and silver ; and the whole furnished with cisterns and reservoirs of water.

Such at least the crusaders found the spot, when in the year 1099, they captured Jerusalem by storm.   A multitude of the Muslim inhabitants took refuge in the sacred enclosure, as a place of strength.   But their hope was vain ; for Tancred and his followers broke in upon them, and committed here the most horrible excesses.   Many who had fled to the roof of the mosk, were shot down with arrows ; others rushed for safety into the cisterns, and

[1] Theophanes Chronogr. p. 281. ed. Paris. Eutychii Annales, Oxon. 1658, Tom. II. p. 284 sq. Will. Ty. 1. 2 Hist of Jerus. by Mejr ed-Din, Fundgruben des Orients, V. p. 161.—It must be borne in mind, that of all the writers who profess to give an account of these events, whether Franks or Orientals, the earliest lived nearly or quite two centuries afterwards.

[2] Will. Tyr. 1. 2. ib. 8. 3 Abulfed. Syria, ed. Köhler, p. 87. Comp. Wilken's Gesch. der Kreuzzüge I. p. 21 sq.

[3] Abulfed. ibid. p. 87. Hist. of Jerusalem in Fundgr. des Orients V. pp. 158, 162. The object of Abd el-Melek, in build-

ing the mosk, is said to have been, to prevent the necessity of pilgrimages to Mecca ; Fundgr. des Orients, ibid. p. 162. Eutychii Annales, II. p. 364.—Yet some of the historians of the crusades refer the building of this same mosk or temple to Christians ! So Albertus Aquensis 6. 24, in Gesta Dei p. 281 ; Jac. de Vitriaco, c. 62.

[4] Fundgr. des Orients II. p. 84. Ali Bey's Travels II. p. 217. Comp. Richardson's Travels II. pp 304, 306. In the circumstance of Omar's praying in this place during his visit to Jerusalem, lies a further proof that the building itself is of a more ancient date ; Fundgr. des Or. l. c.

i. 440, 441

there perished by drowning or the sword.[1] More than ten thousand Muslims, according to the admission of Christian writers, were massacred within the sacred precincts ; neither sex nor age was spared ; and the whole area was covered ankle deep with blood.[2] Arabian writers give the number of those here slain at seventy thousand.[3]

So soon as order was restored, the city cleared of the dead, and a regular government established by the election of Godfrey as king ; one of the first cares of the sovereign was to dedicate anew to Jehovah the sacred place, where of old His presence had been wont to dwell. A regular chapter of canons was established in the great mosk, now converted into a temple of the Lord ; as well as in the church of the Holy Sepulchre. These were endowed with all the immunities and privileges which belonged to the cathedrals of the west ; and dwellings were assigned to them around the building.[4] The Christians erected a choir and altar within the edifice, over the sacred rock ; which itself was covered over with marble.[5] The historians of the crusades all speak of the great mosk es-Sûkhrah, as the *Templum Domini;* they describe its form and the rock within it ; and know it by no other name.[6] To the other large edifice on the southern side of the enclosure, they give indiscriminately the name of *Palatium, Porticus, seu Templum Salomonis,* the palace, portico, or temple of Solomon ;[7] and these names it appears to have retained among the Franks down to the sixteenth century.[8] A portion of this edifice was assigned by king Baldwin II, in A. D. 1119, to a new order of knights ; who from this circumstance took the name of the knights Templars.[9] The accounts we have of this structure are not very distinct. The king himself would seem to have dwelt in it ; whence perhaps the appellation *palace;* and it very probably had many side buildings, and was perhaps more exten-

---

[1] Fulcher. Carnot. in Gesta Dei, p. 398. Albert. Aq. 6. 20 sq. ibid. p. 280. Will. Tyr. 8. 20.

[2] Will. Tyr. 8. 20. Fulcher. Carnot. ibid. p. 398. Raimund de Agiles frankly says: "Tantum hoc dixisse sufficiat, quod in templo et porticu Salomonis equitabatur in sanguine usque ad genua et usque ad frenos equorum ; " Gesta Dei, p. 179.

[3] So Abulfeda Annal. Muslem. A. H. 492. Comp. Wilken Comment. de Bellor. Cruc. ex Abulf. Historia, pp. 31, 32.

[4] Will. Tyr. 8. 3.

[5] Will. Tyr. 8. 3. Reinaud Extr. des Historiens Arabes, 1829, p. 217.

[6] Will. Tyr. 8. 2. ib. 12. 7. Jac. de Vitriac. c. 62.

[7] So *Palatium* Salomonis, Albert. Aq.

6. 20, 22 ; in Gesta Dei, p. 280. Will. Tyr. 12. 7. *Porticus* Salomonis, Raim. de Ag. in Gesta Dei, p. 179. *Templum,* Will. Tyr. 8. 3. Jac. de Vitr. c. 62. This latter writer says, it was perhaps called *Templum Salomonis* to distinguish it from the other, or Templum Domini.

[8] Brocardus calls it *Palatium Regis,* c. 8; Marinus Sanutus *Templum Salomonis,* Secret. fidel. Cruc. 3. 14. 9. Breydenbach and Fabri speak of it in A. D. 1483 as *Porticus Salomonis,* Reissb. des h. Landes, pp. 111, 251. So too Lud. de Suchem in the 14th century, and Baumgarten A. D. 1507, p. 86.

[9] Will. Tyr. 12. 7. Jac. de Vitr. c. 65. Comp. Benjamin of Tudela, I. p. 69, ed. Asher.

sive than the present mosk el-Aksa.[1] The Templars built a
wall before the *Mihrâb* or niche of prayer ; and used this part
of the building as a granary.[2]

In A. D. 1187, the celebrated Egyptian Sultan Salâh ed-Din
(Saladin) became master of Jerusalem ; and the order of things
was again reversed. The sacred precincts of the temple fell back
once more to the uses of Islam ; the golden cross upon the lofty
dome was cast down and dragged along the ground, and the crescent elevated in its place ; the erections and ornaments of the
Christians were all removed ; and the edifices purified throughout
with rose water brought for the occasion from Damascus. The
voice of the Mu'edh-dhin was again heard proclaiming the hour
of prayer ; and Saladin himself was present in a solemn assembly,
and performed his devotions in both the mosks es-Sûkhrah and
el-Aksa.[3] From that time onward to the present day, the precincts of the ancient temple, with one slight exception, have remained in the hands of the Muslims ; and seem to have experienced no important changes, except such as are incidental to the
lapse of time.

The rock es-Sûkhrah beneath the great dome, with the excavated chamber under it, is one of the most venerated spots of Muslim tradition and devotion. Even the Christians of the middle
ages regarded it as the stone on which Jacob slept when he saw
the vision of angels ; and also as the spot where the destroying
angel stood, when about to smite Jerusalem for the sin of David.[4]
Some regarded it likewise as having existed anciently under the
most holy place of the Jewish temple ; and as still containing in
itself the ark and other sacred things.[5] The followers of Muhammed have loaded this rock with legends respecting their prophet ; until it has become in their eyes second alone to the sacred
Ka'beh of Mecca. Their writings are full of the praises of the
Sûkhrah and of Jerusalem. Even the false prophet himself is
reported to have said : " The first of places is Jerusalem, and the
first of rocks is the Sûkhrah ;" and again : " The rock es-Sûkhrah
at Jerusalem is one of the rocks of Paradise."[6] The mosk el-Aksa is
perhaps even more respected. Indeed the two are regarded as form-

---

[1] Jac. de Vitriaco describes it as being "immensæ quantitatis et amplitudinis." c. 62.

[2] Reinaud Extr. des Historiens Arabes, 1829, p. 215.

[3] Wilken Gesch. der Kreuzz. III. ii. p. 311 sq. Reinaud Extr. des Historiens Arabes, 1829, p. 214 sq.

[4] Gen. 28, 11 sq. 2 Sam. 24, 16. Pho-cas de Locis Sanct. 14. Will. Tyr. 8. 3, fin.

[5] Albert. Aq. 6. 24. p. 281. Fulcher. Carn. c. 18. p. 397.—This is probably the
i. 443, 444

stone mentioned by the *Itiner. Hieros.* in A. D. 333, near the two statues of Adrian : "Est non longe de statuis lapis pertusus, ad quem veniunt Judæi singulis annis, et ungnent eum, et lamentant se cum gemitu, et vestimenta sua scindunt, et sic recedunt."

[6] Hist. of Jerusalem by Mejr ed-Din, Fundgr. des Orient. II. p. 384. See also the account of two Arabic Mss. of similar import, in the Royal Library at Paris ; Notices et Extraits des Mss. etc. Tom. III. pp. 605, 610.

ing together one great temple; which, with their precincts, is now commonly called el-Haram esh-Sherif; but which in earlier Arabian writers bears the general name of Mesjid el-Aksa, 'the remotest' of the holy places, in distinction from Mecca and Medina.[1] This grand temple or mosk they regarded as the largest in the world, except that at Cordova in Spain.[2]

The walls around, and even the ground itself, bear evidence of being in part composed of the materials of former structures. Fragments of marble columns and masses of rubbish are visible in places where the ground is turned up or the sward broken;[3] and the famous seat of Muhammed, where he is to sit and judge the world, is nothing more than the broken shaft of a column, built in horizontally across the upper part of the eastern wall, instead of a square stone. Being longer than the thickness of the wall, it projects somewhat externally and overhangs the valley of Jehoshaphat; thus affording an occasion for the legend.[4] Other similar fragments are seen in various parts of the wall.

We heard much of the large reservoirs or cisterns which are said to exist under the surface of the Haram; and which have been often mentioned by travellers.[5] The Muslim worship, with its many ablutions, requires an abundant supply of water in or near the mosks; and the construction of cisterns was here almost a matter of course. The ancient subterranean vaults in this quarter, appear to have been in part used for this purpose. These cisterns are filled, as in the private houses of the city, partly by rain water from the roofs of the buildings; and partly also by the aqueduct which brings water from Solomon's pools. At the time of our visit, this was dry. Between the mosks es-Sûkhrah and el-Aksa there is a marble basin or fountain, bordered with olive, orange, and cypress trees; apparently connected with the tank or cistern described here in the times of the crusaders, which had a basin and a dome supported by columns, and furnished water

[1] The *Jámi'a* el-Aksa is the mosk alone; the *Mesjid* el-Aksa is the mosk with all the sacred enclosure and precincts, including the Sûkhrah. Thus the words *Mesjid* and *Jámi'a* differ in usage somewhat like the Greek ἱερόν and ναός. See *Hist. of Jerus.* in Fundgr. des Or. II. p. 93. Comp. Ibn el-Wardi, in Abulf. Syria, ed. Köhler, p. 180.

[2] Ibn el-Wardi, l. c. Edrisi, p. 343, ed. Jaubert.—The most complete oriental account of the Haram is in the History of Jerusalem by Mejr ed-Din, already so often quoted, Fundgr. des Or. II. pp. 81, 118, 375. V. p. 157. Less important is the History of the Temple by Jelâl ed-Din, translated by Reynolds, Lond. 1836. See also Ali Bey's Travels, Vol. II. c. 16.

p. 214 sq. Richardson's Travels, II. p. 285 sq. Bonomi in Hogg's Visit to Alexandria, Jerusalem, etc. II. p. 272 sq.

[3] Richardson's Travels, II. p. 312.

[4] Bonomi in Hogg's Visit to Alexandria, pp. 282, 283.

[5] Niebuhr Reisebeschr. Bd. III. Anh. p. 141. Ali Bey's Travels, II. p. 226.—So Tacitus describes the ancient temple as having within its enclosure " piscinæ cisternæque servandis imbribus;" Hist. 5. 12. Comp. Aristæus in Appendix to Havercamp's Josephus, Vol. II. p. 112. So too the *Itin. Hieros.* A. D. 333, speaks thus of the site of the temple: " Sunt ibi exceptoria magna aquæ subterraneæ et piscinæ magno opere ædificatæ."

i. 444–446

for the besieged and their cattle.[1]   In the lower part of the city, around the enclosure of the mosk, are several public fountains of Muslim construction, which appear once to have been fed from the cisterns of the Haram; but they have long ceased to flow.

The spacious crypts or vaults, which are known to exist beneath the mosk el-Aksa and the southern part of the enclosure, are a matter of intense interest; and we may hope that the time is not far distant, when they will become more accessible to a complete examination.   They are mentioned by travellers, who heard of them as early as the fifteenth century.[2]   An Arabian writer of about the same age speaks of a structure beneath the mosk, which was called the "ancient temple," and was referred to Solomon on account of its massive architecture.[3]   In A. D. 1697, Maundrell appears to have seen these vaults, and describes them as extending one hundred feet or more under Mount Moriah on the south side, and consisting of columns of a single stone, each four feet in diameter, and arched over with very large stones. How he can have seen these from the outside, from any point *within* the city wall, is to me inexplicable; unless there may have been at the time a breach in the wall.   At present there is no trace of any door or entrance on this part.   A few small holes or windows high up, are all the openings now visible.[4]   So far as I know, the only Frank travellers who have been permitted to descend into the vaults from within, are Richardson in 1818, and Messrs Bonomi, Catherwood and Arundale in 1833.[5]   The usual entrance from above is at the southeast corner of the enclosure, where a flight of steps leads down to "a square subterraneous chamber, in the middle of which, laid on the floor, is a sculptured niche" in the form of a sarcophagus, with a canopy above.   This is called the cradle of Jesus.   "From this chamber," Mr Bonomi says, "we descended a staircase to a spacious crypt, or series of vaults, extending beneath a considerable portion of the enclosure.— These noble substructions consist entirely of Roman arches of large dimensions and admirable workmanship, probably of the age of Herod."[6]   Richardson remarks, that the stones of which

---

[1] Albert. Aq. 6. 22, in Gesta Dei, p. 280.

[2] Breydenbach, A. D. 1483, relates that they could contain 600 horses; Reissb. p. 111. Fabri in the same year says, they were held to have been the stables of Solomon; and he entered them through a hole in the outer wall; ibid. p. 279. Baumgarten in A. D. 1507 heard of them as spacious and magnificent, and capable of receiving many thousand men; Peregrinatio, p. 86.

[3] History of Jerusalem, etc. Fundgr. des Or. II. p. 95.

[4] Maundrell's Journey, etc. Apr. 5. De i. 446. 447

Bruyn (le Brun) appears to speak of the same vaults a few years before. He calls them the *Temple of the Presentation*; they were under a mosk and could be seen only with lights; Voyage, etc. p. 262. Morison also entered the vaults from below; p. 879.

[5] Richardson's Travels, II. p. 308 sq. Bonomi in Hogg's Visit to Alexandria, etc. II. p. 281 sq. Ali Bey also heard of the vaults, but did not visit them; Travels II. p. 227.

[6] Bonomi, l. c. II. pp. 281, 282. I have since had the pleasure of receiving

the square columns are composed, are five feet long and are bevelled at the ends and corners ; they are disintegrated, and have a
much older appearance than the arches which they support.[1]

From information and plans kindly communicated to me by
Mr Catherwood, who with his companions examined and measured these subterranean structures without hindrance in 1833, it
appears that these vaults, so far as they are now accessible to
strangers, were originally formed by some fifteen rows of square
pillars measuring about five feet on a side, built of large bevelled
stones, and extending from the southern wall northwards to an

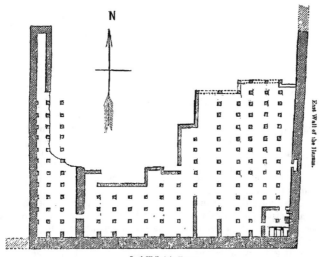

South Wall of the Haram.

unknown extent.   The intervals between the rows are usually,
though not entirely, regular ; and the pillars of some of the ranges are of a somewhat larger size.   In each row the pillars are
connected together by semicircular arches ; and then the vault,
resting upon every two rows, is formed by a lower arch, consisting
of a smaller segment of a circle.   The circumstance mentioned
by Richardson, that the pillars have a much older appearance
than the arches which they support, was not noticed by the
three artists.   From the entrance at the southeast corner of the

from Mr Bonomi himself a full confirma-   [1] Travels, II. pp. 309, 310.
tion of the account given in the text.

i. 447, 448

Haram for about one hundred and twenty feet westward, these
ranges of vaults extend northwards nearly two hundred feet;
where they are shut up by a wall of more modern date. For
about one hundred and fifty feet further west, the vaults are
closed up in like manner at less than a hundred feet from the
southern wall; and to judge from the wells and openings above
ground, it would seem as if they had thus been walled up, in order that the northern portion of them might be converted into
cisterns.   Beyond this part, towards the west, they again extend
still further north.   They are here terminated on the west, before reaching el-Aksa,[1] by a like wall filling up the intervals of
one of the rows of pillars.   How much further they originally
extended westward, is unknown; not improbably quite to the
western wall of the enclosure, where are now said to be immense
cisterns.[2]

The ground in these vaults rises rapidly towards the north;
the southernmost columns with the double arches being about
thirty-five feet in height; while those in the northern parts are
little more than ten feet high.   The surface of the ground is
everywhere covered with small heaps of stones; the memorials of
innumerable pilgrims who have here paid their devotions.   It is
a singular circumstance, that the roots of the large olive trees
growing upon the area of the Haram above, have in many places
forced their way down through the arches, and still descending
have again taken root in the soil at the bottom of the vaults.—
The accompanying plan of these vaults is from the skilful pencil
of Mr Catherwood; and was made out from his own very full
and exact measurements.[3]

At about thirty feet in front of el-Aksa, just on the east of
its principal porch or door, a passage leads down by steps through
the pavement and under the mosk, and continues to descend
partly by steps and partly without, until it terminates in a noble
ancient gateway adjacent to the southern wall of the enclosure.
This gateway is forty-two feet in breadth by fifty or sixty feet in
length from south to north.   It is described by Mr Catherwood
as entirely similar in its character and architecture to the Golden
gateway spoken of above,[1] except that it would seem to be of a

---

[1] The distance from the southeast corner of the Haram to the eastern wall of
el-Aksa, according to Mr Catherwood's
plans, is about 475 feet; while from the
same corner to the western side of the
vaults now open to visitors, is only about
820 feet.

[2] The vaults described by Maundrell
i. 448—450

would seem to have been on the west of
el-Aksa.

[3] This language refers to the cut in the
former edition. The present cut is from
Ferguson's Essay on the Ancient Topography of Jerusalem, Plate V.; for which
it was likewise furnished by Mr Catherwood.

somewhat earlier date ; the same groined roof and marble columns of the Corinthian order, indicating a Roman origin or at
least a Roman style. Like that too it is a double gateway ; and
the middle row of columns extends up through the whole passage.[1]

There can be little question, that this is the ancient gate
mentioned by Josephus, in the middle of the southern side of the
temple area.[2] It may have been erected, or at least decorated
by Herod ; and perhaps rebuilt by Adrian or at the same time
with the church under Justinian. At present the floor of it is
about fifteen or twenty feet above the ground on the outside.
Probably an external flight of steps originally connected it with
the part of the city below. The present southern wall, here
wholly modern, entirely covers this gateway from view ; so that
a person by merely looking at the outside, would have no suspicion of its existence ; although to one already acquainted with
it, certain traces in the wall serve to mark its place. This is
just on the east of the spot, where the city wall, coming up from
the south, meets the wall of the Haram ; it is consequently very
near the middle of the southern side of the ancient temple area.
At present neither this gateway, nor the passage leading down
to it, have any communication with the vaults above described.—
The existence of this ancient gateway goes to confirm indubitably
the view already taken, that the present southern wall of the
Haram occupies the identical site of the same wall of the ancient
temple area.[3]

The crypts too are doubtless ancient ; and may be referred,
partly perhaps to the vaulted substructions which were built up,
or very probably only repaired, for the area of Justinian's church;[4]
and partly either to Herod, or with greater probability to a still
earlier date. Herod indeed appears not to have meddled to any
great extent with the substructions of the temple ; except perhaps so far as to construct a subterraneous passage to it from
the fortress Antonia.[5] In doing this he doubtless made use in
part of older vaults or excavations ; and we know from Josephus,

---

[1] See the description of the Golden gateway above, p. 296.
[2] Joseph. Ant. 15. 11. 5.
[3] See above, p. 289. The reader, I am
sure, will join with me in thanking Mr
Catherwood for this very specific and valuable information respecting the vaults and
this subterranean gateway. The very existence of such a gate now becomes known
to the public for the first time. Besides
the preceding plan of the vaults, the same
gentleman has in his possession similar

measurements and plans of the subterranean and Golden gateways ; as well as of
both the mosks el-Aksa and el-Sâkhrah,
and of the Haram in general. It is greatly
to be desired, that these too may be given
to the public.—This hope has never been
fulfilled, and probably never will be. The
lamented Catherwood perished in the ca-
tastrophe of the ill fated Arctic, in 1854.
[4] See above, p. 297.
[5] See above, p. 283. Joseph. Antiq. 15.
11. 7.

i. 450–452

that such existed in connection with the temple. This historian relates,[1] that near the close of the siege of Jerusalem by Titus, Simon, one of the Jewish tyrants in the upper city, withdrew with a company of friends and stonecutters, furnished with tools and provisions, into a subterraneous cavern, with the hope of being able through connecting passages and by occasional mining, to make their escape without the walls of the city. In this purpose however they were frustrated; their provisions failed; and after Titus had departed from the city, Simon, arraying himself in white and purple, emerged from the ground on the spot where the temple had stood, in the vain hope of terrifying the guards who were there stationed, and thus making his escape. He was however seized, and reserved for the triumph of Titus.—This account implies at least, that there had been subterranean vaults or passages beneath the temple, corresponding to the *cavati sub terra montes* of Tacitus.[2]

Of the living fountain deep under the site of the temple, mentioned perhaps by Aristæus and apparently referred to by Tacitus, I shall speak in another place, in treating of the waters of Jerusalem.

VI. TOWER OF HIPPICUS, AND OTHER TOWERS.

Having thus obtained, in the substructions of the former temple, a fixed and definite point in the ancient topography of Jerusalem; and having found in the same a specimen and standard of the Jewish mural architecture; we afterwards turned our attention to other like remains, in the hope of being able to determine the places and the direction of some of the ancient towers and walls, which stood in connection with those of the temple.

Hippicus. The most important spot in a topographical respect yet to be ascertained, was the exact situation of the ancient tower Hippicus; which Josephus, as we have seen, assumed as the starting point in his description of all the city walls; and which was to be sought for at the northwest corner of the upper city or Mount Zion.[3] Of this tower the historian has left us a tolerably minute description.[4] It was built by the first Herod, and named after a friend of his who had fallen in battle. The form was a quadrangle, twenty-five cubits on each side; and built up entirely solid to the height of thirty cubits. Above this solid

[1] Joseph. B. J. 7. c. 2.

[2] So Jos. B. J. 5. 3. 1, *εἰς τοὺς ὑπονόμους.* Tacit. Hist. 5. 12, "Templum in modum arcis,—fons perennis aquæ, cavati sub terra montes, et piscinæ cisternæque servandis imbribus." See generally on this subject an essay of J. D. Michaelis, which exhibits much more of hypothesis than of i. 452. 453

proof, entitled: *Von den Gewölbern unter dem Berge Zion und des Tempels,* in his Zerstreute kl. Schriften, p. 427 sq. Münter Antiquarische Abhandlungen, p. 87 sq.

[3] See above, pp. 279, 280. Joseph. B. J. 5. 4. 2.

[4] Ibid. 5. 4. 3, 4.

part was a cistern twenty cubits high ; and then, for twenty-five cubits more, were chambers of various kinds ; with a breastwork of two cubits and battlements of three cubits upon the top. The altitude of the whole tower, accordingly, was eighty cubits. The stones of which it was built, were very large, twenty cubits long by ten broad and five high ; and (probably on the upper part) were of white marble.—It must here be borne in mind, that Josephus (as above mentioned) probably had no such specific measurements ; he was writing, after the lapse of years, at Rome ; and the numbers here given must therefore be regarded only in the light of conjectural estimates.[1]　On the other hand, the solidity of the lower part of the tower is a circumstance so remarkable, and was probably of such publicity, that it cannot well be referred to the imagination of the historian.

On the same northwestern part of Zion, a little south of the Yâfa gate, lies at present the fortress or citadel of the modern Jerusalem. It is an irregular assemblage of square towers, surrounded on the inner side towards the city by a low wall ; and having on the outer or west side a deep fosse. The towers which rise from the brink of the fosse, are protected on that side by a solid sloping bulwark or buttress, which rises from the bottom of the trench at an angle of about 45° This part bears evident marks of antiquity ; and this species of sloping bulwark, of which we saw several other specimens in Palestine, I am disposed to ascribe to the times of the Romans. In respect to the present instance, Adrian, in rebuilding and fortifying the city, would very naturally build up again a citadel upon the commanding site of the former one ; and to his age I am inclined to refer these massive outworks.—At the capture of Jerusalem by the crusaders in A. D. 1099, this fortress was the strongest part of the city, and the last to be surrendered.[2]　The historians of those times speak of it under the name of the tower or citadel of David ; and describe it as built of large hewn stones and of immense strength.[3] When the walls of the city were thrown down A. D. 1219 by the Muslims, this fortress was spared ;[4] and continued to bear among Franks only the name of the tower of David down to the sixteenth century.[5]　It then apparently began also to be called the castle of the Pisans ; in consequence, it is said, of having formerly been rebuilt or repaired by citizens of the Pisan republic.[6]

[1] See above, p. 277.
[2] Will. Tyr. 8. 24.
[3] Will. Tyr. 8. 3. ib. 9. 8. Jac. de Vit. c. 60, "ex lapidibus quadris cœmento et plumbo fusili quasi indissolubiliter compaginatis constructam."
[4] Wilken Gesch. der Kreuzz. VI. p. 238.
[5] So Marin. Sanut. A. D. 1321, Secr.

fid. Cruc. 3. 7. 2.　F. Fabri in 1483 ; Reissb. p. 215.
[6] *Pisanum Castellum, Pisanorum Castrum*, Adrichomius, p. 156. Cotovicus in 1598, Itin. p. 279.—The use of this name appears to have grown up in the sixteenth century. I find it first in the Itinerary of B. Salignac, who travelled in A. D. 1522, i. 453–455

Within this fortress, as the traveller enters the city by the Yâfa gate, the northeastern tower attracts his notice ; and, even to the unpractised eye, bears strong marks of antiquity. The upper part is apparently modern, and does not differ from the other towers and walls around ; but the lower part is built of larger stones, bevelled at the edges ; and apparently still occupying their original places. Among the Franks this is now known as the tower of David ; while they sometimes give also to the whole fortress the name of the castle of David.

Judging from the external appearance of this tower, and its situation in respect to Zion and the ancient temple, it early occurred to us, that the antique lower part of it was very probably a remnant of the tower of Hippicus erected by Herod ; which, as Josephus informs us, was left standing by Titus, when he destroyed the city.[1] This impression was strengthened as we daily passed and repassed the fortress, and became more at home in the topography of the city ; and especially was this the case, after we had discovered the remains of the ancient bridge connected with the temple. We now repaired to the citadel, as already related ;[2] and, from a careful inspection and measurements, found our former impressions confirmed.

This tower has been built up at the top like the other towers, in later times ; and is of about the same altitude as the rest. It is quadrangular, though not a square ; the eastern side measuring 56 feet 4 inches ; and the southern side, 70 feet 3 inches. The bearings of the sides, taken from the southeast corner, are N. 11° W. and W. 11° S. The height of the antique portion is 40 feet, but there is much rubbish in the fosse at the bottom ; and an allowance must be made of several feet more on this account. The large stones of which this part is built, have evidently never been disturbed ; they have neither been thrown down nor relaid ; and the general impression which they make upon the beholder, is precisely like that of the remains of the ancient walls around the temple. One of these stones measured 9¾ feet long, 4½ feet broad, and 3 feet 10 inches high ; another, 10 feet 2 inches long, 4 feet 1 inch high ; a third, 12¾ feet long, 3 feet 5 inches broad. They are therefore smaller than the stones of the temple walls ; and although like them bevelled, yet the rest of the surface is only roughly hewn. These two circumstances indicate a less massive and less careful style of architecture ; and probably imply a later date.

(Tom. VII. c. 1,) from whom Adrichomius quotes it; and also in Helffrich, A. D. 1565, Reissb. p 717 ; Zuallardo, A. D. 1586, p. 261 ; Cotovicus, as above ; Sandys in A. D. 1610, p. 123, etc.

[1] Joseph. B. J. 7. 1. 1.—I was not aware

i. 455. 456

at the time, that the same suggestion had been made on similar grounds by Scholz, de Golgathæ situ, p. 8. See also Raumer's Palästina, edit. 3. p. 312.   Schubert's Reise, II. p. 532.

[2] See above, p. 245.

The entrance of the present tower is in the western side, about half way up, in the upper or modern part. To the lower or antique part there is no known nor visible entrance, either from above or below; and no one knows of any room or space in it. The officer who accompanied us, said there was a tradition among them, that there was formerly an underground passage leading to it; but no one knew any thing of it now.—We made all our measurements in the presence of the soldiers; and some of them even went so far as to assist us.

All these circumstances, compared with the account of Josephus, and taking into view the conjectural and exaggerated nature of his statements, tally well enough with the description of Hippicus; while the position of the tower and the apparent solidity of the antique part, leave little room to doubt of its identity.

Towers of Phasaëlus and Mariamne. Josephus describes also two other towers,[1] built by Herod in the same general form, but of somewhat larger dimensions; one called Phasaëlus after his friend, and the other Mariamne after his favourite wife. They stood not far from Hippicus, on the first or ancient wall, which ran from the latter tower eastward to the temple, along the northern brow of Zion. This brow was here thirty cubits above the valley of the Tyropœon, and added greatly to the apparent height of the towers. Connected with these towers and Hippicus, was the royal castle or palace of the first Herod, which was enclosed by the said wall on the north, and on the other sides by a wall thirty cubits high. The whole was finished with great strength and regal splendour; and furnished with halls, and galleries, and cisterns, and apartments without number.[2]

But of all this strength and splendour not a vestige now remains, except the lower solid part of Hippicus, as above described. Titus, indeed, on beholding the massive nature of these works, gave orders to let these three towers be left standing, as memorials to posterity of the impregnable nature of the fortifications, which Roman valour had been able to subdue.[3] But not improbably Adrian, while he retained the foundations of Hippicus within his fortress, may have demolished the remains of the others for the sake of their materials.

The Tower Psephinos. Josephus describes a fourth tower, called Psephinos, situated overagainst Hippicus and the other towers towards the north, at the northwest corner of the third or exterior wall of the city.[4] This would seem to have been built by Agrippa, or at least in connection with the third or later wall. It was of an octagonal form, seventy cubits high; and from it could

---

[1] B. J. 5. 4. 3, 4.
[2] Ibid. 5. 4. 4.
[3] Ibid. 6. 9. 1. ib. 7. 1. 1.
[4] Ibid, 5. 4. 2, 3.

i. 456–458

be seen Arabia towards the rising sun, and the inheritance of the Hebrews quite to the sea.[1] All this shows that this tower must have stood upon the high swell of ground which extends up N. N. W. from the northwest corner of the present city. Here, at the distance of 700 feet from that corner, on the highest part of the ridge, (which indeed is higher than Zion,) are traces of ancient substructions, apparently of towers or other fortifications, extending along the high ground for 650 feet further in the same direction. This must always have been an important spot in every siege of the city; and although none of these substructions may perhaps be actually those of Psephinos; yet, in connection with the traces of walls, of which I shall speak hereafter, they serve to render it probable, that the tower in question stood somewhere in this vicinity.

VII. ANCIENT AND LATER WALLS.

We have thus ascertained two fixed points in the ancient topography of the city, viz. the tower of Hippicus and the temple. At the former of these Josephus makes all the walls of the city begin; while they all terminated at or near the latter. An outline of their several courses has already been given.[2]

First or earliest Wall. We follow again the order of Josephus.[3] The first and most ancient wall, beginning at Hippicus on the north, ran first (eastward) along the northern brow of Zion and so across the valley to the western side of the temple area. In this wall were the other two towers Phasaëlus and Mariamne; and adjacent to it on the south were the palace of Herod, the Xystus, and the bridge leading from the upper city to the temple. The length of this wall, between Hippicus and the temple, as near as we could estimate by paces, must have been about 630 yards.

From the tower of Hippicus again, this first or ancient wall on the west ran (southwards) along the western brow of Zion, through a place called Bethso to the gate of the Essenes. Both these are now unknown. Thence it turned along on the south over Siloam; and bending round on the east to Solomon's pool and the place called Ophla, it joined itself to the eastern portico of the temple.[4] This account is not very definite; and whether any traces of this wall remain, is doubtful. Along the western brow of Zion, outside of the present city, is a narrow higher ridge, which may not improbably be composed of rubbish and the

---

[1] This must of course mean the Dead Sea. The Mediterranean is not visible from the mount of Olives; and much less could it be seen from any tower, or any part of the walls, or from any spot what-
i. 458, 459

ever, within or around the city of Jerusalem.
[2] See above, pp. 278, 279.
[3] B. J. 5. 4. 2.
[4] See Note 1, on page 279.

foundations of the ancient wall. Quite at the southwest corner of Zion also, just below the brow, we found detached ledges of rock scarped in several places, as if they had once formed part of the foundation of the wall; and these we could trace for some distance eastward.[1] We were told also, that in digging deeply for the foundations of the new barracks, just south of the castle, many remains of walls and buildings had been discovered; but we were too late to examine this point ourselves; the excavations having been already filled up.—From a remark of Benjamin of Tudela, about A. D. 1165, it would seem that traces of some part of the ancient wall of Zion were visible in his day.[2]

In respect to the wall upon the eastern side, from Siloam to the temple, the question arises, whether it so ran as to include the waters of Siloam and the fountain of the Virgin within the city. On this point there is nothing very definite in Josephus or elsewhere; but it seems hardly probable, that the wall should have been carried close along by the only living fountains in the whole region of the city, and yet exclude them. It would seem too, from a passing notice of Josephus, that the city extended quite down to Siloam; and that there was a wall or fortification around that fountain.[3] This is also more distinctly evident from the language of Nehemiah.[4] From Siloam the wall ran to the pool or reservoir of Solomon; and this cannot well have been any other than the fountain of the Virgin, which is deep and excavated in the rock. At least there is nothing else in all this quarter which answers to that pool; nor is there any other passage in Josephus which can be applied to this ancient fountain.[5] The eastern wall then probably ran along the valley of Jehoshaphat; or else, crossing the point of the narrow ridge northeast of Siloam, swept down into that valley so as to include the fountain.[6] Then, passing by Ophla (Ophel), it ascended and terminated at the eastern portico of the temple. This circumstance serves to show, that the wall did not run along the brow of the ridge above the valley; for in that case it could have terminated only on the southern side of the temple, and not upon the eastern. Indeed, from another passage of Josephus, it would appear, that a portion of the valley of the Kidron was included in this wall.[7] The third wall too, coming from the north towards the temple, is said to terminate, not at the temple itself, but at this ancient wall in the

---

[1] See the account of the English cemetery in Vol. III. Sec. IV.
[2] Benj. of Tud. ed. Asher, I. p. 73.
[3] B. J. 6. 7. 2. ib. 6. 8. 5.
[4] Neh. 3, 15.
[5] This is not improbably the "King's pool" of Neh. 2, 14.
[6] On the narrow ridge north of Siloam

and south of the temple, at the distance of 960 feet from the city wall, are scarped rocks, apparently the foundations of a wall or some other like structure.
[7] Jos. B. J. 5. 6. 1. Here John is said to have held possession of the temple and the parts thereto adjoining, as also Ophla and *the valley of the Kidron.*

valley of the Kidron.[1]—Hence, the place Ophel would appear
to have been situated on the south of the temple, perhaps extending down towards the fountain of the Virgin. It was inhabited by
the Nethinim, who performed the menial offices of the temple and
therefore dwelt in its vicinity.[2]

In the account of the siege of Jerusalem by Titus, it appears,
as we have seen, that after the Romans had got possession of the
lower city, the temple, and all the tract south of it as far as to
Siloam, they were yet unable to enter the upper city, into which
the Jews had withdrawn themselves.[3] We are therefore under
the necessity of supposing a wall along the eastern brow of Zion,
above the Tyropœon, extending from the Xystus probably to a
point near Siloam.[4] Such a wall is not mentioned by Josephus
or any other writer ; but the circumstances of the case obviously
imply its existence.[5]

Second Wall. Josephus' description of the second wall is
very short and unsatisfactory. It began at the gate called Gennath in the first wall, and encircling only the tract lying north,
extended to Antonia.[6] This gate of Gennath in the first wall
doubtless was near the tower of Hippicus ; and was probably not
included within the second wall, in order to allow a direct passage
between the upper city and the country.[7] The two extremities
of this wall are therefore given ; but its course between these
points is a matter of some difficulty to determine.

Did this wall perhaps run from its beginning near the tower
of Hippicus *on a straight course* to the fortress Antonia ? This
question I feel compelled to answer in the negative, for several reasons. First, the express language of Josephus, that it took a
circular course. Secondly, the pool of Hezekiah, which is of high
antiquity and lay within the ancient city, must then have been
excluded. Thirdly, the whole space included in the lower city,
would in this way have been reduced to a small triangle, of about
600 yards on the south side and some 400 yards on the east side.
And lastly, this wall, built for the defence of this part of the city,
would thus have passed obliquely across the very point of the hill
Akra, and have been overlooked and commanded on the west by
every other part of the same hill.

These reasons constrain me to suppose, that the second wall

[1] Joseph. B. J. 5. 4. 2.
[2] Neh. 3, 26. 27. 11, 21. Comp. Jos.
B. J. 5. 6. 1.
[3] Jos. B. J. 6. 6. 2, 3. ib. 6. 7. 2.
[4] Comp. Jos. B. J. 6. 8. 5.
[5] In 2 Chr. 33, 14, king Manasseh is
said to have " compassed about Ophel, and
raised it up a very great height." May it
not have been the case, that the more ancient wall on this side included only Zion ;
while this wall of Manasseh ran, as de-
i. 461, 462

scribed by Josephus, from Siloam by Solomon's pool to the eastern side of the temple ?
[6] Jos. B. J. 5. 4. 2, κυκλούμενον δὲ
τὸ προσάρκτιον κλίμα μόνον, ἀνῄει μέχρι τῆς
'Αντωνίας.
[7] It must have been on the east of Hippicus, for the *third* wall began at that
tower. It could not however have been
far distant ; because that part of Zion was
then high and steep. Jos. B. J. 5. 4. 4.

ran first from near Hippicus northwards across the higher and
more level part of Akra; and then sweeping round to the valley
between Akra and Bezetha somewhere in the vicinity of the present Damascus gate, afterwards took a direction across the high
ground of Bezetha down to the northwest corner of Antonia; although the whole of Bezetha certainly was not included by it.—
In favour of this general hypothesis, we have not only the express
language of Josephus, as above quoted, and the fact that it removes all the difficulties just enumerated as incident to a straight
course; but it also receives some support from another incidental
remark of the Jewish historian. Having described the manner
in which the Romans, after many fierce assaults, got possession of
the second wall, he informs us, that Titus immediately caused
all the *northern* part to be thrown down; but placed troops in
the towers along the *southern* part. Had the wall run in a direct
course from Hippicus to Antonia, the writer could well have spoken only of the eastern and western parts.

The same hypothesis seems to receive further confirmation
from a fact which we noticed near the Damascus gate; and which
apparently has not been mentioned by any writer. Every traveller has probably observed the large ancient hewn stones, which
lie just in the inside of that gate towards the east. In looking at
these one day, and passing around them, we were surprised to
find there a square dark room adjacent to the wall; the sides of
which are entirely composed of stones having precisely the character of those still seen at the corners of the temple area,—large,
bevelled, with the whole surface hewn smooth, and thus exhibiting an earlier and more careful style of architecture than those
remaining in the tower of Hippicus. Connected with this room
on its west side is a winding staircase, leading to the top of the
wall, the sides of which are of the same character. Following out
this discovery, we found upon the western side of the gate, though
further from it, another room of precisely the same kind, corresponding in all respects to that upon the eastern side; except
that it had been much more injured in building the present wall,
and is in part broken away. Of the stones, one measured $7\frac{1}{4}$ feet
long by $3\frac{1}{2}$ feet high; and another $6\frac{1}{2}$ feet long by a like height.
Some of them are much disintegrated and decayed; but they all
seem to be lying in their original places, as if they had never been
disturbed or moved from the spot, where they were first fitted to
each other.—The only satisfactory conjecture which I can form
respecting these structures is, that they were ancient towers, of a
date anterior to the time of Herod, and probably the guard-houses
of an ancient gate upon this spot. This gate could have belonged
only to the second wall.[1]

[1] Another conjecture is indeed possible, viz. that when Adrian rebuilt the city, the

Except these, no traces whatever of the second wall are visible, so far as we could discover. Heaps of rubbish out of various centuries, and modern houses, cover the whole ground.[1]

Third Wall. This began also at Hippicus ;[2] ran northwards as far as to the tower Psephinos ; then passed down opposite the sepulchre of Helena ; and being carried along through the royal sepulchres, turned at the corner tower by the Fuller's monument ; and ended by making a junction with the ancient wall in the valley of the Kidron. This wall was commenced by the elder Agrippa under the emperor Claudius ; but he desisted from it for fear of offending that emperor ; and it was afterwards carried on and completed by the Jews themselves, though on a scale of less strength and magnificence.[3] Before the erection of this wall, the buildings of the city had extended themselves far to the north, covering also the hill Bezetha ; and were " wholly naked " of defence.

The tower Psephinos, as we have seen, must have stood upon the high ground N. N. W. of the northwest corner of the modern city. The tomb of Helena, if not identical with the present tombs of the Kings, (as is most probable,) was doubtless near them.[4] The wall is not said to have been carried so far as this monument ; but only passed opposite or overagainst it. Of the other points mentioned, nothing definite is known. The conclusion is a probable one, that the wall passed from Psephinos in an easterly or northeasterly direction to the brow of the valley of Jehoshaphat ; and thence along that valley, until it met the ancient wall coming up from the south on the east of the temple.

In correspondence with this conclusion, we suppose that we found traces of the foundations of Agrippa's wall on its northwest part. I first came upon them accidentally, in returning one evening with Mr Whiting from the tombs of the Kings along the path leading up to the Yâfa gate. A few days after, in passing the same way with Messrs Smith and Lanneau, we examined them more leisurely. On the east of the said path, in the

---

Romans may have taken stones from the ruins of the temple and built these towers. But this seems inconsistent with the style of architecture, the evident fitting of the stones to each other, and also with their decay apparently in their original places. Nor is such a conjecture supported by anything analogous in other parts of the city.

[1] See further upon this second wall in Vol. III. Sec. V.—In describing the siege of Jerusalem by Herod, before the third wall was built, Josephus speaks also of a first and second wall ; Ant. 14. 16. 2. But his *first* wall there is evidently that to i. 464, 465

which the besiegers first came, and which they first took, viz. the second wall of the text above, which was then the exterior wall on this part. By the *second* wall in the same passage, he obviously means the wall around the court of the temple.

[2] Jos. B. J. 5. 4. 2.

[3] As Claudius ascended the throne in A. D. 41, and Agrippa is generally held to have died in A. D. 44, the date of the commencement of this wall is pretty definitely fixed. It was begun ten or twelve years after our Lord's crucifixion.

[4] See " Tombs of the Kings," further on.

field about half way between those tombs and the northwest corner of the city, we noticed foundations, which belonged very distinctly to the third wall ; consisting of large hewn blocks of stone, of a character corresponding to other works of those ages. On the west of the path, and running up the hill in a line with the above, were other similar foundations ; and still further up were stones of the like kind apparently displaced. By following the general direction of these, and of several scarped rocks which had apparently been the foundations of towers or the like, we succeeded in tracing the wall in zigzags in a westerly course for much of the way to the top of the high ground. Here are the evident substructions of towers or other fortifications, extending for some distance ; and from them to the northwest corner of the city, the foundation of the ancient wall is very distinctly visible along the hard surface of the ground. Within the corner of the modern walls is also a trace of the ancient one ; to which we shall recur again presently.[1]

The next day, April 28th, we took measurements of these foundations, so far as we could determine the various points, as follows ; beginning at the northwest corner of the city.

1. N. 26° W. 700 feet.   To the foundations of a large tower.
2. N. 20° W. 650   Across other foundations of towers, etc.
3. N. 10° E. 336   To another point ; the intervening wall not traceable.
4. N.   100   To foundations, etc.
5. E.   400   To the path.
6. N. 20° E. 465   Along the path.
7. N. 75° E. 264   To the end of the large hewn stones first seen.

In the courses No. 5 and 6, there was some uncertainty. Hewn rocks lay to the west in a line with the course No. 7. We therefore returned to the end of No. 4, and measured new courses as follows :

5. N. 40° E.   To hewn rocks, apparently the foundation of a tower.
6. N. 75° E. 200 feet.   To the path, at the end of the former No. 6.
7. N. 75° E. 264   To the hewn stones, as before.

Beyond this point we were unable to trace anything ; unless perhaps the foundation of a tower hewn in the rock towards the northeast, but quite uncertain. A like search along the brow of the valley of Jehoshaphat, was also in vain. Indeed, the level ground on this side of the city has now been ploughed over for ages, and the stones carried off or thrown together to form terraces ; so that all traces of former foundations have nearly disappeared. Many ancient cisterns however still remain ; and marble tesserae are often picked up.

Circumference of the Ancient City. The ancient southern

[1] See below, under " Walls of the Middle Ages."

i. 466, 467

wall, we know, included the whole of Zion ; the eastern wall ran
probably along or near the bottom of the valley of Jehoshaphat ;
while, as we have now seen, the northern wall passed some forty or
fifty rods north of the present city.   Hence I am disposed to allow
full credit to the assertion of Josephus, that the ancient city was
33 stadia in circumference, equivalent to nearly 3⅓ geographical
miles.   The present circumference, as we have seen, is about 2¼
geographical miles ; but the extent of Zion now without the walls,
and that of this tract upon the north, are sufficient to account
for the difference.

Walls of Adrian, and of the Middle Ages.   The new city
of Ælia, erected by Adrian on the ruins of Jerusalem, would appear to have occupied very nearly the limits of the present city.
The portion of Zion which now lies outside, would seem then
also to have been excluded ; for Eusebius and Cyrill in the fourth
century speak of the denunciation of the prophet as having been
fulfilled, and describe Zion as "a ploughed field."[1]   On the north
the extent of the second wall and the remains of the ancient gate
formed an appropriate boundary ; the wall being carried across
to the brow of the valley of Jehoshaphat on the east, so as to include the hill Bezetha, instead of bending southward, as anciently, to the corner of Antonia.

The walls of Adrian appear to have remained until the times
of the crusaders ; having probably been more or less repaired
and strengthened by the Muhammedans, after they became masters of the city.   About A. D. 697, Arculfus speaks of the southern wall as running across the northern part of Zion ;[2] and when
the crusaders came, they also found the greater part of Zion still
without the city.   When they invested Jerusalem, the Count of
Toulouse pitched his camp on this side, between the city and
the church of Zion, which was a bowshot distance from the
wall.[3]

Thus from the time of Adrian onward, even to our day, the
limits of the Holy City appear to have undergone no important
change.   But the walls themselves have been subjected to many
vicissitudes.   Towards the close of the period in which the crusaders had possession of the city, the walls in several parts had
fallen down from age ; and on this account a subscription was
entered into in A. D. 1178, among the princes of Europe both

[1] Mic. 3, 12. Euseb. Demonstr. Evan-
gel. 8. 3. p. 406, edit. Colon. 1688,
" Mons Sion—per viros Romanos in nulla
re a reliqua regione differens aratur et co-
litur, ut nos quoque inspexerimus boum
opera locum arari et seminari."—Cyrill.
Hieros. Catech. 16. 18. p. 253. ed. Touttée : Σιὼν ὡς ἀγρὸς ἀροτριασθήσεται · προ-
i. 467, 468

λέγων τὸ νῦν ἐφ' ἡμῶν πληρωθέν.   The
Itin. Hieros. also implies that Zion was
then without the walls : " Item exeunti
in Hierusalem, ut ascendas Sion," etc.
See above, pp. 264, 265.
[2] Adamnan. ex Arculf. I. 1.
[3] Will. Tyr. 8. 5.

secular and ecclesiastical, in order to rebuild them ; they engaging to pay a sum of money annually until the work should be completed.[1]   This labour was probably in part accomplished ; for in A. D. 1187, the city sustained a siege of several weeks, before it yielded to the power of Saladin.   Some years later, in the beginning of A. D. 1192, Jerusalem being threatened with a siege by Richard of England, Saladin spent the whole winter in strengthening the fortifications.   New walls and bulwarks were erected, and deep trenches cut.   The Sultan himself rode daily around the works to encourage the labourers ; and sometimes brought stones to them upon the saddle of his own horse.   In like manner the high officers and learned men took part in the work ; which was completed in six months, and had all the firmness and solidity of a rock.   Indeed the fortifications were now stronger than ever before ; and the population of the city increased greatly.[2]

In A. D. 1219, the Sultan Melek el-Mu'adh-dhem of Damascus, who now had possession of Jerusalem, ordered all the walls and towers to be demolished, except the citadel and the enclosure of the mosk ; in the fear lest the Franks should again become masters of the city, and thus find it a place of strength. This order occasioned great grief to the Muslim inhabitants, great numbers of whom abandoned the city ; but it was carried into effect during that and the following year.[3] In this defenceless state the city continued, until it was again delivered over to the Christians in consequence of the treaty with the emperor Frederick II. in A. D. 1229 ; with the express understanding, according to Arabian writers, that the walls should not be rebuilt.[4] Yet ten years later, in A. D. 1239, the barons and knights of the kingdom of Jerusalem made no scruple to break the terms of the truce ; and began anew to build up the walls, and erected a strong fortress on the west of the city.[5] Their progress however was interrupted by an assault of the Emir David of Kerak, who seized the city, strangled the Christian inhabitants, and threw down again not only the walls and the fortress just erected, but also dismantled the tower of David, which had before been spared.[6]

Four years later, in A. D. 1243, Jerusalem was again by treaty given over into the hands of the Christians without reserve ; to the great indignation of all good Mussulmans, who now beheld their sacred places again profaned.[7] The fortifications appear to have been immediately repaired ; for they are

[1] Will. Tyr. 21. 25, " propter nimiam vetustatem cum muri jam ex parte corruissent," etc.
[2] Wilken Gesch. der Kreuzzüge, IV. p. 457. VI. p. 236.

[3] Wilken ib. VI. pp. 237, 370.
[4] Ibid. pp. 478, 480.
[5] Ibid. p. 587.
[6] Ibid. p. 596.
[7] Ibid. p. 628.

mentioned as existing in the storm of the city by the wild Kharismian hordes in the next year, A. D. 1244;[1] shortly after which the city reverted for the last time into the hands of its Muhammedan masters, with whom it has remained unto the present day.[2] Of its walls we have no further account ; except the fact of their having been rebuilt, as already described, in A. D. 1542.[3]

These modern walls, as I have already remarked,[4] appear to occupy the site of the former ones ; a slight deviation only being visible around the northwest corner of the city. Here both along the western and northern sides, the remains of a former wall may be traced for some distance on the outside, evidently belonging to the times of the crusades. A more important fragment of the same wall lies on the inside, just within the northwest corner of the present walls, not far from the Latin convent. It consists of a large square area or platform, built up solidly of rough stones, fifteen or twenty feet in height, and paved on the top. This was probably the former northwest bastion of the city.[5] At the southwest corner of this platform are the remains of a higher square tower, built of small unhewn stones cemented together. All these works seem to have been erected on the ruins of a still older wall ; for at the southwest corner of the mass, near the ground, are three courses of large bevelled stones, rough hewn, passing into the mass diagonally, in such a way as to show that they lay here before the tower and bastion were built. These are probably remains of the ancient *third* wall ;[6] the foundations of which we had already traced from near this point on the outside of the city. These ancient stones bore from Hippicus N. 36° W.

VIII. ANCIENT AND LATER GATES.

Ancient Gates. In regard to the gates of ancient Jerusalem, there exists so much uncertainty, that it would seem to be a vain undertaking to investigate the relative positions of them all. Of the ten or twelve gates enumerated in the book of Nehemiah and other parts of the Old Testament, Reland remarks with

---

[1] Chorosini, Chorosmini, Chowarismii; Wilken Gesch. der Kreuzz. VI. pp. 631, 634. Comment. de Bell. cruc. Hist. p. 202.

[2] Wilken. Gesch. der Kreuzz. VI. p. 646.

[3] After these historical notices, it is apparent that the story can be only a fable, which is related by Quaresmius, and also by Le Brun and by Korte, respecting the architect employed by the Sultan to build up the present walls, viz. that he lost his head for leaving out Mount Zion. See i. 470, 471.

Quaresmius, II. p. 41. Le Brun's Voyage etc. p. 298. Kortens Reise, p. 216.

[4] See above, p. 261.

[5] Not improbably the "Tancred's Tower" of the crusaders, which according to William of Tyre (8. 5) was at the northwest angle of the city. The present tradition has transported it to the northeast corner; see Prokesch Reise etc. p. 86.

[6] Unless we take them as having perhaps belonged to the ancient *second* wall.

truth, that it is uncertain, first, whether they all were situated
in the external walls, or perhaps lay partly between the different
quarters of the city itself, as is common even now in oriental
cities; secondly, whether some of them were not gates leading
to the temple, rather than out of the city; and again, whether
two or more of the names enumerated, may not have belonged to
the same gate.[1] Indeed, it is certain, that there must have been
gates forming a passage between the upper and lower city; and
we know that there were several on the western side of the area
of the temple. There must also probably have been a gate and
way leading from Akra to the quarter south of the temple, passing perhaps beneath the bridge. But of all those gates, who
can ascertain the names?

It must however be borne in mind, that all the accounts of
the Old Testament relate to the city only as bounded on the
north, by the *second* wall of Josephus. There can of course be
no allusion to any of the gates of the subsequent third wall.
Hence, for example, the suggestion that the present gate of St.
Stephen may correspond to the ancient Sheep gate, is wholly untenable; since apparently, until the time of Agrippa, no wall existed in that quarter.

The chief passages relating to the gates and walls of the ancient city, are found in the book of Nehemiah;[2] and these are
occasionally illustrated by other incidental notices. It is obvious
in the account of the rebuilding of the walls by Nehemiah, that
the description begins at the Sheep gate; and proceeds first
northwards, and so towards the left around the city, till it again
terminates at the same gate.[3] This gives the probable order in
which the ten gates there mentioned stood; and the other two
named elsewhere can be easily inserted.[4] But where was the
beginning, or what the intervals between, or where the positions
of the several gates? These are questions which can never be
answered, except in a general and unsatisfactory manner.

Yet in regard to the probable position of a few of the gates,
we may arrive at some more definite conclusion. Thus the Fountain gate, without much doubt, was situated near to Siloam;[5] and
was not improbably the same as the "gate between two walls," by

[1] Reland Pal. p. 855.
[2] Neh. 2, 13–15. 3, 1–32. 12, 31–40.
[3] Neh. 3, 1. 32.
[4] The ten gates mentioned in Nehem.
c. 3, are the following: Sheep gate, vs. 1,
32; Fish gate, vs. 3; Old gate, vs. 6;
Valley gate, vs. 13; Dung gate, vs. 14;
Fountain gate, vs. 15; Water gate, vs. 26;
Horse gate, vs. 28; East gate, vs. 29; Gate
Miphkad, vs. 31. Also in 12, 39, we find
the Prison gate, perhaps the same with

Miphkad; and the gate of Ephraim. Then
again mention is made of the Corner gate,
2 Chr. 25, 23; and the gate of Benjamin,
Jer. 37, 13. The latter is probably the
same as the gate of Ephraim.—Josephus
mentions further the gate called Gennath,
near the tower of Hippicus; and that of the
Essenes on the south part of the city; B.
J. 5. 4. 2.

[5] Neh. 3, 15. 12, 37.

which king Zedekiah attempted to escape.[1] There was also
doubtless upon the northern side of the city a gate leading towards
the territory of Benjamin and Ephraim ; and this would naturally take the name of those tribes. It may very probably have
been the ancient gate, which we found upon the site of the present
Damascus gate. The notices of the Valley gate and Dung gate
are less distinct. In passing around the city towards the left,
they are mentioned before reaching the Fountain gate or Siloam;
and are therefore to be sought probably on the western or southern part of Zion. Now the northwestern corner of Zion lies
just at the bend of the valley of Gihon or upper part of Hinnom ;
and here would naturally be, and so far as we know always has
been, a gate, the Gennath of Josephus. Here probably stood the
Valley gate, overagainst the Dragon fountain or Gihon.[2] We must
look then for the Dung gate on the southern part of Zion ; and
as the nature of the ground in this part does not admit of frequent
gates, there seems good reason for regarding it as identical with
the gate of the Essenes mentioned by Josephus.[3]

In this way the course of Nehemiah during his night excursion becomes plain. Issuing from the Valley gate on the west, he
followed down the valley of Hinnom and around to Siloam and
the King's (Solomon's) pool, or fountain of the Virgin. Beyond
this the narrow valley was full of ruins, so that there was "no
place for the beast that was under him to pass." He therefore
went up " by the brook " on foot, and then returned by the same
way.[4]

Further than this, I would not venture to advance. The notices respecting the other gates are too indefinite to enable us to
determine anything more, than that some of them probably did
not belong to the external city wall. Thus the Horse gate evidently lay between the temple and the royal palace ;[5] and the
Water gate was apparently on the western part of the area of
the temple.[6]

[1] 2 K. 25, 4.
[2] Neh. 2, 13.
[3] Josephus says the wall ran from Hippicus through the place called Bethso to
the gate of the Essenes, and thence on the
south to Siloam ; B. J, 5. 4. 2. This would
fix the probable site of this gate on the
southwest part of Zion. The name Bethso
(Βηθσώ) which Josephus does not translate,
seems to be the Hebrew בֵּית צוֹאָה, 'Dung
place ;' and not improbably marks the spot
where the filth of this part of the city was
thrown down from Zion into the valley
below. From this circumstance, the adjacent gate might naturally receive the
synonymous name שַׁעַר הָאַשְׁפֹּת 'Dung
gate."
i. 473, 474

[4] Neh. 2, 13–15.
[5] 2 K. 11, 16.   2 Chr. 23, 15.
[6] Neh. 8, 1. 3. Comp. 3, 26.—Of the
Fish gate, Jerome says that it led to Diospolis and Joppa, and of course was on the
west or northwest side of the city ; but this
is inconsistent with the order in Nehemiah
c. 3. See Hieron. in Sophon. 1, 10.—The
different hypotheses respecting the ancient
gates may be seen in Bachiene's Palast.
Th. II. § 94–107. Faber's Archäol. der
Heb. I. p. 336. Hamelsveld Bibl. Geogr.
II. p. 75 sq. Rosenmueller Bibl. Geogr.
II. ii. p. 216. Gesen. Thesaur. Heb. art.
שַׁעַר, page 1460.

Gates of the Middle Ages. Of the gates erected by Adrian in his new city Ælia, we have no account. As however the walls of that city apparently occupied very nearly the same place as the present ones, the nature of the ground renders it almost certain that there must have been, as now, one or more gates on the west, north, and east ; and probably also on the south.

The earliest mention of gates in the subsequent ages, is by Adamnanus, from the information of Arculfus, about A. D. 697.[1] Then follow the notices of both Christian and Arabian writers in the times of the crusades and later.

On the *west* side there appears to have been formerly two gates. The first and principal was the *Porta David*, Gate of David, mentioned by Adamnanus, and also by the historians of the crusades.[2] At that period it was called by the Arabs *Bâb el-Mihrâb*.[3] This corresponds to the present Yâfa gate or Bâb el-Khûlil.— The second was the *Porta Villæ Fullonis*, Gate of the Fuller's field, of Adamnanus.[4] It seems to have been the same which Brocardus calls *Porta Judiciaria* in the wall of those days, somewhere overagainst the church of the Holy Sepulchre, leading to Silo (Neby Samwil) and Gibeon. Probably also it was the same which Arabian writers call *Serb*.[5] There is no trace of it in the present wall.—There would seem also to have been a small portal contiguous to the Armenian convent in the southwest.[6]

On the *north*, there were also two gates ; and all Christian writers speak of the principal one in those days as being called the gate of St. Stephen. There can be no question on this point; for they all, from Adamnanus down to Ludolf de Suchem (A. D. 1336–50), mention this gate and the place of St. Stephen's martyrdom, as upon the north side of the city.[7] The tradition of the monks on this point, was changed apparently about that time and before the middle of the fifteenth century ; since they now, as we have seen, call the eastern gate of the city by this name, and show the place of martyrdom near it.[8] The same northern gate is also sometimes called the gate of Ephraim, in reference to its

---

[1] Lib. 1. 1, "Portas bis ternas, quarum per circuitum civitatis ordo sic ponitur. 1. Porta David ad occidentalem partem montis Sion. 2. Porta villæ Fullonis. 3. Porta S. Stephani. 4. Porta Benjamin. 5. Portula, hoc est parvula porta, ab hac per gradus ad vallem Josaphat descenditur. 6. Porta Tecuitis."

[2] Gesta Dei, p. 572. Will. Tyr. 8. 5.

[3] Edrisi about A. D. 1150, ed. Jaubert, I. p. 341. Hist. of Jerusalem in Fundgr. des Or. II. p. 129.

[4] So called from Isa. 7, 3.

[5] Brocardus, c. 8. fin. Mejr ed-Din Hist. of Jerus. in Fundgr. des Or. II. p. 129.

[6] Mejr ed-Din, l. c.

[7] Adamnanus l. c. Will. Tyr. 8. 5, "porta quæ hodie dicitur *Sancti Stephani*, quæ ad Aquilonem respicit." 9. 19. Gesta Dei, p. 572. Marin. Sanut. 3. 14. 8.— That Stephen was here stoned, is expressly said; Will. Tyr. 3. 2, "a Septentrione . . . ubi usque hodie locus in quo protomartyr Stephanus a Judæis lapidatus." Gesta Dei, p. 572. Brocardus c. 8. fin. Lud. de Suchem, p. 83, and in Reissb. p. 846.—Yet Sir J. Maundeville, about 1325, speaks of a church of St. Stephen, where he was stoned, as already existing on the east of the city by the valley of Jehoshaphat; p. 80. The tradition had begun to waver.

[8] St. Stephen's gate appears on the east

i. 474–476

probable ancient name.[1] Arabic writers give it the name of *Bâb 'Amûd el-Ghurâb;*[2] of which the present Arabic form, Bâb el-'Amûd, is only a contraction.—Further east was the *Porta Benjaminis,* Gate of Benjamin,[3] corresponding apparently to the present gate of Herod.

Towards the *east* there seem to have been also at least two gates. The northernmost, corresponding to the present gate of St. Stephen, is described by Adamnanus as a " small portal from which steps led down into the valley of Jehoshaphat." The crusaders called it the gate of Jehoshaphat, from the valley.[4] Arabian writers mention it as *Bâb el-Usbât,* gate of the Tribes, another form of the modern Arabic name Bâb es-Sûbât.[5] The four lions sculptured over the present gate on the outside, as well as the architecture, show that this structure did not proceed from the Muhammedans, and must be older than the present walls. Not improbably the earlier " small portal" on this spot was rebuilt on a larger scale and thus ornamented by the Franks, when they built up the walls of the city, either about A. D. 1178 or in A. D. 1239.[6]—The other gate on this side is the famous Golden gate, *Porta aurea,* in the eastern wall of the Haram esh-Sherîf ; now called by the Arabs Bâb ed-Daharîyeh, but formerly named by the Arabian writers *Bâb er-Rahmeh,* Gate of Mercy.[7] The name *Porta aurea* as applied to this gate, I have not been able to trace back further than to the historians of the crusades.[8] It probably comes from some supposed connection with one of the ancient gates of the temple, which are said to have been covered with gold.[9] We have seen above, that it is apparently of Roman origin.[10] This gate was already closed up in the times of the cru-

---

side of the city, as at present, in the journals of Steph. von Gumpenberg, A. D. 1449 ; Tucher, A. D. 1479 ; Breydenbach and F. Fabri, A. D. 1483, etc. See Reissb. des h. Landes, pp. 444, 665, 111, 252.—Quaresmius gravely undertakes to remove the idea of any change of place, by supposing that the present gate formerly faced towards the north ! Elucid. II. p. 295.

[1] Brocardus c. 8, fin. Marinus Sanutus calls it, probably erroneously, the gate of Benjamin ; de Secret. 3. 14. 8.

[2] Edrisi ed. Jaubert, p. 341. Hist. of Jerus. in Fundgr. des Or. II. p. 129.

[3] Adamnanus, as above. Brocardus c. 8, fin. The latter writer calls it also *Porta Anguli.* Comp. De Salignaco, Tom. VIII. c. 5. It is not mentioned by Edrisi. Mejr ed-Din in his Hist of Jerusalem speaks here of two gates ; Fundgr. des Orients, II. p. 129.

[4] Will. Tyr. 11. 1. Gesta Dei, p. 572. Benj. of Tudela ed. Asher, I. pp. 70, 71.

i. 476, 477

—Brocardus speaks of another gate further north, which he calls the Dung gate ; c. 8, fin.

[5] Edrisi ed. Jaubert, I. p. 344. Hist. of Jerus. in Fundgr. des Or. II. p. 129.

[6] See above. pp. 316, 317.

[7] Edrisi ed. Jaubert, I. pp. 341, 344. Hist. of Jerus. in Fundgr. des Or. II. p. 96.

[8] Will. Tyr. 8. 3. Gesta Dei, p. 572.—Quaresmius professes to quote Jerome for the name, but gives no reference whatever ; Elucid. II. p. 336. The name *Porta aurea* occurs indeed in Hegesippus *de Excidio Hieros.* lib. 5. c. 42, in the Biblioth. Max. Patrum, Tom. V. p. 1203. But the author is there obviously speaking of a gate of the ancient interior temple or fane itself.

[9] Joseph. B. J. 5. 5. 3. It may perhaps have been regarded as the ancient *Porta orientalis ;* see Lightfoot Opp. I. p. 555 sq.

[10] See above, p. 296.

sades ; but was thrown open once a year on Palm Sunday, in celebration of our Lord's supposed triumphal entry through it to the temple.[1] It remains still walled up ; because (according to the Franks) the Muhammedans believe that a king is to enter by it, who will take possession of the city and become Lord of the whole earth.[2] But Muhammedan writers describe it as having been closed up for the security of the city and sanctuary ; because it is on the side towards the desert, and there would be no great advantage in having it open. Some say it was walled up by Omar ; and will not be opened again until the coming of Christ.[3]

On the *south* side were likewise two gates. Of the easternmost, the present Dung gate of the Franks, I find no mention earlier than Brocardus, about A. D. 1283, who regards it as the ancient Water gate.[4] It may have been the *Porta Tecuitis* of Adamnanus. An Arabian writer speaks of it in the fifteenth century as the Bâb el-Mughâribeh, its present native name.[5]—Further west, between the eastern brow of Zion and the Porta David (Yâfa gate), there was according to Adamnanus, no gate in his day.[6] Yet the crusaders found one here, which they called the gate of Zion, corresponding to that which now bears the same name.[7] It is also called by Arabian writers, Bâb Sahyûn ;[8] though the present native usage gives it the name of David.[9]

Thus it appears, that before the rebuilding of the walls of Jerusalem by Suleimân in the sixteenth century, the principal gates of the city were much the same as at the present day.

IX. SUPPLY OF WATER.

Jerusalem lies in the midst of a rocky limestone region, throughout which fountains and wells are comparatively rare. In the city itself, little if any living water is known ; and in its immediate vicinity are only the three small fountains along the lower part of the valley of Jehoshaphat. Yet with all these disadvantages of its position, the Holy City would appear always to have had a full supply of water for its inhabitants, both in ancient and in modern times. In the numerous sieges to which in all ages it has been exposed, we nowhere read of any want of water within the city ; while the besiegers have often suffered severely, and have been compelled to bring water from a great distance. During the siege by Titus, when the Jews, pressed with famine,

[1] Gesta Dei, p. 572. xxiv. Edrisi ed. Jaubert, p. 541.
[2] Quaresmius II. p. 340.
[3] Hist. of Jerusalem in Fundgr. des Orients, II. p. 96.
[4] Brocardus c. 8, fin.
[5] Hist. of Jerus. l. c. p. 129.
[6] Adamn. ex. Arculf. 1. 1.

[7] Will. Tyr. 8. 6, 19. Gesta Dei, p. 572.
[8] Edrisi ed. Jaubert, p. 341. Hist. of Jerus. l. c. p. 129.
[9] In Wilken's Geschichte der Kreuzz. III. ii. p. 315, mention is made of a gate of St. Lazarus in the southern wall ; but of this I have found no other notice.

had recourse to the most horrible expedients, and thousands
daily died of hunger, there is no hint that thirst was added to
their other sufferings.[1] Yet when Antiochus Pius had previously
besieged the city, his operations were at first delayed for want of
water ; and Josephus regards it as the result of a divine interposition, that the Romans under Titus were not in like manner
straitened.[2] So too in the siege by the crusaders, A. D. 1099, the
inhabitants were well supplied ; while the besiegers were driven
to the greatest straits by thirst under the burning sun of June.[3]
Thus in every age the truth of Strabo's brief description has been
manifest : "Jerusalem, a rocky well-enclosed fortress ; within
well-watered, without wholly dry."[4]

It becomes therefore a matter of some historical importance,
as well as interest, to ascertain as far as possible, how this supply of water has been furnished to the city. To this inquiry I
address myself here, in giving an account of the Cisterns, the Reservoirs, and the Fountains, in and around the city, with some
notices of the aqueduct from Solomon's pools.

CISTERNS. The main dependence of Jerusalem for water at
the present day is on its cisterns ; and this has probably always
been the case. I have already spoken of the immense cisterns
now and anciently existing within the area of the temple ; supplied partly from rain water, and partly by the aqueduct.[5]
These of themselves, in case of a siege, would furnish a tolerable
supply. But in addition to these, almost every private house in
Jerusalem, of any size, is understood to have at least one or more
cisterns, excavated in the soft limestone rock on which the city
is built. The house of Mr Lanneau, in which we resided, had no
less than four cisterns ; and as these are but a specimen of the
manner in which all the better class of houses are supplied, I subjoin here the dimensions :

	Length.	Breadth.	Depth.
I.	15 Feet.	8 Feet.	12 Feet.
II.	8	4	15
III.	10	10	15
IV.	30	30	20

This last is enormously large, and the numbers given are the

[1] Jos. B. J. 5. 12. 3.   ib. 5. 13. 4, 7.
[2] Jos. Ant. 13. 8. 2.   B. J. 5. 9. 4. p.
350. ed. Havers.
[3] Albert. Aq. 6. 22, in Gesta Dei, p.
280. Will. Tyr. 8. 7, "Interea siti fatiga-
batur exercitus vehementissimus.—Augebat
denique sitis importunitatem, et angoris
geminabat molestiam, æstatis inclementia
et ardens Junius," etc. The distress of
the host appears to have been very great.
On the other hand, the inhabitants, he
i. 479. 4

says, were abundantly supplied, both with
rain water and that brought by aqueducts
from abroad ; in which way two immense
reservoirs (maximæ quantitatis) near the
enclosure of the temple were supplied ; 8.
4 fin. Comp. also 8. 24.
[4] Strabo's still briefer text is as follows :
16. 2. 40, τὰ Ἱεροσόλυμα—ἦν γὰρ πετρῶδες
εὐερκὲς ἔρυμα· ἐντὸς μὲν εὔυδρον, ἐκτὸς δὲ
παντελῶς δίψηρόν.
[5] See above, p. 301.

least estimate. The cisterns have usually merely a round opening at the top, sometimes built up with stonework above, and furnished with a curb and a wheel for the bucket ; so that they have externally much the appearance of an ordinary well. The water is conducted into them from the roofs of the houses during the rainy season ; and, with proper care, remains pure and sweet during the whole summer and autumn.—In this manner most of the larger houses and the public buildings are supplied. The Latin convent in particular is said to be amply furnished ; and in seasons of drought is able to deal out a sufficiency for all the Christian inhabitants of the city.[1]

Most of these cisterns have undoubtedly come down from ancient times ; and their immense extent furnishes a full solution of the question, as to the supply of water for the city. Under the disadvantages of its position in this respect, Jerusalem must necessarily have always been dependent on its cisterns ;[2] and a city which thus annually laid in its supply for seven or eight months, could never be overtaken by a want of water during a siege. Nor is this a trait peculiar to the Holy City ; for the case is the same throughout all the hill country of Judah and Benjamin. Fountains and streams are few, as compared with Europe and America ; and the inhabitants therefore collect water during the rainy season in tanks and cisterns in the cities, in the fields, and along the high roads, for the sustenance of themselves and of their flocks and herds, and for the comfort of the passing traveller.[3] Many, if not the most of these are obviously antique ; and they exist not unfrequently along the ancient roads which are now deserted. Thus on the long forgotten way from Jericho to Bethel, " broken cisterns " of high antiquity are found at regular intervals.—That Jerusalem was thus actually supplied of old with water, is apparent also from the numerous remains of ancient cisterns still existing in the tract north of the city, which was once enclosed within the walls.

A few wells are occasionally found, both in and around the city ; but they are either dry, or the water is low and bad. One of these has been already mentioned near the tombs in the valley of Jehoshaphat ; and another near the wall on mount Zion.[4]

---

[1] According to Scholz, the Latin convent has 28 cisterns ; Reise, p. 197. So also Salzbacher, Erinnerungen II. p. 95.

[2] Such was also the case during the times of the crusades. Will. Tyr. 8. 4, " Est autem locus in quo civitas sita est, aridus et inaquosus, rivos, fontes ac flumina non habens penitus, cujus habitatores aquis tantum utuntur pluvialibus. Mensibus enim hybernis in cisternis quas in civitate habent plurimas, imbres solent sibi colligere, et per totum annum ad usus necessarios conservare." So too Jac. de Vitriaco, c. 55. Benjamin of Tudela, ed. Asher, p. 71.

[3] So Jerome, writing at Bethlehem, says : " In his enim locis in quibus nunc degimus, præter parvos fontes omnes cisternarum aquæ sunt; et si imbres divina ira suspenderit, majus sitis quam famis periculum est." Comm. in Amos 4, 7.

[4] See above, pp. 236, 238.

There is also a well of bad water just out of the Damascus gate, not used for drinking; and another, somewhat better, just by the tombs of the Kings. The reason why so few wells exist, is doubtless to be referred to the small quantity and bad quality of the water thus obtained.

But although the cisterns of Jerusalem thus afford apparently an abundant supply, yet as a matter of convenience and luxury, water is brought during the summer in considerable quantity from fountains at a distance from the city. The principal of these is 'Ain Yâlo, a small fountain in Wady el-Werd, several miles southwest of Jerusalem. The water is transported in skins, on the backs of asses and mules; and is sold for a trifle for drinking, to those who prefer it to rain water. It was even said, that one of the baths is supplied with water in this way during a part of the season.

RESERVOIRS. The same causes which led the inhabitants of Judea to excavate cisterns, induced them also to build, in and around most of their cities, large open reservoirs for more public use. Such tanks are found at Hebron, Bethel, Gibeon, Bireh, and various other places; sometimes still in use, as at Hebron, but more commonly in ruins. They are built up mostly of massive stones; and are situated chiefly in valleys where the rains of winter could be easily conducted into them. These reservoirs we learned to consider as one of the least doubtful vestiges of antiquity in all Palestine; for among the present race of inhabitants such works are utterly unknown.

With such reservoirs Jerusalem was abundantly supplied; to say nothing of the immense pools of Solomon beyond Bethlehem, which no doubt were constructed for the benefit of the Holy City. In describing these tanks or pools, I begin with those lying without the walls on the west side of the city. Here are two very large reservoirs, one some distance below the other in the valley of Gihon or Hinnom, and both unquestionably of high antiquity. Now as the prophet Isaiah speaks of an upper and lower pool, the former of which at least lay apparently on this side of the city, I venture to apply these names to the two reservoirs in question.[1]

Upper Pool. This is commonly called by the monks *Gihon,* and by the natives *Birket el-Mamilla.*[2] It lies in the basin forming the head of the valley of Hinnom or Gihon, about 700 yards W. N. W. from the Yâfa gate. Our first visit to it has

---

[1] Is. 7, 3. 36, 2. 2 Kings 18, 17.— Is. 22, 9.

[2] Quaresmius II. p. 715. Hist. of Jerus. in Fundgr. des Or. II. p. 181. The crusaders called it *Lacus Patriarchæ;* Will. Tyr. 8. 2.—The monk Bernhard in A. D. i. 482, 483

870, mentions in this quarter a church of St. Mamilla, in which were preserved the bodies of many martyrs slain by the Saracens. Hence perhaps the Arabic name of the reservoir. Bernh. Mon. de Locis Sanct. 16. See too Eutych. Annal. II. p. 213.

already been described, and the small rude conduit mentioned, which carries the water from it down to the vicinity of the Yâfa gate and so to the pool of Hezekiah within the city.[1] The sides are built up with hewn stones laid in cement, with steps at the corners by which to descend into it. The bottom is level. The dimensions are as follows:

Length from east to west	.	.	.	316 Engl. feet.
Breadth at the west end	.	.	.	200
" at the east end	.	.	.	218
Depth at each end	.	.	.	18

We noticed no water-course or other visible means by which water is now brought into the reservoir;[2] but it would seem to be filled in the rainy season by the waters which flow from the higher ground round about. Or rather, such is its present state of disrepair, that it probably never becomes full; and the small quantity of water which it at first retains, soon runs off and leaves it dry.

The upper pool of the Old Testament was situated near the "highway of the Fuller's field," and had a trench or conduit.[3] This indeed is indefinite; but we are also told that there was "an upper out-flow of the waters of Gihon" on the west of the city.[4] Taking these two circumstances together, the upper pool and the upper out-flow or water-course of Gihon, it seems most probable that this reservoir is intended; and that it anciently had some connection with the fountain of Gihon in the neighbourhood. This conclusion is strengthened by the fact, that nowhere else in or around Jerusalem are there traces of other ancient reservoirs, to which the names of the upper and lower pool can be applied with any like degree of probability.[5]

Lower Pool. This name is mentioned only by Isaiah; and that without any hint of its locality.[6] I venture to give it to the large and broken reservoir lower down on the west side of the city, called by the Arabs *Birket es-Sultân.* Monkish tradition is here somewhat at fault; some calling it the pool of Bersaba; others of Bathsheba;[7] while others again give the latter name to a small tank just within the Yâfa gate. The accounts of travellers exhibit a like diversity. The probable identity of this tank

---

[1] See above, p. 238.

[2] Quaresmius says there are two channels, perhaps subterranean, by which water flows into the reservoir; one on the north, and the other on the south side. Elucid. II. p. 716. But nothing of the kind is seen at present.

[3] Is. 7, 3. 36, 2. 2 Kings 18, 17. Of the Fuller's field, Eusebius and Jerome merely say, that it was shown in their day in the suburbs of the city; Onom. art. *Ager Fullonis.*

[4] 2 Chr. 32, 30. I follow here the Hebrew, which the English version does not fully express.

[5] Pococke also assumes these as the Upper and Lower pool; Descr. of the East, II. i. pp. 25, 26.

[6] Is. 22, 9.

[7] Quaresmius Elucidat. II. p. 596 sq.

i. 484. 485

with the lower pool of Isaiah, rests upon its relative position in
respect to the upper pool just described ; and upon the fact,
that no other reservoir is anywhere to be found, to which this
scriptural name can so well be applied.

This reservoir is situated in the valley of Hinnom or Gihon,
southward from the Yâfa gate. Its northern end is nearly upon
a line with the present southern wall of the city, which here lies
about 100 feet above it. The pool was formed by throwing
strong walls across the bottom of the valley ; between which the
earth was wholly removed ; so that the rocky sides of the valley are
left shelving down irregularly, and form a narrow channel along
the middle. The wall at the south end is thick and strong like
a dam or causeway ; those along the sides are of course comparatively low and much broken away ; that on the north is also in
part thrown down. A road crosses on the causeway at the southern
end ; along which are fountains erected by the Muslims, and once
fed from the aqueduct which passes very near. They were now
dry. The following are the measurements of this reservoir :

Course of the two sides	. . . . .	S. 10° W.
" of the north end, taken from the east	.	W. 10° N.
" of the south end, do.	. . .	W.
Length along the middle	. . .	592 Engl. feet.
Breadth at the north end	. . . . .	245
" at the south end	. . . . .	275
Depth at north end, including about 9 feet of rubbish		35
" at south end, including about 3 feet of rubbish		42

This reservoir was probably filled from the rains, and from the
superfluous waters of the upper pool. It lies directly in the natural channel by which the latter would flow off ; but is now in
ruins.

Besides these two large reservoirs, we find further without
the walls, the comparatively small and unimportant tank just
north of St. Stephen's gate, called by the natives *Birket el-Hammâm Sitty Meryam.* It seems to have been little regarded by
the monks, and we did not find that it had among the Franks a
name ; though some, as we were told, hold it to be the pool of Bethesda.[1] There is also the small cistern-like tank in the trench
near the gate of Herod on the northeast part of the city.[2] My
impression is, that both these receptacles are filled only by the
rain water, which flows in winter from the higher ground on the
west and northwest into and along the trench.[3] They have no
appearance of great antiquity.—The pool of Siloam, also without
the walls, will be described in another place.

---

[1] See p. 233, above.
[2] See p. 234, above.
[3] Scholz in 1821 says, that water was
i. 485, 486

then carried from the reservoir outside of
St. Stephen's gate to a bath within the city
Reise, p. 271. The same is true now.

Within the walls of the city there are *three* reservoirs; two of which are of large size.

Pool of Bathsheba. The smallest of the reservoirs, which indeed is rather a mere pit, lies just within the Yâfa gate, on the north side of the street, overagainst the castle. It is now called by the Franks the pool or bath of Bathsheba, on the supposition that David dwelt in the castle opposite; though it has long had to dispute its claim to this appellation with the large lower pool outside.[1] We did not hear of any Arabic name. It was now dry, nor did we learn that it ever becomes full.[2]

Pool of Hezekiah. The reservoir now usually so called, lies some distance northeastward of the Yâfa gate, just west of the street that leads north to the church of the Holy Sepulchre. A line of houses only separates it from this street; and as it is not far from the said church, it was formerly called by the monks the pool of the Holy Sepulchre.[3] The natives now call it *Birket el-Hammâm*, from the circumstance that its waters are used to supply a bath in the vicinity. Its sides run towards the cardinal points. Its breadth at the north end is 144 feet; its length on the east side about 240 feet, though the adjacent houses here prevented any very exact measurement. The depth is not great. The bottom is rock, levelled and covered with cement; and on the west side the rock is cut down for some depth. The reservoir is supplied with water during the rainy season, by the small aqueduct or drain brought down from the upper pool, along the surface of the ground and under the wall near the Yâfa gate. When we last saw it in the middle of May, it was about half full of water; which however was not expected to hold out through the summer.

In searching in this quarter for traces of the second wall of the ancient city, we came to the Coptic convent, situated at the northern end of the reservoir. This had been recently rebuilt and was not yet completed. On inquiring of the master mason, who had charge of the whole work, in respect to the excavations which had been made, he informed us, that in digging to lay the foundation of the new wall, running from east to west, they had come upon an old wall of large hewn stones parallel to the present north wall of the reservoir, and 57 feet distant from it

[1] Doubdan Voyage, etc. p. 138. Quaresmius in his zeal for the other location does not even mention this spot. Maundrell drily remarks, that the one has probably the same right to the name as the other; Apr. 6th.

[2] Monro calls it "an oblong pit, twenty feet deep, lined coarsely with small stones;" Summer Ramble, I. p. 107. Schubert remarks that "the architecture and the size of the stones seem to belong to the works of the ancient Jerusalem;" Reise II. p. 532. I am not able to say which of these is most correct.—Mr Wolcott says: "The former [Monro] is correct; there is nothing large or ancient about it." Biblioth. Sac. 1843, p. 33.

[3] *Piscina S. Sepulchri*, Quaresmius II. p. 717.

towards the north. This wall, he said, was ten or twelve feet thick, laid in cement, and also plastered over on the south side with cement, like the wall of a reservoir. The bottom below was rock, which was also covered towards the south with a coating of small stones and cement several inches thick, like the bottom of the present pool. In laying the foundations of another part of the convent, he had also dug down along a part of the present northern wall of the pool, which he found to be built of small stones ; so small indeed that he had been compelled to remove them and build up the wall anew. All these circumstances led him to the conclusion, that the pool of Hezekiah once extended further north, as far as to the old wall above described. To this conclusion we could only assent ; for the stones thus dug out were still lying around, and bore every mark of antiquity. They were not indeed large, like those of the temple walls ; but were bevelled, and obviously of ancient workmanship.

We are told of king Hezekiah, that he "made a pool and a conduit, and brought water into the city ;" and also that "he stopped the upper water-course of Gihon, and brought it straight down to the west side of the city of David."[1] From this language we can only infer, that Hezekiah constructed a pool within the city on its western part. To such a pool, the present reservoir, which is doubtless an ancient work, entirely corresponds ; and it is also fed in a similar manner. The pool must of course have been situated within the second wall of Josephus ; and its present position serves therefore to determine in part the probable course of that wall.[2] It is, doubtless, also the pool Amygdalon of Josephus, about thirty cubits distant from the monument of the highpriest John.[3]

Bethesda. Sheep Pool. In the Gospel of John we are informed, that "there was at Jerusalem, by the Sheep [gate], a pool, which was called in the Hebrew tongue Bethesda, having five porches."[4] This pool the monks and many travellers have chosen to find in the deep reservoir or trench on the north side of the area of the great mosk. They give to it the different names of Bethesda and the Sheep pool ; and in the two long vaults at its southwest corner, they profess to find two of the five ancient porches.[5] The natives call it *Birket Isrâil.* There is not the slightest evidence that can identify it with the Bethesda of the New Testament. Eusebius and Jerome, and also the *Itin. Hieros.* do indeed speak of a *Piscina Probatica* shown in their day as

[1] 2 Kings 20, 20. 2 Chr. 32, 30. Comp. also Sirac. 48, 17.
[2] See above, p. 312.
[3] Κολυμβήθρα 'Αμύγδαλον, Jos. B. J. 5. 11. 4.
[4] John 5, 2. The ellipsis in the Greek i. 488, 489

text is to be supplied by πύλη *gate*, from Neh. 3, 1. See Bos Ellips. Graec. art. πύλη. Lightfoot Opp. II. p. 587. Comp. next page, Note I.
[5] Quaresmius calls it *Piscina Probatica ;* but seems to doubt about the porches ;

Bethesda, a double pool, one part of which was filled by the winter rains, and the other was reddish as if formerly tinged with bloody waters.[1] But neither of these writers gives any hint as to the situation of the pool. The name has doubtless been assigned to the reservoir in question comparatively in modern times, from its proximity to St. Stephen's gate, which was erroneously held to be the ancient Sheep gate.[2] The dimensions of the reservoir have already been given ; and the reasons assigned why I hold it to be the ancient fosse, which protected the fortress Antonia and the temple on the north.[3] That it was formerly filled with water, is apparent from the lining of small stones and cement upon its sides. But from what quarter the water was brought into it, I am unable to conjecture ; unless perhaps it may have been fed from the pool of Hezekiah, or more probably from the superfluous waters formerly collected from the aqueduct and elsewhere, in the cisterns of the adjacent Haram es-Sherif. The reservoir has now been dry for more than two centuries ; during which its deep bottom has been in part a receptacle of filth, and in part occupied as a garden of herbs and trees.[4]

FOUNTAINS. The only sources, or rather receptacles, of living water now accessible at Jerusalem, are three in number. They are all situated without the present walls, in and along the deep valley of Jehoshaphat. We begin with that lowest down the valley.

Well of Nehemiah or Job. This is the deep well situated just below the junction of the valley of Hinnom with that of Jehoshaphat. The small oblong plain there formed, is covered with an olive grove, and with the traces of former gardens extending down the valley from the present gardens of Siloam. Indeed this whole spot is the prettiest and most fertile around Jerusalem. Franks call this the well of Nehemiah, supposing it to be the same in which the sacred fire is said to have been hid during the Jewish captivity, until again recovered by that leader of the exiles.[5] But

---

II. p. 98 sq. Comp. Cotovic. Itin. p. 258. Maundrell Apr. 9th.

[1] Onomast. art. *Bethesda.*—These fathers supplied the ellipsis in the Greek text so as to read : "There was in Jerusalem by the Sheep [pool], a pool which was called," etc. They thus make here a double pool.

[2] See above, p. 319. I have not found the name *Piscina Probatica* distinctly applied to this reservoir earlier than Brocardus A. D. 1283, (c. 8,) and Marinus Sanutus A. D. 1321, lib. 3. 14. 10. These writers speak also (especially Brocardus l. c.) of a large reservoir adjacent to the church of St. Anne, called *Piscina interior,* now apparently destroyed. This latter seems to have been the *Piscina Probatica* of the earlier historians of the crusades ; see Gesta Dei, p. 573. Will. Tyr. 8. 4, fin. Jac. de Vitr. c. 63. They mention indeed the present reservoir as "lacus quidam," but give it no name ; Gesta Dei, p. 573. Will. Tyr. l. c. Sir John Maundeville in the 14th century places the *Piscina Probatica* within the church of St. Anne ; Lond. 1839, p. 88. Comp. also F. Fabri and Rauwolf in Reissb. des heil. Landes, pp. 252, 609.

[3] See above, pp. 293, 294.

[4] Cotovic. Itin. p. 258. Quaresmius II. p. 98. Comp. p. 233, above.

[5] 2 Macc. 1, 19-22. Formerly also *Puteus ignis ;.* see Quaresmius II. p. 270

i. 489—491

I have not found this name in any writer earlier than the close
of the sixteenth century. Those who mention the well before
that time, speak of it only as the En-Rogel of the old Testament.[1] The native inhabitants call it *Bir Eyûb*, the well of
Job.[2]

It is a very deep well, of an irregular quadrilateral form, walled up with large squared stones, terminating above in an arch
on one side, and apparently of great antiquity. There is a small
rude building over it, furnished with one or two large troughs or
reservoirs of stone, which are kept partially filled for the convenience of the people. The well measures 125 feet in depth ; 50
feet of which was now full of water. The water is sweet, but not
very cold ; and is at the present day drawn up by hand. An
old man from Kefr Selwân was there with his cord and leather
bucket, and drew for us. He said the water was good and would
sit lightly on the stomach. In the rainy season the well becomes
quite full, and sometimes overflows at the mouth. More usually,
however, the water runs off under the surface of the ground, and
finds an outlet some forty yards below the well. Here, the old
man said, it commonly flows for sixty or seventy days in winter,
and the stream is sometimes large. An Arabian writer describes
the Bir Eyûb as built up with very large stones ; and as having
in its lower part a grotto or chamber walled up in like manner,
from which the water strictly issues. It might be inferred, perhaps, from the same account, that in a season of drought, the Muhammedans had sunk this well to a greater depth.[3]

It is singular that the earlier historians of the crusades make
no mention of this well ; although on account of the abundance
of its living water, it must have been of great importance to the
Franks.[4] That it existed before their day is obvious ; for it is
mentioned by Brocardus in A. D. 1283, as being one of the fountains of the Old Testament. It may not improbably have been
filled up ;[5] and thus have remained unknown to the first crusaders.
It is apparently of high antiquity ; and there can be little doubt,

sq. Cotovic. p. 292. Doubdan Voyage, p.
136.

[1] So Brocardus c. 8. Marinus Sanutus
3. 14. 9. De Salignac in A. D. 1522, Itin.
Tom. X. c. 1. Cotovicus in 1598 calls it
Puteus ignis ; and Quaresmius seems to
be the first to give it the name of Nehemiah.

[2] I know not the occasion of this name ;
yet it occurs in Mejr ed-Din in A. D. 1495,
as if already of long standing ; Fundgr.
des Or. II. p. 130. It is found also in the
Arabic version of Joshua in the Paris and
London Polyglotts, for En-Rogel, Josh. 15,
7. The Jewish Itinerary published by
Hottinger in his *Cippi Hebraici,* says this
well is properly that of Joab, though the

Gentiles call it the well of Job ; p. 48. ed.
2. This does not at all help the matter.
And besides, this Itinerary cannot be older
than the last half of the sixteenth century ;
since it speaks of the building of the walls
by Sultan Suleimân ; p. 34.

[3] Mejr ed-Din Hist. of Jerus. in Fundgr.
des Or. II. p. 130.

[4] Jac. de Vitriaco says expressly of
Jerusalem, "fontes autem non habet, excepto *uno,* qui Siloü nominatur ; c. 55. But
he probably would not regard this well as
a fountain.

[5] See the story related in the work ascribed to Hugo Plagon, respecting an ancient well below Siloam, which was dis-

that it was rightly regarded by Brocardus as identical with the En-Rogel of Scripture ; though probably it may have been enlarged and deepened in the course of ages.

The fountain En-Rogel is first mentioned in the book of Joshua, in describing the border between the tribes of Judah and Benjamin.[1] This border began at the northwest corner of the Dead Sea, and passed up westward through the mountains to En-Shemesh ; which may very possibly have been the fountain near St. Saba. Thence it came to En-Rogel ; and went up the valley of Hinnom on the south side of the Jebusites (Jerusalem); and so to the top of the hill overagainst the valley of Hinnom westward, at the north end of the valley of Rephaim or the Giants. Thence it was carried on to the waters of Nephtoah, perhaps one of the several fountains in Wady el-Werd. It needs but a glance at the plan, to see that this description applies most definitely and exactly to the present well of Nehemiah. The border probably came up along the lower part of the valley of Jehoshaphat to this well ; and then continued up the valley of Hinnom and across the hill to the valley of Rephaim.[2] One other notice goes also to fix the place of the fountain Rogel in the same vicinity. When Adonijah caused himself to be proclaimed king, he assembled his friends and made a feast at En-Rogel ; or, as Josephus records it, "without the city at the fountain which is in the king's garden."[3]

Siloam. The name Siloah or Siloam,[4] which has obtained such celebrity in the Christian world, is found only three times in the Scriptures as applied to waters ; once in the prophet Isaiah, who speaks of it as running water ; again as a pool in Nehemiah ; and lastly also as a pool in the account of our Lord's miracle of healing the man who had been born blind.[5] None of these passages afford any clue as to the situation of Siloam. But this silence is amply supplied by the historian Josephus, who makes frequent mention of Siloam as a fountain ;[6] and says expressly, that the valley of the Tyropœon extended down to Si-

---

covered and cleared out about A. D. 1184, and furnished an abundant supply of water. Hug. Plag. Contin. Gallicæ Historiæ Guil. Tyr. in Martini et Durand Collect. ampl. Tom. V. p. 889 sq. Wilken's Gesch. der Kreuzz. III. ii. p. 248.

[1] Josh. 15, 7. 8.   18, 16. 17.

[2] The site of Jerusalem lay of course wholly within the original limits of the tribe of Benjamin.

[3] 1 Kings 1, 9. Joseph. Ant. 7. 14. 4. Comp. 2 Sam. 17, 17. We have seen above, that the Arabic version in Josh. 15, 7 has 'Aïn Eyûb for En-Rogel; see the preceding page, Note 2.

[4] The Arabic form of this name is *Selwân.*

[5] Isa. 8, 6 שִׁלֹחַ. Neh. 2, 15 שֶׁלַח. John 9, 7. 11. The Hebrew word in the two passages of the Old Testament is indeed written with different vowels; but there is no reason to doubt the identity of the name. It signifies *sent, a sending,* etc. The Greek form is Σιλωάμ, both in the N. T. and in Josephus. There was probably both a fountain and a reservoir, as at the present day. Hence the diversity in different writers.—A tower of Siloam is also mentioned, Luke 13, 4.

[6] B. J. 5. 4. 1, 2. ib. 5. 9. 4. p. 350, Havere.

i. 492–494

loam ; or in other words, Siloam was situated in the mouth of the Tyropœon, on the southeast part of the ancient city ; as we find it at the present day.[1] Its waters, he says, were sweet and abundant. There can also be no room for question, that the Siloam of Josephus is identical with that of the Scriptures.

Of the same tenor is the account of the *Itin. Hieros.* A. D. 333, that to those going out of the city in order to ascend Mount Zion, the " pool" of Siloam lay below in the valley on the left. More definite is the testimony of Jerome about the close of the same century. ᷍ This father says expressly that " Siloam is a fountain at the foot of Mount Zion ; whose waters do not flow regularly, but on certain days and hours ; and issue with a great noise from hollows and caverns in the hardest rock." Again, in speaking of Gehenna, he remarks that " the idol Baal was set up near Jerusalem at the foot of Mount Moriah, where Siloam flows."[2] Moriah must here be taken as including the ridge which runs from it towards the south ; and the mention of the idol Baal limits the position of Siloam to the gardens at the mouth of the Tyropœon and valley of Hinnom ;[3] which also corresponds to the language of Josephus.   In the account of Jerome, we have the first correct mention of the irregular flow of the waters of Siloam.[4]

Siloam is mentioned both as a fountain and pool by Antoninus Martyr early in the seventh century ; and as a pool by the monk Bernhard in the ninth.[5] Then come the historians of the crusades ; who also place Siloam as a fountain in its present site, near the fork of two valleys. William of Tyre mentions its irregular flow ; and another speaks of it both as a fountain and a pool.[6] According to Benjamin of Tudela about A.D. 1165, there

---

[1] B. J. 5. 4. 1, ἡ δὲ τῶν Τυροποιῶν προσαγορευομένη φάραγξ—καθήκει μέχρι Σιλωάμ· οὕτω γὰρ τὴν πηγήν, γλυκεῖάν τε καὶ πολλὴν οὖσαν, ἐκαλοῦμεν. Comp. B. J. 5. 4. 2. It is chiefly from a misapprehension of this latter passage, that Reland and other modern commentators have transferred the place of Siloam to the valley on the southwest part of Zion ; see above, p. 279, Note 1.

[2] Hieron. Comment. in Esa. 8, 6 " Siloë autem fontem esse ad radices montis Sion, qui non jugibus aquis, sed in certis horis diebusque ebulliat, et per terrarum concava et antra saxi durissimi cum magno sonitu veniat, dubitare non possumus ; nos præsertim, qui in hac habitamus provincia." Comm. in Matt. 10, 28 " Idolum Baal fuisse juxta Jerusalem ad radices montis Moria, in quibus Siloë fluit, non semel legimus."

[3] See above, p. 274.

i. 494, 495

[4] The *Itin. Hieros.* magnifies this circumstance into a flowing for six days and nights and a resting on the seventh day. Isidore of Spain, in the seventh century, copies the account of Jerome ; Etymolog. 13. 13. 9. The same legend probably existed long before ; and gave occasion to the language of Pliny, H. N. 31. 2, "In Judæa rivus sabbathis omnibus siccatur." Comp. Wesseling's note upon this legend, *Itiner. Hieros.* p. 592.

[5] Antonini Mart. Itin. 24. Bernh. Mon. de Locis Sanct. 15.

[6] Will. Tyr. 8. 4, " Juxta urbem tamen, a parte Australi, ubi duæ valles prædicatæ se continuant, quasi milliario distans ab urbe, fons est quidam famosissimus, Siloë.—Fons quidem modicus, et qui nec sapidas, nec perpetuas habet aquas ; interpolatum enim habens fluxum, die tantum tertia aquis dicitur ministrare." Jac. de Vitriaco c. 55. Comp. also Gesta

was then here an ancient edifice ; and Phocas in 1185 says the
fountain was surrounded by arches and massive columns, with
gardens below.[1] Then follow Brocardus A. D. 1283, and Marinus Sanutus A. D. 1321, who both speak of the fountain and
the pool ; and the latter does not forget its irregular flow. A few
years later Sir John Maundeville mentions it as a " welle " at the
foot of Mount Zion towards the valley of Jehoshaphat, " clept
natatorium Siloë."[2]

Thus far, all the historical notices refer only to the present
Siloam, in the mouth of the valley of the Tyropœon, which still
exhibits both a fountain and a reservoir ; and they all have no
reference to the fountain of the Virgin further up the valley
of Jehoshaphat ; with which, as we have seen, the waters of
Siloam stand in connection. The mention of gardens around Siloam, and of its waters as flowing down into the valley of the
Kidron, is decisive on this point; for neither of these circumstances
could ever have been applicable to the other fountain. Indeed,
singular as the fact must certainly be accounted, there seems to
be nothing which can be regarded as an allusion to the fountain of
the Virgin, during the long series of ages from the time of Josephus
down to the latter part of the fifteenth century. At that time
Tucher (A. D. 1479), Breydenbach and F. Fabri, as also Zuallart and Cotovicus a century later, mention distinctly the two
fountains of Siloam and the Virgin ; but appear to have no knowledge of their connection.[3] This seems to have been first brought
to notice by Quaresmius in the beginning of the seventeenth century.[4] The hypothesis that the fountain of the Virgin is the
true *fountain* of Siloam, and the other merely the *pool* of Siloam,
which has found favour in modern times among the Franks,
seems to have sprung up only in the early part of the eighteenth
century, and is destitute of all historical foundation. The first
mention of it which I find, is in a suggestion of Pococke, A. D.
1738 ; and the same is expressed more definitely by Korte about
the same time.[5]

The general features of Siloam have already been described ;
a small deep reservoir in the mouth of the Tyropœon, into which
the water flows from a smaller basin excavated in the solid rock
a few feet higher up ; and then the little channel by which the

Dei, p. 573; "Ad radicem hujus montis
Syon exoritur fons aspectu liquidissimus,
sed gustu amarus, quem dicunt *natatoria
Siloë*; qui emittit rivulum suum in alveo
ubi torrens Cedron fertur in hyeme cursu
rapidissimo."
    [1] Benj. of Tud. ed. Asher, p. 71. Pho-
cas de Loc. Sanct. 16.
    [2] Brocard. c. 8. Mariu. San. de Secr.

fid. Cruc. 3. 14. 9. Maundeville's Travels,
1839, p. 92.
    [3] See Reissbuch des h. Landes, ed. 2.
pp. 666, 113, 256. Zuallart Viaggio, pp.
135, 149. Cotovici Itin. pp. 292, 293.
Sandys' Travels, pp. 146, 147.
    [4] Quaresmius, Elucid. II. p. 289 sq.
    [5] Pococke, II. i. pp. 23, 24. Kortens Reise,
pp. 111, 112.

stream is led off along the base of the steep rocky point of Ophel, to irrigate the terraces and gardens extending into the valley of Jehoshaphat below.[1] The distance from the eastern point of Ophel nearest this latter valley to the said reservoir, is 255 feet. The reservoir is 53 feet long, 18 feet broad, and 19 feet deep; but the western end is in part broken down. Several columns are built into the side walls; perhaps belonging to a former chapel, or intended to support a roof; but there is now no other appearance of important ruins in the vicinity. No water was standing in the reservoir as we saw it; the stream from the fountain only passed through and flowed off to the gardens.

The smaller upper basin or fountain is an excavation in the solid rock, the mouth of which has probably been built up, in part, in order to retain the water. A few steps lead down on the inside to the water, beneath the vaulted rock; and close at hand on the outside is the reservoir. The water finds its way out beneath the steps into the latter. This basin is perhaps five or six feet in breadth, forming merely the entrance, or rather the southern termination, of the long and narrow subterranean passage beyond, by which the water comes from the fountain of the Virgin. Our examination of this passage, and the character and irregular flow of the water, will be described in speaking of that fountain further on.

A rude path which follows along the west side of the valley of Jehoshaphat, crosses the mouth of the Tyropœon upon a causeway near the ancient mulberry tree, which marks the legendary site of Isaiah's martyrdom.[2] Just above this causeway, the ground is lower, forming a sort of basin, which is now tilled as a garden. Here, according to the reports of travellers near the close of the sixteenth century, was formerly another larger reservoir, in the form of a parallelogram rounded off at the western end. It was dry in that age, and was probably not long after broken up; inasmuch as Quaresmius makes no distinct mention of it. Brocardus speaks also of two reservoirs, which in his day received the waters of the fountain of Siloam. Not improbably both were ancient.[3]

The Muhammedans, like the Christians, have a great veneration for this fountain; and their prophet is reported to have declared: "Zemzem and Siloah are two fountains of Paradise."[4] Yet in Christian lands the name is consecrated by stronger and holier associations; and the celebrity of

[1] See above, p. 231.
[2] See above, p. 232. This tree is mentioned as "antichissimo" by Zuallart in A. D. 1586; Viaggio, p. 135. Comp. Cotovic. Itin. p. 292. Sandys' Travels, p. 146.

[3] See Zuallart Viaggio, p. 135. Cotovic. p. 292. Quaresmius II. p. 285. Brocardus c. 8.
[4] Hist. of Jerus. in Fundgr. des Orients, II. p. 130.

> " Siloa's brook that flowed
> Fast by the oracle of God,"

is co-extensive perhaps with the spread of Christianity itself.

Fountain of the Virgin. On the west side of the valley of Jehoshaphat about twelve hundred feet northward from the rocky point at the mouth of the Tyropœon, is situated the fountain of the Virgin Mary ;[1] called by the natives *'Aïn Um ed-Deraj,* " Mother of Steps." In speaking of Siloam I have already brought into view the singular fact, that there is no historical notice later than Josephus which can be applied to this fountain, before near the close of the fifteenth century ; and have also mentioned the more modern hypothesis, which regards it as the *fountain* of Siloam, in distinction from the pool of that name.[2] Others have held it to be the Gihon, the Rogel, and the Dragon well of Scripture ; so that in fact it has been taken alternately for every one of the fountains, which anciently existed at Jerusalem. It is unquestionably an ancient work ; indeed there is nothing in or around the Holy City, which bears more distinctly the traces of high antiquity. I have already alluded to the reasons which make it not improbable, that this was the " King's pool" of Nehemiah, and the " pool of Solomon" mentioned by Josephus, near which the wall of the city passed, as it ran northwards from Siloam along the valley of Jehoshaphat to the eastern side of the temple.[3]

The cavity of this fountain is deep, running in under the western wall of the valley ; and is wholly excavated in the solid rock. To enter it, one first descends sixteen steps ; then comes a level place of twelve feet ; and then ten steps more to the water. The steps are on an average each about ten inches high ; and the whole depth therefore is about 25 feet ; or some ten or fifteen feet below the actual bottom of the valley. The basin itself is perhaps 15 feet long by 5 or 6 feet wide ; the height is not more than 6 or 8 feet. The bottom is strewed with small stones ; and the water flows off by a low passage at the interior extremity, leading under the mountain to Siloam. There is now no other outlet for the water ; and apparently a different one never existed.

This subterranean passage is first mentioned by Quaresmius, writing about A. D. 1625.[4] He relates the unsuccessful attempt of his friend Vinhouen to explore it ; and says that a Pater Julius had passed through it a few years before. But he

---

[1] The legend by which this name is accounted for, relates that the Virgin frequented this fountain before her purification, in order to wash her child's linen ; " ad abstergendos filii sui Jesu panniculos" (clouts), as Quaresmius has it ; Vol. II. p. 290.

[2] See p. 335, above.

[3] See p. 311, above. Neh. 2. 14. Jos. B. J. 5. 4. 2.

[4] There seems to be an allusion to the same canal in *Anselmi Descript. Terrœ Sanct.* A. D. 1509, in Basnage Thesaur. Monumentor. Tom. IV. pp. 791, 792. i. 498–500.

gives no definite information respecting the canal ; and is unable
to say, whether the waters of Siloam come from the fountain of
the Virgin.[1] Notwithstanding this tolerably full notice, the canal
seems to have been again forgotten, or at least overlooked, for
another century. Monconys, Doubdan, le Brun, and Maundrell,
all of whom were no careless observers, are wholly silent as to its
existence ; although they describe both the fountains.[2] Slight
and imperfect notices of it again appear in the eighteenth century, and more in the nineteenth.[3] All these however are so
confused and unsatisfactory, that the latest and most successful
investigator of the topography of Jerusalem, declares in A. D.
1839, that the question is yet undecided, whether the water
flows from the Virgin's fountain to Siloam or *vice versa*.[4]

We found it to be the current belief at Jerusalem, both
among natives and foreigners, that a passage existed quite
through between the two fountains ; but no one had himself explored it, or could give any definite information respecting it.
We therefore determined to examine it ourselves, should a fit opportunity occur. Repairing one afternoon (April 27th) to Siloam,
in order to measure the reservoir, we found no person there ; and
the water in the basin being low, we embraced this opportunity
for accomplishing our purpose. Stripping off our shoes and
stockings and rolling our garments above our knees, we entered
with our lights and measuring tapes in our hands. The water
was low, nowhere over a foot in depth, and for the most part not
more than three or four inches, with hardly a perceptible current.
The bottom is everywhere covered with sand, brought in by the
waters. The passage is cut wholly through the solid rock, everywhere about two feet wide ; somewhat winding, but in a general
course N. N. E. For the first hundred feet, it is from fifteen to
twenty feet high ; for another hundred feet or more, from six to
ten feet ; and afterwards not more than four feet high ; thus
gradually becoming lower and lower as we advanced. At the
end of 800 feet, it became so low, that we could advance no further without crawling on all fours, and bringing our bodies close
to the water. As we were not prepared for this, we thought it

---

[1] Quaresmius Elucid. Terr. Sanct. II.
pp. 289, 290.

[2] Von Troilo in 1666 speaks of the irregular flow of Siloam, and says, that the
water comes through hidden pipes under
ground; but in attempting to account for
this, it does not even occur to him that
there is any connection with the Virgin's
fountain. Reisebeschr. Dresd. 1676, pp.
260-262.

[3] Van Egmond and Heyman make the
water flow from Siloam to the other foun-
i. 500. 501

tain; Reizen, etc. I. p. 392. Comp. Po-
cocke's Deser. of the East, II. i. pp. 23, 24.
Kortens Reise, p. 112. Chateaubriand
Itin. Paris 1837, II. p. 32. Buckingham's
Travels, p. 188. Richardson's Travels, II.
p. 357. O. v. Richter's Wallfahrten, p. 31.
Sieber's Reise, p. 65. Hogg's Visit, etc.
II. p. 237.

[4] Crome, in Ersch u. Gruber's Encyclop.
art. *Jerusalem*, p. 281. Comp. Rosenmueller's Bibl. Geogr. II. ii. p. 251.

better to retreat, and try again another day from the other end. Tracing therefore upon the roof with the smoke of our candles the initials of our names and the figures 800, as a mark of our progress on this side, we returned with our clothes somewhat wet and soiled.

It was not until three days afterwards, (April 30th,) that we were able to complete our examination and measurement of the passage. We went now to the fountain of the Virgin ; and having measured the external distance (1200 feet) down to the point east of Siloam, we concluded, that as we had already entered 800 feet from the lower end, there could now remain not over four or five hundred feet to be explored. We found the end of the passage at the upper fountain rudely built up with small loose stones, in order to retain the water at a greater depth in the excavated basin. Having caused our servants to clear away these stones, and having clothed (or rather unclothed) ourselves simply in a pair of wide Arab drawers, we entered and crawled on, hoping soon to arrive at the point which we had reached from the other fountain. The passage here is in general much lower than at the other end ; most of the way we could indeed advance upon our hands and knees ; yet in several places we could only get forward, by lying at full length and dragging ourselves along on our elbows.

The sand at the bottom has probably a considerable depth, thus filling up the canal in part ; for otherwise it is inconceivable, how the passage could ever have been thus cut through the solid rock. At any rate, only a single person could have wrought in it at a time ; and it must have been the labour of many years. There are here many turns and zigzags. In several places the workmen had cut straight forward for some distance, and then leaving this, had begun again further back at a different angle ; so that there is at first the appearance of a passage branching off. We examined all these false cuts very minutely, in the hope of finding some such lateral passage, by which water might come in from another quarter. We found, however, nothing of the kind. The way seemed interminably long ; and we were for a time suspicious, that we had fallen upon a passage different from that which we had before entered. But at length, after having measured 950 feet, we arrived at our former mark of 800 feet traced with smoke upon the ceiling. This makes the whole length of the passage to be 1750 feet ; or several hundred feet greater than the direct distance externally,—a result scarcely conceivable, although the passage is very winding. We came out again at the fountain of Siloam.[1]

[1] Vinhouen, the correspondent of Quaresmius, gives a very similar account of this passage, as far as he saw it. He entered from the upper end, creeping on his
i. 501–503

In constructing this passage, it is obvious that the workmen commenced at both ends, and met somewhere in the middle. At the upper end, the work was carried along on the level of the upper basin; and there was a tendency to go too far towards the west under the mountain; for all the false cuts above mentioned are on the right. At the lower end, the excavation would seem to have been begun on a higher level than at present; and when on meeting the shaft from the other end, this level was found to be too high, the bottom was lowered until the water flowed through it; thus leaving the southern end of the passage much loftier than any other part. The bottom has very little descent; so that the two basins are nearly on the same level; the upper one ten feet or more below the valley of Jehoshaphat, and the other some forty feet above the same valley. The water flows through the passage gently and with little current; and I am unable to account for the "great noise" of which Jerome speaks, unless he refers perhaps to the time of the irregular ebullition of the waters.[1]

The purpose for which this difficult work was undertaken, it is not easy to discover. The upper basin must obviously have been excavated at an earlier period than the lower; and there must have been something to be gained, by thus carrying its waters through the solid rock into the valley of the Tyropœon. If the object had been merely to irrigate the gardens which lay in that quarter, this might have been accomplished with far less difficulty and expense, by conducting the water around upon the outside of the hill. But the whole looks as if the advantage of a fortified city had been taken into the account; and as if it had been important to carry this water from one point to the other in such a way, that it could not be cut off by a besieging army. Now as this purpose would have been futile, had either of these points lain without the ancient fortifications; this circumstance furnishes an additional argument, to show that the ancient wall probably ran along the valley of Jehoshaphat, or at least descended to it, and included both Siloam and this upper fountain; which then either constituted or supplied the " King's pool," or "pool of Solomon."[2]

The water in both these fountains, then, is the same; notwithstanding travellers have pronounced that of Siloam to be

hands and knees, and sometimes at full length; until in a low spot his candle went out, and he could neither strike a light nor turn round except with great difficulty. At length he extricated himself and returned, " licet bene madidus et sordibus plenus." He entered again the next day at the lower end; but did not succeed in passing through the whole length. Quaresmius Elucidat II. pp. 289, 290.

[1] See above, p. 334, Note 2.—This subterraneous passage corresponds entirely to the proper etymological signification of the name Siloah in Hebrew, sent, viz. missio aquae, an aqueduct.

[2] See above, pp. 311, 337.

bad, and that of the upper fountain to be good. We drank of it often in both places. It has a peculiar taste, sweetish and very slightly brackish, but not at all disagreeable. Later in the season, when the water is low, it is said to become more brackish and unpleasant. It is the common water used by the people of Kefr Selwân.[1] We did not learn that it is regarded as medicinal, or particularly good for the eyes, as is reported by travellers; though it is not improbable that such a popular belief may exist.[2]

The irregular flow of the water mentioned by writers of the earlier and middle ages as characteristic of Siloam, must of course belong equally to both fountains; except as the rush of the water towards Siloam would be nowadays impeded and diminished, by the dam of loose stones at the upper end of the passage. The earlier writers who speak of this phenomenon, have already been cited.[3] But ever since the fourteenth century, this remarkable circumstance seems to have been almost, if not entirely, overlooked by travellers. I have searched in vain through all the more important writers, from Sir John Maundeville down to the present day, without finding any distinct notice respecting it, derived from personal observation.[4] Quaresmius, who describes most fully both the fountains, is wholly silent as to any irregularity; as are also all the writers on Biblical Geography from Adrichomius and Reland onward to the present time; except so far as they refer to the testimony of Jerome. Yet the popular belief in this phenomenon is still firm among the inhabitants of Jerusalem; our friends had often heard of it; but having themselves never seen the irregular flow, they regarded the story as one of the many popular legends of the country.

We were more fortunate in this respect; having been very unexpectedly witnesses of the phenomenon in question; and we are thus enabled to rescue another ancient historical fact from the long oblivion, or rather discredit, into which it had fallen for so many centuries. As we were preparing to measure the basin of the upper fountain (in the afternoon of April 30th) and explore the passage leading from it, my companion was standing on

---

[1] See above, p. 232.

[2] Monro's Summer Ramble in Syria, I. pp. 199, 200. Comp. Cotovic. Itin. p. 292. De Salignaco in A. D. 1522 describes the water of Siloah as not only good to prevent blindness and ophthalmia, but also for other cosmetic uses: "Porro aqua fontis ipsis etiam Saracenis in pretio est, adeo ut cum naturaliter fœteant instar hircorum, hujus fontis lotione fœtorem mitigant seu depellant." Tom. X. c. 1.

[3] See above, pp. 334, 335.

[4] Surius, Morone, von Troilo, and perhaps others, slightly mention the irregular flow; but leave it uncertain whether they speak from personal knowledge, or merely (as in so many other instances) from traditional report. Surius Pelerin, p. 400. Morone Terra Santa illustr. I. p. 225. Von Troilo's Reisebeschr. Dresd. 1676. p. 261. Nau says the water flows regularly in the fountain of the Virgin; but irregularly and at different hours in Siloam. Voyage, p. 308.

i. 505, 506

the lower step near the water, with one foot on the step and the other on a loose stone lying in the basin. All at once he perceived the water coming into his shoe ; and supposing the stone had rolled, he withdrew his foot to the step ; which however was also now covered with water. This instantly excited our curiosity; and we now perceived the water rapidly bubbling up from under the lower step. In less than five minutes it had risen in the basin nearly or quite a foot ; and we could hear it gurgling off through the interior passage. In ten minutes more it had ceased to flow ; and the water in the basin was again reduced to its former level. Thrusting my staff in under the lower step, whence the water appeared to come, I found that there was here a large hollow space ; but a further examination could not be made without removing the steps.

Meanwhile a woman of Kefr Selwân came to wash at the fountain.[1] She was accustomed to frequent the place every day ; and from her we learned, that the flowing of the water occurs at irregular intervals ; sometimes two or three times a day, and sometimes in summer once in two or three days. She said, she had seen the fountain dry, and men and flocks, dependent upon it, gathered around and suffering from thirst ; when all at once the water would begin to boil up from under the steps, and (as she said) from the bottom in the interior part, and flow off in a copious stream.

In order to account for this irregularity, the common people say, that a great dragon lies within the fountain ; when he is awake, he stops the water ; when he sleeps, it flows. An Arab who was there, whom we had seen at the bath in the city, said that the water comes down from the fountain beneath the great mosk, of which I shall speak immediately. But how, or why ? Was there perhaps originally a small and failing fountain here, to which afterwards other waters were conducted from the temple ? Some supposition of this kind seems necessary, in order to account for the large excavation in this place. Is perhaps the irregular flow to be explained by some such connection with waters from above, the taste of which we found on trial to be the same ? This is a mystery which former ages have not solved ; and which it must be left to the researches of future travellers, under more favourable auspices, fully to unfold.

In the account of the pool of Bethesda, situated near the Sheep [gate], we are told that "an angel went down at a certain season into the pool, and troubled the water ; " and then whosoever first stepped in, was made whole.[2] There seems to have been here no special medicinal virtue in the water itself ; but

---

[1] The women of Kefr Selwân wash clothes in like manner customarily at Siloam. Some days afterwards I found i. 506, 507

parties of soldiers washing their linen at this fountain and also at Siloam.

[2] John 5, 2-7.

only he who *first* stepped in after the troubling, was healed. Does not this " troubling " of the water look like the irregular flow of the fountain just described? And as the Sheep gate seems to have been situated not far from the temple,[1] and the wall of the ancient city probably ran along this valley ; may not that gate have been somewhere in this part, and this fountain of the Virgin have been Bethesda ? the same with the " King's pool " of Nehemiah and the ' Solomon's pool' of Josephus ? I suggest these questions as perhaps worthy of consideration ; without having myself any definite conviction either way upon the subject.[2]

Fountain under the Grand Mosk. Not long after our arrival at Jerusalem, we were informed by our friends, that in conversation with intelligent Mussulmans they had been told of a living fountain under the Haram esh-Sherif ; from which a bath in the vicinity was in part supplied. We took up the inquiry, and received similar information from various quarters. As the Mufti of Jerusalem one day paid a visit to our host, this fountain was mentioned in the course of conversation, and he confirmed the accounts which we had previously heard. On being asked whether we could visit it ; he said there would be no difficulty, and expressed a desire to afford us every facility in our researches.

We now repaired to the bath, (April 28th,) which is situated in a covered passage leading to one of the western entrances of the enclosure of the mosk. It is called Hammâm esh-Shefa, ' Bath of Healing,' and is apparently much used by those frequenting the Haram. We were conducted through the bath, and through several apartments and passages, to the parallel street leading to the southern entrance of the mosk ; and then up a flight of steps on the left to a platform, or rather the flat roof of a low building, eighteen or twenty feet above the level of the street. Here, in a low arched room, we found two men drawing water from a narrow and deep well, in leathern buckets suspended over a pully. The depth of the well, by careful measurement, proved to be 82½ feet, or about 65 feet below the surface of the ground ; the water stood in it three and a half feet deep. The distance from the well to the wall of the area of the mosk, I found to be one hundred and thirty-five feet.

The elder of the two men said that he had often been at the bottom of the well ; and was willing to accompany us, if we would go down. The water he said comes to the well through a passage of mason work, four or five feet high, from under the

---

[1] Neh. 3, I. 32. The Sheep gate was built up by the priests, who of course dwelt in and around the temple. It would seem therefore to have been near the temple.

[2] Comp. the similar conjecture of Lightfoot in regard to this subject ; Opp. II. p. 588. See more on this subject in Vol III. Sect. V.

Sŭkhrah or grand mosk. This passage is entered from the well by a doorway ; and one has to stoop a little in passing through. It leads first through a room of considerable size, arched, and supported by fourteen marble columns with capitals ; and afterwards terminates in a room under the Sŭkhrah about eight or ten feet square, cut out of the solid rock ; which is entered by another similar doorway. Here the water boils up from the rock in a basin at the bottom. He knew of no other passage, open or closed, from this room, nor from the main passage, by which the water could flow off; but said there was at the bottom of the well, a door closed up on the other side, leading no one knew whither. This water in dry seasons ceases to flow out into the well ; and then they are obliged to descend and bring it out from the fountain by hand into the well, in order to supply the bath. There is no known way of access to the fountain, except by descending into this well.[1] They all declared, that when the keeper of the bath takes pay of poor Muslim pilgrims for bathing, the water is miraculously stopped. We drank of the water ; and found that it had the same peculiar taste, which we had remarked in the waters of Siloam and the fountain of the Virgin in the valley below. We inquired whether this fountain had any connection with those in the valley, and were told that there was none ; but when we afterwards saw the same man at the fountain of the Virgin, he declared that there was a connection.—The above account was afterwards confirmed to us by the keeper of the bath.

Had we been prepared at the time to descend into the well and explore the fountain, we should perhaps have met with little difficulty ; or at least a small *bakhshish* would have removed every obstacle. But when we repaired thither again three days afterwards (May 1st), with lights and a stronger rope and pully, they began to think it a matter of importance, and were unwilling to let us go down without authority from their superiors. We therefore deferred our purpose and returned home, after taking more exact measurements than before, and letting down a light into the well, which continued to burn brightly quite to the bottom. The bath-keeper afterwards consulted the Mutawelly of the Haram, who said he would ask the opinion of the council. But as this would give to the matter a greater notoriety than was desirable ; and as the Mufti had already told us, that there would be no objection to our descending ; we preferred making the ap-

---

[1] I have since been informed by Mr Catherwood, that just within the western entrance of the Great Mosk itself, at the right hand, is a deep well, from which water is drawn for ablutions. He suggests, that this well or fountain may possibly have some connection with that described in the text, if it be not the same. But this would not accord with the information received by us from the Mufti and people at the bath, as well as from other independent sources.

i. 509, 510

plication directly to him. He was accordingly waited upon ; but unfortunately at an unpropitious moment, when he was surrounded by several Muhammedan doctors and others ; and his reply was, that the thing was not in his hands, but if we would get permission and a Kawwâs (Janizary) from the governor, there would be no difficulty. Had he been alone, he might perhaps have given a different answer. Perceiving that under the circumstances, it would probably be unavailing to press the matter further at the moment, we thought it better to wait and apply at a later period to the Kâim Makâm, or military governor, who probably would have at once granted our request. But when we afterwards returned to the city from our excursions, the prevalence of the plague and other circumstances combined to hinder us from making the application ; and we were reluctantly compelled to forego the further prosecution of this interesting inquiry.

However imperfect or exaggerated the preceding account may be in several respects, there seemed no reason for doubt as to the main fact, viz. that there was in the heart of the rock, at the depth of some eighty feet underneath the Haram, an artificial fountain ; the water of which has the same essential characteristics as that flowing out at the artificial excavations in the valley below. This fountain naturally reminds us of that mentioned by Tacitus,[1] and still more strongly of the language of Aristæas ; who in describing the ancient temple, informs us that "the supply of water was unfailing, inasmuch as there was an abundant natural fountain flowing in the interior, and reservoirs of admirable construction under ground, extending five stadia around the temple, with pipes and conduits unknown to all except those to whom the service was intrusted, by which the water was brought to various parts of the temple and again conducted off."[2] This account is also doubtless exaggerated. Yet all the circumstances taken together render it not improbable, that there may be some hidden channel, by which the waters of the fountain beneath the mosk are carried down to the valley below. From what quarter they are first brought into this excavated chamber, is a question which presents no less difficulty. There seems little reason to doubt that the whole work is artificial ; and we may perhaps reasonably conjecture, that it stood in some connection with the ancient fountain of Gihon on the higher ground west of the city.

---

[1] " Fons perennis aquæ, cavati sub terra montes ; " Hist 5. 12. See this more fully quoted above, p. 306, Note 2.

[2] Aristæ. de Leg. div. Transl. p. 112, in Joseph. Opp. Tom. II. Append. ed. Havercamp, ὕδατος δὲ ἀνέκλειπτός ἐστι σύστασις, ὡς ἂν καὶ πηγῆς ἔσωθεν πολυῤῥύτου φυσικῶς ἐπιῤῥεούσης κτλ. See also Adricho-

mius, p. 160. Quaresmius II. p. 292. Lightfoot Opp. I. p. 612.—Yet it is perhaps doubtful, whether an actual fountain is here meant in the passage from Aristæas ; or only a constant flow of water from an aqueduct, as if from a natural fountain. Lightfoot understands the language in the latter way.

i. 511, 512

Later investigations have however shown, that no such supposed connection exists.[1]

Fountain of Gihon. The place to which Solomon was brought from Jerusalem to be anointed, was called Gihon ; but the direction of it from the city is not specified.[2] At a later period we are told of king Hezekiah, that he "stopped the upper water-course [or upper out-flow of the waters] of Gihon, and brought it down to the west side of the city of David."[3] It is said too that "he took counsel with his princes and his mighty men to stop the waters of the fountains which were without the city ;—and there was gathered much people together, who stopped all the fountains and the brook that ran through the midst of the land, saying, why should the kings of Assyria come, and find much water?"[4] The Son of Sirach also informs us, that "Hezekiah strengthened his city, and brought in water into the midst of it ; he dug with iron into the rock and built fountains for the waters."[5] Josephus mentions also the fountain of Gihon.[6] From all these passages I am unable to arrive at any other conclusion, than that there existed anciently a fountain Gihon on the west of the city, which was "stopped" or covered over by Hezekiah, and its waters brought down by subterranean channels into the city. Before that time it would naturally have flowed down through the valley of Gihon or Hinnom ; and probably it formed the "brook" which was stopped at the same time.

The fountain may have been stopped and its waters thus secured very easily, by digging deep and erecting over it one or more vaulted subterranean chambers. Something of the very same kind is still seen at the fountain near Solomon's pools beyond Bethlehem ; where the water rises in subterranean chambers, to which there is no access except down a narrow shaft like a well.[7] In this way the waters of Gihon would be withdrawn from the enemy, and preserved to the city ; in which they would seem to have been distributed among various reservoirs and fountains. The present pool of Hezekiah was probably one ; and the fountain under the temple (if one exists) may have been another. Josephus also speaks of an aqueduct apparently, which conveyed water to the tower of Hippicus, and of one connected with Herod's palace on Zion ;[8] both of which would naturally have come from Gihon or its reservoir.

[1] See Wolcott in Biblioth. Sac. 1843, pp. 24–28. Tobler Denkblätter, etc. p. 73 sq. For Dr Barclay's examination see Vol. III. Sect. V.
[2] 1 Kings 1, 33. 38.
[3] 2 Chron. 32, 30. Comp. also 33, 14.
[4] 2 Chron. 32, 3. 4. Similar precau-
i. 512, 513

tions were taken by the Muhammedans on the first approach of the crusaders to Jerusalem ; Will. Tyr. 8. 7.
[5] Sirac. 48, 17. [19.] Cod. Alex.
[6] Joseph. Antiq. 7. 11. 5.
[7] See under date of May 8th.
[8] Joseph. B. J. 5. 7. 3. ib. 2. 17. 9.

All these circumstances, as well as the nature of the ground, seem to leave little room for doubt, that an open fountain did anciently thus exist somewhere in the vicinity of the upper pool on the west of the city ; the waters of which may still continue to flow by subterranean channels down to the ancient temple, and perhaps to Siloam. This fountain of course was Gihon.[1] But to arrive at entire certainty upon the subject, extensive excavations in this part would probably be necessary ; and we may hope that the day is not far distant, when these may be set on foot without hindrance.

The Dragon fountain mentioned by Nehemiah, was over-against the Valley gate ; and there seems therefore good reason to suppose, that this was only another name for the fountain of Gihon.[2]

THE AQUEDUCT. The course of the aqueduct which brings water from Solomon's pools to the great mosk, has already been described, from the point where it crosses the valley of Hinnom and winds around the sides of Zion.[3] We did not ourselves see its termination in the area of the mosk ; but the unanimous testimony both of Muhammedans and Christians leaves no doubt upon this point. It enters the Haram across the mound already described.[4] In passing along the road to Bethlehem, the aque-duct is seen from the plain of Rephaim on the left ; and again on approaching Bethlehem, on the low ridge between Wady Ahmed at the right and the head of another Wady at the left. Here water was running in it. It winds eastwards around the hill on which Bethlehem stands ; and on the southern side, beyond the town, lies at some depth below the surface. Here is a well, or rather reservoir, through which it flows ; whence the water is drawn up with buckets. The channel is usually conducted along the surface of the ground ; and has an appear-ance of antiquity. For some distance from the pools it is laid with earthen pipes enclosed and covered with stones ; but after-wards, apparently, it consists merely of stones laid in cement, forming a small channel of perhaps a foot in breadth and depth.

---

[1] For a similar view, see Crome in Ersch and Gruber's Encycl. art. *Jerusalem*, p. 288. In this way the connection be-tween Gihon and Siloam, which some have assumed, may still be true ; see Gesenius Lex. Heb. art. שִׁלֹחַ. Quaresmius II. p. 288.—Others have regarded Gihon and Siloam as identical ; on the ground that in 1 Kings 1, 33. 38, the Targum of Jonathan substitutes Siloam for Gihon. But as this Targum is held to be not older than the close of the second century after Christ, when the correct tradition was probably lost, this circumstance can weigh little

against the express language of 2 Chron. 32, 30 ; supported as it is by vs. 3. 4. of the same chapter, and by Sirac. 48, 17. [19.] Nor is the expression "*down* to Gihon" in 1 Kings 1, 33 inconsistent with the view in the text ; for in passing from Zion to Gihon on the west, there is first a somewhat steep descent, and then a gradual rise ; and this descent was probably in an-cient times still more marked.

[2] Nehem. 2, 13. See p. 320, above.
[3] See above, p. 265.
[4] See above, p. 267.

Of course, being thus exposed, it could never benefit the city in a time of siege.

That the aqueduct is ancient, is also probable from the character and enormous size of the pools themselves, which could not well have been erected on such a scale for any purpose, except to aid in furnishing the ordinary supply of water for the Holy City. They may indeed have served also to irrigate gardens in the valley below ; but this could hardly have been their main object. Yet there is no mention of them in the Scriptures. Later Jewish writers, however, as cited in the Talmud, speak often of the manner in which the temple was supplied with water by an aqueduct from the fountain of Etam, which lay at a distance from the city on the way to Hebron.[1] This notice could not well have been an invention of their own ; corresponding as it does to the mention of an Etam by Josephus, not far from Jerusalem, which Solomon is said to have adorned with gardens and streams of water.[2] Those writers doubtless refer to an aqueduct which of old, as at the present day, connected those ancient reservoirs with the temple of Jerusalem.

This aqueduct seems not to be mentioned by any of the pilgrims of the earlier centuries, nor by the writers of the times of the crusades.[3] The first direct though imperfect allusion to it, which I have been able to find, is in the Itineraries of William of Baldensel and Ludolph de Suchem (A. D. 1336 50), who speak of the cisterns of Jerusalem as being filled with water brought under ground from Hebron, which however could be seen along the way. A similar allusion occurs in Gumpenberg's Journal A. D. 1449. A fuller notice is given by F. Fabri in 1483 ; but Cotovicus a century later (A. D. 1598), is apparently the first to make known both the pools and aqueduct with tolerable exactness.[4] Since that time the pools have been often described ; while the aqueduct has usually been passed over with a slight notice.[5]

---

[1] See Lightfoot Descr. Templi Hieros. c. 23, Opp. I. p. 612. Ejusd. Disq. chorogr. Joanni præmissa c. v. § 5. Opp. II. p. 589. —In 2 Chr. 11, 6 "Bethlehem and Etam and Tekoa" are placed together. Comp. Reland Palæst. p. 304, 558, *Aitam.*—Josephus also relates, that Pilate expended the sacred treasures in bringing water to the city from the distance of 400 stadia ; B. J. 2. 9. 4.

[2] Antiq. 8. 7. 3.

[3] Perhaps a trace of it may be found in the remark of Adamnanus (1. 17), that w i. 515, 516

in going from the gate of David down the valley, with Mount Zion on the left, there was a stone bridge crossing the valley on arches. This answers to the aqueduct, which here crosses on nine very low arches.

[4] See L. de Such. Itin. p. 74. Reissb. des h. Landes, Ed. 2. pp. 843, 461, 283. Cotovici Itin. pp. 241-243. Zuallart, twelve years earlier, seems to speak only from report ; Viagg. p. 235.

[5] Comp. the art. *Jerusalem* by Crome, p. 280, in Ersch and Gruber's Encycl.

X. CEMETERIES, TOMBS, ETC.

The four Christian cemeteries upon Mount Zion have already been described;[1] as also the three burial places of the Muhammedans; one along the eastern wall of the city next the Haram esh-Sherif; another on the west near the upper pool; and the third over the grotto of Jeremiah on the north.[2] The present cemetery of the Jews lies on the western slope of the mount of Olives, near the foot, just above the tombs of Absalom and Zacharias. Here, overagainst their ancient temple, many wanderers of that remarkable people have come to mingle their bones with those of their fathers; awaiting the great day foretold as they suppose by their prophets, when the Lord shall stand upon the mount of Olives, and the mountain shall cleave asunder, and the dead of Israel shall rise from beneath it, and all nations be judged in the valley, and Israel be avenged.[3] The slope of the mountain is here thickly covered with their graves, each decked simply with a stone laid flat upon it; on which is usually a Hebrew inscription.

SEPULCHRAL MONUMENTS. Under this term I here include only the four tombs or monumental sepulchres situated in the valley of Jehoshaphat, on the east side of the Kidron, and opposite to the southeast corner of the area of the grand mosk. These are commonly described as the tombs of Jehoshaphat, Absalom, St. James, and Zacharias. This I believe to be the most usual order of the names, beginning from the north; but the tradition of the monks, as well as the judgment of travellers, has varied much at different times; so that these names have been frequently applied to the tombs in a different and very uncertain order.[4] Those of Absalom and Zacharias, here so called, are real monuments of rock; the other two are only excavated tombs with ornamented portals.

These tombs are situated in the narrowest part of the valley of Jehoshaphat, where a shelf or ledge of rock extends down from the east, and terminates in an almost perpendicular face just over the bed of the Kidron. The tomb of Zacharias on the south, so called in allusion to the person "slain between the temple and the altar,"[5] lies directly beneath the southeast cor-

---

[1] See above, pp. 229–231.
[2] See above, pp. 232, 234, 239.
[3] Zech. 14, 3–11. Joel 3, [4,] 2. 12. 14. 20. Lightfoot Cent. chor. Matthæo præm. c. 40. Opp. II. p. 201.
[4] The order in the text is that given by Quaresmius, II. p. 249 sq. and also by Van Egmond and Heymann and by Pococke, a century later. The same appears on monastic authority in Catherwood's Plan of Jerusalem, 1835. Cotovicus gives the same order in his text, though there is an error in his engraving; p. 204 sq.— Prokesch on the other hand applies the names of Jehoshaphat and Zacharias to those above called Zacharias and St. James; Reise, p. 70. Comp. Schubert's Reise, II. p. 524, note.
[5] Matth. 23, 35. Luke 11, 51.

ner of the area of the ancient temple, and is wholly hewn out
from the rocky ledge above mentioned. It is a square block,
about twenty feet on each side ; the rock having been cut away
around it so as to form a square niche or area, in which it stands
isolated, leaving a broad passage all around it. The body of the
tomb is about eighteen or twenty feet high, and apparently
solid ; at least no chamber or entrance is known. The sides are
decorated each with two half columns and two quarter columns ;
the latter adjacent to square pilasters at the corners, and all
having capitals of the Ionic order. Around the cornice is an ornament of acanthus leaves, about three feet high ; and above
this the top is formed by an obtuse pyramid of ten or twelve
feet in height. The whole monument has thus an elevation of
about thirty feet ; and, with all its ornaments, is wholly cut out
from the solid rock.[1]

Just north of this is the excavated cavern into which the
apostle James is said to have retired, during the interval between the crucifixion and resurrection of our Lord ;[2] but which
in common parlance bears the name of his sepulchre. The entrance is by an open portal with two Doric columns and two
side columns fronting towards the west, and situated ten or fifteen feet above the ground in the same ledge of rock. The cavern is said to be fifteen feet high and ten broad, and to extend
back some fifty feet. There is another entrance to it from the
niche around the adjacent tomb of Zacharias.[3]

The tomb of Absalom is close by the lower bridge over the
Kidron ; and is a square isolated block hewn out from the rocky
ledge, in the same manner as that of Zacharias, leaving a like
area or niche around it. The body of this tomb is about
twenty-four feet square ; and is ornamented on each side with
two half columns and two quarter columns of the Ionic order,
with pilasters at the corners, like the former tomb. The architrave exhibits triglyphs and Doric ornaments. The elevation is
about eighteen or twenty feet to the top of the architrave, and
thus far it is wholly cut from the rock. But the adjacent rock
is here not so high as at the tomb of Zacharias ; and therefore
the upper part of this tomb has been carried up with mason
work of large stones. This consists first of two square layers ;
of which the upper one is smaller than the lower ; and then a
small dome or cupola runs up into a low spire, which spreads a
little at the top like an opening flower. This mason work is
perhaps twenty feet high ; giving to the whole an elevation of

[1] Prokesch describes this tomb under
the name of Jehoshaphat : see his Reise,
p. 70. Comp. also Turner's Tour in the
Levant, II. p. 251. See Tobler's Golgotha,
p. 280.
   i. 518, 519

[2] Quaresmius Elucid. Terræ Sanctæ, II.
p. 258.
[3] Turner, l. c. p. 252. Prokesch, l. c.
p. 70. Tobler l. c. p. 295.

about forty feet. There is a small excavated chamber in the body of the tomb; into which a hole had already been broken through one of the sides, several centuries ago.[1]

Behind this tomb, at the northeast corner of its niche, is the portal of the excavated sepulchre of Jehoshaphat. It is in the perpendicular face of the niche; and is of course a later work than the tomb before it. The portal is surmounted by a fine pediment resting (I think) on square pilasters. The tomb itself is wholly subterranean.[2]

It is not necessary to waste words here, to show that these tombs never had any thing to do with the persons whose names they bear. The style of architecture and embellishment would seem to indicate, that they are of a later period than most of the other countless sepulchres round about the city; which, with few exceptions, are destitute of architectural ornament. Yet the foreign ecclesiastics who crowded to Jerusalem in the fourth century, found these monuments here; and of course, it became an object to refer them to persons mentioned in the Scriptures. Yet from that day to this, tradition seems never to have become fully settled, as to the individuals whose names they should bear. The *Itin. Hieros.* in A. D. 333 speaks of the two monolithic monuments as the tombs of Isaiah and Hezekiah.[3] Adamnanus, about A. D. 697, mentions only one of these, and calls it the tomb of Jehoshaphat; near to which were the two excavated sepulchres of Simeon the Just and Joseph the husband of Mary.[4] The historians of the crusades appear not to have noticed these tombs. The first mention of a tomb of Absalom, is by Benjamin of Tudela, who gives to the other the name of king Uzziah; and from that time to the present day, the accounts of travellers have been varying and inconsistent.[5]

The intermingling of the Greek orders, and a spice of the massive Egyptian taste, which are visible in these monuments, serve also to show, that they belong to a late period of the Greek and Roman art; and especially to that style of mingled Greek and Egyptian, which prevailed in the oriental provinces of the Roman empire. The chief seat of this style was perhaps at Petra; where it still appears in much of its pristine character, in

---

[1] See Prokesch, I c. p. 70. Tobler l. c. p. 268 sq The hole is mentioned by Quaresmius, II. p. 249.—Chateaubriand's description of this monument exhibits a specimen of his usual inaccuracy. According to him there are six columns on each side, all of the Doric order; while the top, he says, is built up in the form of a triangular pyramid. Itin. II. p. 77. Par. 1837.

[2] Tobler l. c. p. 304 sq.

[3] Itin. Hieros. ed. Wessel. p. 595.

[4] Adamnanus 1. 14.

[5] Benj. de Tud. p. 71. Marinus Sanutus speaks only of the tomb of Jehoshaphat; 3. 14. 9. Lud. de Suchem and Breydenbach name only that of Absalom, etc. See L. de Such. Itin. p. 84 Reissb. des h. Landes, pp. 846, 113. Maundeville mentions the tomb of Jehoshaphat, and further south those of St. James and Zacharias; p. 96. Lond. 1839.

i. 519–521

the very remarkable excavations of Wady Mûsa. When we
visited that place some weeks afterwards, we were much struck
at finding there several isolated monuments, the counterparts of
the monolithic tombs in the valley of Jehoshaphat.[1] The architectural remains of Petra are not held, I believe, to be in general
older than the Christian era; nor is there any reason to suppose
that the Jewish monuments in question, are of an earlier date.
Indeed, if they existed prior to the destruction of Jerusalem,
they are probably to be referred to the times of the Herods; who
themselves were of Idumæan descent, and maintained an intercourse between Petra and Jerusalem.[2] In that age too, as we
know, other foreigners of rank repaired to Jerusalem, and erected
for themselves mansions and sepulchres.[3] It would not therefore
be difficult to account in this way, for the resemblance between
these monuments and those of Petra.

Or, if the entire silence of Josephus and other cotemporary
writers as to these tombs be regarded as an objection to this hypothesis, why may they not perhaps be referred to the time of
Adrian? This emperor appears to have been a patron of Petra;
he also built up Jerusalem; and both these cities were called
after his name.[4] It would therefore not be unnatural, that this
period should be marked in both places by monuments possessing a similar architectural character.

SEPULCHRES. The numerous sepulchres which skirt the valleys on the north, east, and south of Jerusalem, exhibit for the
most part one general mode of construction. A doorway in the
perpendicular face of the rock, usually small and without ornament, leads to one or more small chambers excavated from the
rock, and commonly upon the same level with the door. Very
rarely are the chambers lower than the doors. The walls in
general are plainly hewn; and there are occasionally, though
not always, niches or resting places for the dead bodies. In order to obtain a perpendicular face for the doorway, advantage
was sometimes taken of a former quarry; or an angle was cut in
the rock with a tomb in each face; or a square niche or area was
hewn out in a ledge, and then tombs excavated in all three of
its sides. All these expedients are seen particularly in the
northern part of the valley of Jehoshaphat, and near the tombs
of the Judges. Many of the doorways and fronts of the tombs

[1] See our approach to Wady Mûsa under
May 31st. Also Burckhardt's Travels in
Syria, etc. p. 422. Of these monuments
Laborde has given no account whatever.

[2] Herod the Tetrarch married the daughter of Aretas, king of Arabia Petræa;
but he afterwards repudiated her in order

i. 521. 522

to marry Herodias; Joseph. Ant. 18. 5. 1.
Comp. B. J. 1. 6. 2.

[3] Joseph. Ant. 20. 4. 3. B. J. 5. 6. 1.
ib. 6. 6. 3, 4.

[4] Coins of Petra are found with the
inscription: Αδριανη Πετρα Μητροπολις.
Eckhel Doctr. Numor. vet. Tom. II. p. 503.

along this valley are now broken away, leaving the whole of the interior exposed.

Of this multitude of sepulchres, those on the south of the valley of Hinnom seem to be in general the best preserved ; with the exception of the tombs of the Judges and Kings, which will be described separately. On the north side of the valley of Hinnom, along Mount Zion, there are, I think, no sepulchres; and the same is the case on the west side of the valley of Jehoshaphat, so far as the ancient city extended along it. Nor do they appear anywhere in the latter valley, below the junction of the valley of Hinnom.

Tombs south of Hinnom. These I visited in company with Messrs Smith, Whiting, and Nicolayson, on the 3d of May. Two Jews were with us ; one of whom, called Hillel, had been in the East Indies, and had published a book full of extravagant descriptions of Jerusalem. He professed to have discovered several Hebrew inscriptions among the tombs, and undertook to lead us to them. We went first to the top of the hill, to the villa of Caiphas, so called ; and then descending northwards, and somewhat to the west of the path which passes down from Zion and crosses the valley of Hinnom, we came among the tombs. Here, the side of the hill, as it rises from the valley, is for the most part perpendicular rock, from twenty to forty feet high, with other rocky ledges higher up ; and the face of the hill is full of sepulchres along the whole extent of the valley. One of the first tombs we came to, had on the side of the entrance a long Hebrew inscription, well cut, in the ordinary modern character ; but so defaced by time that only a few separate words could be made out. We could be certain only of the following :

$$. \quad . \quad . \quad . \quad . \quad . \quad . \quad \text{כיום}$$
$$. \quad . \quad . \quad . \quad . \quad . \quad \text{שנח}$$
$$. \quad . \quad . \quad \text{ממשלת אדונו הלמך} \quad . .$$

The next word contained the letter *Sin* (ש), from which our companion Hillel was greatly inclined to make out the name of Solomon. We regretted much that the date had become so hopelessly obliterated. The existence and state of this inscription, and the form of the character, seem to indicate that the Jews must have buried here during the middle ages. Indeed, Benjamin of Tudela seems to allude to these sepulchres, when he speaks of Jewish cemeteries on the same side of the city as Mount Zion ; among which, he says, there were tombs with the date inscribed.[1]

Our guide now took us to another tomb near by, where he

---

[1] Benj. of Tud. p. 72. I presume the inscription in the text is the same which Scholz professes to have copied ; Reise, p. 179. He appears to have made out much more of it than we could.

said there were inscriptions inside in large Hebrew characters.
But what he had taken for Hebrew letters, proved he be only
fortuitous scratches or marks in the rock. A little further down,
we came upon a tomb with a Greek inscription over the entrance,
to which a cross was prefixed:

† *THC AΓIAC*

C I ω N

Not far off was another with the same letters and cross, but much
defaced. Close by the former was also a tomb with a Greek inscription of some length, now illegible; and in this quarter were
two or three others, apparently in the same language, but too
much obliterated to be made out.[1] The inscription in Phenician
characters mentioned by Dr. Clarke, we did not see.[2]

Following down the side of the valley, and passing sepulchres
and caverns without number, we came to the place shown as the
Aceldama or Field of Blood.[3] The tradition which fixes it upon
this spot, reaches back to the age of Jerome; and it is mentioned
by almost every visitor of the Holy City from that time to the
present day.[4] The field or plat is not now marked by any
boundary to distinguish it from the rest of the hill-side; and the
former charnel house, now a ruin, is all that remains to point out
the site. It is a long massive building of stone, erected in front
apparently of a natural cave; with a roof arched the whole length,
and the walls sunk deep below the ground outside, forming a
deep pit or cellar within. An opening at each end enabled us
to look in; but the bottom was empty and dry, except a few
bones much decayed.

This plat of ground, originally bought " to bury strangers in,"
seems to have been early set apart by the Latins and even by the
crusaders themselves, as a place for the burial of pilgrims.[5] Sir
J. Maundeville in the fourteenth century says, that "in that
Feld ben manye Tombes of Cristene Men; for there ben manye
Pilgrymes graven." He is also the first to mention the charnel
house, which then belonged to the hospital of St. John.[6] In the
beginning of the seventeenth century, Quaresmius describes it as
belonging to the Armenians; who sold the right of interment
here at a high price.[7] In Maundrell's day dead bodies were still

---

[1] These are apparently the same of
which Scholz has professedly given copies;
Reise, pp. 179, 180.
[2] Clarke's Travels in the Holy Land,
4to. p. 555.
[3] Matth. 27, 7. 8. Acts 1, 19.
[4] Onomast. art. *Acheldamach.* Eusebius places it on the *north* of the city;
Jerome on the *south.* Whether this discrepancy arises from a change in the tra-

dition, or an error in transcription, cannot
now be determined.—See also Antonin.
Mart. 26. Adamnanus 1. 20. Edrisi ed.
Jaub. p. 345. Will. Tyr. 8. 2. Brocardus,
c. 8. Lud. de Suchem, p. 84. Reissb. pp.
847, 848.
[5] Jac. de Vitr. Hist. Hieros. 64.
[6] Travels, pp. 93, 94. Lond. 1839. Lud.
de Such. pp. 84, 85. Reissb. pp. 846, 847.
[7] Elucid. II. p. 285.

i. 524. 525

deposited in it ; and Korte relates, that in his time it was the usual burial place of pilgrims.[1] Dr Clarke repeats the same story in the beginning of this century ; but at present it has the appearance of having been for a much longer time abandoned.[2] The soil of this spot was long believed to have the power of consuming dead bodies in the space of twenty-four hours. On this account shiploads of it are said to have been carried away in A. D. 1218, in order to cover over the famous Campo Santo in Pisa.[3] Ten years before our visit, I had listened to the same story within the walls of that remarkable cemetery.

Not far from this place, lower down the hill, we came to a tomb which had once been painted in the interior. Traces of the painting still remain upon the ceiling and walls ; but they consist chiefly of glories around the heads of Greek saints, without value either in a historical or archæological respect. I suppose this to be the tomb usually shown by the monks, as the place where the apostles hid themselves after the arrest of Jesus.[4] Still more to the east, and not far from the corner of the hill near the valley of Jehoshaphat, we entered a sepulchre which was said to have been recently opened. The entrance was low under the surface of the ground ; an upright doorway with a descent to it by steps. It led into an ante-room excavated in the rock, having an arched ceiling or dome, with doorways in the three sides, opening into five or six side chambers. In these are seen low sarcophagi, or rather hollow couches, left in the same rock along the sides ; in which were still many bones and skulls, the relics of their former tenants.

In general, it may be said of these sepulchres, as well as of most of those around Jerusalem, that they exhibit little which is remarkable, except their number. In none of them, save in the tombs of the Kings, have regular sarcophagi ever been found, either plain or sculptured. The manner in which the work is executed, exhibits for the most part any thing but skill ; and with the exception of the monuments in the valley of Jehoshaphat and the tombs of the Kings, there is nothing which can be compared, either with the architectural decorations of the sepulchres at Petra, or with the interior magnificence of the ancient Egyptian tombs.[5]

Tombs of the Judges. Passing now from the valley of Hinnom to the very head of the valley of Jehoshaphat, we find there

[1] Maundrell's Journey, Apr. 6th. Kortens Reise, p. 110. See too Pococke II. i. p. 25.
[2] Travels in the Holy Land, 4to. p. 567. That corpses were still thrown into this place so late as 1818, as related by Richardson, is barely possible ; Travels, II. p. 355.

[3] Raumer's Paläst. Edit. 3. p. 270. Pococke's Descr. of the East, II. i. p. 25.
[4] Quaresmius Tom. II. p. 283. Maundrell, Apr. 6th.
[5] See remarks on Dr Clarke in Note XXVIII, end of the volume.

the tombs of the Judges, half an hour distant from the Damascus gate. In approaching them along the valley, the rocks on each side are full of ordinary sepulchres ; and it is not until one has crossed the water-shed, and begins slightly to descend towards the Wady Beit Hanina, that he reaches these tombs.[1] They are situated just on the east of the path ; and are entered by a not large portico under a fine pediment, sculptured with flowers and leaves. From the middle of the portico, a doorway larger than in most sepulchres leads into an ante-chamber eighteen or twenty feet square. In the north side of this room are two rows of deep narrow niches or crypts for dead bodies, one above the other ; the crypts running in perpendicular to the wall, and being just large enough to receive a corpse ; the side of the room, as Sandys says, being " cut full of holes in manner of a dove-house." On the east and south sides of the ante-chamber, small doors lead to two other apartments, each about twelve feet square, in both of which three of the sides have similar crypts below and a larger niche above, as if for a sarcophagus. At the southeast and northwest corners of the ante-room, a few steps lead down through the floor to a lower apartment in each corner, of like form and dimensions. It is not improbable, that similar apartments may exist under the other two corners of the ante-room, the entrances to which are now covered with stones and rubbish.[2] In the chambers now open we counted about sixty of these deep narrow niches or crypts. We took here no measurements and made no minute examination.

I have been able to find no notice of these tombs earlier than the time of Cotovicus, A. D. 1598, who gives them no name. Sandys in A. D. 1611, calls them the " Sepulchre of the Prophets."[3] Quaresmius first describes them under the present name ; and they have not often been mentioned by later travellers.[4] That writer refers them to the Hebrew judges of the Old Testament. But the name, however it arose, more probably had reference to the judges of the Jewish Sanhedrim ; and was applied in consequence of a fancied correspondence between the number of the narrow crypts, and the seventy members who composed that tribunal.

Tomb of Helena, commonly called Tombs of the Kings. About one hundred and seventy-five rods north of the Damascus gate, on the right of the Nâbulus road, just as it begins to

---

[1] See above, pp. 241, 270.
[2] Both Cotovicus and Doubdan seem to say, that there is a chamber still lower down, a third story, which is entered in like manner by steps from the second. Cotovici Itin. p. 317. Doubdan Voyage, etc. p. 116.

[3] Cotovici Itin. p. 317. Sandys' Travels, Lond. 1658, p. 136.
[4] Quaresmius Elucid. Terr. Sanct. II. p. 728. Monconys I. p. 319. Doubdan, p. 114. Pococke Descr. of the East, II. i. p. 48.

. i. 527, 528

descend towards the valley of Jehoshaphat, is situated the remarkable sepulchre usually called the tombs of the Kings.[1]
The construction is as follows. A large square pit or court is
sunk in the solid rock, which here forms the level surface of the
ground.   The direction of the sides, as taken from the south, is
N. by W. measuring 92⅔ feet; while the other two sides
measure eighty-seven feet.   The depth of the court is now eighteen feet; but the bottom is obviously much filled up. In order
to form an entrance to this court, a broad trench of the same
depth, thirty-two feet in width, was cut parallel to the southern
side, leaving between it and the court a solid wall of rock seven
feet thick.   The western end of this trench slopes down very
gradually to the bottom, forming a commodious descent, while
towards the eastern end, an arched passage is cut through the
intervening wall, from the trench into the court.   The sides of
the court are perpendicular, and hewn smooth.

In the western wall of this sunken court, a portico or hall has
been excavated from the solid rock, measuring in the interior
thirty-nine feet long, by seventeen wide and fifteen high.   The
open front or portal was originally twenty-seven feet in length;
but is now broken away in parts for a greater distance.   The
sides of this portal were once ornamented with columns or pilasters; and there were also two intermediate columns now broken
down, dividing the whole portal into three nearly equal parts.
The rock above is elegantly sculptured in the later Roman style.
Over the centre of the portal are carved large clusters of grapes
between garlands of flowers, intermingled with Corinthian capitals and other decorations; below which is tracery-work of flowers
and fruits extending quite across the portal and hanging down
along the sides.   This is the finest specimen of sculpture existing
in or around Jerusalem.

At the south end of the interior portico or hall, near the inner
corner, is the low entrance to the excavated chambers.   If I recollect aright, the top of this entrance is little if any above the
level of the floor; a passage being sunk in the latter by which to
descend and reach it; so that if this passage were filled up to its
former level, all traces of an entrance might be easily concealed.
At present this passage and the door are greatly obstructed by
loose stones casually thrown in, which no one takes the trouble to
clear away; so that the entrance is difficult, affording only room
to pass in upon the hands and knees.

The first room is merely an ante-chamber, 18½ feet by 19,
containing nothing.   The walls here, as in all the other rooms,
consist of the solid rock, hewn smooth but not polished.   The ceiling slopes upwards a little from the two sides, forming a sort of

[1] See above, p. 240.

double roof. On the south side of this room are two low entrances to other apartments ; and on the west side, one. These entrances were once closed by doors of limestone, with carved panels, shutting from within ; the doors have been thrown down and broken, and the fragments still lie around. They were suspended by tenons above and below, fitted to corresponding sockets in the rock ; the lower tenon being of course short. One of these doors was still hanging in Maundrell's day, and "did not touch its lintel by at least two inches."[1]

The first room on the left or southeast from the ante-chamber, measures 11 feet 2 inches by 12 feet. On the eastern and southern sides are small low niches or crypts, three on a side, running in perpendicular to the wall, with narrow entrances, intended as a place of deposit for dead bodies, and exhibiting nothing worthy of particular remark. Along the sides of the room there is a small channel cut in the floor, to carry off the drippings from the damp walls ; and a similar arrangement is found in the other chambers.

The second room on the south of the ante-chamber and adjacent to the one just described, is 13 feet by 13½ ; and has also six small crypts or chambers in its southern and western sides, three in each. But they differ somewhat from those of the former apartment ; the middle crypt on each of the two sides having a higher entrance, being itself larger, and having also beyond it another smaller recess or tomb. Moreover, from one of these, or from a like recess, a few steps lead down to still another and lower tomb, or low square vault, with a large niche on three sides, in which once stood sarcophagi of white marble, elegantly sculptured with flowers and wreaths. These are now broken ; and the fragments strewed around upon the floors.

The third room, on the west of the ante-chamber, was apparently the most important of all. It is 13½ feet square ; and has three crypts on each of its three sides towards the south, west, and north. These are similar to those of the second room ; except that they are somewhat larger. The middle one indeed on each side is quite large, with each an interior recess or tomb as before. From one of these again, (that on the north side,) steps lead down to another low vault, like the former, with similar marble sarcophagi.[2]

---

[1] Maundrell's Journey, March 28th. Similar doors are described by Dr Clarke in the remarkable excavated sepulchres at Telmessus on the southern coast of Asia Minor ; Travels, etc. 4to. Part II. Vol. I. p 252. So also in the sepulchres near Beisân ; Irby and Mangles, p. 302. [92.]

[2] By the kindness of Mr Catherwood, I am enabled to lay before the reader the accompanying plan of these tombs, drawn out from his own measurements in 1833. The lower vault connected with the southwest chamber is not laid down ; the steps leading to it are marked on the north side of the room. The other lower vault on the north of the westernmost chamber, strikes me as being perhaps too large ; but we did not measure it. Only a part of

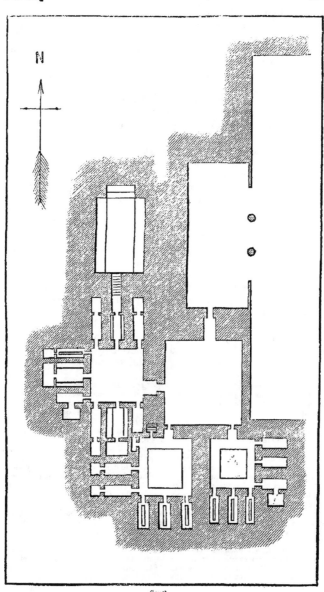

. South.

The four chambers thus described as connected with the present entrance, are all situated at the south end of the portico ; and only the lower vault belonging to the westernmost extends northwards for a distance behind it. Thus all the rock around the northern part of the portico remains apparently unexcavated. The question naturally arose in our minds, whether a work of such magnificence, and of such labour and expense, would probably have been left thus incomplete ; and it occurred to us, whether another like entrance to similar chambers might not exist at the other end of the portico, or in the middle, where the area has been filled up with stones and rubbish apparently for ages. We accordingly set men to work under the direction of our active servant Komeh, to clear away the accumulated rubbish from the northern end ; and frequently visited the spot ourselves. They laboured for several days, and laid bare the floor of rock at the bottom ; but without finding the slightest trace of any entrance. Yet I would not aver that such an entrance may not after all actually exist ; having been perhaps purposely concealed in the manner above suggested.[1]

This splendid sepulchre, with its sunken court, reminded me of some of the tombs of the Egyptian Thebes ; which also it resembles in its workmanship, but not in the extent of its excavations. In its elegant portal and delicate sculpture, it may well bear comparison with the sepulchres of Petra ; though the species of stone in which it is cut, does not admit of the same architectural effect. It has usually, I believe, been considered as unique in Palestine ; yet it is not the only monument of its kind in the vicinity of Jerusalem. It is indeed by far the best preserved ; which has been owing, doubtless, to the difficulty of

---

the sunken court is given ; and no attempt is made to represent the parallel trench on the south. Of former plans of these tombs, Niebuhr's seems to me to be the best ; Reischeschr. Bd. III. But a lower vault (h) which he lays down on the northern side of the anteroom, we did not see. Pococke's plan is less accurate, (Vol. II. p. 21,) and was obviously drawn from recollection. The sketch of Irby and Mangles (p. 332) is copied from Pococke.

[1] It was not until after these pages were written, that I was able to get access at Berlin to the Travels of Irby and Mangles. It is there related, that the same idea of a corresponding entrance at the northern end had also occurred to Mr Bankes ; and that so thoroughly was he convinced of it, that when at Constantinople he used every exertion to procure a firmán authorizing him to excavate and ascertain the fact ; but in vain. In the

spring of 1818, these travellers with others being at Jerusalem, endeavoured to obtain permission from the governor to dig on the same spot, but also without success. They therefore undertook the excavation themselves secretly by night, viz. Messrs Bankes, Legh, Irby, Mangles, and Corry, with five servants. They came in the morning to a large block of stone on the spot where they expected to find an entrance. They succeeded during the day in breaking the stone, but their proceedings were discovered and prohibited by the authorities. P. 332 sq. [101.] Times have now changed. We asked no leave ; and although we wrought openly for several days, we experienced no hindrance from any man.—See also the Life and Adventures of G. Finati, edited by Mr Bankes, II. pp. 219–234. —Mr Wolcott renewed the attempt in 1842 ; but with no better success. See Biblioth. Sac. 1843, p. 35 sq.

i. 532–534

entrance, and to the utter darkness that reigns within. One day as I was returning from this spot to the city with a friend, we kept along the brow of the valley of Jehoshaphat, in order to search for traces of Agrippa's wall. Of the wall we found nothing; but at some distance southeast from the tombs of the Kings, and near the brow of the valley, we came upon another sepulchre constructed on the same plan with the former; a square sunken court, with a portico and entrance upon its western side. But here the rock had been less judiciously chosen, and in some parts the sides of the court had been built up with masonry. The portal too was less ornamented and more broken away. The low entrance was here in the middle of the portico; and led into chambers of considerable size, but of less skilful workmanship. Indeed the whole appearance was less imposing; partly perhaps on account of the greater decay. Several other sepulchres of a similar character are to be traced in this quarter; but they are still more broken down and indistinct.

The sepulchre above described, has long borne among the Franks the name of the tombs of the Kings; probably on account of its remarkable character, which naturally led to the idea of a regal founder. It has been commonly referred to the ancient Jewish kings; on the supposition, that some of them may have been here entombed. The sepulchres of David and his descendants, as we know, were upon Zion;[1] they were called apparently the sepulchres of the Sons of David, and also of the kings of Israel;[2] and were still extant in the times of the Apostles.[3] Four of the Jewish kings, indeed, are said not to have been brought into those sepulchres; but there is no evidence to show that they were buried out of the city, and least of all in this quarter.[4] Josephus too mentions the tomb of Helena queen of Adiabene, (who embraced the Jewish religion and lived for a time at Jerusalem,) on the north of the city; and speaks also of royal grottos or sepulchres in the same quarter, near which ran the third or Agrippa's wall.[5] In another place the same writer speaks of monuments or tombs of Herod, situated apparently near this wall in the same quarter.[6] This circumstance suggests the inquiry, Whether

---

[1] 1 Kings 2, 10. 11, 43. etc.

[2] 2 Chron. 32, 33. 28, 27.

[3] Acts 2, 29.

[4] Uzziah was buried *with his fathers,* but not within their sepulchres, he being a leper; 2 Chron. 26, 23. Ahaz was buried within the city, but not in the same sepulchres; 2 Chron. 28, 27. Manasseh and Amon were buried in the garden of their own house, in the garden of Uzza, probably on Zion; 2 Kings 21, 18. 26.

[5] Joseph. B. J. 5. 4. 2.

[6] Ibid. 5. 3. 2. Titus caused the whole interval to be levelled from Scopus to the walls, or as it is also said, to the monuments (sepulchres) of Herod, μέχρι τῶν Ἡρώδου μνημείων. These would seem therefore to have been in the plain and near the northeast part of the city; not certainly upon the high land further west. But in another place, (B. J. 5. 12. 2,) a single monument (τὸ μνημεῖον) of Herod

these royal sepulchres of Josephus and these tombs of Herod
may not be identical ; and refer perhaps to sepulchres constructed
by the Idumæan princes for members of their own family ?   A
further inquiry also arises : Whether perhaps these tombs with
sunken courts, so different from all the rest around Jerusalem,
and situated not like the others in the rocky sides of the valleys,
but on the level ground above, may not have been a style
appropriated to royalty?   In that case, the dilapidated sepulchres of that kind which we found along the brow of the valley,
near where the ancient wall must have passed, would answer
well to the royal grottos or sepulchres of Josephus ; and the
present tombs of the Kings above described, would then correspond to the monument of Helena.

The latter part at least of this hypothesis, is probably well
founded.   Josephus thrice mentions the sepulchre prepared for
herself by Helena during her residence at Jerusalem ; once as
constructed with three pyramids at the distance of three stadia
from the city ; again on the approach of Titus to the city from
the north in order to reconnoitre, where it is said to be overagainst the gate on that side ; and lastly, where he describes the
third northern wall as passing overagainst it.[1]   Eusebius also
relates that Helena constructed a tomb, of which the "famous stelæ" or cippi were still pointed out in his day in the
suburbs of Jerusalem.[2]   More definite is the passing notice of
Jerome, who relates that as Paula approached the city from the
north, the mausoleum of Helena lay upon the left or east.[3]
Now the great northern road at present is unquestionably the
same that it ever was ; the very nature of the ground not
admitting the supposition of any material variation.   Thus
then, according to the ancient accounts, the tomb of Helena
lay on the east of this road, three stadia distant from the ancient
northern wall ; and we have seen above that the present sepulchre lies on the same side of the way, at the distance of a little
more than half an English mile or four stadia from the modern
Damascus gate.   But the ancient northern wall, as we know,
ran a stadium or more further north than the present one ; and
we have therefore here a very exact coincidence.   This fact,
taken in connection with the circumstance that the tomb of
Helena was celebrated of old, just as the sepulchre in question
is to this day the most remarkable object of antiquity round
about Jerusalem, seems amply sufficient to establish their
identity.

is mentioned, which lay south of the Roman
camp ; and of course on the west side of
the city.
[1] Joseph. Antiq. 20. 4. 3. B. J. 5. 2. 2.
ib. 5. 4. 2.
   i. 535–537

[2] Hist. Eccles. 2. 12, στῆλαι διαφανεῖς.
See also the note of Valesius on this passage.
[3] Hieron. ad Eustoch. Epitaph. Paulæ :
"Ad lævam mausoleo Helenæ derelicto,—

The same conclusion is further strengthened by an historical notice from another quarter, where we should hardly look for any illustration of Jewish antiquities. The Greek writer Pausanias in the second century, in speaking of the sepulchres that he had seen, mentions two as being worthy of particular admiration, viz. that of king Mausolus in Caria, and that of Helena at Jerusalem.[1] This latter he describes as remarkable for its door, which was of the same rock, and was so contrived that it could only be opened when the returning year brought round a particular day and hour; it then opened by means of mechanism alone, and after a short time, closed again; had one tried to open it at another time, he must first have broken it with violence. In this exaggerated account, we may nevertheless recognise the carved doors above described in these excavated tombs, and found here in this sepulchre alone; while the passage also shows the celebrity which the tomb of Helena had obtained in foreign lands. Taking all the circumstances together, there seems therefore little room for doubt, that the excavations so long known in modern times as the tombs of the Kings, ought henceforth to reassume their ancient celebrity as the sepulchre of Helena.

The three pyramids or stelæ by which the tomb was anciently surmounted, were probably small, and erected over the portal on the level ground above; and could hardly be expected to have survived the ravages of time and of barbarous hands. The earlier pilgrims, before the period of the crusades, make no mention of this tomb; probably because it still bore the name of Helena and was not to them a consecrated object. The same was perhaps the case with the writers of the age of the crusades, who have all passed it over in silence. Only Marinus Sanutus, A. D. 1321, slightly mentions the sepulchre of Helena on the north of the city; so slightly indeed that it is difficult to say, whether the same tomb is meant; though from its remarkable character this is most probable.[2] After this writer, there seems to be no allusion whatever to this sepulchre until near the close of the sixteenth century, when it is again brought into notice as the tombs of the Kings, in the tolerably full descriptions of Zuallart, Villamont, and Cotovicus.[3] From that

---

ingressa est Jerusolymam urbem." Opp. Tom. IV. ii. p. 673, ed. Martianay.

[1] Pausan. Græciæ Descript. Lib. VIII. c. 16 fin. See Note XXIX, end of the present volume.

[2] Secreta fidel. Crucis 3. 14. 9, "contra orientem descendit torrens Cedron, collectis simul omnibus aquis, quas secum trahit de partibus superioribus: scilicet Rama, Anathoth, sepulcro Reginæ Jabe-

norum," etc. Further on, the writer again refers to this tomb in connection with that of the Virgin in the valley of Jehoshaphat: "De sepulcro vero *Helenæ* Reginæ, dictum est supra," etc.

[3] Zuallart, A. D. 1586; Viaggio, p. 264. Villamont in A. D. 1589; Voyages, Liv. II. c. 31. Cotovicus in A. D. 1598; Itin. p. 304.

i. 537. 538

time onward the place has been described by almost every traveller down to the present day.   Pococke was the first to suggest,
that it might be the tomb of Helena ; but without reference to
the exact specification of Josephus and Jerome, and only as a
matter of conjecture.[1]   This was strengthened by Chateaubriand
and Dr Clarke by a reference to the passage of Pausanias above
cited ; although the former adopts in the end a different conclusion.[2]

Tombs of the Prophets.   The excavations commonly known
under this name, are situated on the western declivity of the
mount of Olives, a little south of the footpath leading over
from St. Stephen's gate to Bethany.   Pococke describes them
as "very large, having many cells to deposit bodies in ; the
further end of them they call the labyrinth, which extends a
great way ; I could not find the end of it ; this part seems to
have been a quarry."[3]   Doubdan compares them with the
tombs of the Judges and Kings ; but says the chambers are not
square, as in these, but consist of two large and high galleries
cut strictly one within the other in a continued curve ; the
holes or niches for the bodies being on a level with the floor.[4]
These sepulchres are not often mentioned by travellers, and no
exact description of them seems to exist.   I regret therefore the
more, that we did not visit them.[5]

[1] Pococke Descr. of the East, II. i. p.
20.—Doubdan speaks also of a tomb of
Helena, but distinct from the tombs of the
Kings and on the other side of the road ;
Voyage, p. 258.   See also Van Egmond
and Heyman, Reizen I. p. 347.   Quaresmius knew nothing of any tomb of Helen
in his day ; II. p. 734.

[2] Chateaubriand Itin. II. p. 79 sq. Paris 1837.   Clarke's Travels, etc. 4to. Part
II. Vol. I. p. 599.   See Note XXIX, at the
end of the volume.—See more on this
tomb in Vol. III. Sec. V.

[3] Descr. of the East, II. i. p. 29.

i. 538, 539

[4] Voyage, etc. p. 285.—See further
Quaresmius II. p. 305.   Chateaubriand
Itin. II. p. 37, Paris 1837.   I am not sure
whether these belong among the "certain
subterraneous chambers" mentioned by
Dr Clarke on the mount of Olives ; Travels,
4to. II. i. p. 577.   The "subterraneous
pyramid" upon the pinnacle of the mountain, which he holds to be a work of pagan
idolatry, we did not see ; but according to
his description, it answers well to one of
the ordinary subterranean magazines so
common in the villages of Palestine.

[5] See more in Vol. III. Sect. V.

SECTION VIII.

JERUSALEM.

HISTORY, STATISTICS, ETC.

I. HISTORICAL NOTICES.

It is not my purpose here to enter into any critical discussion; but merely to bring together a few historical notices of the Holy City, which may aid in throwing light upon some of the preceding details. They relate chiefly to the early centuries after the Christian era.

The picture which Josephus has given us of the siege and overthrow of Jerusalem by Titus, is drawn in gloomy colours; and presents a fearful succession of disease, famine, suffering, and slaughter. The Romans had besieged the city at a time when multitudes of the Jews were collected in it to celebrate the passover. First came pestilence, and then famine and the sword; so that, according to the same historian, there perished during the siege not less than eleven hundred thousand persons; while ninety-seven thousand more were made captives.[1] The devastation of the temple and the city was terrific; and in a sense complete. The former was burned with fire; and the walls of both, with the exceptions hereafter to be mentioned, were levelled with the ground; so that a passer-by would not have supposed that the place had ever been inhabited.[2]

Yet amid all this destruction and the insatiable fury of the Roman soldiers, there is no evidence that it was the intent of Titus to lay a ban upon the city, and devote it to perpetual desolation. This indeed was sometimes done by the Romans in respect to conquered cities; the plough was made to pass over

[1] Jos. B. J. 6. 9. 3. This is doubtless a greatly exaggerated estimate. The destruction of life was at any rate immense; though an estimate approaching to correctness could hardly be made.
[2] Joseph. B. J. 7. 1. 1.

their ruins, as a symbol of exauguration ; and they might then never be again built up.[1] But Jerusalem was not thus made a doomed site ; no plough was passed over its ruins, as has sometimes been reported ; and no superstitious curse rested upon its future renovation. Josephus, the eyewitness and participator in all those scenes, who describes in minute detail the events and consequences of the siege, is wholly silent as to any such desecration. The report in question has no doubt arisen in modern times, from confounding a notice relating to the time of Adrian with the events which occurred under Titus.[2]

The destruction of Jerusalem, however terrible, was nevertheless not total. Josephus expressly relates,[3] that by order of Titus the whole western wall of the city, and the three towers Hippicus, Phasäelus, and Mariamne, were left standing ; the former as a protection for the troops that remained here in garrison, and the latter as a memorial to posterity of the strength of the fortifications, which Roman valour had overcome. Titus stationed here at his departure the whole of the tenth legion, besides several squadrons of cavalry and cohorts of foot.[4] For these troops and their attendants there of course remained dwellings ; and there is no reason to suppose, that such Jews as had taken no part in the war, or perhaps also Christians, were prohibited from taking up their abode amid the ruins, and building them up so far as their necessities might require. But, on the other hand, the language of Eusebius is no doubt exaggerated, when in commenting upon a prophecy of Zechariah,[5] he assumes, in order to explain it, that the city was only half destroyed under Titus.[6] The remark of Jerome is probably nearer the truth, that " for fifty years after its destruction, until the time of Adrian, there still existed remnants of the city."[7] This accords also with other subsequent accounts.

---

[1] Servius ad Virg. Æn. 5. 755, " Nam ideo ad diruendas vel exaugurandas urbes aratrum adhibitum, ut eodem ritu, quo conditæ, subvertantur." So Horat. Carm. I. Od. 16 :

　　" et altis urbibus ultimæ
　Stetere causæ cur perirent
　Fundisæ, inprimæretque houris
　Hostile aratrum everitus insidens."

See also Seneca de Clementia I. c. 26. Deyling de Æliæ Capitol. Origine et Hist. § 6, in Deyling's Observat. Sacr. P. V. p. 448.

[2] The assertion in question seems first to have been made by Joseph Scaliger in a hap hazard manner in his Animadv. ad Euseb. Chron. p. 211. It is repeated by Valesius in his notes on Eusebii Hist. Ecc. 4. 6. p. 61 ; by Witsius, Miscell. Sacr. II. Exerc. 12. 8 ; and by several other writers. ii. 2, 3

Scaliger evidently confounded the later alleged passing of the plough over the site of the temple by Titus Annius Rufus, with the desecration of Jerusalem itself; and has even changed the name of the person to Musonius Tyrrhenus. See a full exposure of the error in Deyling l. c. p. 450 sq.

[3] B. J. 7. 1. 1.

[4] Ibid. 7. 1. 2.

[5] Zech. 14, 2 " And half of the city shall go forth into captivity, and the residue of the people shall not be cut off from the city."

[6] Demonstr. Evang. 6. 18, Τότε μὲν οὖν εἰκὸς τὸ ἥμισυ τῆς πόλεως ἀπολωλέναι τῇ πολιορκίᾳ, ὥς φησιν ἡ προφητεία. Compare Jerome on the same passage.

[7] Hieron. Epist. ad Dardanum, Opp. ed. Mart. II. p. 610, " Civitatis usque ad Had-

For half a century after its destruction, there is no mention of Jerusalem in history. The Jews in Egypt had revolted under Trajan, and had been subdued.[1] That emperor died in A. D. 117, and was followed by Adrian, who spent the greater part of his reign in journeying through the provinces of his vast empire. He appears to have been in Palestine about A. D. 130;[2] up to which time, with slight exceptions, the Jews had remained quiet, though waiting doubtless for a favourable opportunity of shaking off the yoke of Roman oppression, and reasserting their national independence. The emperor could not but be aware of the state of feeling prevalent among them; and it was natural that he should adopt precautionary measures to secure the fidelity and quiet of the province. One of these was to disperse the remaining Jews in colonies in various parts, especially along the northern coast of Africa.[3] A measure more important in its consequences, was the rebuilding of Jerusalem as a fortified place, by which to keep in check the whole Jewish population.

This determination of Adrian is assigned by the historian Dio Cassius, as the cause of the subsequent revolt and war of the Jews; who could not bear that foreigners should dwell in their city, nor that strange gods should be set up within it.[4] Eusebius, on the other hand, relates, that the city was rebuilt and the colony founded by Adrian, after the revolted Jews had been once more subdued.[5] These accounts are easily reconciled; the works had probably already been commenced, when they were broken off by the rebellion, and after this was quelled, they were again resumed and completed.[6]

The undertaking of this renovation, then, was the signal for the Jews to break out into open revolt, so soon as the emperor had forsak enthe east, apparently about A. D. 132.[7] The long smothered embers of hatred and discontent now burst forth into a flame, which overran and consumed both the land and the people with terrible desolation. The leader of this war was the celebrated though mysterious Barcochba, "Son of a Star." His success at first was great; the Jews of Palestine all flocked

---

rianum principem per quinquaginta annos mansere reliquæ." When Chateaubriand asserts that the Christians returned from Pella to Jerusalem soon after its destruction by Titus, this is nothing more nor less than a mere figment of imagination; Itineraire, Introd. p. 124. Paris 1837.

[1] See generally, Münter's Jüdischer Krieg unter Trajan und Hadrian, 1821, p. 13, etc.

[2] Münter l. c. pp. 29, 30.

[3] Colonies of Jews sent by Adrian to Libya are mentioned by several historians; see Münter l. c. p. 35.

[4] Dio Cass. 69. 12.

[5] Hist. Ecc. 4. 6.

[6] So Basnage Hist. des Juifs Tom. V. p. 1117, Rotterd. 1706. Münter l. c. p. 39.—The year in which the building of the new city was begun is very doubtful. According to the *Chron. Paschale seu Alexandr.* it would appear to have been in A. D. 119. But this seems quite too early; as Adrian was not in Palestine until about A. D. 130, and the war did not break out until after his departure. Münter, pp. 73, 74.

[7] Münter, l. c. p. 45.

to his standard ; the Christians also were tampered with, but re-
fusing to join him were afterwards treated with horrid cruelty.[1]
He appears to have soon got possession of Jerusalem. This is
evident from the fact of the subsequent recapture of the city by
the Romans ; and it would seem also, that coins (some of which
are still extant) were struck by him in the Holy City.[2] The
Romans at first made light of the rebellion, and disregarded the
efforts of this despised people ; and it was not until the spirit of
revolt had spread among the Jews throughout the empire, and
the whole world (as Dio expresses it) was moved, that Adrian
awoke from his apathy. The rebel Jews had already got possession of fifty fortified places, and nine hundred and eighty-five
important villages. The emperor now collected troops from various quarters,[3] and took measures to prosecute the war in earnest. He despatched his best officers into the revolted country ;
and recalling his most distinguished general, Julius Severus,
from Britain, sent him to take charge of the war in the east.
The struggle was long and desperate. The Jews were numerous, and fought with the bravery of despair. Julius attacked
their smaller parties ; cut off their supplies of provisions ; and
thus was able, more slowly indeed, but also with less danger,
to wear out their strength and finally destroy them.[4]

It is singular that the siege and capture of Jerusalem by the
Romans during this war, is nowhere described, and only once
mentioned, by a cotemporary writer. The historian Appian in
the same century gives it a passing notice ;[5] but all we know
further is from the slight mention of it by Eusebius and later
authors, the earliest of whom wrote two centuries after the
event.[6] The writings of the Rabbins, the repositories of Jewish
tradition, are silent as to the siege ; though they speak of the
desecration of the site of the temple. Yet the various testimonies, although scattered, are too numerous and definite to admit
of doubt as to the fact. Jerusalem must naturally have been
one of the chief points of Jewish defence ; and the possession of

---

[1] Justin. Mart. Apol. 1. 31. Euseb.
Chron. ad. An. xviii Hadriani. Orosii
Histor. 7. 12. See Münter l. c. p. 55.

[2] Münter, l. c. pp. 62, 63.

[3] An inscription now at Rome records,
that even the Gætuli in Mauritania furnished troops for this expedition against
the Jews ; Münter, p. 84.

[4] Dio Cass. 69. 13, 14. Münter, p. 66
sq.

[5] Appian. de Reb. Syriac. 50. ed. Tauchn.
II. p. 69, Ἱερουσαλήμ... ἣν δὲ καὶ Πτολε-
μαῖος ὁ πρῶτος Αἰγύπτου βασιλεὺς καθῄρῃ,
καὶ ὁ Οὐεσπασιανὸς αὖθις οἰκισθεῖσαν κατέ-
σκαψε, καὶ Ἀδριανὸς αὖθις ἐπ' ἐμοῦ.

[6] Euseb. Demonstr. Evang. 6. 18, as

ii. 5, 6

quoted above, p. 366, Note 6, where he continues : μετ' οὐ πολὺν δὲ χρόνον κατὰ
Ἀδριανὸν αὐτοκράτορα κινήσεως αὖθις Ἰου-
δαϊκῆς γενομένης τὸ λοιπὸν τῆς πόλεως
μέρος ἡμῖσυ πολιορκηθὲν αὖθις ἐξελαύνεται,
ὡς ἐξ ἐκείνου καὶ εἰς δεῦρο πάμπαν ἄβατον
γενέσθαι τὸν τόπον. So also Chrysost.
Orat. III. in Judæos, Tom. I. p. 431. Frkf.
1698. Hieron. Comm. in Joel 1, 4 "Ælii
quoque Hadriani contra Judæos expedi-
tionem legimus, qui ita Jerusalem muros-
que subvertit,"etc. Ejusd. Comm. in Ezech.
5, 1 ; in Habac. 2, 12-14. etc. etc. See
these and other writers cited in Deyling l.
c. p. 455. Münter l. c. p. 69-71.

it one of the main objects of the Roman policy. Of the circumstances of the siege and capture we have no account. It was not now, as under Titus, the scene of the last great struggle of the war ; for this took place in the siege of the strong but now unknown city of Bether, described as situated not far from Jerusalem.[1] Here the bloody tragedy was brought to a close, in the eighteenth year of Adrian, A. D. 135.[2] Thousands and thousands of the captive Jews were sold as slaves ; first at the terebinth near Hebron, where of old the tent of their forefather Abraham had stood, and where there had long been a frequented market; afterwards at Gaza ; and then the remainder were transported in ships as slaves to Egypt.[3] By a decree of Adrian, the Jews were henceforth forbidden even to approach their holy city ; and guards were stationed to prevent them from making the attempt.[4]

Several of the writers who allude to the capture of Jerusalem under Adrian, speak of the city as having been laid a second time in ruins, and utterly destroyed.[5] But this circumstance stands in direct contradiction with the known purpose of Adrian to rebuild the former city ; a purpose which he afterwards accomplished, and which he had probably begun to carry into execution before the war broke out ; since this is assigned as the very cause of the war.[6] It must also be remembered, that the writers who thus speak, all lived some three centuries or more after the event. Nor does a greater degree of credit seem due to the relation of Jewish writers, which is also repeated by Jerome, that the governor of the province, Titus Annius Rufus, caused the plough to be passed over the site of the ancient temple in order to desecrate it forever.[7] There is no evidence, that the

---

[1] Euseb. Hist. Ecc. 4. 6. The usual Talmudic name is בֵּיתַר. See Lightfoot Opp. II. p. 143, 208. Reland Palæst. p. 639. Münter l. c. p. 77 sq. See more in Vol. III. Sect. VI.

[2] Münter, p. 79.

[3] Hieron. Comm. in Zachar. 11, 4 "Legimus veteres historias et traditiones plangentium Judæorum, quod in tabernaculo Abrahæ, ubi nunc pe annos singulos mercatus celeberrimus exercetur, post ultimam eversionem quam sustinuerunt ab Adriano, multa hominum millia venundata sint, et quæ vendi non potuerint, translata in Ægyptum, tam naufragio et fame quam gentium cæde truncata." Ejusd. Comm. in Jerem. 31, 15. Chronicon Paschale seu Alexandr. A. D. 119, p. 253. Sozom. Hist. Ecc. 2. 4. See Reland Palæst. p. 715. Münter l. c. p. 85 sq.

[4] Justin. Mart. Apol. I. 47, ὅτι δὲ φυλάσσεται (Ἱερουσαλὴμ) ὑφ' ὑμῶν, ὅπως μηδεὶς ἐν αὐτῇ γένηται, καὶ θάνατος τοῦ καταλαβομένου Ἰουδαίου ἐσιόντος ὥρισθαι, ἀκριβῶς ἐπίστασθε. Euseb. H. E. 4. 6. Ejusd. Chron. ἔνθεν εἴργονται πάντη τῆς πόλεως ἐπιβαίνειν προστάξει θεοῦ καὶ Ῥωμαίων κράτει. Sulpic. Severi Hist. Sac. 2. 45, " Militum cohortem custodias in perpetuum agitare jussit, quæ Judæos omnes Hierosolymæ aditu arceret."

[5] Jerome is the earliest ; Comm. in Ezech. 5, 1 " Post quinquagenta annos sub Ælio Hadriano usque ad solum incensa atque deleta est, ita ut pristinum quoque nomen amiserit." Eusebius, nearly a century earlier, merely says, that " the place became inaccessible to the Jews ;" see Note 6, on p. 368, above. Münter p. 69 sq.

[6] See p. 367, above.

[7] The Rabbins call him Turanus Rufus ; Eusebius simply Rufus, Hist. Ecc. 4. 6. See Gemara Taanich c. 4, " quando aravit Turanus Rufus impius porticum," etc. Mai-

Romans ever applied this symbol of perpetual doom to the sites of single edifices. And further, Adrian himself is expressly said to have erected a temple to Jupiter upon the same spot,[1] a circumstance entirely inconsistent with such a desecration ; and Julian, two centuries later, the zealous protector of ancient superstitions, encouraged the Jews themselves to undertake the rebuilding of their temple.—Both these accounts, therefore, would seem rather to belong to the legendary inventions of a later age.

The work of rebuilding the city would appear to have been resumed immediately after the close of the war, if not before. In A. D. 136, the emperor Adrian celebrated his *Vicennalia*, on entering upon the twentieth year of his reign. On such occasions, which heretofore only Augustus and Trajan had lived to see, it seems to have been customary to build or consecrate new cities, or also to give to former cities new names.[2] At this time the new Roman colony established upon the site of the former Jerusalem, received the names of *Colonia Ælia Capitolina ;* the former after the prænomen of the emperor, Ælius Adrianus ; and the latter in honour of the Jupiter Capitolinus, whose fane now occupied the place of the Jewish temple.[3] The place became to all intents a Roman and pagan city ; Jupiter was made its patron god ; and statues of Jupiter and Venus were then or later erected on sites, which afterwards were held to be the places of the crucifixion and resurrection of our Lord.[4] The city was probably strongly fortified. Of its citadel and the apparent extent of its walls, we have already spoken.[5]

The ancient capital of the Jews was henceforth long known only as Ælia ; and coins bearing in their inscription the name COL. AEL. CAP. are still extant from the time of Adrian to Hostilian about A. D. 250.[6] The name Jerusalem went out of use ; and was indeed to such a degree forgotten, that when a martyr at Cæsarea under Maximin mentioned Jerusalem as his birthplace, (meaning the heavenly city,) the Roman governor Firmilianus inquired, What city it was and where it lay ?[7] In

monides in Bartoloc. Biblioth. Rabb. III. p. 679. Hieron. Comm. in Zachar. 8, 19 " Capta urbs Bethel (Bether), ad quam multa millia confugerant Judæorum ; aratum templum in ignominiam gentis oppressæ, a Tito Annio Ruffo." Münter l. c. p. 71.

[1] See Note 3, below.

[2] Pagi Critica Antibaroniana ad Ann. Chr. 132, 135.

[3] Dio Cass. 69. 12, Ἐς δὲ τὰ Ἱεροσόλυμα πόλιν αὐτοῦ ἀντὶ τῆς κατασκαφείσης οἰκίσαντος, ἣν καὶ Αἰλίαν Καπιτωλίναν ὠνόμασε, καὶ ἐς τὸν τοῦ ναοῦ τοῦ θεοῦ τόπον, ναὸν τῷ Διΐ ἕτερον ἀντεγείραντος κτλ. Euseb. ii. 8. 9

Hist. Ecc. 4. 6, Hieron. Comm. in Esai. 2, 8 " Ubi quondam erat templum et religio Dei, ibi Hadriani statua et Jovis idolum collocatum est." See also above, p. 296.

[4] Hieron. Ep. 49, ad Paulin. ed. Mart. Tom. IV. ii. p. 564. Sozomen, II. E. II. 1.

[5] See above, pp. 307, 316.

[6] Münter Jüdischer Krieg, etc. p. 94. The coins of Ælia are found in Rasche's Lexicon Tom. I, and the first Supplement. Sestini Descript. Nummor. vet. p. 544. Mionnet Médailles Ant. Tom. V. p. 516 sq.

[7] Euseb. de Martyrib. Palæstinæ, c. 11

the days of Constantine the ancient name became again more current; though that of Ælia still remained in use; as is shown by the writings of Eusebius and Jerome.[1] Even so late as A. D. 536, the name of Ælia appears in the acts of a synod held in Jerusalem itself;[2] and it afterwards passed over also to the Muhammedans, by whom it was long retained.[3]

The history of Jerusalem from the time of Adrian until Constantine, presents little more than a blank. The Christians, who, as individuals or perhaps communities, had suffered so greatly from the atrocities of Barcochba and his followers, had become more distinctly separated from the Jews; and while the latter (as we have seen) were now prohibited on pain of death even from approaching Jerusalem, the latter would seem to have resided in it without special molestation from the Romans. At this period probably, if ever, the former church of Jerusalem, which as a body is said to have withdrawn before the siege by Titus to Pella beyond the Jordan,[4] re-established itself in the new city; and in order to lay aside as far as possible every appearance of a Jewish character, elected its bishop Marcus and his successors from among the Gentile converts.[5] Between Marcus and Macarius in the time of Constantine, twenty-three bishops are enumerated; respecting whom, however, little is known.[6] Narcissus, in the beginning of the third century, under Severus, is related to have wrought miracles;[7] and Alexander, his successor, founded a library in Jerusalem, which was still extant in the days of Eusebius, nearly a century later.[8] Yet both these bishops, as well as other Christians, were exposed to persecutions on account of their faith; and the Christian church existed in Jerusalem, as elsewhere, only by sufferance.

The severe prohibition against the Jews appears not to have been relaxed during all this interval of nearly two centuries; and they continued to be shut out from the land of their fathers, and deprived even of the common rights of strangers upon its soil.[9] In the days of Constantine they were first allowed again

---

[1] Particularly in their specifications of the distances of places from this city; see the Onomast. art. *Bethel*, and elsewhere.

[2] " In Colonia Ælia metropoli, sive Hierosolymis;" Harduin. Concil. II. p. 1412. Labbe Concil. V. p. 275.

[3] Eutychius relates that the name Ælia was in use among the Arabs in his day; Annales I. p. 354. It is mentioned also by Edrisi, ed. Jaub. p. 341; by Ibn el-Wardi in Abulf. Syr. ed. Köhler, p. 179; and also by Mejr ed-Dîn so late as A. D. 1495; Fundgr. des Orients, II. p. 136.— It is found likewise in Adamnanus, about A. D. 697; de Locis Sanct. 1. 21.

[4] Euseb. H. E. 3. 5. Epiphanius (ob. 403) de Mensurib. et. Pond. 15. p. 171. ed. Petav. Eusebius is silent as to their return; but it is affirmed by Epiphanius.

[5] The election of Marcus is related by Eusebius under the 18th year of Adrian; H. E. 4. 6. Le Quien Oriens Christ. III. p. 145.

[6] Le Quien, l. c. p. 146 sq.

[7] Euseb. H. E. 5. 12. ib. 6. 9, 10.

[8] Euseb. H. E. 6. 20.

[9] Tertull. c. Judæos, c. 15. Apol. c. 21, " quibus [Judæis] nec advenarum jure terram patriam saltem vestigio salutare conceditur." Euseb. Demonstr. Evang. 6. 18, ii. 9–11

to approach the Holy City ; and at last, to enter it once a year, in order to wail over the ruins of their ancient sanctuary.[1]

Meantime the influence and the limits of Christianity were continually increased and extended, as well in Palestine itself as in other parts of the Roman empire. The hearts of Christians in other lands yearned to behold the sacred city, and the scenes of so many great events and hallowed recollections ; and in that age of pilgrimages, the Holy Land did not of course remain unvisited. Even early in the third century, two pilgrimages of this kind are recorded ; one that of Alexander, then bishop in Cappadocia, who became the successor of Narcissus in the see of Jerusalem ;[2] and the other, that of a female mentioned in a letter to Cyprian.[3] In the beginning of the fourth century, these journeys had become more common ; for Eusebius, writing about A. D. 315, speaks of Christians who came up to Jerusalem from all the regions of the earth ; partly to behold the accomplishment of prophecy in the conquest and destruction of the city ; and partly to pay their adorations on the mount of Olives where Jesus ascended, and at the cave in Bethlehem where he was born.[4]

In the conversion of Constantine, Christianity obtained a worldly triumph, and became henceforth the public religion of the state. The difficulties which had formerly beset the way of pilgrims to the Holy City, were now removed. The number of the pilgrims increased ; and an example of high influence was set by Helena, the mother of the emperor. At the age of nearly fourscore years, but with a youthful spirit, she repaired in person to Palestine in the year 326, to visit the holy places, and render thanks to God for the prosperity of her son and family. Having paid her adorations at the supposed places of the nativity and ascension, and being sustained by the munificence of her son, she caused splendid churches to be erected on those spots, viz. in Bethlehem and on the mount of Olives ; which were afterwards still further adorned by sumptuous presents from Constantine himself.[5] She returned to Constantinople ; and died there at the age of eighty, about the year 327 or 328.[6]

In the mean time, after the transactions connected with the council of Nicea, as Eusebius informs us, the emperor Constantine (not without a divine admonition) became desirous of per-

---

as quoted above on p. 368, Note 6. The remark in the text applies of course only to Judea; the Jews continued to reside in Galilee in great numbers.

[2] See above p. 237. Itin. Hieros. p. 591. ed. Wesseling. Hieron. Comm. in Sophon. 1, 15.

[3] Euseb. H. E. 6. 11, τὸν πορείαν ἐπὶ τὰ ii. 11, 12

[1] Ἱεροσόλυμα εὐχῆς καὶ τῶν τόπων ἱστορίας ἕνεκεν πεποιημένον.

[3] Cyprian. Epist. 75.—Cyprian died A. D. 258.

[4] Euseb. Demonstr. Evang. 6. 16. ib. 7. 4.

[5] Euseb. Vit. Const. 3. 42, 43.

[6] Ibid. 3. 46. Tillemont Mémoires pour servir à l'Hist. Eccl. Tom. VII. p. 16.

forming a glorious work in Palestine, by beautifying and rendering sacred the place of the resurrection of our Lord. For hitherto, according to the same writer, impious men, or rather the whole race of demons through their instrumentality, had used every effort to deliver over that illustrious monument of immortality to darkness and oblivion. They had covered the cave[1] with earth brought from other quarters; and then erected over it a sanctuary of Venus, in which to celebrate the impure rites and worship of that goddess. All these obstructions Constantine caused to be removed, and the Holy Sepulchre to be purified. Not content with this, he gave directions to build a magnificent temple or place of prayer over and around the sepulchre. His letter on this subject to the bishop Macarius is preserved by Eusebius; and presupposes the recent and joyful discovery of the " sign (or monument) of the Saviour's most sacred passion, which for so long a time had been hidden beneath the earth."[2] This discovery the emperor regards as a miracle, which it is beyond the capacity of man sufficiently to celebrate, or even to comprehend.[3] The church was completed and dedicated in the thirtieth year of Constantine, A. D. 335. On this occasion a great council of bishops was convened by order of the emperor from all the provinces of the empire, first at Tyre, and then at Jerusalem. Among them was Eusebius himself, who took part in the solemnities, and held several public discourses in the Holy City.[4]

In like manner Constantine gave orders to erect a church on the site of the terebinth of Mamre, where Abraham had dwelt; and where, as was supposed, the Saviour had first manifested his presence in Palestine. The emperor wrote on the subject to Eusebius, who has preserved the letter. This church is also mentioned by the Bordeaux pilgrim and by Jerome.[5]

Such is the account which Eusebius, the cotemporary and eyewitness, gives of the churches erected in Palestine by Helena and her son Constantine. Not a word, not a hint, by which the reader would be led to suppose, that the mother of the emperor had any thing to do with the discovery of the Holy Sepulchre, or the building of a church upon the spot. But, as I have already remarked, this was the age of credulous faith as well as of legendary tradition and invention, if not of pious fraud; and

---

[1] Eusebius everywhere speaks of the sepulchre as a cave, ἄντρον. De Vit. Const. 3. 26, 33.

[2] Euseb. Vit. Const. 3. 30, τὸ γνώρισμα τοῦ ἁγιωτάτου ἐκείνου πάθους ὑπὸ τῇ γῇ πάλαι κρυπτόμενον.

[3] See in general Euseb. Vit. Const. 3. 25-40.

[4] Euseb. Vit. Const. 4. 43-47. Sozomen 2. 26. Tillemont Mémoires, etc. VII. p. 12.—The site of the Jewish temple appears to have been left untouched by Constantine; see above, p. 296.

[5] Euseb. Vit. Const. 3. 51-53. Itin. Hieros. p. 599, ed. Wess. Hieron. Onomast. art. Arboe.

this silence of the father of Church History respecting Helena, was more than made good by his successors. All the writers of the following century relate as with one voice, that the mother of Constantine was from the first instigated by a strong desire to search out and discover the Holy Sepulchre and the sacred cross on which the Saviour had suffered. A divine intimation had pointed out to her the spot; and on her arrival at Jerusalem, she inquired diligently of the inhabitants. Yet the search was uncertain and difficult, in consequence of the obstructions by which the heathen had sought to render the spot unknown. These being all removed, the sacred sepulchre was discovered, and by its side[1] three crosses, with the tablet bearing the inscription written by Pilate. The tablet was separated from the cross; and now arose another dilemma, how to ascertain which of these three was the true cross. Macarius the bishop, who was present, suggested an appropriate means. A noble lady of Jerusalem lay sick of an incurable disease; the three crosses were presented to her in succession. The first two produced no effect; but at the approach of the third, she opened her eyes, recovered her strength, and sprang from her bed in perfect health.—In consequence of this discovery, Helena caused a splendid church to be erected over the spot where the crosses were found. The same writers relate also the erection, by Helena, of the two churches at Bethlehem and on the mount of Olives.[2]

Leaving out of view the obviously legendary portions of this story, it would seem not improbable, that Helena was the prime mover in searching for and discovering the sacred sepulchre; and that through her representations her son was induced to undertake the erection of the church; which in this way might still be appropriately ascribed to her. The emperor's letter to Macarius, as we have seen above, seems to presuppose some such event.[3] Yet how are we then to account for the entire silence of Eusebius as to any such discovery by Helena; supported as it is by the like silence of the pilgrim of Bordeaux, A. D. 333?[4] Possibly Eusebius, the flatterer of Constantine, may have chosen

[1] Theodoret. Hist. Ecc. 1. 17.

[2] Rufinus, ob. circa 410, lib. 1. (11.) 7, 8. Theodoret, fl. c. 440, lib. 1. 18. Socrat. fl. c. 440, lib. 1. 17. Sozomen, fl. c. 450, lib. 2. 1. Rufinus speaks of a divine intimation as well as of minute inquiry; and so Sozomen, and apparently Socrates. Sozomen also mentions the story of a Jew as one of the chief actors; but rejects it. The story of torture and the like, belongs apparently to a later age. Comp. Paulin. Nolan. Epist. XI. Marinus Sanutus in Gesta Dei per Francos, II. p. 121. Adrichomius, p. 176.

[3] Page 373, above.

[4] The Itin. Hieros. merely speaks of the church erected by Constantine over the sepulchre; and says not one word of Helena or of the cross. Even the churches of Bethlehem and the mount of Olives, which Eusebius ascribes to Helena, are referred by the pilgrim to Constantine; pp. 595, 597, 599, ed. Wesseling.

to ascribe all to the piety and magnanimity of his patron ; and while the church was building under the emperor's auspices for six or seven years after Helena's death, her participation in it may have been unknown or overlooked by the pilgrim.

However this may be, and notwithstanding the silence of Eusebius, there would seem to be hardly any fact of history better accredited, than this alleged discovery of the true cross. All the historians of the following century relate the circumstances as with one voice, and ascribe it to the enterprise of Helena. But this is not all. Cyril, who was bishop of Jerusalem from A. D. 348 onward, only some twenty years after the event, and who frequently speaks of preaching in the church erected by the munificence of Constantine, mentions expressly the finding of the cross under that emperor, and its existence in his own day.[1] So too Jerome, describing in A. D. 404 the journey of Paula, relates that in Jerusalem she not only performed her devotions in the Holy Sepulchre, but also prostrated herself before the cross in adoration.[2] Yet neither of these fathers makes mention of Helena in any connection with either the cross or sepulchre. It would seem, however, to be as little reasonable to doubt the existence of the alleged true cross at that early period, as it would be to give credit to the legendary circumstances related of its discovery. It was probably a work of pious fraud.

In the writings and traditions of succeeding centuries, the name of Helena became more prominent. Her memory and her deeds were embalmed and magnified in story as successive ages rolled on ; until, in the fourteenth century, not less than thirty churches were ascribed to her within the limits of Palestine.[3] And to the present day, almost every remaining church in that country, of any antiquity, is in like manner referred in monastic tradition to the munificence of Helena. Yet if we adhere, as we must, to the testimony of all the writers near her time, the only churches which she can be regarded as having built, are those at Bethlehem and on the mount of Olives ; except so far as she may have taken part in the construction of those connected with the Holy Sepulchre.

---

[1] So in his Epist. ad Constantium 3, Opp. ed. Touttée, p. 352, ἐπὶ μὲν γὰρ τοῦ . . . . Κωνσταντίνου τοῦ σοῦ πατρός, τὸ σωτήριον τοῦ σταυροῦ ξύλον ἐν Ἱεροσολύμοις ηὕρηται. Also in Cat. X. 19. p. 146, τὸ ξύλον τὸ ἅγιον τοῦ σταυροῦ μαρτυρεῖ, μέχρι σήμερον παρ' ἡμῖν φαινόμενον. In other places he speaks of portions of the true cross as already distributed throughout the world. Catech. IV. 10. p. 57. Cat. XIII. 4. p. 184.

[2] Hieron. Epist. 86, ad Eust. Epitaph. Paulæ, Opp. T. IV. ii. p. 673. ed. Mart.

[3] So Nicephorus Callistus, fl. about A. D. 1300, Hist. Ecc. 8. 30. p. 595 sq. ed. Ducæo. This writer enumerates by name seventeen churches as built by Helena : and then says at the close, that she erected more than thirty in all. It is hardly necessary to remark, that his authority can weigh nothing against the silence of all the writers of the fourth and fifth centuries.

The Christian temple thus erected over the holy places at Jerusalem, according to the description of Eusebius, had little resemblance to the structure which exists there at the present day.[1] The first care of Constantine was to erect a chapel or oratory over the sacred cave or sepulchre itself. This edifice was decorated with magnificent columns and ornaments of every sort. No mention is made of its magnitude or elevation, as is the case in respect to the neighbouring Basilica; whence we may infer that the chapel was not large. Before this, on the east, was a large open court or area ornamented with a pavement of polished stones; and surrounded on three sides by long porticos or colonnades. This place was apparently held to be the garden near which Christ was crucified; and as such it is also mentioned by Cyril as having been beautified by regal gifts.[2] The eastern side of this court was shut in by the *Basilica*, or church, erected over the spot where the cross was found, if not also over the rock held to be Golgotha.[3] This edifice is described as of great extent both in its length and breadth, and of immense altitude. The roof was covered with lead; the interior overlaid with variegated marbles; the ceiling decorated with carved work; and the whole glittered in every part with burnished gold. Beyond this Basilica, still towards the east, was another court, with porticos or colonnades on the sides, and gates leading to the city; "beyond which, in the very midst of the street of the market, the splendid *Propylæa*, or vestibule of the whole structure, presented to those passing by on the outside the wonderful view of the things seen within."[4]—It was this large church to which the name of the *Martyrion* was strictly applied, as standing upon the place of the Saviour's passion.[5] The chapel over the sepulchre was called

---

[1] See in general, Euseb. Vit. Const. 3. 33–39. Touttée Deser. et Hist. Basilicæ S. Resurrect. in Cyril. Hieros. Opp. p. 418.
[2] John 19, 41. Cyril. Hieros. Catech. 14. 5. p. 206. ed. Touttée.
[3] Comp. Cyril. Catech. 10. 19. Catech. 13. 23. ed. Touttée. The fact of a large court between the sepulchre and this Basilica, and also that later a chapel was erected over Golgotha, between the two, seems to favour the idea, that at this time the rock or *monticule* of Golgotha was left uncovered in the midst of this splendid court. Eucharius seems also to testify to the same effect; see Touttée l. c. § 6.— From this rock or *monticule* was doubtless derived the epithet *mount* as applied to the present Golgotha or Calvary. Hence the expression "Mount Calvary" has been adopted almost without question into every language of Christendom. Yet in the New Testament there is no hint that Golgotha

was in any sense a hillock; Matt. 27, 33. Mark 15, 22. Luke 23, 33. John 19, 17. Neither Eusebius, nor Cyril, (except as made to say so by the Latin translator,) nor Jerome, nor the historians of the 4th and 5th centuries, speak of it as a mount. Yet the expression must have early become current, perhaps among the pilgrims; for the *Itiner. Hieros.* speaks of it as "monticulus Golgotha." Rufinus has the expression "Golgothana rupes," Hist. Ecc. 9. 6. Antoninus and Adamnanus make no allusion to a mount; but Bernhard again has "Mons Calvariæ." At that time the usage appears to have become fixed; and is found in all later pilgrims and writers.
[4] Euseb. l. c. 3. 39, ἐπ' αὐτῆς μεσῆς πλατείας ἀγορᾶς.
[5] Cyril. Hieros. Cat. 14. 6. ed. Touttée. Compare Euseb. de Laud. Const. c. 9, sub. fine.

ii. 17, 18

the *Anastasis* or Resurrection.[1] But both these names seem also to have often been applied indiscriminately to the whole structure and to its various parts.[2]

The high example of Helena, the supposed discovery of the sacred places, and the erection of all these splendid churches, conspired to draw, in a still greater degree, the attention and the longings of the Christian world towards Jerusalem. Pilgrimages were now multiplied, as the dangers and difficulties were diminished; and one of the most important documents of the age, is the Itinerary of a palmer from Bordeaux in A. D. 333.[3] The dedication of the church of the Holy Sepulchre in A. D. 335, was afterwards celebrated annually by a festival, which continued for a week, and was resorted to by multitudes from all parts of the world.[4] Towards the middle of the same century, Hilarion first introduced the monastic life from Egypt into Palestine and Syria;[5] which, finding there a congenial soil, at once took deep root, and spread itself rapidly abroad throughout the land.

The Jews, as we have seen,[6] in the age of Constantine, were again permitted to approach Jerusalem, and apparently to dwell once more upon their native soil. They had never been driven out from Galilee; and under the reign of his successor Constantius, they formed the chief population of Diocæsarea (Sepphoris) and other towns; and felt themselves in sufficient strength to take up arms in rebellion against the Romans. But they were soon subdued; and in A. D. 339, this city was levelled to the ground.[7] The emperor Julian, in abandoning Christianity, endeavoured as a matter of policy to win the confidence of the Jews. He showed them favour; granted them privileges; and gave them permission to return to Jerusalem, and rebuild their sacred temple. They accordingly began to lay the foundations about A. D. 362; but the attempt, according to cotemporary writers, was rendered abortive by supernatural hindrances.[8]—Under the successors of Julian, the edicts would seem to have been renewed, which prohibited the Jews from residing in Jerusalem; for Jerome relates, that in his day they were still forbidden to enter the city, except once a year, to wail over the temple.[9] Thus

---

[1] The Arabic name of the present church is still *el-Kiyâmeh*, the Resurrection.

[2] Tillemont Mémoires, etc. Tom. VII. p. 11.

[3] Itiner. Hieros. seu Burdigalense.

[4] Sozomen 2. 26.

[5] Hieron. Vita Hilar. Sozom. 3. 14. Tillemont Mém. Tom. VII. p. 565. Neander K. G. III. p. 458 sq. ed. 2.

[6] See above, p. 371 sq.

[7] Socrates H. E. 2. 33.   Theophan. Chronogr. p. 33, Paris. See Reland Pal.

p. 1000. For the Jews in Galilee, see in Sec. XV, under Tiberias.

[8] Ammian. Marcell. 23. 1, " metuendi globi flammarum prope fundamenta crebris assultibus erumpentes, fecere locum exustis aliquoties operibus inaccessum; hocque modo, elemento destinatius repellente, cessavit inceptum." Socr. H. E. 3. 20. Sozom. 5. 22. Tillemont Mémoires, etc. VII. p. 409 sq.

[9] Hieron. Comm. in Zephan. 1, 15, " usque ad præcentem diem perfidi coloni

ii. 18–20

they continued to struggle on for a residence in the land and city
of their fathers; objects of contumely and oppression on every
side, and with little change in their general situation; until at
length the Muhammedan conquest gave them the opportunity of
acquiring larger privileges, both in Jerusalem and throughout
Palestine.

In the latter part of the fourth century, A. D. 384, Jerome,
the celebrated father, took up his residence in Palestine, where
he remained as a monk in the convent at Bethlehem until his
death in A. D. 420. At this time monasteries and communities
of anchorites (*laurae*) were numerous;[1] and the whole of Palestine swarmed with monks and hermits. Jerome speaks expressly of "the great multitude of brethren and the bands of monks,"
who dwelt in and around Jerusalem.[2] Even Paula, a noble Roman matron, the friend of Jerome, first made a pilgrimage to the
holy places, and then retired to Bethlehem; where she erected
four monasteries, one for monks and three for nuns.[3] Nor was
the throng of strangers and pilgrims, who came from every quarter of the globe to visit the holy places and adore the cross, less
remarkable. The same father relates that devotees "streamed
to Jerusalem from every part of the world; so that the city was
crowded with persons of both sexes and of every class."[4] From
Gaul, Britain, Persia, India, Ethiopia, Egypt, and the whole
east, princes and nobles thronged to the Holy City; believing
themselves to have less of religion, less of science, and not to have
attained the highest point of virtue, unless they had paid their
adorations to the Saviour in the very places, where the Gospel
first shone forth in splendour from the cross.[5] Nor did the pilgrims limit their holy veneration to Palestine. Egypt was
equally thronged; and many also travelled into Arabia, the supposed country of Job, to visit the dunghill and kiss the ground,
on which the man of God had suffered with such patience.[6] Indeed, after the fourth and fifth centuries, there are comparatively
few of the more distinguished saints of the calendar, among

(Judæi) .... excepto planctu prohibentur ingredi Jerusalem." Then follows the pas-sage quoted above, p. 238, Note.

[1] A community of anchorites, dwelling near each other in separate cells, was call-ed λαύρα, *laura*, i. e. a street, village. See Neander K. G. III. p. 459 sq. ed. 2. Bol-land in Acta Sanctor. Jan. Tom. II. p. 298.

[2] "Tantam fratrum multitudinem et monachorum choros;" Ep. xxxvii, ad Pammach. Tom. IV, ii. p. 308. ed. Mart.

[3] Hieron. Ep. lxxxvi, ad Eustoch. Ep-itaph Paulæ.

[4] "De toto huc orbe concurritur. Ple-ii. 20. 21

na est civitas universi generis hominum et tanta utriusque sexus constipatio, etc." Ep. 49, ad Paulin. Tom. IV. P. II. p. 565. ed. Mart. So Chrysost. in Ps. 109. § 6, ἡ οἰκουμένη συντρέχει.

[5] See the Epistle under the name of Paula and Eustochium, Hieron. Opp. Tom. IV. P. II. pp. 550, 551.

[6] So Chrysost. Homil. V. de Statuis §1. Tom. II. p. 59, Πολλοὶ νῦν μακράν τινα καὶ διαπόντιον ἀποδημίαν στέλλονται ἀπὸ τῶν περάτων τῆς γῆς εἰς τὴν Ἀραβίαν τρέχοντες, ἵνα τὴν κοπρίαν ἐκείνην ἴδωσι, καὶ θεασάμε-νοι καταφιλήσωσι τὴν γῆν.

whose merits one or more pilgrimages to the Holy Sepulchre are not enumerated.[1]

In such state of things, it cannot be a matter of wonder, that the end should often be forgotten in the means ; that a pilgrimage to Jerusalem, instead of being resorted to merely as a means of elevating and purifying the religious feelings, and quickening the flame of devotion, should come to be regarded as having in itself a sanctifying and saving power ; and so the mere performance of the outward act, be substituted for the inward principle and feelings.   That such was actually the case, is obvious from the language of Jerome and other fathers, who strove against this tendency.   The former declares that " the places of the cross and of the resurrection of Christ can benefit only those who bear his cross, and who with Christ rise daily.   From Jerusalem and from Britain, the celestial halls are equally open."[2]   And he goes on to relate of Hilarion, who spent much of his life as an anchorite in Palestine, that he only once visited Jerusalem and the sacred places.[3]   To the same effect is the language of Gregory of Nyssa ;[4] who justly appeals to the corruption and licentiousness which prevailed in Jerusalem, as a proof, how little such external impressions can contribute in themselves to the purification of the heart.

The effects which would naturally follow from all these circumstances in respect to the topography of the Holy Land, have already been pointed out in the beginning of the preceding section.   Almost as a matter of course, every place celebrated in the Bible was sought after by the credulous piety of monks and pilgrims, and its site definitely assigned.   Whether this were done correctly, was not often with them a matter of strict inquiry.   Yet, during the fourth century, there is less reason for regret and complaint in this respect, than in the succeeding ages.   Eusebius had composed his Onomasticon in Greek, apparently about A. D. 330, after the sites of the holy places in Jerusalem had been determined ;[5] and this was now translated and revised by Jerome during his residence in Palestine, before the mass of foreign tradition, which afterwards spread itself abroad, had taken root or cast its darkening shadows over the land.   This important work serves to show the state of topographical tradition as it then

---

[1] See the Indices to the many volumes of the *Acta Sanctorum* of Bolland, art. *Peregrinatio*, etc. Some of these holy men made no less than three pilgrimages to the Promised Land. So St. Cadocus bishop of Beneventum, and Theodosius bishop of Anastasiople, in the sixth century ; Acta Sanctor. Jan. Tom. I. p. 604. April. T. III. p. 32 sq.

[2] Ep. 49, ad Paulin. Tom. IV. P. II. p. 564.

[3] Hieron. l. c.

[4] Gregor. Nyss. Epist. ad Ambrosium et Basilisam. Compare Neander Kirchengeschichte, III. p. 643, ed. 2. II. p. 342, Engl.

[5] See the art. Γολγοθά, *Golgotha*, the site of which had already been fixed.

existed ; and often stands in direct contradiction to the specifications of later ages.[1]

During the centuries after the destruction of Jerusalem, the
metropolitan see of Palestine was at Cæsarea ; to which the see
of Jerusalem was subject like the rest.[2]   But when in the fourth
century the holy places at Jerusalem became known, and were
decorated with splendid edifices, and the Holy City began to
reassume its importance in the Christian world, its bishops were
not slow to bring forward its claims to a higher rank, as the
original seat of the apostolic church. Even so early as at the council of Nicea, A. D. 325, its traditional claims had been acknowledged and affirmed ; saving however the dignity of the then
metropolitan see.[3]   Cyril as bishop of Jerusalem contended long
with Acacius of Cæsarea for the supremacy ; though he was at
last compelled to yield to the authority of the primate, by whom
he was deposed.[4]   His successor, John, claimed also to be independent of Cæsarea, and appealed to the patriarch of Alexandria ;
for which he is censured by Jerome.[5]   The following bishop,
Praylus, was a meek and holy man, and apparently avoided such
controversies.   But Juvenal, his successor, who held the chair of
Jerusalem from about A. D. 420 to 458, exerted himself to the
utmost to establish the authority of his see, not only as superior
to Cæsarea, but as independent of the patriarch of Antioch.   It
was not however until the council of Chalcedon, A. D. 451–453,
that he was able after long efforts to effect his purpose.   It was
there decreed, that Jerusalem should be thenceforth an independent patriarchate, comprising the three Palestines ; while Antioch
should retain the two Phenicias and northern Arabian.[6]

Amid all the religious or rather theological controversies, which
agitated the oriental churches during these centuries, it was hardly
to be expected that Palestine, crowded as it was with ecclesiastics and monks, should remain in peace.   On the contrary, it
actually became one of the chief seats of strife and fierce conten-
tion, which were not in all cases appeased without bloodshed.   In
the fourth century, the Arian controversy had much to do with
the repeated depositions of Cyril from the see of Jerusalem.[7]   In
A. D. 415 Pelagius himself appeared before two tumultuous

---

[1] See more above, p. 254.

[2] So Jerome, as if addressing himself to
John, bishop of Jerusalem, and referring
him to the council of Nicea, exclaims:
" Ni fallar, hoc ibi decernitur, ut Palæs-
tinæ metropolis Cæsaræa sit, et totius ori-
entis Antiochia ; " Hieron. Ep. xxxviii, ad
Pammach. Tom. IV. P. II. p. 330. ed.
Mart.

[3] Concil. Nic. Can. VII, Ἐπειδὴ συνήθεια
κεκράτηκε καὶ παράδοσις ἀρχαῖα ὥστε τὸν ἐν
ii. 23, 24

Ἀλλίᾳ ἐπίσκοπον τιμᾶσθαι, ἐχέτω τὴν ἀκο-
λουθίαν τῆς τιμῆς, τῇ μητροπόλει σωζομένου
τοῦ οἰκείου ἀξιώματος. Labb. Concil. Tom.
I. p. 47.
[4] Theodoret. H. E. 2. 26. Sozom. 4. 25.
[5] Hieron. l. c.
[6] Concil. Chalcedon. Act. VII. Labb.
Tom. IV. p. 613. See also Le Quien
Oriens Christ. Tom. III. p. 110 sq.
[7] Sozom. H. E. 4. 25.

synods at Jerusalem and Diospolis (Lydda).[1] About the same
period we find in and around Jerusalem the germ of the controversy, which a century later raged with such vehemence against
the Origenists.[2]

The declaration of the council of Chalcedon (A. D. 451) in
favour of the doctrine of the two distinct natures of Christ, was
the signal for the outbreak of violence on the part of the Monophysites, its opposers ; whose chief seat at first was in Palestine
and Egypt. Theodosius, a fanatical monk, who had already
excited tumults in the council, returned to Jerusalem ; and having
ingratiated himself with Eudocia, the widow of the late emperor
Theodosius II, who resided in Palestine, he soon obtained influence throughout the convents, and raised a fierce party against
the decision of the council. His partisans took possession of the
church of the Holy Sepulchre, deposed the patriarch Juvenal,
drove him from the country, and elected Theodosius in his stead.
The orthodox bishops and moderate men were now everywhere
deposed ; some were slain ; and their places filled by unworthy
persons and even malefactors. The emperor Marcian, on hearing
of these events, took measures to replace the exiled patriarch in
his station, and restore things to their former order ; but this could
only be done after fierce conflicts ; since both parties (as Eva-
grius expresses it) acted only according to the dictates of their
rage. Theodosius retired secretly to Mount Sinai ; where he was
followed by a letter missive of the emperor, to which we have
already alluded in another place.[3]

The controversy continued to rage in Egypt, accompanied
with many tumults ; and the successive emperors, themselves
weak-minded or vacillating men, were unable to quench the
flames of discord. Under Anastasius I, who began to reign in
A. D. 491, and was himself opposed to the decree of the council
of Chalcedon, the monophysite party acquired new strength, and
gave occasion to new disturbances, under its two distinguished
leaders, Xenaja or Philoxenus, and Severus.[4] The tumults broke
out first at Antioch ; where Flavianus, the mild but orthodox
patriarch, was assailed in A. D. 512 by a host of fanatic monks
from the neighbourhood, who forced their way into the city, and
demanded that he should anathematize the acts of the council of
Chalcedon. The people of the city however sided with the patriarch, rose upon the monks, and slew a large number, who found

---

[1] Neander K. G. IV. p. 1092 sq. ed. 2.
II. p. 581 sq. Engl.
[2] Neander l. c. p. 1264 sq. or p. 678 sq.
Engl.
[3] See above, p. 124. For the general
history of this tumult, see *Vita St. Eu-
themii* No. 73, in Cotelerii Monum. Eccl.

Græcæ, Tom. II. p. 261 ; Lat. in Acta
Sanctor. Jan. T. II. p. 313 Evagrii Hist.
Eccl. II. 5. Le Quien Oriens Christ. III. p.
166.
[4] Neander K. G. IV. p 1002 sq. ed. 2.
II. p. 530 sq. Engl.

their only sepulchre in the waves of the Orontes. The monks of
Cœle-Syria also, among whom Flavianus had lived, hastened to
Antioch to tender him their services and protection. Yet he was
ultimately deposed in the same year, and driven into exile at
Petra. He was succeeded in his office by the monophysite leader
Severus.[1]

The patriarchate of Jerusalem was at this time held by Elias ;
whose influence among the monks and clergy of Palestine, however great, was yet less than that of the celebrated anchorite, St.
Sabas, the founder of several *lauræ* and monasteries ; and among
them, of that which still bears his name in the desert between
Jerusalem and the Dead Sea. In the very same year, A. D. 512,
Severus of Antioch sent messengers to Elias, who refused to acknowledge him. The message was repeated in May, A. D. 513,
accompanied by several clergy and some of the emperor's troops.
This roused the indignation of Sabas in his holy retreat ; he
repaired with other abbots to Jerusalem ; expelled the messengers of Severus from the city ; and collecting a multitude of
monks before Calvary, pronounced anathemas against Severus and
all those of his communion, in the presence of the magistrates
and of the officers and troops whom the emperor had sent. Still,
the power of the state at length prevailed. The emperor sent
Olympius, who then held the command in Palestine, with a body
of troops to Jerusalem ; and as Elias still refused to disavow
allegiance to the decrees of Chalcedon, he was deposed and banish-
ed to Ailah. There he died in A. D. 518 ; being visited in his
last moments by Sabas.[2]

His successor in the patriarchate, John III, who was expected
to anathematize the council of Chalcedon, not only did not do
this, but took at first a neutral course, and afterwards made common cause with the orthodox party. Disputes and fierce passion
continued to prevail among the ecclesiastics and monks of Palestine ; but they seem not to have broken forth into deeds of
open violence. The accession of the orthodox emperor, Justin I,
in A. D. 518, was hailed with triumph by Sabas and his disciples.
The new decrees of this emperor in favour of orthodoxy were no
sooner known in Jerusalem, than an infinite multitude of monks
and laymen collected in that city ; the holy Sabas and a council
of bishops hastened to assemble ; and at a festival celebrated on
the 6th of August, the imperial decrees were openly promulgated.

Justinian, who ascended the throne in A. D. 527, was the
still more decided and despotic friend of the orthodox faith. Sabas died about A. D. 532, in the odour of sanctity, at the great

[1] Evagr. H. E. 3. 32.   Græc. T. III pp. 308-10, 324. Le Quien
[2] Cyrill. Scythop. Vita Sabæ 56, 60 ;   Oriens Christ. III. p. 181 sq.
Gr. et Lat. in Cotelerii Monum. Eccles.
ii. 26, 27

age of ninety-four years.[1] Not long after his decease, new troubles and dissensions broke out among his immediate disciples and flock. The unquiet spirit of oriental monachism, which had hitherto expended itself in the monophysite controversy, or been controlled by the predominance of a master spirit, or felt the influence of the imperial despotism, now began to manifest itself in a different form. The tendency and doctrines of the Origenists were again broached, especially by Nonnus in the 'new laura founded by Sabas near Tekoa, and in several others. The same doctrines found admission also among many of the members of the principal laura of Sabas ; but the great body remained faithful to the orthodox doctrine, and expelled the others to the number of forty from the community. These retired to the laura near Tekoa ; and the united band of the Origenists now attempted to get possession of various monasteries. They even attacked the chief laura of Sabas, with force and violence, but without success.[2]

In A. D. 536, at the suggestion of the Roman bishop, Agapetas, then at Constantinople, and of Mennas patriarch of that city, the patriarch Peter of Jerusalem held a synod composed of the bishops of the three Palestines ; at which not only the decrees of the synod of Constantinople in the same year against the Monophysites were confirmed, but the dogmas of Origen were also publicly subjected to anathema. This measure caused great indignation among the followers of Nonnus, and gave rise to further tumults.[3] The edict of the synod was however subscribed by all the bishops and abbots of Palestine, except one ; which so enraged Nonnus and the other chiefs of the Origenists, that they renounced the communion of the orthodox ; and withdrawing from the laura near Tekoa, dwelt in the plain. After long negotiation they returned to the laura, retaining still great bitterness against the inmates of the laura of Sabas ; which they manifested by open and violent attacks. They succeeded at length in obtaining possession for a time of this chief laura ; and an Origenist was installed as abbot in the seat of the holy Sabas.[4] This however did not long continue. The holy Conon was afterwards made abbot ; Eustochius (about A. D. 545) succeeded to the patriarchate of Jerusalem ; and, by command of the emperor, the military force was employed to drive out the Origenists from their stronghold, the new laura (so called) near Tekoa. From this time peace appears to have been restored.[5]

[1] Cyrill. Scyth. Vita Sabæ, in Cotelerii Monum. Eccl. Græc. Tom. III p. 353 sq. Le Quien Oriens Chr. III. p. 194 sq.

[2] Cyrill. ibid. p. 360-2. Baronius Ann. A. D. 532. viii, sq. Le Quien ibid. p. 196-200.

[3] Labb. Concil. Tom. V. p. 275-87.

Baronius Ann. A. D. 536. xciv. Cyrill. Vita Sabæ l. c. p. 365. Le Quien l. c. p. 204 sq. Neander K. G. IV. p. 1014 sq. ed. 2. II. p. 537 sq. Engl.

[4] Cyrill. Scyth. Vit. Sabæ, ibid. p. 370.

[5] Cyrill. ibid. p. 375 sq. Evagr. H. E. 4. 38.

I have dwelt the longer upon these gloomy details, in order to show the extent, as well as the character and spirit, of that body of monks and ecclesiastics with which Palestine was thronged ; and who for so many centuries were the only persons to investigate the Scriptures, and fix the traditional topography of the Holy Land.

Despotic as Justinian was in behalf of orthodoxy, he was no less a passionate builder of churches and monasteries, as well as of fortresses ; and to such an extent was this passion carried out during his long reign, that the cotemporary historian Procopius has left us a work in six books, treating solely of the edifices erected by this emperor.[1] In Constantinople itself, the church of St. Sophia remains to this day a monument of his taste and public munificence. With the convent erected by him at Sinai we have already become acquainted.[2] In Palestine the Samaritans made insurrection against Justinian, as they had formerly done under the emperors Zeno and Anastasius ; slaughtered the Christians of Neapolis ; and destroyed their churches. They were however speedily subdued ; and the emperor rebuilt the churches and erected a new one strongly fortified on Mount Gerizim. This was in the third year of Justinian, A. D. 529.[3] In the same connection, and as if occurring about the same time, Procopius describes the erection of a large church at Jerusalem by Justinian in honour of the Virgin, on which great expense and labour were bestowed in order to make it one of the most splendid in the world. This church, as we have seen, was apparently the edifice now known as the mosk el-Aksa, on the southern part of the site of the temple.[4] The same writer ascribes to this emperor the building of not less than ten or eleven monasteries in and around Jerusalem and Jericho, a Xenodochium or hospital for pilgrims at Jericho, and also the building up of the walls of Bethlehem and other cities.[5] Eutychius in the ninth century relates the same general facts respecting Justinian ; and adds that he erected also a hospital for strangers in Jerusalem.[6]

This public provision for the accommodation of pilgrims in the Holy Land, serves to show, that their numbers at this period

[1] Περὶ τῶν τοῦ δεσπότου Ἰουστινιανοῦ κτισμάτων, De Ædificiis Justiniani, etc. in the Corpus Scriptor. Historiæ Byzant.

[2] See above in p. 124 sq.

[3] Procop. de Ædific. 5. 7.   Chron. Paschale seu Alexandrin. pp. 325, 326. ed. Ducange, Paris 1688.

[4] See above, p. 296 sq. Procop. de Ædif. 5. 6.

[5] Procop. de Ædificiis Justiniani, 5. 9.

[6] Eutychii Annales, Arab. et Lat. ed Pococke, Oxon. 1658. Tom. II. pp. 158, ii. 29, 30

159 sq.—Of the church built by Justinian in Jerusalem, Eutychius merely says, "he completed the church of Helena which had been begun by the patriarch Elias;" of course in the same century ; Ibid. p. 108. Eutychius also relates, that Justinian at the same time caused the church in Bethlehem to be rebuilt; and being displeased at the manner in which his legate had constructed the edifice, he ordered his head to be struck off. Both these accounts have an air of the fabulous.

were not diminished. On the contrary, the pilgrims from the west would appear to have increased ; and it was regarded as a pious duty of occidental princes and wealthy individuals, to make further provision for their wants. At the close of this century, Gregory the Great of Rome (A. D. 590-604) is said to have sent the abbot Probus with a large sum of money to Jerusalem, where he too erected a splendid hospital for the reception of pilgrims.[1] To such an extent was this feeling of duty at length carried, that in the following centuries there was scarcely a city of note in France or Italy, in which the charity of Christians had not provided a hospital for the pious wanderer to Rome and the Holy Land ; while in Constantinople, at least in the ninth century, there were several establishments of the same character.[2]

To the close of the sixth century belongs also the Itinerary of Antoninus Martyr, or Antoninus Placentinus ; for he is called by both names. His description of the church of the Holy Sepulchre corresponds with that of Eusebius as above given. Of the author, nothing further is known.

The journey of the pilgrims to Jerusalem was also facilitated, and the interest taken by all in the Holy Land was cherished and augmented, by the commercial intercourse, which at this period was kept up with the east by several cities along the coasts of the Mediterranean. The merchants of Marseilles in the sixth and seventh centuries sent their ships to Alexandria and the coasts of Syria ; and received from thence paper, oil, and the silks and spices of the remoter east.[3] In the sixth century, at the court of king Guntram of Burgundy, the wine of Gaza was regarded as the highest delicacy.[4]—In like manner the merchants of Syria and the east travelled with their wares into the occident, and extended their wanderings throughout the greater part of France and Spain.[5]

Another motive which served at this period and later to encourage and multiply pilgrimages to the Holy Land, was the desire of obtaining the relics of saints and holy persons ; among which not a few were alleged to have appertained to our Saviour himself. About this time the bones and other remains, especial-

---

[1] Acta Sanctor. Mart. Tom. II. p. 157. Possibly this hospital or that of Justinian may have been the edifice still used by the Muslims as a hospital, where food is daily distributed to the poor. It is called by the Franks the Kitchen of Helena, and is situated on the street in which we resided, running down eastward below the church of the Holy Sepulchre. Its portal, if I remember right, exhibits an architecture of the Byzantine type. See

Turner's Tour in the Levant, II. p. 268. Schubert's Reise, II. p. 585. The Arabic name is et-Tekiyeh.

[2] Muratori Antiq. Ital. med. ævi, Tom. III. p. 575. Acta Sanctor. Mart. T. II. p. 298. Wilken Gesch. der Kreuzz. I. p. 10.

[3] Gregor. Turonensis, 5. 5. Wilken Gesch. der Kreuzzüge, I. p. 17.

[4] Gregor. Tur. 7. 29.

[5] Greg. Tur. 4. 38. Wilken l. c. pp. 17, 18.

ii. 30-32

ly of those who had suffered martyrdom, became an object of idolatrous veneration. Churches and convents held it to be necessary to possess (if possible) the skeletons or other memorials of their patron saints; or at least those of other saints of holy renown; in order to increase their own authority and consideration with the people. Among the laity too, the most sacred oath was that taken upon the relics of a saint; and the possession of a relic was regarded as a protection against every species of evil.[1] Hence such relics were sought for with avidity, and purchased at a high price. They were indeed to be found in great numbers in the west; for the saints of France and Spain, and especially those of Italy, did not fail to leave behind them memorials possessing a wonder-working power. Yet relics from the Holy Land enjoyed nevertheless the pre-eminence; and those churches and convents were especially venerated, which could boast of possessing some relic of the Saviour or of his cotemporary followers.[2] The shrewdness of the oriental clergy was not slow to take advantage of this superstition; and the pilgrims who sought in Jerusalem and elsewhere for relics, were seldom necessitated to seek in vain. The common people at length manufactured them according to the demand;[3] although, in practising this fraud, they did not go beyond that of the priests both of the east and the west, in distributing to all the world pieces of the true cross.[4]—These relics from Palestine were sold in the west to clergy and laity at a high profit; and thus a pilgrimage to Jerusalem often became a source, not only of spiritual renown, but also of emolument. So profitable, indeed, did this trade in relics become, that Syrian merchants repaired with them to Europe for sale.[5]

Thus had now rolled on the first six centuries after the

---

[1] Capitular. Caroli Magn. lib. VI. c. 209, "Omne sacramentum in ecclesia et super reliquias juretur. . . Sic illum Deus adjuvet et illi Sancti, quorum istæ reliquiæ sunt, ut veritatem dicat." Charlemagne also took relics with him in time of war. So too the Byzantine Greeks. See Wilken, l. c. p. 12. Du Fresne in Villahardouin Hist. de l'Empire de Constantinople, Paris 1657. fol. p. 311-13.

[2] Wilken l. c. p. 12.

[3] Thus in A. D. 1027 a common man in France made a regular trade of such fabricated relics, prepared mostly from the bones of persons recently dead. Several bishops patronized the cheat, and shared the gains. See Rodolph. Glaber, Francor. Hist. 4. 3; in Du Chesne Scriptores Hist. Franc. Tom. IV. Bouquet's Recueil, Tom. X.

[4] The trade in pieces of the true cross ii. 32, 33

commenced very early; for Cyril of Jerus. (c. 350,) mentions that they were already dispersed throughout the world; see above, p. 375, Note 1. The sacred cross was alleged to have an inherent power of reproduction; so that when a portion was taken away, it was again immediately replaced: "In materia insensata vim vivam tenens, ita ex illo tempore innumeris pæne quotidie hominum votis lignum suum commodat, ut detrimenta non sentiat, et quasi intacta permaneat," etc. See Paulin. Nolan. (ll. A. D. 400,) Epist. 11 seu 31. Very many abbeys and convents had portions of the cross to show; see Wilken, l. c. p. 13.—In like manner, Charles the Bald founded a convent in Aquitaine, "in quo posuit præputium Domini Jesu Christi;" Chron. Sithiense ad Ann. 875, in Martene Thesaur. nov. Anecdot. Tom. III.

[5] Gregor. Tur. 8. 31. Wilken, l. c. p. 15.

Christian era. For half of this long period Jerusalem had remained in darkness, beneath the oppressive sway of heathen domination. During the other half, she had again reassumed her station as the Holy City of the Christian world ; and the relations in which she stood towards the west, if not always of the holiest character, were nevertheless such as to excite even in worldly minds a deep interest in her fortunes. Another period of longer and deeper darkness was now about to commence ; and Jerusalem, " the joy of the whole earth," was once more to be trodden down by the barbarian hordes of a false religion, under a thraldom from which even yet she is not emancipated.

The Persians under Chosroes I, had already made inroads upon the Roman empire during the reign of Justinian, and had extended their conquests into the heart of Syria, as far as to Antioch and the shores of the Mediterranean. Under Chosroes II, the war was renewed against the emperor Phocas and his successor Heraclius. The Persians penetrated into Syria ; captured Damascus in A. D. 613 ; and then directed their victorious progress southwards towards Jerusalem. They were joined on the way by the Jews of Tiberias, Nazareth, and the mountains of Galilee. In the month of June, A. D. 614, the Holy City was invested and taken by storm ; many thousands of the clergy, monks, consecrated virgins, and other inhabitants were slain ; the splendid churches were thrown down, and that of the Holy Sepulchre burned with fire ; while the patriarch Zacharias with the true cross, and multitudes of the inhabitants were carried away into captivity.[1]

Many fugitives from Palestine and Syria now retired to Alexandria, where they were cherished by the bounty of the patriarch John Eleemon (the compassionate). This munificent patron also sent large supplies of provisions to the miserable inhabitants who remained in Jerusalem. And when, not long after, Modestus was appointed as the vicar of Zacharias during his exile, the same patriarch furnished him with a large sum of money and a thousand labourers from Egypt, to aid in rebuilding the Holy City and its churches.[2]

Although Palestine and Syria remained under the yoke of

---

[1] The particulars of this siege and its consequences are related by a cotemporary writer in the Chronicon Paschale seu Alexandrinum, p. 385, ed. Paris. Also by Antiochus, at that time abbot of the convent of St. Saba, in Biblioth. vet. Patrum, Tom. I. p. 1023 sq. Later writers are : Theophanes Chronographia, p. 252, ed. Paris. Eutychii Annal. II. p. 213. Comp. le Quien Oriens Christ. III. p. 250 sq.— Theophanes gives the number of the slain at ninety thousand ; and Eutychius ascribes the slaughter to the Jews. The Saracens or Arabs would appear also to have acted with the Persians ; they plundered the monastery of St. Saba, and massacred forty-four of the monks. Antiochus, l. c. Le Quien III. p. 252.

[2] See the life of St. John Eleemon by Leontius, a cotemporary Cyprian bishop ; Lat. in Acta Sanctor. Jan. Tom. II. p. 500. Le Quien III. p. 250 sq.

the Persians, yet Modestus appears not to have been hindered
in the work of restoration. He proceeded to build up again
from their foundations the churches of the Resurrection and of
Calvary, as also a church of the Assumption.[1] Whether in doing
this he changed the form of the buildings around the Holy Sepulchre, we are not told ; but the description of Arculfus, as
given by Adamnanus at the close of the century, seems not to
tally with the accounts of Eusebius. According to him, the
Holy Selpulchre was covered by a small *tegorium* (tugurium ?)
cut from the same rock, and standing in the midst of a large
circular church constructed over it.[2] The Basilica or Martyrion
of Constantine was situated as before. Adamnanus further describes a church of Golgotha between the Basilica and the sepulchre ; but this is not mentioned by Bernhard two centuries
later.[3] Both these writers however speak of a church of St.
Mary, adjacent to the buildings of the sepulchre on the south ;
and this is not improbably the church of the Assumption restored by Modestus.

After years of discomfiture and disaster, the tide of victory
turned at length in favour of Heraclius. He routed the armies
of the Persians, put their monarch to flight, and pursued them
into their own territory. Early in A. D. 628, Chosroes was deposed and murdered by his son Siroes ; who immediately concluded an inglorious peace with the Roman emperor. The patriarch Zacharias and other captives were restored after fourteen
years of exile, and the true cross was given up. The emperor
returned first to Constantinople, where he made a triumphal
entry ; and in the following year repaired in person to Jerusalem, which he entered on foot, bearing the true cross upon his
shoulder.[4]

But the restoration of the Holy City to the dominion of the
Christians, was not of long duration. Jerusalem had indeed
been freed from the yoke of the disciples of Zoroaster ; but only
in order to be speedily subjected to the more galling and permanent bondage of the followers of Muhammed. The arms of
the false prophet and his companions had already subdued Arabia, Syria, and Egypt ; and in A. D. 636 the troops of the Khalif Omar appeared before Jerusalem. The city was bravely de-

---

[1] Antiochi Epist. in Biblioth. vet. Patr.
Græc. Tom. I. p. 1023 sq. Le Quien l. c.
p. 259. Baron. Annal. A. D. 616. vi.—
Antiochus describes Modestus as a second
Bezaleel, or at least a Zerubbabel.

[2] "Valde grandis ecclesia . . . . . super
illud constructa;" Adamn. 1. 2.

[3] See the description and plan of Adamnanus, 1. 2 sq. Bernhard de Locis Sanct.
10.
:: 25 26

[4] Chron. Paschal. p. 398 sq. ed. Paris.
Theophan. Chronogr. p. 273, ed Paris.
Baronii Annal. A. D. 628. i, ii. Le Quien
l. c. p. 257.—In A. D. 634, Heraclius retiring before the Muhammedans, carried
with him the true cross to Constantinople,
where it was seen and described by Arculfus at the close of the century. Theophan.
Chronogr. p. 280. Adamnan. de Loc.
Sanct. 3. 3.

fended by the patriarch Sophronius. After a long siege,[1] the Khalif himself repaired to the camp ; and the patriarch at length surrendered to him the Holy City in A. D. 637, on condition that the inhabitants should be secured as to their lives, their families, their property, and their churches. The latter were neither to be destroyed nor appropriated to the Muhammedans. The gates were opened ; and Omar entered in a garment of camel's hair, the common apparel of his countrymen. He was not very cordially received by the patriarch ; who, on seeing him in this garb, exclaimed : "This is of a truth the abomination of desolation spoken of by Daniel the prophet, standing in the holy place !"[2] The Khalif honourably fulfilled his promises ; and performed his devotions only on the steps of the Basilica ; in order that his followers might have no pretext to claim possession of the church after his departure, under the pretence that he had worshipped in it.[3] The further proceedings of Omar and his successors in erecting a mosk upon the site of the Jewish temple, have already been narrated.[4]

From this time onward until the era of the crusades, a period of four and a half centuries, the history of Jerusalem again presents little more than a blank. A few scattered notices drawn from the itineraries of pilgrims and the cotemporary works of European authors, with the traditions recorded by later oriental writers, furnish all the materials which exist for such a history ; and. strange as it may appear, even these have never yet been fully collected and arranged.[5] The names of the successive patriarchs are indeed preserved ; but the chronicle of their lives illustrates the progress of theological controversy, rather than the history of Jerusalem.[6] We can here, of course, only touch upon some of the principal events.

The remainder of the seventh century, as well as the greater portion of the eighth, is barren of incidents relating to Jerusalem. The Muslims extended their conquests ; subdued the

---

[1] Christian writers say the siege continued two years; Arabian writers, four months.

[2] In allusion to Matth. 23, 15. Theophanes Chronograph. p. 281, ed. Par.

[3] The earliest writers who describe these events are Theophanes l. c. and Eutychius Annal. II. p. 284 sq. The former lived apparently nearly or quite two centuries after the event ; and the latter about A. D. 870. The Arabian writers Elmacin (el-Makin), Abulfeda and Abulfaragius (Bar Hebræus), who give still more particulars, are all of the thirteenth century.

[4] See above, pp. 297, 298.

[5] The notices of Jerusalem during this period are best given by Wilken (whom I

have in part followed) in his introduction ; Gesch. der Kreuzz. I. p. 1 sq. See also Michaud Hist. des Croisades, Tom. I The work of Gibbon contains some of these notices. Witsius in his professed history of Jerusalem utterly passes over this whole period ; Miscell. Sac. Tom. II. Exerc. XII. 40, 41.—William of Tyre wrote a work entitled *de Gestis orientalium Principum*, covering the time from the conquest of Jerusalem to the era of the crusades ; but it is unfortunately lost. Will. Tyr. 1. 3, fin.

[6] See Pappebroch Patriarchar. Hieros. Hist. chronol. prefixed to the Acta Sanctor. Maii Tom. III. Le Quien Oriens Christ. III. pp. 280-500.

northern coast of Africa and the kingdom of Spain ; and threatened to advance into France and Italy.　Meanwhile the Christian pilgrims to Palestine resumed their wonted course, apparently in peace ; and the Holy City, which the Arabians also called el-Kuds (the Holy), became likewise a place of pilgrimage for the Muhammedans.[1]　These pilgrimages were still connected with the spirit of trade.　Arculfus, who visited Jerusalem about A. D. 697, relates that a fair was held there annually on the fifteenth day of September, which was attended by an innumerable multitude from every quarter, for the purposes of mutual traffic and intercourse.[2]

Towards the middle of the eighth century, the sceptre of the Khalifs, after a long and bloody struggle, was transferred from the race of the Ommiades to that of the Abassides.[3]　About A. D. 750, Almansor (el-Mansûr), the second of his race, founded the city of Bagdad, and removed the seat of the Khalifate from Damascus to his new capital on the banks of the Tigris.　During this century, earthquakes were frequent in Syria and Palestine.[4] The situation also of the Christians in the east appears to have become more difficult and less secure.　Patriarchs and bishops were deposed and driven from their homes, at the caprice of their Muhammedan rulers ; and exactions and oppressions were the natural consequence of the existing relations of society.[5]　Yet the pilgrims from the west seem in general to have been looked upon with favour ; and they seldom suffered harm in their persons or hindrance in their pursuits.　Among them at this period was St. Madelveus, bishop of Verdun in France, who made a strong impression upon the patriarch Eusebius by his piety and fervent devotion.[6]　About A. D. 786, St. Willibald, bishop of Eichstädt, with seven companions, made the pilgrimage to the Holy Land, which they traversed in all directions ; visiting Jerusalem no less than four times, and Emesa and Damascus twice. They first passed through Emesa (Hums) on their way to Jerusalem ; and the inhabitants, not being accustomed to the sight of pilgrims, and ignorant whence they came, wondered at their

---

[1] Eutych. Annal. II. p. 364.　D'Herbelot Biblioth. Or. art. *Cods.*

[2] Adamnan. de Locis Sanct. I. 1.

[3] The general history of this change may be seen in Gibbon, Chap. LII.

[4] Violent earthquakes, which destroyed churches, convents, and even whole cities, are mentioned by Theophanes in A. D. 746, 749, 756.　Chronogr. pp. 354, 357, 361, ed. Paris.

[5] So the patriarchs of Antioch and Jerusalem ; Elmacin Hist. Sarac. lib. I. 17. p. 82. Lugd. Bat. 1625.　See too the letter of the Syrian monks to the second council of Nicea, A. D. 787, in Labb. Concil. Tom. VII. p. 170 sq.　Le Quien Or. Christ. III. p. 297 sq. 304.　Also Acta Sanctorum, Jul. Tom. III. pp. 531, 537, 551.—In A. D. 757, the Khalif increased the tribute, stripped the churches, and compelled the Jews to purchase the spoils; Theophan. Chronogr. p. 361, ed Paris.

[6] St. Madelveus was made bishop in A. D. 753, and died about A. D. 776.　See the Chron. Virdunense by Hugo Flaviniacensis, in Labb. Nov. Bibiloth. Manuscr. Tom. I. p. 110 sq.　Le Quien l. c. p. 300 sq.　Acta Sanctor. Oct. Tom. II.

strange appearance, and regarded them as spies. They were brought before a wealthy Sheikh to be examined ; who after inquiry, said : "I have often seen men from their part of the world ; they seek no harm, and only wish to fulfil their law." Yet they were kept for some time in prison, though treated with great courtesy ; until, through the influence of a Spaniard, the Emir of the city ordered them to be set at liberty.[1]

Just at the close of the same century, a furious civil war raged in Palestine among the various tribes of Saracens or Arabs inhabiting the country. In A. D. 796 the monastery of St. Saba was again pillaged and many of the monks slain. The fortunes of the war also laid waste the cities of Gaza, Askelon, and Sariphæa, and converted Eleutheropolis into a desert.[2]

In the latter part of the eighth and the beginning of the ninth century, amid the general darkness of those ages, it is interesting to meet with two cotemporary monarchs, lords of the Orient and Occident, who both exerted a mighty influence upon their respective quarters of the globe, and are still the heroes of many a romantic tale, and landmarks in the history of the world. In the east, Hârûn er-Rashid (Aaron the Just), who swayed the sceptre from A. D. 786 to 809, is celebrated as the ideal of Arabian justice, magnanimity, and splendour ; and procured for the empire of the Khalifs a renown, both in learning and in arms, unequalled in its previous or later history. In the west, Charlemagne was the sagacious founder of a new and still more powerful empire, which he governed with equal wisdom and justice for the long period of some forty years ; having reigned from A. D. 771 to A. D. 814. The interjacent position of the Byzantine empire, prevented these two sovereigns from becoming rivals or enemies ; and there was too much of nobleness in the character of both, not to awaken a mutual sentiment of respect and good will.

Another motive also prompted the monarch of the west to set on foot and cultivate an interchange of courtesies and friendship. His compassion for Christians in poverty and suffering was not confined to the wide limits of his own realms ; but was likewise awakened for those languishing under the oppression of the followers of the false prophet, both in Africa and Asia.[3] The situation of the Holy Land could not, of course, but excite his sympathy. He sent ambassadors to distribute alms in the Holy City ; and they were also charged with presents and a message to the Khalif, to intercede with him in behalf of

[1] St. Willibaldi Hodœporicon, in Mabillon Acta Sanct. Ord. Benedict. Sæc. III. P. II. p. 373.

[2] See the account of these civil wars and massacres, by Stephen, a cotemporary monk of St. Saba, in Acta Sanctor. Mart. Tom. III. p. 167 sq. Le Quien l. c. p. 313.

[3] Eginhardi Vita Car. Magni VIII vel XVI.

his Christian subjects.   Hârûn received the messengers with
courtesy ; immediately granted all their requests ; and even went
so far as to make over to Charlemagne the jurisdiction of the
Holy Sepulchre and its appurtenances.[1]   The ambassadors on
their return were accompanied by those of the Khalif, bringing
rich presents of vestments and spices and the choicest products
of the eastern world ; and bearing to the emperor the keys of the
Holy Sepulchre and of Calvary, as the symbol of possession.   A
few years before, the Khalif, at the emperor's request, had sent
him the only elephant he happened to possess.[2]   Indeed, so strong
was the mutual admiration of the two monarchs, that according
to Eginhard, the biographer of Charlemagne, this emperor preferred the friendship of Hârûn to that of all the kings and princes of the world ; and regarded him alone as worthy to be distinguished with honours and magnificence.[3]   To the end of his
life Charlemagne continued to send alms to the Christians in
Jerusalem, in aid of the poor and for the rebuilding of churches;
and his example was followed by his son Lewis the Pious, and
by his grandson Lewis the German.[4]

These of course were palmy days of pilgrimage ; but after the
death of Hârûn er-Rashîd the prospect was again clouded.   The
dissensions among his sons spread also through the provinces ;
the people were divided into factions ; and each party rejoiced in
the opportunity to wreak its fury on the Christians.   The Holy
City did not escape the storm ; churches were destroyed and convents pillaged ; and among the latter, the monastery of St. Saba,
which seems ever to have been a special object of vengeance, was
again plundered and the monks massacred in A. D. 812.[5]

The remainder of the ninth century presents no important
incident in the history of Jerusalem, save the visit and Itinerary
of the monk Bernhard and his two companions, about A. D.
870.[6]   His account is very brief ; but the description of the Holy

---

[1] " Sed etiam sacrum illum et salutarem
locum, ut illius potestati ascriberetur, con-
cessit ;"   Eginh. l. c. v.

[2] Eginhardi Vita Car. Magni v.   The
presents of the Khalif are described in the
Annales Mettenses ad Ann. 807, in Bouquet's Recueil des Hist. Fr. Tom. V. p. 354.
The elephant arrived in A. D. 802 ; Annal.
Loiseliani ad h. Ann. in Duchesne Tom.
II. p. 24 sq.   The keys are sometimes
said to have been sent by the patriarch of
Jerusalem ; but as Eginhard expressly
says, that the Holy Sepulchre was made
over to Charlemagne by the Khalif, the
keys were also probably sent by his order.
See generally, Le Quien Oriens Christ. III.
p. 318 sq. 346.

[3] " Cum Aaron . . . . . . talem habuit
in amicitiæ concordiam, ut is gratiam ejus
ii. 41. 42

omnium qui in toto orbe terrarum erant
Regum ac Principum amicitiæ praeponeret,"
etc.   Eginhard l. c.

[4] So late as A. D. 810, there is a Capitu-
larium of Charlemagne entitled :   " De
eleemosyna mittenda ad Hierosolymas,
propter ecclesias Dei restituandas."   Capit.
I. Ann. 810. c. 17.   Monach. Sangall. II.
c. 14.   Wilken l. c. p. 27.—For the later
legend, which relates that Charlemagne
himself repaired to Palestine, see Wilken
l. c. I. Anh. p. 3.

[5] Theophanes Chronogr. p. 409. ed.
Paris.   Baronii Annal. A. D. 812. xt.

[6] The writer was cotemporary with pope
Nicholas I, who died A. D. 867 ; and with
Theodosius, who was patriarch of Jerusa-
lem from A. D. 867 to A. D. 879.

Sepulchre and its appurtenances is quite distinct. He speaks indeed of four churches round about it, though he enumerates only three, viz. that of the Sepulchre itself upon the west, that of St. Mary on the south, and the Basilica on the east, forming three sides of an open court, and all connected by walls. Adjacent to the church of St. Mary, there was already a hospital, in which all the Latin pilgrims were received. This traveller is the first to mention the jugglery of the Greek holy fire; and he also speaks of a library founded by Charlemagne in the church of St. Mary.

The renown of the house of the Abassides lingered long in its decay. The munificence of Almamon (el-Mamûn) the son and second of the successors of Hârûn, who held the sceptre for thirty years (A. D. 813–843), and the patronage which he gave to learning, sustained for a time the waning glory of his race. Under him the Christians still enjoyed favours, and were found among his officers of trust and the attendants of his person.[1] But his successors held the reins of empire with a feeble hand; the various provinces were distracted with feuds and bloody wars; and the Christian subjects became every day more and more exposed to violence and oppression. The empire was torn with dissensions; and the Holy Land was again made the scene of battles and bloodshed, during the long wars waged by the Khalifs, either against the various factions and revolted governors of cities, or against new heretical sects, which strove to propagate their tenets by the sword.[2] One province after another was thus wrested from the sway of the Khalifs. At length in A. D. 969, Mu'ez, of the race of the Fatimites, whose ancestors for sixty years had reigned as Khalifs at Kairwân (Cyrene) over a great part of Africa, extended his conquests throughout Egypt and Syria, and transferred the seat of his empire to the new city of Musr el-Kâhirah, the present Cairo.

The Holy City had now fallen into the hands of new masters, who were inclined to pay little regard to the stipulations or usages which had found place under the former dynasties. The church of the Holy Sepulchre is said again to have been set on fire; and the patriarch John was committed to the flames.[3] The Christians were subjected to new oppressions and afflictions; against which they would seem to have complained bitterly to their brethren of the west. A letter of the pope Sylvester II,

---

[1] Eutychii Annal. II. pp. 431, 432.

[2] See a sketch of some of these wars and factions in Gibbon, Chap. LII. More fully in Desguignes Hist. des Huns, Tom. II. De Sacy, Exposé de la Réligion des Druzes, Tom. I. Introd.—The Karmathiaus were a new and powerful religious sect, A. D. 890. Syria and Egypt were twice dismembered from the empire, first by the Tulunides, A. D. 868; and then by the Ikshides, A. D. 934.

[3] Cedreni Histor. Compend. p. 661. ed. Par. Le Quien l. c. p. 466.

(A. D. 999–1003,) is still extant, intended to rouse the western church to active sympathy in behalf of her oriental sister.[1] The ships of Pisa actually made descents upon the African coasts; and not improbably, the necessity of a general war against the followers of the prophet and in behalf of the Holy Land, had already begun to occupy the minds of men.[2]

Yet in the oppression of the Egyptian Khalifs there was a pause; and the Christians of the Holy Land, either from a habit of suffering or the policy of their oppressors, obtained a breathing-spell.[3] The pilgrims from the west, and especially the western merchants, were not unwelcome guests; for the tolls and exactions to which they were subjected, contributed to fill the coffers of the Muslim rulers. The merchants of Amalfi in Italy were particularly favoured; and were able to purchase many commercial privileges. As they often visited the Holy City in their peregrinations, they obtained from the Khalif permission to erect there a domicile, which they might call their own. They accordingly founded a monastery with a church in honour of the Virgin, at the distance of a stone's throw from the Holy Sepulchre, in which all the services were performed in the Latin tongue; and which, for this reason, took the name of *St. Mary de Latina.* Adjacent to this a nunnery was not long afterwards erected, in honour of Mary Magdalene; in which the nuns devoted themselves to the care of the poor female pilgrims. But as even in those perilous times the numbers and the need of pilgrims continued to increase, so that even both these convents were insufficient to receive them, the monks procured a Xenodochium or hospital to be built within the same precincts, in which the poor and the sick found a shelter, and were fed from the fragments of the monastic tables. This hospital was dedicated to St. John Eleemon, the former patriarch of Alexandria; and in it, at a later period, arose the celebrated order of the Hospitalers, or knights of St. John of Jerusalem.[4]

The third of the Fatimite Khalifs in Egypt was el-Hâkim,

Mabillon refers this letter to A. D. 986; Acta Sanctor. Ord. Bened. T. IV. p. 39. It has often been printed; e. g. in Bouquet's Recueil T. X. p. 426. The genuineness of the letter is doubted; but not the fact of such an appeal. Wilken l. c. p. 28.

[2] Wilken l. c. p. 29.

[3] Will. Tyr. l. 4, "Sub quo principatu [Egyptiorum], sicut captivis solent aliquando tempora indulgentiora concedi, a suis anxietatibus coepit aliquantulum esse remissius," etc.

[4] The founding of the church and monastery of St. Mary de Latina by the merchants of Amalfi, is related two centuries after by William of Tyre, 18. 4, 5; and by Jacob de Vitr. c. 64. But a church of St. Mary is mentioned in the same place by Adamnanus, A. D. 697; and in Bernhard's time, A. D. 870, the same church was still in existence, and also a hospital for Latin pilgrims. Not improbably these may have been destroyed at the capture of Jerusalem under Mu'ez, and again rebuilt by merchants of Amalfi. This may perhaps be the destruction of buildings around the Holy Sepulchre, which is mentioned by Cedrenus as above quoted; see N. 3 on preceding page.

ii. 44, 45

who mounted the throne at the age of eleven years in A. D. 996. He became a wild and visionary fanatic, who gave himself out as the prophet of a new religion; and his whole reign was a series of violence and inconsistencies.[1] By Arabian writers he is described as a compound of atheism and insanity.[2] About A. D. 1010, prompted by suspicion or some motive equally unworthy, he became jealous of the Christians who had hitherto enjoyed tranquillity and even honours under his reign,[3] and set on foot a furious persecution against them both in Egypt and Palestine. Disregarding the claims of usage and the concessions of his predecessors, he imposed upon his Christian subjects and upon the pilgrims enormous contributions and taxes; and forbade the celebration of the Christian worship in the churches. But this was not all. The houses of Christians were broken open, and the inmates hurried off, without accusation or trial, to death by the cross and by impalement. Sons and daughters were torn from the houses of their parents, and compelled, sometimes by the bastinado and sometimes by blandishments, to apostatize from their faith, or were delivered to the cross. No one was secure in his property or life; the former was confiscated and plundered at will. To crown this exhibition of hatred towards the Christian name, the Khalif gave orders to demolish the church of the Holy Sepulchre; and this order was fully carried into execution by the governor of Ramleh, to whom it was directed. The building was razed to the foundations; and much labour was expended to deface and destroy the sepulchre itself.[4]

The news of these atrocities was carried by the pilgrims to Europe; and awakened universal indignation and grief.[5] Yet instead of combining to take vengeance on the direct authors of these calamities, a report was spread abroad that the Jews had been the cause of this persecution, by secretly informing the Khalif of a proposed warlike expedition against Jerusalem;

---

[1] This Khalif el-Hâkim, is regarded as the prophet of the Druzes. He built a mosk in Cairo, which is still standing; and in an inscription over one of the doors, bearing date in A. H. 393, (A. D. 1003,) he is already treated as a prophet. See Wilkinson's Thebes, etc. p. 547, ed. 1. Gibbon, Chap. LVII.

[2] Elmacin Hist. Saracen. 3. 6. p. 260.

[3] Christians even enjoyed the office of Vizier; Bar Hebr. Chron. Syr. p. 211.

[4] " Prædicta ecclesia usque ad solum diruta," are the words of William of Tyre. The above description is drawn chiefly from this writer; lib. I. c. 4, 5. See also Elmacin lib. III. 5, 6. Ademarus in Labb. Nov. Biblioth. Manuscr. T. II. p. 174; and

in Bouquet T. X. p. 152. Albericus as quoted in le Quien Or. Christ. III. p. 475 sq. Baronii et Pagii Annales, etc. A. D. 1009.—The mother of el-Hâkim was a Christian; her brother Orestes was at this very time patriarch of Jerusalem, and was put to death. The extravagancies of the Khalif had probably been referred to his Christian origin and propensities; and, according to William of Tyre, it was to clear himself from this calumny, that he set on foot this persecution. Will. Tyr. I. 4.

[5] "Eodem anno (1010) Radulphus, Petragoriæ episcopus, Hierosolymis rediens, retulit quæ ibi viderat nefanda;" Chron. Ademari in Labb. Nov. Biblioth. II. p. 174.♦ Bouquet Tom. X. p. 153.

ii. 45, 46

thus instigating him to set on foot the cruel proceedings against the
Christians. The Jews themselves now became the sufferers, and
throughout all France were subjected to violent persecution;
which, if perhaps less bloody than that which it was intended to
avenge, was at least equally unjust.[1] Yet the Khalif himself,
with an inconstancy common to weak and insane minds, afterwards repented of his violence; he allowed the multitudes who had
apostatized from Christianity to return to their former faith; and
gave permission to rebuild the churches which had been destroyed.[2] This concession would seem to have been long inoper-
ative, or at least slowly acted upon; for, although el-Hâkim
died in A. D. 1021, it was not until ten years afterwards, and on
the application of the Greek emperor Romanus, that his successor edh-Dhaher confirmed the permission, so that the rebuilding of the church of the Holy Sepulchre could be commenced.[3]
The successor of Romanus granted aid in the work.[4] Then there
was joy throughout the Christian world; and pilgrims flocked ex-
ulting to Jerusalem, bearing gifts for the restoration of the house
of God.[5] The church of the Sepulchre was completed in A. D.
1048; but instead of the former magnificent Basilica over the
place of Golgotha, a small chapel only now graced the spot.[6]

The increase of pilgrims had indeed become very great; and
it is not improbable that a dread of their power and vengeance,
may have had an influence on the conduct of el-Hâkim and his
successor. A wild idea had prevailed in some minds, that the
Saviour's second coming was to take place in the year 1000;
and others now saw in the disorders of the times a prognostic
of the near approach of Antichrist.[7] Under the influence of
these circumstances, and perhaps of the concessions of the Khalifs, multitudes of all ranks and classes flocked to the Holy City.
It was no longer single pilgrims with staff and scrip, a monk or
an abbot, or even perhaps a bishop with a few companions, who
wended their way to the Promised Land, and were sustained
wholly or in part by the alms of the pious; but henceforth also
the common people and laity in great numbers, and especially
noblemen and princes, often with a large retinue of armed followers, assumed the garb of pilgrims, and found their way into
the east. Even noble ladies did not shrink from the hardships

[1] Rod. Glaber Histor. III. 7; in Bouquet
T. X. Duchesne T. IV. Chron. Ademari,
in Bouquet T. X. p. 152. Le Quien l. c.
pp. 478, 480.
[2] Elmacin Hist. Sarac. 3. 6. p. 260.
Chron. Ademari l. c. Will. Tyr. 1. 6. Bar
Hebr. p. 216.
[3] Will. Tyr. 1. 6. Albericus in le Quien
III. p. 493. Cedrenus, p. 731, ed. Par.
Comp. Baronii et Pagii Annal. A. D. 1031.
ii. 47, 48

[4] Will. Tyr. ibid.
[5] "Tunc quoque de universo terrarum
orbe incredibilis hominum multitudo ex-
ultanter Hierosolymam pergentes, domui
Dei restaurandæ plurima detulerunt mu-
nera." Rod. Glaber 3. 7.
[6] "Oratoria valde modica;" Will. Tyr.
8. 3.
[7] Rod. Glaber. 4. 6.

and dangers of the pilgrimage. Many of the pilgrims desired to find their death in the Holy Land.[1] It was perhaps in order to keep back these throngs, or more probably in order to derive the greater profit from them, that the Muslims about this time demanded of every pilgrim the tribute of a piece of gold, as the price of entrance into the Holy City.[2]

Among the remarkable pilgrimages of this period, was that of Robert duke of Normandy, the father of William the Conqueror, which was undertaken in A. D. 1035, in spite of the remonstrances of his barons.[3] Having settled the succession upon his illegitimate son William, and leaving him under the protection and guardianship of the French king, he set off with a large retinue of knights, barons, and other followers. He himself, like every pilgrim, went barefoot and in palmer's weeds, with staff and scrip. In passing through cities, he sent his train forwards ; himself following alone in the rear in all humility, and bearing patiently the insults of the rabble. He took the way through Italy to Constantinople, where his piety and charity obtained for him the respect of the emperor and the Greek nobles. The former tendered him presents, and forbade his subjects to receive payment for articles furnished to the Norman duke ; but the pilgrim refused the gifts, and ordered his people to pay for every thing. The emperor commanded that no wood should be furnished to him, in order that he might be compelled to receive it free from the royal magazines ; but Robert purchased a large quantity of nuts, the shells of which he used as fuel. During his journey through Asia Minor he fell sick, and caused himself to be transported in a litter by Saracens. Meeting a Norman pilgrim, who was returning home and inquired if he had any message to send : " Tell my people," said he, " that thou hast met me where I was borne of devils into Paradise." Before the gates of Jerusalem Robert found a crowd of needy pilgrims, too poor to pay the entrance money, and awaiting the arrival of some wealthy and generous fellow-pilgrim, who might open for them the Holy City. For each of these he paid a golden byzant. The Muslims admired his devotion and munificence ; and an Emir caused

---

[1] " Anno D. 1033, ex universo orbe tam innumerabilis multitudo cœpit confluere ad Sepulchrum Salvatoris Hierosolymis, quantam nullus hominum prius sperare poterat. Primitus enim ordo inferioris plebis; deinde vero mediocres; posthæc permaximi quique, reges, comites, ac præsules ; ad ultimum vero, quod nunquam contigerat, mulieres multæ nobiles cum pauperioribus illuc perrexit. Pluribus enim erat mentis desiderium mori priusquam ad propria reverterentur." Rod. Glaber, 4. 6.

[2] *Aureus, Bisantium aureum*, a gold Byzant, equivalent to about five Spanish dollars. First mentioned in the *Gesta Consulum Andegavensium*, in d'Achery Spicileg. Tom. III. p. 252. fol. William of Tyre mentions the imposition of the *aureus* in this century, but not the exact time ; Hist. 1. 10.

[3] Described in the cotemporary *Chronique de Normandie*, in Bouquet's Recueil Tom. II. p. 326 sq. Wilken Gesch. der Kr. I. p. 37.

all that he had paid for the pilgrims to be restored to him ; but
Robert immediately distributed it among the poor pilgrims, and
made to the Muslims also costly presents. He died on his way
home, at the city of Nicea ; and the relics that he had collected,
were deposited in the abbey of Cerisy, which he had founded.

About this time the conversion of the Hungarians to Christianity, which took place gradually at the close of the tenth and
in the first half of the eleventh centuries, opened a new route for
pilgrims to the Holy Sepulchre ; since they could now traverse
the whole distance to Constantinople by land, through a Christian
country. One of the first to avail himself of this route, was the
bishop Lietbert of Cambray in A. D. 1054. He was attended by
so great a company of pilgrims, that the party was called "exercitus Domini," the Lord's host. The king of Hungary at first
distrusted the intentions of this numerous body; having been
but little accustomed to the sight of pilgrims ; but he afterwards
treated them with kindness. The pilgrims travelled by land as
far as to Laodicea in Syria ; and then took ship on account of the
insecurity of the country. But being driven back by a storm,
and learning from other pilgrims, that the Christians were then
excluded from the holy places in Jerusalem, and treated with
indignity, the bishop and his companions returned to France.[1]
The same route was followed by Count William of Angouleme,
about A. D. 1062, attended by some of his counsellors, several
abbots, and a large company of noblemen. They too were treated with great courtesy by the king of Hungary, in their passage
through his dominions.[2]

But the most celebrated pilgrimage of this period was that of
several German bishops in A. D. 1065, which is mentioned by
all the chroniclers of that age.[3] The party was composed of
Siegfried, archbishop of Maintz, and the bishops Günther of
Bamberg, Otho of Ratisbon, and William of Utrecht ; followed
by no less than seven thousand persons both rich and poor.
Among these was Ingulphus, the English secretary of William
the Conqueror, who with others joined the party from Normandy,
attracted by the fame of the immense preparations. The bishops
travelled with great pomp ; carrying with them dishes and ves-

---

[1] Vita Dom. Lietberti Episc. Camerac.
in d'Achery's Spicilegium Tom. II. p. 138
sq. c. 29-43. This temporary exclusion of
the Christians from the church of the Holy
Sepulchre is also mentioned in the life of
the cotemporary St. Wulframnus, A. D.
1056, in Acta Sanct. Mart. T. III. p. 157,
fin. Pagii Critica, etc. A. D. 1056. VI.

[2] "Magna caterva nobilium," Chron.
Ademari in Bouquet Tom. X. p. 162. Labb.
nov. Biblioth. T. II.

ii. 50, 51

[3] Most fully in the chronicles of Lam-
bertus Schafnaburgensis and Marianus Sco-
tus, both printed in Pistorii Scriptores Rer.
Germanic. Tom. I. pp. 172, 452, Francof.
1613 ; or Tom. I. pp. 332, 651, ed. Struve.
Likewise by Ingulphus, who was himself
among the pilgrims, in his History ; see
Scriptores Rer. Angl. ed. Fell. p. 73. ed.
Savill. p. 513. See also Baronii Annal. A.
D. 1064. XLIII-LVI.

sels of gold and silver, and also costly tapestry, which was hung up around their seats whenever they made a halt.[1] Bishop Günther of Bamberg, was celebrated for his personal beauty, as well as for his talents and learning; so that wherever the pilgrims came, a crowd ran together to get a sight of the handsome bishop; and made sometimes so much disturbance, that his companions had to urge him to show himself to the people. They set off in the autumn of A. D. 1064, taking the route through Hungary to Constantinople; and reached Syria in safety. But the rumour of their wealth and the pomp with which they travelled, had preceded them, and excited the cupidity of the wandering predatory hordes with which Palestine has ever been infested. On the day before Easter they were attacked by a large body of these Arabs in the vicinity of Ramleh; and after losing many of their companions, were compelled to take refuge in a neighbouring village, where was a decayed castle or place enclosed by a wall, in which they could defend themselves, and where they were besieged by the Arabs.[2]

On the third day, exhausted by hunger and thirst, they made known their readiness to capitulate. The chief Sheikh with sixteen others was admitted into the castle; but rejected all proposals for the purchase of their freedom and safe escort, and would hear of nothing but an unconditional surrender. Unwinding his turban and making with it a noose, he threw it around the neck of bishop Günther, exclaiming that he was his property, and he would suck his blood and hang him up like a dog before the door. The bishop felled him to the earth with a blow; the Sheikh and his followers were seized and bound; and the pilgrims, elated by this turn of affairs, continued the contest with renewed vigour. The prisoners were exposed upon the walls, where the combat was hottest and the shower of arrows thickest; and a person with a drawn sword was stationed by each, threatening to cut off his head, if the Arabs did not cease from the attack. The son of the chief Sheikh now held back his followers, in order to save his father's life; and meantime the governor of Ramleh came up with a force in aid of the pilgrims; at whose approach the Arabs fled. The prisoners were delivered over to the governor; and he recognised with pleasure in the Sheikh a rebel chief, who had for many years given great trouble to the Egyptian Khalif, and several times defeated the forces sent against him. The

---

[1] "Ubi episcopi sedebant, dorsalia pallia pendebant; scutellas et vasa aurea et argentea portabant;" Mar. Scot.

[2] "Quoddam castellum nomine Carvasalina;" Mar. Scot. Lambert of Aschaffenburg speaks only of a village and a "maceria" just ready to tumble down of itself. The pilgrims held this place to be Capernaum, from the supposed similarity of the name. A closer analogy is supplied by the ancient name Capharsaluma (Καφαρσαλαμά), which Josephus describes as a village in or near Judea. 1 Macc. 7, 31. Joseph Antiq. 12. 10. 4.

ii. 51–53

governor now caused the pilgrims to be escorted in safety to Jerusalem, and back again to the sea ; receiving for his civility and aid a present of five hundred gold byzants. But of the original host of seven thousand pilgrims, only two thousand lived to return to their native land ; and the bishop Günther also died on the way back in Hungary. Ingulphus and others returned through Italy ; and he observes of his own companions, " that they sallied from Normandy, thirty stout and well appointed horsemen ; but that they repassed the Alps, twenty miserable palmers, with the staff in their hand, and the wallet at their backs."[1]

But another revolution was now impending over Syria, still more disastrous in its immediate consequences to the Christians of the east ; and destined to kindle up at last those holy wars, which for nearly two centuries deluged the soil of Palestine with the choicest blood of Europe.

Ever since the conquest of Syria by the Fatimite Khalifs of Egypt in A. D. 969, the dynasty of the Abassides had still continued nominally to reign at Bagdad, in the possession of a mere shadow of honour and power ; while their chief commanders, under the title of Emîr el-Omara, ruled with unlimited authority both the Khalif and his realms. This high post had now been held for a century by the race of the Buides,[2] when the Turkish or Turkman leader Togrul Beg, of the family of Seljûk, came with a large army from Khorasan to Bagdad, and extended his conquests to the Euphrates. This conqueror drove the Buides from the post of Emir el-Omara, which he took upon himself ; deprived the Khalif of even the remaining shadow of temporal power ; and reigned as Sultan over all the lands of the Khalifat. His nephew, Alp Arslan, penetrated into Asia Minor as far as to Iconium ; took prisoner in battle the Greek emperor Romanus Diogenes in A. D. 1071 ; and carried consternation to the gates of Constantinople. He was succeeded in A. D. 1072 by his son Melek Shah ; who, following out the rude feudal system of the Turkmans, bestowed on his kinsman Suleimân, Asia Minor and the adjacent countries west of the Euphrates, which he was to conquer and hold as a fief under the Sultan of Bagdad. Suleimân was successful in his operations, and established in A. D. 1073 the Seljûk kingdom and dynasty of Rûm, extending from the Euphrates to the shores of the Bosphorus, and having its metropolis first at Nicea, and afterwards at Iconium.[3]

While Suleimân was thus establishing his dominion in Asia Minor, Melek Shah despatched another of his generals, Atsiz the

[1] This is Gibbon's pompous paraphrase of the simpler language of Ingulphus : " Et tandem de triginta equitibus, qui de Northumannia pingues exivimus, vix viginti pauperes peregrini et omnes pedites macie   multi attenuati reversi sumus." Ingulph. l c.
[2] Deguignes Hist. des Huns, T. I. i. p. 406. II. i. pp. 168, 170.
[3] Deguignes, l. c. lib. XI.
ii 53 54

Kharismian, to make war upon the Syrian possessions of the Egyptian Khalif. He took the city of Damascus after a long siege in A. D. 1075 ; the inhabitants having been compelled to surrender by famine. During the two following years he subdued the greater part of Syria, marched against Egypt, and penetrated almost to Cairo. The Khalif trembled and fled by night ; but his people rallied, defeated the invader, and drove him back upon Syria. Atsiz retired to Damascus, taking the route by Ramleh and Jerusalem, which he pillaged, A. D. 1077.[1] In consequence of this defeat, Melek Shah now bestowed the Syrian provinces as a fief upon his brother Tutush ; who in A. D. 1078 laid siege to Aleppo ; got possession of Damascus by treachery ; and carrying his victorious arms from Antioch to the borders of Egypt, established the Seljûk kingdom of Syria or Aleppo ; which he held under the nominal sovereignty of his brother, the Sultan of Bagdad.[2]

Following out the same system of feudal reward, these Turkman leaders bestowed also upon their officers the hereditary command, or rather the property, of particular cities and districts, as a recompense for the services of themselves and their followers. In this way, in A. D. 1083 or 1084, the Holy City was made over by Tutush to his general Ortok, the chief of a Turkman horde serving under his banner. This chieftain continued to hold the city as Emír of Jerusalem until his death in A. D. 1091 ; when it passed into the hands of his two sons, Ilghâzy and Sukmân.[3]

The permanent approach of the savage Turkman hordes to the shores of the Bosphorus, spread dismay not only among the Christians of the Byzantine empire, but also throughout Europe. The Greek emperor wrote letters to the western Christians, imploring their aid against the terrific progress of the Turks.[4] The impetuous Hildebrand, as pope Gregory VII, for a time took up the cause of his eastern brethren ; and in A. D. 1074 wrote letters exhorting the western church in general, and also individuals, to take arms in behalf of the emperor and the churches of the east. He even held out the hope, that he himself would bear them company in this holy expedition.[5] But his attention was soon divert-

---

[1] Deguignes, Tom. II. p. 216.—William of Tyre affirms that Jerusalem was subject to the Turks for thirty-eight years; which would give A. D. 1060 or 1061, for the time of their first conquest; Hist. l. 6. ib. 7. 19. This must at any rate be an error; for in the year 1065, when the pilgrim bishops visited the Holy City, it was still under the Egyptian Khalif.

[2] Deguignes, lib. XII.—A summary and chronology of all the four or five Seljûk dynasties, is given by Deguignes, Tom. I. i. p. 241 sq.

[3] Abulfedæ Annales, ed. Adler, Tom. III. pp. 260, 280; comp. p. 253. Deguignes Hist. des Huns, Tom. II. ii. p. 134.

[4] One of these letters is preserved by Guibert "verbis tamen vestita meis," as he frankly says; Guibert Abbot. Hist. Hieros, in Gesta Dei, pp. 475, 476.

[5] The general letter is found in Gregor. Epist. lib. II. 37 ; and a particular one to Count William of Burgundy, ibid. I. 46. See, generally, Mansi Collect. Concil. Tom. XX.

ed from the dangers of the east, and absorbed in his own strug-
gles for supremacy over the monarchs of the west. His successor
Victor III, was actuated by similar views; but as the unbelievers
of Africa at this time often ravaged the Italian coasts, he first
turned the vengeance of the Christians against them. In A. D.
1086 he caused a crusade to be preached in Italy against the African Muslims, promising to all who should take part in it the full
absolution of their sins. A Christian host was collected and proceeded to Africa, under the standard of St. Peter; where it desolated the chief cities of the Arabs, and is said to have destroyed a hundred thousand of the inhabitants. This was a pre-
lude worthy of the approaching crusades in the Holy Land.[1]

The dominion of the Turkmans in Palestine, these fierce sons
of the eastern deserts, could only render the condition of the
Christians and pilgrims still more deplorable. These wild hordes
knew no law and no right, save that of the sword; they neither
knew nor cared for ancient usage nor stipulation; and in their
rage for gain and their rude fanatic zeal for the religion of the
false prophet, they perpetrated every species of cruelty and outrage
against the followers of the cross. In Jerusalem especially, under
the dominion of Ortok and his sons, the native Christians and pilgrims were overwhelmed with insult and driven to extremity.
Troops of these savage oppressors often forced their way into the
churches during divine service; terrified the worshippers by their
wild noise and fury; mounted upon the altars; overturned the
sacred cups; trod under foot the consecrated vessels; broke in
pieces the marble ornaments; maltreated the clergy with contumely and blows; seized the patriarch himself by the hair and
beard, and dragged him from his seat headlong to the ground;
and several times threw him into prison, in order that the Christians might redeem him with large sums of money.[2]

It might be supposed that this state of things, when known in
Europe, would have served to allay the rage for pilgrimage, and
have deterred the Christians of the west from exposing themselves to dangers and contumelies hitherto unparalleled. But the
custom had become too firmly established, and pilgrimages during
this century had been too frequent, to be at once broken off.
Multitudes of pilgrims still flocked to the Holy City; and as the
Turkmans were now more rigorous in exacting the price of
entrance, than the governors of the Egyptian Khalifs formerly
had been, thousands of pilgrims, who had consumed or lost their
all upon the way, were compelled to lie waiting before the gates.
Here many of them died, worn out with famine and nakedness.

[1] Chronicon Casinum auct. Leone Os-
tiensi, in Muratori Scriptores Rerum Itali-
carum, Tom. IV. p. 480.
ii. 56, 57

[2] Will. Tyr. 1. 10. Comp. also the same
writer, 1. 8.

Whether living or dead, the pilgrims were now an intolerable burden to the inhabitants. If admitted into the city, they were the source of continual dread to the Christians, lest by their incautious behaviour they should excite the fury of their oppressors. So great also were their numbers and penury, that the convents and hospitals were unable to receive more than a small part of them ; and the care of the remainder fell upon the citizens. Not one pilgrim in a thousand had the means of self-subsistence.[1] The Christians of the east now repaired to Europe, lamenting their misery and imploring help. The pilgrims who returned, confirmed their accounts, and supported their appeal for aid.[2]

It was in the midst of these calamities, that the celebrated Peter the hermit repaired as a pilgrim to Jerusalem, in A. D. 1093 and 1094.[3] His soul was filled with indignation at the horrors he beheld ; and his spirit roused to vengeance. He reproached the patriarch for his pusillanimity, and exhorted him no longer to submit to such indignities ; but the patriarch had no power to break the chains of oppression, and could only commission Peter to go forth as his ambassador, to awaken the energies of Europe in behalf of their suffering fellow Christians. Peter hastened to Rome ; obtained the ready sanction and support of the pope Urban II ; and traversed Italy and France, proclaiming to high and low the miseries of their brethren in the east, and urging them to arise for the deliverance of the Holy City and to take vengeance on the infidels. His efforts were crowned with wonderful success ;[4] for, as we have seen, the ground was already prepared and the seed sown. The pope urged the cause with all his eloquence at the crowded councils of Placentia and Clermont in A. D. 1095 and 1096 ; and Christian Europe roused itself in frenzy, for a crusade against the oppressors of the Holy Land.

The first host of these pilgrim warriors set off at once by way of Hungary under the guidance of Peter himself ; without preparation, without discipline, and without supplies. After many hardships and much turbulent dissension, they succeeded in reaching Constantinople ; but had hardly set foot on the shores of Asia Minor, when the whole host was annihilated by the Turks. This was in A. D. 1097. A second and better appointed army was already on the way, under leaders of more renown and

---

[1] Will. Tyr. 1. 10.

[2] Baldrici Archiepisc. Hist. Hieros. in Gesta Dei, p. 86. Wilken's Gesch. der. Kr. I. p. 45.

[3] The authorities for the following narrative, are found in all the historians of the crusades.

[4] In such veneration was Peter held by the people at large, that they even plucked hairs from his mule and preserved them as relics; "præsertim cum etiam de ejus mulo pili pro reliquiis raperentur ! " Guibert Abbot. 2. 8, in Gesta Dei.

greater experience. They marched to Constantinople; and
after many hindrances and several battles, succeeded in reaching
Antioch, and encamped before that city on the 18th of October,
A. D. 1097. After a long siege of nearly nine months, they
became masters of the city by treachery, July 3, A. D. 1098.
Scarcely were they in possession, when an immense Muslim host
appeared before the walls, to which they gave battle on the
10th of July, and gained a complete victory. This opened to
them the whole of Syria; and there was now nothing to hinder
their advance upon Jerusalem. But the dissensions and inde-
cision of the princes delayed the impatient warriors still four
months; until at length, on the 24th of November, they broke
up from Antioch, and proceeded on their march for the deliverance of the Holy City.

During the progress of these events, the affairs of Syria and
Palestine had assumed a new aspect. On the death of the
Sultan Melek Shah in A. D. 1092, his brother Tutush of Syria
aspired to the empire of the Seljucides; made war upon his
nephew Borkiaruk the son of Melek Shah; but was defeated
and slain in battle, A. D. 1095.[1] Dissensions arose between his
sons Rûdhwân and Dekak for the succession in Syria; and the
Emirs of the several cities and districts took occasion of the
anarchy, to make themselves for the time independent. Such
was the case with the sons of Ortok in Jerusalem; to which
Rûdhwân unsuccessfully laid siege in A. D. 1096.[2] In like
manner the Fatimite Khalif of Egypt, el-Mustâly, profiting at
length by the distracted state of Syria and the dissensions of
the Seljûk princes, despatched an army into that country under
his vizier Afdal, in order to reduce it again to his own dominion.
Afdal marched through the land; summoned Rûdhwân to
acknowledge the Khalif of Egypt; took possession of Tyre;
and having besieged Jerusalem for forty days, received the
surrender of the city from the inhabitants.[3] The two sons of
Ortok, Ilghâzy and Sukmân, retired to the region of Edessa,
established themselves afterwards at Maredin and Haifa, where
they founded the two dynasties of the Ortocides, which became
famous in the wars of the crusades. The surrender of Jerusalem took place after the famous battle of Antioch.[4] The city

[1] Deguignes Hist. des Huns, T. I. i. p.
247, II. ii. p. 83.

[2] Abulfedæ Annales ad A. H. 488. Deguignes l. c. Tom. I. i. p. 247. II. ii. pp.
84, 85. Kemaleddin in Wilken's Gesch.
der Kr. Bd II. Beyl. p. 28 sq.

[3] Abulfedæ Annal. ad. A. H. 492. Deguignes l. c. T. II. ii. p. 134. I. i. p. 249
sq.

[4] So William of Tyre and Guibert expressly; Will. Tyr. 7, 19. Guib. Abb. 7, 3.
p. 533. The former writer also says that
the Egyptians had been only eleven months
in possession of the city; 9, 10. Yet
Abulfeda places the Egyptian conquest two
years earlier, in A. D. 1096; in which he
is followed by Deguignes, Tom. II. ii. p.
134. See Wilken Comment. de Bell. Cruc.
Hist. pp. 30, 31.

ii. 59, 60

was left in charge of the Emîr Iftikar ed-Daulch ; who had now governed it for eleven months in the name of the Egyptian Khalif, when on the 7th of June, A. D. 1099, the host of the crusaders appeared before its walls.[1]

It is not my province here to recount the events of this siege, nor the history of Jerusalem in general during the crusades. Suffice it to say, that after an investment of nearly forty days, the Holy City was taken by storm on the 15th day of July. Some of the frightful scenes which then ensued I have already had occasion to describe.[2]

After order was restored and the city purified, one of the first cares of the Christian warriors was to establish churches according to the Latin rites and constitution. It was also not long, before convents of Latin monks and nuns sprung up in Jerusalem and in various parts of the country ; and thus the mass of foreign tradition, of which the oriental church had long laid the foundation, was now built up and decorated anew, by the fresher zeal and lore of their western brethren.

The Christians retained Jerusalem for eight and eighty years ; until it was again wrested from their hands by Saladin in A. D. 1187. During this long period they appear to have erected several churches and many convents. Of the latter, few if any traces remain ; of the former, save one or two ruins, the church of the Holy Sepulchre is the only memorial that survives in the Holy City, to attest the power or even the existence of the Christian kingdom of Jerusalem. The crusaders found the buildings connected with the sepulchre as they had been completed in A. D. 1048 ; a round church with an open dome over the sepulchre itself, and a small separate chapel covering Calvary and the other sacred places. These edifices were regarded by the crusaders as too contracted ; and they accordingly erected over and in connection with them a stately temple, inclosing the whole of the sacred precincts ; the walls and general form of which probably remain unto the present day. The grand entrance then, apparently, as now, was from the south.[3]—To the southward of this church, the site of the hospital or palace of the knights of St. John continues to this day unoccupied, an open field in the heart of the city ; where the foundations and a few broken arches alone remain to testify of its former solidity and splendour.

Of the conquest of Jerusalem by Saladin, the subsequent demolition of the walls, the two successive surrenders of it by

---

[1] Deguignes, Tom. II. ii. p. 99. Will. Tyr. 8. 5.
[2] See above, pp. 298, 239.
[3] Will. Tyr. 8. 3. The time when this edifice was erected is not mentioned ; but it appears to have been after A. D. 1103; for Sæwulf, who visited Jerusalem in that year, speaks only of the former church, which some held to be the work of Justinian ! p. 260.

i. 60–62

treaty to the Christians, and its varying fortunes until it finally reverted to the Muhammedans in A. D. 1244, I have already spoken, in tracing the changes which have taken place in the walls of the city.[1] In that year the forces of the Sultan Nijm ed-Dín Eyûb of Egypt, the seventh of the Eyubite dynasty established by Saladin, took possession of the Holy City, after the defeat of the combined forces of the Christians and Syrian Muslims at Gaza. From that time onwards Jerusalem appears to have sunk in political and military importance ; and its name scarcely occurs in the slight histories we have of the two successive Memlûk dynasties, the Baharites and the Circassians or Borgites, who reigned over Egypt and the greater part of Syria during the fourteenth and fifteenth centuries.[2] In all their wars in Syria, the nature of the country led the great and frequent military expeditions between Egypt and Damascus to take the route along the coast and the adjacent plains ; and rarely did a Sultan turn aside to visit the neglected sanctuary in the mountains.[3] The pilgrims and travellers who found their way to Jerusalem during this long period, make no mention of its immediate masters, nor of any military changes.

In A. D. 1517, Jerusalem with the rest of Syria and Egypt passed under the sway of the Ottoman Sultan Selim I ; who paid a hasty visit to the Holy City from Damascus after his return from Egypt.[4] From that time until our own days, Palestine and Syria have continued to form part and parcel of the Ottoman empire. During this period Jerusalem has been subjected to few vicissitudes ; and its history is barren of incident. Suleimân, the successor of Selim, erected its new walls in A. D. 1542 ; and so recently as A. D. 1808, the church of the Holy Sepulchre was partially consumed by conflagration. A fire which commenced in the Armenian chapel on the 12th of October, destroyed the great dome, the Greek chapel, and various other parts, as well as many of the marble columns. The edifice was rebuilt by the Greeks; and after twelve months of labour and an enormous expense, was completed in September A. D. 1810. The funds were collected from the contributions of Christians in various countries. The stranger who now visits this imposing temple, remarks no obvious traces of its recent desolation.[5]

In A. D. 1832, Syria became subject to the dominion of Muhammed Aly, the powerful Pasha of Egypt ; and the Holy City

---

[1] See above, pp. 317, 318.

[2] Deguignes Hist. des Huns, Tom. IV. lib. 21, 22.

[3] Two visits of the Borgite Sultan Sheikh Mahmûd or Abu en-Nâsr, are recorded in A. D. 1414 and 1417. Deguignes, Hist. des Huns, Tom. IV. pp. 310, 313.
ii. 62, 63

[4] v. Hammer Gesch. des Osmanische Reiches, II. p. 526.

[5] Turner's Journal of a Tour in the Levant, Vol. II. p. 165. See also the general account of the fire drawn up in Italian by the Latin monks, Turner ibid. Appendix, p. 597.

opened its gates to the victor without a siege. During the insurrection in the districts of Jerusalem and Nâbulus in A. D. 1834, the Fellâhîn seized upon Jerusalem, and held possession of it for a time; but under the stern energy of the Egyptian government, order was soon restored, and the Holy City returned to its allegiance upon the approach of Ibrahim Pasha with his troops.[1] In 1840 it again reverted to the Sultan.

II. CHURCH OF THE HOLY SEPULCHRE.

The circumstances connected with the discovery of the Holy Sepulchre in the fourth century, and the erection of edifices over and around it under the auspices of Constantine and his mother Helena, have already been detailed.[2] In tracing the further history of the city of Jerusalem, we have also noted some of the changes to which this spot has been exposed. Twice, at least, the church of the Holy Sepulchre appears to have been totally destroyed; once in the seventh and again in the eleventh century; besides the various partial desolations to which it has been subjected.[3] After all the preceding details, topographical and historical, we are now prepared to enter upon the discussion of another question of some interest; I mean the genuineness or probable identity of the site thus ascribed to the Holy Sepulchre.

The place of our Lord's crucifixion, as we are expressly informed, was without the gate of the ancient city, and yet nigh to the city.[4] The sepulchre, we are likewise told, was nigh at hand, in a garden, in the place where Jesus was crucified.[5] It is not therefore without some feeling of wonder, that a stranger, unacquainted with the circumstances, on arriving in Jerusalem at the present day, is pointed to the place of crucifixion and the sepulchre in the midst of the modern city, and both beneath one roof. This latter fact, however unexpected, might occasion less surprise; for the sepulchre was nigh to Calvary. But beneath the same roof are further shown the stone on which the body of our Lord was anointed for burial, the fissure in the rock, the holes in which the crosses stood, the spot where the true cross was found by Helena, and various other places said to have been connected with the history of the crucifixion; most of which it must have been difficult to identify even after the lapse of only three centuries; and particularly so at the present day, after the desolations and numerous changes which the whole place has undergone.

---

[1] See the Report of the Rev. Mr Thomson, etc. Missionary Herald, 1835, pp. 44–51. Marmont's Voyage, etc. Tom. II, III. Mengin's Histoire de l'Egypte, de l'an 1823 à l'an 1838, Paris 1839, p. 73 sq.

[2] See above, p. 372 sq.
[3] See above, pp. 387, 393, 395.
[4] Heb. 13, 12. John 19, 20. The same is also implied in John 19, 17. Matt. 27, 32.
[5] John 19, 41. 42.

The difficulty arising from the present location in the heart
of the city, has been felt by many pious minds, from the days of
St. Willibald and Jacob de Vitry to our own time; but it has
usually been evaded, by assuming that the city was greatly enlarged under Adrian towards the north or west; or, sometimes,
that the ancient city occupied a different site.[1]

The first to take an open stand against the identity of these
holy places, was Korte the German bookseller, who visited Jerusalem in A. D. 1738, at the same time with Pococke.   While
the learned Englishman slightly passes over this topic, entering
into no discussion and expressing no opinion,[2] the honest simplicity of the unlearned German led him to lay before his countrymen a plain account of the impression made upon his own
mind, and his reasons for distrusting the correctness of the common tradition.   Unacquainted with the historical facts, he confines himself solely to a common sense view of the case; and
urges the impossibility that the present site could have been without the ancient city, because of its nearness to the former area
of the Jewish temple.[3]   The reasoning of Korte seems to have
made a considerable impression among the Protestants of the con-
tinent; and is often referred to.[4]   But he had no follower among
the travellers of the last century; though in the present, the
voices of powerful assailants and defenders are heard among both
Catholics and Protestants.   Chateaubriand led the way in a most
plausible defence; and Dr. Clarke, a later writer though an
earlier traveller, followed with a violent attack.   In later years
the parties have been reversed.   Scholz, Catholic professor at
Bonn, declared that the place of the crucifixion cannot have been
where it is now pointed out, because this spot must have been
within the ancient city; though he strangely enough admits the
identity of the sepulchre.[5]   On the other hand, several Protestant travellers and writers take sides with the tradition, and support the genuineness both of the sepulchre and Golgotha.[6]

A true estimate of this long agitated question must depend

---

[1] St. Willibaldi Hodœpor. ed. Mabillon,
p. 375. Jac. de Vitriac. Hist. Hieros. c. 60.
Will. de Baldensel, ed. Canis. p. 348. Monconys was not satisfied with this solution;
Tom. I. p. 307. Quaresmius disposes of
the objections of "nonnullos nebulones oc-
cidentales hæreticos" in a summary way,
but without making any new suggestion,
II. p. 515.—The absurd hypothesis of Dr.
Clarke, which transports Zion across the
valley of Hinnom, serves as the fit basis of
Buckingham's solution; Travels in Pal. pp.
284, 287.

[2] Pococke Descr. of the East, Vol. II. i.
p. 15 sq.

ii. 65, 66

[3] Jonas Kortens Reise, etc. pp. 210, 212.
[4] The work of Plessing, "Ueber Golgotha und Christi Grab," Halle 1789, dis-
cusses the subject on historical grounds in
connection with the report of Korte.   The
author exhibits great diligence, and has
collected many good materials; but they
are wrought up in such a way as to become
' a kernel of wheat in a bushel of chaff.'
[5] Scholz Reise, etc. p. 190. De Gol-
gothæ situ, Bonn 1825. 4.
[6] So Berggren, Buckingham, Elliott II.
p. 449, etc. Also Raumer in his Palästina
p. 267, ed. 3; followed by Schubert, Reise,
etc. II. p. 503 sq.

on two circumstances. As there can be no doubt, that both Golgotha and the sepulchre lay outside of the ancient city, it must first be shown that the present site may also anciently have been without the walls. Or, should this in itself appear to be impossible, then it must be shown, that there were in the fourth century historical or traditional grounds for fixing upon this site, strong enough to counterbalance such an apparent impossibility. The following observations may help to throw some light on both these points.

Our preceding investigations respecting the temple and the ancient walls of Jerusalem, seem to show conclusively, that the modern city occupies only a portion of the ancient site; a part of Zion and a tract upon the north, which were formerly included in the walls, being now left out. The nature of the ground and the traces of the ancient third wall which we found,[1] demonstrate also that the breadth of the city from east to west is the same now as anciently. There can therefore be no question, that the site of the present Holy Sepulchre falls within the ancient city as described by Josephus. But as the third or exterior wall of that writer was not erected until ten or twelve years after the death of Christ,[2] it cannot here be taken into account; and the question still arises, whether the present site of the sepulchre may not have fallen without the *second* or interior wall; in which case all the conditions of the general question would be satisfied.

This second wall, as we have seen, began at the gate of Gennath, near the tower of Hippicus, and ran to the fortress Antonia on the north of the temple.[3] Of the date of its erection we are nowhere informed; but it must probably have been older than the time of Hezekiah, who built within the city a pool, apparently the same which now exists under his name.[4] We have then three points for determining the probable course of this wall; besides the general language of Josephus and the nature of the ground. We repaired personally to each of these three points, in order to examine there this very question; and the first measurement I took in Jerusalem, was the distance from the western side of the area of the temple or great mosk to the church of the Holy Sepulchre. I measured from the western entrance of that area on a direct course along the street by the hospital of Helena, to the street leading north from the bazar; and then from this street to a point in front of the great entrance of the church. The whole distance proved to be 1223 feet, or about

---

[1] See above, pp. 314, 315, 318.
[2] See above, p. 314, n. 3.
[3] See above, p. 312 sq.
[4] See above, pp. 329, 330. This second wall was also apparently the northern wall attacked by Antiochus, adjacent to which there was a level tract or plain. Jos. Ant. 13. 8. 2.

407 yards ; which is 33 yards less than a quarter of an English mile.

On viewing the city from the remains of the ancient Hippicus, as well as from the site of Antonia, we were satisfied that if the second wall might be supposed to have run in a straight line between those points, it would have left the church of the Holy Sepulchre without the city ; and thus far have settled the topographical part of the question.[1] But, it was not less easy to perceive, that in thus running in a straight course, the wall must also have left the pool of Hezekiah on the outside ; or, if it made a curve sufficient to include this pool, it would naturally also have included the site of the sepulchre ; unless it made an angle expressly in order to exclude the latter spot. And further, as we have seen, Josephus distinctly testifies that the second wall ran *in a circle* or curve, obviously towards the north.[2] Various other circumstances also, which go to support the same view, such as the nature of the ground and the ancient towers at the Damascus gate, have already been enumerated.[3] Adjacent to the wall on the north, there was a space of level ground on which Antiochus could erect his hundred towers.[4] All this goes to show that the second wall must have extended further to the north than the site of the present church. Or again, if we admit that this wall ran in a straight course, then the whole of the lower city must have been confined to a small triangle ; and its breadth between the temple and the site of the sepulchre, a space of less than a quarter of an English mile, was not equal to that of many squares in London and New-York. Yet we know that this lower city at the time of the crucifixion was extensive and populous ; three gates led from it to the temple ; and ten years later Agrippa erected the third wall far beyond the limits of the present city, in order to shelter the extensive suburbs which before were unprotected. These suburbs could not well have arisen within the short interval of ten years ; but must already have existed before the time of our Lord's crucifixion.

After examining all these circumstances repeatedly upon the spot, and as I hope without prejudice, the minds of both my companion and myself were forced to the conviction, that the hypothesis which makes the second wall so run as to exclude the alleged site of the Holy Sepulchre, is on topographical grounds untenable and impossible. If there was prejudice upon my own mind, it was certainly in favour of an opposite result ; for I went to Jerusalem strongly prepossessed with the idea, that the alleged site might have lain without the second wall.

[1] The reader will be able easily to follow the details upon the plan of Jerusalem.

[2] Κυκλούμενον. See above, p. 312. ii. 68, 69

[3] See above, p. 313.

[4] Jos. Ant. 13. 8. 2.

But even if such a view could be admitted, the existence of populous suburbs on this part is strongly at variance with the probability, that here should have been a place of execution with a garden and sepulchre. The tombs of the ancients were not usually within their cities, nor among their habitations; and excepting those of the kings on Zion, there is little evidence that sepulchres existed in Jerusalem.

Let us now inquire whether there were probably, in the time of Constantine, any such strong historical or traditional grounds for fixing upon this site, as to counterbalance the topographical difficulties, and lead us on the whole to a different conclusion.

Chateaubriand has furnished us with the clearest and most plausible statement of the historic testimonies and probabilities, which may be supposed to have had an influence in determining the spot; and from him later writers have drawn their chief arguments.[1] I give an epitome of his remarks. The first Christian church, he says, at Jerusalem, was gathered immediately after the resurrection and ascension of our Lord; and soon became very numerous. All its members must have had a knowledge of the sacred places. They doubtless also consecrated buildings for their worship; and would naturally erect them on sites rendered memorable by miracles. Not improbably the Holy Sepulchre itself was already honoured in this manner. At any rate there was a regular succession of Jewish-Christian bishops, from the Apostle James down to the time of Adrian, who could not but have preserved the Christian traditions;[2] and although during the siege by Titus the church withdrew to Pella, yet they soon returned and established themselves among the ruins. In the course of a few months' absence, they could not have forgotten the position of their sanctuaries; which, moreover, being generally without the walls, had probably not suffered greatly from the siege. And that the sacred places were generally known in the age of Adrian, is proved incontestably by the fact, that in rebuilding Jerusalem, that emperor set up a statue of Venus upon Calvary and one of Jupiter over the Holy Sepulchre.[3] Thus the folly of idolatry, by its imprudent profanation,

---

[1] Itineraire, Second Mémoire, Tom. I. p. 122 sq. Par. 1837.

[2] Even here the usual looseness and inaccuracy of the French writer does not abandon him. He himself assigns A. D. 35 as the first year of James, and A. D. 137 as the beginning of the new succession of bishops from the Gentiles under Adrian; and then gravely affirms, that the succession of fifteen Jewish bishops, between these two dates, occupied a space of 123 years, "cent vingt-trois ans!" pp. 123, 125.

[3] Yet in another part of the same work (Vol. II. p. 17), Chateaubriand refers with approbation to the *Epitome Bellorum Sacrorum* for the rather remarkable circumstance, that Adrian at the request of the Christians enclosed the Holy Sepulchre and the adjacent sacred places with walls; and this is quoted by Prokesch (p. 54) as a permission granted by Adrian to erect a church over the Sepulchre!—The Epitome in question is a legendary tract of the fifteenth century; and is found in Canisii Thesaur. Monumentor. Eccl. ed. Basnage, ii. 69–71.

only made more public "the foolishness of the cross." From that time onward till the reign of Constantine, there was again a regular succession of bishops of Gentile origin; and the sacred places could not of course have been forgotten.

Such is the general case, as stated by Chateaubriand; and I am not aware of having in any particular weakened the strength of his argument. It is indeed a strong one at first view; and at one time made a deep impression on my own mind; though this impression was again weakened and in part done away, when he afterwards goes on to admit the alleged miracles, which are said to have accompanied the finding of the cross. The long list of subsequent testimonies which he adduces, has no bearing on the question, and is a mere work of supererogation; for who has ever doubted the identity of the present site with that selected under Constantine?[1] Let us now examine the argument more closely.

That the early Christians at Jerusalem must have had a knowledge of the places where the Lord was crucified and buried, there can be no doubt; that they erected their churches on places consecrated by miracles, and especially on Calvary and over our Lord's sepulchre, is a more questionable position. There is at least no trace of it in the New Testament nor in the history of the primitive church. The four Gospels, which describe so minutely the circumstances of the crucifixion and resurrection, mention the sepulchre only in general terms; and although some of them were written thirty or forty years after these events, yet they are silent as to any veneration of the sepulchre, and also as to its very existence at that time. The writers do not even make in behalf of their Lord and Master the natural appeal, which Peter employs in the case of David, "that he is both dead and buried, and his sepulchre is with us unto this day."[2] The great Apostle of the Gentiles too, whose constant theme is the death and resurrection of our Lord and the glory of his cross, has not in all his writings the slightest allusion to any reverence for the *place* of these great events or the instrument of the Saviour's passion. On the contrary, the whole tenor of our Lord's teaching and that of Paul, and indeed of every part of the New Testament, was directed to draw off the minds of men from an attachment to particular times and places, and to lead the true worshippers to worship God, not merely at Jerusalem or in Mount Gerizim, but everywhere "in spirit and truth."[3]—The position that the Christian churches in the apostolic age were without

Tom. IV. p. 423 sq. The passage referred to is on p. 446.

[1] See however Ferguson's ancient Topogr. of Jerus. Lond. 1847; in which he takes the ground, that the present mosk,

ii. 71. 72

Kubbet es-Sûkhrah, is the church erected by Constantine.

[2] Acts 2, 29. Comp. Gen. 35, 20.
[3] John 4, 21. 23.

the walls of the city, is a mere fancy springing from the similar location of the sepulchre; and still more fanciful and absurd is the assertion, that those churches, if any such there were, might have escaped destruction during the long siege by Titus.

The alleged regular succession of bishops, from the time of St. James to the reign of Adrian, is also a matter of less certainty perhaps than is here represented. Eusebius, the only authority on the subject, lived two centuries afterwards; and says expressly, that he had been able to find no document respecting their times, and wrote only from report.[1]

More important is the circumstance related in connection with Adrian, that this emperor erected heathen temples on Golgotha and over the sepulchre about A. D. 135. Could this be regarded as a well ascertained fact, it would certainly have great weight in a decision of the question. But what is the evidence on which it rests? The earliest witness is again Eusebius, writing after the death of Constantine; who merely relates that a temple of Venus had been erected over the sepulchre by impious men, but says not one word of Adrian. The historians of the following century relate the same fact in the same manner.[2] It is Jerome alone, writing about A. D. 395, or some sixty years later than Eusebius, who affirms that an idol had stood upon the spot from the time of Adrian.[3] There is moreover a discrepancy in the accounts. Eusebius and the other historians speak only of a temple of Venus over the sepulchre. Jerome on the other hand places the marble statue of Venus on the "rock of the cross" or Golgotha, and an image of Jupiter on the place of the resurrection. Here the Latin father is probably wrong; for Eusebius was an eyewitness; and the former is therefore equally liable to have been wrong in ascribing these idols to Adrian.

What then after all is the amount of the testimony relative to an idol erected over the place of the resurrection, and serving to mark the spot? It is simply, that writers *ex post facto* have mentioned such an idol as standing, not over the sepulchre known of old as being that of Christ, but *over the spot fixed upon by Constantine as that sepulchre*. Their testimony proves conclusively that an idol stood upon *that* spot; but it has no bearing to show that this spot was the true sepulchre. Eusebius, the co-

---

[1] Euseb. H. E. 4. 5, Τῶν γε μὴν ἐν Ἱεροσολύμοις ἐπισκόπων τοὺς χρόνους γραφῇ σωζομένους οὐδαμῶς εὗρον· κομιδῇ γὰρ οὖν βραχυβίους αὐτοὺς λόγος κατέχει γενέσθαι. τοσοῦτον δ᾽ ἐξ ἐγγράφων παρείληφα, ὡς μέχρι τῆς κατὰ Ἀδριανὸν Ἰουδαίων πολιορκίας, πεντεκαίδεκα τὸν ἀριθμὸν αὐτόθι γεγόνασιν ἐπισκόπων διαδοχαί.—So too speaking of the same bishops before the time of Adrian, Demonstr. Evang. 3. 5, fin. p.

Vol. I.—35*

124, Par. 1628: λέγονται γοῦν οἱ πρῶτοι κατὰ διαδοχὴν προστάντες αὐτόθι ἐπίσκοποι Ἰουδαῖοι γεγονέναι, ὧν καὶ ὀνόματα εἰσέτι νῦν παρὰ τοῖς ἐγχωρίοις μνημονεύεται.—Perhaps this last passage may aid in explaining the ἐξ ἐγγράφων of the former.

[2] Euseb. Vit. Const. 3. 26. Socrat. H. E. 1. 17. Sozom. 2. 1.

[3] Hieron. Ep. xlix, ad Paulin. Tom. IV. ii. p. 564. ed. Martiany.

ii. 72-74

temporary and eyewitness, makes no mention of any tradition connected with the idol. Jerome sixty years later is the only one to ascribe it to Adrian; and Sozomen in the middle of the fifth century is the first to remark, that the heathen erected it in the hope, that Christians who came to pay their devotions at the sepulchre, would thus have the appearance of worshipping an idol.[1] Yet from these slender materials, the skilful pen of Chateaubriand has wrought out a statement so definite and specious, that most readers who have not had an opportunity of investigation, have probably regarded the matter as a well established fact.

Thus then the positive proofs alleged in favour of an earlier tradition respecting the Holy Sepulchre, vanish away; and there remains only the possibility, that a fact of this nature might have been handed down in the church through the succession of bishops and other holy men. Yet there are also various circumstances, which militate strongly even against such a probability.

One of these is the utter silence of Eusebius and of all following writers, as to the existence of any such tradition. Nor is this all; for the language both of Eusebius and of Constantine himself, seems strongly to imply, that no such former tradition could have been extant. Eusebius relates, in speaking of the place of the resurrection, that "hitherto impious men, or rather the whole race of demons through their instrumentality, had made every effort to deliver over that illustrious monument of immortality to darkness and oblivion." They had covered it with earth, and erected over it a temple of Venus; and it was this spot, thus desecrated and wholly "given over to forgetfulness and oblivion,"[2] that the emperor, "not without a divine intimation, but moved in spirit by the Saviour himself," ordered to be purified and adorned with splendid buildings.[3] Such language, certainly, would hardly be appropriate, in speaking of a spot well known and definitely marked by long tradition. The emperor too, in his letter to Macarius, regards the discovery of "the token of the Saviour's most sacred passion, which for so long a time had been hidden under ground," as "a miracle beyond the capacity of man sufficiently to celebrate or even to comprehend."[4] The mere removal of obstructions from a well known spot, could hardly have been described as a miracle so stupendous. Indeed, the whole tenor of the language both of Eusebius and Constantine goes to show, that the discovery of the Holy Sepulchre was held to be the result, not of a previous knowledge derived from tradition, but of a supernatural interposition and revelation.

I have already alluded to the silence of Eusebius respecting

---

[1] Sozomen, H. E. 2. 1.
[2] Λήθῃ τε καὶ ἀγνοίᾳ παραδιδομένον.
[3] Euseb. Vit. Const. 3. 25, 26.
[4] Ibid. 3. 30. It may here be doubt-
ii. 74, 75

ful, whether the word γνώρισμα (sign) refers to the sepulchre or to the cross; most probably to the latter. See above, pp. 372–374.

the part which Helena bore in these transactions; and have detailed the circumstances under which, according to later writers, she was enabled to find and distinguish the true cross.[1] We have also seen that this supposed cross was certainly in existence so early as the time of Cyril, only some twenty years after its alleged discovery by Helena.[2] It would seem therefore to be a necessary conclusion, that this main circumstance in the agency ascribed to Helena, must have had some foundation in fact; and, however difficult it may be to account for the silence of Eusebius, it would also appear not improbable, that these later accounts may be in the main correct, at least so far as they ascribe to Helena the chief agency in searching for and discovering the supposed Holy Sepulchre. Yet even in these accounts, she is nowhere said to have acted in consequence of any known tradition; but only to have received a "divine suggestion," and also to have inquired diligently of the ancient inhabitants, and especially, according to some, of the Jews.[3] At any rate, therefore, the place of the sepulchre was not then a matter of public notoriety; and the alleged miracle, which attended her discovery of the true cross, serves at least to show the degree of ready credulity with which the search was conducted.

Thus far the balance of evidence would seem to be decidedly against the probable existence of any previous tradition. But we are now prepared to advance a step further; and to show, that even were it possible to prove the existence of such a prevailing tradition, still this would not have been of sufficient authority to counterbalance the strength of the topographical objections.

The strongest assertion which can be made in the case, as we have seen, is the general probability, that such a tradition might have been handed down for three centuries in the church, through the succession of bishops and other holy men. But for the value of such a tradition, supposing it to have existed, we have a decisive test, in applying the same reasoning to another tradition of precisely the same character and import. The place of our Lord's ascension must have been to the first Christians in Jerusalem an object of no less interest than his sepulchre, and could not but have been equally known to them. The knowledge of it too would naturally have been handed down from century to century, through the same succession of bishops and holy men. In this case, moreover, we know that such a tradition did actually exist before the age of Constantine, which pointed out the place of the ascension on the summit of the mount of Olives. Eusebius, writing about A. D. 315, ten years or more before the

---

[1] See above, p. 374.
[2] See p. 375.

[3] See the account and the authorities, as given above, pp. 374, 375.

journey of Helena, speaks expressly, (as we have already seen,) of the many Christians who came up to Jerusalem from all parts of the earth, not as of old to celebrate a festival, but to behold the accomplishment of prophecy in the desolations of the city, and to pay their adorations on the summit of the mount of Olives, where Jesus gave his last charge to his disciples, and then ascended into heaven.[1] Yet notwithstanding this weight of testimony, and the apparent length of time and unbroken succession through which the story had been handed down, the tradition itself is unquestionably false ; since it is contradicted by the express declaration of Scripture. According to Luke, Jesus led out his disciples as far as to Bethany, and blessed them ; and while he blessed them, he was parted from them, and carried up into heaven.[2]—Yet Helena erected a church upon the mount of Olives ; and assuredly there could have been no tradition better accredited in respect to the Holy Sepulchre. Indeed, the fact that no pilgrimages were made to the latter, goes strongly to show that there was no tradition respecting it whatever.

We arrive at a similar, though less decided result, in following up another parallel tradition of the same kind. The cave of the Nativity, so called, at Bethlehem, has been pointed out as the place where Jesus was born, by a tradition which reaches back at least to the middle of the second century. At that time Justin Martyr speaks distinctly of the Saviour's birth, as having occurred in a grotto near Bethlehem.[3] In the third century, Origen adduces it as a matter of notoriety, so that even the heathen regarded it as the birthplace of him whom the Christians adored.[4] Eusebius also mentions it several years before the journey of Helena ;[5] and the latter consecrated the spot by erecting over it a church. In this instance, indeed, the language of Scripture is less decisive than in respect to the place of the ascension ; and the evangelist simply relates that the Virgin " brought forth

---

[1] Τῶν εἰς Χριστὸν πεπιστευκότων ἁπάντων πανταχόθεν γῆς συντρεχόντων, οὐχ ὡς πάλαι κτλ. . . καὶ [ἕνεκα] τῆς ἐπὶ τὸ ὄρος τῶν ἐλαιῶν προσκυνήσεως . . ἔνθα [τοῦ λόγου] τοῖς ἑαυτοῦ μαθηταῖς ἐπὶ τῆς ἀκρωρείας τοῦ τῶν ἐλαιῶν ὄρους τὰ περὶ τῆς συντελείας μυστήρια παραδεδωκότος, ἐντεῦθέν τε τὸν εἰς οὐρανοὺς ἄνοδον πεποιημένου. Euseb. Demonstr. Evang. 6. 18. p. 128. Colon. 1688.

[2] Luke 24, 50. 51. See more above, p. 254. n. 1.

[3] Γεννηθέντος δὲ τότε τοῦ παιδίου ἐν Βηθλεέμ, ἐπειδὴ Ἰωσὴφ οὐκ εἶχεν ἐν τῇ κώμῃ ἐκείνῃ ποῦ καταλῦσαι, ἐν δὲ σπηλαίῳ τινὶ σύνεγγυς τῆς κώμης κατέλυσε · καὶ τότε αὐτῶν ὄντων ἐκεῖ, ἐτετόκει ἡ Μαρία τὸν Χριστόν, καὶ ἐν φάτνῃ αὐτὸν ἐτεθείκει. Justin. ii. 77, 78

tin. Mart. Dial. cum Tryph. 78. p. 175. Hag. Com. 1742.

[4] Origen. c. Celsum 1. 51. Opp. Tom. 1. p. 367. ed. Delarue.

[5] Euseb. Demonstr. Evang. 7. 2. p. 343. Col. 1688. In this passage, instead of διὰ τῆς τοῦ ἀγροῦ δείξεως, it should doubtless read διὰ τῆς τοῦ ἄντρου δείξεως. Comp. the τῆς γεννήσεως ἄντρον as used of the same cavern, Euseb. Vit. Const. 3. 43.—Jerome, seventy years later, affirms, that from the time of Adrian onwards Adonis was worshipped in this cavern ; but as all the earlier writers are silent as to any such desecration, it is perhaps nothing more than a rhetorical parallel to the statue of Venus in Jerusalem. Hieron. Ep. xlix, ad Paulin. Opp. Tom. IV. ii. p. 564, ed Mart.

her first born son, and laid him in a manger; because there was no room for them in the inn."[1]　But the circumstance of the Saviour's being born in a cave would certainly have not been less remarkable, than his having been laid in a manger; and it is natural to suppose, that the sacred writer would not have passed it over in silence. The grotto moreover was and is at some distance from the town; and although there may be still occasional instances in Judea, where a cavern is occupied as a stable, yet this is not now, and never was, the usual practice, especially in towns and their environs. Taking into account all these circumstances,—and also the early and general tendency to invent and propagate legends of a similar character, and the prevailing custom of representing the events of the gospel history as having taken place in grottos,[2]—it would seem hardly consistent with a love of simple historic truth, to attach to this tradition any much higher degree of credit, than we have shown to belong to the parallel tradition respecting the place of our Lord's ascension.

The two traditions which we have now examined, both present a much stronger case, than any thing which ever has been or can be urged in behalf of the supposed Holy Sepulchre. Yet one of them at least, and probably both, have no foundation in historic truth. On this ground then, as well as on all others, the alleged site of the sepulchre is found to be without support.[3]

Thus in every view which I have been able to take of the question, both topographical and historical, whether on the spot or in the closet, and in spite of all my previous prepossessions, I am led irresistibly to the conclusion, that the Golgotha and the tomb now shown in the church of the Holy Sepulchre, are not upon the real places of the crucifixion and resurrection of our

---

[1] Luke 2, 7; comp. vs. 12. 16.

[2] On the subject of grottos, I subjoin the very apposite remarks of Maundrell, Journey, Apr. 19th. "I cannot forbear to mention in this place an observation, which is very obvious to all that visit the Holy Land, viz. that almost all passages and histories related in the Gospel, are represented by them that undertake to show where every thing was done, as having been done most of them in grottos; and that, even in such cases where the condition and the circumstances of the actions themselves seem to require places of another nature. Thus, if you would see the place where St. Anne was delivered of the blessed Virgin, you are carried to a grotto; if the place of the Annunciation, it is also a grotto; if the place where the blessed Virgin saluted Elizabeth; if that of the Baptist's or of our Saviour's nativity; if that of the agony, or that of St. Peter's repentance, or that where the Apostles made the creed, or this of the Transfiguration; all these places are grottos. And in a word, wherever you go, you find almost every thing is represented as done under ground. Certainly grottos were anciently held in great esteem, or else they could never have been assigned, in spite of all probability, for the places in which were done so many various actions. Perhaps it was the hermit-way of living in grottos from the fifth or sixth century downward, that has brought them ever since to be in so great reputation." The historical notices in the text, show that this practice is of much earlier date than is here assigned.

[3] After this discussion, it would be of little avail, to dwell upon the arguments usually drawn from the form and condition of the present sepulchre, against its antiquity.

Lord.   The alleged discovery of them by the aged and credulous
Helena, like her discovery of the cross, may not improbably have
been the work of pious fraud.   It would perhaps not be doing injustice to the bishop Macarius and his clergy, if we regard the
whole as a well laid and successful plan for restoring to Jerusalem its former consideration, and elevating his see to a higher
degree of influence and dignity.

If it be asked, Where then are the true sites of Golgotha and
the sepulchre to be sought?   I must reply, that probably all
search can only be in vain.   We know nothing more from the
Scriptures, than that they were near each other, without the
gate and nigh to the city, in a frequented spot.[1]   This would
favour the conclusion, that the place was probably upon a great
road leading from one of the gates; and such a spot would only
be found upon the western or northern sides of the city, on the
roads leading towards Joppa or Damascus.

III.   STATISTICS.

The details in the preceding pages have extended themselves
far beyond the limits originally proposed; and will at least prove
to the reader, that during our sojourn in Jerusalem, our attention was directed more to the topography and antiquities of the
Holy City, than to its present social and political relations.   The
facts, however, which we gleaned upon these latter points, may
not be devoid of interest; and may help to fill out or correct the
accounts of other writers.

The glory of Jerusalem has indeed departed.   From her ancient high estate, as the splendid metropolis of the Jewish com-
monwealth and of the whole Christian world, the beloved of nations and 'the joy of the whole earth,' she has sunk into the
neglected capital of a petty Turkish province; and where of old
many hundreds of thousands thronged her streets and temple,
we now find a population of scarcely as many single thousands
dwelling sparsely within her walls.   The cup of wrath and desolation from the Almighty has been poured out upon her to the
dregs; and she sits sad and solitary in darkness and in the dust.
The Saviour " beheld the city and wept over it, saying, If thou
hadst known, even thou, at least in this thy day, the things
which belong unto thy peace! but now they are hid from thine
eyes!"[2]   He wept at the calamities and the doom which were
then coming upon the city, and which now for almost eighteen
centuries have bowed her heavily to the ground.   That which
our Lord wept over in prospect, we now see in the terrible reality.

---

[1] John 19, 20.   [2] Luke 19, 41 sq.
    ii. 80, 81.

Long since have the days come, when "her enemies cast a trench about her, and compassed her round, and kept her in on every side, and have laid her even with the ground, and her children within her ; and have not left in her one stone upon another !" How fearfully, and almost to the letter, this ' burden ' of Jerusalem has been accomplished upon her, the preceding pages may serve to testify.

Under the Egyptian rule in Syria, the former Pashaliks of 'Akka and Aleppo have been done away. The whole country is united under one civil government, the seat of which is at Damascus ; while the independent military command is intrusted to Ibrahim Pasha. The same system is also followed in the several districts into which the country is divided. Thus in the district of Jerusalem, which includes the hill country around the city from Sinjil on the north to about half way to Hebron on the south, there is a Mutesellim or civil governor, residing in the city, and likewise a military commander. The powers of these two chiefs, perhaps from policy, are not very distinctly marked, nor separated by any very definite line. The former, however, seems to be the responsible person for the due administration of justice; and he too was the actor in disarming several villages while we were there, which would seem to fall more naturally under the jurisdiction of his colleague. The district of Hebron is subordinate to that of Jerusalem, and is administered only by a deputy governor. The Bedawin tribes around Hebron and in the deserts further south, were under the superintendence of Sheikh Sa'id, the civil governor of Gaza ; who collected from them the tribute, and controlled their predatory excursions against other tribes.—The little intercourse which we had occasion to seek with the two governors of Jerusalem, has already been mentioned.[1]

A considerable body of troops usually lay in garrison at Jerusalem ; but the number was variable, and we did not learn the average amount. They were at this time mostly Syrian troops, taken by force as soldiers in the country itself; and of course exceedingly discontented with the service. Shortly before our visit, a mutiny had occurred among them ; a large number had deserted, many of whom had been retaken ; while others were still wandering about as outlaws and robbers. It was the usual policy of the Egyptian government to remove the Syrian regiments from their own soil to Egypt or other places, where they would be less reminded of their bondage ; and during our stay in Jerusalem a large detachment of its garrison was sent off to Yâfa, intended for a more distant service. The troops we saw, were in general composed of fine looking young men. They are lodged

[1] See above, pp. 244, 246.

ii. 81–83

in Jerusalem in the citadel, adjacent to which new barracks had recently been erected; and also in the former house of the governor of the city, on the north of the Haram, now converted into a barrack. A military guard was regularly kept at each of the city gates. We saw also several times parties of soldiers at the fountains and wells round about the city, washing their garments and spreading them upon the ground to dry.

The population of Jerusalem has been variously estimated according to the fancy of different travellers from 15,000 up to nearly 30,000.[1] No doubt the number has varied much at different times; and entire certainty can never be hoped for under an oriental government, where a census of the whole population is a thing unknown. Indeed, until within the last few years, there would appear to have been no data whatever accessible to a traveller, on which to found a calculation. The more common estimate of late years among the Franks, has been the round number of 15,000 inhabitants; of which the greater part have been supposed to be Muhammedans. We found, however, reason to distrust the accuracy of both these statements.

The introduction of the Egyptian system of taxation and military conscription into Syria, has led to the enumeration and registry of all the *males* who are of an age to be taxed or to bear arms. We could not learn that this age is very exactly defined; but it is usually reckoned as commencing at about eighteen or twenty years. According to the proportion generally assumed, this enumeration may thus be regarded as a loose census of one fourth of the population. As this measure was a great innovation, and led to consequences which excited much alarm and oppositon, the number of persons thus registered in the different cities and villages became everywhere an object of interest to the inhabitants, and was very generally known. On our inquiring of different individuals respecting the number enrolled in a particular place, the answer given was almost uniformly the same. We found this therefore to be the best, and indeed the only positive basis, on which to found an estimate of the population of any city or village. Yet even this enumeration is not always correct; as the partiality or negligence of the authorities often causes the list to fall below the actual number. Among the multitudes belonging to different sects, there are always eyes keen enough to watch and detect the errors arising from this source; and we not unfrequently received two reports, one according to the official registry, and the other according to the alleged truth.—I have dwelt the longer upon this topic here; because these re-

---

[1] Turner 26,000, Vol. II. p. 263. Richardson 20,000, Vol. II. p. 256. Scholz 18,000, p. 271. Jowett 15,000, p. 238. Salzbacher (in 1837) not less than 25,000, Vol. II. p. 119.

ii. 83 84

marks apply not only to Jerusalem, but to all our subsequent travels in Palestine.[1]

The inhabitants of Jerusalem dwell in separate quarters according to their religion, Christian, Jewish and Muhammedan. The Christian quarter extends along the upper or western part of the city, between the Latin convent at the northwest corner, and the great Armenian convent in the southwest, including also the church of the Holy Sepulchre. The Jewish quarter occupies the northeastern part of Zion and extends upwards so as to include the greater portion of the hill lying within the walls. The Muhammedans are in the middle and lower parts of the city. After careful inquiry, the information which we found most worthy to be relied upon, amounted to the following.

I. The MUHAMMEDANS are reckoned in the government books at 750 men; but amount really to 1,100. This gives at the utmost a round number of 4,500.

II. Of the JEWS, only 500 males are enrolled; but there are actually many more. According to the careful estimate of the Rev. Mr. Nicolayson, who has a better opportunity of judging than any other person, the whole number of the Jews at this time was about 3,000. In former years the number had sometimes amounted to 5,000.

III. CHRISTIANS. The *Greeks* are reckoned by the government at 400, but are actually 460; the *Latins* at 260; the *Armenians* at 130. Total 850 males, indicating a population of about 3,500 in all.—Hence

Muhammedans	4,500
Jews	3,000
Christians	3,500
Total population	11,000

If to this we add something for possible omissions, and for the inmates of the convents; the standing population of the city, exclusive of the garrison, cannot well be reckoned at over 11,500 souls. The Muhammedans, it will be seen, are more numerous than either the Jews or Christians alone; but fewer in number than these two bodies united.[2]

---

[1] In regarding this partial enumeration as the only existing basis for a general estimate, I am happy to have the concurrence of my friend Dr. Bowring; whose researches into the resources and statistics of Egypt and Syria during the same year, as the accredited agent of the British government, were carried on under facilities and to an extent to which ours could make no pretension.

[2] I have more recently learned, (Oct. 1840,) that some of our friends in Jerusalem, on the strength of later information, have been led to estimate the number of the Muhammedans at about 1,500 higher, or 6,000 in all; and the Jews at 7,000, according to the reported enumeration obtained by Sir Moses Montefiore in A. D. 1839. This would give for the whole population of the city about 17,000 souls. But

Of all this native population, as well as throughout Syria and Egypt, the Arabic is the vernacular language; as much so as the English in London or the French in Paris. The Jews are for the most part not natives of the country; and speak a corrupt medley of tongues among themselves. Among the other foreigners, the Greek, Armenian, and Italian languages are also found; but whoever desires to obtain access to the common people, whether Muhammedans or Christians, can do it only through the medium of the Arabic.

Of the Jews now resident in Palestine, the greater number are such as have come up to the land of their fathers, in order to spend the remainder of their lives and die in one of the four holy places, Jerusalem, Hebron, Tiberias, or Safed. Those in Jerusalem desire to lay their bones in the valley of Jehoshaphat.[1] They come hither from all parts of the Levant, and especially from Smyrna, Constantinople, and Salonika; in which cities there are many thousands of this people. Two years before our visit, the Jews were said to have flocked in great numbers to Syria, and particularly to Damascus and Tyre, where formerly they were not permitted to reside. But subsequently, as the high prices of provisions and of living in general increased, this circumstance prevented the coming of more, and compelled the return of many; so that the number of Jews in Jerusalem had been much diminished. They live here, for the most part, in poverty and filth. A considerable amount of money is collected for them by their emissaries in different countries; but as it comes into the hands of the Rabbins, and is managed by them without responsibility, it is understood to be administered without much regard to honesty; and serves chiefly as a means of increasing their own influence and control over the conduct and consciences of their poorer brethren.

Most of the Jews now in Palestine appear to be of Spanish or Polish origin; very few are from Germany, or able to speak the German language. The very motive which leads them thus to return to the land of Promise, shows their strong attachment

---

I have yet to learn, that the new sources of information as to the Muhammedans, were more correct than ours. As to the Jews, the enumeration in question was made out by themselves, in the expectation of receiving a certain amount of alms for every name returned. It is therefore obvious, that they here had as strong a motive to exaggerate their number, as they often have in other circumstances to underrate it. Besides, this number of 7,000 rests merely on report; Sir Moses himself has published nothing on the subject; nor could his agent in London afford me any ii. 86, 87

information so late as Nov. 1840. The Scottish deputation of clergymen in 1839, as I learned from some of its members, estimated the Jews in Jerusalem at 5,000 souls; while Mr. Calman, who accompanied them, himself a converted Jew, still supposed them not to exceed 3,000 in all.— The estimate of the British consul at Beirût, who makes the whole population of Jerusalem only 10,000, is on the other hand certainly too low. See Dr. Bowring's Report on Syria, p. 7.

[1] See above, p. 349.

to their ancient faith ; and would of itself point *a priori* to the conclusion, which is found to be true in fact, viz. that the Jews thus resident in Palestine are of all others the most bigoted, and the least accessible to the labours of Christian missionaries. The efforts of the English mission have as yet been attended with very slight success ; and it remains to be seen, whether the erection of a Jewish-Christian church in Jerusalem will add to the influence and prosperity of the mission. The site was purchased during our stay in the city ; and the building has been since completed.

The Christians of the Latin rite live around the Latin convent, on which they are wholly dependent. They are native Arabs ; know no other language than the Arabic ; and are said to be descended from Catholic converts in the times of the crusades. They are in number about 1,100 souls, according to the preceding estimate ; and live partly by carving crosses and beads for rosaries, and partly on the alms of the convent.[1]—The Latin convent in Jerusalem, like all those in the Holy Land, is in the hands of the Franciscans, or Minorites, of the class termed *Fratres Minores ab Observantia.* I have already mentioned their former residence on Mount Zion, and their removal to the present building in A. D. 1561.[2] This convent contains at present between forty and fifty monks, half Italians and half Spaniards ; and takes rank of all the other Catholic monasteries in the east. In it resides the intendant or principal of all the convents, with the rank of an abbot, and the title of "Guardian of Mount Zion and Custos of the Holy Land."[3] He is always an Italian ; and is appointed or at least confirmed at Rome every three years. The same individual is sometimes reappointed. There is also a vicar, called likewise president, who takes the place of the guardian in case of his absence or death. He is chosen in like manner for three years ; and may be an Italian or a Spaniard.[4] The procurator, who manages the temporal concerns, is always a Spaniard ; and is elected for life. The executive council, called *discretorium,* is composed of these three officials, and of three other monks, *patres discreti.*

The cost of maintaining the twenty convents belonging to the establishment of the "Terra Santa," is rated at 40,000 Spanish dollars per annum. They are said to be very deeply in debt, contracted in former years, when the wars in Europe cut off for a time their usual eleemosynary supplies. Under the Egyptian

---

[1] Salzbacher gives the number at 1,500. Other native Catholics are found also in connection with the Latin convents at Bethlehem and Nazareth.

[2] See above, p. 242. n. 5.

[3] "Guardianus sacri Montis Sion et Cus-

tos (Præsul) Terræ Sanctæ;" Quaresmius, Tom. I. p. 465.

[4] "Vicarius sive Præses;" Quaresmius I. p. 468. Formerly the vicar was usually a French monk; but this seems no longer to be the case. Scholz, p. 195.

government, they are freed from the numerous exactions to which they were formerly subjected from the caprice and greediness of pashas and governors ; and pay a regular tax for the property which they possess. For their buildings and lands in and around Jerusalem, including the holy places, the annual tax is said to be 7,000 piastres, or about 350 Spanish dollars.[1]

The Christians of the Greek rite (not monks) are all native Arabs ; have their own native priests ; and enjoy the privilege of having the service in their churches performed in their own mother tongue, the Arabic. They amount in Jerusalem to nearly 2,000 souls.—The Greek convents are tenanted by foreigners, all Greeks by birth, mostly from the Archipelago, speaking only the Greek language. There are eight convents for men, containing in all about sixty monks, viz. the great convent of Constantine near the church of the Sepulchre, in which most of the monks and the officials reside ; and those of Demetrius, Theodorus (Arabic Tâdrus,) George, Michael, Nicolas, Johannes, and George in the Jewish quarter. All these minor establishments are chiefly used for the accommodation of pilgrims, and are kept by only one or two monks and lay brethren. There are also five convents of Greek nuns, containing about thirty-five in all, who are foreigners like the monks ; viz. those of the Holy Virgin (Panagia, Arabic es-Seideh), Basil, Catharine, Euthymius, and another of the Virgin Mary. In the vicinity of Jerusalem the Greeks have also the convents of the Holy Cross (Deir el-Musüllabeh) about three quarters of an hour W. S. W. of the city ; that of Mâr Elyâs towards Bethlehem ; one at the grotto of the Nativity at Bethlehem ; and the renowned monastery of Mâr Sâba, founded about the beginning of the sixth century, and situated on the continuation of the valley of the Kidron, as it runs off to the Dead Sea.

All these Greek convents in and around the city are under the government of three vicars (Arab. *Wakil*) of the patriarch of Jerusalem, who himself resides at Constantinople. The present vicars were the Greek bishops of Lydda, Nazareth, and

[1] See Scholz Reise, p. 194 sq. Salzbacher Erinnerungen, II. p. 92 sq. The amount of the present tax is given on the authority of the latter writer ; who as canon of St. Stephen's cathedral at Vienna, and a Catholic pilgrim of rank, may be supposed to have had access to the best information. Yet I am not sure that this alleged sum of 7,000 piastres (like so many other things) is not copied by him from Scholz, who was there in A. D. 1821 ; p. 197.—The following list of the Catholic convents now connected with that of Jerusalem, is from the same authority : Beth-

lehem ; St. John's in the Desert, an hour and a half southwest of Jerusalem ; Ramleh, Yâfa, Haifa, 'Akka, Nazareth, Sidon, Beirût, Tripolis, Larissa, Aleppo, Damascus, and one on Mount Lebanon ; also in Alexandria, Rosetta, and Cairo in Egypt ; and in Larnaka and Nicosia on the island of Cyprus. In Jerusalem, Bethlehem, and Nazareth, half the monks are Italians and half Spaniards ; in Yâfa, Ramleh, and St. John, they are all Spaniards ; and in the other convents all Italians. The whole number of monks is about two hundred.

Kerak (Petra). They were assisted by the bishops of Gaza, Nâbulus, es-Salt (Philadelphia), and Sebaste ; who with the archimandrites form a council. The vicars, with the concurrence of the council, appoint the superiors of the several convents ; and all the priests within these dioceses are ordained at Jerusalem. Indeed, all the bishops above named live there permanently, in the great convent near the church of the Sepulchre. The Greek bishop of 'Akka alone was said to reside in his own diocese.[1]

The Armenians have their large monastery on Mount Zion, said to be the wealthiest in the city, with the splendid church of St. James. Not far off is a convent of Armenian nuns, called ez-Zeitûny. Outside of the city, on Mount Zion, the pretended house of Caiaphas serves as a smaller convent and is occupied by monks.[2] The Armenians are for the most part not natives ; and those not attached to the convents, are usually merchants.

The Coptic Christians consist only of monks in their convent of es-Sultân, situated on the north side of the pool of Hezekiah. At the time of our visit, it had just been rebuilt.[3] There is also a convent of the Abyssinians ; and we were likewise told of one belonging to the Jacobite Syrians.[4]

Of these Christian sects, the Greeks, Latins, Armenians, and Copts, have their own chapels in the church of the Holy Sepulchre ; and the three former have also convents or dwellings within the walls of the church, for the monks who are shut up here to perform the regular offices day and night.[5] Along the walls of the circular church around the sepulchre itself, are niches with altars for several of the minor sects ; as the Abyssinians, Jacobites, Nestorians, Maronites, and others ; but their service is performed in these chapels only occasionally. It is well known that a deep hatred exists among all these possessors of the Holy Sepulchre towards each other. Especially is this the case between the Greeks and Latins ; in whom it seems to be irreconcilable, and gives occasion for constant intrigues and bitter complaints on either side. The Greeks have indeed the advantage in their greater cunning ; in the far greater number of their pilgrims ; and in their proximity to the regions whence their resources are derived. They are consequently enabled to prosecute their purposes more systematically and with greater effect. During

---

[1] Scholz, p. 205. The preceding information respecting the Greek Christians and convents was obtained from intelligent natives of that persuasion.

[2] See above, p. 243.

[3] See above, pp. 329, 330. See more in Vol. III. Sec. IV.

[4] Scholz, p. 275.

[5] These monks are confined to the church, provisions being brought to them daily from their respective convents. The Latin monks are relieved every three months. In 1837, there was only one Copt thus residing in the church. Salzbacher, Vol. II. pp. 77, 82.

the wars in Europe the Latins were comparatively forgotten ; their pilgrims dwindled away to nothing ; and their resources were in a measure cut off.

The Greeks took occasion of these circumstances to get possession by degrees of many of the holy places, in and around the churches of the Sepulchre and at Bethlehem, which had formerly been in the hands of the Latins ; and notwithstanding all the efforts of the latter, these have not yet been recovered. Near the close of the year 1836, the prince de Joinville, son of the king of France, visited the Holy City ; and one of the first requests of the Latin fathers was, that the influence of the French monarch might be employed to recover for them all the sacred places, which the Greeks had so unjustly wrested from them ever since the crusades. The prince promised his support ; and a representation is said actually to have been made by the French cabinet to the Turkish court, through their ambassador at Constantinople. A firmân was granted, commanding the Greek patriarch to deliver up to the Latins the possession of the sacred places in question ; but still the Greek spirit of intrigue was able to evade the execution. A timely present of some 500 purses [1] to the governor of Syria, is said to have stayed all proceedings. Further negotiations were set on foot at Constantinople ; but they appear to have led to no result. [2]

The kings of France have ever been the protectors of the Catholics in the east ; and the French ambassador at Constantinople has always acted, and still acts, as their patron and advocate with the Porte. When we were in Jerusalem a splendid salver of gold for the presentation of the host, had just arrived, a present from the queen of the French to the convent. They possess also the portrait of king Louis Philip, a gift from himself.

Formerly all the Christians of Jerusalem paid their taxes to the government through their respective convents ; that is to say, the monasteries became the collectors of the taxes ; a system which gave opportunity for great extortion on the part of the convents. The Egyptian government has done away this system ; and apportions and collects its own taxes from all the Christian sects, except the Latins. For these the Latin convent pays the *Kharaj* or extra tax for Christians ; they being very poor. No *Firdeh* or ordinary capitation tax is paid by any of the inhabitants of Jerusalem, whether Muslims, Christians, or Jews ; because it is regarded as a sacred place, and because of the poverty of the people. The inhabitants of the villages pay

---

[1] A *purse* is equivalent to 500 piastres, or about 25 Spanish dollars.

[2] Salzbacher II. p. 98 sq.—In all such questions the Egyptian government declines to interfere ; and gravely refers the parties to the Sultan at Constantinople, as the highest tribunal.

ii. 92, 93

the Firdeh, as well as the Kharaj and other taxes.[1]—At the same
time, the Pasha of Egypt has abolished the tolls and tribute,
which under the name of *el-Ghûfr* were formerly so oppressive
to the pilgrims and travellers.   Even the entrance money, which
for so many centuries was paid for admission to the church of the
Sepulchre, is in like manner done away.

From these facts, however, it must not be inferred, that the
exactions of the Pasha are in themselves less oppressive than those
of the Sultan.   The preference lies rather in the more equal
manner in which the extortions are now conducted.   The burdens to be endured are more definitely known ; and no distinction is made, as formerly, between the Christian and the Mussulman.   Yet the whole mode of proceeding, as well as the enormous
amount of taxation, is sufficiently oppressive ; as we had abundant occasion to see in the course of our subsequent journies.
While we were at Jerusalem, the value of the Turkish gold coins
of twenty piastres, which had always been the common currency of the country, was by a decree of the Egyptian government
at once cut down to 17¼ piastres, a loss of nearly fourteen per
cent.   It would be natural to suppose, that a measure of this sort
would have been fixed to go into operation on a particular day ;
and that this day would have been publicly made known.   Yet
nothing of the kind took place.   The measure was proclaimed on
different days in different places, and in each went immediately
into operation.   In Beirût and in Yâfa, it was known and acted
upon for nearly a fortnight before it was proclaimed in Jerusalem.   It was said that the authorities of the latter city had a
large quantity of this coin on hand, of which they wished first to
rid themselves by paying it away at its full value.   The consequence was the greatest confusion among the tradesmen, and the
impossibility of guarding against loss.

The bazars have been already alluded to, as situated in the
middle of the city, on and near the principal street running
north to the Damascus gate.   They consist of two or three narrow lanes roofed over, with open shops on each side, occupied by
merchants and sedentary artisans.   They appeared not to be
well furnished, even for an oriental city.   The markets are supplied by the peasants from the neighbouring villages.   There
seemed to be no gardens of any importance round about the city ;
except those below Siloam.   Wheat would appear not to grow
well around Jerusalem, but is brought from other quarters.   In
one of our journies northward, we met a small caravan of camels
belonging to Bethlehem, loaded with wheat from Nâbulus.   The

[1] The *Firdeh* is a tax laid upon every male inhabitant from 15 years upwards; varying from 15 to 500 piastres according to the supposed ability of the individual.   The *Kharaj* is a similar extra tax on Christians and Jews, a species of toleration-tax.   Compare Bowring's Report on Syria, p. 112.

ii. 93-95

exhausted situation of the country arising from the maintenance of an immense army, the forced export of wheat to Egypt, and the general discouragement to labour and enterprise, have naturally caused an enormous increase in the cost of the necessaries of life. In 1838 the cost of living in Jerusalem had become threefold. To this succeeded the plague, which prevailed more or less for some years ; and then the suspense and miseries of actual war ; so that the prices of provisions, as I am informed, had in 1839 advanced to the quadruple of what they were only four or five years since.

Jerusalem has few manufactures; and no exports, except what is carried away by the pilgrims. The manufacture of soap is one of the principal. For this there are nine establishments, which appear to have been long in existence. The mounds of ashes which they have thrown out at some distance from the city on the north, have almost the appearance of natural hills.[1] At Easter large quantities of perfumed soap are said to be sold to the pilgrims.[2] Oil of sesame is made to a considerable extent ; for this there are nine presses. There is also a large tannery for leather, just by the eastern entrance to the court before the church of the Sepulchre. All these establishments are private property, not controlled by the government ; and are in the hands of the Muslims.

The chief articles manufactured by the Christians, both here and at Bethlehem, are rosaries, crucifixes, models of the Holy Sepulchre, and the like, carved in olive wood, the fruit of the Dôm palm said to be brought from Mecca, mother of pearl, or sometimes in the species of black shining stone found near the Dead Sea. Some of these are neatly executed. The concourse of pilgrims at Easter converts the city into a sort of toy shop or fair ; and immense quantities of these tokens are carried away, after having been duly consecrated by the priests. Merchants also resort hither at that season from Damascus and other places, bringing their wares of various kinds ; so that the whole city then wears an air of bustle and business, strikingly in contrast with its stillness and listlessness during the remainder of the year. The wares find a ready sale among the pilgrims ; and the annual Easter fair of Jerusalem is relatively not much less important, than those of Leipzig and Frankfort.

IV. CLIMATE.

The climate of the mountainous tract on which Jerusalem is situated, differs from that of the temperate parts of Europe and

---

[1] For these mounds, see Vol. III. Sec. IV, fin.   [2] Comp. Turner, Vol. II. p. 265.
ii. 95. 96

America, more in the alternations of wet and dry seasons, than in the degrees of temperature. The variations of rain and sunshine, which in the west exist throughout the whole year, are in Palestine confined chiefly to the latter part of autumn and the winter; while the remaining months enjoy almost uninterruptedly a cloudless sky.

The autumnal rains, the early rains of Scripture, usually commence in the latter half of October or beginning of November; not suddenly, but by degrees; which gives opportunity for the husbandman to sow his fields of wheat and barley. The rains come mostly from the west or southwest,[1] continuing for two or three days at a time, and falling especially during the nights. Then the wind chops round to the north or east, and several days of fine weather succeed. During the months of November and December the rains continue to fall heavily; afterwards they return only at longer intervals and are less heavy; but at no period during the winter do they entirely cease to occur. Snow often falls in Jerusalem in January and February to the depth of a foot or more; but does not usually lie long.[2] The ground never freezes; but Mr Whiting had seen the pool back of his house (Hezekiah's) covered with thin ice for one or two days.

Rain continues to fall more or less through the month of March, but is rare after that period. During the present season, there had been little or none in March, and indeed the whole quantity of rain had been less than usual. Nor is there at the present day any particular periods of rain, or succession of showers, which might be regarded as distinct rainy seasons. The whole period from October to March now constitutes only one continued season of rain, without any regularly intervening term of prolonged fair weather. Unless therefore there has been some change in the climate since the times of the New Testament, the early and the latter rains, for which the husbandman waited with longing, seem rather to have implied the first showers of autumn, which revived the parched and thirsty earth and prepared it for the seed; and the later showers of spring, which continued to refresh and forward both the ripening crops and the vernal products of the fields.[3]

During the whole winter the roads, or rather tracks, in Palestine, are muddy, deep, and slippery; so that the traveller at this season is subjected to the utmost discomfort and inconve-

---

[1] Luke 12, 54, "When ye see a cloud rise out of the west, straightway ye say, There cometh a shower; and so it is." These words were spoken by our Lord at Jerusalem.

[2] So Shaw in 1722. Brown near the close of the century found here very deep snow for several days. Comp. Scholz, p. 138. The information in the text is derived from our resident friends.

[3] James 5, 7. Prov. 16, 15.

nience. When the rains cease, the mud soon disappears, and the roads become hard, though never smooth. Whoever therefore wishes to profit most by a journey in Palestine, will take care not to arrive at Jerusalem earlier than the latter part of March. During the months of April and May, the sky is usually serene, the air mild and balmy, and the face of nature, after seasons of ordinary rain, still green and pleasant to the eye. Showers occur occasionally; but they are mild and refreshing. On the 1st of May we had showers in the city; and at evening there was thunder and lightning, (which are frequent in winter,) with pleasant and reviving rain. The 6th of May was also remarkable for thunder and for several showers, some of which were quite heavy. The rains of both these days extended far to the north; and overtook our missionary friends who were returning from Jerusalem to Beirût. But the occurrence of rain so late in the season, was regarded as a very unusual circumstance. Morning mists however are occasionally seen at a still later period.

In ordinary seasons, from the cessation of the showers in spring until their commencement in October or November, rain never falls, and the sky is usually serene. If during the winter there has been a sufficiency of rain, the husbandman is certain of his crop; and is also perfectly sure of fine weather for the ingathering of the harvest.[1] The high elevation of Jerusalem secures it the privilege of a pure atmosphere; nor does the heat of summer ever become oppressive, except during the occasional prevalence of the south wind, or Sirocco.[2] During our sojourn from April 14th to May 6th, the thermometer ranged at sunrise from 44° to 64° F., and at 2 P. M. from 60° to 79° F. This last degree of heat was felt during a Sirocco, April 30th. From the 10th to the 13th of June at Jerusalem, we had at sunrise a range from 56° to 74°; and at 2 P. M. once 86°, with a strong northwest wind. Yet the air was fine, and the heat not burdensome. The nights are uniformly cool, often with a heavy dew; and our friends had never had occasion to dispense with a coverlet upon their beds during summer. Yet the total absence of rain soon destroys the verdure of the fields; and gives to the whole landscape the aspect of drought and barrenness. The only green thing which remains, is the foliage of the scattered fruit trees, and occasional vineyards and fields of millet. The deep green of the broad fig leaves and of the millet, is delightful to the eye in the midst of the general aridness; while the foliage of the

---

[1] "Snow in summer and rain in harvest" were things incomprehensible to a Hebrew; Prov. 26, 1. Rain in wheat harvest occurred only by a miracle; 1 Sam. 12, 17. Compare Amos 4, 7, and &c. &c. &c.

Jerome's Commentary upon the same passage.
[2] Luke 12, 55, "And when ye see the south wind blow, ye say, There will be heat; and it cometh to pass."

olive, with its dull grayish hue, scarcely deserves the name of verdure.

The harvest upon the mountains ripens of course later than in the plains of the Jordan and the sea coast. The barley harvest precedes the wheat harvest by a week or fortnight. On the 4th and 5th of June the people of Hebron were just beginning to gather their wheat ; on the 11th and 12th the threshing-floors on the mount of Olives were in full operation. We had already seen the harvest in the same stage of progress on the plains of Gaz aon the 19th of May ; while at Jericho, on the 12th of May, the threshing-floors had nearly completed their work. The first grapes ripen in July ; and from that time until November, Jerusalem is abundantly supplied with this delicious fruit. The general vintage takes place in September. We found ripe apricots at Gaza in May ; and they are probably brought to Jerusalem, though I do not recollect to have seen any there. The fine oranges of Yâfa were found in abundance both at Jerusalem and Hebron.

In autumn the whole land has become dry and parched ; the cisterns are nearly empty ; the few streams and fountains fail ; and all nature, physical and animal, looks forward with longing to the return of the rainy season. Mists and clouds begin to make their appearance, and showers occasionally to fall ; the husbandman sows his seed; and the thirsty earth is soon drenched with an abundance of rain.

V. BETHANY

It was on one of the last days of our stay at Jerusalem, (June 11th,) that mounting the spirited mules we had engaged for our journey northwards, and accompanied by our friend Mr Lanneau, we rode out to Bethany. Passing along the wall from the Damascus gate to that of St. Stephen's, we then descended and crossed the bridge in the valley, and followed the camel road which ascends obliquely the side of the mount of Olives back of the village of Siloam, and crosses the ridge at a lower spot some distance south of the summit. It then winds north around the head of a Wady running off southeast, and after crossing another lower ridge, passes on towards Jericho. Here, on the eastern slope, (strictly of the mount of Olives,) in a shallow Wady, lies the village of Bethany ; in a direction about E. S. E. from Jerusalem. We reached it in three quarters of an hour from the Damascus gate. This gives a distance of a little less than two Roman miles from the eastern part of the city ; corresponding well to the fifteen furlongs of the Evangelist.[1] On the W. N. W.

[1] John 11, 18.

is a hill partially separated from the higher ridge of the mount of Olives by a deep valley; the head of which we went round in returning over the summit of the mount. Just south of the village is a very deep and narrow Wady or ravine running down towards the east; and on its further side on higher ground, southeast from Bethany, about one third of a mile distant, is seen the deserted village of Abu Dîs.

Bethany is a poor village of some twenty families; its inhabitants apparently are without thrift or industry. In the walls of a few of the houses there are marks of antiquity, large hewn stones, some of them bevelled; but they have all obviously belonged to more ancient edifices, and been employed again and again in the construction of successive dwellings or other buildings. The monks, as a matter of course, show the house of Mary and Martha, that of Simon the leper, and the sepulchre of Lazarus. The latter is a deep vault, like a cellar, excavated in the limestone rock in the middle of the village; to which there is a descent by twenty-six steps.[1] It is hardly necessary to remark, that there is not the slightest probability of its ever having been the tomb of Lazarus. The form is not that of the ancient sepulchres; nor does its position accord with the narrative of the New Testament, which implies that the tomb was not in the town.[2]

The Arab name of the village is el-'Azirîyeh, from el-'Azir, the Arabic form of Lazarus. The name Bethany is unknown among the native inhabitants. Yet there is no reason to question the identity of the place. The distance from Jerusalem and the situation on the road to Jericho are sufficiently decisive. The *Itin. Hieros.* in A. D. 333, already mentions here the crypt of Lazarus; and Jerome some seventy years later speaks of a church as having been built over it.[3] In the seventh century it is further mentioned by both Antoninus Martyr and Arculfus; at that time the church (Basilica) was standing over the supposed sepulchre, and a large monastery had been established.[4]

About A. D. 1132, Melisinda, the queen of king Fulco of Jerusalem, wishing to found a nunnery over which her younger sister Iveta might preside as abbess, selected Bethany as the site, and obtained it from the canons of the Holy Sepulchre in exchange for Tekoa. She then established here a convent of Black nuns professing the rule and institutes of St. Benedict; the same order of which her sister was already a member in the

---

[1] In the days of Cotovicus there were twenty-two steps; Itin. p. 276.
[2] John 11, 31. 38.
[3] Itin. Hieros. ed. Wesseling, p. 596.
ii. 101, 102

Hieron. Onomasticon, art. *Bethania.* Eusebius does not mention it.
[4] Adamnanus 1. 24.

nunnery of St. Anne in Jerusalem.[1] The new convent was more richly endowed than any other in Syria ; and for its protection, the queen caused a strong tower of hewn stones to be erected at a great expense. The buildings were not completed until near the death of king Fulco in A. D. 1143. An aged matron of approved piety was made the first abbess ; who was soon succeeded by the high born Iveta.[2] Two centuries later, this convent was no longer in existence.[3] Brocardus in the thirteenth century does not allude to it ; and Ludolph de Suchem in the fourteenth speaks only of three churches, one of which was used by the Arabs as a stall for cattle. In A. D. 1484 Felix Fabri found only the church over the sepulchre of Lazarus ; and this in the days of Cotovicus had been converted into a mosk. Since then the place is often mentioned by travellers ; and has been gradually falling more and more into decay.

Of the village of Bethphage no trace exists. In coming from Jericho our Lord appears to have entered it before reaching Bethany ;[4] and it probably therefore lay near to the latter, a little below it towards the east. Of course, it could not well have been where Abu Dis now stands ;[5] and still less on the spot which the monks assign to it, half-way between Bethany and the summit of the mount of Olives, where there is nothing to show that a village ever stood.

We returned to Jerusalem by the somewhat shorter route over the summit of Mount Olivet.

---

[1] See above, p. 233.

[2] Will. Tyr. 15. 26. Jac. de Vitriaco 58. Wilken Gesch. der Kreuzz. II. pp. 616, 617.

[3] Vertot relates, without citing his authority, that in A. D. 1254, the pope granted the castle (fortified convent) of Bethany, to the knights Hospitalers; the nuns after the destruction of Jerusalem having retired to Europe. Histoire des Chev. Hospit. de St. Jean, etc. I. p. 400.

[4] Matt. 21, 1. Luke 19, 29.

[5] Schubert suggests that Abu Dis may have been the site of the ancient Bahurim; Reise III. p. 70. This of course is a mere conjecture; though Bahurim was not far from Jerusalem, beyond the mount of Olives; 2 Sam. 16, 5. Joseph. Ant. 7. 9. 7. Yet as David came to Bahurim on his way to the Jordan, after passing over the summit of the mount of Olives, it would seem that this place must have stood further north than Abu Dis. 2 Sam. 16, 1. 5.

SECTION IX.

EXCURSION FROM JERUSALEM TO BETHEL, ETC.

HAVING thus been for several weeks diligently occupied in investigating the antiquities and interesting features of the Holy City, the time had now arrived, when, according to our plan, it became necessary to extend our researches to other parts of the country. We still regarded Jerusalem as our head-quarters; as the central point from which to make excursions; and by varying our routes in going and returning to and from different points, we were enabled to see much more of the country, than would have been possible by merely travelling once or twice along the same road. Our routes often crossed each other; but I do not recollect that we ever passed for any distance over the same ground twice, excepting the short interval between Jerusalem and Bethlehem, and one or two like instances. Three times, for example, we were in Hebron; but in no instance did we enter or leave the town by the same route a second time.

Before entering upon the account of our further travels, I must beg the reader to recall to mind the remarks already made upon the mass of foreign ecclesiastical tradition, which has been fastened not only upon Jerusalem and its environs, but also upon the whole country west of the Jordan.[1] Besides this, many travellers have exercised their own discretion, (not always the most enlightened,) in assigning the ancient Scriptural names of places to such sites as they might happen to fall in with or hear of; without stopping to inquire, whether some other place might not have an equal or better claim to the proposed appellation.[2] Others, and especially the older travellers, professedly give

---

[1] See the beginning of Sect. VII. p. 251, above.

[2] An instance of this is furnished by Dr. Clarke; who is very much disposed to convert the fortress Sânûr, (which he writes Santorri,) between Nâbulus and Jenin, into the ancient city of Samaria; because *he* saw no other appropriate site for the latter town upon that route. Yet, as he admits, Maundrell and others had a century before found the name of Sebaste (Samaria), and described its site upon another route. The same is mentioned by Maundeville and William of Baldensel in the 14th century;

a description of the various parts of the Holy Land ; but in
such a way, that it is usually difficult and often impossible to
distinguish what they have actually visited and seen, from that
which they have only heard or read of, or relate perhaps merely
from conjecture. Very rarely do they mention the modern
names of the places, which they thus call only by Scriptural
appellations ; so that when the same ancient name has a
diversity of application, as is often the case, it is only by close
attention to minor circumstances, that we can determine what
modern place is meant. Thus, for instance, under the name of
Shiloh, it is difficult to tell whether a writer is speaking of Neby
Samwîl, or of one of the various other points which have been
assumed as its site. The true site appears to have been visited
by no traveller.[1]

I have made these observations in order to draw the reader's
attention to the confusion and discrepancies which prevail among
the books of travels in Palestine ; and also in order to found
upon them this further remark, viz. that if a traveller at the
present day is unable to find many of the ancient places
mentioned and described by earlier writers, the reason often lies
not in his own ill success ; but in the fact, that those writers
have described places which they never visited, and which in
all probability no longer existed in their day.

As a preparation for our further journies in Palestine, my
companion had taken great pains to collect from various quarters
the native names of all the places in those parts which we
hoped to visit. This practice he had commenced so early as the
year 1834, during a journey through Haurân and the northern
parts of Syria ; and had afterwards continued it with express
reference to our proposed investigations in Palestine. In Jerusalem itself, there was frequent opportunity of making the
acquaintance of intelligent Sheikhs and other persons from the
towns and villages in that and other districts ; and they were in
general ready to communicate all they knew respecting the
places in their own neighbourhood. This mode of obtaining
information we preferred to a direct application to the government ; not wishing in any way to awaken distrust or risk a
denial. The lists of names thus made out, were in some respects
more complete than any which the government could have
furnished ; inasmuch as the latter has to do only with inhabited
towns and villages, while our attention was directed, in at least
as great a degree, to the deserted sites and ruined places of

and also by several other travellers.
Clarke's Travels, etc. 4to. Part II. Vol. I.
p. 504

[1] These remarks apply particularly to
the tract of Brocardus, the travels of Breydenbach, and other like works. Even
Cotovicus is not wholly free from the same
fault ; and Pococke's writings must be used
with great caution, as he thus often gives
an opinion instead of facts.

which the country is so full. The lists thus obtained were afterwards enlarged and corrected by our own observations and further inquiries ; and subsequently revised and copied out by my companion. In this form, although far from complete, they were nevertheless more so than anything of the kind which had hitherto been attempted in Palestine and Syria ; and by the advice of eminent scholars they were subjoined in an appendix to the first edition of this work. They could be regarded only as the first step towards a collection, which may hereafter become of great importance to biblical geographers.[1]

Our first excursion from Jerusalem was towards the northeast, into a region which, so far as I know, had never been visited by any Frank traveller. We returned on the second day by a more western and better known route. Our friends had heard, that villages existed in the former quarter, bearing names which might be regarded as the Arabic forms of Anathoth, Geba, and Bethel ; but none of them had ever yet visited these places. They had however become acquainted in Jerusalem with some of the native Christian priests from Taiyibeh, a large village three hours or more northeast of el-Bireh, and from Râm-Allah, another village just west of the latter place. It was therefore proposed, that some of our friends should join us in the excursion, in order that while they thus afforded us countenance and aid, they might also return the visits of the priests, and awaken in them an interest for the distribution of books and the diffusion of instruction. The party, as at length made up, consisted of Messrs Lanneau, Nicolayson, Paxton,[2] and ourselves ; in all six persons, besides one of our servants. We were all on horseback, with an extra mule for the tent and baggage, and two attendants (Mukârin, muleteers) on foot, who had charge of the animals.[3]

Friday, May 4th. We intended to have set off this morning with the rising sun ; but the arrangements for a large party delayed us ; so that it was seven o'clock before all was ready. Then occurred various other delays ; some of the party went out at St. Stephen's gate, and others by that of Damascus ; and it was not until 7½ o'clock that we mustered at the northeast corner of the city wall and took our departure. The road descends obliquely into the valley of Jehoshaphat, and then crosses the ridge

---

[1] These Arabic lists, corrected and enlarged, it is proposed soon to publish in a separate volume. 1856.

[2] The Rev. J. D. Paxton, also an American, resided for nearly two years at Beirût, and afterwards published a work entitled : *Letters on Palestine and Egypt, written during a residence there in the years* 1836–7–8. Lexington, Ky. 1839, 8vo. Reprinted Lond. 1839.—In his Letters, Mr Paxton makes ii. 106–108

no allusion to his excursion with us; but introduces the names of the places which he now saw for the first time, into a letter dated Oct. 1836 ; thus leaving upon the mind of the reader the impression, that he became acquainted with them nearly two years earlier. Lett. XV. p. 169. Lond.

[3] The Mukâry is indiscriminately the owner or provider and driver of camels, horses, asses, mules, etc.

extending between the mount of Olives and Scopus, at a point just at the left of the northern summit of the former. We reached the top of the ridge in twenty-five minutes. This point, and more especially the adjacent summit, presents, I think, the finest view of Jerusalem anywhere to be found. The city is seen diagonally; and the view thus includes the great mosk and the deep valley, which are not seen so well from the Damascus road; while, at the same time, the domes and minarets are here exhibited to the eye with far better effect than from the other summit of Olivet. The Dead Sea was also visible, and the little village el-'Isâwiyeh in a valley below us about a quarter of an hour distant, bearing N. 70° E. Far in the north was the high village er-Râm, the ancient Ramah, on the east of the Nâbulus road. Before us was a wide prospect of broken hills and valleys, extending to the plain of the Jordan.

Our course thus far had been N. 25° E. The way now became more winding, but in the general direction northeast. We lost sight of Jerusalem, and descending rather steeply came in twenty minutes to the bottom of Wady es-Suleim, here running east by south to join Wady Sidr further down, and afterwards the Fârah. In the same direction we were told of the ruins of a convent, called Deir es-Sidd. We thus left el-'Isâwiyeh on the right behind a ridge; and crossing the valley obliquely, ascended another ridge skirting it on the north; beyond which runs also a deep parallel valley, called Wady es-Selâm. We kept along upon this ridge, which becomes gradually wider; and at 8¾ o'clock reached 'Anâta, situated on the same broad ridge at the distance of one hour and a quarter from Jerusalem. There can be no question that this is the ancient Anathoth, the birthplace of the prophet Jeremiah; which Josephus describes as twenty stadia distant from Jerusalem, and which Eusebius and Jerome also place in the tribe of Benjamin about three miles from the same city towards the north.[1] Ecclesiastical tradition, as is well known, has selected for Anathoth another site, at the village of Kuryet el-'Enab on the road to Ramleh, a distance of three hours from Jerusalem.[2]

'Anâta seems to have been once a walled town and a place of strength; but I do not find it directly mentioned by any writer since the days of Jerome.[3] Portions of the wall remain,

[1] Jer. 1, 1, et Hieron. Comm. in loc. "qui habitabant contra septentrionalem Jerusalem in tertio miliaro et viculo Anathoth." Onomast. art. *Anathoth.* Joseph. Ant. 10. 7. 3. See the other authorities collected by Reland, Palæst, p. 561.

[2] Adrichomius, p. 14. Cotovicus, p. 146. Quaresmius II. p. 15.

[3] Brocardus indeed mentions Anathoth, but places it close by Ramah of Benjamin; c. 7. p. 179. He had probably heard of the name 'Anâta, without knowing its exact position. Breydenbach copies Brocardus. In like manner Nau has merely the passing remark, that Anathoth lies a league east of Jerusalem; Voyage, p. 49.

built of large hewn stones, and apparently ancient ; as are also the foundations of some of the houses. One of our party found the fragments of a column or two among the ruins. The houses are few, and the people seemed poor and miserable, amounting only to a few scores. The village lies where the broad ridge slopes off gradually towards the southeast. On this side are tilled fields, and we had passed several others on our way. The grain was still standing ; the time of harvest not having yet come. Fig trees and olive trees are also scattered around. From the vicinity of 'Anâta a favourite species of building-stone is carried to Jerusalem ; and we met several troops of donkeys loaded in this manner with the materials of future dwellings ; a hewn stone being slung upon each side of the poor animal. Larger stones are transported on camels.

From this point there is an extensive view over the whole eastern slope of the mountainous tract of Benjamin ; including also the valley of the Jordan and the northern part of the Dead Sea. The region before us was that alluded to by the prophet Isaiah, near the end of the tenth chapter, where the approach of Sennecharib towards Jerusalem is described ; and from the spot where we now stood, several of the places there mentioned were visible. Thus er-Râm (Ramah) bore N. N. W. on its conical hill ; and Jeba' (Geba) was before us, bearing N. 10° E. The nearest village was Hizmeh N. 20° E. and far in the distance we could distinguish Taiyibeh lying N. N. E.$\frac{1}{4}$N. on a lofty hill, which was to be the limit of our excursion.

The whole tract over which we were now about to pass, is made up of a succession of deep rugged valleys running towards the east ; with broad ridges of uneven table land between, often broken and sometimes rising into high points. These terminate towards the east in high cliffs overhanging the plain of the Jordan. I have already remarked, that the great northern road from Jerusalem to Nâbulus passes along the water-shed of the mountainous country ; where the heads of the valleys running off in opposite directions often interlap.[1] Our present road lay at some distance further east ; so that the valleys, where we crossed them, had now become very deep. The sides of these Wadys indeed are here so steep and high, that in descending into them, we were usually obliged to dismount from our horses. The whole district is a mass of limestone rock ; which every-where juts out above the surface, and imparts to the whole land an aspect of sterility and barrenness. Yet wherever soil is found among the rocks, it is strong and fertile ; fields of grain are seen occasionally ; and fig trees and olive trees are planted everywhere

---

[1] See above, p. 258.

among the hills. Lower down the slope, towards the Jordan valley, all is a frightful desert.

With some difficulty we obtained a guide at 'Anâta to conduct us to Taiyibeh. Our object in this was not so much to learn the way ; for that was tolerably plain ; but rather to have a person always at hand, of whom we could inquire respecting the various villages and features of the country, as they came into view. We continued this practice during our future journies, so far as possible ; and found it generally necessary to obtain a new guide at the end of every few miles ; inasmuch as the peasants, though well acquainted with the immediate neighbourhood of their own villages, seldom know much of the country at a distance from their homes.

Our route now led us to Hizmeh. Leaving 'Anâta at 9.10, we descended very steeply in ten minutes to the bottom of Wady es-Selâm, which, with the Suleim, runs into Wady el-Fârah further down. Crossing a low ridge and a small shallow Wady, we ascended again more gradually, and came at 9.50 to Hizmeh, situated on the top of the next high ridge, with a deep valley on the north. Its position is similar to that of 'Anâta ; though the ridge is not so high. The village is about as large as 'Anâta and was now deserted ; the inhabitants having about two months before all fled across the Jordan to escape the conscription, leaving their fields of wheat and their olive and fig trees with none to attend them. The houses are solidly built of stone ; but we saw here no appearance of antiquity ; nor do I know of any ancient name to which the form Hizmeh corresponds.

Here, as on all the high points we crossed, there was a wide view over the whole slope quite to the Jordan and its valley, including the Dead Sea and the eastern mountains. We could trace the course of the Jordan by the green trees along its banks. The transparency of the atmosphere rendered distant objects very distinct ; so that the plain of the Jordan seemed not more than two hours distant, though its real distance was not less than four or five hours. In that direction we could see Wady el-Fârah as it ran off towards the plain, bearing S. 85° E.[1] From this point er-Râm bore N. 55° W. ; and Jeba', the next village on our route, due north. A high conical hill near the Nâbulus road, called Tuleil el-Fûl, with a large heap of stones upon the top, was everywhere a sightly object, and bore from Hizmeh S. 70° W.

Leaving Hizmeh at 10 o'clock, it took us again ten minutes to descend into the deep valley on the north, which I suppose to

---

[1] The name of this Wady might suggest a coincidence with the Parah of Benjamin ; Josh. 18, 23. But these names come from different roots ; the Hebrew word meaning 'a heifer,' while the Arabic signifies 'a mouse.' We could hear of no village called Fârah, as related by Buckingham. Travels, 4to. p. 312.

ii. 111, 112

be the Fârah.   Here are enclosures of fig trees ; and on the projecting point of a low hill at the right of the road, are a few ancient walls, some broad as if for terraces, and others apparently
foundations ; but there are not enough of them to be regarded
as the ruins of a town or village.   Our guide called them Ma'dâd.[1]
Ascending, again, we now came out upon the table land of the
next ridge, and reached Jeba' at 10.40.   It lies upon a low conical, or rather a round, eminence on the broad ridge, which shelves
down like all the rest toward the Jordan valley, and spreads out
below the village into a fine sloping plain with fields of grain
now in the milk.   The views of the Dead Sea and Jordan and
of the eastern mountains were here still more extensive ; while
across the deep ravine on the north we could see the next village
on our route, Mŭkhmâs, the ancient Michmash, lying directly
overagainst Jeba' in a direction about northeast.

The village of Jeba' is small, about the size of those already
described ; and is half in ruins.   Among these are occasionally
seen large hewn stones indicating antiquity.   There is here the
ruin of a square tower, almost solid ; and a small building having the appearance of an ancient church.   Two nights before
our visit, robbers had entered the village ; and breaking into the
houses of the principal inhabitants, wounded them with swords.
To-day the men were all out on the search ; and we found only
women.

Besides Mŭkhmâs, we could here see several other villages,
viz. Deir Duwân N. by E.   Taiyibeh N. 20° E.   Burka lying this side of Deir Duwân N. 9° W.   el-Kudeirah N. 3° E.
Rŭmmôn N. N. E.¼ E.   This latter village forms a remarkable
object in the landscape ; being situated on and around the summit of a conical chalky hill, and visible in all directions.   There
can be little doubt of its being the identical rock Rimmon, to
which the remnant of the Benjamites fled after the slaughter of
the tribe at Gibeah.   A place of this name is also mentioned by
Eusebius and Jerome, as existing in their day fifteen miles north
of Jerusalem.[2]

The name Jeba' corresponds exactly to the Hebrew *Geba* in
the Old Testament, a city of Benjamin assigned to the priests.[3]
It lay on the northern border of the kingdom of Judah ;[4] overagainst Michmash, from which it was separated by a " passage,"
meaning the deep valley between.[5]   Here Saul and Jonathan
encamped against the Philistines in Michmash ; and here between
the two places was the scene of Jonathan's remarkable adven-

---

[1] See more on this tract in Vol. III, under May 10. 1852.

[2] Judg. 20, 45. 47. 21, 13. Onomast.
art. *Remmon.*

ii. 112-114

[3] Josh. 18, 24. 21, 17.

[4] 1 K. 23, 8.   Zech. 14, 10.

[5] Heb. מַעֲבָר, 1 Sam. 13, 23. Is. 10,
29.

ture.[1]   All these circumstances accord perfectly with the situation of Jeba'.   At a later period king Asa built up Geba and Mizpah with stones brought from Ramah.[2]   The exiles returned again to Geba after the captivity ; and the name is simply mentioned by Eusebius and Jerome.[3]   But from that time till the present day, there is no further trace of Geba in history.[4]

We left Jeba' at 11.10 for Mûkhmâs.   The descent into the valley was steeper and longer than any of the preceding.   The path led down obliquely, and we reached the bottom in half an hour.   It is called Wady es-Suweinît.   It begins in the neighbourhood of Beitîn and el-Bîreh ; and as it breaks through the ridge below these places, its sides form precipitous walls.   On the right, about a quarter of an hour below where we crossed, it again contracts and passes off between high perpendicular precipices, which (our guide said) continue a great way down and increase in grandeur.   In one of them is a large cavern called Jâîhah.   This Wady was said to run into another called the Fûwâr coming more from the north, which receives also the Fârah and then empties into Wady el-Kelt.   This latter issues out upon the plain not far from Jericho.   We doubted at the time the correctness of this information ; but our own subsequent observations tended to confirm it.

This steep precipitous valley is probably "the passage of Michmash," mentioned in Scripture.[5]   In the valley, just at the left of where we crossed, are two hills of a conical or rather a spherical form, having steep rocky sides, with small Wadys running up behind each so as almost to isolate them.   One is on the side towards Jeba', and the other towards Mûkhmâs.   These would seem to be the two rocks mentioned in connection with Jonathan's adventure ;[6] they are not indeed so 'sharp' as the language of Scripture would seem to imply ; but they are the only rocks of the kind in this vicinity.   The northern one is connected towards the west with an eminence still more distinctly isolated.   This valley appears to have been at a later time, the dividing line between the tribes of Benjamin and Ephraim.[7]

Crossing the valley obliquely, and ascending with difficulty

---

[1] 1 Sam. 13, 15. 16. 14, 5. 16.   In all these passages the English version wrongly has *Gibeah.*   In the first three, the Heb. reads *Geba;* and the same should evidently be read in c. 14, 16.   Elsewhere also there is some confusion in the writing of these two names : e. g. in Judg. 20, 10. 33, Geba is obviously put for Gibeah ; comp. vv. 4, 5, 9, 36.   This arose probably from copyists, who might easily thus interchange the masculine and feminine forms of the same word.   The error of the English translators is less easily to be accounted for.

[2] 1 K. 15, 22. 2 Chr. 16, 6. Jos. Antt. 8. 12. 4.
[3] Neh. 7, 30.   Onomast. art. *Gabe.*
[4] In the former edition of this work, Jeba, was wrongly held to be Gibeah.
[5] 1 Sam. 13, 23.   Compare Isa. 10, 29.
[6] 1 Sam. 14, 4. 5.
[7] Geba on the south side of this valley was the northern limit of Judah and Benjamin, 2 Kings 23, 8 ; while Bethel on its north side further west was on the southern border of Ephraim ; Josh. 16, 1. 2. 18, 13. Judg. 1, 22–26.

for fifteen minutes, we came upon the slope on which Mŭkhmâs stands, a low ridge between two small Wadys running south into the Suweinît ; the ground rising towards the north beyond, to the still higher land which extends to Deir Duwân. The rocks here by the side of the path were cut away in several places. We reached the village at 12 o'clock. It was even more desolate than Anathoth ; but bears marks of having been a much larger and stronger place than any of the others we had passed. There are many foundations of large hewn stones ; and some columns were lying among them. Here the prospect towards the east and north is cut off by higher ground. We could look back upon Jeba' ; and er-Râm bore S. 70° W.

There seems to be no reason for any doubt as to the identity of Mŭkhmâs with the Michmash of Scripture. Eusebius and Jerome describe the latter as a large village nine miles distant from Jerusalem, and not far from Ramah.[1] We were nearly three and a half hours in reaching it, over a very rough and difficult road.

Passing on without stopping, and taking a more northerly course, we ascended gradually and soon crossed the high broad swell of land before us. We now struck upon the eastern side of a narrow but deep side valley running south into the Suweinît nearly at right angles. This we followed up to its head at Deir Duwân. Opposite the point where we came upon it, at the bottom of the valley, in the steep western wall, are several sepulchres excavated in the rock. The path keeps along the verge of the high ground, gradually approaching the bottom of the valley as the latter ascends. At 12.35 we were opposite the village of Burka, bearing W. N. W. across the valley, high up on the hillside, a quarter of an hour distant. The high point of Neby Samwil had also been for some time in sight, and now bore W. S. W. The village of Kudeirah lay N. 18° W. and Deir Duwân N. 10° E. At 12.50 the valley had become more shallow ; and tombs and quarries appeared again in its bottom on the left, near the low point of a hill between the valley, and a more western branch. On this low hill, as we were afterwards told, there are traces of an ancient site, which we explored more fully at a later period.[2] We reached Deir Duwân at 1.05, in an hour and five minutes from Mŭkhmâs.

This is a large and tolerably wealthy place, compared with all the others we had seen to-day. It lies in an uneven rocky basin, at the head of the valley we had followed up ; and its position is high, although shut in by hills. This is shown by the rapid

<hr/>

[1] Onomast. art. *Machmas.*—The monks have usually transferred the site of Michmash to el-Bireh; Brocardus, c. 7. Quaresmius II. p. 786. That was for them a more convenient location.
ii. 117. 118
[2] See under May 14th, 1838.

ascent of the small Wady from the south ; while on the north
the place is skirted by another very deep and rugged valley running towards the east.　The declivities around were now covered
with grain, olive, and fig trees, all growing among the rocks as
before ; and everything appeared thrifty.　The place is said to
produce large quantities of figs ; and we had hoped to have obtained here some of the dried fruit ; but their stock of it was
exhausted.　As we rode into the town, we were welcomed by a
company of twenty or thirty men, who conducted us to the flat
roof of a house and treated us with great civility.　They had
never before seen a Frank among them.　Their village, they said,
was anciently situated on the low hill towards the south, where
there are ruins ; and on the present site was then a convent.　But
I apprehend that this is nothing more than a mode of accounting
for the name Deir (convent).　There are no marks of antiquity
about the present village.

　　About an hour from Deir Duwân towards the northwest,
lies Beitîn, the ancient Bethel, not in sight ; and it follows from
the scriptural account and from the nature of the country, that
the city of Ai, destroyed by Joshua, must have been somewhere
in the vicinity of the spot on which we now were.[1]　The name
however has utterly perished ; we inquired diligently after it
throughout the whole region, but without finding the slightest
trace.　The city might have been situated perhaps upon the site
with ruins south of Deir Duwân ; or upon a rocky Tell (hill)
bearing from the village N. 46° W. and overlooking the deep
northern valley.　Another place of ruins, el-'Alya, was also
pointed out, bearing N. 50° E. at some distance across the same
valley.　But our researches to-day respecting Ai were so unsatisfactory, that we renewed them at a later period ; though with
not much better success.[2]

　　From this place Taiyibeh, our next stage, bore N. 23° E.
situated on very high ground.　The village of Kudeirah bore S.
50° W. er-Râm S. 40° W. Jeba' S. 12° W. and Rŭmmôn on its
lofty rock E. N. E. ½ N.

　　Having remained for half an hour at Deir Duwân, we set
off again at 1.35 for Taiyibeh ; although our guide was very desirous of proceeding directly to Beitîn.　His reason probably was
the much shorter distance of the latter place.　After five minutes
we began to descend the very rugged wall of the valley on the
north, the steepest and longest descent we had yet made.　The
valley here cannot well be less than two hundred and fifty or
three hundred feet in depth.　We dismounted as usual, the
path being very difficult for the horses, even without a load.
Before us, towards the right, was Rŭmmôn, on a naked conical

---

[1] Josh. c 7 and 8.　　　　　[2] See under May 14th.

point of the ridge, rising steeply on the north side of the valley ; the houses being apparently built in terraces around the hill from the top downwards. It took us thirty minutes to reach the bottom of the valley. This seemed to have here more than one name. Some called it el-Mŭtyâh ; while another spoke of it as Wady el-'Asas. It is the great drain of the adjacent tract ; and passes down to the plain of the Jordan, issuing from the mountains at some distance north of Jericho under the name of Wady Nawâ'imeh, where we afterwards encountered it again.

We now entered a narrow branch valley which comes into Wady el-Mŭtyâh from the north nearly at right angles. It is called Wady el-'Ain, from a spring of water which descends into it further up, from the western hill. The region is very rocky ; and we advanced by a rugged and often dangerous path. During the whole day we saw very little grass ; the chief herbage everywhere was the furzy plant Bellân ; and in this valley I was struck with the frequent appearance of the common sage of our gardens, interspersed with the fragrant Za'ter. At 2.25, we came upon the fountain which gives name to the Wady ; a pretty spring issuing from the rocky wall upon our left. The valley extends quite up to Taiyibeh, having its head in a basin on the northwest of the hill, on which that place is situated.

Instead of following the direct road up the valley, which would have brought us to the village in one hour from the fountain, or at 3.25, the guide at about half way mistook the path, and led us up a side Wady on the right, to the high open country lying between Rŭmmôn and Taiyibeh. Discovering the mistake, we now struck across the fields towards the north without a path, passing over a high hill which afforded a wide prospect, and at length reached Taiyibeh ; losing about twenty minutes by this *détour*.

The village of Taiyibeh crowns a conical hill, on the highest ridge or tract of land which we had yet crossed. On the very summit of the hill are the ruins of a tower, once similar apparently to those we had seen in almost all the villages. From these ruins the houses extend down the sides of the hill, chiefly towards the southeast. On the west and north are fertile basins of some breadth, forming the beginning of Wadys ; and these are full of gardens of olive and fig trees. Many olive trees are also scattered upon the hills around. From the site of the old tower there is a splendid view over the whole eastern slope, the vale of the Jordan or el-Ghôr, the Dead Sea, and the eastern mountains comprising the districts of the Belka and of Jebel 'Ajlûn. In the latter, towards the E. N. E. a break was seen, where the valley of the Zerka comes down ; and just north of

ii. 120, 121

it, the ravine of 'Ajlûn with the Saracenic castle, Kŭl'at er-Rŭbŭd, perched on a lofty rock high up in the mountains, and bearing N. 55° E.[1] Further south the site of Nimrin was pointed out.[2] On the east of the sea the mountains seemed to come down in precipices close to the water; so that apparently no road could pass. Occasional ravines were visible in the naked rocks. Towards the south the view took in the Frank Mountain (el-Fureidis) beyond Bethlehem. Neither Jerusalem nor the mount of Olives was visible. Near at hand was Rŭmmôn, now below us. The landscape exhibited little of verdure or beauty; yet its stern and desert features were strongly impressive.[3]

Close by Taiyibeh, S. E.¼E. on the top of a lower hill, sixty or eighty rods distant, are the ruins of a small church of St George; of which the walls are still partially standing.

The inhabitants of Taiyibeh are all native Christians of the Greek rite. Their priests had visited the missionaries in Jerusalem, and we now found here friends, who seemed exceedingly glad to welcome us to their village. As we wished, if possible, to proceed further to-day, Mr Smith and myself repaired immediately to the ruined tower, taking with us one or two of the inhabitants to point out and name to us the various objects in view. On returning, we found our companions sitting with the priests and others before the *Medâfeh*,[4] sipping coffee out of small cups in the oriental style. The Mukârys had concluded to stop here for the night, and without asking leave had unloaded the horses; so that we were in a measure compelled to remain.

A place was now selected and the tent pitched; and we obtained a supply of mats, lights, and eatables from the village. We took this course both because we preferred our tent to the small and uncomfortable dwellings of the inhabitants, infested as they are with vermin; and because too we hoped thus to have more the command of our own time. But in this latter

[1] Burckhardt visited and describes this castle; Travels in Syria, pp. 266, 267. Compare Irby and Mangles' Travels, p. 306. [93.] From the inscriptions, it appears to have been built under Saladin; and so Abulfeda, Tab. Syr. ed. Köhler, pp. 18, 92. The same district was visited by my companion Mr Smith, in 1834.

[2] See further under May 13th.

[3] Here we took, among others, the following bearings: Rŭmmôn S. 5° W. Frank Mountain S. 17° W. er-Râm S. 36° W. Neby Samwil S. 50° W. el-'Alya S. 60° W. Khân Hŭdhrûr, a ruined Khân on the way from Jerusalem to Jericho, S. 15° E. Dead Sea, northwest bay, S. 35° E. North

end of the sea S. 44° E. Wady Zerka, mouth, N. 60° E. Kŭl'at er-Rŭbŭd N. 55° E. Deir Jerûr, a small Muslim village near Taiyibeh, N. 5° E.

[4] The Medâfeh is a sort of public house, set apart for the reception of travellers. Each village has one or more. In those parts of the country not yet corrupted by the frequency of foreign travellers, the stranger is hospitably entertained by the inhabitants, without the expectation of a reward. Of this we found several instances; see at Beit Nettif under May 17th. See also Burckhardt's Travels in Syria, pp. 295, 351, 384.

particular we reckoned without our host. The inhabitants crowded about us with their Sheikh and three priests, until the tent was completely full, besides a multitude standing around the door. Mr Lanneau distributed among them several books and tracts in the Arabic language ; and they became quite clamorous for more. They were especially delighted with the psalters ; and each of the priests obtained the promise of a bible, for which they were to come or send to Jerusalem. The Sheikh we did not like ; he was shy, though cringing in his manner ; and almost from the first, as he accompanied us to the ruined church, began to inquire about his *bakhshish*. Afterwards in the tent, he declared himself an American ; and to convince us of it, drank milk in a cup of tea before the priests, although it was on Friday and therefore unlawful. It was only by ordering the people away that we could get room to eat ; and it was quite late before we could even think of sleep.

At length, however, we made shift to arrange our couches within our somewhat narrow limits, and laid ourselves down. The captain or responsible guard of the village himself kept watch by our tent, accompanied by two or three others ; and to beguile the night and keep themselves awake, they one after another repeated tales in a monotonous tone of voice. This served their own purpose ; and had too the further effect of aiding to keep us awake ; so that, what with the voices of the Arabs, the barking of dogs, the crawling of fleas, and the hum of mosquitos, we were none of us able to get much sleep all night. —Two or three nights before, robbers had entered the village and stolen several sheep. The desert towards the Dead Sea was said to be full of them.

Taiyibeh contains seventy-five taxable inhabitants, showing a population of from three to four hundred souls. The only other villages north of Jerusalem within the province, containing Christians, were said to be Râm-Allah and Jifneh, which we afterwards visited ; and the smaller ones of Bir Zeit and 'Ain 'Arik, each with twenty-five Christian men and the rest Muslims. The land at Taiyibeh is held by the peasants in freehold ; except that in a certain sense the whole village belongs to the Haram esh-Sherîf, to the Mutawelly of which it pays annually seventy-five *Mids* (measures) of barley and wheat. The *Mid* is equal to sixteen *Sâ'a*, or twelve *Ruba'* of Egypt.[1] Besides this there are paid in taxes to the government for each olive and fig tree one piastre ; for each she goat and ewe one piastre ; and for each ox seventy-five piastres, which is intended rather as a tax upon the land ploughed, than upon the oxen. Each man also pays one hundred piastres as *Firdeh* or capitation-tax ; and being all

---

[1] The Egyptian *Ruba'* is the twenty-fourth part of an *Ardeb*.

ii. 123, 124

Christians and free from the military conscription, each pays an additional tax of twenty-five piastres, which is reckoned to the *Kharaj* or toleration tax.[1] The village was said to pay in all, not far from seventy-five purses annually, equivalent to 1875 Spanish dollars.—The *Sheikh el-Beled*, literally the "elder of the village," is here as elsewhere the chief man, and the medium of communication with the government.

The remarkable position of Taiyibeh would not probably have been left unoccupied in ancient times ; but I was formerly unable to identify it with any earlier site, unless with the Ophrah of Benjamin. This city, according to Eusebius and Jerome, lay five Roman miles east of Bethel ; which accords with the situation of et-Taiyibeh.[2]

There arises, however, the further question, whether this Ophrah is not the same with the *Ephron* or *Ephraim* of the Old Testament ; a place which Abijah king of Judah took from Jeroboam along with Bethel and Jeshanah.[3] Josephus speaks also of a small city *Ephraim*, which Vespasian took along with Bethel.[4] All these appear to be names of one and the same city, identical with Ophrah.[5] With the same, too, we may well identify the city *Ephraim* of the New Testament, which was "near to the wilderness," and to which our Lord withdrew with his disciples after the raising of Lazarus.[6] Thence he returned to Jerusalem by crossing the Jordan, and passing down through Perea to Jericho.[7] With all these circumstances the position of et-Taiyibeh well corresponds.

Saturday, May 5th. Taking with us a guide from Taiyibeh, we set off at 4.50 for Beitin, intending to visit on our way the ruins at el-'Alya. We followed down the narrow valley by the road of yesterday for forty minutes. Here we turned W. N. W. up another branch, and then passed up an ascent, reaching the top at 6 o'clock. From this point el-'Alya lay ten minutes towards the south. We found there only a few ruins of small houses on a high plateau, with a deep valley on the west and southwest, but no traces of antiquity. Not far off towards the east is a spring of water, called 'Ain el-'Alya, 'upper spring,' to distinguish it from that in the valley below, which we passed yes-

---

[1] See above, p. 427. n. 1.

[2] Heb. עָפְרָה, Josh. 18, 23. 1 Sam. 13, 17. Euseb. et Hieron. Onomast. art. *Aphra.*

[3] 2 Chr. 13, 19. Heb. עֶפְרוֹן Keth. עֶפְרָיִן Keri; Sept. 'Εφρών.

[4] Joseph. B. J. 4. 9. 9.

[5] The Heb. names עָפְרָה *Ophrah* and עֶפְרוֹן *Ephron* differ strictly only in termination; and the same difference is also found in the proper name *Salmon*, e. g. שַׂלְמָה and שַׂלְמוֹן Ruth 4, 20. 21.

[6] John 11, 54.

[7] See the author's Harmony of the Gospels in Greek, p. 201.—See also generally, ibid. p. 203 sq. Biblioth. Sacra, 1845. p. 398 sq.

terday. The village probably derived its name from the fountain.[1]

Returning to the point where we had left our road, we now proceeded again at 6.40, on the same general course towards Beitîn. We soon crossed a broad shallow Wady, running nearly south, apparently one of the heads of that passing down on the north side of Deir Duwân ; and at 7.10, reached the eastern branch of the great Nâbulus road on the higher land beyond. Hence Taiyibeh bore N. 76° E. and el-Bireh S. 40° W. Descending gradually by this road southwest, we came to the site of Beitîn at 7½ o'clock, just at the left of the path ; making a distance of two hours from Taiyibeh. The ruins lie upon the point of a low hill, between the heads of two shallow Wadys, which unite below and run off S. S. E.½S. into the deep and rugged valley es-Suweinit, which passes down between Jeba, and Mûkhmâs. The spot is shut in by higher land on every side ; so that the only places we could see distinctly from the ruins were el-Bireh S. 48° W. and Sha'fât S. 10° W.

Perceiving however some ruins across the valley S.½E. on the higher ground, we immediately proceeded thither, and came in eight minutes to what the Arabs called Burj Beitîn and also Burj Makhrûn, 'Castle of Beitîn or Makhrûn.' It is the ruin of a small square fortress of hewn stones, including a Greek church. Several columns were lying among the ruins, on one of which a cross was carved in relief.—Proceeding still in the direction S. by E.½E. we came in ten minutes more to the ruins of another larger Greek church, situated on the highest spot of ground in the vicinity. The lower walls are still very distinct, and many columns are lying about ; though it seems to have been long ago destroyed. To this ruin one of the Greek priests at Taiyibeh, who had been delving a little into biblical history, had chosen to give the name of Ai ; and we found the same name among some of the people of that village. But there is not the slightest ground for any such hypothesis. There never was any thing here but a church ; and Ai must have been further off from Bethel, and certainly not directly in sight of it.[2]

We now returned to the site of Beitîn, and took a nearer survey of its ruins. They occupy the whole surface of the hillpoint, sloping towards the southeast, and cover a space of three or four acres. They consist of very many foundations and halfstanding walls of houses and other buildings. On the highest

---

[1] From 'Alya, Deir Duwân bore S. 5° W. Bir Zeit near Jifna N. 55° W. 'Atâra beyond Jifna N. 30° W. 'Ain Yebrûd on the Nâbulus road N. 20° W. Tell 'Asûr with a Wely N. 15° E. For several of these places as seen from Jifna and the vicinity, see under June 13th, on our journey northwards.

[2] From this church Beitîn bore N. N. W. ½ W. Taiyibeh N. E. by E. 'Alya N. 54° E. Deir Duwân S. 65° E. er-Râm S. 20° W.

ii. 125, 126

part, towards the N. N. W. are the remains of a square tower ; and near the southern point, the walls of a Greek church, standing within the foundations of a much larger and earlier edifice built of large stones, part of which have been used for erecting the later structure. The broken walls of several other churches are also to be distinguished. In the western valley are the remains of one of the largest reservoirs we saw in the country ; measuring 314 feet in length from northwest to southeast and 217 feet in breadth from northeast to southwest. The walls were built of massive stones ; the southern one is still entire ; those upon the sides are partly gone, while the northern one has almost wholly disappeared. The bottom was now a green grass-plat, having in it two living springs of good water. Here we spread our carpets on the grass for breakfast, by the side of these desolations of ages. A few Arabs, probably from some neighbouring village, had pitched their tents here for the summer, to watch their flocks and fields of grain ; and they were the only inhabitants. From them we obtained milk and also butter of excellent quality, which might have done honour to the days, when the flocks of Abraham and Jacob were pastured on these hills. It was indeed the finest we found anywhere in Palestine.

There is little room for question, that both the name and site of Beitin are identical with those of the ancient Bethel. The latter was a border city between Benjamin and Ephraim ; at first assigned to Benjamin, but conquered and afterwards retained by Ephraim.[1] According to Eusebius and Jerome, it lay twelve Roman miles from Jerusalem, on the right or east of the road leading to Sichem or Neapolis (Nâbulus).[2] From Beitin to el-Bîreh we found the distance to be forty-five minutes, and from Bîreh to Jerusalem three hours, with horses. The correspondence therefore in the situation is very exact ; and the name affords decisive confirmation. The Arabic termination *in* for the Hebrew *el*, is not an unusual change ; we found indeed several other instances of it entirely parallel.[3] Yet the name has been preserved solely among the common people. The monks appear for centuries not to have been aware of its existence ; and have assigned to Bethel a location much further towards the north.[4]

[1] Josh. 16, 1. 2. 18, 13. 22. Judg. 1, 22-26. 1 Kings 12, 29.

[2] Onomast. art. Βαιθήλ *Bethel*, 'Αγγαί *Agai*, Λουζάν *Luza*. See the other notices collected by Reland from Josephus and elsewhere, Palæst. p. 636.

[3] Thus for Heb. *Jezreel* we have *Zer'in* ; instead of Wady *Isma'il* (Ishmael), we heard Wady *Isma'in* ; and the name *Beit Jibrin* also occurs in Arabic writers under the form *Beit Jibril*, i. e. Gabriel.

[4] Brocardus places Bethel two leagues south of Samaria on the way to Sichem (Nâbulus) upon a high mountain; c. 7. p. 177. Eugesippus sets it a mile from Sichem on a part of Mount Gerizim; see in L. Allatii Symmikta, Col. Agr. 1653, pp. 111, 112. See also Breydenbach, Reissb. p. 127; and Quaresmius, Tom. II. pp. 792, 793. Maundrell looked for Bethel near Sinjil; March 25th. Schubert supposed himself to be near Bethel, 2½ hours north of el-Bîreh; Reise III. p. 129.

Our friends the Greek priests at Taiyibeh had also recognised the identity of Beitin and Bethel ; and had endeavoured to bring into use the Arabic form *Beitil* as being nearer to the original ; but it had found currency only within the circle of their own influence.   From them the missionaries in Jerusalem had heard of the place and had learned the name Beitil ; though from others they had heard only of Beitin.[1]

Bethel is celebrated in the Old Testament.   Abraham first pitched his tent in Palestine on the high ground eastward of this spot, still one of the finest tracts for pasturage in the whole land.[2]   Here Jacob slept on his way to Haran, and saw in his dream the ladder and the angels of God ascending and descending upon it ; and hither he afterwards returned and built an altar, and called the place Beth-el, ' House of God.'[3]   Samuel came once a year to Bethel to judge the people.[4]   In later times it became notorious as a seat of idolatrous worship, after Jeroboam had erected here one of his golden calves.   This was denounced at the time by a prophet of the Lord, who then transgressed and was destroyed by a lion.[5]   Bethel came afterwards into the possession of Judah ; and king Josiah destroyed its altars and idols, burning upon them dead men's bones from the sepulchres.[6]   After the exile, the place was again inhabited by the returning Jews ; and was fortified by Bacchides the Syrian in the time of the Maccabees.[7]

In the New Testament Bethel is not mentioned ; but it still existed, as we learn from Josephus ; and was captured by Vespasian.[8]   Eusebius and Jerome describe it as a small village in their day.[9]   This is the last notice of Bethel as an inhabited place.   The name is indeed mentioned by writers of the times of the crusades ; but apparently only as a place known in Scripture history, and not as then in existence.[10]   Yet the present ruins are greater than those of a small village ; and show that after the time of Jerome, the place must probably have revived and been enlarged.   The ruined churches upon the site and beyond the valley, betoken a town of importance even down to the middle ages ; and i certainly is matter of surprise, that no allus(i)on to the place as then existing occurs in the historians of

---

[1] Elliott, travelling here with Mr Nicolayson in 1836, saw this spot, and writes the name erroneously *Betheel*. Travels, Vol. II. p. 411.

[2] Gen. 12, 8.

[3] Gen. 28, 10–19.   31, 1–15.

[4] 1 Sam. 7, 16.

[5] 1 Kings 12, 28–33. c. 13. 2 Kings 10, 29.   17, 28.

[6] 2 Chr. 13, 19. Joseph. Ant. 8. 11. 3. —2 Kings 23 15–18. We did not remark ii. 128, 129

any sepulchres in the vicinity ; but they may very probably exist in the deep rocky valley south of the town.

[7] Ezra 2, 28. Neh. 7, 32. 11, 31.—1 Macc. 9, 50. Joseph. Antiq. 13. 1. 3.

[8] Joseph. B. J. 4. 9. 9.

[9] Onomast. art. *Agai*. Jerome's words are: " Bethel . . . usque hodie parvus licet vicus ostenditur."

[10] Will. Tyr. 8. 1. Brocard. c. 7, p. 179.

the crusades. The site would seem already to have been forgotten in ecclesiastical tradition. During the following centuries, Bethel was sought for near to Sichem ;[1] and it is only within the last three or four years that its name and site have been discovered among the common people, by the Protestant missionaries in Jerusalem. The monks even now know nothing of it ; and the traveller who communicates only with them, is still led to believe, that Bethel and its very name have perished.[2]

We left Bethel at 9¾ o'clock, and ascending from the western Wady entered the Nâbulus road, and proceeded towards el-Bîreh. The path soon begins gradually to descend into the broad valley north of Bireh, which runs off E. S. E. forming the principal head of Wady es Suweinît between Jeba' and Mükhmâs. We soon passed a fountain on our left, called 'Ain el-'Akabah ; and not long after a cavern on the right, supported by two columns, and serving as a reservoir for water ; being apparently supplied by a spring within. The bottom of the broad valley is cultivated, and seemed fertile. We reached Bîreh at half past ten, situated on the ridge running from west to east which bounds the northern prospect as seen from Jerusalem and its vicinity. A shallower valley has its head just on the south, which also runs east and joins the northern one further down at the end of the ridge.

Bireh may be seen at a great distance both from the north and south. The houses are low ; and many of them half under ground. Many large stones and various substructions testify to the antiquity of the site. Here are also the remains of a fine old church with pointed arches, which mark it as being of the time of the crusades. It was probably erected by the knights Templars, who then owned the place.[3] The walls, the recess of the altar, and the sacristies, are still standing ; the former measured ninety feet in length by thirty-five in breadth. On the southern edge of the village is a Khân in ruins ; and a few minutes further southwest on the right side of the Jerusalem road, is a fine flowing fountain, with a trough of stone, connected with a small Muslim building or place of prayer. Here several females were employed in washing. The water was anciently conducted into two large reservoirs a little below on the other side of the path ; in one of which, portions of two of the sides still remain tolerably entire, while the other is more in ruins.

Bireh, as we were afterwards informed, now contained one hundred and thirty-five taxable persons ; and sixty more had been taken away as soldiers. This gives a population of some

[1] So Brocardus, Eugesippus, Breydenbach, and many others; see above, p. 449. n. 4.

[2] So Lord Lindsay, Letters, etc. Schubert, Reise III. p. 129.

[3] Brocardus, c. 7, p. 178.

seven hundred souls, all Muhammedans.   The first seizure of soldiers took place after the rebellion in 1834.   At that time all
such as failed to produce the arms which the government required them to surrender, were at first imprisoned in Jerusalem,
and then marched off to Yâfa, where all who were fit to serve as
soldiers, were transferred to the army.   Since that time there
had been three regular conscriptions.   The Nâzir (warden) of
the sub-district in which el-Bîreh is situated, resided at this time
at Beit Iksa, and was one of the former Sheikhs.

From el-Bireh, Jerusalem (the city) bore S. 4° W. and el-
Jîb (Gibeon) S. 32° W.[1]—The distance from Jerusalem is reckoned at three hours with horses or mules ; although with fast
travelling it may be passed over in 2¾ hours.   From Bireh to el-
Jîb we travelled in an hour and a half by way of Râm-Allah ;
the direct route would occupy about fifteen or twenty minutes
less.

I hold el-Bireh to be the Beer or Beeroth of Scripture, unless these were names of two distinct places ;[2] and in that case
el-Bireh corresponds to the latter, Beeroth.   The correspondence
of the names is in itself sufficiently decisive.   And further, according to Eusebius, Beeroth was seen by the traveller in passing
from Jerusalem to Nicopolis ('Amwâs), at the seventh Roman
mile.   This road was the present camel-path from Jerusalem to
Ramleh passing near el-Jîb ; and to this day the description of
Eusebius holds true.   The traveller on emerging from the hills
into the plains around el-Jîb, sees el-Bireh on his right after
a little more than two hours from Jerusalem.[3]   From the
time of Jerome to the crusades there is no further mention of
Beeroth.   Brocardus first again speaks of *Bira*, which was regarded by the crusaders and later ecclesiastics as the site of

---

[1] Other bearings from el-Bîreh were:
Sha'fât S. 4° W.   Neby Samwil S. 30° W.
Râm-Allah about west.   Kefr Murr (ruins)
N. 25° E.   Tell 'Asûr N. 42° E.

[2] Beer is mentioned only once in Scripture, as the place to which Jotham fled,
Judg. 9, 21.   It is merely the same word
in the singular, ' well,' of which Beeroth is
the plural, ' wells.'   Yet Eusebius and Jerome place Beer in the great plain ten
miles north of Eleutheropolis (Onomast.
art. Βηρά *Bera*); and I find in our lists a
deserted village el-Bireh at the present
day, adjacent to the mouth of Wady el-
Surâr, not far from the site of Beth-she-
mesh.

[3] Onomast. art. Βηρώϑ *Beeroth.*   In the
corresponding article of Jerome, a false
translation, or more probably a corruption
of the text, has occasioned great difficulty.

ii. 131, 132

Eusebius says that Beeroth was ὑπὸ τὴν
Γαβαών, i. e. belonged to the Gibeonites, as
related in Josh. 9, 17.   This Jerome trans-
lates " *sub colle Gabaon*," as if Beeroth
was situated under the hill on which Gibeon stood.   Yet in the article Χεφεῤῥά
Chephira, also one of the Gibeonitish cities,
he correctly renders the very same phrase,
πόλις ὑπὸ τὴν Γαβαών by " vicus *ad civita-
tem pertinens Gabaon.*"   The former instance therefore, is either an error in translation, or a corruption.—Instead of Nicopolis, the text of Jerome also has *Neapolis;* making Beeroth to be seven miles
from Jerusalem on the road to the latter
city.   This is also an error; for the actual
distance is three hours, equivalent to nine
Roman miles.   The text of Eusebius is
here in every respect the correct one.   See
further Reland Palæst. p. 618.

Michmash. At that time it belonged to the knights Templars, who probably erected here the church now in ruins. Maundrell seems to have been the first to remark its coincidence with the ancient Beer.[1]

Leaving el-Bireh at 11.10, we crossed the low ridge or swell west of the fountain, and came in twenty minutes to Râm-Allah. This swell forms here the dividing line between the waters running to the Jordan and those of the Mediterranean. On our right, as we approached the village, was a deep rugged Wady running southwest and issuing from the mountains (as we afterwards found) not far from the lower village of Beit 'Ûr, the ancient Beth-horon. Râm-Allah itself lies on high ground, though there are higher swells in the vicinity, especially towards the southeast. It overlooks the whole country towards the west, including portions of the great plain, as far as to the sea; which latter was in sight for a long distance. The hills of white sand which skirt the shore south of Yâfa were distinctly visible.[2]

The inhabitants of Râm-Allah are all Christians of the Greek rite; and are reckoned at two hundred taxable men, giving a population of eight or nine hundred souls. The priests had heard from Jerusalem of our coming; and as we entered the house of the principal priest, the large room was speedily filled with guests, who came to bid us welcome. They soon ranged themselves along the walls, squatting upon their feet or sitting cross-legged; while we were accommodated with mats and a carpet by the side of the priest, and permitted to stretch our limbs at full length. Coffee was served round to all; and was brought to us by a young man, who was in training for the priesthood. The conversation became animated, and was well sustained by the priests. The staff which I had brought from Sinai, excited great curiosity, as coming from one of their holiest places, and as being professedly of the same species of wood with Moses' rod. It was a festival day; and the inhabitants seemed all to be well-dressed and in good circumstances. Indeed the village had more the appearance of thrift and wealth, than any we had yet seen. The houses are substantially built, and are all modern; there being here apparently no traces of antiquity. The country around is fertile and well cultivated, yielding grain, olives, figs, and grapes in abundance.

---

[1] Brocardus, c. 7, p. 178. Maundrell's Journey, Mar. 25th. See above, p. 442, and Note.

[2] From Râm-Allah we obtained the following bearings: Mount of Olives S. 11° E. Rifât S. 11° W. Neby Samwîl S. 18° W. Biddu a vill. S. 37° W. Beit Unia S. 60° W. Deir Kadis N. 62° W. Râs Kerker, a castle towards the plain, N. 57° W. el-Jânieh N. 55° W. Deir Abu Mesh-'al N. 45° W. (For this and the three preceding places, see other bearings which determine their position, under June 9th at Beit 'Ûr el-Fôka and Um Râsh.) Abu Shukheidim, ruins, N. 12° W. 'Atâra N. by E.½E. Tell 'Asûr N. 50° E.

ii. 133. 134

Râm-Allah belongs, like Taiyibeh, to the Haram, or great mosk; to which it annually pays about three hundred and fifty mids of grain.[1] Besides this, it was said to pay to the government for each olive tree one and a quarter piastres; for each ass ten piastres; for each ox seventy-five piastres; and on every *feddân* (acre) of figs and grapes thirty piastres. For each man, the *Firdeh* was sixty-five piastres; and the *Kharaj* from thirty to sixty piastres.

We now bent our course towards el-Jib, lying S. by W.½W. Leaving Râm-Allah at 12½ o'clock, and crossing first a swell of land which forms the watershed, we then followed down the shallow and somewhat winding Wady ed-Deir among low hills. Our friend the priest had furnished us with a guide, who proved to be the schoolmaster of Râm-Allah. He had however only five or six boys under his care; and considered their education as completed, when they had read through the Arabic psalter. His pay consisted in fifty piastres received for each boy thus carried through his education; besides ten paras (¼ piastre) every Saturday, and three piastres on finishing each of the seven lessons of the psalter.

As we were following down the Wady just mentioned, we were disturbed by a loud quarrel between our Muslim muleteer and a Christian of Râm-Allah, who had joined the party. The latter showed a bloody face; having been beaten, he said, by a Muslim in a neighbouring village. He was in a state of great excitement; and said he was going to take us to his enemy, that we might beat him in return. His claim on us was founded solely on the fact of his being a Christian; and it was some time before he could be persuaded, that it was none of our business to interfere in his quarrel.

We left Beit-Ûnia at some distance on the right; and at 1.10 passed near a village (Râfât?) on our left. Here we came upon a beautiful plain, which extends far west, nearly to the brow of the mountains, and also towards the east and south; in which direction it is bounded by the lofty ridge of Neby Samwil. In this plain towards the south, separated from the base of Neby Samwil by a narrow fertile tract, is the isolated oblong hill or ridge on which el-Jib is situated. It is composed of horizontal layers of limestone rock, forming almost regular steps, rising out of the plain; in some parts steep and difficult of access, and capable of being everywhere very strongly fortified. The camel-road from Jerusalem to Ramleh leads along the northern side of the hill, passing onwards across the plain till it divides and descends the mountain both at Beit 'Ûr and through Wady Suleimân. In the west is spread out the fine meadow-like plain,

[1] See above, p. 446 sq.

with a large neglected well at some distance, called Bîr el-'Özeiz. The hill may be said to stand in the midst of a basin, composed of broad valleys or plains, cultivated and full of grain, vineyards, and orchards of olive and fig trees. It was decidedly the finest part of Palestine, that I had yet seen.

Indeed the whole tract west of the main water-shed, seems to be less rocky and sterile than that along the eastern slope. The rock is apparently softer, and is more easily disintegrated into soil. The open tract or basin around el-Jib, however, lies upon a secondary division of the waters; those of its western end descending directly towards the Mediterranean; while those of the middle and eastern parts flow round the northern end of the ridge of Neby Samwil into the deep valley, which runs off southeast between that ridge and Jerusalem to the western plain.

We reached the village of el-Jib situated on the summit of this hill at a quarter before 2 o'clock. It is of moderate size; but we did not learn the number of souls. The houses stand very irregularly and unevenly, sometimes almost one above another. They seem to be chiefly rooms in old massive ruins, which have fallen down in every direction. One large massive building still remains, perhaps a former castle or tower of strength. The lower rooms are vaulted, with round arches of hewn stones fitted together with great exactness. The stones outside are large; and the whole appearance is that of antiquity. Towards the east the ridge sinks a little; and here, a few rods from the village, just below the top of the ridge towards the north, is a fine fountain of water. It is in a cave excavated in and under the high rock, so as to form a large subterranean reservoir. Not far below it, among the olive trees, are the remains of another open reservoir, about the size of that at Hebron; perhaps 120 feet in length by 100 feet in breadth. It was doubtless anciently intended to receive the superfluous waters of the cavern. At this time no stream was flowing from the latter.[1]

It is not difficult to recognise in el-Jib and its rocky eminence the ancient *Gibeon* of the Scriptures, the Gabaon of Josephus; although the specifications which have come down to us respecting the position of that place, are somewhat confused.[2] There

---

[1] From el-Jib, Neby Samwil bore S. 21° W. Biddu S. 70° W. Râm-Allah N. by E.½E. Jedireh N. 60° E. Kulûndia N. 65° E. Bir Nebâla S. 77° E.

[2] Josephus in one place gives the distance of Gabaon from Jerusalem, at fifty stadia, and in another at forty stadia; B. J. 2. 19. 1. Antiq. 7. 11. 7. This shows that both are merely conjectural estimates.

Eusebius places Gibeon at four Roman miles west of Bethel; while the corresponding article of Jerome sets it at the same distance on the east; Onomast. art. Γαβαών *Gabaon*. The text of Jerome is here probably corrupted. The nearest route between el-Jib and Jerusalem by Neby Samwil is about 2½ hours or sixty stadia (7½ Roman miles); while the camel-

is however enough, in connection with the name, to mark the
identity of the spot. The name *Jib* in Arabic is merely the
abridged form of the Hebrew Gibeon ; and presents perhaps the
most remarkable instance that occurred to us, in which the *'Ain*
of the Hebrew, that most tenacious of letters, has been dropped
in passing over into the Arabic.[1] In respect to the site of Gibeon
the Scriptures are silent ; but Josephus relates, that Cestus,
marching from Antipatris by way of Lydda, ascended the mountains at Beth-horon, and halted at a place called Gabaon, fifty
stadia from Jerusalem.[2] Jerome also relates of Paula, that passing from Nicopolis, she ascended the mountains at Beth-horon,
and saw upon her right as she journied, Ajalon and Gabaon.[3] This
ascent at Beth-horon is on the present camel-road from Jerusalem
to Ramleh and Yâfa, which now passes along on the north side
of el-Jib, as it anciently in like manner passed by Gibeon. These
circumstances taken together, leave little room for doubt as to
the identity of the two places.[4]

Gibeon is celebrated in the Old Testament ; but is not mentioned in the New. It was "a great city, as one of the royal
cities ;" and to its jurisdiction belonged originally the towns of
Beeroth, Chephirah, and Kirjath-Jearim.[5] The city is first mentioned in connection with the deceit practised by its inhabitants
upon Joshua ; by which, although Canaanites (Hivites), they
induced the Jewish leader not only to make a league with them
and spare their lives and cities ; but also in their defence to make
war upon the five kings by whom they were besieged. It was in
this great battle that "the sun stood still on Gibeon."[6] The
place afterwards fell to the lot of Benjamin, and became a Levi-
tical city ;[7] where the tabernacle was set up for many years
under David and Solomon.[8] Here the latter youthful monarch
offered a thousand burnt offerings ; and in a dream by night
communed with God, and asked for himself a wise and understanding heart instead of riches and honour.[9] Here too it was,
that Abner's challenge to Joab terminated in the defeat and flight
of the former, and the death of Asahel ; and here also at a later
period Amasa was treacherously slain by Joab.[10]—The notices of

road cannot well be less than three hours,
or some seventy stadia.—See further notices in Reland Palæst. p. 810.

[1] See above, p. 255. n. 2.
[2] Joseph. B. J. 2. 19. 1.
[3] Hieron. Ep. 86, ad Eustoch. Epitaph.
Paulæ. Opp. T. IV. ii. p. 673. ed. Mart.
[4] Pococke saw el-Jib from Neby Samwil, and also held it to be Gibeon ; Descr.
of the East, II. i. p. 49. fol. So too Von
Troilo in 1666 ; Reisebeschr. p. 290.
[5] Josh. 10, 2. 9, 17.
[6] Josh. c. 9. c. 10, 1–14.

ii. 137, 138

[7] Josh. 18, 25. 21, 17. In these passages the three towns Gibeon, Geba, and
Gibeah (Gibeath), are distinctly enumerated ; comp. 18, 24. 28. These names,
however, were sometimes confounded ; e.
g. Gibeon for Geba, 1 Chron. 14, 16.
Comp. 2 Sam. 5, 25.
[8] 1 Chron. 16, 39. 21, 29. 2 Chron. 1.
3.—The ark at this time was at Jerusalem ;
2 Chron. 1, 4.
[9] 1 K. 3, 4–15. 2 Chr. 1, 3–13.
[10] 2 Sam. 2, 12–32. 20, 8–12. The
'Pool of Gibeon,' mentioned in the story

Gibeon by Josephus, and by Eusebius and Jerome, have already been referred to in the preceding paragraph. The name Gabaon is mentioned by writers of the times of the crusades, as existing in the present spot ; and among the Arabs it already bore the name el-Jib.[1] It seems afterwards to have been overlooked by most travellers ; until in the last century the attention of Pococke was again directed to it.

We left el-Jib at 2.25, descending on the southern quarter through orchards of pears, apples, figs, and olives, and also vineyards, into the narrow strip of plain which skirts the hill upon this side. We now had before us the elevated ridge of Neby Samwil ; which, beginning at no great distance on the left, rises rapidly towards the southwest into the highest point of land in the whole region ; and then sinks off gradually in the same direction into lower and less marked hills and ridges. Its general course is thus from northeast to southwest. The elevation cannot be less than some 500 feet above the plain ; and is apparently greater than that of the mount of Olives. The waters of the plain are drained off eastward by a valley around its northern end ; and here passes also a road to Jerusalem which we took at a later period.[2] Our way now led us directly to the summit, up the steep but not difficult ascent of the northwestern side. The top is crowned by a small miserable village and a neglected mosk. This point we reached at 2.55, in half an hour from el-Jib ; and found ourselves upon the most sightly spot in all the country.

The mosk is here the principal object ; and is regarded by Jews, Christians, and Muhammedans, as covering the tomb of the prophet Samuel. It is now in a state of great decay. We were admitted without ceremony to every part of it ; ascended to its flat roof and minaret ; and examined, so far as we chose, the pretended tomb in a more private apartment. This is only a box of boards. The building was evidently once a Latin church, built up on older foundations in the form of a Latin cross ; and probably dates from the time of the crusades. There are few houses now inhabited ; but many traces of former dwellings. In some parts, the rock, which is soft, has been hewn away for several feet in height, so as to form the walls of houses ; in one place it is thus cut down apparently for the foundation of a large building. Two or three reservoirs are also in like manner hewn in the rock. These cuttings and levellings extend over a considerable space.

of Abner, may well be the waters of the fountain or reservoir described in the text ; and these are also probably ' the great (or many) waters in Gibeon,' spoken of in Jer. 41, 12.

[1] Will. Tyr. 8. 1. Benj. of Tud. I. p.

68. Brocard. c. 9. p. 184. Mariu. Sanut. p. 249. Breydenbach copies Brocardus. Bohaeddin mentions el-Jib ; Vita Saladin. p. 243.

[2] See under June 9th.

The view from the roof of the mosk is very commanding in every direction. Below in the southeast is the deep Wady Beit Hanina stretching off towards the southwest ; and further in the former direction are seen Jerusalem, the mount of Olives, the Frank mountain, and a large portion of the eastern slope, with the mountains beyond the Jordan and Dead Sea. In the northwest the fertile plain of el-Jib lies immediately below ; and further on, the eye embraces a large extent of the great lower plain along the coast, as well as of the Mediterranean itself. In a clear day Yâfa may be distinctly seen ; a slight haze now intercepted it from our view. A large number of villages were visible on every side.[1]

The tradition that here is the tomb of the prophet Samuel, necessarily includes the supposition that this spot is the Ramah or Ramathaim-Zophim of the Old Testament, the birthplace, residence, and burial-place of that prophet.[2] That this was a different city from the Ramah near Gibeah of Saul (now er-Râm) on the east of the Nâbulus road, is obvious ; for the latter is only half an hour from Gibeah, Saul's residence ; and its situation does not at all accord with the circumstances of his first visit to Samuel when in search of his father's asses, nor with David's subsequent flight to Samuel for refuge.[3] But the same difficulties lie with almost equal force against the supposition, that the present Neby Samwîl can be the Ramah of the prophet. As such, it could not well have been unknown to Saul ; since as being the highest point in the country and hardly an hour distant from his native place, with no intervening hills, it must have been continually in full view before his eyes.

But there are still greater difficulties. It is usually supposed, that the visit of Saul to Samuel, above alluded to, took place in Ramah, where the prophet entertained him in his own house. At his departure in order to return to Gibeah, the prophet anoints him as king, and describes his way home as leading him "by Rachel's sepulchre in the border of Benjamin."[4] This circumstance is decisive against the identity of Neby Samwîl with such a Ramah. We have already seen that the site of Rachel's tomb cannot well be called in question ;[5] and therefore the Ramah of

---

[1] The most important bearings which we got here, were the following : Mount of Olives S. 40° E. Jerusalem S. 35° E. Frank mountain S. 10° E. el-Kûstûl S. 50° W. Sôba S. 54° W. Ramleh N. 66° W. el-Jib N. 21° E. el-Bireh N. 30° E. Taiyibeh N. 50° E.—Other bearings of minor places were : Beit Hanina across the valley below, S. 72° E. Sha'fât S. 60° E. Lifta, in the great valley, S. 12° E. Mâr Elyâs, south of Jerusalem, S. 7° E. Bethlehem S. 1° E. Beit Iksa, below us on the hills, S. 4° W. 'Ain Kârim with ii. 140, 141

the convent of St John, S. 20° W. Deir Yesin S. 57° W. Beit Dukkah N. 77° W. Biddu N. 48° W. Beit Unia N. 4° W. Râm-Allah N. 18° E. Jedireh N. 37° E. Kulûndia N. 44° E. Bir Nebâla N. 51° E. Rûmmôn N. 55° E. er-Râm N. 75° E.

[2] 1 Sam. 1, 1. 19. 2, 11. 8, 4. 19, 18. 25, 1. 28, 3.

[3] 1 Sam. c. 9. c. 19, 18.

[4] 1 Sam. 10, 1. 2.

[5] See above, pp. 218 sq. 254.

the prophet must have been so situated, that a person going from
it to Gibeah would naturally, or at least without difficulty, pass
near to the present sepulchre northwest of Bethlehem. But from
Neby Samwil, Gibeah lies about E. S. E. and hardly more than
one hour distant; while the tomb of Rachel bears directly south
at the distance of nearly three hours. Hence, every step taken
from Neby Samwil towards the sepulchre of Rachel, only carries
a person away from Gibeah.—I shall have occasion hereafter to
speak again of the Ramah of the prophet; my sole object here
has been to show, that it could not have been the present Neby
Samwil.

The true site of the Ramah of Samuel seems to have been
early forgotten; since both Eusebius and Jerome place it, with
still less probability, in the plain near Diospolis or Lydda.[1] Yet
the present tradition as to the prophet's tomb must have sprung
up not long after their day; for apparently Procopius alludes to
this spot, when he relates that Justinian caused a well and a
wall to be constructed for the (monastery of) St. Samuel in Palestine.[2] At the close of the seventh century Adamnanus describes the ground north of Jerusalem as rocky and rough, as far
as to the city of Samuel or Ramah.[3] The crusaders found here
the name of St. Samuel; and with little regard to consistency, held
the place to be also the Shiloh of Scripture; or as Brocardus
expresses it, "Mount Shiloh, which is now called St. Samuel."[4]
Here stood a Latin convent of the order of Præmonstrants;
which was plundered by the troops of Saladin as he was preparing
to besiege Jerusalem in A. D. 1187.[5] To the same period probably belongs the Latin church now converted into a mosk. From
that time onward to the present day, the natives have known the
place only as Neby Samwil; while the monks and travellers have
varied in describing it either as Shiloh or Ramah. In later centuries the name of Ramah has predominated.[6] Most travellers have

[1] Onomast. art. *Armatha Sophim.*

[2] Procop. de Ædific. 5. 9.

[3] De Loc. Sanct. 1. 21.

[4] " *Mons Silo,* qui nunc *ad St. Samuel-
em* dicitur;" Brocardus c. 9. p. 184. Will.
Tyr. 8. 1.—The true Shiloh lay north of
Bethel towards Shechem or Nâbulus; Judg.
21, 19.

[5] Rad. Coggesh. Chron. Anglican. in
Martene et Durand Coll. ampl. Tom. V. p.
565. Wilken Gesch. der Kreuzz. III. ii.
pp. 298, 299.—Benjamin of Tudela also
has the name *St. Samuel of Shiloh;* and
relates the legend, that when the Edomites
(Christians) took Ramleh from the Ishmaelites, they found there near the Jews'
synagogue the tomb of Samuel, from which
they transferred his body to the present

St. Samuel, after erecting there a large
church; Benj. of Tud. I. p. 78. Nothing
of all this is found in any of the historians
of the crusades, who would not have been
likely to overlook such a transaction;
while too, as we have seen, the present
name is older than the time of the crusades. Besides, Jerome relates, that the
bones of Samuel were removed to Thrace
under the emperor Arcadius; Hieron. adv.
Vigilant. p. 283. Reland Palæst. p. 965.

[6] Thus we find *Shiloh* in Marin. Sanut.
p. 249. Breydenbach in Reisb. pp. 130,
136. Nau, p. 501. Zuallart names it
both Shiloh and Ramah, Viaggio p. 119.
Quaresmius gives it as *Ramah,* II. p. 727;
and so Von Troilo, p. 290. Pococke II.
i. p. 48. Elliott, Travels II. p. 412.

been contented to adopt the information of their monastic guides ; although a few have ventured to call in question its accuracy.[1]

As however Neby Samwîl is one of the most marked places in the vicinity of Jerusalem, and was unquestionably the site of an ancient town, it became to us a matter of interest, to ascertain, if possible, what city of antiquity had occupied this sightly spot. Among the scriptural names, after which we made diligent search in this region, though without success, was that of Mizpeh, a city of Benjamin renowned in the Old Testament ; where the tribes often assembled ; where Samuel offered sacrifice and judged the people ; where Saul was chosen king by lot ; and where under the Chaldeans, Gedaliah the governor resided and was assassinated.[2] The position of this city is nowhere described, neither in the Old Testament nor by Josephus ; and we only know that it must have lain near Ramah of Benjamin ; since king Asa fortified it with materials brought from the latter place.[3] The name, too, which signifies "a place of look out, watch tower," implies that it was situated on an elevated spot.

On these grounds, as well as from the traces of an ancient town upon it, I am inclined to regard Neby Samwîl as the probable site of Mizpeh. Further, the writer of the first book of Maccabees describes Mizpeh as situated "overagainst Jerusalem," implying that it was visible from that city ;[4] a description which is true of Neby Samwîl. Eusebius also and Jerome describe Mizpeh as lying near to Kirjath-Jearim, which must have been on the west of Gibeon, probably at Kuryet el-'Enab ; and this too points to Neby Samwîl rather than to any other hill.[5]

From Neby Samwîl we bent our course towards Jerusalem. The distance is reckoned at two hours ; but as our horses were now travelling homewards, we accomplished it in one hour and fifty minutes. Leaving at 3¾ o'clock we descended along smaller spurs and ridges towards the great valley ; the declivity on this side being in general much less steep than the ascent from el-Jib. We had here on the left Beit Hanina across the valley ; and on the right Beit Iksa on the hills ; while before us low down in the Wady, on its eastern side, was seen the village of Lifta, where many mules are kept. Here, somewhere towards the right, is situated apparently the fountain of St. Samuel men-

---

[1] Cotovicus appears to confound this spot with Sôba ; his description of Sôba applies only to the present Neby Samwîl ; pp. 316, 317. Doubdan, following the authority of Jerome, transfers the tomb to Ramleh ; pp. 488, 489 ; comp. p. 114. Sandys also questions the report of his monkish guides, p. 135. Lond. 1658.

[2] Josh. 18, 26. Judg. 20, 1. 21, 1. i. 143–145

1 Sam. 7, 5–16. 10, 17 sq. 2 K. 25, 22–25. Jer. c. 40. 41.

[3] 1 Kings 15, 22. 2 Chr. 16, 6.

[4] Κατέναντι Ἱερουσαλήμ, 1 Mac. 3, 46.

[5] Onomasticon, art. Μασσηφά Massefa. Both writers confound here the Mizpeh of Gilead, where Jephthah dwelt (Judg. 11, 34), with the Mizpeh of the text. Comp. also Jer. 41, 10. 12. 16.

tioned by travellers, in a sort of grotto.[1] At 4.20 Beit Hanîna bore N. 45° E. and Lifta S. 10° W.

We reached the bottom at 4.40, which is here narrow and very stony, but planted with fine vineyards and orchards of fig and olive trees. This valley has two main heads; one coming from the plain around el-Jîb, down which passes a different road to Jerusalem; and the other from near er-Râm. They unite just below Beit Hanîna which stands on the ridge between, and gives its name to the Wady below, as it passes off towards the southwest.[2] We crossed the bottom very obliquely, having over us on the right a little village with green gardens around it; and began immediately to ascend by a small branch Wady on the opposite side. After ten or fifteen minutes we left its bed, and passed up the very rocky slope to the tombs of the Judges and head of the valley of Jehoshaphat. This point we reached at 5.05; and came in another half hour to the Damascus gate. Here we found a quarantine guard stationed, to watch against the entrance of persons coming from Yâfa, where the plague was now raging. In Jerusalem itself no new cases had occurred; and we hoped the alarm was over.

One of the two Mukâriyeh who accompanied us on this excursion, was from Kŭlônieh, a village overhanging the western side of the great valley below Lifta, at the point where it is crossed by the direct road from Jerusalem to Ramleh.[3] As we came from Neby Samwil, he gave us the following account. The village of Kŭlônieh belongs to Omar Effendi,[4] to whom it pays 110 Mids of grain annually. The tax to the government consists of one piastre for every ewe and she goat, ten piastres for every ass, twenty for every horse and mule, thirty for every camel, and seventy-five on every ox; one piastre for every olive tree, and thirty-five on each feddân of fig trees or vineyards. The Firdeh or capitation-tax the preceding year was sixty-nine piastres. As fast as men are taken away for soldiers, or die, the Firdeh is divided among the remainder; so that the government takes care to lose nothing. Our attendant had been taken as a soldier; but proved unfit and was therefore released. Yet he had to pay thirty dollars to procure a man to serve in his place.

---

[1] Most distinctly by Doubdan, p. 114. Also by Quaresmius, II. p. 728. Von Troilo, p. 291. Pococke II. p. 48. fol.

[2] For the lower part of this valley, see under May 17th. Ecclesiastical tradition regards it as the valley of Elah (Terebinth), in which David slew Goliah, 1 Sam. 17, 2 sq. Hence travellers usually give it the name of the Terebinth valley. But the scene of that battle was unquestionably in a different place; see further on, under May 18th.

[3] Kŭlônieh is an hour and a half from Jerusalem. From the convent of St. John ('Ain Kârim), it bears N. 10° E. The part of the great valley between, is broad and planted with trees. Prokesch Reise, p. 120. —See more in Vol. III. Sect. III, penult.

[4] Apparently the same personage who figures in Richardson, Vol. II. p. 239 sq.

To raise this sum he sold an ox and several sheep ; and after they were sold, had to pay taxes upon the proceeds.

The price of our horses and mules on this and other excursions was fifteen or sixteen piastres a day for each animal ; or if at any time we chose to lie by, the half of this price only was to be paid for every such day of rest. With the keeping of the animals or attendants, we had no concern ; nor was any thing extra paid for the men. The horses we had now and afterwards, were slender and active, and also exceedingly hardy. They were fed usually only at night ; commonly on barley or other grain, with straw ; and occasionally when there was a scanty herbage around the tent, they were suffered to crop it. Their gait is a fast walk ; never a trot ; for upon the mountains the state of the roads renders this for the most part impossible. They are surefooted, and exceedingly sagacious in picking their way among the rocks ; and we found little difference in this respect between horses and mules. These remarks apply of course only to horses for hire ; and not to the sleek and well-fed animals (usually mares) of the Sheikhs and wealthy individuals ; which with equal hardiness, exhibit a wonderful degree of activity and fleetness.

The caparison of the animals for hire is also not very splendid. Arab riding saddles with stirrups are sometimes given ; but they are usually narrow and hard ; so that we at last came to prefer the common huge pack-saddles. These are very long and broad, stuffed with a large mass of straw ; and cover almost the whole of the poor animal, from whose back they are seldom removed. We had our own stirrups ; and usually were able (though not always) to muster a bridle for each of ourselves ; while our servants were quite contented, if they made out to obtain a halter.

Our rate of travel with horses and mules appears to have been on the average very nearly three Roman miles the hour ; which is equivalent to 2.4 geographical miles of 60 to the degree, or 2.78 (nearest 2¾) English miles.[1] This would apply, I think, very accurately, during our present excursion, to the distance passed over between Beitîn and el-Jîb. But on the other hand, between 'Anâta and Taiyibeh, where we had to cross several very deep and rugged valleys, and found the whole road rough, a considerable allowance must be made from this average. On the plains again, where the roads were level and smooth, the rate of travel naturally rose somewhat above the average.

This excursion was to us deeply interesting, and we returned

[1] The Roman mile is usually reckoned at 75 to the degree. See more in Note VII, end of the volume.
ii. 146–148

from it highly gratified. It had led us through scenes associated with the names and historic incidents and deeds of Abraham and Jacob, of Samuel and Saul, of Jonathan and David and Solomon ; and we had been able to trace out the places where they had lived and acted, and to tread almost in their very footsteps. True, in Jerusalem itself the associations of this kind are still more numerous and sacred ; but there they are so blended together, as to become in a measure indistinct and less impressive ; while here in the country, they stand forth before the soul in all their original freshness and individuality. It was like communing with these holy men themselves, to visit the places where their feet had trod, and where many of them had held converse with the Most High. I hope that in this respect the visit was not without its proper influence upon our own minds ; at any rate, it served to give us a deeper impression of the reality and vividness of the Bible history, and to confirm our confidence in the truth and power of the sacred volume.

The region through which we passed on the first day, as I have already remarked, was that described by the prophet Isaiah as the scene of Sennecharib's approach to Jerusalem.[1] This approach is portrayed in the most vivid colours ; indeed, the whole description is the highly wrought poetic expression of a prophetic vision. Every thing lives and moves ; the various towns upon the conqueror's route, tremble and cry aloud and flee away in terror. All this is probably to be viewed in the light of a divine threat or prophetic warning ; for although Sennecharib at a later period actually invaded Judea, yet he himself did not come against Jerusalem ; but sent Rabshakeh thither from Lachish with an army.[2] The route too which the prophet describes, can never have been a common way of approach to Jerusalem. It presupposes, that the monarch and his army, instead of keeping along the great feasible northern road to the city, turned off at or near Bethel towards Ai, situated doubtless in the vicinity of the present Deir Duwân ; from which point to Jerusalem by Michmash and Anathoth, they would have to cross not less than three very deep and difficult valleys.

However this may be, the route itself is very distinctly traced, and we were able in a great measure to follow it out. Of the probable site of Ai, I have already spoken ; we ourselves visited Michmash, Geba, Ramah, and Anathoth ; and Gibeah of Saul was almost ever in sight. Of the other places mentioned, no further trace remains. Migron must have been situated somewhere between Deir Duwân and Michmash ; and Gallim and Laish, Madmenah and Gebim, were probably further south and

[1] Isa. 10, 28-32.   [2] Is. c. 36. 37.   2 K. c. 18. 19.
ii. 148, 149

nearer to Anathoth.[1] Arrived at Nob, the Assyrian makes a
halt ; and "shakes his hand against the mount of the daughter
of Zion."   This language implies that the holy city was in sight
from Nob ; which therefore must have been situated somewhere
upon the ridge of the mount of Olives, northeast of the city.[2]
We sought now and afterwards all along this ridge, from the
Damascus road to the summit opposite the city, for some traces
of an ancient site which might be regarded as the place of Nob ;
but without the slightest success. This was probably the city
of the priests destroyed by Saul ; for although there appears to
have been another Nob near the plain towards Lydda, yet the
ark of God after its return from the Philistines in the days of
Samuel, seems never again to have departed from the mountains.[3]

As one result of this excursion, as well as of our subsequent
researches, the remark presents itself, that while very many of
the ancient Hebrew names have in this way perished, there exists
at the present day a class of names, which, although not occurring in the Scriptures, are nevertheless probably of Hebrew
origin, and have come down from the earliest times.   Thus, I
apprehend that all (or nearly all) those appellations in which
the Arabic word *Beit* appears as a component part, are only the
successors of ancient Hebrew names with *Beth* (house), whether
found in the Scriptures or not.   Many of these indeed do thus
occur, as Bethlehem, Bethel, Beth-horon, and the like ; but a
still larger number exist at the present day, of which the Bible
makes no mention.   Such are Beit Hanîna, Beit Iksa, Beit
Ûnia,[4] Beit Jâla, which have been already noticed, and very
many others.   The same is true of names like el-Hismeh, Tell
'Asûr, 'Atâra, and others similar ; which although apparently of
Hebrew origin, are not distinctly found in connection with the
district in which they now exist.[5]

[1] All these places obviously lay within
this tract, and almost within sight of each
other. It is contrary to all the circumstances of the case, to connect this Laish
with that on the northern border of Palestine ; Judges 18, 7. 29. It more probably had some relation to the person of that
name, a native of Gallim ; 1 Sam. 25, 44.
[2] So Jerome professedly from Hebrew
tradition : "Stans in oppidulo Nob et pro-
cul urbem conspiciens Jerusalem ;" Comm.
in Esa. x. 32. Nob is also mentioned as
one of the cities of Benjamin near to Anathoth, Neh. 11, 32.
[3] 1 Sam. c. 6, c. 21, 1–9. 22, 9–19.
Jerome mentions a *Nobe* not far from
Lydda ; probably the Beit Nûba of the
crusaders and of the present day ; see un-
ii. 150, 151

der June 9th.   Hieron. Ep. 86, ad Eustoch. Epitaph. Paulæ, p. 673.
[4] This name might be supposed to correspond to the Hebrew Bethulia ; but the
Bible mentions no such place in this region.   See Reland Pal. pp. 658, 639.
[5] Does Tell 'Asûr perhaps correspond to
the *Azor* of Benjamin, which is mentioned
with Ramah and Anathoth ? Neh. 11, 33.
If so the Hebrew ר has passed over into
the Arabic *'Ain*, as in Beit 'Ur for Beth-
horon. We saw Tell 'Asûr from el-'Alya,
el-Bireh, and Jifna.—'Atâra is the Heb.
Ataroth, but seems hardly to correspond
to the place so called on the border of Ephraim, Josh. 16, 5. 7. See more under May
15, and June 13.

That such should be the general fact, is not surprising ; although so far as I know, it has never been distinctly brought into notice. The Bible does not claim to be a geographical work, nor to enumerate all the towns and villages of the Promised Land. Indeed, in most of the recorded lists of Hebrew cities, we find the express addition of " their villages," and sometimes of "their towns and villages," of which no names are given.[1] Among these unknown names, were doubtless many of those which have survived to our time.

Another trait of the ancient Hebrew topography is the repeated occurrence of the same name. Thus there were several Ramahs and Gibeahs, two Carmels, two Mizpehs, two Aroers, two Socohs, and many similar instances. The same trait appears also in respect to the Arabic names of the present day. We found not less than three Jeba's, three or four Taiyibehs, two el-Birehs, two 'Atâras, two Shuweikehs (Socoh), two Râfâts, and many other like examples.

[1] So Josh. 15, 32. 36. 41. 47. etc.   18, 24. 28.   19, 7. 8. 16. 23. etc.   1 Chr. 8, 12.   Neh. 11, 25–31.

ii. 151

SECTION X.

WE remained in Jerusalem after our return, only so long as was necessary to make preparations for another journey. Our former excursion had led us along the eastern slope of the mountains on the north of the Holy City; and we now proposed to explore the continuation of the same tract on the south, comprising the district lying between the Hebron road and the Dead Sea, as far south at least as to the place called 'Ain Jidy; and then along the western shore of that sea to the Jordan. A prominent object in my own mind, was to find (if possible) somewhere upon or near the coast two high points, from which we might obtain a view of the whole extent of the Dead Sea, and make observations in order to determine its length and breadth. In this, however, we were only partially successful; the nature of the country and the basin of the sea turning out to be very different from what I expected.

The districts we were now about to visit, are usually regarded as among the most insecure in Palestine. The desert along the sea is inhabited, if at all, only by a few Bedawin, of whom we heard the worst reports as thieves and robbers. The tract was said now also to be full of deserters and outlaws, who lay here concealed, and subsisted by thieving and robbery; as was likewise the case on the north of Jerusalem.[1] Whether this reputation of the country was well founded or not, I will not undertake to decide; but certainly the district had a right to it by ancient prescription; for it is the very same region into which David with his band of six hundred adventurers withdrew from the pursuit of Saul, and dwelt long in the caves and lurking-places.[2] The plain of the Jordan too, around Jericho, was con-

---

[1] See under Jeba' and Taiyibeh, pp. 440, 446. [2] 1 Sam. 23, 13-26. c. 24.

ii. 152, 153

sidered as very unsafe; partly because of the thievish character of the inhabitants, and partly as being exposed to excursions from the lawless Arabs of the eastern mountains. Three weeks before this time, some of our friends had accompanied the annual caravan of pilgrims to the Jordan; and had there spoken with several merchants from Damascus, who were going to es-Salt and Kerak. The very next day, these merchants were shot dead and their goods plundered.

As our intended journey became known, our ears were filled with stories of this kind; and we were urged to take with us a guard of soldiers from the governor of Jerusalem. For this we had no sort of inclination; partly because we must then have been in a measure under their control, and not they under ours; and partly because, with such a guard, we could only expect to excite the ill will and perhaps the hostility of the Arabs we might fall in with; and thus frustrate in a degree the very object of our journey. Still, as it was not prudent to travel without some escort, we thought it more advisable to obtain the services of the supposed robbers themselves, or of persons on good terms with them, who might at the same time act both as guards and guides. Sheikh Mustafa, the head of a wandering tribe of half Derwishes who frequent the vicinity of Jericho, was spoken of; but was not then to be found at Jerusalem. Another person was then recommended, who had been a leader in the rebellion of 1834; a price was set upon his head, and he had been ever since an outlaw, but had never been taken. He was known to be often in Jerusalem, and was on good terms with the convent in Bethlehem. Indeed, a few days before, he had been guide and escort to a party of our friends, including several ladies, during an excursion from that convent to several places in the vicinity of Bethlehem. As he was of course on good terms with all the other outlaws and Arabs, and could thus protect us from any attack, we commissioned our Arab-Greek friend and agent Abu Selâmeh, to find him out and engage him. The latter applied to the Greek convent at Bethlehem, which readily undertook the matter; but they afterwards sent word, that as the country was now very unsafe, it would be prudent to take a larger escort, and not trust ourselves to the care of a single person. They accordingly sent to us the Sheikh of the Ta'âmirah, a tribe of Arabs living south-east of Bethlehem towards the Dead Sea, and noted as being among the foremost on occasions of rebellion and robbery. He was a noble-looking man, and we at once made a bargain with him, that he should accompany us with three of his men. We were to pay him ten piastres a day for himself, and five or six piastres for each of his attendants. He fulfilled his contract honourably; and we had no reason to repent of our choice.

ii. 153, 154

The Christian Sabbath passed away in quiet enjoyment ; and Monday was occupied in writing out our journals and various other preparations. We hoped for a time that Mr Whiting would have accompanied us ; but it was not convenient for him ; so that the party was limited to ourselves, with our two servants. We engaged six horses, including one for the tent and luggage ; with the condition that they should be accompanied by three men, in order to render our party as large as possible. At evening our Sheikh came and slept in the house ; having appointed his men to join us at Bethlehem.

Tuesday, May 8th. The horses were brought between 6 and 7 o'clock ; but with only two men and without bridles. We demurred to this state of things ; and a difficulty arising, they went off again, leaving their earnest-money in our hands. While we were endeavouring to procure other horses, Abu Selâmeh came in, and immediately set off after the men to bring them back ; as the owner of the horses seemed to be his particular friend. In this he succeeded, as he said ; the men and the horses came back, and a brother of the owner with them. But we found that our Arab friend had gone a little beyond his instructions in the terms of conciliation ; we were indeed to have the bridles, but the owner was to send only the two men ; the third was to be furnished by our Sheikh from his tribe, and we were to pay for him. We thought it best on the whole to submit to this imposition, rather than to lose more time ; and accordingly got all things in readiness to mount. We took our tent as before ; but carried all our bedding and blankets upon our own saddles. Our provisions and utensils were distributed in small sacks ; which were then deposited in capacious saddle-bags, slung across the horses of our servants.

But another delay now arose ; the brother of the owner and the muleteers all affirming, that in order to visit Jericho, where there is a small garrison, it was necessary to have a *Tezkirah* from the governor. We doubted the fact, and afterwards found that we were right ; yet in order to be on the safe side, we sent Komeh with our Firmân to the governor, accompanied by the owner's brother, in order to obtain the desired paper. This latter was a man of enterprise and daring ; some ten years before, he had combined with a few others and suddenly got possession of the citadel, turning out the garrison and afterwards closing the gates of the city for a time against the Turkish government. As our messenger he was now courteously received by the governor ; and it so happened that the Aga in command at Jericho was present. The governor immediately gave him verbal orders to receive us at Jericho, and attend to all our wants ; and also

ii. 154–156

to send with us an escort of soldiers to the Jordan. This latter
kindness we afterwards took care to avoid.

All these matters being at length arranged, we left the Yáfa
gate at ten minutes before 10 o'clock, on our way to Bethlehem,
across the valley of Hinnom and along the plain of Rephaim, by
the same route by which we had first approached Jerusalem.[1]
At 10 o'clock we were opposite to Wady el-Werd, leading out
between high hills from the southwest corner of the plain. It
here runs W. by S. and is joined further down by the Wady
Ahmed. In this valley, in sight of our road, lies the village of
Beit Súfáfa ; and further off in the same direction, esh-Sheráfát,
on the southern hill. Both of these now bore west. On the
northern hill, overagainst the latter place, we could see the village el-Málihah, bearing N. 70° W. Further down the valley,
out of sight, lies 'Ain Yâlo,[2] a fountain, from which water is often brought to Jerusalem. At 10.45 Sheráfát bore N. 80° W.
and Málihah N. 55° W.[3] When we reached the gate leading
to the Greek convent Már Elyás, ten minutes later, these villages were already shut out from view by intervening hills.

We had lingered on the way, so that we were now as long in
passing over this interval to the convent with horses, as we formerly had been with camels. It is usually reckoned one hour.
The convent lies in the fields at some distance from the road, on
the verge of the ridge, having a wide prospect across the deep
valleys on the south.[4]

From this point two paths lead to Bethlehem ; one direct,
descending and crossing the deep valley on the south ; the other
passing more to the right around the head of the valley, and so
by Rachel's tomb. We took the latter, now as before ; and at
11.10 Már Elyás behind us bore N. 44° E. and Beit Jála S. 60°
W.—At 11.20 there was a little ruin on the right, called el-
Khamís.[5] We came to Rachel's tomb in five minutes more,
which has already been described.[6] The Muslims keep the tomb
in order ; and those of Bethlehem were formerly accustomed to
bury around it. The whole tract before us was full of olive
groves, especially in Wady Ahmed and on the slopes of Beit Jála,
and also in the valleys on the east of the low swell or water-shed ;
while towards Bethlehem were likewise many orchards of fig
trees.

[1] See above, p. 219.

[2] See p. 326. For this and other fountains
in Wady el-Werd, see Vol. III. Sec. VI.

[3] Prokesch passed from Beit Súfáfa to
Málihah in half an hour ; and thence to
the village of St. John ('Ain Kárim) in three
quarters of an hour. Reise, pp. 118, 119.

[4] From the well at the gate leading to
the convent, we took the following bear-

ings : Jerusalem N. 25° E. Neby Samwíl
N.¼W. Bethlehem S. 15' W. Convent
of Bethlehem S. 10° W. Beit Sáhúr S.
50' E. Frank mountain S. 16° E.

[5] See more in Vol. III. Sec. VI.

[6] See above, p. 218.—From Rachel's
tomb Bethlehem bears S. 5° E. distant 25
minutes ; and Beit Jála S. 85° W. distant
about 20 minutes.

Passing on towards Bethlehem, we met a mule laden with water, said to be from Bethlehem for the Armenian convent in Jerusalem. We took this at first as a confirmation of the excellence of the water longed for by David ;[1] but we were afterwards able to find no well in Bethlehem, and especially none "by the gate," except one connected with the aqueduct on the south. That to which the monks give the name of the 'Well of David,' is about half or three quarters of a mile N. by E. of Bethlehem, beyond the deep valley which the village overlooks ; it is merely a deep and wide cistern or cavern now dry, with three or four narrow openings cut in the rock.[2]

At 11.35 we came upon. the aqueduct from Solomon's pools ; which having wound far to the east around the ridge on which Bethlehem and the convent stand, curves here again to the west in order to preserve its level. It had lately been repaired, and the water was now flowing in it at this point. Crossing the low water-shed, we now ascended gradually towards Bethlehem around the broad head of a valley running northeast to join that under Mâr Elyâs. The town lies on the E. and N. E. slope of a long ridge ; another deep valley, Wady Ta'âmirah, being on the south side, which passes down north of the Frank mountain towards the Dead Sea, receiving the valley under Mâr Elyâs not far below.[3] Towards the west the hill is higher than the village, and then sinks down very gradually towards Wady Ahmed.

We reached Bethlehem at ten minutes before noon, in just two hours from Jerusalem. As we entered the gate, we were met by a procession or party of armed Bedawîn on horseback, passing through the town apparently towards Jerusalem. Some had firearms, and the rest swords and long spears. They seemed much disposed to be on good terms with us ; saluted us courteously ; and some of them in passing reached us their right hand. We hardly knew what to make of all this ; and our Sheikh was too much of a diplomatist to inform us at the time ; but we afterwards found that they belonged to a larger party of the Tiyâhah and Jehâlin, who were on their way to cross the Jordan, on a marauding expedition against their enemies, under the sanction of Sheikh Sa'îd governor of Gaza. The result we learned at a later period from the Jehâlin.[4]

We proceeded directly through the town, and stopped for fifteen minutes on the level part of the ridge between it and the convent. The latter is some thirty or forty rods distant from the village towards the east, and overlooks the deep valley on the north.

---

[1] 2 Sam. 23, 15–17. 1 Chr. 11, 17–19.   speaks of it expressly as a *cisterna;* c. 9.
[2] Quaresmius II. p. 614.   Maundrell,   p. 184.
Apr. 1. Turner's Tour in the Levant, II. p.   [3] See more under May 11th.
270.   Monro I. pp. 251, 252.—Brocardus   [4] See under May 26th.
ii. 158, 159

It is occupied by the Greeks, Latins, and Armenians ; and encloses the church built by Helena over the alledged cave of the Nativity. The monks had now shut themselves up in quarantine on account of the plague ; so that we did not enter the convent. We were expecting at the time to visit Bethlehem again, and examine it more at leisure ; but this hope was afterwards frustrated ; and I am therefore able to add little to the stock of information already known.[1]

No one has ever doubted, I believe, that the present Beit Lahm, 'House of Flesh,' of the Arabs, is identical with the ancient Bethlehem, 'House of Bread,' of the Jews ; and it is therefore not necessary here to dwell upon the proofs.[2] Not only does the name coincide ; but the present distance of two hours from Jerusalem corresponds very exactly to the six Roman miles of antiquity. Tradition moreover has never lost sight of Bethlehem ; and in almost every century since the time of the New Testament, it has been visited and mentioned by writers and travellers.[3] Helena built here a church, which appears to have been the same that still exists.[4] Jerome afterwards took up his residence in the convent, which early sprung up around it ; and the Roman matron Paula came and erected other convents, and spent here the remainder of her days.[5] As to the value of the early tradition, which fixes the birthplace of the Saviour in a cavern at some distance from the village, I have already expressed a judgment.[6] Although in this respect I felt no desire to visit the spot ; yet it would have been gratifying to have seen it, as the place where Jerome lived and prepared his version of the Bible and so many other works. His cell or cave is still professedly shown.[7]

The crusaders, on their approach to Jerusalem, first took possession of Bethlehem, at the entreaty of its Christian inhabitants. In A. D. 1110, king Baldwin I erected it into an episcopal see, a dignity it had never before enjoyed ; but although this was confirmed by pope Pascal II, and the title long retained in the Romish church, yet the actual possession of the see appears

---

[1] From this point, between the town and convent, we took the following bearings : Frank Mountain S. 27° E. Beit Ta'mar, the village of the Ta'amirah, S. 40° E. Beit Sâhûr S. 55° E. Deir Ibn 'Obeid not far from Mâr Saba, S. 80° E. This seems to be the Der-Bendibede of Pococke, on the way to Mâr Saba ; II. i. p. 34.

[2] They may be seen in Reland Palæst. p. 642. Euseb. et Hieron. Onomast. art. *Bethlehem*.

[3] By Justin Martyr in the second century ; by Origen in the third ; and then by Eusebius, Jerome, the Bourdeaux pilgrim, and so on by hundreds to the present day.

For the general character of this tradition, see above, p. 416 sq.

[4] One of the churches, that of St. Catharine, is supposed by Quaresmius to have been built by Paula ; but he assigns no better reason than mere conjecture ; II. pp. 675, 676. He is followed by some later writers. Early history, so far as I know, makes no mention of any such fact.

[5] See above, p. 378.

[6] See above, p. 417.

[7] The monks have fixed the spot, where the angels appeared to the shepherds, in a valley about half an hour eastward from Bethlehem.

not to have been of long continuance.[1] In A. D. 1244, Bethlehem like Jerusalem was desolated by the wild hordes of the
Kharismians.[2]

The present inhabitants of Bethlehem are all Christians; and
are rated at eight hundred taxable men, indicating a population
of more than three thousand souls. There was formerly a Muhammedan quarter; but, after the rebellion in 1834, this was
destroyed by order of Ibrahim Pasha. The town has gates at
the entrance of some of the streets; the houses are solidly built,
though not large. The many olive and fig orchards and vineyards
round about, are marks of industry and thrift; and the adjacent
fields, though stony and rough, produce nevertheless good crops
of grain. Here indeed was the scene of the beautiful narrative
of Ruth, gleaning in the fields of Boaz after his reapers; and it
required no great stretch of imagination to call up again those
transactions before our eyes.[3] The present inhabitants, besides
their agriculture, employ themselves in carving beads, crucifixes,
models of the Holy Sepulchre, and other similar articles, in olive
wood, the fruit of the Dôm palm, mother of pearl, and the like,
in the same manner as the Christians of Jerusalem.[4] Indeed the
neatest and most skilfully wrought specimens of all these little
articles, come from Bethlehem.

The Bethlehemites are a restless race, prone to tumult and
rebellion, and formerly living in frequent strife with their neighbours of Jerusalem and Hebron.[5] In the rebellion of 1834 they
naturally took an active part; and the vengeance of the Egyptian government fell heavily upon them. The Muslim quarter
was laid in ruins; and all the inhabitants, like those of other
towns and villages, disarmed. The manner in which this disarming of the population is carried into effect, is highly illustrative
of the character of oriental despotism. A town or village is required to surrender, not what arms they may actually have; for
this would hardly be effectual, and many might be concealed;
but a requisition is made upon them, and rigidly enforced, to
deliver up a certain amount of muskets and other weapons,
whether they have them in possession or not. The consequence
is, that the people of a place are often compelled to search out
and purchase arms elsewhere at an enormous price, in order thus
to deliver them up; or, if unable to do this, they are thrown into
prison, and sometimes marched off as conscripts.[6] In either case
the intentions of the government are answered.

[1] Will. Tyr. 11. 12. Le Quien Oriens
Christ. III. p. 1275 sq. Wilken Gesch. der
Kreuzz. II. p. 366.
[2] Wilken Gesch. der Kreuzz. VI. p.
635.
[3] Ruth c. 2-4.
    ii. 161. 162.

[4] See above, p. 428.
[5] Such was the case in Hasselquist's day
A. D. 1751; Reise, p. 170. See too Ali
Bey's Travels, Vol. II. p. 231.
[6] See the case of el-Bireh above, p. 451 sq.

When this process was going on at Bethlehem after the rebellion, an interesting circumstance took place, which serves to illustrate an ancient custom. At that time, when some of the inhabitants were already imprisoned, and all were in deep distress, Mr Farran, then English consul at Damascus, was on a visit to Jerusalem, and had rode out with Mr Nicolayson to Solomon's pools. On their return, as they rose the ascent to enter Bethlehem, hundreds of the people, male and female, met them, imploring the consul to interfere in their behalf, and afford them his protection ; and all at once, by a sort of simultaneous movement, "they spread their garments in the way" before the horses.[1] The consul was affected unto tears ; but had of course no power to interfere. This anecdote was related to me by Mr Nicolayson ; who, however, had never seen or heard of any thing else of the kind, during his residence in Palestine.

Bethlehem is celebrated in the Old Testament as the birthplace and city of David ; and in the New, as that of David's greater son, the Christ, the Saviour of the world. What a mighty influence for good has gone forth from this little spot upon the human race, both for time and for eternity ! It is impossible to approach the place, without a feeling of deep emotion, springing out of these high and holy associations. The legends and puerilities of monastic tradition may safely be disregarded ; it is enough to know that this is Bethlehem, where Jesus the Redeemer was born. Generation after generation has indeed since that time passed away, and their places now know them no more. For eighteen hundred seasons the earth has now renewed her carpet of verdure, and seen it again decay. Yet the skies and the fields, the rocks and the hills, and the valleys around, remain unchanged ; and are still the same, as when the glory of the Lord shone round about the shepherds, and the song of a multitude of the heavenly host resounded among the hills, proclaiming "Glory to God in the highest, and on earth peace, good will toward men."[2]

We were joined at Bethlehem by the remainder of our escort ; and left the place five minutes past noon, for Solomon's pools ; taking the path which follows the aqueduct around the hills, considerably to the eastward of our former route. Going down the steep descent from the town, we came after a few rods to what seemed at first to be two wells ; but they proved to be only openings over the aqueduct, which here passes through a sort of deep vault or reservoir, from which the water is drawn up about twenty feet. Many females were drawing water, and bearing it away in skins upon their shoulders. They assured us, that there is no well of living water in or near the town.

[1] Matt. 21, 8. Mark 11, 8. Luke 19, 36. [2] Luke 2, 8-14.

The Wady Ta'âmirah, into which we now descended, has its head just at the right ; the aqueduct is carried around it.   The declivities are full of gardens and vineyards and fine olive trees. Ascending upon the other side, at 12.20, Bethlehem behind us bore N. 30° E.   Ten minutes later we struck the aqueduct again, and followed it now quite to the pools, along and around the eastern and southern sides of a steep hill, looking down on the south into the deep Wady Ŭrtâs, which also runs towards the east.   At 12.50 the ruined village Ŭrtâs was on the declivity below us, with a fine fountain and streamlet, which waters many gardens in the valley.   A few minutes higher up, the valley divides ; one branch comes in from the S. S. W. which I suppose to be the continuation of Wady et-Tuhcishimeh ;[1] the other leads westward directly up to the pools.   Just at the foot of these, it is joined by another small parallel valley from the left with an aqueduct.[2]   Above the fountain at Ŭrtâs all these valleys are comparatively sterile.

We reached the pools, called by the Arabs el-Burak, at ten minutes past 1 o'clock.   These three huge reservoirs, built of squared stones and bearing marks of the highest antiquity, lie one above another in the steep part of the valley, though not in a direct line ; and are so situated that the bottom of the one is higher than the surface of the next below, rising one above another towards the west.   The top of the side walls is not entirely level ; for the water-mark extending from the lower end along the sides, strikes several feet below the top as it reaches the upper end.   The upper pool was by no means full, though the whole of the bottom was covered with water.   In the two others, water stood only in the lower part.   In these the bottom is formed by the naked shelving rock, which constitutes the steep sides of the valley, leaving only a narrow channel through the middle, and having several offsets or terraces along each side. The inside walls and bottoms of all the reservoirs, so far as visible, are covered with cement ; and the lower one had been recently repaired.   Flights of steps lead down in various places into all the pools.

Our first business was to measure the several pools ; and the following is the result in English feet.

I. LOWER POOL.

Length 582 feet.   Breadth $\begin{cases} \text{East end 207 feet.} \\ \text{West end 148 "} \end{cases}$

Depth at east end 50 feet; of which 6 feet water.
Direction of north side N. 45° W.

---

[1] See above, p. 217.   [2] See ibid.
    ii. 164, 165

II. MIDDLE POOL.

Distance above lower pool 248 feet.

Length 423 feet.　　　　Breadth $\begin{cases} \text{East end 250 feet.} \\ \text{West end 160 "} \end{cases}$

Depth at east end 39 feet; of which 14 feet water.
Direction of south side W. N. W.

III. UPPER POOL.

Distance above middle pool 160 feet.

Length 380 feet.　　　　Breadth $\begin{cases} \text{East end 236 feet.} \\ \text{West end 229 "} \end{cases}$

Depth at east end 25 feet; of which 15 feet water.
Direction of north side, N. 65° W.

The road by which we had formerly come from Hebron, passes along at the western end of the upper pool ; adjacent to which on the north stands the old Saracenic fortress already mentioned.[1] The main source from which these reservoirs have always been supplied, (when supplied at all,) appears to be a sunken fountain, situated in the open and gradually ascending fields, about forty rods northwest of the castle. Here one sees only the mouth of a narrow well, which at this time was stopped by a large stone, too heavy for us to remove. This is the entrance to the fountain below, which my companion had formerly explored. It cannot perhaps be better described than in the words of Maundrell : "Through this hole you descend directly down, but not without some difficulty, for about four yards ; and then arrive at a vaulted room fifteen paces long and eight broad. Joining to this is another room of the same fashion, but somewhat less. Both these rooms are covered with handsome stone arches very ancient, and perhaps the work of Solomon himself. You find here four places at which the water rises. From these separate sources it is conveyed by little rivulets into a kind of basin ; and from thence is carried by a large subterraneous passage down to the pools."[2]

This passage terminates at the northwest corner of the upper pool ; not in the pool itself, but in a sort of artificial fountain just above, so arranged that the water here divides. A part now passes off through a small aqueduct, which runs along the northern side of the pools ; while another part is turned down a descent into a vaulted subterranean chamber, twenty-four feet long and five or six feet wide ; at the further end of which it runs off through a square passage in the side, apparently to the adjacent pool. The aqueduct above mentioned continues along on

[1] See above, p. 218.
[2] Maundrell's Journey, Apr. 1st.—In a similar way the fountain of Gihon was probably "stopped" by Hezekiah; see above, p. 346. The monks hold the fountain here described to be the "sealed fountain" of Cant. 4, 12. Quaresmius II. p. 764.

ii. 165, 166

the north side of all the reservoirs ; giving off in like manner a
portion of its waters to the middle pool, and another portion to
the lower one.   It then passes down a steep declivity to join a
similar channel issuing from the lower end of the lower pool.

This main supply of water, however, was originally not the
only one.   The aqueduct which we had formerly seen in the parallel valley on the south,[1] is brought down across the point of
the southern hill, and descends steeply to the lower pool, one
hundred feet west of its southeast corner.   We traced this up
for some distance, and found that still another branch joined it
above.   We were told in Jerusalem, that the principal source
was in this southern valley ; but that two or three years ago a
large mass of rock fell into the fountain and stopped it, or at
least diverted its waters from the aqueduct, which was now dry.
We doubted the truth of the story ; for the aqueduct in question
seemed to have been long neglected.—The southern valley itself
comes in just below the lower pool ; and along or near its bed
passes another similar aqueduct, which we traced up.   There is
here a well of some depth, across the bottom of which the water
was seen running ; it then flows down and joins the channel
coming from the lower pool.

At the eastern end of the lower pool, a large abutment is built
up, in which is a passage and a chamber extending under the
massive wall of the reservoir quite up near to the water.   The
manner in which the water is drawn out or let off, we could not
distinguish, as we had no lights ; but it seemed to trickle out in
a small stream, and passed off below in a narrow channel.[2]

Thus the aqueduct which leads from hence to Bethlehem and
Jerusalem is here formed by the union of three branches, viz. first,
that coming from the fountain northwest of the castle along the
north side of the pools ; second, that from the eastern end of the
lower pool ; and third, that from the mouth of the small southern
valley.   It would seem, however, to have been the original intention, that the aqueduct should be ordinarily and mainly supplied
from the fountain above the castle ; its superabundant waters being
turned off at three points as above described, in order to aid in
filling these great reservoirs ; while these latter again, in time of
need, could be drawn off gradually to supply the aqueduct.   They
thus form all together an immense work, which is still of incal-
culable importance to Bethlehem, and might easily be made so
to Jerusalem.—The form and general course of the aqueduct, and
its termination in Jerusalem, have already been described ; and

---

[1] Vol. I. p. 217.

[2] In 1853 a vaulted room of considerable size was discovered underneath the
eastern end of the lower pool.   It would
ii. 166–168

seem to be similar to the subterranean
chambers above described at the fountain
above the pools, and at the northwest corner of the upper pool.

all the historical traces that I have been able to find relating either to the aqueduct or the pools, have in like manner been given.[1]

We left the pools at 3¼ o'clock for the Frank mountain ; returning for ten minutes by the way we came, and then striking down to the ruined village of Úrtâs near the bottom of the valley, which we reached at 3.35. The place is still inhabited, though the houses are in ruins ; the people dwelling in caverns among the rocks of the steep declivity. Here are manifest traces of an ancient site,—the foundations of a square tower, a low thick wall of large squared stones, rocks hewn and scarped, and the like. If we are to look anywhere in this quarter for Etam, which was decorated by Solomon with gardens and streams of water, and fortified by Rehoboam along with Bethlehem and Tekoa ; and whence too, according to the Rabbins, water was carried by an aqueduct to Jerusalem ; I know of no site so probable as this spot.[2] The fountain here sends forth a copious supply of fine water, and forms a beautiful purling rill along the bottom of the valley. This to me, was the more delightful, as being the first I had seen in Asia.

After stopping here five minutes, we passed down the valley on a general course about E. S. E. along the streamlet, and through the midst of gardens and fields fertilized by its waters. In the valley and on the hills were flocks of sheep and goats mingled together ; and this would seem to have been also the patriarchal mode of pasturage.[3] The sheep of Palestine are all of the broad-tailed species ; the broad part being a mere excrescence of fat, with the proper tail hanging out of it. A few camels were also seen, and many neat cattle, all looking in fine case ; thus showing that this is a good grazing district, however rocky and sterile it may be in appearance. The little stream was soon absorbed in the thirsty gravelly soil of the valley, and the gardens ceased.

Our Sheikh had been all day unwell, and now became quite ill ; so that we persuaded him to mount the horse of one of our servants. At a quarter past four, the valley turned more to the right, and we sent off our servants and baggage with the Sheikh to the encampment of his tribe, where we had concluded to pass the night. The Sheikh had told us that he would kill a sheep for us, if we would do him this honour. Taking with us the other attendants, we now struck up the hill-side on the left to the high table land above, and so continued our course towards

---

[1] See above, pp. 347, 348.

[2] See the historical references on p. 348, above.—The monks make the gardens below to be the *hortus conclusus*, 'garden en-closed,' of Cant. 4, 12. Quaresmius II. p. 764.

[3] Gen. 30, 35 sq.

the Frank mountain. Crossing another small Wady running down southeast to the Ùrtâs, we had at 4.50 the foundations of a ruined village on our left, called el-Munettisheh. The hills around, though now desolate and arid, had once been built up in terraces and cultivated. At 5.10, we reached the base of the mountain; which bears in Arabic, for what reason I know not, the name el-Fureidis, a diminutive of the word signifying Paradise.

The mountain here rises steep and round, precisely like a volcanic cone, but truncated. The height above the base cannot be less than from three to four hundred feet; and the base itself has at least an equal elevation above the bottom of Wady Ùrtâs in the southwest; towards which there is a more gradual descent. There are traces of terraces around the foot of the mountain, but not higher up; and these would seem to have been intended for cultivation rather than for defence. We did not notice any road to the top, nor any fosse upon the south, as described by Pococke;[1] though our attention was not particularly drawn to these points. Indeed the sides of the mountain above, present now no appearance of any thing artificial.—Just on our left, in the direction N. N. W. from the mountain, a large tract had once been levelled off and built up on the eastern side with a wall. In the midst of this tract was a large reservoir, some two hundred feet square, now dry; and in the middle of it a square mound like an island. There seemed also to be ancient foundations round about; though we did not remark the church of which Pococke speaks; and traces of an aqueduct were seen coming from the north.

Leaving here our horses, a steep ascent of ten minutes brought us to the top of the mountain, which constitutes a circle of about seven hundred and fifty feet in circumference. The whole of this is enclosed by the ruined walls of a circular fortress, built of hewn stones of good size, with four massive round towers standing one at each of the cardinal points. Either the ruins have formed a mound around the circumference, or the middle part of the enclosure was once excavated; it is now considerably deeper than the circumference. The tower upon the east is not so thoroughly destroyed as the rest; and in it a magazine or cistern may still be seen.[2]

This mountain commands, of course, a very extensive view towards the north; less so towards the south and west; while on the east, the prospect is bounded by the mountains of Moab beyond the Dead Sea. A slight haze prevented us from distinguishing the site of Taiyibeh and also Kerak. In the view of the Dead Sea I was greatly disappointed. I had hoped to have got

---

[1] Descr. of the East, II. i. p. 42.
[2] The Frank mountain has not usually been ascended by travellers. Among the ii. 169-171

few who speak of having been upon it, are Von Troilo, Nau, le Brun, Pococke, Irby and Mangles, and some others.

sight here perhaps of both its extremities ; or at least to have
ascertained some other high points from which that would be
possible ; but we found that very little more of its surface is
visible from this spot, than is seen from the mount of Olives.
The mountain is too far from the sea to command a view over it ;
and other mountains intervene, which, though rugged and desolate, are low ; so that while they serve to shut out the prospect,
they present among themselves no better point of view.[1]

The present name of the "Frank mountain" is known only
among the Franks ; and is founded on a report current among
them, that this post was maintained by the crusaders for forty
years after the fall of Jerusalem.[2] But, to say nothing of the
utter silence of all the historians of the crusades, both Christian
and Muhammedan, as to any occupation whatever of this post by
either party, it is justly remarked by Irby and Mangles, that
" the place is too small ever to have contained half the number
of men, which would have been requisite to make any stand in
such a country ; and the ruins, though they might be those of a
place once defended by the Franks, appear to have had an earlier
origin, as the architecture seems to be Roman."[3] The present
appellation appears to have sprung up near the close of the seventeenth century.[4] Before that time most travellers who mention
the mountain, call it Bethulia, and give the same name to the
ruins at its foot ;[5] though on what conceivable ground this latter
name was adopted, I have not been able to discover.

The earliest direct mention of the mountain in modern times,
as well as of this story of the Franks, is apparently by Felix
Fabri in A. D. 1483. According to him the Franks had plenty
of water in cisterns, and land enough within the fortress to raise
corn and wine and fruits sufficient for each year ; and they might
have held out indefinitely, had not a pestilence broken out among
them after thirty years, and destroyed most of the men and all
their wives and daughters ; after which the remnant withdrew

---

[1] We took on the Frank mountain the
following bearings : Abu Nujeim, a Wely,
W. Bethlehem N. 27° W. Beit Sâhûr N.
21° W. (This is the Bethsaon of Pococke,
II. p. 34.) Beit Ta'mar N. 20° W. Mâr
Elyâs N. 16° W. Neby Samwîl N. 10°
W. Mount of Olives N. 10° E. Abu Dis,
near Bethany, N. 20° E. Khûreitûn S.
15° W. Tekû'a S. 50° W. Beit Feijâr
S. 77° W.

[2] Some say by the knights of St. John.
Most travellers who mention the report,
seem to doubt its truth. Von Troilo, p.
314. Pococke II. i. p. 42.

[3] Travels, p. 340, [103.]

[4] I have not found it in any writer earlier than le Brun, Voyage p. 279. So

Maundrell's Journey, Mar. 31st. Morison,
p. 487.

[5] So Felix Fabri in 1483, Reissb. p. 287.
Znallart Viagg. p. 218. Quaresmius II. p.
687. Doubdan, p. 366. Von Troilo, p.
313. Morison has both names, p. 487.
Rauwolf, and also Cotovicus, confound this
mountain with Tekoa ; Reissb. p. 645.
Cotovic. p. 225.—Brocardus speaks of a
" collis Achillæ " overagainst Tekoa, c. 9.
p. 184. This Breydenbach and Adrichomius refer to the site of Masada on the
Dead Sea ; Reissb. p. 132. Adrichom. p.
38. De Salignaco on the contrary seems
to make it the Frank mountain ; Tom. X.
c. 2. I have not been able to trace this
name any further.

to other lands.[1] Subsequent travellers have repeated this report
in different forms; but all the circumstances lead only to the
conclusion, that it is in all likelihood a legend of the fifteenth
century.[2]

More probable is the suggestion, that the spot is the site of
the fortress and city Herodium, erected by Herod the Great.
According to Josephus, that place was situated about sixty stadia
from Jerusalem, and not far from Tekoa.[3] Here on a hill of
moderate height, having the form of the female breast, and which
he raised still higher or at least fashioned by artificial means,
Herod erected a fortress with rounded towers,[4] having in it royal
apartments of great strength and splendour. The difficult ascent
was overcome by a flight of two hundred steps of hewn stone.
At the foot of the mountain he built other palaces for himself
and his friends; and caused water to be brought thither from a
distance, in large quantity and at great expense. The whole
plain around was also covered with buildings, forming a large
city, of which the hill and fortress constituted the acropolis.[5] So
important indeed was the city, that one of the toparchies afterwards took the same name; and Ptolemy also mentions it as a
town of note.[6] To the same place, apparently, the body of Herod
was brought for burial, two hundred stadia from Jericho, where
he died.[7]—All these particulars, the situation, the mountain, the
round towers, the large reservoir of water and the city below, correspond very strikingly to the present state of the Frank mountain; and leave scarcely a doubt, that this was Herodium, where
the Idumean tyrant sought his last repose.[8]

An earlier mention of this mountain, or indeed any mention
of it in the Scriptures, cannot be assumed with the like certainty.
Pococke indeed suggests, that it may have been the Beth-hac-

[1] Reissb. des h. Landes, p. 287. Morison in 1698 makes this story refer to the
time of the conquest by Selim in 1517!
Relat. p. 487. I cannot find that Quaresmius mentions the story.

[2] Compare the similar legend relative
to the leaving out of Zion at the rebuilding
of the walls of Jerusalem in 1542; see
above, p. 318. n. 3.

[3] Joseph. Antiq. 15. 9. 4. B. J. 1. 21. 10.
Also in B. J. 4. 9. 5, it is related, that
Eleazar, who had laid siege to Tekoa, sent
messengers "to the garrison in Herodium,
which was near," πρὸς τοὺς ἐν Ἡρωδίῳ φρου-
ροὺς, ὅπερ ἦν πλησίον.

[4] Κυκλωτερέσι πύργοις, Ant. 15. 9. 4.
Στρογγύλοις πύργοις, B. J. 1. 21. 10.

[5] See generally, Joseph. Antiq. 15. 9. 4.
B. J. 1. 21. 10.

[6] Joseph. B. J. 3. 3. 5.   Ptolem. 5. 14.

ii. 172-174

See the authorities collected in Reland
Pal. p. 820.

[7] Joseph. Ant. 17. 8. 3. B. J. 1. 33. 9.—
Another castle of the same name was built
by Herod on a mountain of Arabia; Joseph.
B. J. 1. 21. 10.

[8] The first suggestion as to the identity
of the Frank mountain with Herodium, so
far as I have been able to find, is in Mariti;
Viaggi, etc. Germ. p. 545. He relates
that the Greek monks of St. Saba, who accompanied him towards Bethlehem, pointed out on a mountain towards the south,
the castle of Herod, which they called Ero-
dion. This seems to have been the Frank
mountain; though Mariti does not name it
and perhaps did not recognise it. The
same suggestion is made by Berggren, Resor etc. III. p. 50. Stockh. 1828. Then
by Raumer, Paläst. p. 220.

ccrem of the prophet Jeremiah, where the children of Benjamin were to "set up a sign of fire," while they blew the trumpet in Tekoa.[1] Jerome also says that there was a village Bethacharma, situated on a mountain between Tekoa and Jerusalem.[2] All this accords well enough with the position and character of the Frank mountain ; but is too indefinite to warrant anything more than conjecture. And besides, if Beth-haccerem was indeed succeeded by the fortress and city of Herod, it is difficult to see why Jerome, who usually employs the Greek names by preference, should here and elsewhere make no allusion to the later and more important Herodium.

Mounting again at 4 o'clock, and descending from the table land towards the southwest, we came in twenty minutes to the bottom of Wady Ûrtâs. There another valley joins it from the southwest, which we now followed up for some distance. The former Wady here runs about southeast, passing at some distance south of the Frank mountain ; and soon contracts into a narrow picturesque gorge, with high precipitous walls upon each side. High up on the southern side, at some distance below the entrance of the ravine, are the remains of a square tower and village, called Khûreitûn, which we had seen from the mountain ; and further down among the rocks on the same side, is an immense natural cavern, which my companion had formerly visited, but which we were now prevented from examining by the lateness of the hour. The mouth of the grotto can be approached only on foot along the side of the cliffs. My friend's description accorded well with the account of Irby and Mangles ; according to whom, the cave "runs in by a long, winding, narrow passage, with small chambers or cavities on either side. We soon came to a large chamber with natural arches of a great height ; from this last there were numerous passages, leading in all directions, occasionally joined by others at right angles, and forming a perfect labyrinth, which our guides assured us had never been thoroughly explored ; the people being afraid of losing themselves. The passages were generally four feet high, by three feet wide ; and were all on a level with each other. There were a few petrifactions where we were ; nevertheless the grotto was perfectly clear, and the air pure and good."[3]—The valley here takes the same name, and is known as Wady Khûreitûn.

This remarkable cavern is regarded in monastic tradition, reaching back to the time of the crusades, as the cave of Adullam, in which David took refuge after leaving Gath of the Phi-

---

[1] Jer. 6, 1. Pococke II. i. p. 42. fol.
[2] Hieron. Comm. in Jer. 6, 1. Neither Eusebius nor Jerome mention Herodium, nor elsewhere Beth-haccerem.

[3] Travels, pp. 340, 341, [103, 104.] See also Pococke II. i. p. 41. Turner's Tour in the Levant, II. p. 238.

listines.[1] But Adullam is enumerated among the cities of the
plain of Judah; and Eusebius and Jerome place it in the vicinity
of Eleutheropolis, west of the mountains.[2]

Following up the branch valley among the open hills, and
then gradually ascending the higher ground towards the left, we
came in twenty minutes (at 6.40) to the encampment of the
Ta'âmirah belonging to our guides; where we found our tent
already pitched, and our home for the night prepared. The situation was high, lying on the northern declivity of the high land
around Tekoa; and overlooking a large tract of country towards
the north.[3]

The Ta'âmirah were said to muster in all about three hundred men. The limits of their territory are not very distinct;
but they may be said to occupy, in general, the district lying between Bethlehem, Tekoa, and the Dead Sea; the eastern part
of which is a mere desert. At the place where we now were,
there were only six tents; the rest of the tribe being dispersed in
other similar encampments. They have but a single village,
Beit Ta'mar, and this is rarely inhabited; here they store their
grain in subterranean magazines like cisterns, as is common in
other villages. The Ta'âmirah occupy indeed a sort of border
ground, between the Bedawin and Fellâhîn; between the wandering tenants of the desert who dwell only in tents, and the
more fixed inhabitants of the villages. Hence, being acknowledged by neither and distrusted by all, they are regarded as a
sort of Ishmaelites whose "hand is against every man;" and
have acquired for themselves a notorious character as restless and
daring robbers and rebels. As a matter of course, they took part
in the insurrection of 1834; and at the capture of Jerusalem,
our Sheikh was said to have been the first man who entered the
city.

They also held out till the very last against the government.
Fearing the consequences of their activity in the rebellion, and
dreading especially the thought of being subjected to the conscription, they retired into the desert and encamped near the
Dead Sea. In order to bring them to terms, the Mudir of 'Akka
came with several thousand men and encamped in their territory
for some months; and it was only when they saw their flocks
and stores seized, their crops destroyed, and famine staring them
in the face, that they returned and submitted. They were disarmed, and compelled to pay an annual capitation-tax of one
hundred piastres for each man; but no soldiers were taken from
them, nor as yet had any other tax been demanded in any form.

[1] 1 Sam. 22, 1. 2 Sam. 23, 13.—Will.
Tyr. 15. 6.   Quaresmius II. p. 766.
[2] Josh. 15, 35. Onomast. art. *Adollam.*
ii. 175–177

[3] From the encampment the Frank
mountain bore E. N. E. Bethlehem N.
Tekû'a S. 6° E. distant 25 minutes.

But during the very last year, orders had come from Ibrahim Pasha to take of them for soldiers; upon which all the young men immediately fled to the east side of the Dead Sea. The Sheikh made representations to the authorities at Jerusalem, and the orders were recalled; though in the mean time five men had been already seized, some of whom were now dead, and the others not yet given up.

Such were the character and circumstances of the tribe, in the midst of whom we now were, and into whose care and keeping we had committed ourselves. But we had already learned enough of common reports, to know that they were in general exceedingly exaggerated; and we felt ourselves quite as secure here as within the walls of Jerusalem. To judge from our own intercourse of eight days with the Ta'âmirah, they are much like other Bedawin; though I think braver, and more faithful and trustworthy in danger. The Sheikh and his four men who accompanied us, were personally brave, and would probably have laid down their lives at any moment in our defence. Yet, like most Arabs, they have no regard for veracity, whenever there is the slightest personal motive to tell a lie; and like most Arabs too, their notions of *meum* and *tuum* are not very strictly defined, except towards one another, and towards those to whom they are bound in honour. In this particular, we at least had no occasion for complaint.

Our Sheikh was in every respect something more than a common Arab. In stature he was more than six feet high, well built and finely proportioned; and there was in his movements a native dignity and nobleness, which we did not find in other Bedawin. His countenance was intelligent, and had a mild and pensive cast; indeed there was a seriousness and earnestness about him, which could not but give him influence in any situation. He was also more than an ordinary Sheikh; he could read and write; and was likewise the Khatib or orator and Imâm of his tribe. In this capacity he was very regular in the performance of the Muslim devotions, and often chanted long prayers aloud. This seemed indeed to be his chief character, and he was addressed only as 'Khatib;' so that we hardly heard him called by his real name, Muhammed. There was said to be one or more other Sheikhs of the tribe; though we saw no one but him. The learning of the tribe is confined to the Khatib, no other individual being able to read or write; but as even this is an exception to Bedawy custom, the Ta'âmirah stand degraded by it in the eyes of their brethren.

As the Khatib was unwell, we saw no more of him that night. When we sent forward our servants, we had given them a hint to evade (if possible) the sheep, which the Sheikh had proposed to kill in our honour; for which, we were told in Jerusalem, a present of not less than two dollars to the Sheikh's wife would be a necessary acknowledgment. This they had been able to do without difficulty. The Sheikh had indeed brought to the tent, not the proffered sheep, but a kid, to be killed as a present; and our servants had told him rather unceremoniously, that we did not eat goat's flesh, and counselled him to take it away again; which he did.

It was now late; and in the bright light of the moon, the scene was highly romantic. We were here on the lofty hill-side, looking out upon the dark mass of the Frank mountain and the sacred region of Bethlehem; while around us were the black tents, the horses picketed, and the numerous flocks of sheep and goats, all still like the silence of the desert.

We had noticed on our arrival a fine mare with many trappings picketed near the tents; and were told the animal belonged to a Sheikh of the Jehâlin, who was here on a visit. He came to our tent during the evening, and proved to be Defa' Allah, the chief Sheikh of that tribe. He was gaily dressed, and wore red boots, which he kicked off with some difficulty on entering our tent. As we were expecting to visit Wady Mûsa with an escort from his tribe, we were glad to meet him here and obtain the necessary preliminary information. He had lately been there himself; having accompanied Lord Prudhoe thither directly across the desert from Suez. He said they were accustomed to take travellers from Hebron either on horses or dromedaries; but the latter were preferable, because in case of necessity they were fleeter, and could hold out longer. He was quite talkative, and seemed good natured and spirited; but as I could not follow his talk, and was exceedingly weary, I could not resist falling into a deep sleep as I leaned on my couch; however little honour this might reflect upon my courtesy. He however did not take it ill; and after some weeks we met again as old acquaintances at Hebron.

The object of Defa' Allah's visit here we did not learn at the time; but it afterwards turned out, that he belonged to the warlike party we had met in Bethlehem, and had come hither to induce the Ta'âmirah to join in the expedition. But they had already suffered enough from war, and were too wary to make any movement, which might draw upon them the notice of the Egyptian government; so that the Sheikh of the Jehâlin did not effect his purpose, and left the encampment during the night to overtake his party. But the Khatib was still too much of a diplomatist not to keep all this for the present to himself; and it was only after our return to Jerusalem, that he gave us this information.

Wednesday, May 9th. We rose soon after 4 o'clock, and
ii. 178–180

looked about upon the encampment. All was already in motion at this early hour. There were about six hundred sheep and goats, the latter being the most numerous; and the process of milking was now going on. They have few cows. The six tents were arranged in a sort of square; they were made of black hair-cloth, not large; and were mostly open at one end and on the sides, the latter being turned up. The tents formed the common rendezvous of men, women, children, calves, lambs, and kids. The women were without veils, and seemed to make nothing of our presence. Here we had an opportunity of seeing various processes in the housekeeping of nomadic life. The women in some of the tents were kneading bread, and baking it in thin cakes in the embers or on iron plates over the fire. Another female was churning the milk in a very primitive way, which we often saw afterwards in different parts of the country. The churn consists of a common water-skin, i. e. the tanned skin of a goat stripped off whole and the extremities sewed up. This is partly filled with the milk; and being then suspended in a slight frame, or between two sticks leaning against the tent or house, it is regularly moved to and fro with a jerk until the process is completed.

In another tent a woman was kneeling and grinding at the hand-mill. These mills are doubtless those of scriptural times; and are similar to the Scottish *quern.* They consist of two stones about eighteen inches or two feet in diameter, lying one upon the other, with a slight convexity between them and a hole through the upper to receive the grain. The lower stone is fixed, sometimes in a sort of cement, which rises around it like a bowl and receives the meal as it falls from the stones. The upper stone is turned upon the lower, by means of an upright stick fixed in it as a handle. We afterwards saw many of these mills; and saw only women grinding, sometimes one alone and sometimes two together. The female kneels or sits at her task, and turns the mill with both hands, feeding it occasionally with one. The labour is evidently hard; and the grating sound of the mill is heard at a distance, indicating (like our coffee-mills) the presence of a family and of household life. We heard no song as an accompaniment to the work.[1]

As we were looking round upon this scene of busy life, the sun rose gloriously over the wide prospect, and shed his golden light upon a landscape, not rich indeed in appearance, for all is rocky and sterile to the view; yet fertile in pasturage, as was testified by the multitude of flocks. The curling smoke ascend-

[1] " Two women shall be grinding at the mill; the one shall be taken and the other left;" Matt. 24, 41. Luke 17, 35. Comp. Ex. 11, 5.—"Moreover I will take from them the voice of mirth and the voice of gladness, the voice of the bridegroom and the voice of the bride, the sound of the mill-stones and the light of the candle;" Jer. 25, 10. Compare Rev. 18, 22. 23.

ing from various Arab encampments in the distance, added to
the picturesque effect of the landscape.

We left the encampment at 6.10 for Teků'a, keeping along
the eastern brow of the high ground. The Khatib had shaken
off his illness during the night; and now marched as our leader
with vigour and spirit. As his tribe had been disarmed, our
guides could lawfully carry no better weapons than short clubs
and staves; but they prided themselves on bearing our muskets
and pistols; and took with them also a gun of their own, which
was clandestinely kept among them.

We reached Teků'a at 6.35. It lies on an elevated hill, not
steep, but broad on the top, and covered with ruins to the extent
of four or five acres. These consist chiefly in the foundations of
houses built of squared stones, some of which are bevelled. At
the northeast part are the remains of a large square tower or
castle, still the highest point of all. Near the middle of the site
are the ruins of a Greek church; among which are several fragments of columns, and a baptismal font of rose-coloured limestone verging into marble. The font is octagonal, five feet in
diameter on the outside, four feet on the inside, and three feet
nine inches deep. There are many cisterns excavated in the
rocks; and not far off is a living spring from which our Arabs
brought us fine water. The ruins of a church lying a mile further
south, as mentioned by Pococke, we did not see.[1]

The high position of Teků'a gives it a wide prospect. Toward
the northeast the land slopes down towards Wady Khŭreitûn;
on the other sides the hill is surrounded by a belt of level table
land; beyond which are valleys and then other higher hills. This
belt is tilled to a considerable extent, and there were now several
fields of grain upon it. On the south at some distance, another
deep valley runs off southeast towards the Dead Sea. The view
in this direction is bounded only by the level mountains of Moab,
with frequent bursts of the Dead Sea, seen through openings
among the rugged and desolate intervening mountains. In the
E. S. E. were seen also two small isolated towers, Kŭsr 'Antar
and Kŭsr Um el-Leimôn, between Teků'a and the continuation
of Wady Khŭreitûn; but there seemed to be nothing remarkable
about them.[2]

Here then are the remains of the Tekoa of the Old Testament; whence Joab called the "wise woman" to plead in behalf
of Absalom; and which, fortified by Rehoboam, was afterwards

---

[1] Probably the fountain is that mentioned by Pococke, as being in a grotto towards
the northwest. Vol. II. i. p. 41.

[2] At Teků'a we obtained the following
bearings: Frank mountain N. 50° E.
Mount of Olives N. 15° E. Sûr Bâhil, a
ii. 181-183

village towards Jerusalem, N. 13° E. Mâr
Elyâs N. 5° E. Bethlehem N. Neby Samwil N. 2° W. Abu Nujeim N. 15° W.
Beit Fejjâr S. 85° W. esh-Shiyûkh, a
well-built village, S. 51° W.

the birthplace of the prophet Amos, and gave its name also to the adjacent desert on the east.[1] Not only is the present name decisive ; but the ancient specifications as to its site are equally distinct. Eusebius and Jerome describe Tekoa as lying twelve miles from Jerusalem and six miles from Bethlehem towards the south ; and the latter further remarks, that from Bethlehem he had Tekoa daily before his eyes.[2] We did not indeed travel the direct route between these two places ; but the distance is still reckoned at two hours.[3] In the beginning of the sixth century, the holy Sabas established in this vicinity a new *laura*, in connection with the greater one which still bears his own name ; and this became afterwards a seat of strife and controversy, as has already been related.[4] About A. D. 765, Tekoa was visited by St. Willibald ; it was then a Christian place and had a church.[5] In the time of the crusades it was still inhabited by Christians, who afforded aid to the crusaders during the siege of Jerusalem ; and the place was afterwards assigned by king Fulco to the canons of the church of the Holy Sepulchre in exchange for Bethany.[6] In A. D. 1138, Tekoa was sacked by a party of Turks from beyond the Jordan ; but the inhabitants had mostly taken refuge in the cavern above described at Khûreitûn, which was held to be that of Adullam.[7]

Whether Tekoa ever recovered from this blow, we are not informed ; nor do we know anything further as to the time of its abandonment.[8] In the days of Quaresmius it was, as now, desolate, and was not visited for fear of the Arabs ; though Morone in the same century mentions the baptismal font among the ruins.[9] A few years later (A. D. 1666) Von Troilo visited the spot; and describes its appearance much as it exists at present.[10] Since that time travellers have not unfrequently passed this way ; sometimes on their route between Bethlehem and Hebron.[11]

We had been hesitating, whether to go from Tekoa to Hebron, about four hours distant ; or to keep upon the hills more towards the left, and thus explore the country between us and

[1] 2 Sam. 14, 2. 2 Chr. 11, 6. Am. 1, 1. 2 Chr. 20, 20. 1 Macc. 9, 33.

[2] Onomast. art. *Elthei*, 'Εκθεκυέ. Hieron. Comm. in Amos Procem. Comm. in Jerem. vi 1, "Thecuam quoque viculum in monte situm . . . . . quotidie oculis cernimus." See the authorities collected in Reland Palæst. p. 1028.—Jerome in the Onomasticon gives the distance of Tekoa from Jerusalem at nine miles; which is inconsistent with Eusebius and with himself, and is probably a corruption.

[3] Comp. Turner's Tour, II. p. 240.

[4] See above, p. 383.

[5] Hodœporicon, p. 377, ed. Mabillon.

[6] Will. Tyr. 8. 7. ib. 15. 26. See p. 432, above.

[7] Will. Tyr. 15. 6. Wilken Gesch. der Kr. II. p. 682. See above, p. 481 sq.

[8] Brocardus and Marinus Sanutus mention Tekoa; but merely as an ancient place. Broc. c. 9. p. 184. Marin. Sanut. p 247. So too Breydenbach, Reissb. p. 132. Rauwolf mistakes the Frank mountain for it; ibid. p. 645.

[9] Quaresmius II. p. 687. Morone, p. 298.

[10] Reisebeschr. p. 314. Dresd. 1676.

[11] E. g. le Brun, p. 279. Morison, p. 487. Pococke II. i. p. 41. Turner II. p. 240. Irby and Mangles and party, p. 341. [104.] ii. 183, 184

'Ain Jidy more thoroughly. Adopting the latter course, as presenting a route hitherto untrodden by travellers, we proceeded on our way at 7.40, descending towards the southwest. We soon struck upon a small Wady, and followed it down in the same direction until ten minutes past eight. Here the larger Wady 'Arrûb comes in from the southwest, and the united valley, under the name of Wady Jehâr, now runs off towards the southeast to join the great Wady el-Ghâr, which empties into the Dead Sea a short distance south of 'Ain Jidy. Following up the Wady 'Arrûb, we took the branch that leads to a small village called Sa'ir,[1] being also the usual road to Hebron. At 9 o'clock, before reaching this village, (which lies half an hour beyond, or two hours from Tekoa,) we turned to the left into a side valley; and following it upwards to its head, we then passed up a steep ascent. The valleys along which we thus travelled, and the sides of the hills around, were sprinkled and sometimes covered with arbutus, dwarf oaks, small firs, and other bushes, with an abundance of the Za'ter; presenting the same general features as the country around Hebron.

At the top of the ascent, which we reached at 9.20, is a cistern marked by two or three trees. The spot is called Bir ez-Za'ferâneh.[2] The country before us was now a high rocky tract, exhibiting on our left no appearance of cultivation, though there are occasional traces of its having been formerly inhabited. A few villages appeared at a distance on our right. Fifteen minutes from Bir ez-Za'ferânch (at 9.40), while this place bore N. 50° E. and Shiyûkh S. 86° W. the next point of our route, Beni Na'im, came in sight, bearing S. 9° W. But instead of proceeding directly towards it, we were compelled to make a great *detour* towards the west, in order to pass around the heads of several branches of the Wady el-Ghâr, which lay between us and Beni Na'im, and were said to be so deep and rugged as to be nearly impassable for horses.—At the point where we now were, we saw traces of former foundations; and at ten o'clock there were ruins of small square towers on our left. At half past ten, we crossed a low sharp ridge, from which Bir ez-Za'ferânch bore about N. 70° E. and at 10.40 we halted for ten minutes in the shallow valley beyond. From hence our Mukârîyeh went with one horse to Hebron to purchase barley; to rejoin us again at Beni Na'im. They had neglected to bring a supply, thinking they could so manage as to induce us to go to Hebron.

Starting again at ten minutes before eleven o'clock, we began from this point to take a more direct course towards Beni Na'im,

---

[1] Probably the same which Irby and Mangles call Sipheer; p. 342. [104.]
[2] From this spot Tekoa bore N. E. by

N. Beit Feijâr N. 25° W. Shiyûkh S. 81° W.

ii. 184–186

proceeding first for half an hour in a direction nearly south. We soon came upon the brow of a very deep valley on our right; which, commencing further to the north, here runs towards the south, and passing to the eastward of Dhoheriyeh goes to join Wady es-Seba'. After receiving the Wady in which Hebron lies, it takes the name of Wady el-Khûlîl; and is the great drain of all the region around. At 11.20 we saw Nebi Yûnas, or Hûlhûl, on the high ridge beyond this valley, bearing N. 35° W. We had formerly seen it from the other side.[1] Near by us was a "broken cistern" in the rocks, well covered on the inside with cement. A ruin called Beit 'Ainûn was pointed out, bearing N. 40° W. Hebron, as near as we could judge, bore about S. 50° W. and was not far from an hour distant. The direction of Beni Na'im was here S. 50° E. towards which we now shaped our course.

We were thus travelling along the dividing line between the waters of the Dead Sea and the Mediterranean; and although we now diverged from the great valley on our right, yet it continued to be the drain of all the country on that side during the whole day. As we approached Beni Na'im, the traces of cultivation increased; and the level spots of any size were sown with barley or millet. Towards the west, olive trees and small vineyards appeared occasionally. All the tillage belongs to the few scattered villages which we saw.

The whole slope towards the Dead Sea on this side of Jerusalem, resembles in its general features the same slope on the north of that city. But it has even less of fertility; the desert region extending further up from the Dead Sea towards the water-summit. Still, even in those parts where all is now desolate, there are everywhere traces of the hand of the men of other days, as we saw both yesterday and to-day; terraces, walls, stones gathered along the paths, frequent cisterns, and the like. Most of the hills indeed exhibit the remains of terraces built up around them, the undoubted signs of former cultivation.

After a long ride we reached Beni Na'im at twenty minutes past noon, where we made a halt of several hours. This is a village with a mosk, lying on very high ground, to which the ascent is gradual on every side, forming a conspicuous object to all the region far and near. It overlooks the country around Hebron; and is therefore not improbably the very highest point in all the hill country of Judah. According to the Muslims this is the burial-place of Lot; and the mosk professedly covers his tomb.[2] It is a well built structure, much in the shape of an ordinary Khân, surrounding a court with chambers and porticos around

---

[1] See p. 216, above.

[2] Sir John Maundeville mentions the tomb of Lot as shown in his day two miles from Hebron; Travels, p. 68. Lond. 1839. ii. 186. 187

the inside. The flat roof over these forms a terrace along the wall, which is furnished with loop-holes for muskets ; and thus the building answers also the purpose of a fortress. Some of the houses of the village are built of large hewn stones, indicating antiquity. Most of them were in good repair, but none of them now inhabited ; all the people being abroad, dwelling in tents or caves, in order to watch their flocks and fields of grain. This is the custom of the peasants in this part of Palestine, during the months of pasturage in spring and until the crops are gathered ; while in autumn and winter they inhabit their villages.[1] Cisterns excavated in the solid rock testify also to the antiquity of the site ; and the exterior of the rocks is in many places hewn smooth or scarped. Over most of the cisterns is laid a broad and thick flat stone, with a round hole cut in the middle, forming the mouth of the cistern. This hole we found in many cases covered with a heavy stone, which it would require two or three men to roll away.[2]

From the roof of the mosk at Beni Na'im we had an extensive view on every side, and especially towards the east and south. The prospect towards the north was limited by the high tract over which we had just passed ; and towards the west and southwest by the hills around Hebron. The mountains beyond the Dead Sea were very distinct ; but the sea itself was not visible except through gaps in the western mountains, by which the eye could penetrate into its deep bosom. One of these was said to be near the pass of 'Ain Jidy ; and through another, further south, we could perceive what appeared to be a large sand-bank in the sea. Towards the south the land sinks down gradually to an extensive basin or plain, having many villages and ancient sites, with which we afterwards became better acquainted. We now remarked the ancient fortress of Kurmul (Carmel), and beyond it a dark mountain ridge beginning not far to the left and running off W. S. W.[3]

In respect to the place which anciently stood here, we can be guided only by conjecture. Jerome relates of Paula, that, departing from Hebron, she stopped upon the height of *Caphar Barucha*, 'Village of Benediction ;' to which place Abraham accompanied the Lord, and where of course he afterwards looked

[1] See above, p. 212. We afterwards met with other like instances.
[2] Gen. 29, 2. 3, " a great stone was upon the well's mouth ; and thither were all the flocks gathered ; and they rolled the stone from the well's mouth, and watered the sheep, and put the stone again upon the well's mouth in his place." We afterwards saw many illustrations of this passage in the fields ; the cisterns being very often thus covered with a stone, which is removed only at particular times.
[3] From the mosk we took bearings: esh-Shiyûkh N. 5° W. Pass of 'Ain Jidy S. 65° E. Wady el-Mojib beyond the sea, N. 80° E. Kurmul S. 23° W.—Hebron bears S. 82° W. distant about an hour and a half. This we were able afterwards to ascertain from the hill west of Hebron. See Hebron, May 25th.

ii. 188, 189

towards Sodom and Gomorrah and beheld the smoke of their burning.[1]   Here Paula looked out upon the wide desert, the land of Sodom and Gomorrah, and the regions of Engaddi and Zoar; and here she remembered Lot and his sin.[2]   She then returned to Jerusalem by way of Tekoa.   All these circumstances accord exactly with the situation of Beni Na'im, and with no other spot; and the mention of Lot in this connection, may help to account for the origin of the present Muhammedan tradition.— This of course was a different place from the *Valley* of Berachah (benediction) in the direction of Tekoa, where Jehoshaphat celebrated the miraculous overthrow of the Moabites and Ammonites.[3] Yet even of this perhaps a trace remains in the name *Bereikût*, which stands on Seetzen's map, and is found also in our lists.[4]

On arriving at Beni Na'im we quietly took possession of the court of the mosk; spread our carpets in the northern portico; and our servants having kneaded and baked unleavened bread for the first time, we enjoyed our repast and made ourselves very comfortable.   The weather was bright and pleasant, with a mid-day temperature of 67° F.   After two hours the Mukâriyeh arrived from Hebron; bringing with them their barley, and also oranges and other fruit for us.

We had before been undecided what route to take from Beni Na'im; but the sight of Kurmul, and a report of names like Zîf, Ma'in, and Yûtta, in that region, induced us to bend our steps that way.   Near Tekoa we had fallen in with two of the Arabs Rashâideh, who dwell around 'Ain Jidy; and as this point lay out of the territories of our guides of the Ta'âmirah, we had taken up one of these Arabs, both as a further guide for that portion of the western coast of the Dead Sea, and likewise in order to insure a good reception from such Arabs of his tribe, as we might happen to fall in with.   In going to Kurmul we entered also the territory of the Jehâlîn.

We left Beni Na'im at half past 3 o'clock, descending gradually; and in twenty minutes came in sight of Yûtta on the distant hills, bearing S. 55° W.   This is doubtless the Juttah of the Old Testament; we afterwards saw it much nearer, and I shall again recur to it.[5]   At the same time Beni Na'im bore N. 40° E. and Yûkîn S. 5° W.   The latter is a Muhammedan Makâm (station), where they say Lot stopped after his flight from Sodom.   At 4.10 we passed close by it; and continued to

---

[1] Gen. 18, 33. 19, 27. 28.

[2] "Altera die stetit in supercilio *Caphar Barucha*, id est, *villæ benedictionis;* quem ad locum Abraham Dominum prosequutus est. Unde latam despiciens solitudinem, ac terram quondam Sodomæ, etc. Recordabatur speluncæ Lot, etc." Hieron. Ep.

86, ad Eustoch. Epitaph. Paulæ, T. IV. ii. p. 675. ed. Mart. See also Reland Palæst. pp. 356, 685.

[3] 2 Chron. 20, 1. 2. 20. 26. 27.

[4] See more in Vol. III. Sec. VI.

[5] Josh. 15, 55. 21, 16. See under June 4th.

descend gradually towards the plain.   At 4¾ o'clock we reached
the western base of Tell Zif (hill of Zif) a round eminence
situated in the plain, a hundred feet or more in height.   Here
we fell into the road from Hebron to Kurmul.

The proper ruins of Zif, the Ziph of the Old Testament, lie
about ten minutes east of this point, on a low hill or ridge between two small Wadys, which commence here and run towards
the Dead Sea.   We ran thither on foot along the north side of
the Tell, which is separated from the ruins by one of the Wadys.
There is here little to be seen except broken walls and foundations, most of them of unhewn stones, but indicating solidity
and covering a considerable tract of ground.   In the middle is a
low massive square building, constructed of squared stones and
vaulted within with pointed arches ; showing that the place
must have been inhabited long after the Muhammedan conquest.
Cisterns also remain ; and in the midst of the ruins is a narrow
sloping passage cut down into the rock, terminating at a door
with a subterranean chamber beyond, which may have served as
a tomb or more probably as a magazine.—On the top of Tell Zif
is a level plot apparently once enclosed by a wall ; and here too
are several cisterns.[1]

Ziph is mentioned by Jerome as existing in his day eastward
from Hebron.   From that time to the present, there is no trace
of the name in history.[2]

Mounting again at ten minutes past 5 o'clock, we proceeded
upon the Hebron road towards Kurmul.   The region around,
and especially upon our right, was the finest we had yet seen in
the hill country of Judah.   The great plain or basin spread itself
out in that direction, shut in on every side by higher land or hills,
except upon the east, where it slopes off towards the Dead Sea.
The elevation of this plain, though not so great as that of Dhoheriyeh, cannot be less than fifteen hundred feet or more above
the level of the Mediterranean.   Its waters apparently flow off
in both directions, partly towards the Dead Sea, and partly towards Wady es-Seba'.   The surface of the plain is waving, and
almost free from rocks ; indeed, even the smaller stones are less
abundant than usual.   At present the whole tract was almost
covered with fine fields of wheat, belonging to persons in Hebron
who rent the land of the government.   Watchmen were stationed

[1] From this Tell, some fifteen rods east
of our road, the ruins of Zif bore N. 78° E.
distant about ten minutes.   Beni Na'im N.
39° E. Kurmul S. 7° W. Hebron about N.
by W.

[2] Onomast. art. *Ziph.* Eusebius does
not mention it.—Jerome says it was eight
miles from Hebron towards the east.   It
ii. 191, 192

is indeed somewhat east of south ; but the
distance is not quite an hour and three
quarters with camels, or less than five Roman miles.   Jerome had no personal knowledge of this region, and his estimates of
distances are here very loose.   See under
May 26th.

in various parts, to prevent cattle and flocks from trespassing upon
the grain. The wheat was now ripening ; and we had here a
beautiful illustration of Scripture. Our Arabs "were a hun-
gered," and going into the fields, they "plucked the ears of corn,
and did eat, rubbing them in their hands."[1] On being questioned, they said this was an old custom, and no one would speak
against it ; they were supposed to be hungry, and it was allowed
as a charity. We saw this afterwards in repeated instances.

In the first ten minutes we noticed two small sites of ruined
foundations on our left, for which our guides knew no name ;
but which the Jehâlin, as we afterwards passed this way, included under the name of Zif. At 5.40 there were other ruins upon
a low hill at our left, called Um el-'Amad, 'mother of the pillar.'
Foundations and heaps of stones with some cisterns cover a small
tract of ground ; while two or three coarse columns mark the
site probably of a village church, and give occasion for the name.[2]
Beyond this point, the land which was not ploughed, was covered
with the herbs Za'ter and Bellân (or *Netsh*), which afford fine
pasturage for sheep and goats ; the latter preferring it even to
grass. The tower of Semû'a was occasionally in sight.

We came to the ruins of Carmel at twenty-five minutes past
six ; and were about to pitch our tent by the reservoir in the
deep head of the valley, when an Arab peasant came and warned
us against it, saying there were *wanderers* (robbers) round about,
and inviting us to go on to Ma'in to an encampment of peasants
from Yûtta. This we consented to do, more for the sake of seeing the place and the people, than from any apprehension of
danger ; for our escort was not of a kind which robbers would
be likely to attack. Accordingly, after five minutes' delay, we
went on, and reached the place at five minutes before seven
o'clock. Here we encamped by a sheepfold near a cavern. It
was now dark and a strong chill wind was blowing from the west ;
so that we rejoiced in the protection of our tent, and enjoyed
also the blazing fire of our Arabs beneath the shelter of a rock.

A band of peasants from Yûtta were here, keeping their
flocks and dwelling in caves amid the ruins of Ma'in. They
gathered around us, astonished at our appearance among them ;
but their shyness seemed rather to proceed from timidity, than
from any disposition to be uncivil. They answered our questions
at first with suspicion, but with apparent honesty ; and their
distrust soon passed away.—The encampment was on the northern declivity of the conical hill of Ma'in, five minutes' walk below the summit. This hill rises gradually not less than some
two hundred feet above the site of Carmel.

---

[1] Matt. 12, 1. Mark 2, 23. Luke 6, 1.　　　[2] We visited this spot afterwards, May
Comp. Deut. 23, 25.　　　　　　　　　　　　26th.

Thursday, May 10*th.* We repaired to the top of the hill, from which there is an extensive prospect towards the north and over the broad plain on the west. The sun rose in his strength, and poured a flood of golden light upon the plain and the hills beyond ; so that every object was distinctly seen. The summit is crowned with ruins of no great extent ; foundations of hewn stone ; a square enclosure, the remains probably of a tower or small castle ; and several cisterns. The view is fine, including on the east the region towards the Dead Sea ; and extending on the north to Beni Na'im and Hebron, which was distinctly seen in its valley ; and on the west to Dhoheriyeh and beyond. Towards the south the view was interrupted by the mountain ridge already mentioned, about half an hour distant, running off nearly W. S. W. We could not learn that it had any special name ; it certainly is not called the mountain of Kurmul, or Mount Carmel ; unless sometimes because of its vicinity to that place.[1]

From Ma'in we could distinguish quite a number of places ; the bearings of which are given in the note below.[2] Of these places several are of unquestionable antiquity. Ma'in is without doubt the Maon of Nabal.[3] Semú'a we had formerly seen from Dhoheriyeh, and it probably corresponds to the ancient Eshtemoa.[4] 'Attîr suggests the Jattir of Scripture ;[5] and Sûsieh is a tract of ruins in the middle of the plain, said to be large, with many columns, though there seemed to be no houses standing. 'Anâb is of course the ancient name Anab without change ;[6] and in Shuweikeh, the diminutive form of Shaukeh, we may recognise the Socoh of the mountains of Judah.[7] In Yûtta and Kurmul we have the Juttah and Carmel of antiquity. Most of these places we afterwards saw again, in returning by a more western route from Wady Mûsa.

Here then we found ourselves surrounded by the towns of the mountains of Judah ; and could enumerate before us not less than nine places still bearing apparently their ancient names :

[1] Seetzen gives it this name ; Zach's Monatl. Corresp. XVII. p. 134.

[2] Bearings from Ma'in : Semú'a S. 86° W. 'Attîr, further south. Sûsieh N. 88° W. 'Anâb with a small tower N. 86½° W. Shuweikeh, a small ruin, N. 85° W. Dhoheriyeh on the hills N. 83° W. Mejd el-Bâ'u, a ruin on a hill, N. 71° W. Yûtta, a large village on a hill sloping east, N. 40° W. Hebron N. 4° W. Kurmul, the castle, one mile distant, N. 10° E. Beni Na'im N. 22° E.

[3] 1 Sam. 25, 2.

[4] Josh. 21, 14. 15, 50. The Hebrew name has the Hithpael form, which might easily pass over into the Arabic name with the article, es-Semú'a. Compare the simii. 194, 195

ilar case of el-'Âl for the Hebrew Elealeh. We visited Semú'a in returning from Wady Mûsa, June 4th.—A city Shema is also mentioned in the south of Judah ; too far south indeed to correspond to Semú'a ; Josh. 15, 26.

[5] Josh. 15, 48. There is here a difficulty in supposing a change of Yodh into 'Ain, of which there seems to be no other instance.—Raumer confounds Jattir with Ether in the plain, Josh. 15, 24 ; see his Paläst. ed. 3, p. 171.

[6] Josh. 11, 21. 15, 50.

[7] Josh. 15, 48. We afterwards found another Shuweikeh corresponding to the Socoh in the plain, Josh. 15, 35.

"Maon, Carmel, and Ziph, and Juttah;" Jattir, Socoh, Anab, and Eshtemoa; "and Kirjath Arba, which is Hebron."[1] The feelings with which we looked abroad upon these ancient sites, most of which had hitherto remained unknown, were of themselves a sufficient reward for our whole journey.

Of Ziph I have already spoken. Eusebius and Jerome enumerate Anab, Eshtemoa, Jattir, and Juttah, as large villages in their age ; though the specifications they give of their sites are very indefinite. Maon was then desolate ; and the Socoh of the mountains is not mentioned by them.[2] Carmel existed, as we shall see immediately. But from the days of Jerome, until the present century, not one of these names, except Carmel, occurs in history, or has been known as being still in existence. The crusaders seem not to have penetrated into this region, except in one or two military excursions around the south end of the Dead Sea. In March, 1807, Seetzen passed through this tract in the same direction ; and although his letter makes mention only of the mountain south of Carmel, yet his map contains the names of Kurmul, Semû'a, Yûtta, and Shuweikeh.[3] In 1818, Irby and Mangles and their companions travelled by this route from Hebron to the south end of the Dead Sea ; but none of them mention any of these names. Irby and Mangles speak of what may indeed have been Kurmul, near a well called "Albaid."[4] Within the last few years, travellers on the direct route from Wady Mûsa to Hebron have passed through Semû'a ; but seem to have heard nothing of these other ancient places.[5]

While we were taking our observations, many of the peasants gathered around us, and seemed gratified to hold our telescopes and render other little services ; although they wondered at our employment. The opinion was expressed among themselves, that we were each noting down his own estate in the lands around. Indeed, there seems to be a current impression, that ever since the country was in the hands of the Franks, their descendants still have deeds of all the land ; and when travellers come here, their presumed object is to look up their estates. These poor people, however, seemed well pleased at the idea of our coming to take possession ; hoping in this way to be themselves freed from the oppression of Muslim misrule.

We now returned on foot down the hill towards Kurmul, leaving our animals to follow when loaded. Here are more extensive ruins than we yet had anywhere seen, unless perhaps at Bethel. On the way, about a quarter of a mile south of the

[1] Josh. 15, 48–55.
[2] Onomast. arts. *Anab, Esthemo (Astemae?)*, *Jether* for Jattir, *Jetham* for Juttah, *Maon, Socoh*.
[3] Seetzen in Zach's Monatl. Correspond.

XVII. p. 133 sq. His map is found in the same work, Vol. XXII.
[4] Travels, p. 348. [106.]
[5] Stephens, Lord Lindsay, Schubert, etc.

castle, are the remains of a church standing quite alone. The whole length of the foundations is one hundred and fifty-six feet; the building having consisted apparently of two parts. The easternmost of these, the proper church, with columns, measures sixty-nine feet in length by forty-six feet broad; the western part, eighty-seven feet long by forty-eight feet broad; but the purpose to which the latter was applied we could not determine. On the south side is a square reservoir sunk in the rock.

The ruins of the town lie around the head and along the two sides of a valley of some width and depth; the head of which forms a semicircular amphitheatre shut in by rocks. From this the valley runs for some thirty or forty rods S. S. E. and then bends northeast towards the Dead Sea. The bottom of the amphitheatre is a beautiful grass plat, with an artificial reservoir in the middle, measuring one hundred and seventeen feet long by seventy-four feet broad. The spring from which it is supplied, is in the rocks on the northwest where a chamber has been excavated. The water is brought out by an underground channel, first to a small basin near the rocks, and then five or six rods further to the reservoir. No water was now flowing down the valley.

The main ruins are on the level ground west of the amphitheatre; and here stands the castle. They consist chiefly of the foundations and broken walls of dwellings and other edifices, scattered in every direction, and thrown together in mournful confusion and desolation. Most of the stones were only roughly hewn, or else have been worn away by time and exposure. In the western part are the remains of a smaller church, surrounded by those of very many houses. Here is also an open passage leading down into a narrow cavern apparently natural, which may have been used as a tomb or magazine, like the one we saw at Zif. A similar artificial cave, about twenty feet square, is seen just east of the castle.

The castle itself is a remarkable ruin, standing on a swell of the ground in the midst of the town. It is quadrangular, the sides measuring sixty-two feet by forty-two and facing towards the cardinal points. The height now remaining is about thirty feet. The external wall is evidently ancient; and has on the northern and western sides a sloping bulwark, like the citadel in Jerusalem.[1] The stones are bevelled; and though not so large as those of the tower of Hippicus, yet the architecture is of the same kind; leaving little room for doubt that it is the work of Herod or of the Romans. There is a lower and an upper story, both once arched; but the upper arch is gone. The walls are nine feet ten inches thick. On entering the building, the first thing which struck me was the pointed arches, indicating a later

---

[1] See above, p. 307.

ii. 197, 198

and Saracenic architecture, utterly inconsistent with the external appearance. But on looking further and examining particularly the windows, it was obvious, that the interior part had been built up at a later period within the more ancient exterior walls.— On the north side of the castle, at the distance of a few feet, are the foundations of what would seem to have been a round tower, measuring twenty-eight and a half feet in diameter from outside to outside, with a wall six feet thick. There would seem to have been a subterranean, or at least a covered passage from this building into the castle.—Adjacent to the castle on the east was also a small church.[1]

On the eastern side of the valley, opposite to the castle, was apparently a less important part of the town, perhaps a suburb. There is here also a small tower on the brink, with a like sloping bulwark rising up out of the valley. On the point of a hill about one third of a mile northeast from the castle, are the ruins of another large church and of a few other buildings.[2]

I have already used the names Kurmul and Carmel interchangeably; because there is no room for question, that this is the Carmel of the mountains of Judah; where Saul set up the trophy of his victory over Amalek, and where Nabal was shearing his sheep when the affair took place between him and David, in which Abigail bore so conspicuous a part.[3] No further mention of this Carmel occurs in the Scriptures; but Eusebius and Jerome describe it in their day as a village ten miles from Hebron, verging towards the east, with a Roman garrison.[4] From that time onward we hear no more of Carmel until the year 1172; when Saladin invaded the country on the east and south of the Dead Sea, where the crusaders had fortresses; and king Amalrich, having marched against him without effect, at length drew back and encamped at Carmel. Here he found a pool, and water in plenty for his army. Whether the place was then in ruins, we are not informed.[5] That it had been of old, and even not long before, a place of importance, is manifest from the Roman garrison, and from the rebuilding of the castle by the Saracens; if indeed the latter did not occur at a still later period. When and how Carmel became desolate, no record tells; and its

---

[1] Mr Wolcott in 1842, observed a Greek cross distinctly inscribed on the outer south wall several feet from the ground. He regarded the structure as erected out of the ruins of another; and supposes the sloping bulwark belonged originally to a larger structure. Biblioth. Sac. 1843, p. 60.

[2] From the castle of Kurmul we obtained the following bearings: Beni Na'îm N. 23° E. Hebron N. 5° W. Yûtta N. 48° W. Mejd el-Bâ'a N. 80° W. 'Anâb W. Shuweikeh S. 87° W.

[3] Josh. 15, 55. 1 Sam. 15, 12. 25, 2 sq.

[4] Onomasticon, art. Carmelus. The distance of ten miles here assigned is too great; and was probably put only as a round number. We afterwards travelled from Hebron to Carmel with camels in three hours, which gives at the most a distance of about 8 Roman miles. See May 26th.

[5] Will. Tyr. 20. 30. Wilken Gesch. der Kreuzz. III. ii. p. 151.

name was again forgotten until the present century. Seetzen, as we have seen, has given its position upon his map, and wrongly assigned its name to the mountain-ridge upon the south; but since his day no travellers appear to have recognised it.[1]

We were here in the midst of scenes memorable of old for the adventures of David, during his wanderings in order to escape from the jealousy of Saul; and we did not fail to peruse here, and with the deepest interest, the chapters of Scripture which record the history of those wanderings and adventures.[2] Ziph and Maon gave their names to the desert on the east, as did also En-gedi;[3] and twice did the inhabitants of Ziph attempt to betray the youthful outlaw to the vengeance of his persecutor.[4] At that time David and his men appear to have been very much in the condition of similar outlaws at the present day; for "every one that was in distress, and every one that was in debt, and every one that was discontented, gathered themselves unto him; and he became a captain over them; and there were with him about four hundred men."[5] They lurked in these deserts, associating with the herdsmen and shepherds of Nabal and others, and doing them good offices, probably in return for information and supplies obtained through them.[6]

Hence, when Nabal held his annual sheep-shearing in Carmel, David felt himself entitled to share in the festival; and sent a message recounting his own services, and asking for a present: "Wherefore let the young men find favour in thine eyes; for we come in a good day; give, I pray thee, whatsoever cometh to thine hand unto thy servants, and to thy son David."[7] In all these particulars we were deeply struck with the truth and strength of the biblical descriptions of manners and customs, almost identically the same as they exist at the present day. On such a festive occasion near a town or village, even in our own time, an Arab Sheikh of the neighbouring desert would hardly fail to put in a word, either in person or by message; and his message, both in form and substance, would be only the transcript of that of David.

We left Carmel at ten minutes past 7 o'clock, following down at first the small valley, but soon leaving it and passing more to the right on a general course E. by S. The ruins of et-Tawâneh were soon seen on the side of a hill not far distant on the right, and at 7.40 bore S. 20° W. The Wady from Carmel, and others on the right and left, go to form the Khûbarah,

[1] See above, p. 494. Berton passed this way a few weeks before us, and saw Carmel and Tell Zif.
[2] 1 Sam. 23, 13 sq. cc. 24. 25. 26.
[3] So Ziph as a desert, 1 Sam. 23, 14. 26, 2. Maon as a desert, 23, 25. En-gedi as a ii. 199–201

desert, 24, 1. That is, portions of the desert.
[4] 1 Sam. 23, 19. 26, 1.
[5] Ibid. 22, 2. These were afterwards increased to six hundred, 23, 13.
[6] Ibid. 25, 7. 14–16.
[7] Ibid. 25, 8. 9.

which runs down to the Dead Sea not far south of 'Ain Jidy.
Our road for a great distance was along these Wadys; sometimes in one, sometimes in another, and sometimes on the ridges
between. At 7.55 the small ruin Deirât appeared on the left,
bearing N. 10° W. On a ridge at 8¼ o'clock we stopped for
about ten minutes, and took bearings to ascertain our course.[1]

The country continued to be cultivated and fertile. Our
Arabs, as we passed among the fields of wheat, were constantly
"plucking the ears of grain, and eating, rubbing them with
their hands."[2] The tillage, however, soon became less frequent.
At 9 o'clock we passed near a large encampment of the Arabs
el-Ka'âbineh, situated in a broad open valley on our left. Their
black tents, to the number of twenty or thirty, were pitched in
a large oval. They were said to number about one hundred
men; and occupy in part the same territory with the Jehâlin
(Jehâliyeh), whose encampment at present was nearly two hours
southeast of Carmel. These Arabs also usually encamp further
south; but they were now pasturing in this vicinity, and we
found their flocks and camels among the hills and valleys for a
long distance as we advanced.

Our descent was constant; and in proportion to it, the heat
increased, and the country began to assume more the appearance
of the desert. We had left the grass green at Carmel; by 9
o'clock it was dried up. At 9.20 we came upon two deep cisterns in the rock, with rain water, directly in the path, belonging to the Jehâlin and Ka'âbineh. By 11 o'clock we were completely in the midst of the desert. The country is everywhere
entirely of limestone formation; but the rocks contain a large
mixture of chalk and flint, alternating with the limestone of the
region above. All around were naked conical hills, and also
ridges from two hundred to four hundred feet high, running down
mostly towards the sea. At first the hills as well as the valleys
were sprinkled with shrubs; but further down these disappeared
from the hills; and only a dry stunted grass remained, the growth
of winter. We recognised among the shrubs many old acquaintances of the southern desert, the 'Ajram, the Retem, and several
others; and found ourselves thus in an hour transported back
into the scenes of our former journey.

At 11½ o'clock we reached another cistern, or rather a reservoir of rain water by the side of a water-course. It was originally hewn out under a rock with a roof and a column to support
it; but the roof is now broken away. It is called Bîr Selhûb.
Before we were aware, our Sheikh and two of his men were plung-

---

[1] These were as follows: Ma'in S. 72°
W. Kurmul S. 87° W. Beni Na'im N.
4° W.—At 8.30 the small ruin of Zûrtût

bore N. 5° W.—Our bearings in this region were of course few.
[2] See above p. 493.

ing into the water to cool themselves. Three or four precipitous
hills around are called es-Sûfra. We had thus far been gradually
crossing the tributaries of Wady el-Khûbarah, leaving them running more to the right, in which direction that valley enters the
sea by a deep ravine just south of Wady el-Ghâr. At that point
there was said to be a foot-pass, leading down the south side of
this ravine to the shore ; but our Arabs knew of no other pass
for a great distance in that direction.

Leaving Bir Selhûb at 11.40, we crossed what seemed on that
side to be merely a low ridge ; and came immediately upon a
descent of nearly two hundred feet, along the steep face of a hill
of scaly friable limestone. At 11.10, another steep descent of
five minutes brought us to a difficult pass along the brink of a
deep precipitous valley on our left, which proved to be Wady el-
Ghâr ; here very narrow and running between walls of perpendicular rock, at a depth of more than a hundred feet. We descended by a very rugged and somewhat dangerous path ; and
reached the bottom at twenty minutes past noon.

In the course of the day we had already started a gazelle ; and
had seen also a jackal, which at a distance might be mistaken
for a fox ; though his colour is more yellow, and his movements
less wily. As we now came in view of the ravine of the Ghâr, a
Beden (mountain-goat) started up and bounded along the face
of the rocks on the opposite side. Indeed we were now in the
"wilderness of En-gedi ;" where David and his men lived among
"the rocks of the wild goats ;" and where the former cut off the
skirts of Saul's robe in a cave.[1] The whole scene is drawn to
the life. On all sides the country is full of caverns, which might
then serve as lurking-places for David and his men, as they do
for outlaws at the present day.

Our path now followed down the bottom of the valley for
some distance ; which is here just wide enough to be the bed of
a torrent, sometimes scarcely fifty feet, between perpendicular
precipices rising in some parts hundreds of feet on each side. In
the cliffs above, multitudes of pigeons were enjoying their nests
undisturbed. Here was again the Retem, growing very large ;
and other shrubs of the desert. Further down, the valley contracts and becomes impassable. It enters the sea just south of
'Ain Jidy. Near its mouth, as our Sheikh informed us, is a fine
fountain, and large willow trees, from which Arab bowls are
made ; and there too it was said to bear the name of Wady el-
'Areijeh.

We left the Ghâr at 12.35, and turned up a steep and rocky
pass northeast along a side valley, which brought us out in fifteen minutes upon the rough and desert table land above. At

[1] 1 Sam. 24, 1-4.

ii. 203. 204

1.35 we could see Carmel and Beni Na'im very distinctly; the former bearing N. 85° W. and the latter N. 67° W. Fifteen minutes later we fell into the road from Jerusalem to 'Ain Jidy. At five minutes before two, we had the first view of the Dead Sea, lying low and still in its deep bed; and at length, fifteen minutes later, reached the brow of the pass leading down to the shore.

For the last two or three hours of the way, we had been subjected to continual disappointment. At every moment we had expected to obtain some glimpse of the sea, and to arrive at the shore nearly upon a level with its waters. But the way at every step seemed longer and longer; and it was now only after nearly seven hours of travel, that we arrived at the brow of the pass. Turning aside a few steps to what seemed a small knoll upon our right, we found ourselves on the summit of a perpendicular cliff overhanging 'Ain Jidy and the sea, at least fifteen hundred feet above its waters. The Dead Sea lay before us in its vast deep chasm, shut in on both sides by ranges of precipitous mountains; their bases sometimes jutting out into the water, and again retreating so as to leave a narrow strip of shore below. The view included the whole southern half of the sea, quite to its extremity; and also, as we afterwards found, the greater portion of the northern half; although the still higher projecting cliff el-Mersed intervened on our left, to prevent our seeing the extremity of the sea in that direction.

One feature of the sea struck us immediately, which was unexpected to us, viz. the number of shoal-like points and peninsulas which run out into its southern part, appearing at first sight like flat sand-banks or islands.[1] Below us on the south were two such projecting banks on the western shore, composed probably of pebbles and gravel, extending out into the sea for a considerable distance. The larger and more important of these is on the south of the spot called Birket el-Khŭlil, a little bay or indentation in the western precipice, where the water, flowing into shallow basins when it is high, evaporates, and deposites salt.[2] This spot is just south of the mouth of Wady el-Khŭbarah. Opposite to this, nearly in the middle of the sea, is a long low narrow bank, also apparently composed of pebbles and gravel, running from northeast to southwest, and joined towards the south end to the eastern shore by an isthmus of some breadth. This long peninsula extends towards the south beyond the western shoal or point above described; so that from the spot where

---

[1] Burckhardt also, from the eastern mountains, "had a fine view of the southern extremity of the Dead Sea, which presented the appearance of a lake, with many islands or shoals covered with a white saline crust." Travels in Syria, p. 393.

[2] Described in Dr. Anderson's Geol. Report, p. 176.

ii. 204. 205

we now stood, they seemed to interlock, and we saw the end of
the peninsula across the point of the shoal.

Towards the southern extremity of the sea, a long low mountain was seen running out obliquely towards the S. S. E. extending from near the western cliffs apparently to the middle of the
Ghôr. This our Arabs called Hajr Usdum, 'Stone of Sodom ;' [1]
and said it was composed wholly of rock-salt, too bitter to be fit
for cooking, and only used sometimes as a medicine for sheep.
The sea washes the base of this mountain, and terminates opposite to its southeast extremity as here seen ; though as we were
still unacquainted with the features of that region, the water
seemed to us to extend further south and to wind around the
end of the mountain. This appearance, as we afterwards found,
must have arisen from the wet and slimy surface of the ground
in that part ; which, by reflecting the rays of the sun, presented
the optical illusion of a large tract of water, and deceived us as to
the extent of the sea in that direction.

The mountains on both sides of the sea are everywhere precipitous ; those on the east were now very distinct, and obviously
much higher at some distance from the shore, than those upon
the west. Across the isthmus of the low peninsula towards the
southeast, we could look up along a straight ravine descending
from the eastern chain ; at the head of which Kerak with its
castle was visible, situated on a high precipitous rock, far up near
the summit of the mountains. Opposite to us was Wady el-
Môjib ; and further north, Wady ez-Zerka.[2] At the foot of
these mountains, there is a passage along the eastern shore for
the whole distance on the south of the peninsula ; but further to
the north this would seem to be impossible. From the spot
where we stood, the line of the western cliffs ran in the direction
about S. by W.¼W. with a passage along the shore all the way
south of 'Ain Jidy. At nearly one half the distance towards
Usdum, just south of Wady es-Seyâl, the next beyond the Khûbarah, a ruin was pointed out on a high pyramidal cliff, rising
precipitously from the sea, to which our guides gave the name of
Sebbeh.[3]

---

[1] The form *Usdum* is probably a traditional reminiscence of the name Sodom.
Galen says the mountains around the lake
were in his day called Sodom. Instead of
Hajr Usdum, we afterwards heard from
our guides of the Jehâlin the name
Khashm Usdum. See more under May
29th. Galen de Simpl. Med. Fac. 4. 19. Reland Palæst. p. 243.

[2] The Zerka Ma'in of Burckhardt, Travels in Syria, p. 369 sq. For the Môjib, see
the same work, p. 371 sq.

ii. 206, 207

[3] From the cliff over 'Ain Jidy we took
the following bearings : 'Ain Jidy deep below, S. 70° E. Peninsula, north end, S.
38° E. Penins. south end, S. 4° E. Isthmus S. 26° E. • Point of western shoal S.
5° E. Hajr Usdum, southeast point, S. 6°
W. Do. middle S. 10° W. Course of western cliffs to near the north end of Usdum,
S. 15° W. Kerak S. 40° E. Mouth of the
Môjib S. 85° E. Mouth of the Zerka Ma'in
N. 60° E.

The features now described, together with the flat shores, give to the whole southern part of the sea the appearance, not of a broad sheet of water, but rather of a long winding bay, or the estuary of a large river, when the tide is out and the shoals left dry. Only a comparatively narrow channel remained covered with water. This channel of the sea (so to speak) is in some parts quite narrow, and winds very much. Between the point of the western shoal and the peninsula, the distance cannot certainly be more than one fourth or perhaps one sixth of the whole breadth of the sea; if so much. The direction of the peninsula, and then that of Usdum, causes the channel apparently to sweep round first towards the west and afterwards towards the east; giving to this portion of the sea a very irregular form. Our Arabs, both the Ta'âmirah and Rashâideh, knew of no place where the sea could be forded.[1] As we looked down upon it from this lofty spot, its waters appeared decidedly green, as if stagnant; though we afterwards saw nothing of this appearance from below. A slight ripple was upon its bosom; and a line of foam was seen along and near the shore, which looked like a crust of salt.

We remained on the cliff until three quarters past two o'clock, and then began to work our way down the terrific pass. This was no easy labour. The path descends by zigzags, often at the steepest angle practicable for horses, and is carried partly along ledges or shelves on the perpendicular face of the cliff, and then down the almost equally steep debris. Much of the rock is a compact reddish or rose-coloured limestone, like the baptismal font at Tekoa; smooth as glass, yet with an irregular surface. Looking back upon this part from below, it seemed utterly impossible that any road could exist there; yet by a skilful application of zigzags, the path is actually carried down without any insuperable difficulties; so that even loaded camels often pass up and down. Some few spots are very bad; because not kept in repair. Indeed there is very little of art about it; in a few places only is the way rudely built up and the stones removed from the track. In one part, not long ago, a Bedawy woman fell off and was killed; when picked up she was found to have brought forth a child. My companion had crossed the heights of Lebanon and the mountains of Persia; and I had formerly traversed the whole of the Swiss Alps; yet neither of us had ever met with a pass so difficult and dangerous. Of those which I had seen, that of the Gemmi resembles it most; but is not so high, and the path is better.

As we were descending the pass, we saw upon the water before us another optical illusion, which may serve to explain the

[1] See "The Ford," further on.

ii. 207, 208

supposed appearance of *islands* in the sea, remarked by some
travellers. In the direction east from us, near the opposite shore,
we saw what seemed to be another long dark-coloured shoal or
sand-bank. On looking further, however, it proved to be a spot
of calm smooth water, around which the rest of the sea was
covered with a ripple; and the dark brown eastern mountains
being reflected in this mirror, gave to it their colour. Yet for
the moment, the illusion was complete, that a long dark yellow
sand-bank or island lay before us.[1]

After a descent of forty-five minutes, we reached at 3½ o'clock
the beautiful fountain, 'Ain Jidy, bursting forth at once a fine
stream upon a sort of narrow terrace or shelf of the mountain,
still more than four hundred feet above the level of the sea.
The stream rushes down the steep descent of the mountain below; and its course is hidden by a luxuriant thicket of trees
and shrubs, belonging to a more southern clime. We stopped
at the fountain, expecting to continue our descent and encamp
on the shore; but here we learned with dismay, that in order to
proceed northward, it would be necessary to climb again the
whole of the fearful ascent; since all passage along the shore
was cut off by a projecting cliff not far remote. Till now we
had always understood the Arabs, that there was a path below;
but they had probably spoken at random, as is common, and
meant nothing more than a path along the cliffs and table land
above. Under these circumstances, we thought it better to encamp by the fountain, and visit the shore at our leisure during
the afternoon.

While thus engaged in pitching the tent, our Arabs were
alarmed at seeing two men with guns coming down the brow of
the pass. The idea of robbers was uppermost in their minds;
and two scouts were hastily despatched to meet them, and ascertain their character and purpose. But a few minutes afterwards,
there appeared on the brow above a troop of peaceful donkeys;
and now all alarm vanished in a loud laugh. The strangers
proved to be Fellâhîn from the village Deir Ibn 'Obeid near Mâr
Sâba, coming to this part of the Dead Sea after salt. They
rested for a time at the fountain; and then proceeded to the
Birket el-Khŭlil. The poor animals had afterwards to ascend

---

[1] Irby and Mangles saw a similar appearance from the eastern mountains near
Rabba. "This evening, about sunset, we
were deceived by a dark shade on the sea,
which assumed so exactly the appearance of
an island, that we did not doubt of it, even
after looking through a telescope." They
had seen similar appearances before. Travels, p. 457. [141.]—Seetzen, as he ascend-
ii. 208-210

ed from the southwestern part of the sea
by the pass of Zuweirah, thought he discovered in it a considerable island. This
was probably the peninsula above described; he not having remarked the isthmus
from that more distant point. See his letter in Zach's Monatl. Correspond. XVIII.
p. 438.

this difficult pass with heavy loads. The salt is used for cooking, after being washed.[1]

Here at the fountain are the remains of several buildings apparently ancient; though the main site of the town seems to have been further below. .The fountain itself is limpid and sparkling, with a copious stream of sweet water; but warm. The thermometer stood in it at 81° F. Kept in vessels over night, we found it delightfully cool and refreshing. Issuing from the limestone rock, it is of course strongly impregnated with lime, and does not take soap well. In the fountain itself are great quantities of small black snails.

Among the trees below the fountain, making part of the thicket along the stream, were the Seyâl, producing gum-arabic, our old acquaintance of the southern deserts; the Semr,[2] and the thorny Nûbk (lote tree) of .Egypt, called also Sidr,[3] and by our Arabs Dôm, bearing a small acid fruit like a thorn-apple, which our Egyptian servants enjoyed greatly; the 'Osher, which will be described more particularly below; and another large tree with long beautiful clusters of whitish blossoms, which our Arabs called *Fustak* (Pistacia), and which we then supposed to be the *Pistacia vera;* though we were afterwards led to doubt whether they had given us the right name.[4] Not a palm tree now exists there; though the place seems anciently to have been famous for them. The thicket is rendered almost impenetrable by a regular cane brake, flourishing luxuriantly along the watercourse. Of smaller plants, the egg-plant nightshade, or mad apple, was growing here in abundance;[5] and also occasionally an herb called by the Arabs Hûbeibeh, with a smooth shining reddish stalk and small glass-like leaves, the ashes of which are called *el-Kûli* (alkali), from their peculiar alkaline properties.[6]

We set off for the shore about 5 o'clock, and reached it in some twenty-five minutes; descending along the thicket by the brook. The declivity is here still steep, though less so than the

[1] Galen mentions that in his day also, the inhabitants used this salt for the various purposes to which common salt is applied. De Simpl. Med. fac. IV. c. 19. Reland Pal. p. 241.

[2] *Mimosa unguis cati*, Forskal Flor. Ægypt. p. 176.

[3] *Rhamnus nabeca*, Forskal Flor. Ægypt. p. LXIII. *Zizyphus lotus*, Sprengel Hist. Rei herb. I. p. 251. Lane's Mod. Egyptians II. pp. 288, 296.—The name Nûbk belongs strictly to the fruit of this tree. The *Dôm* in Egypt is the Dôm palm; but the name is also properly applied to the Nûbk. See Freytag's Lex. Arab. II. p. 73.

[4] Schubert says he found the *Pistacia*

vera at Hebron in full blossom in April; Reise II. p. 478. It would naturally blossom here still earlier. It has since occurred to me, whether this tree may not be the *el-Henna* of the Arabs, the 'camphire' of the English Bible, (*Lawsonia inermis* Linn.) which is described as having similar flowers, and for which the spot was anciently celebrated. Cant. 1, 14. Hasselquist, p. 502. See especially Celsii Hierobot. I. p. 222.—Seetzen also has here the name *Fustak*, but with no explanation; Reisen II. p. 231; more fully p. 237.

[5] *Solanum melongena.*

[6] Apparently one of the numerous species of *Salsola.*

pass above.   The whole of this descent was apparently once
terraced for tillage and gardens ; and on the right near the foot
are the ruins of a town, exhibiting nothing of particular interest.
Few of the stones appear to have been hewn.   From the base of
the declivity, a fine rich plain slopes off very gradually nearly
half a mile to the shore.   The brook runs across it directly to
the sea ; though at this season its waters were absorbed by the
thirsty earth long before reaching the shore.   So far as the water
extended, the plain was covered with gardens, chiefly of cucumbers, belonging to the Rashâideh.

These Arabs were now encamped in the tract called Hûsâsah
towards Tekoa ; and had only watchmen stationed here to protect the gardens.   The soil of the whole plain is exceedingly
fertile, and might easily be tilled and produce rare fruits.   In
various parts of it are traces of unimportant ruins.   The length
of the plain is little more than half a mile, it being nearly a
square ; terminated on the south by the Wady el-Ghâr, which
here enters the sea between lofty precipices ; and on the north
by Wady Sudeir, a comparatively short ravine breaking down
from above through the cliffs, between banks almost equally lofty
and precipitous.   Indeed, the cliff upon its northern side, called
el-Mersed, just beyond the plain, is perhaps the highest and
most inaccessible along the whole western coast ; and its base,
projecting into the sea, cuts off all further passage along the
shore.[1]   The precipice upon which we had stood near the brow
of the pass, is situated somewhat further back, and stands like a
gigantic bastion between these Wadys, overlooking and almost
overhanging the plain.

The approach to the sea is here over a bank of pebbles, six
or eight feet higher than the level of the water as we saw it.
These are covered with a shining crust, as of salt, or rather of an
oily appearance.[2]   The water has a slightly greenish hue, and is
not entirely transparent ; but objects seen through it, appear as
if seen through oil.   It is most intensely and intolerably salt ;
and leaves behind a nauseous bitter taste, like Glauber's salts.
It is said that common salt thrown into it, will not even be dissolved ; we did not try the experiment, but such would seem
very likely to be the fact.[3]   The water is exceedingly buoyant.
Two of us bathed in the sea ; and although I could never swim
before, either in fresh or salt water, yet here I could sit, stand,

---

[1] Yet there does exist a narrow and very
difficult path along the base of this cliff; it
was traversed by Seetzen in 1806; but this
was in December, when the level of the sea
was lower ; Roisen II. p. 239 ; comp. pp.
257, 258.

ii. 211-213

[2] Soetzen describes this appearance as an
incrustation of lime or gypsum.   Zach's
Monatl. Corresp. XVIII. p. 440.

[3] Dr. Marcet's experiments seem to show
the contrary ; Philosoph. Transact. 1807.
p. 299.

lie, or swim in the water, without difficulty.[1] The shore in this part shelved down very gradually; so that we waded out eight or ten rods before the water reached our shoulders. The bottom was here stony, but without mud or slime. After coming out, I perceived nothing of the salt crust upon the body, of which so many speak. There was a slight pricking sensation, especially where the skin had been chafed; and a sort of greasy feeling, as of oil upon the skin, which lasted for several hours. The bath proved exceedingly refreshing, after the heat and burden of the day.—There was much drift-wood along the shore; brought down into the sea, doubtless, from the Wadys in the adjacent mountains.

We now measured a base upon the plain near the shore, beginning at the mouth of the little stream from the fountain, and extending N. 19° E. for 1500 feet or 500 yards. From the northern end of this base we took with our large compass the bearings recorded in the note below.[2] The point of the western shoal lay here nearly in a line with the southern extremity of the peninsula.

The geographical position of 'Ain Jidy is: Lat. N. 31° 27′ 55″; Long. E. from Greenwich 35° 28′.[3]

We returned much exhausted to our tent; and spent the evening, until quite late, in writing up our journals on the spot. The beams of the full moon lay upon the sea below us, diffusing a glow of light over the darkness of death.

During the day, as we travelled down the declivity of the eastern slope, we had found the heat continually increase; and here in the chasm of the sea, we encountered an Egyptian climate and Egyptian productions. At Carmel the thermometer at sunrise had stood at 51° F.; at 2 o'clock P. M. near the brow of the cliffs it stood at 82°; and at sunset on the shore at 80° F. The next morning at sunrise, it was at 68° F. Indeed, shut in as this deep caldron is, between walls of rock, the heat of the burning summer-sun cannot be otherwise than very great. And such is the richness of the soil, both along the descent below the fountain and on the little plain, and such the abundance of water, that nothing but tillage is wanting, to render this a most prolific spot. It would be admirably adapted to the cultivation of tropical fruits.

---

[1] So Tacitus: "Periti imperitique nandi perinde attolluntur;" Hist. 5. 6. This buoyancy is mentioned by many ancient writers; e. g. Aristot. Meteorol. 2. 3. Plin. H. N. 5. 12. Joseph. B. J. 4. 8. 4. See these and other notices collected in Reland Pal. p. 249 sq.

[2] Bearings from the N. end of the base on the shore at 'Ain Jidy: Mouth of Wady

el-Mójib opposite, S. 82¼° E. Kerak S. 35¼° E. Peninsula, north end, S. 28¾° E. Penius. south end, S. 1° W. Usdum, west end, S. 10½° W. Cliff at southwest corner of the sea, S. 13¼° W. Sebbeh S. 21¾° W. Rás el-Feshkhah near the northwest corner of the sea, N. 18° E.

[3] Lynch's Off. Report, 1852, p. 68.

We had no question at the time, nor have we any now, that
this spot is the ancient En-gedi. With this name the present
'Ain Jidy of the Arabs is identical ; and like it also signifies the
'Fountain of the Kid.' The more ancient Hebrew name was
Hazezon-Tamar. As such it is first mentioned before the destruction of Sodom, as being inhabited by Amorites and near to
the cities of the plain. Under the name En-gedi it occurs as a
city of Judah in the desert, giving its name to a part of the desert to which David withdrew for fear of Saul.[1] At a later
period, bands of the Moabites and Ammonites came up against
king Jehoshaphat, apparently around the south end of the Dead
Sea as far as to En-gedi ; by the very same route, it would seem,
which is taken by the Arabs in their marauding expeditions at
the present day, along the shore as far as to 'Ain Jidy, and then
up the pass and so northwards below Tekoa.[2] According to Josephus, En-gedi lay upon the lake Asphaltis, and was celebrated
for beautiful palm trees and opobalsam ; while its vineyards are
likewise mentioned in the Old Testament.[3] From it towards
Jerusalem there was an ascent "by the cliff Ziz," which seems
to have been none other than the present pass.[4] In the days of
Eusebius and Jerome, En-gedi was still a large village on the
shore of the Dead Sea.[5]

I find no mention of En-gedi in the historians of the crusades; but Brocardus, about A. D. 1283, speaks of the mountains
of En-gedi in such a way, as to show that their character was
then known. They were on the west side of the sea, lofty, and
so precipitous as to threaten to fall down into the valley beneath ;
and were ascended by a pass. But the site of En-gedi itself he

[1] Gen. 14, 7.—Josh. 15, 62. 1 Sam. 24,
1-4. See above, p. 500.
[2] 2 Chr. 20, 1. 2. 20. Joseph. Ant. 9.
1. 2. See more upon this road under May
11th.
[3] Joseph. l. c. Cant. 1, 14. Plin. H. N.
5. 17. Josephus here gives the distance
of En-gedi from Jerusalem at 300 stadia
or 37½ Roman miles, which is by far too
great.
[4] Heb. יָצִיא הַצֵּלָה מַעֲלֵה, Josephus ἀναβά-
σεως λεγομένης ἐξοχῆς. 2 Chr. 20, 16.
Joseph. Antiq. 9. 1. 2.
[5] Onomasticon, art. Engaddi. Both
writers here say that En-gedi was situated
in Aulone Hierichus; and this has led
Reland and others to place it at the north
end of the Dead Sea. But the Aulon is
described by the same writers, as the great
valley of the Jordan, in which Jericho and
the Dead Sea are situated, extending south
to the desert of Paran; Onomast. art.
ii. 214, 215

Aulon.—Jerome elsewhere seems to say
that En-gedi was at the south end of the
sea, "ubi finitur et consumitur;" Comm.
in Ezech. 47, 10. But this does not necessarily imply any thing more, than that
in relation to En-gallim, it lay towards the
southern part of the sea. In like manner
both Eusebius and Jerome connect Hazezon-Tamar with the desert of Kadesh;
but this is only because they are so connected in Gen. 14, 7; and implies nothing
more than a general proximity. Onomast.
art. Hazazon-Thamar. The "wilderness
of Judah" in which En-gedi was situated,
was doubtless the desert along the western
side of the Dead Sea, extending from the
north end of the sea to the desert of Kadesh on the south ; Josh. 15, 61. 62 ; comp.
vs. 6. 18, 18. All this goes to show, that
there was only one En-gedi. See generally Reland Palæst. p. 763. Raumer Pal. p.
170, ed. 3.

seems to place above upon the mountains.[1] Since that day no traveller appears to have visited the region until the present century. Succeeding writers copied Brocardus; and the imagination of the monks drew En-gedi nearer and nearer towards Bethlehem, until Quaresmius places it at six miles from Bethlehem and seven from the Dead Sea, apparently on the way to Mâr Sâba.[2] He speaks also of its vineyards as formerly connected with Bethlehem; and these are probably the same which Hasselquist regarded as the vineyards of Solomon at En-gedi.[3] The present name and site of 'Ain Jidy were first found out by Seetzen in A. D. 1806, and are given upon his map; but whether he actually visited the spot, or only obtained his information from the Arabs, we were then nowhere told.[4] At any rate, the preceding pages contain, I believe, the first account of this place from personal observation, which has been given to the public for many centuries.[5]

THE DEAD SEA.

A few general remarks upon the character and phenomena of the Dead Sea, arising out of our observations at 'Ain Jidy, and during the two following days, may here find their proper place. In our later excursion from Hebron to Wady Mûsa, we visited the south end of the sea; and I shall there have occasion to make some further remarks upon that portion of it, as well as upon the geological structure of the whole region, and the destruction of the cities of the plain.

Length and Breadth of the Dead Sea. The general breadth of the sea is very uniform; except where it is contracted near the extremities, by Usdum on the south and by Râs el-Feshkhah on the north. According to Lieut. Lynch the north end of the Dead Sea is in Lat. 31° 46' 20"; and the south end in Lat. 31° 5' 20".

In constructing a new map of this region, a minute and very careful comparison of all the bearings taken by us at various points along the whole western coast of the Dead Sea, as well as of the distances travelled upon our several routes, resulted in fixing the *breadth* of the sea at 'Ain Jidy at about *nine* geogra-

---

[1] Brocardus, c. 7. pp. 179, 180.
[2] Elucid. II. pp. 692, 693. Compare Von Troilo, p. 327. Pococke II. i. p. 38.
[3] Elucid. II. p. 620. Hasselquist's Reise, p. 156.
[4] No mention is made of 'Ain Jidy in any of Seetzen's papers, formerly printed. But in the recent edition of his travels, (Reisen, Berlin 1854,) his visit to 'Ain Jidy

is fully described; II. p. 226 sq.—'Ain Jidy was likewise for a considerable time the camping-ground of Lieut. Lynch and his exploring party in 1848.
[5] 'Ain Jidy is mentioned by the Arabian writer Mejr ed-Din about A. D. 1495, as on the eastern border of the district of Hebron. Fundgr. des Or. II. p. 142.

phical miles. The same minute comparison and cautious construction, gave likewise for the *length* of the Dead Sea about *thirty-nine* of the like miles ; 'Ain Jidy being situated nearly at the middle point of the western coast.[1]

There will therefore be no very essential error in estimating the whole length of the Dead Sea at THIRTY-EIGHT or FORTY geographical miles. The length appears to vary not less than two or three miles in different years or seasons of the year, according as the water extends up more or less upon the flats towards the south.[2]

From the same point on the shore, we estimated the height of the western cliffs at 1500 feet, as above mentioned ; and that of the highest ridges of the eastern mountains lying back from the shore, at from 2000 to 2500 feet above the water.

Form and Character of the Shores. Burckhardt relates, that " the mountains which enclose the Ghôr, or valley of the Jordan, open considerably at the northern extremity of the Dead Sea, and encompassing it on the west and east sides, approach again at its southern extremity, leaving [afterwards] only a narrow plain between them."[3] This account is not correct ; that intelligent traveller did not himself visit the sea, and was probably misled by the information of the Arabs. The bed of the Dead Sea is only a portion of the Ghôr or great valley, which here retains its usual breadth, and does not spread out into an oval form or to a larger compass, as is the case around the lake of Tiberias. Its breadth at 'Ain Jidy is much the same as opposite to Wady Mûsa ; certainly not greater. Around Jericho indeed, the mountains do thus retire on both sides ; so that the valley at that point is not less than eleven or twelve miles wide ; but they again approach each other before they enclose the sea. So far as we could perceive, the eastern mountains run in nearly a straight course along the whole length of the sea. From the western mountains, Râs el-Feshkhah and the adjacent cliffs project obliquely towards the northeast near the northern end of the sea, giving to the shore in that part the same direc-

---

[1] Mr Legh, and also Irby and Mangles, who saw the whole extent of the Dead Sea several times from the eastern mountains, give their judgment of its length, the former at not over forty miles, and the two latter at thirty. But the transparency of the atmosphere in these regions, and the want of any known fixed points as a standard, render any mere judgment of this kind liable to great uncertainty. See Legh in Macmichael's Journey, Chap. IV. Irby and Mangles' Travels, p. 459. [141.]—Josephus gives the length of the Dead Sea at 580 stadia or 72½ Roman miles ; and the breadth at 150 stadia or 18¾ Roman miles ; B. J. 4. 8. 4. This is another specimen of the inexactness of that writer's estimates.

[2] See under May 29th ; also Anderson's Geol. Rep. p. 182.—According to the Map of Lieut. Lynch, the length of the Dead Sea, is 40 geogr. miles ; and the breadth 9 to 9½ geogr. miles. Several circumstances indicate, that at the time of his visit (1848) the sea was fuller and extended further south, than when we saw it ten years earlier. See also Note XXX, end of the volume.

[3] Travels in Syria, p. 390.

ii. 217-219

tion, and contracting the breadth both of the sea and valley. At the southern end a like contraction is occasioned by Hajr Usdum, as above described. Between el-Feshkhah and Usdum, the western cliffs run in a tolerably direct course, about S. 15° W.

The phenomena around the Dead Sea are such as might naturally be expected from the character of its waters and of the region round about, a naked solitary desert. It lies in its deep caldron, surrounded by lofty cliffs of naked limestone rock, and exposed for seven or eight months in each year to the unclouded beams of a burning sun. Nothing therefore but sterility and deathlike solitude can be looked for upon its shores; and nothing else is actually found, except in those parts where there are fountains or streams of fresh water. Such is the case at 'Ain Jidy, in the Ghôr near the southeast corner of the sea, and on the isthmus of the peninsula; to say nothing of the Jordan and the fountains around Jericho on the north. In all these places there is a fertile soil and abundant vegetation; nor have I ever seen a more luxuriant growth than at 'Ain Jidy. Here too were birds in great numbers in the thicket; and we saw them frequently flying over the sea. The fountain of 'Ain Jidy appears to be the main source of sweet water upon the western coast;[1] but further towards the north are the brackish fountains 'Ain Terâbeh, el-Ghuweir, and el-Feshkhah, (the last very copious,) in the midst of marshy ground along the shore covered with canes and reeds, and furnishing a retreat to an abundance of frogs. The coasts of the sea have also been inhabited from time immemorial, and are yet so in a degree; Jericho, 'Ain Jidy, and the southern Ghôr are still the abodes of men; and if this is now less the case than formerly, the cause is to be sought rather in the altered circumstances and relations of social life, than in the nature of the country or the sea.

I have adduced all these particulars in order to show, that the stories so long current of the pestiferous nature of the Dead Sea and its waters, are a mere fable.[2] We were for five days in the vicinity of its shores; and nowhere perceived either noisome smell or noxious vapour arising from its bosom.[3] Our Arabs too had never seen or heard of any such appearance. Smoke we had

---

[1] There is a fountain near the mouth of the Wady el-Ghâr, already mentioned; and another in Wady Sudeir just north of 'Ain Jidy, running into the sea. The water of both was said to be sweet.

[2] "Mare illud semper fumum reddere, et nebulam in modum camini infernalis.— Quocunque vapor a mari illo ascendens impellitur, ibi terræ nascentia non secus quam si a pruina fuissent tacta emoriuntur;" Brocardus c. 7. p. 179. "Stagnum

fœtidissimum, infernalis nigredinis, tetrum habens odorem;" Willeb. ab Oldenborg sub fine. Even Quaresmius had good sense enough to deny all this on the testimony of his own senses; Tom. II. p. 760.

[3] Seetzen perceived in some places a bad smell; arising, however, from decayed plants which had been brought down from the Jordan or by other streams into the sea, and then cast upon the shore; Reisen II. p. 211.

indeed often seen on the high ground above, proceeding from Arab encampments or the preparation of charcoal. There must also naturally be an immense evaporation from the sea itself, in consequence of its depressed position and exposure to the summer heats; and this again cannot but occasionally affect the clearness of the atmosphere around. But the character of this evaporation cannot well be different from that of any other lake in similar circumstances.[1]

The Egyptian heat of the climate, which is found throughout the whole Ghôr, is in itself unhealthy; and, in connection with the marshes, gives rise in summer to frequent intermittent fevers; so that the Ghawârineh, or proper inhabitants of the Ghôr, including the people of Jericho, are a feeble and sickly race. But this has no necessary connection with the Dead Sea, as such; and the same phenomena might probably exist, in at least an equal degree, were the waters of the lake fresh and limpid, or even were there here no lake at all.

The mineral productions around the sea have often been described. The body of the mountains is everywhere limestone; excepting Usdum, which is of rock-salt and will be hereafter described.[2] I am not aware that the dark basaltic stones, so frequent around the lake of Tiberias, have ever been discovered in this vicinity. There is however a black shining stone, found at the northern extremity of the sea, which partially ignites in the fire and emits a bituminous smell. We saw some of this in descending from Râs el-Feshkhah to the plain. It is used in Jerusalem for the manufacture of rosaries and other little articles.[3] Sulphur is found in various parts; we picked up pieces of it as large as a walnut near the northern shore; and the Arabs said it was found in the sea near 'Ain el-Feshkhah in lumps as large as a man's fist. They find it in sufficient quantities to make from it their own gunpowder. Near Usdum we afterwards

---

[1] "As soon as we came to the pass, which commands an extensive prospect of the Dead Sea, we could observe the effect of the evaporation arising from it, in broad transparent columns of vapour, not unlike waterspouts in appearance, but very much larger;" Irby and Mangles, p. 447, [137.]

[2] Irby and Mangles mention "fragments of red and gray granite; gray, red, and black porphyry," and many other kinds of stone scattered along the shore at the southeast corner of the Dead Sea, which they supposed to be fragments from the mountain above; Travels, p. 358, [109.] But in the Life of Giov. Finati, edited by Mr. Bankes, it is said, that there were no rocks of the same nature discernible, from which these fragments could have fallen; Vol. II. p. 240.—According to Seetzen, the mountain near the southeast corner of the sea, not farn orth of Wady el-Ahsy, consists of brownish sand-stone; Zach's Montl. Corr. XVIII. p. 435. Seetzen found here large blocks of most beautiful breccia and conglomerate of various colours; also blocks of dark olive green jasper, etc. These blocks he supposes were brought down from the ravines by the torrents. Reisen. II. p. 354.

[3] The "stink-stone" of Burckhardt, p. 394. Maundrell, March 30. Pococke II i. p. 37. Hasselquist describes it as "quartz in the form of slate, one of the rarest minerals he met with in his travels." Reise, p. 153. [Engl. p. 131.]

ii. 220-222

picked up small lumps of nitre.[1] All these circumstances testify
to the volcanic nature of the whole region ; and this is also confirmed by the warm fountains of 'Ain Jidy and el-Feshkhah on
the west, and the hot sulphur springs of the ancient Callirrhoë
on the eastern coast.[2] Three weeks before, one of our friends,
the Rev. Mr Hebard, had picked up a large piece of pumice-stone
on a small knoll near the mouth of the Jordan.

One of the most singular circumstances in the character of
the Dead Sea, is the deep depression of its level below that of
the Mediterranean. This has been detected only within the
last few years. Messrs Moore and Beke were the first to notice
it in March, 1837, by means of the boiling point of water ; in
this way they found the depression to be about 500 English feet.[3]
A month or two later the barometrical measurements of Schubert gave the depression of the sea at 598.5 Paris feet ; that of
Jericho being 527.7 feet.[4] The very great descent which we
found from Carmel to the cliffs over 'Ain Jidy, and the immense
depth of the sea below, point to a like result. But so great is
the uncertainty in all such partial measurements and observations, (as evinced in the like case of the Caspian Sea,) that the
question can never be decided with exactness, until the intervening country shall have been surveyed and the relative level
of the two seas trigonometrically ascertained.[5] To such an undertaking no great obstacle would probably exist.[6]

Character of the Waters. The buoyancy of the waters of
the Dead Sea, according to our experience, has already been
described ; and this shown to accord with 'the testimony of ancient writers.[7] It is occasioned by the great specific gravity of
the water, arising from the heavy solution of various salts contained in it, chiefly those of magnesia and soda. But the weight
and proportions of this solution, and of course the specific gravity,
would seem to vary somewhat in different parts of the sea, and

[1] Irby and Mangles found also " lumps
of nitre and fine sulphur from the size of a
nutmeg up to that of a small hen's egg,"
upon the western shore of the long peninsula ; Travels, p. 453. [139.] See also
Seetzen, Reisen, II. p. 352.
[2] Ibid. p. 467–469. [143--145.] Legh
in Macmichael's Journey, Chap. IV. See-
zen, Reisen II. p. 336 sq.
[3] Journal of the Royal Geogr. Soc. Vol.
VII. 1837. p. 456. Vol. IX. 1839. p.
lxiv.
[4] Reise, Vol. III. p. 87. Berghaus' Al-
manach für 1840. p. 481. Russegger and
Bertou in 1838 first make the depression
of the sea amount to more than 1,300 Paris feet. See Berghaus' Annalen, etc. Feb.
and März 1839. p. 432. Bulletin de la
Société de Géogr. Octobre, 1839. p. 161.

[5] The case of the Caspian Sea furnishes
a striking instance of the uncertainty of
such barometrical measurements. Eleven
different series of observations between A.
D. 1782 and A. D. 1836, gave for the depression of that sea below the sea of Azof,
different results, varying from about 100
Paris feet as the least, to about 366 Paris
feet as the greatest. The true depression
as determined by geometrical survey in
A. D. 1836, is 76 Paris feet. See Monats-
bericht der Berliner Gesellsch. für Erdkunde, Bd. I. pp. 167, 168.
[6] This was accomplished in 1848 by the
U. S. Expedition, under Lieut. Lynch.
See the results in Note XXX, end of the
volume.
[7] See p. 506, above.

at different seasons of the year. A portion of water taken from near the mouth of the Jordan, might be expected to be at all times less strongly saturated, than another from the vicinity of 'Ain Jidy ; and during the winter season, when the sea is filled by the rains and its level raised several feet, its waters are naturally more diluted than in autumn, after having been for months subjected to the process of evaporation under a burning sun.[1] These considerations may serve to account in part for the different results, which have been obtained by chemical analysis.

Of the seven analyses of the water of the Dead Sea, which have hitherto been published, the four following seem to deserve the preference, both for their greater exactness and coincidence, and as marking in some measure the progress of chemical discovery ; viz. that of Dr Marcet of London, 1807 ; Gay-Lussac of Paris, about 1818 ; Prof. C. G. Gmelin of Tübingen, 1826 ; and Dr Apjohn of Dublin, 1839.[2] It will be seen that the *amount* of salts is in general nearly equal ; while the relative proportions assigned to the different salts, are exceedingly diverse. The standard of comparison for the specific gravity, is distilled water at 1000 ; and the density of the water of the Dead Sea is supposed to be greater than that of any other natural water known.

		Dr Marcet.	*Gay-Lussac.*
Specific gravity		1211	1228
Muriate of Lime	(Chloride of calcium)	3.920	3.98
" of magnesia	(" of magnesium)	10.246	15.31
" of soda	(" of sodium) . .	10.360	6.95
Sulphate of lime[3]	. . . . .	0.054	——
		24.580	26.24
Water		75.420	73.76
		100	100

[1] Galen also remarks, that the water was more bitter in summer than in winter ; De Simpl. Med. fac. 4. 19. Reland Pal. p. 242.

[2] These seven analyses are as follows : I. By Macquer, Lavoisier, and Le Sage in Paris, Memoirs de l'Acad. des Sciences, 1778.—II. By Dr Marcet, with a small quantity of the water, Philosoph. Transact. 1807. p. 296 sq.—III. By Klaproth of Berlin, with water brought to Europe by Mariti fifty years before ; Beiträge, Vol. V. p. 139. Berliner Magazin, 1809. p. 139.—IV. By Gay-Lussac, with a large quantity of the water brought home by Count Forbin ; see Forbin's Voyage, etc. Annales de Chimie et de Phys. T. XI. p. 197.—V. By Hermstädt of Berlin about 1822 ; Schweigger's Journal, Vol. XXXIV. ii. 223, 224.

p. 153.—VI. By Prof. Gmelin of Tübingen, who first discovered the existence of bromium in the water ; Würtemb. naturwissensch. Abhandl. Vol. I. iii. p. 1. Poggendorff's Journal, 1827, Vol. IX. p. 177 sq. —VII. By Dr Apjohn, in a paper read (1839) before the Royal Irish Academy. A report of this paper was published in the London Athenæum for June 15th, 1839.—One of the specimens of fossil salt brought away by me from the mountain of Usdum, at the south end of the sea, was analyzed by Prof. Rose of Berlin. It contained a small mixture of lime and magnesia, but no trace of bromium.

[3] Gay-Lussac remarks, that he found also a small quantity of chloride of potassium, and traces of a sulphate probably of lime.

	Prof. Gmelin.	*Dr. Apjohn.*	
Specific gravity . .	1212	1153	Boiling point 221° F.
Chloride of calcium .	3.2141	2.438	
" of magnesium	11.7784	9.370	
Bromide of magnesium .	0.4393	0.201	
Chloride of potassium .	1.6738	0.852	
" of sodium .	7.0777	9.830	
" of manganese .	0.2117	0.005	
" of aluminum .	0.0896	——	
" of ammonium	0.0075	——	
Sulphate of lime .	0.0527	0.075	
	24.5398	18.780	
Water	75.4602	81.320	
	100	100	

The water analyzed by Dr. Apjohn was taken half a mile from the mouth of the Jordan, near the close of the rainy season; and exhibits a less amount of salts, and a less specific gravity, than occurs in either of the other analyses. He could detect no trace of either alumina or ammonia.[1]

I have already alluded to the fact, that the level of the waters of the Dead Sea is higher during and after the rainy season, than in the summer and autumn, after they have been for months evaporated under the burning heat of an unclouded sun. The high bank of pebbles and gravel at 'Ain Jidy has been mentioned; and we afterwards saw at the southern end of the sea traces of its high-water mark, more than an hour south of its limit at the time; indicating that its level must be sometimes ten or fifteen feet higher than when we now saw it in May.[2] This is readily accounted for by the vast quantity of water brought into it during the rainy season, not only from the north, but also from the south and from the mountains along its sides. The quantity of rain which falls in Palestine varies greatly in different years; and according to this the basin of the Dead Sea becoming more or less full, is subjected to great variation in a course of years. When the rainy season is at an end, the evaporation is sufficiently powerful to more than counterbalance the influx from the Jordan, and thus again reduce the level of the sea. During the preceding winter, less rain had fallen than is usual.

The strong evaporation from the sea also causes it to deposit

---

[1] See another later analysis in Note XXX, end of the volume.

[2] Irby and Mangles noticed the high-water mark, on some parts of the Peninsula, a mile or more above the water's edge; p. 455. [140.] Pococke also remarks, that in his day (1738) "there had been very extraordinary inundations of this sea over its lower banks, and such as had not happened in many years before." He saw trees that had been killed by its overflowing, and says the water seemed of late years to have gained on the land. This was at the northwest part. Vol. II. i. p. 35. See further on, *The Peninsula* and *Ford*.

its salts, particularly in summer, on various parts of the shore ; from which the Arabs obtain their chief supply for their families and flocks. That obtained in the Birket el-Khŭlil south of 'Ain Jidy has already been mentioned ; [1] and a place was afterwards pointed out to us at the northwest corner of the sea, where it is also gathered. Irby and Mangles found Arabs on the north side of the isthmus of the peninsula, "peeling off a solid surface of salt several inches in thickness, and loading it on asses." [2] The same deposit is doubtless found on other parts of the coast.

According to the testimony of all antiquity and of most modern travellers, there exists within the waters of the Dead Sea no living thing; no trace indeed of animal or vegetable life. [3] Our own experience, so far as we had an opportunity to observe, goes to confirm the truth of this testimony. We perceived no sign of life within the waters. Yet occasionally, travellers have seen shells upon the shore ; which has led to the supposition, that small muscles or periwinkles may after all exist in the sea. Maundrell "observed among the pebbles on the shore two or three shells of fish, resembling oyster-shells, at two hours distance from the mouth of the Jordan." [4] Hasselquist notes also *cochleœ* and *conchœ* as common on the banks near the Jordan ; and Mr Legh saw on the northern shore "in the water several small shell-fish, not unlike periwinkles." [5] Irby and Mangles on the peninsula "searched for shells, but found none excepting snail-shells, and a small spiral species, invariably without any fish, or the appearance of having had any for a long time. [6]

These testimonies seem at first view strongly to favour the hypothesis, that at least some species of shell-fish may exist in the sea. But the shells seen by Maundrell may after all have come from the Jordan, or have been dropped here by some Arab or pilgrim ; and the accounts of Hasselquist and Legh, I apprehend, are explained and more than counterbalanced by the more exact and cautious testimony of Seetzen. "I dismounted," he says, "and followed for a time the shore of the sea, to look for conchylia and sea-plants ; but found none of either. And as fish live upon these, it might naturally be expected that no tenants of the waters would exist here ; and this is confirmed by

---

[1] The salt pools are found for two miles south of Birket el-Khŭlil ; Anderson's Geol. Report, p. 177.

[2] Travels, p. 451. [139.]

[3] Tacit. Hist. 5. 6, "neque pisces aut suetas aquis volucres patitur." Galen. de Simpl. Med. IV. c. 19, φαίνεται ἐν ἐκείνῳ τῷ ὕδατι μήτε ζῶον ἐγγιγνόμενόν τι, μήτε φυτόν. Hieron. ad Ezech. 47, 8 "Mare mortuum, in quo nihil poterat esse vitale. Re vera, juxta literam huc usque nihil quod ii. 226. 227

spirat et possit incedere, præ amaritudine nimia in hoc mari reperiri potest. Abulfeda Tab. Syr. ed. Köhler, pp. 12, 156.— The absence of all water-fowl is readily accounted for, by the absence of fish and other animals which constitute their food.

[4] Journey, March 30th.

[5] Hasselquist's Reise, p. 558. Legh in Macmichael's Journey, Chap. IV.

[6] Travels, p. 454. [140.]

the experience of all whom I have inquired of, and who could know about it.—Snails and muscles I have not found in the lake ; some snails that I picked up on the shore, were *land-snails.* I was particularly attentive to this point ; but must remark, that I was able to examine only a part of the lake."[1]—The shells which other travellers have met with, were probably in like manner those of land animals. Or, if they actually belonged to the lake, they probably have existed in it only near the mouth of the Jordan, where there is a large intermixture of fresh water, or in the vicinity of the various fountains which enter the sea.

As we were leaving Palestine, we saw in the possession of two English travellers, a small flat fish, about the length of a man's little-finger, which was put into their hands as having been taken in the Dead Sea, and as proving that the sea was actually inhabited by fish. But the report added further, that the fish was found on the northern shore at some distance from the mouth of the Jordan ; and, when caught, was in an exhausted and dying state. It would seem therefore much more probable, that this was a wanderer from the Jordan, who paid for his temerity with his life ; furnishing a further example of the truth of Jerome's remark, that "when the Jordan swollen by the rains sometimes carries down fish into the Dead Sea, they die immediately and float upon the sluggish waters."[2]

Asphaltum. Our Arabs picked up along the shore small pieces of bitumen, asphaltum, (Arabic *el-Hummar,*) which we brought away. Our Sheikh of the Ta'àmirah told (as a report) the same story of its origin, which was heard by Seetzen and Burckhardt, viz. that it flows down the face of a precipice upon the eastern shore, until a large mass is collected, when from its weight or some shock it breaks off and falls into the sea.[3] The Sheikh of the Jehâlin, who afterwards accompanied us to Wady Mûsa, related the same report ; assigning the place on the north of the peninsula. It cannot of course be south of the isthmus ; for the road travelled by Irby and Mangles and their party passes all the way at the foot of the rocks along the shore. Nor is it probable that any such spot exists further north ; we had the

[1] Seetzen in Zach's Monatl. Corr. XVIII. pp. 437, 441. So too in Reisen, II. pp. 241, 242.

[2] Hieron. in Ezech. xlvii. 8, "Denique si Jordanes auctus imbribus pisces illuc influens rapuerit, statim moriuntur et pinguibus aquis supernatant." Galen also affirms, that fish caught in the river and thrown into the lake, die immediately ; de Simpl. IV. 19. Reland Palæst. p. 243.— Since the above remarks were written, I am happy to find my views confirmed by

the naturalist Schubert. "Fish or snails," he says, "do not indeed live in this super-salt sea ; the *melastoma* which we found on the shore, as well as the small dead fishes, of which we saw and picked up several thrown out by the waves upon the strand, are brought down by the Jordan or accompany voluntarily his flood ; but they soon pay for this love of wandering with their lives." Reise III. p. 86.

[3] Seetzen in Zach's Monatl. Corr. XVIII. p. 441. Burckhardt, p. 394.

eastern coast very distinctly in sight for two days, as we travelled
along the western shore, and examined it continually with our
glasses; so that any such marked point upon the rocks would
hardly have escaped our notice. All agreed, that there was
nothing of the kind upon the western coast.

More definite and trustworthy was the account which the
Arabs gave us of the appearance of the bitumen in the sea.
They believe that it thus appears only after earthquakes. The
Sheikhs above mentioned, both of the Ta'âmirah and Jehâlin,
related that after the earthquake of 1834, a large quantity of
asphaltum was cast upon the shore near the southwest part of the
sea, of which the Jehâlin brought about sixty *Kuntârs* into
market.[1] My companion also remembered, that in that year a
large amount had been purchased by the Frank merchants at
Beirût. During the last year also, after the earthquake of Jan.
1st, 1837, a large mass of bitumen (one said like an island, another like a house) was discovered floating on the sea, and was
driven aground on the west side, not far to the north of Usdum.
The Jehâlin and the inhabitants of Yûtta swam off to it; and
cut it up with axes, so as to bring it ashore. The Ta'âmirah
heard of it, and went to get a share. They found seventy men
already upon and around it. It was carried off by camel-loads,
partly up the pass of 'Ain Jidy; and sold by the Arabs for four
piastres the *Rutl* or pound. The share of the Ta'âmirah brought
them more than five hundred dollars; while others sold to the
amount of two or three thousand dollars.—Except in those two
years, the Sheikh of the Jehâlin, a man fifty years old, had
never known of bitumen appearing in the sea, nor heard of it
from his fathers.

The above information may serve to illustrate the account of
Josephus, that "the sea in many places sends up black masses
of asphaltum, which float on the surface, having the form and
size of headless oxen."[2] Diodorus Siculus also relates, that the
bitumen is thrown up in masses, covering sometimes two or
three *plethra*, and having the appearance of islands.[3]

The Peninsula. Seetzen, in his first journey around the
Dead Sea, took a direct course from Kerak to the southern extremity, descending there from the mountain by a very difficult
pass. He seems to have observed the peninsula only from the
western mountain; and mistook it for an island.[4] In a later
journey, he visited the peninsula; and it is laid down upon his

---

[1] The *Kuntâr* is about 98 lbs. English.
Lane's Mod. Egypt. II. p. 372.

[2] Joseph. B. J. 4. 8. 4.

[3] Diod. Sic. 2. 48.—Some further remarks on the probable source of the asphaltum of the Dead Sea, and its apparent

connection with the destruction of the
cities of the plain, see near the end of
Sect. XII.

[4] Zach's Monatl. Corr. XVIII. p. 438.
Reisen I. p. 429.

map, though not in its true form.[1]—In the year 1818, Irby and Mangles travelled with Messrs Bankes and Legh from Hebron to Kerak by the usual road ; descending to the south end of the sea by the pass of ez-Zuweirah, then keeping along upon the shore as far as to the isthmus, and ascending to Kerak along the Wady which comes down upon the isthmus from near that place.

From the cliff over 'Ain Jidy, we could look across the isthmus and up this Wady to Kerak ; the direction being about S. E. by S. Irby and Mangles call it the Dara, properly Wady ed-Dera'ah ; we heard for it only the name of Wady Kerak. Burckhardt has both names.[2] The same travellers, after their return from Wady Mûsa, descended again from Kerak to the peninsula, and traversed the whole of it ; and to them we are indebted for the first published account of this remarkable feature of the Dead Sea. They have added a plan of the peninsula and of the part of the sea further south, which they call the " backwater ;" but it seems to have been drawn only from recollection, and does not, according to my impressions, exhibit the present form either of the sea or of the peninsula.[3]

We had the opportunity of looking down upon the peninsula and the whole of this part of the sea from two different high points ; first, from the cliff over 'Ain Jidy looking towards the southeast and again from a cliff near the pass ez-Zuweirah looking towards the east and northeast. As we saw it, the isthmus was comparatively much narrower than is represented on the plan of Irby and Mangles ; and not only did the peninsula extend in a long horn towards the north, leaving a bay behind it ; but also in a shorter horn towards the south, forming likewise a smaller bay behind. Nor was the narrow part or strait of the sea, between the peninsula and the western shoal, so very narrow as they represent it ; although they judge it to be only about a mile in width.[4] These discrepancies may be accounted for partly from the difficulty of sketching such a plan from recollection after so long an interval ; and still more by the supposition, that the waters of the Dead Sea in 1818 were much lower than in 1838. That this was actually the case, I am inclined to believe, not only from the representation of the plan in question ; but also from the accounts of the Arabs, which will be given further on in speaking of the ford.

---

[1] Reisen II. p. 350 sq. Seetzen's map is found in Zach's Monatl Corr. Vol. XXII ; also reduced in Klöden's Palæstina, Berl. 1817.
[2] Travels, p. 390.
[3] Since the above was written, I have had the pleasure of a personal acquaintance with Capt. Mangles, who informs me,

that the supposition in the text is quite correct ; the plan in question not having been sketched until after an interval of several months, when the travellers had already left Palestine ; and then only from recollection. This note is added at the suggestion of Capt. Mangles himself.
[4] Travels, p. 454. [140.]

From the Wady Kerak a never failing stream issues upon the isthmus, and enters the bay on its northern side ; fertilizing here a tract of level ground, which is scattered over with thickets of acacia (Seyâl) and the Dôm (Nûbk) with other trees ; among which is found the 'Öshcr. Further north, nearer the bay, are tamarisks and a cane brake or jungle. In the thicket, according to Irby and Mangles,[1] the hare and the partridge of the desert abound ; and portions of it are cleared and cultivated. In the very heart of it, not visible in any direction beyond a few yards, unless by the smoke arising from it, is the village of the Ghawâ-rineh, who cultivate this tract. Their abode has much the appearance of a village in India or the South Seas. This tract, as we were told, is called Ghôr el-Mezra'ah ; it is so marked on Seetzen's map, and is said by Burckhardt to be much frequented by the people of Kerak, who buy here the tobacco which they smoke.[2]

The peninsula itself, as seen from the western side of the sea, appears much like a long low sand-bank. But according to the same travellers, who passed quite around its northern horn, and then along its western edge nearly or quite to its southern extremity, such is not its general character. Its middle part consists of "a steep white ridge running like a spine down the centre. This ridge presents steep sloping sides, seamed and furrowed into deep hollows by the rains, and terminating at the summit in sharp triangular points, standing up like rows of tents ranged one above another. The whole is of a substance apparently partaking of the mixture of soft and broken chalk and slate, and is wholly unproductive of vegetation. The height of the eminence varies from ten to about thirty feet, becoming gradually lower towards its northern extremity."[3] The opposite sides of this cliff present faces of similar appearance and equal height ; while adjacent to the isthmus it spreads out into broader table land.[4]

The length of the peninsula on the eastern side, from the head of the northern bay to the northern extremity, they found to be one hour and twelve minutes ; and on the western side, from the north end to the strait, or the point overagainst the western shoal, two hours and forty minutes. The breadth of the peninsula and isthmus, from the strait to the stream of the Dera'ah, was also two hours. The breadth of the strait they estimated at one mile ; which, I apprehend, is much too small. —At the foot of the high ground, or cliff, all around, "is a con-

[1] Travels, p. 449. [138.]   See generally ibid. pp. 448–455. [138–140.]
[2] Burckhardt, p. 391.   Irby and Mangles, p. 449. [138.]   Seetzen, Reisen II. p. ii. 232. 233
350 sq.—See more further on, under May 29th.
[3] Irby and Mangles, p. 452. [139.]
[4] Ibid. pp. 453, 455. [139, 140.]

siderable margin of sand, which varies in length and breadth according to the season ; being much wider in summer than in winter, when there is reason to suppose that the waves almost wash the base of the cliff." [1]   This becomes broader towards the strait, and here " a very considerable level is left, which is encrusted with a salt that is but half dried and consolidated, appearing like ice in the commencement of a thaw.   All this space is soft, and gives way nearly as deep as the ankle, when it is trod on." [2]

Along the shore of the northern bay also, the travellers found deposites of salt, and persons gathering it ; and near the northern point of the peninsula they collected lumps of nitre and fine sulphur, apparently brought down by the rains from the low cliff above. [3]—Around the southern end of the peninsula, where we saw a short horn and a bay beyond, " the high-water mark was at this season a mile distant from the water's edge." [4]   This was on the 2d of June. [5]

The Ford.   The first notice of a ford near the south end of the Dead Sea is also from Seetzen.   He describes it from the information of the Arabs, as practicable only in summer, and as requiring five hours for the passage. [6]   In his map, it is laid down as leading from the peninsula to the northern part of Usdum, south of the pass of Zuweirah.   Burckhardt heard the same report of a ford, which might be crossed in three hours and a half. [7]   As however the Arabs have no notion of hours, both these specifications are of little value.   In the plan of Irby and Mangles the ford is laid down across the narrowest part or strait, between the peninsula and the western shoal or tongue of land ; where indeed we should naturally look for it.

So remarkable a feature of the sea of course engaged our attention ; and we made all the inquiries in our power respecting it.   The Arabs who were with us at 'Ain Jidy, both of the Ta'âmirah and the Rashâideh, who dwell chiefly towards Tekoa and Bethlehem, knew nothing of any ford.   Our Sheikh of the Jehâlin, who was with us at the south end of the sea, affirmed that the water in the strait, between the peninsula and the opposite tongue of land, was very deep, and never fordable.   But from the southwest part of the sea, he said, (apparently from near the pass of Zuweirah,) to the south side of the peninsula, he himself had forded the lake many years ago ; although now, and since several years, the water was too deep to be forded.   This account

[1] Irby and Mangles, p. 452. [139.]
[2] Ibid. p. 453. [140.]
[3] Ibid. pp. 451, 453. [139.]
[4] Ibid. p. 455. [140.]
[5] For a geological description of the peninsula, see Anderson's Geol. Report, p.

184 sq.   Its extreme length according to Lynch's map, is nearly eleven miles.
[6] Zach's Monatl. Corr. XVIII. p. 437 Reisen. II. p. 358.
[7] Travels, p. 394.

corresponds to the ford as laid down on Seetzen's map ; and at the time, we had no reason to distrust its accuracy. But Irby and Mangles relate that in descending from Kerak to the peninsula, they fell in with a small caravan going to Hebron by way of the ford ; and while the travellers were examining the northern part of the peninsula, this caravan crossed it to the strait, which they forded. The travellers soon after arrived at the same point ; saw the ford "indicated by boughs of trees;" and observed the caravan just landed on the opposite side. They could discern the species of animal, as well as the people on their backs; and as there were asses of the party, the depth could not be great.[1]

These varying accounts I am not able to reconcile ; except by supposing, as above, that the waters of the Dead Sea, as seen by those travellers in the year 1818, were at their very lowest ebb. In this way, perhaps, they might admit here for the time a ford not known or not remembered by the Arabs of the western coast ; and give to the peninsula and the adjacent shoals a different form.

Apples of Sodom. One of the first objects which attracted our notice on arriving at 'Ain Jidy, was a tree with singular fruit ; which, without knowing at the moment, whether it had been observed by former travellers or not, instantly suggested to our minds the far-famed fruits

"which grew
Near that bituminous lake where Sodom stood."

This was the 'Osher of the Arabs, the *Asclepias gigantea v. procera* of botanists,[2] which is found in abundance in Upper Egypt and Nubia, and also in Arabia Felix ; but seems to be confined in Palestine to the borders of the Dead Sea. We saw it only at 'Ain Jidy ; Hasselquist found it in the desert between Jericho and the northern shore ; and Irby and Mangles met with it of large size at the south end of the sea, and on the isthmus of the peninsula.[3]

We saw here several trees of the kind, the trunks of which were six or eight inches in diameter ; and the whole height from ten to fifteen feet.[4] It has a grayish cork-like bark, with long oval leaves ; and in its general appearance and character, it might be taken for a gigantic perennial species of the milk-weed

[1] Irby and Mangles, p. 454. [140.]
[2] Sprengel Hist. Rei Herbar. I. p. 252.
[3] Hasselquist Reise, p. 151. Irby and Mangles' Travels, pp. 354, 450. [108, 138.] Comp. Seetzen in Zach's Monatl. Corr. XVIII. p. 442. Reisen, I. p. 422. II. p. 231. Burckhardt, p. 392.
ii. 235, 236

[4] Irby and Mangles found them "measuring, in many instances, two feet or more in circumference, and the boughs at least fifteen feet in height; a size which far exceeded any they saw in Nubia." P. 450. [138.]

or silk-weed found in the northern parts of the American States. Its leaves and flowers are very similar to those of the latter plant; and when broken off, it in like manner discharges copiously a milky fluid. The fruit greatly resembles externally a large smooth apple or orange, hanging in clusters of three or four together; and when ripe is of a yellow colour. It was now fair and delicious to the eye, and soft to the touch; but on being pressed or struck, it explodes with a puff, like a bladder or puff-ball, leaving in the hand only the shreds of the thin rind and a few fibres. It is indeed filled chiefly with air, like a bladder, which gives it the round form; while in the centre a small slender pod runs through it from the stem, and is connected by thin filaments with the rind. The pod contains a small quantity of fine silk with seeds; precisely like the pod of the silk-weed, though very much smaller; being indeed scarcely the tenth part as large. The Arabs collect the silk and twist it into matches for their guns; preferring it to the common match, because it requires no sulphur to render it combustible.[1]

The most definite account we have of the apples of Sodom, so called, is in Josephus; who, as a native of the country, is a better authority than Tacitus or other foreign writers.[2] After speaking of the conflagration of the plain, and the yet remaining tokens of the divine fire, he remarks, that "there are still to be seen ashes reproduced in the fruits; which indeed resemble edible fruits in colour, but on being plucked with the hands, are dissolved into smoke and ashes."[3] In this account, after a due allowance for the marvellous in all popular reports, I find nothing which does not apply almost literally to the fruit of the 'Ôsher, as we saw it. It must be plucked and handled with great care, in order to preserve it from bursting. We attempted to carry some of the boughs and fruit with us to Jerusalem; but without success.[4]

[1] Gregory of Tours would seem to have heard of this tree: "Prope Jericho habentur arbores, quæ lanas gignunt; exhibent enim poma in modo cucurbitarum, testas in circuitu habentia duras, intrinsecus autem plena sunt lanæ." Of this wool, he says, fine garments were made. Gregor. Turon. Mirac. lib. I. c. 18.

[2] The Bible speaks only of the "vine of Sodom;" and that metaphorically. Deut. 32, 32.

[3] Joseph. B. J. 4. 8. 4, Ἔστι δὲ κἂν τοῖς καρποῖς σποδιὰν ἀναγεννωμένην, οἳ χρόαν μὲν ἔχουσι τοῖς ἐδωδίμοις ὁμοίαν, δρεψαμένων δὲ χεροῖν εἰς καπνὸν ἀναλύονται καὶ τέφραν.—Tacitus is still more general: Hist. 5. 6, "Terramque ipsam specie torridam vim frugiferam perdisse. Nam cuncta

sponte edita, aut manu sata, sive herbæ tenues aut flores, ut solitam in speciem adolevere, atra et inania velut in cinerem vanescunt."

[4] Seetzen was the first, I believe, to suggest the 'Ôsher (which he writes Aoschâr) as producing the apples of Sodom; Zach's Monatl. Corr. XVIII. p. 442. He describes the plant; Reisen. II. p. 231 sq. According to Irby and Mangles "there is very little doubt of this being the fruit of the Dead Sea often noticed by the ancients," etc. p. 450. [138.]—I am not sure that Brocardus does not refer to the same plant when he says that "under Eu-gedi, by the Dead Sea, there are beautiful trees; but their fruit on being plucked is found full of smoke and ashes;" c. 7. p. 180. Fulcher ii. 236, 237

Hasselquist finds the apples of Sodom in the fruit of the *Solanum melongena*, (nightshade, mad-apple,) which we saw in great abundance at 'Ain Jidy and in the plain of Jericho. These apples are much smaller than those of the 'Osher; and when ripe are full of small black grains. There is here however nothing like explosion, nothing like " smoke and ashes ; " except occasionally, as the same naturalist remarks, " when the fruit is punctured by an insect (Tenthredo), which converts the whole of the inside into dust, leaving nothing but the rind entire, without any loss of colour."[1] We saw the Solanum and the 'Osher growing side by side ; the former presenting nothing remarkable in its appearance, and being found in other parts of the country;[2] while the latter immediately arrested our attention by its singular accordance with the ancient story, and is moreover peculiar in Palestine to the shores of the Dead Sea.

Friday, May 11th. We rose with the dawn, awakened by the voice of the Khâtib, who as priest of his tribe was chanting his prayers in a monotonous tone by the fountain. As we looked down from 'Ain Jidy upon the sea, the sun rose in glory, diffusing a hue of gold upon the waters, now agitated by a strong ripple from the influence of an eastern breeze. We could perceive the dense evaporation rising and filling the whole chasm of the lake, and spreading itself as a thin haze above the tops of the mountains. We were also not less surprised than delighted, to hear in the midst of the solitude and grandeur of these desolations, the morning song of innumerable birds. The trees and rocks and air around were full of the carols of the lark, the cheerful whistle of the quail, the call of the partridge, and the warbling of many other feathered choristers ; while birds of prey were soaring and screaming in front of the cliffs above.

While the rest were busy in packing the tent and luggage and loading the animals, I set off on foot and ascended the pass alone. Three quarters of an hour brought me to the top of the cliff, whence we had yesterday enjoyed our first view of the sea. Here I sat down upon the brink of the precipice, and looked abroad again upon the sea and its wild craggy shores, to fix more deeply the impressions of the preceding day. The

---

Carnot. seems to mean the 'Osher, when in describing the productions around Segor (Zoar) he says : " Ibi vidi poma in arboribus, quæ, cum corticem rupissem, interius, esse pulverulenta comperi et nigra ; " Gesta Dei, p. 405.

[1] " Quod pulvere intus repleta sint, verum est nonnunquam, sed non semper accidit; ii. 238, 239

nempe in nonnullis, quod Tenthredine pungantur, quæ substantiam totam internem in pulverem redigit, et corticem solum egregie coloratum integrum relinquit ; " Hasselquist Reise, p. 560. See also Seetzen, Reisen, II. p. 234.

[2] Hasselquist mentions it at Râs el-'Ain near Tyre, p. 556.

ripple on the sea created a gentle surge upon the shore below; the sound of which as it rose upon the ear, was exceedingly grateful in this vast solitude. Lovely the scene is not; yet magnificently wild, and in the highest degree stern and impressive. Shattered mountains and the deep chasm of the rent earth are here tokens of the wrath of God, and of his vengeance upon the guilty inhabitants of the plain; when, "turning the cities of Sodom and Gomorrah into ashes, he condemned them with an overthrow, making them an ensample unto them that after should live ungodly."[1]

After dwelling for a time on these and the like associations, my attention was particularly directed to the ruin called by the Arabs Sebbeh, already mentioned as situated towards the south upon a pyramidal cliff rising precipitously from the sea, just beyond Wady es-Seyâl.[2] The truncated summit of the lofty isolated rock forms a small plain apparently inaccessible; and this is occupied by the ruin. We had been greatly struck by its appearance; and on examining it closely with a telescope, I could perceive what appeared to be a building on its northwest part, and also traces of other buildings further east. We had heard of this place on the way, and made inquiry respecting it of the peasants at Ma'in; but they knew only the name and had never visited the spot. Our guide of the Rashâideh had been there, as he said; he described the ruins as those of a city, with columns scattered among them; and the place as wholly inaccessible to horses and beasts of burden. Only footmen, he said, could ascend to it.

This spot was to us for the time a complete puzzle; we thought at first it might perhaps be the ruin of some early convent. But subsequent research leaves little room to doubt, that this was the site of the ancient and renowned fortress of Masada, first built by Jonathan Maccabæus, and afterwards strengthened and rendered impregnable by Herod the Great, as a place of refuge for himself.[3] Josephus describes it as situated on a lofty rock of considerable circuit overhanging the Dead Sea, surrounded by profound valleys unfathomable to the eye; it was inaccessible to the foot of animals on every part, except by two paths hewn in the rock. One of these, the least difficult, was on the west; the other, on the east, was carried up from the lake itself by zigzags cut along the crags of the precipice, and was exceedingly difficult and dangerous.[4] The sum-

---

[1] 2 Pet. 2, 6.
[2] See above, p. 502.
[3] The main passage is Joseph. B. J. 7. 8. 2 sq. Compare also B. J. 4. 7. 2. Antiq. 14. 11. 7. ib. 14. 13. 9. ib. 14. 14. 6.

[4] Josephus gives the length of this eastern ascent at thirty stadia or 3¾ Roman miles; which, including the many turns and zigzags, would not be very greatly exaggerated. B. J. 7. 8. 3.

ii. 239–241

mit was a plain surrounded by a wall seven stadia in circuit. Besides the fortifications, and immense cisterns hewn in the rock for a full supply of water, Herod built here a palace, with columns and porticos and baths and sumptuous apartments, situated on the west and north of the plain.

The fortress was dependent solely on its cisterns for water, as there was no fountain near ; and the interior part of the area was left free of buildings and was cultivated, in order to guard against the possibility of famine.[1] Here Herod had laid up an immense store both of arms and provisions, sufficient to supply ten thousand men for many years. Not long before the siege of Jerusalem by Titus, the *Sicarii* or robbers, so notorious in the later Jewish history, had got possession of the fortress and its treasures by stratagem ; and laid contribution upon the country far and near, attacking and plundering among the rest the adjacent town of En-gedi.[2] After the destruction of Jerusalem, the fortresses of Masada, Herodium, and Machærus, all in the hands of the robbers, were the only posts not yet subdued by the Romans.[3] The two latter afterwards surrendered to the procurator Lucilius Bassus ;[4] and his successor, Flavius Silva, at length laid siege to Masada. Here occurred the last horrible act of the great Jewish tragedy. The whole garrison, at the persuasion of their leader, Eleazar, devoted themselves to self-destruction, and chose out ten men to massacre all the rest. This was done ; and nine hundred and sixty persons, including women and children, perished. Two females and five boys alone escaped.[5]

This description of Josephus corresponds very exactly with the character of Sebbeh as seen from a distance ; and there is little doubt that future travellers, who may visit its site, will find other and more definite traces of its ancient strength. The building now visible on the northwest, and the columns described by the Arabs, are not improbably the remains of Herod's palace. So far as I know, the place is mentioned by no writer since Josephus, either as Masada or Sebbeh ; though the latter name is found on Seetzen's map.[6]

The rest of the party having ascended the pass, we set off from the brow at 8.10, returning upon our path of yesterday for twenty minutes to the fork of the Jerusalem road already mentioned. This we now took at 8½ o'clock for ten minutes,

[1] Josephus B. J. 7. 8. 2, 3.
[2] Ibid. 7. 8. 4. ib. 4. 7. 2.
[3] Ibid. 4. 9. 9.
[4] Ibid. 8. 6. 1.
[5] Ibid. 8. 9. 1.
[6] The first suggestion as to the identity of Sebbeh with Masada, I owe to my companion, Mr Smith, while in Leipzig. The place has since been visited and described, first by Messrs Wolcott and Tipping, in 1842 ; Bibliotheca Sac. 1843, pp. 61–67. Again by Lieut. Lynch and party in 1848 ; see Anderson's Geol. Report, p. 177 sq. Also by De Saulcy in 1851 ; Narrat. I. p. 211 sq.
ii. 241, 242

when it went off more to the left towards Tekoa. At 9 o'clock we crossed Wady Sudeir, here only the shallow bed of a small torrent; although as it breaks down through the cliffs to the sea, it becomes a deep and frightful gulf. The high projecting cliff Mersed forms its northern bastion; along the precipitous southern side of which, we could perceive a foot-path ascending from the shore to the high land above, and falling into our route further on. On the south side of this Wady, where we crossed it, are a few graves, called the Graves of the Dawâ'irah; some of whom were killed here many years ago by the soldiers of the governor of Hebron. These Dawâ'irah are Arabs of the northern Ghôr, composed of several tribes. They are a sort of Fûkirs or Derwishes, much respected by the Arabs and peasants of these regions; so that whoever puts himself under their protection for travelling, is safe. This slaughter of them was by mistake; they having been taken for other Arabs.

Before us lay a long naked mountain ridge, with several peaks, running down southeast towards the sea and terminating apparently in or near Râs el-Mersed. We crossed this chain by a gap at 9.20. Like all the hills and ridges of the region, it consists of friable limestone. A large tract of table land now succeeded, called el-Hûsâsah, from a Wady on its northern side. Indeed, the whole region along the sea, where not either mountain ridge or deep valley, is high table land sloping gradually towards the east; entirely desert, as described yesterday, with only a few scattered shrubs; and without the slightest trace of ever having been tilled. In this tract el-Hûsâsah, the Rashâideh were now encamped towards Tekoa; and also another division of the Ka'âbineh living north of Wady el-Ghâr, who are of the Yemen party, while those further south, whose encampment we passed yesterday, are Keisîyeh.[1] The Rashâideh number about sixty men. They still retain their arms; and pay only about fifty piastres each as Firdeh to the government. None of them can read, and few know how to pray.—The tract el-Hûsâsah is intersected by several small Wadys; one of which called Mudhebbih Sa'îd 'Obeideh we crossed at 9.50, and another called Shukaf half an hour beyond. In the former was a small pool of rain water. At 10.50, we had a view of the north end of the sea, and obtained the following bearings: Frank mountain N. 33° W. Tekoa N. 48° W. Mount of Olives N. 19° W. Mount Gilead, near es-Salt, N. 34° E.[2]

[1] See at Beit Nettif under May 17th.
[2] This is the highest point of the mountains east of the Jordan. I suppose it to be the same which Burckhardt calls Jebel Osha, (Ar. Ausha') three quarters of an hour N. N. W. of es-Salt, connected apparently with the ridge Jil'âd, which runs from W. to E. and is about two and a half hours in length. Of Jebel Osha, Burckhardt remarks, that "its summit overtops the whole of the Belka." As seen from the west, the whole cluster appears as one

ii. 242. 243

After a delay of ten minutes, we began to descend gradually towards Wady Derejeh. This, with Wady Hŭsâsah on the south and Wady Ta'âmirah on the north, occupies a somewhat lower region of exceedingly desolate hills and ridges of chalky limestone, hardly surpassed by any part of the desert we had seen. We first came to the Hŭsâsah at 11.40. It rises near Tekoa, and running down southeasterly enters the sea by itself. Near by is a large cistern in the rocks ; but without water. At 12.20 we came upon the bank of Wady Derejeh, here a narrow gulf a hundred feet deep or more, with rugged perpendicular rocky banks ; the bottom of which we reached after a very difficult and somewhat dangerous descent of ten minutes. Here we stopped for rest and refreshment under the shadow of a lofty wall of rock, " a great rock in a weary land." The bed of the valley merely affords a passage for the wintry torrent. This is the continuation of the Wady Khŭreitŭn, which we had followed down from Solomon's pools, and crossed after leaving the Frank mountain.

We set off again at 1.50, and climbing with difficulty the northern bank, came at 2.25, to Wady Ta'âmirah, which rises around Bethlehem and under Mâr Elyâs. Here again was rain water among the rocks, at which we halted for ten minutes. This Wady is a tributary of the Derejeh, and joins it some twenty minutes below, where our guides said there was an immense cave with a cistern and mason-work, called by the Arabs Um el-Hammâm. The whole tract after leaving the Derejeh is a horrible desert, presenting nothing but cliffs of chalky friable limestone without a trace of herbage. We now turned more to the right, and passed, at 2.45, near the junction of the two Wadys. At 3 o'clock we came upon a fork of the road ; one path going to the right leading down to 'Ain Terâbeh on the shore, and the other keeping along upon the high land towards Râs el-Feshkhah. From this point Bîr ez-Za'ferâneh bore N. 78° W.

To descend to 'Ain Terâbeh there is a pass similar to that of 'Ain Jidy, but not so high. We had intended to go down and encamp by the fountain and thence make our way along upon the shore below ; but learning now that we should have to ascend again in order to cross the promontory of el-Feshkhah, we thought it better to remain above upon the cliffs. We therefore passed on and came out at 3.40, a little to the right of the road, upon the summit of a range of cliffs directly overhanging 'Ain Terâbeh and the shore, and commanding a view of the whole of the Dead Sea, including both its northern and southern extremities. This point we judged to be at least one thousand feet

mountain. It is called also Jebel es-Salt. See Burckhardt's Travels, p. 348,
ii. 244, 245

above the sea.[1] It afforded a fine place of encampment; and
our Arabs found rain water in a neighbouring Wady. We were
here much better off, than to have gone down to the fountain.
This is indeed nothing but a little brackish water oozing up
through the sand along the shore, surrounded by a thicket of
reeds, canes, shrubs, and the like. There is no tillage round
about it, as at 'Ain Jidy ; nor do the Arabs ever encamp near
it, except in circumstances when they wish to hide themselves.
The reeds and thicket around the fountain afford a secure retreat
to an abundance of frogs, which were now merrily croaking ;
while pigeons were shooting in rapid flight over the surface of the
sea.

The prospect of the sea and its wild shores from this spot
was magnificent, though stern ; resembling in its general features that from the cliff over 'Ain Jidy, but embracing more of
the sea ; the view in either direction not being here interrupted
by any near projecting cliff. The waters of the sea, as here
seen, assumed the same deep green hue, which we had remarked
from the cliff over 'Ain Jidy. The atmosphere had now become
quite clear ; and we could overlook the whole form of the sea,
and mark its extent both towards the north and south ; although,
as we were still ignorant of its true features at the southern end,
we did not note the point of its termination in that part, so accurately as we might otherwise have done. Kerak was very
distinctly visible.[2]

From the fork of the Carmel and Jerusalem roads, which we
had left this morning, we had travelled somewhat more than five
hours to reach this cliff above 'Ain Terâbeh. Yet so great was
the general curve of our route towards the west, and such the
number of smaller detours we were compelled to make, and of
steep descents and ascents in crossing the deep Wadys, that the
amount of our progress was much less than in ordinary circumstances. Indeed, from calculations founded on the above measurements in connection with those taken at 'Ain Jidy, and from the
general construction of the map, the cliff on which we were now
encamped, appears to be less than eight geographical miles
distant from 'Ain Jidy in a straight line. Had there been a
path along the shore below, I presume the distance between the
two fountains would not have occupied more than three and a

---

[1] The top of the cliffs is in reality about
1300 feet above the sea; see in Note XXX,
end of the volume.

[2] At 'Ain Terâbeh, Lieut. Lynch and
party encamped for a time. See Anderson's Report, p. 166.—We took here above
'Ain Terâbeh, with our large compass, the
following bearings: Usdum, southeastern

point, S. 8¼° W. Peninsula, south end, S.
6° W. Do. north end, S. 10¼° E. Point
of western shoal beyond 'Ain Jidy, S. 8°
W. Râs el-Mersed, base, S. 8° W. Kerak, S. 25° E. Wady el-Mojib, S. 43° E.
Wady ez-Zerka Ma'in, N. 89° E. Mount
Gilead (Jebel Osha) N. 39° E.

half or at the most four hours of travel; making all due allowance for the windings and difficulties of the way.

The road we had been travelling to-day, is the great Arab
track through the desert along the Dead Sea; by which the
Arabs of the southern deserts, and those who come from the
east around the southern end of the sea, are able to penetrate
far to the north, without letting their movements be known to
the tribes or villages further west.   About thirty years before, a
large party of some three hundred and fifty of the Hejâya from
the mountains of Jebâl, south of Kerak, had in this manner
passed along this route quite to Deir Duwân, and stolen and carried off the flocks of the people of that place.   As these people
were in league with the Ta'âmirah, both belonging to the Yemen
party, the latter pursued the Hejâya and overtook them near
Wady Derejeh.   In the attack which ensued, the Hejâya proved
the strongest; they routed the Ta'âmirah, and killed two or
three.   One man, to save his life, leaped off from a precipice into
the valley, and although much hurt, escaped and recovered.
Ever since that time a feud of blood has existed between the two
tribes.—After this the Hejâya came and plundered the convent
of Mâr Sâba.   The door was of wood covered with iron on the
outside; they contrived to burn it away, by pouring on oil and
setting it on fire in the night.   But, as our Sheikh remarked,
Mâr Sâba is a Wely (holy place); and the Hejâya, after they
had done this wickedness, fell to fighting among themselves.

From the south end of the Dead Sea, this great road follows
the shore below as far as to 'Ain Jidy, and then ascends the pass.
Along that part of the sea we heard of no road upon the high
land above.   Indeed such an upper road would be unnecessary;
since it must naturally be longer than that below; and it would
moreover be far less practicable on account of the deep valleys
of the Ghâr, Khûbarah, Seiyâl, and others, which it must cross.
It was doubtless by this same Arab road that the Moabites and
Ammonites came up against king Jehoshaphat, in the incursion
to which we have already had occasion to allude.[1]

The view of this evening from our lofty encampment, was
most romantic.   The whole Dead Sea lay before us; the full
moon rose in splendour over the eastern mountains, and poured
a flood of silvery light into the deep dark chasm below, illumi-
nating the calm surface of the sluggish waters.   All was still as
the silence of the grave.   Our Arabs were sleeping around us
upon the ground; only the tall pensive figure of the Sheikh was
seen sitting before the door of our tent, his eyes fixed intently
upon us as we wrote.   He indeed was ever the last to lie down
at night, and the first to rise up with the dawn. •

---

[1] 2 Chr. 20, 1. 2. See p. 508, above.

ii. 247. 248

Saturday, May 12th. Having a long day's journey before us in order to reach Jericho, we caused the luggage to be mostly packed over night; and rising very early, took our breakfast in the open air on the brink of the cliff, that our servants meantime might pack the tent. The sun rose gloriously above the eastern mountains and the abyss below us, over which a slight mist was now rising; and the song of numerous birds came up sweetly on the ear from the thicket around the fountain.

We set off at 5 o'clock, an earlier start than we had ever yet been able to make in our regular travelling; and proceeded through a desert tract of table land, much like that of yesterday, often intersected by small Wadys, and having a range of chalky mountains on the left. At 5.50 we came to a Wady running to join the gulf by which the next valley, Ghuweir, descends to the shore. On the left were traces of a former encampment of the Ta'âmirah; this being the place to which they retired after the rebellion of 1834.[1] A few minutes further a road from Bethlehem crossed our path, leading to the descent or pass of the Ghuweir on the right. The Ghuweir is a small fountain on the shore at the foot of the precipice, similar to that at 'Ain Terâbeh. At 6.05 we came upon the Wady called Râs el-Ghuweir, which breaks down through the cliffs to the shore near the fountain. It rises in the interior near Deir Ibn 'Obeid, at a pass called el-Kûssâbeh; it was here deep, rugged, and difficult to be crossed. Another Wady was also mentioned, called 'Alya, rising apparently near the same place, and running into Wady er-Râhib, the prolongation of the Kidron.

Proceeding for nearly two hours and a half over a similar tract, surrounded by abrupt chalky hills and cliffs, and crossing many short Wadys, whose banks the animals could hardly descend and ascend, we came at half past 8 o'clock to the deep and almost impassable ravine of the Kidron, coming down by Mâr Sâba, and thence called Wady er-Râhib, "Monk's Valley;" but here bearing also the name Wady en-Nâr, "Fire Valley." At this place it was running nearly E. S. E. in a deep narrow channel between perpendicular walls of rock, as if worn away by the rushing waters between these desolate chalky hills. There was however no water in it now; nor had there apparently been any for a long time. It enters the sea in the angle formed by Râs el-Feshkhah, which here projects from the western cliffs towards the E. N. E. and contracts the north end of the sea by giving to the coast beyond it nearly the same direction.

Turning more to the right, nearly E. N. E. and crossing with difficulty several short Wadys or ravines, we came out at 8¾ o'clock upon Râs el-Feshkhah, the northernmost promontory of

[1] See p. 482, above.

the Dead Sea, still eight hundred or a thousand feet above its waters. Here again we had a perfect view of the north end of the sea and a portion of the Ghôr or valley of the Jordan beyond, with the eastern mountains; and could also distinguish Usdum at the southern end. While we were taking our observations, two ravens and a small hawk were wheeling in rapid flights over the sea.[1]

Beyond the promontory of Râs el-Feshkhah the shore continues to run N. E. by E. quite to the corner of the sea. But the promontory itself on that side, and the mountains further on, retire gradually from the sea in a direction nearly north, leaving between their base and the shore a triangular plain, at first narrow, but afterwards quite wide. The road passes down obliquely along the northern side of the promontory to 'Ain el-Feshkhah at the bottom. The descent is by no means so great nor so steep as at the pass of 'Ain Jidy; but the path itself is worse, the rocks and stones not being at all cleared away. This pass is one of the roads from Mâr Sâba to the Jordan.[2] Sending on the men and horses ahead, we followed on foot at five minutes past nine. When they were about half way down the pass, a shot was heard; and then we saw the Arabs scrambling down the rocks in eager chase. They had fired at a Beden, it was supposed; but after all their pains it turned out to be a poor rabbit. They said however that the Beden are numerous in these mountains, as well as the wild boar.

Meantime the servants and muleteers were left to get on with the horses as they could; and being unacquainted with the way, and the path blind, their progress was attended with some danger. One of the servants' horses, at a steep and difficult place, got out of the road; on attempting to lead him back, he refused to move; and pulling at the bridle, lost his footing and fell backwards ten or twelve feet, down a ledge of the rocks. We were still some distance behind; and I could not help uttering a cry of compassion as the poor animal fell, supposing it impossible that he should not be killed outright, or have at least some legs or bones broken. But he soon got up and went on as before, seeming to make nothing of it. The cooking utensils, which were slung in bags across his back, suffered more; but even they escaped with slighter damage than could have been expected.

[1] From Râs el-Feshkhah we obtained the following bearings: Northwest corner of the Dead Sea and the intervening line of shore, N. E. by E. Mouth of the Jordan E. N. E. Kùsr Hajla, a ruin in the plain of Jericho, N. 28° E. Jebel Jil'âd or J. es-Salt N. 44° E. Mouth of Zerka Ma'in S. 42° E. Do. of el-Mójib S. 21° E. ii. 250, 251

Peninsula, north end, S. Do. south end S. 9° W. Usdum, east end, S. 11° W. Do. west end S. 15° W. Point of western shoal S. 15" W. Râs el-Mersed S. 19° W.

[2] I am not sure whether this was the route taken by Pococke from Mâr Sâba; Vol. II. i. p. 34.

We found here specimens of the well-known black bituminous stone, 'stink-stone,' which has been already mentioned.[1] In one instance it appeared in the form of a casing or crust, enclosing other stones like a sort of conglomerate ; looking much as if it had once flowed down the path in a liquid state, and there become solid among the stones as it cooled.—The lower part of the mountain consists here wholly of conglomerate, containing stones of all sizes ; some of which indeed are large rocks.

We reached the bottom of the descent and the fountain 'Ain el-Feshkhah at 9¾ o'clock. The fountain boils up here near the shore, a very copious stream, or rather streams, of limpid water, beautiful to the eye, but brackish and having a slight taste of sulphuretted hydrogen. Its temperature is 80° F. The wet and marshy ground around the fountain, is covered by a dense thicket of canes, extending for half an hour or more along the shore, showing that the water flows out along this whole distance, or at least moistens the soil. Near the fountain are the foundations of a small square tower and of other small buildings ; whether ancient or not, we could not tell. We stopped here for thirty-five minutes, and found the heat almost intolerable. The cane brake intercepted the sea breeze, while the beams of the burning sun were reflected down upon us from the cliffs above, rendering the spot like an oven. The thermometer stood at 84° F. The cliffs here and further north we estimated at from one thousand to twelve hundred feet in height.[2]

This fountain and those of the Ghuweir and Terâbeh are within the territories of the Ta'âmirah. Besides these and the waters of Wady Sudeir, 'Ain Jidy, and Wady 'Areijeh or the Ghâr, our guides knew of no fountain on the western coast of the Dead Sea ; nor did we anywhere hear of any other.

Leaving 'Ain el-Feshkhah at twenty minutes past ten, we rode between the cane brake and the mountain, passing many masses of conglomerate rocks fallen down from above ; indeed the whole precipice on our left appeared to be of this character. Beyond the brake, the shrubs of the desert again appeared, as also the tamarisk or Tûrfa, and the Ghûrkûd, but all of a large

---

[1] See p. 512, above, for this and other minerals on the shore of the Dead Sea.

[2] At 'Ain el-Feshkhah, and further north along the base of the mountain, M. De Saulcy finds the site of Gomorrah, on the strength of the name of a Wady, which he calls Oumran or Goumran, probably for 'Amrân ; Narrat. I. pp. 56-60, 62-68. He describes these "enormous ruins," (p. 68) that cover a space about four English miles in extent ; p. 66. This would be a much larger city than Jerusalem ever was. We saw there only "masses of conglomerate rocks fallen down from above," as also many "small precipitous hills apparently of marl ;" as in the text. Besides; if Sodom was at Usdum, as M. De S. holds, it seems hardly natural to place Gomorrah at 'Ain el-Feshkhah, 25 or 30 miles distant, with Hazezon-Tamar ('Ain Jidy) between, which too was not destroyed ; Gen. 14, 7.

size. The red berry of the latter was just beginning to ripen.[1] In one of the bushes, at 11½ o'clock, the guides killed an immense lizard, which we at first had taken for a serpent; it measured three feet eight inches from the head to the tip of the tail. The Arabs did not know it; but our Egyptian servants instantly recognised it as the *Waran* of Egypt, the *Lacerta Nilotica* of Hasselquist and Forskal.[2]

Our course was about northeast, inasmuch as we thought, at first, of proceeding directly to Jericho. The plain continued to widen as the mountains and sea diverged; and on our left, towards the cliffs, the whole region was broken up into small precipitous hills, apparently of marl, of singular shapes, as if the intervening earth had been washed away by torrents. Maundrell not inaptly compares the appearance of this tract to that of " places where there have been anciently limekilns."[3] At 12 o'clock the northwest corner of the Dead Sea, forming its northern extremity, bore due east, less than half an hour distant. From it the coast curves off in a general direction southeast quite to the base of the eastern mountains. At the mouth of the Jordan, on its western side, a small tongue of land or low promontory runs out into the sea, forming a bay towards the west. This point now bore east by south. This portion of the sea, as we have seen, is much narrower than the part beyond Râs el-Feshkhah.—At its northernmost part a small peninsula juts out into the sea; a gravelly point with large stones upon it, connected with the main shore by a low narrow neck. When the sea is full, it overflows this isthmus; and then the peninsula must present the appearance of an island.[4]

The earth, as we advanced, was in many places white with a nitrous crust; and we picked up occasionally small lumps of pure sulphur, of the size of a nutmeg or walnut. In some parts the surface was damp, so that the horses slipped; in others it was more like ashes, and they sunk in at every step.

We now found, that we still had enough of the day left to pay a visit to the Jordan before going to Jericho; and as this would be a great saving of time, and we should thereby avoid the inconvenience of an escort from the garrison, we determined to take this course. On proposing it to our guides, some of the younger ones hesitated for fear of robbers; but the Khatib assented at once. We therefore turned more to the right for a time; and then proceeded about N. E. by E. This brought

[1] See above, p. 66.

[2] Hasselquist's Reise p. 361. Forskal Descript. Animalium p. 13.

[3] Journal from Aleppo to Jerusalem, March 30th. ii. 253, 254.

[4] See Lynch's Narrative p. 270. Lands of the Moslem, p. 280. This is doubtless the island seen by Warburton, Crescent and the Cross, II. p. 280; and also by Dr Wilson, Lands of the Bible, II. p. 21.

us in half an hour into the midst of a second thicket of shrubs and canes around the northernmost point of the sea, watered by another brackish fountain called 'Ain Jehâir.   On the flats and shoals along the shore in this part, there is in summer a deposit of salt, as at Birket el-Khûlîl beyond 'Ain Jidy.   We were soon clear of the thicket; and at a quarter before one, crossed a small sluggish stream of salt water running through marshy ground towards the sea.

Beyond this point the plain assumed a new character.   All traces of vegetation ceased, except occasionally a lone sprig of the Hubeibeh or alkaline plant, which we had seen at 'Ain Jidy. The surface was almost a dead level, covered with a thin smooth nitrous crust, through which the feet of men and horses broke and sunk as in ashes, up to the ankles.   The tract continued of this character, with a few gentle swells, until we reached the banks of the Jordan at 1.40, at a ford or crossing place called el-Helu, considerably below the spot usually visited by the pilgrims and travellers.   It is indeed the lowest point where the river is ordinarily crossed.

The upper or outer banks of the Jordan, where we thus came upon it, are not more than one hundred rods apart; with a descent of fifty or sixty feet to the level of the lower valley in which the river flows.   There was here no sign of vegetation along the upper banks, and little, if any, in the valley below; except a narrow strip of canes, here occupying a still lower tract along the brink of the channel on each side.   With these were intermingled occasionally tamarisks, and the species of willow called by the Arabs *Rishrâsh,* the *Agnus castus* of botanists, from which the pilgrims usually carry away branches for staves, after dipping them in the Jordan.   Looking down upon the river from the high upper bank, it seemed a deep, sluggish, discoloured stream, winding its way slowly through a cane brake. Further up the river, we could see that the high upper banks were wider apart, and the border of vegetation much broader, with many trees.[1]

We descended the high outer banks some rods above the crossing place; but found it impossible to reach the channel at that point, partly on account of the thickness of the cane brake, and partly because the stream was now apparently swollen, filling its immediate banks to the brim, and in some places slightly overflowing them so as to cover the bottom of the brake.   At this point, and as far as we could see, this strip of vegetation

---

Among the trees and shrubs higher up are said to be the rhamnus (Nûbk) and oleander. Hasselq. p. 152. Buckingham p. 315. Jacob de Vitry speaks of the canes growing along the Jordan as used for building huts; they are so used at the present day.   "Et ripas idoneas ad arundines seu cannas procreandas, ex quibus tecta domorum tegunt, et parietes contexunt; c. 53. p. 1076.

ii. 254, 255

was itself skirted by offsets or banks five or six feet high. So that here the river might strictly be said to have three sets of banks, viz. the upper or outer ones, forming the first descent from the level of the great valley ; the lower or middle ones enclosing the tract of canes and other vegetation ; and the actual banks of the channel. Further up the river, it is said, the lower tract of cane brake disappears ; and the stream flows between the middle or second banks just described which are there covered with trees and bushes.

We proceeded therefore to the place of crossing, where there was an opening through the canes and trees. Here the low banks of the channel were broken or worn away for the convenience of passing, and were now covered by the water. There was a still though very rapid current ; the water was of a clayey colour, but sweet and delightfully refreshing, after the water to which we had been confined for the last two days since leaving 'Ain Jidy ; either rain water standing in holes in the Wadys and full of animalculæ, or the brackish waters of 'Ain el-Feshkhah. We estimated the breadth of the stream to be from eighty to one hundred feet. The guides supposed it to be now ten or twelve feet deep. I bathed in the river, without going out into the deep channel ; the bottom here (a hollow place in the bank) was clayey mud with also blue clay. I waded out ten or twelve feet, and thus far the water was not over the hips ; but a little further, several of the party who swam across, found it suddenly beyond their depth. The current was so strong, that even Komeh, a stout swimmer of the Nile, was carried down several yards in crossing. This place is strictly not a *ford* ; we understood that the river could never be crossed here by animals without swimming ; and the Aga of Jericho afterwards told us, that he was accustomed to swim his horse in crossing higher up.

The sand-hills which here form the upper banks, are of the same naked character as the desert we had passed over in coming to this spot. From them we could distinguish, some miles higher up the river, the ruined convent of St. John the Baptist, standing upon the brow of the upper bank, or first descent from the plain, near the place where the Latin pilgrims bathe in the Jordan. The Arabs call it Kŭsr el-Yehûd, 'Jews' Castle.' The bathing place of the Greek pilgrims is two or three miles below the convent ; yet each party claims to bathe at the spot where our Lord was baptized by John. Far in the north, a sharp conical peak was seen standing out like a bastion from the western mountains ; our Arabs called it Kŭrn Sŭrtabeh. Opposite to us across the river lay the plains of Moab. The eastern mountains here retire in a small arc of a circle, forming

ii. 255–257

a sort of recess, and leaving the eastern plain much broader
than in any other part.   It is apparently covered with shrubs ;
especially towards the mountains, which seemed to be two or
three miles distant.   Just below the crossing place, the Wady
Hesbân comes in from the same mountains, descending through
a verdant region at their foot, which indeed owes its fertility to
the Wady.   Further north, the similar Wady Sha'ib comes
down from the vicinity of es-Salt, and enters the Jordan nearly
east of Jericho.   At its mouth is the ordinary ford of the river.[1]

THE JORDAN AND ITS VALLEY.

The present Arabic name for the Jordan is esh-Sherî'ah,
' the watering-place ; ' to which the epithet *el-Kebîr*, ' the great,'
is sometimes annexed.[2]   The form *el-Urdun*, however, is not
unknown among Arabian writers.[3]   The common name of the
great valley through which it thus flows below the lake of Tiberias, is *el-Ghôr*, signifying a depressed tract or plain, usually
between two mountains ; and the same name continues to be
applied to the valley quite across the whole length of the Dead
Sea, and for some distance beyond.[4]
   It has so happened, that until the present century, most pilgrims and travellers have visited the valley of the Jordan only at
Jericho ; so that we have had no account of the features of its
upper part in the vicinity of the lake of Tiberias.   Of the
earlier pilgrims indeed, Antoninus Martyr at the close of the
sixth century, and St. Willibald in the eighth, passed down
through the whole length of the valley from Tiberias to Jericho ;
and in the year 1100 king Baldwin I. accompanied a train of
pilgrims from Jericho to Tiberias ;[5] but we have nothing more
than a mere notice of these journeys.   In like manner, the
various excursions of the crusaders across the Ghôr throw no
light upon its character.   In the year 1799 the French penetrated to the south end of the lake of Tiberias, but no further.
In 1806, Seetzen crossed the valley just south of the same lake ;

---

[1] From the high bank near el-Helu, Jebel es-Salt or Gilead bore N. 30° E.   Kûsr
el-Yehud N.   Kûrn Sûrtabeh N. 8° W.
Ain es-Sultân beyond Jericho, about N.
50° W.   Kûsr Hajla N. 70° W.
   [2] To distinguish it from the Sheri'at el-
Mandhûr or Yarmûk, the ancient Hiero-
max, which joins it from the east about two
hours below the lake of Tiberias.   Burckhardt pp. 273, 274.   Edrisi ed. Jaubert
p. 338.   Abulfedæ Tab. Syr. p. 148.
   [3] Abulfedæ Tab. Syr. p. 147   Schultens

Index in Vit. Saladin. art. *Fluvius Jordanes.*
   [4] It thus corresponds to the *Aulon* of
Eusebius and Jerome ; see Onomasticon.—
On the Ghôr, see Edr'si par Jaubert pp.
337, 338.   Schulten's Index in Vit. Salad.
art. *Aljaurum.*   Reland Palæest. p. 365.
Abulfeda says correctly that the same valley extends to Ailah.
   [5] Fulcher. Carnot. 21. p. 402.

but describes it only in very general terms.[1] Burckhardt in
1812 was twice in its northern part ; and travelled along it from
Beisân to a point several hours below, on his way to es-Salt.[2]
Six years later, in the winter of 1818, Irby and Mangles passed
down from Tiberias to Beisân ; thence crossed over into the
country around Jerash ; and returned from es-Salt to Nâbulus,
fording the Jordan several miles above Jericho.[3] About the
same time Mr Bankes, accompanied by Buckingham, crossed
the valley obliquely from Jericho, passing the river apparently
at the same ford (or very near it) as Irby and Mangles.[4]

According to Burckhardt, the Ghôr at the upper end runs
in a course from N. by E. to S. by W. and is about two hours
broad.[5] Opposite Jericho we found its general course to be the
same ; but in consequence of the retiring of the mountains on
both sides, to which I have already alluded, its breadth is here
much greater, being not less than three and a half or four hours.
The Jordan issues from the lake of Tiberias near its southwest
corner, where are still traces of the site and walls of the ancient
Tarichæa.[6] The river at first winds very much, and flows for
three hours near the western hills ; then turns to the eastern,
on which side it continues its course for several hours, to the
district called Kŭrn el-Hemâr, ‘ Horn of the Ass,’ two hours
below Beisân ; where it again returns more to the western side of
the valley.[7] Lower down, the Jordan follows more the middle
of the great valley ; though opposite Jericho and towards the
Dead Sea, its course is nearer to the eastern mountains ; about
two thirds or three quarters of the valley lying here upon its
western side.

A few hundred yards below the point where the Jordan issues
from the lake of Tiberias, is a ford, close by the ruins of a Roman bridge of ten arches.[8] About two hours further down is
another old bridge, called Jisr el-Mejâmi'a, consisting of one
arch in the centre, with small arches upon arches at the sides ;
and also a Khân upon the western bank.[9] Somewhat higher
up, but in sight of this bridge, is another ford.[10] That near Beisân lies in a direction S. S. E. from the town.[11] Indeed, “ the

[1] Zach's Monatl. Corr. XVIII. p. 350.
Reisen I. p. 350 sq.
 [2] Travels, pp. 274, 344 sq.
 [3] Travels pp. 300-305, 326. [91 sq. 99.]
 [4] Buckingham's Travels in Palest. p.
313 sq.
 [5] Page 344.
 [6] Seetzen l. c. p. 350. Irby and Mangles
p. 300. [91.] See Reland's Palæst. p.
1026. Comp. Pococke II. i. p. 70.
 [7] Burckhardt pp. 344, 345. Irby and
Mangles l. c.
    ii. 258-260

[8] Irby and Mangles pp. 296, 301. [90,
91.]
 [9] Irby and Mangles, p. 301. [91.] Seo-
tzen l. c. p. 351. Reisen I. p. 351. Messrs
Smith and Dodge, in connection with their
travels beyond the Jordan, crossed the
river by this bridge in 1834. The Khân
was then in use.
 [10] Buckingham l. c. p. 448. Burckhardt p. 275.
 [11] Burckhardt p. 344.

river is fordable in many places during summer ; but the few spots
where it may be crossed in the rainy season, are known only to
the Arabs."[1]

The banks of the Jordan appear to preserve everywhere a
tolerably uniform character, such as we have described them
above. " The river flows in a valley of about a quarter of an hour
in breadth, [sometimes more and sometimes less,] which is considerably lower than the rest of the Ghôr ; " in the northern part
about forty feet.[2] This lower valley, where Burckhárdt saw it,
was " covered with high trees and a luxuriant verdure, affording
a striking contrast with the sandy slopes that border it on both
sides." Further down, the verdure occupies in some parts a
still lower strip along the river's brink. So we saw it ; and so
also it seems to be described by Pococke near the convent of
St. John.[3]

The channel of the river varies in different places ; being in
some wider and more shallow, and in others narrower and deeper.
At the ford near Beisân on the 12th of March, Irby and Mangles
found the breadth to be one hundred and forty feet by measure ;
the stream was swift and reached above the bellies of the horses.
When Burckhardt passed there in July, it was about three feet
deep.[4] On the return of the former travellers twelve days later
(March 25th), they found the river at a lower ford extremely
rapid, and were obliged to swim their horses.[5] On the 29th of
January in the same year, as Mr Bankes crossed at or near the
same lower ford, the stream is described as flowing rapidly over
a bed of pebbles, but as easily fordable for the horses.[6] Near
the convent of St. John, the stream at the annual visit of the
pilgrims at Easter is sometimes said to be narrow, and flowing six
feet below the banks of its channel.[7] At the Greek bathing
place lower down, it is described in 1815, on the 3d of May, as
rather more than fifty feet wide and five feet deep, running with
a violent current ; in some other parts it was very deep.[8] In
1835, on the 23d of April, my companion was upon the banks
higher up, nearly opposite Jericho, and found the water considerably below them. The lower tract of cane brake did not exist
in that part.[9]

---

[1] Burckhardt p. 345.
[2] Ibid. pp. 344, 345.
[3] " From the high bank indeed of the
river, [meaning the usual level of the lower valley,] there is a descent in many
places to a lower ground, which is four or
five feet above the water, and is frequently
covered with wood ; " Pococke II. i. p. 33.
[4] Irby and Mangles p. 304. [92.] Burckhardt p. 345.
[5] Travels pp. 304, 326. [92, 99.] From

this lower ford the Kŭl'at er-Rŭbŭd bore
N. E. ¼ N.
[6] Buckingham l. c. p. 315.
[7] Maundrell, March 30th. Hasselquist
Reise p. 152.
[8] Turner's Tour, II. p. 224.
[9] For the course and character of the
Jordan and its valley, see more fully,
Lynch's Official Report, and Map. See
also in Note XXX, end of the volume.

These are the most definite notices which I have been able to find respecting the Jordan and its channel ; and I have collected them here, because they have a bearing on another question of some interest, viz. the annual rise and supposed regular overflow of the waters of the river. It is indeed generally assumed that the Jordan of old, somewhat like the Nile, regularly overflowed its banks in the spring, covering with its waters the whole of its lower valley, and perhaps sometimes large tracts of the broad Ghôr itself.[1]

It seems however to be generally admitted, that no such extensive inundation takes place at the present day ; and all the testimony above adduced goes to establish the same fact.   It is therefore supposed that some change must have taken place, either because the channel has been worn deeper than formerly, or because the waters have been diminished or diverted.[2] But although at present a smaller quantity of rain may fall in Palestine than anciently, in consequence perhaps of the destruction of the woods and forests, yet I apprehend that even the ancient rise of the river has been greatly exaggerated.   The sole accounts we have of the annual increase of its waters, are found in the earlier scriptural history of the Israelites ; where according to the English version the Jordan is said to "overflow all its banks" in the first month, or all the time of harvest.[3] But the original Hebrew expresses in these passages nothing more, than that the Jordan " was full (or filled) up to all its banks," meaning the banks of its channel ; it ran with full banks, or was brim-full.   The same sense is given by the Septuagint and Vulgate.[4]

Thus understood, the biblical account corresponds entirely to what we find to be the case at the present day.   The Israelites crossed the Jordan four days before the passover (Easter), which they afterwards celebrated at Gilgal on the fourteenth day of the first month.[5] Then, as now, the harvest occurred during April and early in May, the barley preceding the wheat harvest by two or three weeks.   Then, as now, there was a slight annual rise of the river, which caused it to flow at this season with full banks, and sometimes to spread its waters even over the im-

---

[1] Reland Palæst. p. 273. Bachiene I. p. 140 sq. Raumer Pal. p. 61. Ed. 2.

[2] Maundrell, March 30th.

[3] Josh. 3, 15. 1 Chr. 12, 15. The only other allusion to a rise of the Jordan in harvest is in Sirac. 24, 26 or 36; where however an inundation is not necessarily implied.—The phrase "swelling of Jordan," English version Jer. 12, 5. 49, 19. 50, 44, should be rendered "pride of Jordan," as in Zech. 11, 3, where the original word is the same. It refers to the verdure and thickets along the banks, but has no allusion to a rise of the waters.

[4] Heb. מָלֵא [מִמְלֵא] עַל־כָּל־גְּדוֹתָיו. Sept. ἐπλήρου καθ᾽ ὅλην τὴν κρηπῖδα αὐτοῦ. Vulg. "Jordanis autem ripas alvei sui tempore messis impleverat." Luther also gives the same sense correctly : " Der Jordan aber war voll an allen seinen Ufern."

[5] Josh. 4, 19. 5, 10.

261-263

mediate banks of its channel, where they are lowest, so as in some places to fill the low tract covered with trees and vegetation along its sides.[1] Further than this there is no evidence, that its inundations have ever extended ; indeed the very fact of their having done so, would in this soil and climate necessarily have carried back the line of vegetation to a greater distance from the channel. Did the Jordan, like the Nile, spread out its waters over a wide region, they would no doubt everywhere produce the same lavish fertility.

Although therefore the Jordan probably never pours its floods, in any case, beyond the limits of its green border, yet it is natural to suppose, that the amount of its rise must vary in different years, according to the variable quantity of rain which may annually fall. This consideration will account in a great measure for the various reports and estimates of travellers. It may also appear singular, that this annual increase should (so far as we yet know) take place near the close of the rainy season, or even after it, rather than at an earlier period, when the rains are heaviest. This is sometimes referred to the late melting of the snows on Jebel esh-Sheikh or Hermon ;[2] but at this season these snows have usually long been melted, and only the mighty head of Hermon is decked with an icy crown. The fact however may be easily explained, I apprehend, upon ordinary principles.

In the first place, the heavy rains of November and December find the earth in a parched and thirsty state ; and among the loose limestone rocks and caverns of Palestine, a far greater proportion of the water is under the circumstances absorbed, than is usual in occidental countries, where rains are frequent. Then too the course of the Jordan below the lake of Tiberias is comparatively short ; no living streams enter it from the mountains, except the Yarmûk and the Zerka from the east ; and the smaller torrents from the hills would naturally, at the most, produce but a sudden and temporary rise. Whether such an effect does actually take place, we are not informed ; as no traveller has yet seen the Jordan during the months of November and December. Late in January and early in March 1818, as we have seen, nothing of the kind was perceptible.[3]

But a more important, and perhaps the chief cause of the phenomenon, lies (I apprehend) in the general conformation of the region through which the Jordan flows. The rains which descend upon Anti-Lebanon and the mountains around the

[1] Burckhardt says loosely that the Jordan in winter, (meaning generally the rainy season,) "inundates the plain in the bottom of the narrow valley." But this whole lower plain, where he saw it, was "covered with high trees and a luxuriant verdure." Travels, pp. 344, 345.
[2] Bachiene I. p. 141.
[3] See p. 539, above.

upper part of the Jordan, and which might be expected to produce sudden and violent inundations, are received into the
basins of the Hûleh and the lake of Tiberias, and there spread
out over a broad surface ; so that all violence is destroyed ; and
the stream that issues from them, can only flow with a regulated
current, varying in depth according to the elevation of the lower
lake. These lakes indeed may be compared to great regulators,
which control the violence of the Jordan, and prevent its inundations. The principle is precisely the same, (though on a far
inferior scale,) as that which prevents the sudden rise and overflow of the magnificent streams connecting the great lakes of
North America.—As now the lake of Tiberias reaches its
highest level at the close of the rainy season, the Jordan naturally flows with its fullest current for some time after that
period ; and as the rise of the lake naturally varies (like that of
the Dead Sea) in different years, so also the fulness of the
Jordan.

All these circumstances, the low bed of the river, the absence of inundation and of tributary streams, combine to leave
the lower and greater portion of the Ghôr a solitary desert.
Such it is described in antiquity, and such we find it at
the present day. Josephus speaks of the Jordan as flowing
" through a desert ;" and of this plain as in summer scorched
by heat, insalubrious, and watered by no stream except the Jordan.[1] The portion of it which we had thus far crossed has
already been described ; and we afterwards had opportunity to
overlook it for a great distance towards the north, where it retained the same character. Near the ford five or six miles
above Jericho, the plain is described as " generally unfertile, the
soil being in many places encrusted with salt, and having small
heaps of a white powder, like sulphur, scattered at short intervals over its surface ;" here too the bottom of the lower valley
is generally barren.[2] In the northern part of the Ghôr, according to Burckhardt, " the great number of rivulets which descend
from the mountains on both sides, and form numerous pools of
stagnant water, produce in many places a pleasing verdure, and
a luxuriant growth of wild herbage and grass ; but the greater
part of the ground is a parched desert, of which a few spots
only are cultivated by the Bedawin."[3] So too in the southern
part, where similar rivulets or fountains exist, as around Jericho,

---

[1] Joseph. B. J. 3. 10. 7, Διεκτέμνει τὴν
Γεννησὰρ μέσην, ἔπειτα πολλὴν ἀναμετρού-
μενος ἐρημίαν, εἰς τὴν Ἀσφαλτῖτιν ἔξ-
εισι λίμνην. Ibid. 4. 8. 2, Ἐκπυροῦται δὲ
ὥρᾳ θέρους τὸ Πεδίον, καὶ δι' ὑπερβολὴν
αὐχμοῦ περιέχει νοσώδη τὸν ἀέρα· πᾶν γὰρ
ἄνυδρον πλὴν τοῦ Ἰορδάνου.—In a similar
ii. 264–266

sense Jerome, Comm. in Zech. xi. 3, " Sic
Jordani fluvio . . . fremitum junxit leonum
propter ardorem sitis, et ob deserti viciniam
et latitudinem vastæ solitudinis, et arun-
dineta et carecta."

[2] Buckingham l. c. pp. 313, 314.

[3] Travels, etc. p. 344.

there is an exuberant fertility ; but these seldom reach the Jordan, and have no effect upon the middle of the Ghôr. Nor are the mountains upon each side less rugged and desolate than they have been described along the Dead Sea. The western cliffs overhang the valley at an elevation of a thousand or twelve hundred feet ; while the eastern mountains are indeed at first less lofty and precipitous, but rise further back into ranges from two thousand to twenty-five hundred feet in height.

Such is the Jordan and its valley ; that venerated stream, celebrated on almost every page of the Old Testament as the border of the Promised Land, whose floods were miraculously "driven back," to afford a passage for the Israelites. In the New Testament it is still more remarkable for the baptism of our Saviour ; when the heavens were opened, and the Spirit of God descended upon him, "and lo, a voice from heaven saying, This is my beloved Son !"[1] We now stood upon its shores, and had bathed in its waters, and felt ourselves surrounded by hallowed associations. The exact places of these and other events connected with this part of the Jordan, it is in vain to seek after ; nor is this necessary, in order to awaken and fully to enjoy all the emotions, which the region around is adapted to inspire.

As to the passage of the Israelites, the pilgrims of course regard it as having occurred near the places where they bathe, or not far below. Mistaken piety seems early to have fixed upon the spot, and erected a church and set up the twelve stones near to the supposed site of Gilgal, five miles from the Jordan. This is described by Arculfus at the close of the seventh, and by St. Willibald in the eighth century ; and the twelve stones are still mentioned by Ludolph de Suchem in the fourteenth.[2] In later times, Irby and Mangles remark, that " it would be interesting to search for the twelve stones" near the ford where they crossed, some distance above Jericho.[3] But the circumstances of the scriptural narrative, I apprehend, do not permit us to look so high up ; nor indeed for any particular ford or point, unless for the passage of the ark. " The waters that came down from above, stood, and rose up upon a heap. . . . and those that came down towards the sea. . . . failed and were cut off ; and the people passed over *right against* Jericho."[4] That is, the waters above being held back, those below flowed off and left the channel towards the Dead Sea dry ; so that the people, amounting to more than two millions of souls, were not confined to a single

---

[1] Matt. 3, 13 sq.
[2] Adamnanus ex Arculfo 2. 14, 15. St. Willibaldi Hodœp. 18. Lud. de Suchem p. 91. Reissb. des h. Landes p. 849.
[3] Travels, p. 326. [99.] So too Buckingham, p. 315.
[4] Josh. 3, 16.

point, but could pass over any part of the empty channel directly from the plains of Moab towards Jericho.

We quitted the banks of the Jordan at 2.35 on a course N. W.½ N. for Jericho, intending to visit a fountain on the way, and also the ruin which the Arabs called Kŭsr Hajla. Some of our younger Arabs had affected great fear in remaining so long at the river, as wandering robbers sometimes lie in wait there for travellers. But the Khatib, who seemed not to know fear, rebuked them, exclaiming : " Let come who will, we will all die together." He was indeed a fine specimen of a spirited Arab chief.

Crossing the desert tract for half an hour or more, we came upon a broad shallow water-bed extending from north to south, covered with a forest of low shrubs. Fifteen minutes further we reached another low tract running from west to east towards the former, and occupied by a fine grove of the Rishrâsh or willow (*Agnus castus*).[1] Most of the trees were young ; but some of them old and very large. Within this grove at the upper or western end, we came at 3½ o'clock to the source of all this fertility, a beautiful fountain of perfectly sweet and limpid water, enclosed by a circular wall of masonry five feet deep, and sending forth a stream which waters the tract below. It is regarded as the finest water of the whole Ghôr ; and bears among the Arabs the name of 'Ain Hajla.

This fine fountain I have not found mentioned by any traveller. From it the tower of Jericho bears N. W.¼W. and Kŭsr Hajla S. W. by W. The name Hajla is identical with the ancient name *Beth-Hoglah*, a place on the boundary line between Judah and Benjamin ; which, commencing at or near the mouth of the Jordan, and passing by Beth-Hoglah, went up through the mountains to En-Shemesh and so to En-Rogel and the valley of Hinnom.[2] The position of this spot accords well with such a course ; and as fountains are one of the permanent and most important features of this region, and of course least likely to lose their ancient names, I am disposed to regard this as the site of the ancient Beth-Hoglah. We sought however in vain for traces of ruins in the vicinity of the fountain. Jerome places Beth-Hoglah at two miles from the Jordan towards Jericho ; although he at the same time confounds it with the threshing floor of Atad beyond the Jordan.[3]

---

[1] *Vitex agnus Castus*, Hasselquist Reise p. 555.

[2] Josh. 15, 5. 6. 18, 19. 20. See above, p. 333.

ii. 267, 268

[3] Onomast. art. *Area Atad*. Comp. Gen. 1, 10. 11. Whatever may be the meaning of the phrase "beyond Jordan," in this passage of Genesis, there can be no doubt

The name was then extant ; but is not again mentioned until
the twelfth or thirteenth century, when Eugesippus and Brocardus appear to have heard of it in the same place, as also other
travellers down to the end of the sixteenth century.[1] Since
that time I find no mention of the name until quite recently.[2]—
The name Kûsr Hajla which the Arabs give to the ruin twenty
minutes distant S. W. by W. is doubtless borrowed by them
from the fountain.

Sending our servants forward direct to Jericho, in order to
pitch the tent and prepare for our arrival, we turned off to visit
the ruins just mentioned. It proved to be a Greek convent ;
the walls yet standing in part, and well built of hewn stones.
The chapel is easily made out ; and the pictures of saints are
still to be seen upon its walls. The native Christians now give
it the name of Deir Mâr Yôhanna Hajla, to distinguish it from
the other convent of St. John the Baptist, near the river further
north.[3] From the ruin, the top of Usdum was just visible at the
south end of the Dead Sea, its middle point bearing about S. 15°
W. the direction of the northern Ghôr being at the same time
about N. 15° E. The cliff el-Mersed by 'Ain Jidy bore S. 20°
W. Westward from the north end of the sea, the retreating of
the mountains forms a sort of amphitheatre ; in this part the
mountains are lower, and a break is seen in them, with a pass
leading over to Mâr Sâba. This pass is called Kuneitirah, and
bore S. 60° W.[4] Through the break a low conical peak was
pointed out, bearing S. 58° W. which was said to be the site of
a ruined town called Mird. The town of Jericho bore N. 38° W.

These ruins belong doubtless to one of the many monasteries,
which once stood in the plain of Jericho ; most of which have
been so utterly destroyed as to leave no trace behind. The
earliest and most important of all, appears to have been that of
St. John the Baptist on the banks of the Jordan, the ruins of
which are now called by the Arabs Kûsr el-Yehûd. It existed
before the time of Justinian ; for Procopius relates, that this
emperor caused a well to be constructed in it, and built also
another convent in the desert of Jordan, dedicated to St. Pante-
leemon.[5] The pilgrims of the subsequent centuries speak only
of the former and its church ; and describe it as large and well

[1] that the "trans Jordanem" of Jerome,
writing at Bethlehem, must refer to the
eastern side of the river. Jerome gives
the distance from the ancient Jericho at
five Roman miles.
[1] Eugesipp. in L. Alatii Symmikta, Col.
Agr. 1653. p. 119. Brocardus c. 7. p. 178.
Further Breydenbach in Reissb. p. 129.
B. de Saligniaco Tom. IX. c. 5. Zuallart
Viaggio, p. 240.

[2] Berggren Resor etc. III. p. 13. Stockh.
1828. Germ. III. p. 110.
[3] Maundrell visited these ruins March
30th, but gives them no name. Berggren
heard the name Kûsr Hajla ; l. c.
[4] This road was taken by Schubert from
the Dead Sea to Mâr Sâba ; Reise III. p.
94 sq.
[5] Procop. de Ædif. Just. 5. 9.

built.[1] In that age the annual throng of pilgrims to bathe in the Jordan took place at the Epiphany; nothing is said of Easter.[2] The monk Bernard in the ninth century says there were here many convents.[3] In the twelfth century Phocas speaks of the convent of St. John as having been thrown down by an earthquake, but rebuilt by the liberality of the Greek emperor; while at the same time two other monasteries, those of Calamon and Chrysostom, existed in the vicinity; and a fourth, that of St. Gerasimus, had been undermined and thrown down by the waters of the Jordan.[4] In the fourteenth century, when Ludolf de Suchem visited the monastery of St. John, it was still inhabited by Greek monks; but near the close of the fifteenth, Tucher and then Breydenbach found it in ruins; and such it has continued ever since.[5]

To which of the other convents above named the ruins of the present Kŭsr Hajla may have belonged, or whether to any of them, I am not able to determine. It would seem to have borne among the Arabs the name of Hajla (from the fountain) as early as the fifteenth century; for Breydenbach speaks of Bethagla as a place where Greek monks had formerly dwelt.[6] It was of course already in ruins; though B. de Saligniaco in 1522, says it was then inhabited (perhaps temporarily) by monks of the order of St. Basil.[7] In the same age it was known also to the Latins as the convent of St. Jerome, and was coupled with a legendary penance of that father in the adjacent desert. Under this name it is mentioned by Tucher in 1479; and is also described by Boniface and Quaresmius, as a ruin with pictures of Jerome and other saints upon the walls.[8]

We left Kŭsr Hajla at 4½ o'clock for Jericho, over a beautiful and perfectly level plain of more than an hour in breadth. The whole tract might be tilled with ease; as the soil is light and fertile, like that of Egypt, and needs only the surplus waters around Jericho in order to become exceedingly productive. At present it is merely sprinkled with shrubs like the desert, and with occasional patches of wild grass, now dry and parched. Here we saw tracks of wild swine, and multitudes of holes of the Jerboa.

At 5¼ o'clock, being still in the plain half an hour from the village, we came suddenly upon the remains of a former site,

---

[1] Adamnanus 2. 16.   St. Willibald Hodoep. 17.   Bernard 16.
[2] Antoninus Mart. 11.   St. Willibald ib. 17.
[3] Bernard de Loc. Sanct. 16, " In quibus quoque locis multa consistunt monasteria."
[4] Joh. Phocas de Loc. sanct. 22–24.
[5] L. de Suchem p. 91. Reissb. p. 849. ii. 270, 271

Tucher ibid. p. 670.   Breydenbach ibid. p. 116.
[6] Reissb. des h. Landes p. 129.
[7] Tom. IX. c. 5.
[8] Tucher in Reissb. p. 671.   Quaresmius II. p. 752.   Adrichomius p. 183.   See also Seetzen's Reisen II. p. 302.

exhibiting the foundations of thick walls of well hewn stones. A quadrangular tract of some size seemed to have been surrounded by a wall; within which were the substructions of a large regular building and other smaller ones. About ten or fifteen minutes further south, on a low mound in the plain, we could perceive other ruins apparently of a like kind.[1] Both these sites I am disposed to regard as the substructions of some of the many monasteries above enumerated, which formerly stood upon the plain. Or perhaps one of them may have been the Gilgal mentioned by Eusebius and Jerome and by the pilgrims of the centuries before the crusades, situated two miles from Jericho and five miles from the Jordan, where was a large church held in high repute.[2] The disappearance of the hewn stones is sufficiently accounted for, by the various Saracenic aqueducts still standing in the plain; to say nothing of the repeated constructions of the later village.

After leaving this spot, as we approached the tower or castle (so called) of Jericho, we came upon traces of cultivation, and passed over fields from which crops of maize, millet, indigo, and the like, had been taken apparently the year before. Trees of the Nûbk were scattered around, and also the Zŭkkûm or balsam tree. Crossing the deep bed of a mountain torrent, now dry, which here runs down eastward through the plain, we reached our tent at a quarter before 6 o'clock. We found it already pitched on the northern bank of the Wady, near the castle and village, in a neglected garden among Nûbk and fig trees.

We were glad to take possession of our temporary home. We had had a long and fatiguing day; but a day too of intense and exciting enjoyment; and we now rejoiced to recline our weary limbs upon our couches, and think only of repose. After a week of such toil and excitement, we likewise looked forward with gratification to a day of rest upon the morrow. The village and the Aga were forgotten for the night, and we saw nothing of either. The merry notes of frogs assured us that water was near; and as the darkness gathered around, we listened with delight to the chirping of the cricket and the song of the nightingale. The less welcome music of the musquito was

---

[1] This is probably the spot described by Monro as "a mound with stone substructions, and a large cistern, and the remains of thick walls upon the surface of the soil at no great distance." Summer Ramble I. p. 158. He held it to be the site of Cypros, a fortress so named by Herod in honour of his mother. But according to Josephus, this fortress was situated *over* (ὑπέρ, καδύπερθε) Jericho; and must therefore be sought on or near the western mountain. Antiq. 16. 5. 2. B. J. 1. 21. 4, 9. ib. II. 18. 6.

[2] Euseb. et Hieron. Onomast. art. *Galgala* et *Bunos*. Adamnanus 2. 14, 15. St. Willibald 18. Brocardus transfers this Gilgal to the west side of Jericho near the mountain Quarantana; c. 7. p. 178. The church was therefore probably destroyed before the crusades; indeed that which St. Willibald saw, was small and built only of wood.

also not wanting ; but these insects were not numerous. The thermometer at sunset stood at 78° F.

Sunday, May 13th. We passed the whole day at Jericho ; but in consequence of various circumstances, it had less of the quiet repose of the Christian Sabbath than we could have wished ; while the excessive heat gave us an uncomfortable specimen of the climate of the Ghôr.

As we sat at breakfast, we learned that the Aga had called to pay us a visit ; but had gone away again on hearing that we were at our meal. We thought it better afterwards to return his civility, in order to have done with the matter of official courtesies as soon as possible. We went accordingly, accompanied by our Sheikh, and found the Aga in the narrow court of the castle, by the side of a reservoir, under a temporary shed or bower built up against the wall, preparing to set off in an hour for the country east of the Jordan, where he expected to be absent a week. Several Bedawin of the 'Adwân were present, a tribe inhabiting the tract across the Jordan, from the river to the summit of the mountains as far as to Hesbân. This tribe had so misused and oppressed the Fellâhîn of the district, who dwell in the villages and till the ground in which the government is interested, that they had abandoned their dwellings and fled to the region of Kerak. The Aga had once been over in order to restrain the oppressions of the Bedawin, and induce the peasants to return ; and he had now summoned the 'Adwân whom we saw, to attend him on a second excursion. His purpose was to afford protection to the peasants, so that they might come down from the mountains and reap the harvest in the plain ; both for their own benefit and that of the government.

The Aga received us very courteously, and had his carpet spread for us in a better spot under the shed on the inner side of the basin. He was an active and intelligent Turk, with a thin visage and nose, and a European cast of countenance ; he was probably an Albanian. Although exceedingly civil to us, in respect to whom he had received a personal order from the governor of Jerusalem, yet he certainly looked capable of any deed of cruelty and blood. Two persons were sitting by with their legs chained together ; these were Christians from 'Ajlûn, who had been taken in some misdeed ; they had been examined by the Aga, who had made out his report respecting them to the governor of Jerusalem. An old priest was also present, whom we recognized as one of our former friends at Taiyibeh. The Aga informed us, that the country around es-Salt, 'Ajlûn, and Jerash, was then quiet and safe, so that we could visit it without danger, if we chose ; but the district around Kerak was still disturbed. He seemed gratified to meet with some one who could

speak Turkish with him, and was quite communicative ; gave us
two cups of coffee, a degree of civility quite unusual ; and said
he had been expecting us for several days. He was ready, he
said, to escort us to the Jordan ; a kindness which we were very
glad not to need ; and told his officers to aid us in all we might
desire during his absence. The garrison appeared not to consist
of more than a dozen men, all Albanians.

A poetical traveller might find here materials to make out
quite a romantic description of our visit. Here was the old
tower or castle with its decayed walls, a memorial of the times
of the crusades ; the narrow court with a reservoir and fountain ;
and a bower erected over them to shield off the burning beams
of an oriental sun. On the inside of the cool fountain, beneath
the bower, the Aga and his visitors were seated on costly carpets,
all wearing the Tarbûsh or oriental cap and tassel ; and he with
a splendid sash, with scimetar, pistols, and dagger in his girdle.
Opposite to us, on the other side of the reservoir, stood as silent
spectators the wild fierce looking chiefs of the 'Adwân, attired in
the Kefiyeh and costume of the desert ; near whom in strong
contrast was seen the mild figure of the old priest of Taiyibeh
in his dark robes and blue turban, and our own stately Khatîb
looking on with a subdued expression of scornful independence.
Here and there round about was an officer or soldier with pistols
and scimetar ; behind, on our left, sat the two prisoners, who probably would have told us a far different story of their fortunes ;
one of them an old man with a long beard pounding coffee ;
and near them another old man cutting up the green leaves of
tobacco. Young slaves, some of them jet black, and others
with fair intelligent countenances, were loitering about, bringing coffee and pipes, or presenting the snuff-box of the Aga to
his guests ; maidens came with water skins, and having filled
them at the fountain, bore them off on their shoulders ; while
around the walls of the court, beautiful Arab horses, gaily caparisoned for the warlike expedition, were impatiently champing
the bit and pawing the ground. All was oriental in full measure ;
yet, with the exception of the horses, all was miserable and
paltry in the extreme. The reservoir was a large drinking-
trough for animals in the midst of a stable-yard ; the bower
was a shed of dry cornstalks[1] and straw, resting on rough
crotches ; and the persons and garments of the people were
shabby and filthy. So much for the romance of the scene.

Leaving the Aga, from whose further civilities we were glad
to be relieved so easily, we passed out of the court ; and observing some people threshing wheat a little east of the castle, we
walked towards them. It was truly a scriptural harvest scene,

---

[1] That is, the dry stalks of maize, the Indian corn of the United States.

ii. 275, 276

where the reaping and the threshing go on hand in hand.[1]   The people, we found, were our old acquaintances, the inhabitants of Taiyibeh, who had come down to the Ghôr in a body, with their wives and children and their priest, to gather in the wheat harvest.   They had this year sown all the wheat raised in the plain of Jericho, and were now gathering it on shares ; one half being retained for themselves, one quarter going to the people of the village, and the remaining quarter to the soldiers of the garrison in behalf of the government.   The people of Jericho, it seems, are too indolent, or, as it was said, too weak to till their own lands.

The wheat was beautiful ; it is cultivated solely by irrigation, without which nothing grows in the plain.   Most of the fields were already reaped.   The grain, as soon as it is cut, is brought in small sheaves to the threshing floors on the backs of asses, or sometimes of camels.   The little donkeys are often so covered with their load of grain, as to be themselves hardly visible ; one sees only a mass of sheaves moving along as if of its own accord.   A level spot is selected for the threshing floors ; which are then constructed near each other of a circular form, perhaps fifty feet in diameter, merely by beating down the earth hard.   Upon these circles the sheaves are spread out quite thick ; and the grain is trodden out by animals.   Here were no less than five such floors, all trodden by oxen, cows, and younger cattle, arranged in each case five abreast, and driven round in a circle or rather in all directions over the floor.   The sled or sledge is not here in use, though we afterwards met with it in the north of Palestine.[2]   The ancient machine with rollers, we saw nowhere.[3]   By this process the straw is broken up and becomes chaff.   It is occasionally turned with a large wooden fork, having two prongs ; and when sufficiently trodden, is thrown up with the same fork against the wind, in order to separate the grain, which is then gathered up and winnowed.   The whole process is exceedingly wasteful, from the transportation on the backs of animals to the treading out upon the bare ground. The precept of Moses : "Thou shalt not muzzle the ox when he treadeth out,"[4] was not very well regarded by our Christian friends ; many of their animals having their mouths tied up ; while among the Muhammedans, I do not remember ever to have seen an animal muzzled.   This precept serves to show, that of

---

[1] It brought up before our eyes the scenes of the book of Ruth; cc. 2. 3.
[2] See under June 15th, at Sebûstieh.
[3] Is. 28, 27 sq. Niebuhr found it still in use in Egypt, called Nôrej ; Reisebeschr. I. pp. 151, 152. Lane also describes it ii. 276, 277

under the same name ; Mod. Egyptians II. p. 26. edit. 1.—On the various modes of oriental threshing, see Winer Bibl. Realwörterb. I. p. 324.
[4] Deut. 25, 4.

old, as well as at the present day, only neat cattle were usually employed to tread out the grain.[1]

Thus the wheat harvest in the plain of Jericho was nearly completed on the 13th of May. Three days before, we had left the wheat green upon the fields around Hebron and Carmel ; and we afterwards found the harvest there in a less forward state on the 6th of June. The barley harvest at Jericho had been over for three weeks or more. My companion had visited the place a few years before ; and found the barley then fully gathered and threshed on the 22d of April.

On inquiring of these Christians, Why they thus laboured on the Lord's day ? their only reply was, that they were in the Ghôr away from home, and the partners of Muhammedans. At home, they said, they abstained from labour on that day.

Turning back towards the village, which lies west of the castle along the Wady, we met the Sheikh of the place, watering his young horse at one of the little streams that come down from a large fountain on the west, and irrigate the plain. He seemed intelligent ; and gave us the names of several places in the vicinity. Of a Gilgal he knew nothing. One of the 'Adwân chiefs also came to meet us ; of whom we inquired respecting his country. He pointed out to us again the Wady Hesbân, near which far up in the mountain is the ruined place of the same name, the ancient Heshbon.[2] Half an hour northeast of this lies another ruin, called el-'Âl, the ancient Elealeh.[3] Neither of these places was visible from Jericho. The same Sheikh pointed out also Wady Sha'ib coming down in the northern part of the recess of the eastern mountains, from the vicinity of es-Salt,[4] and passing by the ruins of Nimrin, the Nimrah and Beth Nimrah of Scripture.[5] Here, as I understood, is a fountain, corresponding to the waters of Nimrim.[6] This Wady enters the Jordan nearly E. by N. from Jericho ; and at its mouth is the usual ford of that river ; where, as the Sheikh said, the water was breast high.

---

[1] Comp. Hos. 10, 11.

[2] The celebrated capital of Sihon, king of the Amorites, Num. 21, 25 sq. Euseb. et Hieron. Onomast. art. *Esebon*. Reland Palæst. p. 719. This region was first visited in modern times by Seetzen, who found Hesbân, el-'Âl, and other ancient places; Zach's Monatl. Corr. XVIII. p. 431. Reisen I. p. 407. Then by Burckhardt, Travels p. 365 sq. Afterwards by Irby and Mangles and their party, Travels p. 471. Legh in Macmichael's Journey, ch. IV.

[3] Num. 32, 3. 37. According to Eusebius and Jerome, Elealeh lay one Roman mile from Heshbon; Onomast. art. *Eleale*. The two are mentioned together, Is. 15, 4. 16, 9. Jerem. 48, 34. See the preceding note.—This place seems to be mentioned by Khŭlil Ibn Shâhin, as the northern limit of the province of Kerak, under the name of el-'Aly ; see Rosenmüller Analecta Arab. Pars III. p. 19. fol. p. 39.

[4] See Burckhardt, p. 355.

[5] Num. 32, 3. 36. Josh. 13, 27. Onomast. art. *Nemra*, Νεβρά. Reland p. 650. Burckhardt heard of Nimrin; pp. 355, 391.

[6] Is. 15, 6. Jer. 48, 34. Nimrin in Hebrew is a plural form of Nimrah.

We now returned through the village, which bears in Arabic the name of Erîha, or as it is more commonly pronounced Rîha, a degenerate shoot, both in name and character, of the ancient Jericho.[1] Situated in the midst of this vast plain, it reminded me much of an Egyptian village. The plain is rich, and susceptible of easy tillage and abundant irrigation, with a climate to produce anything. Yet it lies almost desert ; and the village is the most miserable and filthy that we saw in Palestine. The houses, or hovels, are merely four walls of stones taken from ancient ruins, and loosely thrown together, with flat roofs of cornstalks or brushwood spread over with gravel. They stand quite irregularly and with large intervals ; and each has around it a yard enclosed by a hedge of the dry thorny boughs of the Nŭbk. In many of these yards are open sheds with similar roofs ; the flocks and herds are brought into them at night, and render them filthy in the extreme. A similar but stronger hedge of Nŭbk branches, surrounds the whole village, forming an almost impenetrable barrier. The few gardens round about seemed to contain nothing but tobacco and cucumbers. One single solitary palm now timidly rears its head where once stood the renowned " City of Palm trees."[2] Not an article of provision was to be bought here, except new wheat unground. We had tried last evening to obtain something for ourselves and our Arabs, but in vain ; not even the ordinary 'Adas or lentiles were to be found.—Did the palm groves exist here still in their ancient glory, the resemblance to Egypt and its soil would be almost complete ; as the repeated decay and desolations of Rîhah have raised it upon mounds of rubbish, similar to those of the Egyptian villages.

The village was now full of people in consequence of the influx of families from Taiyibeh to the harvest ; many of whom had taken up their abode under the open sheds in the yards of the houses. The proper inhabitants of Rîhah were rated at about fifty men or some two hundred souls ; but the number had been diminished by the conscription. They are of the Ghawârineh, or inhabitants of the Ghôr, a mongrel race between the Bedawy and Hŭdhry, disowned and despised of both. Here indeed they seemed too languid and indolent to do anything. Our Sheikh spoke of them as hospitable and well meaning people, but feeble and licentious, the infidelity of the women being winked at by the men ; a trait of character singularly at variance with the customs of the Bedawin. At our encampment over 'Ain Terâbeh the night before we reached this place, we

[1] Abulfeda writes it with an Alef, *Erîha*, and *Rîha*, ed. Jaubert, p. 338 bis, and Tab. Syr. ed. Köhler p. 35. Edrisi has Note 2.
both forms, with and without Alef, *Erîha*   [2] Deut. 34, 3. Judg. 1, 16.
ii. 279, 280

overheard our Arabs asking the Khatib for a paper or written charm, to protect them from the women of Jericho; and from their conversation, it seemed that illicit intercourse between the latter and strangers who come here, is regarded as a matter of course. Strange, that the inhabitants of the valley should have retained this character from the earliest ages; and that the sins of Sodom and Gomorrah should still flourish upon the same accursed soil.

A streamlet from the fountain flows along between the village and the brink of the Wady on the south, which is here skirted by a thicket of Nûbk and other trees. The rill passed on near our tent, and then entered the court of the castle to supply the reservoir. Around our tent were several large fig trees, whose broad and thick foliage aided to ward off the scorching beams of the sun. Among other trees close by was the Palma Christi (Ricinus), from which the castor oil is obtained; it was here of large size, and had the character of a perennial tree, though usually described as a biennial plant.[1] Another object near our tent also excited our curiosity,—a block of sienite red granite, the fragment of a large circular stone lying partly buried in the earth. It was about two feet thick, and the chord of the fragment measured five and a half feet; the diameter of the stone when whole could not have been less than eight or ten feet. The circular edge was full of small round holes or indentations. Just by are the remains of a circular foundation, on which it perhaps once lay. What could have been the purpose of this stone, or whence it was brought, we could not divine. It had every appearance of the Egyptian sienite; and if such were its origin, it could only have been transported hither across the plain of Esdraelon and so along the Ghôr.—Below the bank of the Wady itself were a few traces of former foundations; but nothing which indicated antiquity.

The climate of Jericho is excessively hot; and after two or three months becomes sickly, and especially unhealthy for strangers. According to our Arabs, the sojourn of a single night is often sufficient to occasion a fever. Indeed, in traversing merely the short distance of five or six hours between Jerusalem and Jericho, the traveller passes from a pure and temperate atmosphere into the sultry heat of an Egyptian climate. Nor is this surprising, when we consider, that the caldron of the Dead Sea and the valley of the Jordan lie thirteen hundred feet below the level of the ocean, and nearly four thousand feet lower than Jerusalem. The sun to-day was sometimes obscured by light

---

[1] Hasselquist also found it here: "Ricinus in altitudinem arboris insignis." Reise p. 555. Comp. Celsii Hierobot. II. p. 273.

Throughout Syria it is understood to be perennial, as in other warm countries.

clouds; but in the intervals his beams were very intense. At 10 o'clock, as I sat writing under a retired and spreading fig tree, near running water, with a refreshing breeze, a thermometer, which hung near me in the shade and in the full current of the breeze, stood at 86° F. A nightingale, "most musical, most melancholy," was pouring forth her song in the branches over my head. The heat in the tent, in spite of all our precautions, and notwithstanding the breeze and the partial obscuration of the sun, became at length insupportable. The thermometer at 2 o'clock rose in it to 102°; while at the same time, another hanging in the shade of a fig tree stood at 91°. We spread our carpets under the fig trees, first under one and then another as their shades changed, and found ourselves in this way much more comfortable.

We did not fail to peruse here the scriptural accounts of Jericho, its remarkable destruction by the Israelites under Joshua, and the perpetual curse laid upon him who should attempt to rebuild its walls.[1] In our devotional exercises, we dwelt particularly upon our Lord's visit to this place; when, on his last journey to Jerusalem, having traversed the country east of the Jordan, he passed through Jericho, healing the blind and honouring the house of Zaccheus with his presence.[2] As we read, we could not but remark, how much fewer, as well as more general and indefinite, are the topographical notices contained in the Gospels, than those preserved to us in the Old Testament.

Towards evening we took a walk to the fountain, whose waters are scattered over the plain; it is the only one near Jericho, and there is every reason to regard it as the scene of Elisha's miracle.[3] It is called by the Arabs 'Ain es-Sultân, and lies N. 35° W. from the village and castle, at the distance of thirty-five minutes, or nearly two miles. We followed up the little brook, which serves to water many fields, and grew larger as we advanced, until it became a mill stream which we crossed with difficulty. Some ten or fifteen minutes from the village, we fell in with the remains of a regular paved Roman road, which we traced for several rods in a direction towards the pass leading up the western mountain to Jerusalem. It was a mere fragment, entirely similar to the Roman roads I had formerly seen in Italy; but we could discover no further trace of it either above or below.[4]

A few minutes beyond this, we came upon foundations, chiefly of unhewn stones, scattered over a considerable tract, and ex-

---

[1] Josh. cc. 2. 6. 7.   c. 6, 26.
[2] Matt. 19, 1.   20, 29-34.   Mark 10, 1. 46-52.   Luke 18, 35-43.   19, 1-10.
[3] 2 K. 2, 19-22.
ii. 282, 283

[4] Buckingham speaks of a similar fragment of a "fine paved way" near the top of the ascent on the road to Jerusalem; p. 293.

tending with few interruptions quite up to the fountain. They are however hardly distinct enough, to be of themselves regarded as the substructions of an ancient city. On our left, as we advanced, were wheat fields, from most of which the grain had been already gathered ; in others the reapers were still at work. On our right, for nearly the whole distance, was a grove of Nûbk, covering a large tract of the plain.

The fountain bursts forth at the eastern foot of a high double mound, or group of mounds, looking much like a tumulus, or as if composed of rubbish, situated a mile or more in front of the mountain Quarantana. It is a large and beautiful fountain of sweet and pleasant water, not indeed cold, but also not warm like those of 'Ain Jidy and the Feshkhah. It seems to have been once surrounded by a sort of reservoir or semicircular enclosure of hewn stones ; from which the water was carried off in various directions to the plain below ; but this is now mostly broken away and gone.[1] The principal stream at this time was that running towards the village ; a part of which is carried across the Wady higher up, by an aqueduct on arches. The rest of the water finds its way at random in various streams down the plain, here decked with the same broad forest of Nûbk and other thorny shrubs.

The mounds above the fountain are covered with substructions of unhewn stone ; and others of the same kind are seen upon the plain towards the southwest. In the same direction, not far off, are the broken pointed arches of a ruined building, which may perhaps have been a Saracenic castle like the one now near the village. Back of the fountain rises up the bold perpendicular face of the mountain Kûrûntûl (Quarantana) ; from the foot of which a line of low hills runs out N. N. E. in front of the mountains, and forms the ascent to a narrow tract of table land along their base.

On this tract, at the foot of the mountains, about an hour distant, N. N. W. is the still larger fountain of Dûk ; the waters of which are brought along the base of Quarantana in a canal to the top of the declivity back of 'Ain es-Sultân, whence they were formerly distributed to several mills, and scattered over the upper part of the plain ; being carried by a second aqueduct, higher up, across the Wady towards the south. This stream is now used only to water a few gardens of cucumbers in the vicinity. The mills are all in ruins ; among them, on the side of the declivity, fifteen minutes back of 'Ain es-Sultân, is a large deserted building, which still bears the name of Tawahin es-Sukkar, or ' Sugar mills.'[2]

---

[1] In Pococke's day six niches were still visible ; II. i. p. 31.

[2] This is most probably the place of the same name mentioned by Burckhardt ; ii. 283-285

Towards the northeast beyond the wood of Nûbk, the plain is again open ; and in this direction, at the mouth of Wady Nawâ'imeh, which here comes out through the line of hills, is seen another aqueduct, once fed by the waters of the same fountain of Dûk, as they flowed down the valley, and were thus scattered over that part of the plain. In this quarter the plain is said to be covered with hewn stones, and the foundations of walls are visible across it.[1]

Here then are traces enough of ancient foundations, such as they are ; but none which could enable us to say definitely : This is the site of ancient Jericho. Around the fountain, where we should naturally look for its position, there is nothing which can well be referred to any large or important building ; nothing, in short, which looks like the ruins of a great city, with a vast circus, palaces, and other edifices. The walls, whose traces are still visible, may very probably have been only the enclosures of gardens and fields ; and this conclusion is indeed strengthened, by the fact of their occurring only below the fountain.

The top of the mound above the fountain commands a fine view over the plain of Jericho, which needs only the hand of cultivation to become again one of the richest and most beautiful spots on the face of the earth. The fountain pours forth a noble stream, which is scattered in rivulets over a wide extent both in front and on the right and left ; while the still more copious streams from Dûk are in like manner distributed higher up, and further towards the north and south. By these abundant waters, fertility and verdure are spread over the plain almost as far as the eye can reach, extending for an hour or more below the fountain. But alas ! almost the whole of this verdure at the present day, consists only of thorny shrubs, or trees of the thorny Nûbk. It is a remarkable instance of the lavish bounty of nature, contrasted with the indolence of man. Where the water does not flow, the plain produces nothing.

In the course of the afternoon, we received a visit from the old Sheikh Mustafa, whom we had tried to obtain as a guide before leaving Jerusalem.[2] He is the head of a tribe, who are considered rather as sacred persons by the Bedawîn and peasants, a sort of derwishes, poor and not given to the acquisition of wealth. They usually encamp around Jericho ; and their tents were now pitched on the way to Dûk. The old man followed us to the fountain ; and after answering our questions, insisted at parting on

which, on the random information of the Arabs, he places on the eastern shore of the Dead Sea ; a most improbable site. Travels, p. 391.

[1] So Monro, who rode into this part of the plain ; Summer Ramble I. p. 161. I

ii. 285, 286

must doubt however whether the stones were actually hewn ; at least this would not accord with what is found elsewhere in the plain.

[2] See above, p. 467.

making us a present of a kid, which he put into the arms of our
Arab attendant to carry to the tent. We of course, as in duty
bound, made him also a present of ten piastres. We had
intended to purchase a kid for our Arabs; so that the present
for once came in good time.—We returned to our tent and
passed the evening in quiet. The thermometer had now fallen
to 76° F.

If we had not yet satisfied ourselves as to the site of the
former Jericho, we had nevertheless been able to ascertain definitely in respect to her ancient neighbour Gilgal, that no trace
either of its name or site remains.[1] Indeed, it may be doubtful,
whether at first this name belonged to a city; though afterwards
there can be little question that Gilgal was an inhabited place.[2]
It seems to have been early abandoned; for there is no certain
trace of it after the exile; nor is it mentioned by Josephus as
existing in his time.[3] The ancient Gilgal was "in the east
border of Jericho," ten stadia from that city and fifty from the
Jordan.[4] This would in all probability bring it somewhere in
the vicinity of the modern village Riha, which is reckoned at
two hours from the river. But there are here no traces of antiquity whatever, unless it be the fragment of sienite granite and
the slight foundations above described. Neither Sheikh Mustafa,
nor the Sheikh of the village, nor any of the Arabs, had ever
heard of such a name in the valley of the Jordan. At Taiyibeh
indeed, the priest who had been delving a little in scriptural
topography, told us that the name Jiljilia still existed in this
vicinity; but when we met him here, he could only point to the
ruined convent of St. John on the bank of the Jordan as the supposed site.

Monday May 14th. This bright morning, before proceeding
on our journey, we repaired to the top of the castle, in order to
enjoy the beautiful view and fix a deeper impression of the surrounding country. It is merely a tower some thirty feet square,
and forty high, in a state of decay verging to ruin. The castle
and modern village lie upon the northern bank of the Wady Kelt,
here the bed of a mountain torrent, at the distance of nearly two
miles from the point where it issues from the western mountains.
This Wady, as we have seen, is the great drain of all the valleys
we had formerly passed in travelling from Jerusalem to Deir

---

[1] The later alleged Gilgal of Eusebius
and Jerome and of the pilgrims, has already been alluded to; see p. 547, above.

[2] Josh. 4, 19. 20. 9, 6. 10, 6. 7. etc.
Afterwards Samuel came to Gilgal in his
annual circuit as judge; and there was
here a school of the prophets; 1 Sam. 7,
16. 2 K. 4, 38.

[3] The Gilgal of Neh. 12, 29, and of 1
Macc. 9, 2, may with more probability be
referred to the place so called in the western plain, near Antipatris. The name is
still extant in that region; and is found in
more than one place.

[4] Josh. 4, 19. Joseph. Ant. 5. 1. 4,
11.

Duwân ; they run first into the Fârah and the Fûwâr, which then unite and go to form the Kelt.[1] It dries up in summer, as was now the case ; but the brook in some seasons continues to run much later.   On the south side of the deep gorge, by which it issues from the mountains, the road to Jerusalem climbs an 'Akabah (pass) in order to gain the higher region above.   Near this road, at some distance within the mountains, is seen a deserted tower or castle, called Kâkôn ; which, as well as the gorge, bore west, from the point where we stood.   So far as it depends upon the name, this Wady Kelt may have been the brook Cherith, where the prophet Elijah hid himself and was fed by ravens.[2]

South of the opening of Wady Kelt, the western mountains retreat very considerably, forming a recess from the plain in the southwest.   Then, sweeping around as they approach the Dead Sea, they end abruptly in the promontory of Ras el-Feshkhah. In this part the mountains are lower and less precipitous.   Here the pass leads over to Mâr Sâba ; and another road also goes up to Jerusalem, south of the former one, passing near the Muslim Wely of Neby Mûsa, the pretended tomb of Moses, which is seen in that direction.[3]   North of Wady Kelt rises the naked and loftier ridge of Quarantana, with its bold precipitous front, and a chapel on its highest point.   Still further north the mountains retreat again, leaving a semicircular recess ; which is separated from the great plain by the line of low hills already mentioned, running north from the base of Quarantana.[4]

The valley of the Jordan is here seen in its broadest part. When on the banks of the river, we had estimated the plains of Moab on the eastern side, at one hour in breadth to the base of the retreating mountain.[5]   From the river to Riha is about two hours ; (we travelled obliquely more than this ;) and thence to the mountains at the opening of Wady Kelt, forty-five minutes.[6]

---

[1] See pp. 439, 441, above.

[2] 1 Kings 17, 3. 7. The Arabic form Kelt and the Hebrew Cherith are indeed not exactly the same ; though the change from Kesh to Lam, and that of Kaph into Koph, are sometimes found. See Gesenius Heb. Lex. under the letters כ, ל, ת. There is also an apparent difficulty in the circumstance, that the brook Cherith is said to be *before* (כלפני) Jordan ; which is usually understood as meaning *east* of Jordan ; so Eusebius and Jerome, Onomast. art. *Chorath*. But the difficulty vanishes, if we translate it *towards* Jordan ; and that this may be done, is shown by Gen. 18, 16. 19, 28, where the angels and Abraham, in the vicinity of Hebron, are said to have "looked *towards* Sodom ; " the expression in Hebrew being the very same as here. So too Judg. 16, 3.

[3] See also Quaresmius II. p. 736. Seetzen, Reisen II. p. 271.

[4] The bearings of various points from the castle of Jericho were as follows : Northeast corner of the Dead Sea, about S. 42° E. Kûsr Hajla S. 39° E.   Ras el-Feshkhah S. 8° W.   Neby Mûsa S. 30° W.   Southern Pass to Jerusalem S. 63° W.   Kâkôn W. Chapel on Quarantana N. 48° W.   Sugar Mills, ruins, N. 40° W.   'Ain es-Sultan N. 35° W.   Aqueduct in Wady Nawâ'imeh N. 5° W.   Easternmost projection of the low hills beyond said aqueduct, N. 3° E. Kûrn Sûrtabeh N. 8° E.

[5] See above, p. 536 sq.

[6] The distance from Jerusalem to Rihah

Taking in the recess further south, the breadth of the valley in this part may be estimated at from three and a half to four hours, or from ten to twelve English miles; being half or three quarters of an hour broader than the basin of the Dead Sea at 'Ain Jidy.

This vast plain, as we have seen, is partly desert; but is for the most part susceptible of being rendered in the highest degree productive, in connection with the abundance of water and the heat of the climate. Indeed its fertility has been celebrated in every age. Josephus, whenever he has occasion to mention Jericho, rarely fails to break forth into praises of the richness and productiveness of its environs. He calls it the most fertile tract of Judea; pronounces it a "divine region;"[1] and in speaking of the fountain, says it watered a tract seventy stadia long by twenty broad, covered with beautiful gardens and groves of palms of various species.[2] The Scriptures call Jericho the "city of Palm trees;" and Josephus everywhere describes those graceful trees as here abundant and very large, and growing even along the banks of the Jordan.[3] The region also produced honey, opobalsam, the Cypros tree or el-Henna, and myrobalanum, as well as the common fruits of the earth in prolific abundance.[4] The sycamore tree likewise grew here, as we learn from Scripture.[5]

Of all these productions, which so distinguished the plain of Jericho, and which it had for the most part in common with Egypt, few now remain. The groves of palms, such as still constitute the pride of Egypt, have here disappeared, and only one solitary palm tree lingers in all the plain. At the close of the seventh century these groves were still in existence.[6] Honey, if found at all, is now comparatively rare; the Henna has entirely disappeared. The sycamore too has retired from Jericho;[7] and the opobalsam, after having been, according to the legend, transferred by Cleopatra to the gardens of Heliopolis, where it continued to flourish for many centuries, is no longer known in either country.[8] The myrobalanum alone appears still to thrive here, being probably identical with the tree called by the Arabs Zûkkûm.

is usually reckoned at about five hours; and to the Jordan seven.

[1] Τὸ τῆς Ἰουδαίας πιότατον B. J. 1. 6. 6. Θεῖον χωρίον 4. 8. 3.

[2] B. J. 4. 8. 3.

[3] Deut. 34, 3. Judg. 1, 16. Joseph. Antiq. 4. 6. 1. ib. 14. 4. 1. ib. 15. 4. 2. B. J. 1. 6. 6. ib. 4. 8. 2, 3.

[4] Joseph. B. J. 4. 8. 3. See also the testimonies of other writers collected by Reland, Palæst. pp. 382–386.—For the Cypros or el-Henna, see above p. 505. n. 4.

[5] Luke 19, 4.

[6] Adamnanus 2. 13.

[7] Hasselquist Reise, pp. 151, 560. This naturalist found it in other parts of Palestine nearer the sea, as at Ramleh; pp. 151, 553. It is now common in Egypt; many of the trees in the fine avenue between Cairo and Shubra are sycamores.

[8] Josephus relates, that Arabia and Judea were bestowed by Antony on Cleopatra, from whom Herod farmed Arabia and the plain of Jericho; Antiq. 15. 4. 1, 2. The legend relates, that she caused slips of the balsam shrub to be carried to Egypt and planted at Heliopolis, where a garden of it is described by the older travellers;

ii. 289–291

The Zŭkkûm is a thorny tree, not large, with greener and smoother bark than the Nŭbk, and like that tree here growing wild, though much less frequent. According to Hasselquist, it is the *Eleagnus angustifolius* of botanists.[1] It bears a green nut, having a very small kernel and a thick shell, covered with a thin flesh outside. These kernels, according to Maundrell, the Arabs bray in a mortar, and then putting the pulp into scalding water, skim off the oil which rises.[2] According to Pococke, they grind the whole nut, and press an oil out of it, as they do out of olives, and call it a balsam.[3] This is the modern balsam or oil of Jericho, highly prized by the Arabs and pilgrims as a remedy for wounds and bruises.[4] When fresh, it is said to resemble, in taste and colour, the oil of sweet almonds. All this accords well with Pliny's description of the myrobalanum, which bore a green nut ; an unguent was prepared from the bark, and a medicinal oil extracted from the bruised nuts by the aid of warm water.[5]

Of other trees forming the natural growth of this region, the Egyptian Nŭbk or Sidr, as we have seen, is the most abundant ; it is here universally called the Dôm.[6] The Ricinus and Agnus castus have likewise already been mentioned. Among the plants, the nightshade or mad apple grows here in profusion.[7] The rose of Jericho, so called, we did not find ; but in this we only trod in the footsteps of Maundrell, Pococke, Hasselquist, and others.[8] The little shrub to which the name is given, a species of *Thlaspi*, has no resemblance to a rose, and according to Belon, does not even grow near Jericho ; indeed he regards the name as merely got up by the monks, in order to have something to correspond with the mention of roses at Jericho by the Son of Sirach.[9]

The feeble and indolent inhabitants of Jericho give them-

---

see Adrichomius p. 47. Brocardus c. 13. p. 192. Breydenbach in Reissb. p. 195. Belon Observations, Par. 1588. p. 246 ; also in Paulus' Sammlung IV. p. 188. In the days of Quaresmius it had already disappeared, II. p. 951. Hasselquist and Forskal also do not mention it.

[1] Reise pp. 555, 559. Oedmann's Sammlungen III. c. 16.

[2] Maundrell, March 30th.

[3] Vol. II. p. 32. Comp. Hasselquist p. 559. Mariti combines both processes.—He saw the Arab women bruise and break the nuts with stones, and then press out the oil with the hands. Afterwards the mass was bruised anew, and thrown into warm water, from which the oil was then skimmed off ; Viaggi, etc. Germ. pp. 414, 415.

[4] The pilgrims call it "Zaccheus' oil ; " because, according to the monks, this was the tree climbed by Zaccheus ; although the Scripture says the latter was a syca-

ii. 291, 292

more. Luke 19, 4. See Hasselquist pp. 151, 559.

[5] "Myrobalanum . . . nascens unguento. —Fructus magnitudine Avellanæ nucis. Unguentarii autem tantum corticem premunt ; medici nucleos, tundentes affusa eis paulatim calida aqua ; " Plin. H. N. 12. 21. § 46. See Rosenmüller's Bibl. Alterthumsk. IV. i. p. 168 sq.

[6] Rhamnus nabeca ; see p. 505. n. 3.

[7] Solanum melongena ; see above, pp. 505, 524.

[8] Maundrell, March, 30th, end. Pococke II. i. p. 32. fol. Mariti, Germ. p. 410. Hasselquist makes no allusion to it.

[9] Sirac. 24, 14. "Une petite herbette que quelques moines trompeurs ont appellée Rose de Jericho ; " Belon Observat. Par 1588. p. 320. Paulus' Sammlung I. p. 265. II. p. 268. See also Rosenmüller's Bibl. Alterthumsk. IV. i. p. 144.

selves little trouble in respect to their agriculture. The fig trees grow large and require little care ; and their fine fields of grain, as we have seen, are sown and harvested by strangers. A few patches of tobacco and cucumbers seemed to be the amount of their own tillage. We saw no fields of maize or millet (Dhurah esh-Shâmy, Dhurah es-Seify) then growing.[1] As we crossed a tract from which a crop of maize had been taken the preceding year, we observed new shoots sprouting from the roots of the old stalks. On inquiry, we were assured that maize is here a biennial plant, yielding a crop for two successive years from the same roots. The same effect of a warm climate is sometimes found in several other plants commonly known as annuals. Cotton is sometimes planted, and flourishes well ; but there was none at present. We saw patches where indigo had been raised a year or two before ; it was said to live for seven or eight years. Edrisi mentions the culture of it here in the twelfth century.[2]

Another plant which formerly was cultivated in abundance in the plains of Jericho, has also disappeared ; I mean the sugar cane. The historians of the crusades inform us, that the earliest crusaders found large tracts of these canes, growing on the coast of the Mediterranean around Tripolis and as far south as Tyre ; yielding a substance called Zuccara or Zucra (sugar) then unknown in western Europe ; and on whose juice the warriors often refreshed themselves under their many sufferings and privations.[3] According to Jacob de Vitry the canes were also cultivated very extensively on the plains of the Jordan around Jericho ; where the many hermits of that region partly lived upon them, regarding the juice as the wild honey of their predecessor John the Baptist.[4]

From all these circumstances it would appear, that in the centuries before the crusades, the Saracens had introduced the culture and preparation of sugar into Syria and Palestine with success, and upon a large scale. To that age and object are probably to be referred the many large aqueducts around Jericho, all of Saracenic construction,[5] intended to spread an abun-

---

[1] Zea mais, Holcus durra, Forskal Flor. Ægypt. pp. lxxv, 174. Lane's Mod. Egyptians II. p. 26.

[2] Edrisi par Jaubert, I. p. 339.

[3] See in Gesta Dei: Albert. Aq. 5. 37. p. 270 Fulch. Carnot. p. 401. Anonym. p. 595.—William of Tyre speaks of the sugar cane as growing abundantly around Ras el-'Ain near the city of Tyre ; Hist. 13. 3. p. 835.

[4] Speaking of the Jordan Jacob de Vitry says, c. 53, p. 1076 : "Campi autem adjacentes ex calamellorum condensa multitudine stillantes dulcedinem, zuccaræ

procreant abundantiam." Ibid. p. 1075 : "Mellis autem ex calamellis maximam in partibus illis vidimus abundantiam. Sunt autem *calamelli* calami pleni melle, id est, succo dulcissimo, ex quo quasi in torculari compresso, et ad ignem condensato prius quasi mel, postbrec quasi zuccara efficitur." See generally Ritter's essay "Ueber die geographische Verbreitung des Zuckerrohrs," in the Transactions of the Berlin Academy, Hist. Phil. Class, 1839.

[5] Buckingham, who saw the northern aqueduct at the mouth of Wady Nawâ'imeh from a distance, says it is of Roman archi-

ii. 292–294

dance of water over every part of the plain ; as also the sugar mills already mentioned, situated upon the acclivity west of 'Ain es-Sultân. At least all writers and travellers subsequent to the times of the crusades, are silent as to the existence of the sugar cane in this region in their day ; and other circumstances which they relate, are at variance with the supposition of its further general culture, and the later construction of the aqueducts. That is to say, there seems to be no later period, when irrigation and cultivation were in like manner and to such an extent, spread out over the plain.[1]

In that age indeed the plain of Jericho would seem to have recovered in part its ancient renown, and to have been considered as the garden of Palestine. When the crusaders took possession of the country, this region was assigned to the church of the Holy Sepulchre as a portion of its possessions ; and it is one of the reproaches brought against Arnulphus, the third Latin patriarch of Jerusalem, that he gave away this district from the endowment of the church, as a portion to his niece on her marriage with Eustache Grenier in A. D. 1111. At that time, the annual revenue arising from this district is said to have been five thousand pieces of gold ;[2] a proof at least of its lavish fertility. It seems soon to have reverted into the power of the church or of the government ; for in A. D. 1138 we find Jericho with its rich fields assigned to the convent of nuns erected by queen Melisinda at Bethany.[3]

To the same period of renovated cultivation I am inclined to refer the origin of the present castle ; which may not improbably have been erected for the protection of the fields and gardens that covered the plain, and was therefore placed in the midst of them, at a distance from the fountain and the former site of Jericho. It is first mentioned by Willebrand of Oldenborg, A. D. 1211 ; it was already in a ruinous state and inhabited by Saracens.[4] A village would naturally spring up around it ; and such an one is mentioned by Brocardus near the close of the same century, which he regarded as the remains of ancient Jericho, consisting only of eight houses and scarcely deserving the name of a village.[5] Subsequent travellers continue to speak of

---

tecture. This is possible ; but the probability is against it. Travels in Pal. p. 310.

[1] Sugar cane is still cultivated around Beirût, and at other places along the coast ; but no sugar is manufactured from it.

[2] Will. Tyr. 11. 15, " cujus hodie redditus annualis quinque millium dicitur esse aureorum." Probably the gold byzant is here intended, equal to about five Spanish dollars ; see above, p. 397. n. 2.

ii. 294, 295

[3] Will. Tyr. 15. 26. See above p. 432. Quaresmius says, there was a suffragan bishop here ; but the authorities he quotes do not bear him out ; II. p. 755.

[4] Willebr. ab. Oldenb. in L. Allatii Symmikta p. 151, Col. Agr. 1653, " Venimus Hiericho, quod est castellum parvum, destructos habens muros, a Saracenis inhabitatum."

[5] Chap. 7. p. 178.

it only as a small Arab village ; in Pococke's day there were here only two or three houses.[1]   In the fifteenth century apparently, the square tower or castle began to pass among the monks and pilgrims as the house of Zaccheus, an honour which it retains among them to the present day.[2]   The house of Rahab, which they also found, seems to have been nearer the fountain and has since disappeared ; unless indeed it be the foundations and broken arches which are still seen in that vicinity.[3]

Having now nothing further to detain us at the castle and village, and not having yet satisfied ourselves as to the site of ancient Jericho, we determined to make a further search along the base of the mountains near the opening of Wady Kelt. Leaving therefore the castle at 5.50 we proceeded along the Wady, and passed the cemetery of the village on the north bank. The graves are built over in the Muhammedan fashion with hewn stones taken from former structures. Crossing the Wady and still following it up, we came in fifteen minutes from the castle to the first aqueduct, carrying a fine full stream of water from 'Ain es-Sultân across to the southern plain. Ten minutes more brought us to the second aqueduct, now in ruins ; but which once conveyed in like manner a stream, apparently from the fountain of Dûk, to a higher portion of the plain. Both these aqueducts are well and solidly built of hewn stones with pointed arches. The Wady itself, both here and below, was full of the Nûbk or Dôm.

We now turned somewhat more to the left, and crossing the Jerusalem track, came at 6.25 to an immense open shallow reservoir, situated near the base of the western mountain, thirty-five minutes from the castle. It measured 657 feet from east to west by 490 feet from north to south. The direction of the eastern or lower wall is S. 10° W. about six feet high and nine feet thick ; all the walls being built of small stones cemented. This reservoir was probably intended to be filled from the waters of Wady Kelt, in order to irrigate this part of the plain in summer ; and it may perhaps have been connected with the aqueduct mentioned by travellers, half an hour up that valley on the Jerusalem road.[4] On the east at a short distance are foundations, apparently of a large square building or block of buildings ; and on the west also are scattered substructions, extending for ten minutes up the gentle slope. At this point are the

[1] Lud. de Suchem p. 88. Reissb. p. 848. Cotovicus p. 311. Quaresmius II. p. 755. Maundrell, March 29. Pococke II. i. p. 31.
[2] First mentioned as such apparently by Tucher 1479, and F. Fabri 1483, Reissb. pp. 670, 268. Quaresm. II. p. 752.—L. de Suchem, W. de Baldensel, and Sir J. Maundeville in the 14th century, make no such allusion to Zaccheus.
[3] See above, p. 555.
[4] Monro I. p. 134. Buckingham p. 293.—From the reservoir the castle at Riha bore N. 73° E. 'Ain es-Sultân N. 15° E. Kâkôn N. 75° W.

remains of several buildings apparently not very ancient ; there is among them no trace of columns, nor hardly of hewn stones. Indeed, in all the foundations in this vicinity, the stones are unhewn and mostly small.

All these remains lie at the foot of the mountain, just south of the Jerusalem road ; and I do not find that the reservoir has ever been noticed by former travellers.—We now proceeded northwards, and found similar substructions extending all the way to Wady Kelt (about ten minutes), and also for some distance on its northern side. Near the southern bank of this Wady is a hill or mound, like a sepulchral tumulus, which one might suppose to be artificial, were there not so many similar ones scattered over the plain below. On its top are traces of former walls ; and a wall seems to have run from it to the Wady. Directly on the bank of the latter are a few remains of some ancient building, faced over with small stones about four inches square, cemented together diagonally, forming a sort of Mosaic. Among the scattered foundations north of the Wady, we noticed the fragment of a column ; the only trace of an architectural ornament we anywhere saw.—This site is not quite five hours from Jerusalem.[1]

About fifteen minutes from Wady Kelt, or half-way towards 'Ain es-Sultân, is another larger tumulus-like hill ; the southern side of which at the top is excavated, either artificially or from natural causes, somewhat in the form of an amphitheatre. If artificial, one might be disposed to regard it as a theatre of Herod ; but as there are others like it in the vicinity, the appearance is more probably natural. Here begin again the traces of similar foundations, apparently connected with those mentioned yesterday around 'Ain es-Sultân. We came to the fountain in half an hour from Wady Kelt, or in about forty minutes from the reservoir further south. All the foundations here described are of unhewn stones, often small and straggling.[2]

After all our search we were disappointed in finding so few traces of work in hewn stones ; nothing indeed, which of itself could at once be referred to any large or important building ; in short, nothing which looks like the ruins of a city of twenty stadia in circumference,[3] with a large hippodrome and palaces. It is true, that the greater part of the materials of these structures may have been swallowed up in the later convents, the many aqueducts, and the renovations of the modern village ; yet nevertheless, one would naturally expect to find some traces of the solidity and splendour of the ancient city. It seems not

---

[1] Comp. Maundrell, March 29.

[2] These remains and hillocks are mentioned by Buckingham ; but his description is, as usual, very greatly exaggerated ; p. 295.

ii. 297, 298

[3] Epiphanius adv. Hær. lib. II. p. 702.

improbable, that with the exception of the royal edifices, the houses of ancient Jericho were small, and built of loose unhewn stones or other perishable materials.

According to the Bourdeaux pilgrim, A. D. 333, the Jericho of that day was at the descent of the mountains, one and a half Roman miles distant from the fountain ; while he places the more ancient city at the fountain itself.[1] I am inclined to adopt this suggestion ; and to regard the remains around the opening of the Wady Kelt, half an hour south of 'Ain es-Sultân, as marking the site of the Jericho of Herod and the New Testament ; while those around the fountain may have belonged to single edifices scattered among the gardens, and to the walls by which the latter were enclosed. The earliest city of all would naturally have been adjacent to the fountain ; and the site of the later Jericho may have been changed in order to evade the curse.[2] But any distinct traces of the former city are now hardly to be looked for.—The site, both at the fountain and at the opening of Wady Kelt, accords entirely with the account of Josephus, that Jericho was sixty stadia distant from the Jordan.[3]

Jericho is often mentioned ; but its varying fortunes are not very definitely described. It was early rebuilt, notwithstanding the curse ; and became a school of the prophets.[4] After the exile its inhabitants returned ; and it was later fortified by the Syrian Bacchides.[5] Pompey marched from Scythopolis along the Ghôr to Jericho, and thence to Jerusalem ; and Strabo speaks of the castles Thrax and Taurus, in or near Jericho, as having been destroyed by him.[6] Herod the Great in the beginning of his career captured and sacked Jericho ; but afterwards adorned and strengthened it, after he had redeemed its revenues from Cleopatra.[7] He appears to have not unfrequently resided here. He built over the city the fortress Cypros ; and between the castle and the former palace, erected other palaces and called them by the names of his friends.[8] There was also here a hippodrome or circus.[9] The cruel tyrant at length closed his career and life at Jericho. It was here, that, the 'ruling passion being still strong in death,' he summoned around him the nobles of the land in great numbers, and having shut them up within the hippodrome, gave a strict charge to his sister Salome to cause them to

[1] Itin. Hieros. ed. Wesseling pp. 596, 597, " A civitate passus mille quingentos est fons Helisei prophetæ.—Ibi fuit civitas Hiericho cujus muros gyraverunt filii Israel," etc.

[2] Josh. 6, 26.

[3] Joseph. Ant. 5. 1. 4. See above, pp. 557, 558.

[4] Judg. 3, 13. 1 K. 16, 34. 2 K. 2, 4. 5.

[5] Ezra 2, 34. Neh. 3, 2. 1 Macc. 9, 50.

[6] Joseph. Ant. 14. 4. 1. Strabo 16. 2. 40.

[7] Jos. Ant. 15. 4. 1, 2. See above, p 559. n. 8.

[8] Joseph. Ant. 16. 5. 2. B. J. I. 21. 4, 9.

[9] Jos. Ant. 17. 6. 5. B. J. 1. 33. 6.

be put to death the moment he expired ; in order, as he said, that his own decease might be commemorated throughout the land by an appropriate mourning. A worthy consummation of an atrocious life ! This charge, however, his sister was wise enough to leave unfulfilled.[1] The palace at Jericho was afterwards rebuilt with greater splendour by Archelaus.[2]

It was this Jericho which our Lord visited, lodging with Zaccheus and healing the blind man.[3] The city became the head of one of the toparchies ; and was visited by Vespasian just before he left the country, who stationed here the tenth legion in garrison.[4] No further mention of Jericho occurs until the time of Eusebius and Jerome in the fourth century ; who relate, that it was destroyed during the siege of Jerusalem by Titus, on account of the perfidy of the inhabitants, and had been again rebuilt.[5] From A. D. 325 onwards five bishops of Jericho are mentioned ; the last of whom, Gregorius, appears among the signers at the synod of Jerusalem in A. D. 536.[6] About the same time, according to Procopius, the emperor Justinian erected here a Xenodochium apparently for pilgrims ; and also a church consecrated to the Virgin. The monastery of St. John near the Jordan was likewise already in existence.[7] This Xenodochium is again mentioned by Antoninus Martyr, before the Muhammedan conquests.[8]

At the close of the seventh century, Adamnanus already describes the site of Jericho as wholly deserted of human habitations, (except the house of Rahab,) and covered with corn and vines. Between it and the Jordan palm groves still existed ; among which were interspersed fields and the dwellings of Canaanites, probably the nomadic inhabitants of the Ghôr.[9] Of this destruction there is no historical account ; as there is none of that of Petra. It is probably to be ascribed to the ravages of the Muhammedan conquerors. In the next century, St. Willibald speaks only of the fountain ; though near the close of the century, there appears to have been a church in the vicinity, perhaps that of Galgala already mentioned.[10] In A. D. 870,

---

[1] Jos. Ant. 17. 6. 5. ib. 17. 7. 1, 2. B. J. 1. 33. 6–8.

[2] Jos. Ant. 17. 13. 1.

[3] Luke 18, 35 sq. 19, 1–7. Matt. 20, 29 sq. Mark 10, 46 sq.

[4] Joseph. B. J. 3. 3. 5. ib. 4. 8. 1. ib. 5. 2. 3.

[5] Onomast. art. *Jericho.* As however Josephus, the cotemporary, is entirely silent as to any such destruction, the fact must be regarded as doubtful. Still more so the modern assertion, that it was rebuilt by Adrian; of which there seems to be no trace in history. Quaresmius II. p. 755.

[6] Labb. Coll. Concil. Tom. V. p. 283. Le Quien Oriens Chr. III. p. 654 sq. See above p. 383.

[7] Procop. de Ædific. Justiniani, 5. 9.

[8] Itinerar. 13.

[9] " Locus vero totius urbis ab humana desertus habitatione, nullam domum habens commorationis, segetes et vincta recepit," etc. Adamnan. de Loc. Sanct. 2. 13.

[10] See above, p. 547. n. 2. Basil, bishop of Tiberias about the close of the eighth or beginning of the ninth century, is said to have previously administered the

Bernard relates that there were already monasteries in the vicinity.[1]—The renovation of the culture of the plain, and the introduction of the sugar cane, which took place apparently about or not long after this time, have already been sufficiently alluded to ; as also the probable origin and history of the castle and the modern village.[2]

On arriving at the fountain 'Ain es-Sultân, we found our servants and the rest of the party waiting ; they having come thither directly from the castle. All was bright and sparkling around, under the refreshing influence of the limpid waters ; and the numerous birds in the groves below had not yet finished their morning song. The old Sheikh Mustafa here joined us again, and afterwards accompanied us for some distance. We were glad of his presence, as being perfectly acquainted with all the region round about.[3]

Leaving the fountain at ten minutes past 8 o'clock, we came in ten minutes to the sugar mills, on the declivity of the low ridge which runs north from Quarantana. They appear to have been once quite extensive and solidly built, though now long deserted. The race or aqueduct which brought the water to them from above, still remains. Five minutes more brought us to the top of the ridge, where we halted for a short time. The water from the fountain of Dûk in the N. N. W. after being conducted along the base of the high mountain in an artificial channel, is here carried through the low ridge by a somewhat deep cut, and distributed by aqueducts to the plain below as already described, after having supplied several mills now in ruins.[4]

We were now at the foot of the mountain Quarantana ; so called, as the supposed place of our Saviour's forty days' temptation. The Arabs have adopted the name under the form of Jebel Kûrûntûl. The mountain rises precipitously, an almost perpendicular wall of rock, twelve or fifteen hundred feet above the plain, crowned with a chapel on its highest point. The eastern front is full of grots and caverns, where hermits are said once to have dwelt in great numbers. At the present day, some three or four Abyssinians are said to come hither annually and pass the time of Lent upon the mountain, living only upon herbs. There is nothing else remarkable about this naked cliff, to distinguish it from the other similar ones along the Ghôr and

---

concerns of the church of Jericho ; Leont. Vit. St. Steph. Sabaitæ 55, in Acta Sanctor. Jul. Tom. III. p. 554. Le Quien l. c. p. 656.

[1] Bern. Sap. de Loc. Sanct. 16. p. 525. ed. Mabillon.

[2] See pp. 560–563, above.

[3] From the mound over the fountain,

we took the following bearings : Castle at Rihu S. 35° E. Kâkûn S. 42° W. Sugar mills N. 60° W. Aqueduct in Wâdy Nawâ'imeh N. 37° E. Mouth of Wady Sha'ib N. 85° E.

[4] Brocardus mentions mills here in his day, probably driven by the same waters ; c. 7. p. 178.

ii. 301–303

the Dead Sea further south.—The tradition which regards the mountain as the place of our Lord's temptation, as well as the name Quarantana, appear not to be older than the age of the crusades.[1]

North of Quarantana the mountains again retreat, sweeping round in the arc of a circle. They thus leave here a broad recess of higher table land, behind the line of low hills which runs out N. N. E. from the foot of Quarantana, and extends nearly across to the mountains further north. The southern part of this higher recess is broken land, as far as to the fountain of Dûk and Wady Nawâ'imeh, which passes down through it ; but further north it forms a fine plain or basin, extending around a low projecting mountain, called 'Esh el-Ghurûb, and watered by another fountain in its northern part, which gives verdure and beauty to the whole tract. Here too in the northern part of the recess, near the said fountain, is a conical hill, and not far off in the plain are the ruins of a town, which like the fountain, now bears the name of el-'Aujeh. This basin seemed to open out directly upon the plain of the Jordan ; the line of hills not extending across its front.—From the point where we now stood, we could overlook the whole of this inner tract between the mountains and the line of hills.[2]

We here also had our last and perhaps most splendid view of the plain of Jericho. It is certainly one of the richest in the world ; enjoying all the rains like the hill country, and susceptible besides of unlimited irrigation from copious fountains, as the numerous aqueducts testify. Here we could see still another aqueduct far to the left in the lower plain, which once perhaps received the waters of the fountain el-'Aujeh. Indeed water is everywhere abundant ; the climate propitious ; the nature of the soil fertility itself ; nothing in short is wanting but the hand of man to till the ground. But the present race of Jericho are only the personification of indolence, misery, and filth.

The principal Wadys and fountains flowing into the Ghôr on both sides, from the Dead Sea northwards as far as to Beisân, so far as we could learn from Sheikh Mustafa and other Arabs, are the following, beginning from the south. On the *west* side :

---

[1] The first mention of this mountain as the place of temptation, seems to be by Sœwulf about A. D. 1103 ; Peregrinat. p. 268. The name Quarantana I first find in William of Oldenborg in 1211 ; he writes it Quaremnia ; Itin. sub fine. Then in Brocardus c. 7. p. 178.—Jacob de Vitry speaks of many hermits attracted to this region as the scene of John the Baptist's preaching ; but says nothing of our Lord's temptation : "Quam plures vero, in solitu-dinibus Jordanis, ubi beatus Joannes Baptista fugiens hominum turmas—ut vivent Deo, quietis sibi sepulchrum elegerunt ;" c. 53. p. 1075.

[2] From this ridge, Jebel es-Salt bore N. 57° E. Kŭsr el-Yehûd S. 64° E. Northeast corner of Dead Sea S. E. Castle of Riha S. 40° E. Neby Mûsa S. 15° W. Kâkôn S. 27° W. el-'Aujeh, ruin, N. 15° W.

ii. 303, 304

Wady Kelt; 'Ain es-Sultân; 'Ain Dûk; Wady Nawâ'imeh, coming from Deir Duwân; Wady el-Abyad; Wady and fountain el-'Aujeh; 'Ain el-Fusâil; Wady el-Ahmar under Kûrn Sûrtabeh; Wady el-Fâri'a north of the Sûrtabeh with a stream of water; Wady el-Mâlih.[1]—On the *east* side; 'Ain es-Suweimeh; Wady Hesbân; Wady Sha'ib; Wady Zerka with a stream; Ghôr el-Wahâdineh.

In the Ghôr, between Jericho and Beisân, the only ruins we could hear of on the *west* side, were es-Sûmrah and el-'Aujeh. The former is in the plain half an hour north of Wady Nawâ'imeh.[2] On the *east* side, beginning from the sea, we heard of ruins at er-Râmeh, in or near Wady Hesbân; el-Keferein;[3] Nimrîn in Wady Sha'ib; Amatah; and the inhabited village el-Arba'în nearly opposite Beisân.[4]

Josephus informs us, that Herod not only erected castles and palaces in and around Jericho, but built also a city called Phasaëlus in the *Aulon* or Ghôr north of Jericho; by which means a tract formerly desert was rendered fertile and productive.[5] The name seems still to have existed in the middle ages; at least Brocardus speaks of a village Phasellum five leagues north of Gilgal; and this name is still to be recognized in 'Ain el-Fusâil.[6] Archelaus, the son of Herod, built also a village in the plain, named from himself Archelaïs.[7] This is placed in the Peutinger Tables at twenty-four Roman miles north of Jericho towards Beisân; and stood probably in or near the opening of Wady el-Fâri'a above mentioned.[8]

During the whole time we were on the coast of the Dead Sea, on the Jordan, and in or near the plains of Jericho, we were much interested in looking out among the eastern mountains for Mount Nebo, so celebrated in the history of the great Hebrew legislator, where he was permitted to behold with his eyes the land of promise, and then yielded up the ghost.[9] But our search was in vain; for although we passed in such a direction as to see the mountains overagainst Jericho from every quarter, yet there seems to be none standing so out from the rest, or so marked, as to be recognised as the Nebo of the Scriptures.

The Wadys Fâri'a and Mâlih are mentioned by Berggren, who saw them higher up in the western hills; the former has a mill stream, the latter a brackish fountain. Reisen, etc. II. p. 267.

[2] It was visited by Rev. E. Smith, in April 1844. Ms. Journal.

[3] Râmeh and el-Keferein are mentioned by Burckhardt; p. 391.

[4] For el-Arba'in and Amatah, see Burckhardt pp. 345, 346. For Amatah (Amathus) see also Reland Palæst. p. 559. Comp.

the similar lists given by Burckhardt of Wadys and places in the Ghôr; p. 344.

[5] Joseph. Ant. 16. 5. 2. ib. 17. 11. 5. ib. 18. 2. 2. B. J. 1. 21. 9. Reland Palæst. p. 953.

[6] Brocardus c. 7. p. 178.

[7] Jos. Ant. 17. 13. 1. ib. 18. 2. 2. Reland Palæst. p. 576; comp. p. 421, Plate.

[8] See more on these places in Vol. III. Sec. VII, under May 11th, 1852.

[9] Deut. 32, 48 sq. 34, 1 sq.

There is no peak or point perceptibly higher than the rest ; but all is apparently one level line of summit without peaks or gaps. The highest point in all the eastern mountains, is Jebel el-Jil'âd or es-Salt, near the city of that name, rising about three thousand feet above the Ghôr ;[1] but this is much too far north to be Mount Nebo, to which Moses ascended from the plains of Moab overagainst Jericho.   Possibly on travelling into these mountains, some isolated point or summit might be found answering to the position and character of Nebo.   Indeed, Seetzen, Burckhardt, and also Irby and Mangles, have all found Mount Nebo in Jebel 'Attârûs, a high mountain which runs southwestward from the bank of the Zerka Ma'in.[2]   This, however, as the latter travellers remark, is " far from opposite Jericho ;" and would be almost as distant, and as little convenient to the plains of Moab as is Jebel es-Salt.   It may perhaps be sufficient to assume, that Moses merely went up from these plains to some high part of the adjacent mountains ; from which he would everywhere have an extensive view over the Jordan valley and the mountainous tract of Judah and Ephraim *towards* the western sea. The Mediterranean itself could never well be visible from any point east of the Jordan.[3]

Our former inquiries respecting the site of Ai, in the vicinity of Deir Duwân, had been so unsatisfactory, that we had now determined to take the route from Jericho to the latter place and so to Bethel, in order further to investigate this and other points, and to trace the ancient road between these cities, so often travelled by kings and prophets of old.[4]   Three roads now lead from Jericho to Deir Duwân.   The first and shortest passes up the face of the cliffs between Quarantana and Wady Kelt, and then follows a direct course over a tract of high shelving table land.   Another goes to Dûk, and crossing the Nawâ'imeh, ascends the mountain on the north leading strictly to Taiyibeh ; but near Rûmmôn a branch goes off and recrosses the valley to Deir Duwân.   The third leaves the preceding road just beyond Dûk, and climbing the mountain on the south side of the Nawâ'imeh, falls into the first road some distance higher up.   Of

[1] See more on this mountain above, p. 527. n. 2.

[2] Seetzen in Zach's Monatl. Corr. XVIII. p. 431.   Reisen II. p. 342.   Burckhardt, p. 370.   Irby and Mangles' Travels, p. 464. [143.]—On the north end of Jebel Attârûs, high above the southern bank of the Zerka Ma'in, Seetzen heard of a ruined fortress now called *Mkaur*; but he did not himself visit it; Reisen II. p. 330. This he regards as the ancient *Machærus*, a fortress of Herod in the Arabian mountains, where according to Josephus (Ant. ii. 306, 307

18. 5. 2), John the Baptist was beheaded. See the description in Josephus, B. J. 7. 6. 1 sq.   Comp. Ritter Erdk. XV. i. p. 577 sq.   But neither Burckhardt nor Irby and Mangles appear to have heard the name.

[3] In our list of the Belka is found the name *Neba*, which may possibly represent the ancient Nebo.   It occurs next to Mâdeba, apparently some distance north of Jebel 'Attârûs.

[4] 1 Sam. 13, 15.   2 K. 2, 3. 4. 23.

these routes the first is the most direct, easiest, and without doubt the ancient road ; but we chose to take the third in order to visit the fountain of Dûk and obtain a more extensive knowledge of the country.

Leaving the height above the sugar mills at 8.40, we passed along the water-course near the base of Quarantana into the recess. We came in a few minutes to the encampment of Sheikh Mustafa, who had accompanied us from the fountain. It consisted of thirty or forty mean tents arranged in a square, most of them open, the sides being thrown up. These people are much darker than the Arabs in general ; and seem to constitute a sort of gypsies among them. Here a large bowl of *lebben* (soured milk) was already prepared for our breakfast ; but as we were neither hungry nor thirsty, we left it to our attendants, by whom it was greedily devoured. We ourselves passed on.

This old Sheikh and his tribe, as already mentioned, are a sort of Derwishes or sacred characters, respected by the Arabs and peasants, and on this account the safest guides for travellers. His full name was Mustafa Abu Yamîn, and his encampment are called the Arabs of Abu Yamîn. Those of another encampment are in like manner called from their Sheikh the Arabs of Abu Nuseir. These two encampments together make out the tribe Ehteim.

Besides the Ehteim, who have gardens at Jericho near the fountain, the following tribes of Arabs also descend more or less into the Ghôr, beginning from the south. On the *west* side : the Ka'âbineh, the Rashâideh, the Ta'âmirah, the Mas'ûdy, the 'Abbâd, the Amîr, the 'Abbâdîn, and the Mushâlikhah. On the *east* side : the 'Adwân, Ibn Ghûnûm, Beni Hasan, the Bahârât, the 'Ajârimeh, Beni Sûkhr, and Beni Hamîdeh.

The hospitable old man sent one of his men to guide us over the broken ground to the fountain of Dûk. At 9 o'clock we came upon Wady Nawâ'imeh, which, after issuing from the mountains just above Dûk, runs here in a southeasterly course, and breaking through the line of lower hills, pursues the same direction to the Jordan. It is the continuation of the Wady el-Mûtyâh between Deir Duwân and Rûmmôn. Water was here flowing in it. We followed it up ; and at 9½ o'clock came to the large and beautiful fountain or rather fountains of Dûk, on the southwestern brink of the same Wady. Here are two very copious sources, besides other smaller ones, all of fine limpid water, like that of 'Ain es-Sultân. The waters naturally all flow down the Wady Nawâ'imeh ; but those of the highest and largest fountain, which springs up at the foot of a large Dôm tree, are carried off by the artificial channel along the base of the mountain, for nearly an hour, to the vicinity of the sugar

ii. 307-309

mills, and thence distributed to the plain. This stream at first is six or eight feet wide and a foot and a half deep. The remaining waters still follow their natural course down the valley ; where they were formerly taken up by the aqueduct at its entrance upon the plain.[1]

Above the fountain are traces of ancient substructions, though not very distinct. Here or in the vicinity of this fountain of Dûk, we are doubtless to look for the site of the ancient castle of Doch near Jericho, in which Simon Maccabæus was treacherously murdered by his son-in-law Ptolemy.[2]

Leaving 'Ain Dûk at 9.35, we passed still along the base of the mountain, overlooking on our right the higher plain or basin within the recess, and having in view the tract of el-'Aujeh, and the smaller Wadys, which descend from the mountains in that part. The plain was covered with verdure, fed by the waters of the fountain of Aujeh. In fifteen minutes we came to the opening of Wady Nawâ'imeh, as it issues a deep ravine from the cliffs ; and immediately began to climb the angle of the mountain on its southern side. The Taiyibeh road crosses the Wady and goes up the mountain further north. The ascent is steep, rugged, and difficult, consisting of two parts. We reached the top of the first and steepest in ten minutes ; and at 10.20 came out upon the head of the pass or summit of the cliff. Here we had our last view back upon the valley of the Jordan.[3]

The way now became in general less steep, though we still had to climb occasionally sharp ascents and pass along the brow of fearful precipices. On our right the Wady Nawâ'imeh occupied the bottom of a broad sunken tract, composed of chalky mountains rising on each side, presenting only the aspect of a terrific desert. All around we could see nought but waves of naked desolate pyramidal and conical mountains, with deep Wadys between, marked only by the narrow tracks of goats, which climb along their sides to crop the few herbs thinly sprinkled over them. It was one of the most truly desert spots we had yet visited. The path led us along the tops and sides of declivities, as nearly perpendicular as they could be without being composed of solid rock. Our general course was S. E. by S. At 11 o'clock we came out upon one of the highest points ;

---

[1] From Dûk, el-'Aujeh bore N. 18° W. Kûrn Sûrtabeh, N. 11° E. Jebel es-Salt N. 60° E.

[2] Δώκ, 1 Macc. 16, 14. 15. Josephus relates the same circumstances ; but moulding the name more after the Greek form, writes it Δαγών, Antiq. 13. 8. 1. B. J. 1. 2. 3.—Dûk is mentioned as a fortress of the knights Templars between Jericho and Bethel, and also by Brocardus ; who, however, places it too far north. Münter Statutenbuch des Ord. des Tempelh. I. p. 419. Brocardus, c. 7. p. 178.

[3] We took here the following bearings : Castle of Jericho, S. 89° E. Mouth of Wady Nawâ'imeh and aqueduct, S. 73° E. Mouth of Wady Sha'ib S. 82° E. Dûk, below, E. Kûrn Sûrtabeh, N. 17° E. el-'Aujeh, in the recess, N. 8° W.

ii. 309 310

where we stopped for a time to breathe, and to survey the surrounding desolation. Here we could distinguish several places
already known to us, as Rŭmmôn, Taiyibeh, and the Mount of
Olives ; showing that we were approaching a region of more
promise.[1]

We now, after fifteen minutes, descended slightly on a course
W. S. W. The land became less broken, a tract of shelving
table land. As we advanced, the scattered herbs of the desert
were more and more interspersed with dried grass ; until at a
quarter past noon we reached a burying place of the Bedawîn
in this lone spot, where the country became more open and even.
Here we struck the southern road from Jericho to Deir Duwân,
coming up from the left ; it having passed, so far as we could
see, through a much more level tract than ours, along the water-
shed between the branches of Wady Nawâ'imeh and those
which go to form Wady Kelt. Our course was now W. by N.
We soon came upon small ploughed patches here and there, belonging probably to the Bedawîn. They had been sown with
wheat ; but the grain, which was now nearly ripe, was thin and
scarcely more than six inches high. The surface became gradually more and more covered with limestone rocks, with the usual
red soil among them ; while vegetation and pasturage increased.

In one place we saw a number of people at some distance
before us ; who on perceiving us became alarmed and ran off in
all haste. Our Arabs called after them to reassure them, and
we afterwards overtook them ; they proved to be several men
and four women from Deir Duwân.

At five minutes past one, we noticed a cistern by the way
side as we ascended a hill ; and two others occurred afterwards ;
all hewn in the rock, and showing this to be an ancient and important route between Gilgal and Bethel. At half past one the
grass and vegetation began to assume a slight appearance of
green ; and the fields of the Fellâhîn were more numerous. At
2 o'clock we got sight of Deir Duwân, bearing northwest. On
our right at 2.35 were the ruins of an ordinary village, called Abu
Sŭbbâh. Shortly before coming to Deir Duwân we sent on our
servants and luggage to that place, which they reached at 3.20 ;
while we turned off to the left to visit the site with ruins on the
south of the village, which had been pointed out to us on our
former visit.[2]

The place is on a low hill or point projecting towards the
south between two shallow Wadys. In the eastern valley are

---

[1] The bearings from this high point were
as follows : Taiyibeh, N. W. Rŭmmôn,
N. 51° W. Tell beyond Deir Duwân, N.
65° W. Mount of Olives, S. 61° W. Abu

Dîs, S. 53° W. Khân Hŭdbrŭr, S. 42°
W. (See under Taiyibeh, p. 445. n. 3.)
Neby Mûsa, S. 5° E.

[2] See above, p. 442.

some excavated tombs. The western valley is the broadest; and
the rocks on that side are precipitous for a few feet. Here are
three reservoirs dug mostly out of the rock, and bearing marks
of antiquity. They measured as follows:

	Length.	Breadth.	Depth.
Upper or Northern	110 feet	32 feet	6 feet
Middle	37	26	12
Lower	88	22	15

On the hill itself are ruins, or foundations of large hewn stones,
in no great number. Many stones have probably been taken
away to build the modern village. While my companions were
measuring the reservoirs, I busied myself in searching for the
small tesseræ of Mosaic work, such as are often found around
Jerusalem ; and picked up a handful within the space of a few
feet. All these circumstances indicate an ancient place of some
importance, but we were not yet satisfied that it was Ai.

We passed through Deir Duwân without stopping, leaving it
at 3.40. The direction of Bethel is about N. W. by W., and the
road leads up from the basin by a hollow way, between a conical
hill or Tell on the right, and another broader hill on the left.
Twenty minutes brought us to the summit of the Tell, from
which we looked directly down into the deep narrow bed of Wady
el-Mûtyâh on the north, where a few excavated sepulchres were
visible. The village we had left bore S. 46° E. and Taiyibeh N.
45° E. We had expected to find here some remains of an ancient
site ; but there was nothing save a cistern, and immense heaps of
unwrought stones, merely thrown together in order to clear the
ground for planting olive trees. The position would answer well
to that of Ai ; and had there been traces of ruins, I should
not hesitate so to regard it. I also went out upon the more
southern hill, but with no better success ; it was wholly covered
with rocks in their natural state.

Ai is chiefly celebrated in Scripture history for its capture and
destruction by Joshua.[1] It lay on the east of Bethel ; Abraham
on his arrival in Palestine pitched his tent between the two
cities ;[2] and they were not so far distant from each other, but
that the men of Bethel mingled in the pursuit of the Israelites,
as they feigned to fly before the king of Ai, and thus both cities
were left defenceless.[3] Yet they were not so near but that
Joshua could place an ambush on the west (or southwest) of Ai,
without its being observed by the men of Bethel ; while he himself remained behind a valley on the north of Ai.[4] At a later

[1] Josh. 7, 2-5. 8, 1-29.   [2] Josh. 8, 17.
[2] Gen. 12, 8. 13, 3.   [4] Josh. 8, 4. 12. Verses 11. 13.
ii. 312, 313

period Ai was again rebuilt, and is mentioned by Isaiah and also after the exile.[1] In the days of Eusebius and Jerome, its site and scanty ruins were still pointed out, not far distant from Bethel towards the east.[2]

After all our search, we could come to no other result, than to assign as the probable site of Ai the place with ruins just south of Deir Duwân. This is an hour distant from Bethel ; having near by on the north the deep Wady el-Mûtyâh ; and towards the southwest other smaller Wadys, in which the ambuscade of the Israelites might easily have been concealed.

After remaining for twenty minutes on and around the Tell, we proceeded across the high and beautiful plain, on which Abraham of old must have pitched his tent. The path led us by the ruins of Burj Beitin. We reached Bethel at 5 o'clock ; and encamped for the night on the green grass, within the area of the ancient reservoir, where we had formerly breakfasted.

Tuesday, May 15th. The Arabs encamped at Bethel brought us this morning a young gazelle, which we purchased, intending it as a present for our friend Mr Lanneau. Our servants carried the little animal in their arms, or on the saddle before them, all the way to Jerusalem ; but it seemed to have been in some way injured, and lived only a few days.

We left Bethel at 5.50, and reached the fountain southwest of el-Birch in just an hour, passing this time on the west of the village, without entering it. These waters, as already remarked, flow off in a valley towards the east. We now took the Jerusalem road ; and leaving the fountain at 7 o'clock passed in five minutes the low water-shed, which brought us to the beginning of another Wady running south ; one of the minor heads of the great Wady Beit Hanîna. The path follows down this Wady, along a sort of hollow way, having on the west an isolated hill of considerable height. My companion ascended this hill in passing ; here are merely the foundations apparently of a tower, with heaps of unwrought stones, and fragments of pottery strowed about. Towards the northwest not far off, are a few foundations called Suweikeh ; but we could learn no name for the hill itself. Beyond the hill, in the plain near its southern base, we came at 7.40 to larger ruins containing some arches ; above them, on the side of the hill, are two ancient reservoirs, perhaps one hundred feet in length by forty feet in breadth. These ruins are called 'Atâra, a name which answers to the Hebrew Ataroth. Two places of this name are mentioned in Scripture, on the border between Benjamin and Ephraim ;[3] but the site in question cannot well be

---

[1] Is. 10, 28. Ezra 2, 28. Neh. 7, 32. 11, 31.   [2] Onomast. art. *Agai.*
[3] Josh. 16, 5. 7. 18, 13.

regarded as either of these, since it lies too far within the territory of Benjamin.[1]

We soon turned off from the Jerusalem road, passing obliquely through the fields towards er-Râm, which we reached at 8.25. It lies upon a high hill about ten minutes east of the road in a direct line. The tract upon the north, as well as upon the west and south, declines towards Wady Beit Hanîna ; here indeed begins one of the main heads of that great valley. Râm is a miserable village, with few houses, and these now in summer mostly deserted. There are here large squared stones, and also columns scattered about in the fields, indicating an ancient place of some importance. A small mosk with columns seems once to have been a church. The situation of er-Râm is very conspicuous and commands a wide prospect.[2]

I have already spoken of er-Râm, as without doubt marking the site of the ancient Ramah of Benjamin.[3] Both the name and position are here decisive. Ramah lay near Gibeah, six Roman miles from Jerusalem towards Bethel.[4] The present er-Râm is a short hour north from Gibeah, and two hours north of Jerusalem. Ramah was again inhabited after the exile ; and in the days of Jerome was a small village.[5] In the thirteenth century Brocardus speaks of it correctly as a village south of el-Bîreh, situated on a hill east of the road leading to Jerusalem.[6] But notwithstanding this distinct notice, the place seems to have been again forgotten in monastic tradition for centuries ; and of course is not mentioned by travellers. Cotovicus saw the spot, but held it to be Gibeah of Saul.[7] Quaresmius speaks only of Ramah as at Neby Samwîl ; and hence probably even the sharp-sighted Maundrell failed to notice er-Râm, and saw Ramah only at the prophet's tomb.[8] Indeed, I have been able to find no

[1] Eusebius and Jerome speak of two Ataroths in their day in the tribe of Benjamin, not far from Jerusalem ; Onomast. art. *Ataroth* 'Αταρώθ. To one of these this place doubtless corresponds.—From this spot the village of Kulûndia bore S. 38° W. Neby Samwîl S. 43° W. Also er-Râm about S. 15° E. distant three quarters of an hour.

[2] The following among other bearings, were taken at er-Râm : Taiyibeh N. 36° E. Mûkhmâs N. 70° E. Deir Duwân, N. 38° E. 'Anâta S. 24° E. Tuleil el-Fûl, S. 10° W. Neby Samwîl, S. 75° W. el-Jîb, W. Kefr 'Akab, ruins about 45 minutes distant, N. 5° W. Erha, ruins, S. 12° E. These last ruins are just across a small Wady running down towards Anathoth.

[3] See above, pp. 437, 458.

[4] Judg. 19, 13. Euseb. et Hieron.

ii. 315, 316

Onom. art. *Rama*. Hieron. Comm. in Hos. v. 8, "Rama, quæ est juxta Gabaa in septimo lapide a Jerosolymis sita." Josephus places it at 40 stadia from Jerusalem. Antiq. 8. 12. 3.

[5] Ezra 2, 26. Neh. 7, 30. Hieron. Comm. in Zephan. 1, 15. 16, "Rama et Bethoron et reliquæ urbes nobiles a Salomone constructæ parvi viculi demonstrantur."

[6] Brocardus, c. 7. p. 178. Breydenbach copies Brocardus, Reissb. p. 128. Sir John Maundeville, (p. 105,) and William de Baldensel place Ramah somewhere north of Shiloh ; p. 353. ed. Basnage.

[7] Itin. p. 331. Fürer von Haimendorf speaks of it in A. D. 1566, and says it was called Ramula ; p. 202. Nurnb. 1646.

[8] Quaresm. II. p. 727. Doubdan, p. 489. Maundrell, Mar. 25th.

further mention of er-Râm until the present century, and that only in one or two travellers.[1]

Jeba', half an hour east of er-Râm, is not visible from it, on account of broad intervening swells of ground. We went out upon these hills half-way to Jeba', where we had a full view of both these villages, and examined the ground carefully in all directions, to see whether there might not be some ancient site between the two. But our search was fruitless; no trace of ruins or of substructions is anywhere to be seen; the surface of the ground being mostly covered with large rocks in their natural position.

We left er-Râm at 10 o'clock, and came in ten minutes to the Jerusalem road, at a place called Khūrâib er-Râm, "Ruins of er-Râm," on the west of the path, bearing from that place S. 55° W. Here are some eight or ten ruined arches in a line parallel to the road: and the foundations of as many more, parallel to these. They may probably have belonged to a large Khân for travellers and caravans. There are also several cisterns. Here we stopped nearly ten minutes, and then proceeded along the great road. The waters of this tract all run towards Wady Beit Hanina. At 10¾ o'clock, near the foot of the ascent leading to the table land north of Scopus, we passed the junction of the camel road from Yâfa to Jerusalem, coming by el-Jîb; and not far beyond, we came upon ancient substructions, large unhewn stones in low massive walls.

We now left the road again, in order to pass over the high Tell on the left, called Tuleil el-Fûl, "Hill of Beans," six or eight minutes from the path, with a large heap of stones upon it. We reached the top at 11 o'clock. There seems to have been here originally a square tower, fifty-six feet by forty-eight, built of large unhewn stones and apparently ancient; this has been thrown down; and the stones and rubbish falling outside, have assumed the form of a large pyramidal mound. No trace of other foundations is to be seen. The spot is sightly and commands a very extensive view of the country in all directions, especially towards the east; in this respect it is second only to Neby Samwil.[2]

It seemed to us at the time, as if this sightly spot must have been connected with some ancient place; but it was not until 1843, that I was able to identify it with the ancient *Gibeah of Saul*. In that year, Mr Gross, a young German theologian,

[1] First apparently in Turner's Tour, II. p. 160. Neither Richardson, nor Scholz, nor Monro, nor Schubert, mention the name, although they passed on this route.

[2] From the Tell, er-Râm bore N. 10° E. Neby Samwil, N. 70° W. Jerusalem, S. 10° W.

since deceased, took the ground, that Gibeah must have lain south of Ramah ; and he conjectured, that it might have been at Tuleil el-Fûl.[1] But he overlooked the passage of Josephus, which affords historical demonstration to the correctness of the hypothesis.

Josephus relates, that Titus, advancing to the siege of Jerusalem, halted for a night at Gophna ; and then, after another day's march, encamped at a place called the Vale of Thorns, near by a certain village named Gabath-Saul, which signifies ' Hill of Saul,' distant from Jerusalem about thirty stadia. During the night a legion coming from Emmaus (Nicopolis) joined the main army ; and the next morning Titus moved forward and encamped at Scopus.[2] In this account, the day's march from Gophna, the thirty stadia from Jerusalem, and the arrival of a legion coming from Nicopolis, all go to fix the encampment of Titus at or near the junction of the camel road from Yâfa, as above mentioned. The conclusion, then, is irresistible, that the Hill of Saul, or Gibeah, was the lofty and isolated Tuleil el-Fûl. Not improbably the limits of the city extended down so as to include the walls and substructions in the road, as above mentioned.

The same conclusion is confirmed by a passage of Jerome. This father, in narrating the journey of Paula, describes her as ascending to Jerusalem by way of the lower and upper Bethhoron ; on her right she sees Ajalon and Gibeon ; she stops a little at Gabaa (Gibeah), then levelled to the ground, calling to mind its ancient crime and the concubine cut in pieces ; and then leaving the mausoleum of Helena on her left, she enters Jerusalem.[3] Now this very road is the present great camel road from Yâfa to Jerusalem, and falls into the great northern road, as we have seen, just north of Tuleil el-Fûl. Gibeah therefore must have lain upon this road somewhere between Gibeon and Jerusalem.

With all this accords likewise the narrative of the Levite and his concubine in the book of Judges. The Levite declined to spend the night in Jebus (Jerusalem) ; but passed on in order to lodge at Gibeah or Ramah. The sun went down upon them near Gibeah ; and they turned aside to lodge in that city.[4] This

---

[1] Theol. Stud. u. Kritiken, 1843, p. 1082. Biblioth. Sac. 1844, p. 598.

[2] Jos. B. J. 5. 2. 1, πρός τινι κώμη Γαβαθσαούλη καλουμένη· σημαίνει δὲ τοῦτο λόφον Σαούλου, διέχοντα ἀπὸ τῶν Ἱεροσολύμων ὅσον ἀπὸ τριάκοντα σταδίων.—In another passage (Ant. 5. 2. 8) Josephus has been supposed to fix the distance from Jerusalem to Gibeah at twenty stadia. But he is there speaking only of the Le-

vite's purpose to go on some twenty stadia beyond Jerusalem.

[3] " Inde proficiscens ascendit Bethoron inferiorem et superiorem ;—ad dexteram aspiciens Ajalon et Gabaon. In Gabaa urbe usque ad solum diruta, paulum substitit, recordata peccati ejus, et concubinae in frustra divisae," etc. Hieron. Epitaph. Paulae, Opp. ed. Martianay, IV. ii. 673.

[4] Judg. 19, 10-15.

shows that Gibeah was south of Ramah; and fixes it, in concurrence with Josephus, at Tuleil el-Fûl.[1]

Gibeah is often mentioned in Scripture. Here was the seat of that abominable transaction, which led in its consequences to the almost total destruction of the tribe of Benjamin.[2] Saul was born here, and continued to make Gibeah his residence after he became king.[3] It was in Gibeah that the Gibeonites hanged up the seven descendants of Saul; and this was followed by the touching maternal tenderness of Rizpah, who "took sackcloth and spread it for her upon the rock, from the beginning of harvest until water dropped upon them out of heaven, and suffered neither the birds of the air to rest upon them by day, nor the beasts of the field by night."[4] Jerome mentions Gibeah as being in his day level with the ground;[5] and since that time it appears to have remained unvisited by travellers. Benjamin of Tudela indeed mentions it, and Brocardus speaks of it as *Gabaa Saulis;* but neither of them knew its exact position.[6]

We remained here half an hour; and then at half past 11 o'clock descended, and regaining the road, proceeded across the high level tract. In fifteen minutes we were opposite Sha'fât, a small village five minutes on the right, where the remains of an old wall are visible; and at five minutes past noon, we came upon the brow of Scopus, overlooking the valley of Jehoshaphat and Jerusalem beyond. The view of the city from this spot is celebrated; here Titus first beheld it and admired the magnificence of its temple.[7] The distance of this spot from the Damascus gate is about twenty or twenty-five minutes.

We now turned to the left along the ridge, having continually fine views of the city, and searching everywhere for ruins which might be regarded as the site of Nob. We came at 12.20 to the 'Anâta road. Our search was without fruit; and afterwards in returning from Bethany, I traversed the ridge from the church of the Ascension northwards to the same spot, with the like ill success.[8] We now turned directly towards Jerusalem; and as we descended the mount of Olives, the Khatib sent off one of his men with the musket of the tribe along the side of the hill, not caring to have it seen within the city. We reached St. Stephen's gate at 12.40; having lost about twenty minutes by

---

[1] See generally, Biblioth. Sac. 1844, pp. 598–602. See also under Jeba' (Geba) above, p. 441. n. 1.
[2] Judg. 19, 14 sq.
[3] 1 Sam. 10, 26. 11, 4. 15, 34. 23, 19. 26, 1.
[4] 2 Sam. 21, 6–10.

[5] See p. 578. n. 3.
[6] Benj. of Tud. p. 78. Brocardus, c. 7. p. 178. Cotovicus mistook er-Râm for Gibeah; Itin. p. 331.
[7] See above, Vol. I. p. 276.
[8] See more on Nob above, p. 464.

ii. 317 318

the *detour*. Our friends we were happy to find all well; although the city was still filled with alarm.

Thus, through the kind providence of God, we had been preserved during a most interesting journey, through what has ever been considered the worst and most dangerous part of all Palestine, —as the retreat of robbers and outlaws ever since the most ancient times. Yet under the care of our Sheikh of the Ta'âmirah and his four men, we had not suffered the slightest let or hindrance; nor felt the slightest degree of insecurity, more than in Jerusalem itself. The Khatîb had fulfilled his pledge, and had given us entire satisfaction. We were able to dismiss him likewise satisfied; and parted from him not without feelings of respect, and also of regret, at the idea of meeting him no more.[1]

With the two Mukâriyeh (drivers, muleteers) we had less reason to be satisfied. They were lazy and careless; as well as utterly indifferent to the welfare and accommodation of those, whom they had undertaken to serve. We of course had nothing to do with their subsistence; yet they took nothing with them, and contrived to spunge their meals out of us and our guides. Knowing the stern law of Bedawîn hospitality, that whoever is present at a meal must be invited to partake, whether there be little or much, they were impudent enough always to put themselves in the way of the guides, and thus deprive them of a part of their slender pittance. Indeed, the Mukâriyeh of Jerusalem are notorious for their insolence and bad faith; and we determined, so far as possible, to have nothing more to do with them.

[1] The American missionaries afterwards kept up an acquaintance with Sheikh Muhammed, and visited his people. He too showed himself faithful, and also grateful for various slight services, which they were able to do in his behalf.

ii. 318, 319

NOTES.

NOTE I.—Page 15.

DIOCLETIAN'S COLUMN. See Wilkinson's Thebes and Egypt, Lond. 1835, p. 289; 1843, I. p. 151. Handbook for Egypt, p. 92. " The pillar of Diocletian has an inscription at its base, and was probably once surmounted by an equestrian statue; as four cramps are still visible on its summit.—The length of the shaft is seventy-three feet [a solid block of granite]; the total height ninety-eight feet nine inches; the circumference twenty-seven feet eight inches; and the diameter of the top of the capital sixteen feet six inches. The shaft is elegant and of good style; but the capital and pedestal are of inferior workmanship, and have the appearance of being of a different period. Indeed it is probable that the shaft was of a Greek epoch; and that the unfinished capital and pedestal were added to it, at the time of its erection in honour of Diocletian."—The inscription, as copied by Wilkinson, " by means of a ladder and chalking out the letters," is as follows; the last word being doubtful:

TON TIMIΩTATON AΥTOKPATOPA
TON ΠOΛIOΥXON AΛEΞANΔPEIAC
ΔIOKΛHTIANON TON ANIKHTON
ΠOΥBΛIOC EΠAPXOC AIΓΥΠTOΥ
EΠAΓAΘΩ ?

NOTE II.—Page 19.

IRRIGATION. On the different machines for raising water in Egypt, see Niebuhr's Reisebeschr. I. p. 148, and Tab. XV. For the *Shadûf*, see Lane's Mod. Egyptians, II. p. 24.—The water-wheel, *Sakieh*, is usually turned by an ox, and raises the water by means of jars fastened to a circular or endless rope, which hangs over the wheel. The *Shadûf* has a toilsome occupation. His instrument is exactly the well-sweep of New England in miniature, supported by a cross-piece resting on two upright posts of wood or mud. His bucket is of leather or wicker work. Two of these instruments are usually fixed side by side, and the men keep time at their work, raising the water five or six feet. Where the banks are higher, two, three, and even four couples are thus employed, one above another.

There is nothing now in Egypt which illustrates the ancient practice of " watering with the foot," alluded to in Deut. 11, 10. This is sometimes referred to the mode of distributing water when already raised, among the channels of a field, by making or breaking down with the foot the small ridges which regulate its flow. But this explanation seems not to reach the point; for the passage in question evidently refers to the mode of *supplying* water, not of distributing it. Possibly in more ancient times the water-wheel may have been smaller, and turned not by oxen, but by men pressing upon it with the foot, in the same way that water is still often drawn from wells in Palestine, as we afterwards saw. Niebuhr describes one such machine in Cairo, where it was called *Sâkieh tedâr bir-rijl*, "a watering machine that turns by the foot," a view of which he also subjoins. The labourer sits on a level with the axis of the wheel or reel, and turns it by drawing the upper part towards him with his hands, pushing the rounds of the under part at the same time with his feet one after another. In Palestine the wheel or reel is more rude; and a single rope is used, which is wound up around it by the same process.

Note III.—Page 20.

Thebes. The Sea. Nahum 3, 8. The "sea" referred to in this passage is the river Nile, which to the present day in Egypt is named *el-Bahr*, "the sea," as its most common appellation. Our Egyptian servant, who spoke English, always called it "the sea." Comp. Wilkinson's Mod. Egypt, II. p. 164.—In Egypt the word *el-Bahr*, implying the Mediterranean sea, is also commonly used for North; a north wind is called "sea-wind," as coming from the Mediterranean. This shows the fallacy of an argument sometimes used to prove, that the Hebrew was the original language of Palestine, viz. that the word *sea* (ים) is also the Hebrew term for West. If for this reason the Hebrew language were original in Palestine, then also the Arabic must have been so in Egypt.—In like manner in Syria the word *Kibleh*, referring to Mecca, is now universally employed for South.

Note IV.—Page 22.

Theban Tombs. Among the Tombs of the Kings, that marked by Wilkinson as No. 2, has become a sort of album for travellers. The name of Sheikh Ibrahim (Burckhardt) appears twice in 1813, both on his way upward to Dongola, and on his return: *Ibrahim—post reditum suum à limitibus regni Dongolæ.* The names of Belzoni, Irby and Mangles, Rüppell, and many other travellers, are also there. In a corner adjacent—an American corner—we added our names to those of several of our countrymen; some of whom have already found their graves in distant lands.

All these tombs are entirely exposed to the depredations of the Arabs and of travellers; and are every year becoming more and more defaced. The tomb marked by Wilkinson as No. 35, near the foot of the hill Sheikh Abd el-Kûrneh, which he justly regards as "by far the most curious of all the tombs in Thebes," was occupied at the time of our visit by an Arab family with their cattle. The walls were already black with smoke, and many of the paintings destroyed. See Wilkinson's Mod. Egypt, II. p. 234. Handbook for Egypt, p. 383.

Note V.—Page 24.

CAIRO. Lane's Manners and Customs of the Modern Egyptians, 2 vols. Lond. 1836 and later.—Through our friend, the Rev. Mr Lieder, we made the acquaintance of the bookseller so amusingly described by Mr Lane in his preface. He visited us several times at our rooms, bringing with him books which had been inquired for. In this way we were able, my companion especially, to purchase several valuable Arabic works.

The magician who has become so famous in Europe through Mr Lane, (Vol. I. p. 347,) we did not see. But we learned enough on the subject to persuade us, that the whole matter depends on a certain *proneness to believe* on the part of the spectator, and a series of leading questions on the part of the operator. We were further informed on good authority, that he exhibits his art only before Franks; and that the native Egyptians know little or nothing of the matter.

Note VI.—Page 30.

EGYPT. For the traveller in Egypt, the two works so often referred to in the text, are indispensable, viz. WILKINSON's *Topography of Thebes and General View of Egypt*, Lond. 1835; reprinted and enlarged in two volumes, *Modern Egypt and Thebes*, Lond. 1843; and condensed in his *Handbook for Egypt*, Lond. 1847, etc. Also LANE's *Account of the Manners and Customs of the Modern Egyptians*, 2 Vols. Lond. 1836, and later editions. If the traveller wish to know how the Egyptians of old lived, he may best add WILKINSON's *Account of the Manners and Customs of the Ancient Egyptians*, 5 Vols. Lond. 1837. If further he be desirous of comparing the contradictory accounts and theories of former travellers, he may take along the volumes of the *Modern Traveller* in Egypt.

The best works on the present condition and statistics of Egypt, are the following: MENGIN, *Histoire de l'Egypte sous le Gouvernement de Mohammed Aly . . . . avec des notes par MM. Langlès et Jomard*, 2 Tom. Paris 1823; also a continuation of the same work, " de l'an 1823 à l'an 1838," Paris 1839. ST. JOHN, *Egypt and Mohammed Ali, or Travels in the Valley of the Nile*, 2 Vols. Lond. 1834. MARMONT, (Duc de Raguse) *Voyage en Hongrie etc. . . . en Syrie, en Palestine, et en Egypte*, 5 Tom. Paris, 1837. I was however assured, on very high authority, that the statistical accounts in these works were not wholly to be relied on. The most condensed and accurate account of Egypt and Muhammed Aly which I have yet seen, is contained in the preliminary sections of RÜPPELL's *Reise in Abyssinien*, Frankf. 1838. Perhaps the most authentic document is BOWRING's *Report on Egypt*, containing the statistics of the country in 1838, printed by order of Parliament, Lond. 1840.

Note VII.—Page 46.

RATE OF TRAVEL. During our journey, we several times measured the ordinary rate of our camels' walk; and found it to be on an average nearest to $2\frac{1}{2}$ English miles the hour, when in full progress. But there are always little delays; sometimes the animals browse more; or a load is to be adjusted; or an observation to be taken; so that the preceding estimate would be too high for a whole day's march. If, therefore, we assume the hour with camels at *two* geographical miles, or nearly $2\frac{1}{3}$ English miles, we shall obtain a near approximation to the truth. The statement in the text is founded on this estimate. According to Wilkinson, the direct distance from Cairo to Suez is about 73 English miles, and about 79 by our road. Mod. Egypt, I. p. 305.

The rate of the camel's walk, and of course the distance passed over in an hour, varies somewhat according to the nature of the ground. On the gravelly plains of the desert it is naturally greater than in mountainous and rocky districts. The following rates upon subsequent parts of our journey, were deduced by Berghaus from a comparison of our routes with the known geographical distances between the given points:

Between Suez and Sinai, G. M.	2,090	
" Sinai and 'Akabah	1,837	
" 'Akabah and Hebron	2,130	

Mean rate 2,019

The rate of travelling with horses and mules in Palestine is considerably faster than the above; and is usually assumed at *three* English miles the hour. But some allowance must be made from this; and, besides, the rate is far more variable than with camels in the desert; owing partly to the character of the animals, and partly to the state of the roads and the uneven nature of the country. Under all the circumstances, I can fix on no better mean rate for the hour with horses and mules, than 2.4 geogr. miles, which is equivalent to about $2\frac{3}{4}$ Engl. miles or exactly 3 Roman miles. But the rate which would be quite correct between Gaza and Ramleh, for example, would be much less so between Ramleh and Jerusalem; the former distance being nearly level, and the latter mountainous and difficult.

Note VIII.—Page 47.

Suez. The present town of Suez appears to have sprung up in the first half of the sixteenth century. The early Arabian writers speak only of Kolzum, which Abulfeda (born A. D. 1273) describes as a small city; Reiske's Transl. in Büsching's Magazin, Th. IV. p. 196. Ludolf de Suchem, who travelled here about 1340, speaks of a castle of the 'Soldan' on this part of the Red Sea, probably the remains of Kolzum; but he gives it no name. Tucher of Nürnberg was here in 1480, and mentions the "mountain of Suez" at the end of the Gulf, meaning probably 'Atâkah. He says there was here a landing-place, to which spices and wares were brought from Althor (et-Tûr) and so carried to Cairo and Alexandria. Breydenbach and Felix Fabri passed in 1484, but give no name, and speak only of the remains of the canal. In 1516 it is mentioned still as a landing-place by Ben-Ayas, an Arabian writer; and in 1538 a fleet was built here by Suleimân, who sailed hence on an expedition against Yemen. See Notices et Extraits des Mss. etc. Tom. VI. p. 356. Ritter's Erdkunde Th. II. p. 231. ed. 1818. Belon about 1546 describes Suez; and says an old castle lay near it upon a small hill, doubtless Tell Kolzum. Löwenstein and Wormbser in 1561, and Helffrich in 1565, speak of Suez as a fortress, near which vessels lay; and the latter describes it as consisting of several block-houses built of the trunks of palm trees, and filled in with earth, with a few dwelling-houses. In 1647, according to Monconys, (I. p. 209,) it was a small place in ruins, inhabited chiefly by Greek Christians. In Niebuhr's time it was still without walls; Reisebeschr. I. p. 219.—For the older travellers above cited, see Reissbuch des heiligen Landes, fol.

The head of this gulf has always been a place for building fleets. Ælius Gallus in his celebrated expedition into Arabia Petræa, built at Cleopatris a fleet, first of 80 large galleys, and then 130 smaller vessels; Strabo 16. 4. 23. During the crusades also, the brother of Saladin caused a fleet to be hastily built at Kolzum against the Christians who had attacked Ailah. See Wilken's Geschichte der Kreuzzüge, III. ii. p. 223.

Note IX.—Page 50.

WADY TAWARIK. Our guides of the Tawarah, and also intelligent natives of Suez, knew no other name for the valley south of Jebel 'Atâkah, than Wady Tawârik. By the French engineers, and also by some writers before them, it is called Wady er-Ramliyeh, 'the Sandy.' Niebuhr and a few earlier travellers speak of the part near the gulf under the name of Bedea; though the former says his Arab guides did not know this name. See Le Père in Descr. de l'Egypte, Et. Mod. I. p. 47. Niebuhr's Beschr. von Arabien, p. 409.

The name Wady et-Tîh, 'Valley of Wandering,' which has sometimes been given to the same valley by travellers, seems not now to be known; and if it ever actually existed among the Arabs, it was probably of Christian origin. Monconys in 1647 travelled through the valley, but did not hear this name. Pater Sicard, the Jesuit missionary in Egypt, who wrote an essay to prove that the Israelites passed by way of this valley, (which he himself visited in 1720,) does not mention the name Tih; although it would have afforded him so opportune an argument from tradition in support of his theory. The name therefore probably did not exist at that time; and may perhaps have come into partial use among the Latins and their Arab dependents in consequence of this very theory. Yet neither Pococke nor Niebuhr has the name, as applied to this valley. The latter indeed gives the name Etti to the part of the desert plain opposite to its mouth, on the east side of the gulf; of which however no trace now exists. Reisebeschr. I. pp. 229, 251. See Nouv. Mém. des Missions, T. VI. p. 1 sq. in Paulus' Sammlung der Reisen, Th. V. p. 210 sq.

Note X.—Page 51.

VALLEY OF THE SEVEN WELLS. In February, 1827, the Rev. Mr Smith, my companion, travelled with a caravan by the direct route from Belbeis to el-'Arîsh, passing by the well of Abu Suweirah. The following is an extract from a letter written by him at the time, describing the valley of the Seven Wells. "We passed," he says, "one tract of land, the features of which were so distinctly marked as to excite considerable curiosity. It was a sort of valley a little lower than the surrounding country, into which we descended at a place with ruins about ten and a half hours from Belbeis. It extends northwest and southeast, descending towards the Nile, and narrowing in this direction. We were told that the Nile occasionally flows up this valley to the spot where we crossed it. Towards the southeast it gradually ascends, and widens into an immense plain, the limits of which in that direction we could not discern. From this plain, the eastern extremity of the Suez mountain ['Atakah] which now showed itself for the first time, bore S. by E. The soil of this tract was a dark mould. I do not doubt that water might be found in any part of it, by digging a few feet. Indeed after travelling upon it four and a half hours, we came to a well only twelve or fifteen feet deep, but sufficiently copious to water the [200] camels, and fill the water-skins, of the whole caravan, and containing the only sweet water that we found in the desert; all the other wells being brackish. It is called *Abu Suweirah.* Having seen how extensively artificial irrigation is practised in Egypt, I was easily persuaded that this whole tract might once have been under the highest cultivation." They passed the mounds of the ancient canal on the north side of this valley; and saw, on their right, tracts covered apparently with salt, like those mentioned by Seetzen; see Note XI.

Note XI.—Page 51.

ANCIENT CANAL. FRENCH MEASUREMENTS. The statements in the text, here and elsewhere, respecting the country along the ancient canal, are founded on the results obtained by the French engineers, as recorded in the great work on Egypt; and in a more convenient form in the article of Mr Maclarin, Edinb. Philos. Journal, 1825, Vol. XIII. p. 274 sq. It is proper to mention, however, that strong doubts exist as to the accuracy of these results. I have been informed, that a learned foreigner [A. von Humboldt] when in Paris once endeavoured to get access to the original notes and measurements, in order to submit them to a re-examination; but without success.

The French found the level of the Red sea at Suez to be at high water $30\frac{1}{7}$ Fr. feet above the level of the Mediterranean; and at low water, 25 Fr. feet; giving a mean of $27\frac{1}{2}$ Fr. feet. The height of the Nile at Cairo, they found to be in ordinary floods $39\frac{1}{2}$ Fr. feet above the Mediterranean; and at its lowest point, 16 Fr. feet; giving a mean of $27\frac{1}{7}$ Fr. feet. Hence it appears that the *mean* height of the Nile at Cairo, is the same with that of the gulf of Suez; while at ordinary times the Nile sinks several feet below the level of the gulf.—But the tolerably accordant testimony of ancient writers, and especially that of Strabo, who wrote as an eyewitness, shows pretty conclusively, that the canal was supplied with water wholly from the Nile, and that *the water of that river flowed through the whole length of the canal into the Red sea.* See the extract from Strabo in Note XIII. The testimony of Arabian historians as to the opening of the canal under the Khalif Omar, about A. D. 640, goes to support the same view; see especially Makrizi in Notices et Extraits des Mss. etc. Tom. VI. p. 333 sq.—This however would obviously be incompatible with accuracy in the French measurements, except at the height of the inundation of the Nile.

In A. D. 1810 Seetzen travelled with camels along the track of the ancient canal; and his notices of it are found in Zach's Monatl. Correspondenz, Vol. XXVI. p. 385 sq. He calls the valley of the Seven Wells, *Wady Sho'aib;* and the Crocodile Lakes, *el-Memlah.* The marshes further east he speaks of as a salt plain of a white appearance, bounded in some parts by precipitous hills.

The mounds of the ancient canal commence, as we saw them, about an hour and a half north of Suez. From this point Seetzen traced them two hours and a half with camels; and then travelled an hour and a half further, to the border of the salt plain. This accords well with the distance from Suez to the Bitter Lakes as given by the French, viz. 11¼ geogr. miles nearly. From this spot to *el-Arbek,* the point which the water of the Nile reaches in high inundations, Seetzen found the distance to be two hours; and the whole distance from Suez, eight hours; l. c. p. 389. This traveller seems not to have been aware, that the French had found the level of this tract to be lower than that of the gulf of Suez; for he remarks, that " this plain has everywhere a slight declivity towards the salt lake el-Memlah, which annually receives water from the Nile;" l. c. p. 388.

The mounds of the canal now remaining are described as being from one or two feet to fifteen or twenty feet in height; the space between them being generally about thirty or forty yards.

Note XII.—Page 52.

Pelusiac Nile. The Pelusiac arm of the Nile has usually been assumed as navigable, in consequence of a passage in Arrian, where he is describing the expedition of Alexander against Memphis; Exp. Alex. 3. 1. 4. From Pelusium, he says, Alexander ordered part of his troops to sail with the fleet up the river to Memphis; while he with the remainder marched through the desert to Heliopolis, having the Nile on the right hand. Ὁ δὲ εἰς μὲν Πηλούσιον φυλακὴν εἰσήγαγε, τοὺς δὲ ἐπὶ τῶν νεῶν ἀναπλεῖν κατὰ τὸν ποταμὸν κελεύσας, ἔς τε ἐπὶ Μέμφιν πόλιν, αὐτὸς ἐφ' Ἡλιουπόλεως ᾔει, ἐν δεξιᾷ ἔχων τὸν ποταμὸν Νεῖλον, καὶ . . . . διὰ τῆς ἐρήμου ἀφίκετο ἐς Ἡλιούπολιν. But this language certainly does not necessarily imply, that the fleet sailed up the Pelusiac branch, or that it did not proceed for some distance along the coast and then ascend another branch. Just as at the present day, when it is said that a vessel sails from Alexandria up the river to Cairo, we do not understand that it follows the canal or the old Canopic arm, instead of running along the shore to the Rosetta or Damietta branch. All ancient writers appear to be silent as to the magnitude of the eastern arm of the Nile; nor is there any thing in the nature or appearance of the country, to show that it was formerly very much larger than the modern canal which occupies its place. The most definite mention of it is by Strabo 17. 1. 4. Compare Rennell's Geogr. Syst. of Herodot. II. p. 171 sq.

Note XIII.—Page 55.

Heroopolis. See on this whole subject the Mémoires of Le Père and Du Bois Aymé in Descr. de l'Egypte, Et. Mod. I. p. 21 sq. p. 187 sq. Also of Rozière, ibid. Antiq. Mém. I. p. 127 sq. Ritter's Erdkunde II. p. 234 sq. 1818.

One passage of Strabo is too remarkable and decisive not to be inserted here: 17. 1. 25, 26, ᾿Αλλη δ᾿ ἐστιν [διώρυξ] ἐκδιδοῦσα εἰς τὴν ᾿Ερυθρὰν καὶ τὸν ᾿Αράβων κόλπον, καὶ [κατὰ] πόλιν ᾿Αρσινόην, ἣν ἔνιοι Κλεοπατρίδα καλοῦσι. Διαρρεῖ δὲ καὶ διὰ τῶν πικρῶν καλουμένων λιμνῶν, αἳ πρότερον μὲν ἦσαν πικραί· τμηθείσης δὲ τῆς διώρυγος τῆς λεχθείσης, μεταβάλλοντο τῇ κράσει τοῦ ποταμοῦ· καὶ νῦν εἰσιν εὔοψοι, μεσταὶ δὲ καὶ τῶν λιμναίων ὀρνέων. —— Πλησίον δὲ τῆς ᾿Αρσινόης καὶ ἡ τῶν ᾿Ηρώων ἐστὶ πόλις καὶ ἡ Κλεοπατρὶς, ἐν τῷ μυχῷ τοῦ ᾿Αραβίου κόλπου τῷ πρὸς Αἴγυπτον κτλ. "Another [canal] empties into the Red Sea and Arabian gulf [at] the city Arsinoë, which some call Cleopatris. It also flows through the Bitter Lakes so called, which indeed were formerly bitter; but the said canal being cut, they were changed by the mixture of the river, and are now full of fish and water-fowl.—Near to Arsinoë is also Heroopolis and Cleopatris, at the corner of the Arabian gulf next to Egypt." In two other passages the same position is assigned to Heroopolis; 16. 4. 2, 5. Hence it very naturally gave name to the Gulf, *Sinus Heroopoliticus*.

At first view, the position here given to Heroopolis might seem inconsistent with the language of the Seventy and Josephus, who make Joseph go up (probably from Memphis) as far as to Heroopolis to meet Jacob, as he comes to Egypt from Beersheba; Sept. Gen. 46, 28. 29. Joseph. Ant. 2. 7. 5. But this difficulty is only apparent; for we found at a later period of our journey, that the present usual caravan route from Hebron by way of Beersheba to Cairo, still passes by 'Ajrûd.

Note XIV.—Page 105.

Israel at Sinai. There were two main reasons, which led us to believe in 1838, that the tract on the south of Sinai was not the position occupied by the Israelites when before the mount. One was the distance from the base of the mountain to the nearest point where the people could have stood. This distance is nowhere less than half a mile; and for the most part is much greater. All this conflicts with the representation of Scripture; see Ex. 19, 10–13. 17. 23. The other reason was the rough and impassable character of the ground, consisting of abrupt, gravelly or (as some say) *granite* hills, accumulated apparently around the base of the mountain in irregular masses of low broken cliffs; precluding all idea of easy approach, or of the setting of bounds.

This general view appeared to us so convincing, that we neglected to examine more particularly the immediate base of Sinai on this southern side. But it has since come to light, that there is here a deep ravine between the mountain proper and the low adjacent cliffs, completely separating them and the more open ground beyond from the mountain; thus demonstrating still more strongly the correctness of our view. Such a valley Ritter infers (XIV. p. 592) from the language of

Schimper; who speaks of passing in his botanical excursions quite around the ridge of Sinai, by following several irregular valleys with only some hills between. It is however more fully described by Mr Kellogg in the New York Literary World of Feb. 19, 1818; accompanied by a sketch on wood, which is not only "inaccurate," as he admits, but is also greatly exaggerated.

Mr K. had ascended the southwestern face of Jebel ed-Deir, in order to obtain a good view of the peak of Jebel Mûsa, which he was anxious to sketch. "Here," he says, "close at my right, arose almost perpendicularly the holy mountain. . . . Clinging around its base was a range of sharp upheaving crags from one to two hundred feet in height, which formed an almost impassable barrier to the mountain itself from the valley adjoining. *These crags were separated from the mountain by a deep and narrow gorge;* yet they must be considered as forming the projecting base of Sinai." * * * "I remained at work until nearly sunset, when I discovered people coming towards me through the deep ravine between the mountain of Sinai [Jebel Mûsa] and the craggy spurs, which shoot up around its base. I feared they might prove to be unfriendly Arabs; but as they came nearer, I discovered them to be my companions and their guides, who were returning from Mount St. Catharine."

Returning next day to the same spot with a companion, Mr K. continues: "From Wady es-Sebâ'iyeh we crossed over the granite spurs, in order to pass around the southern border of Sinai into Wady Leja. These spurs are of sufficient size to have separate names among the Arabs. Around them were generally deep and rugged gorges and ravines or water courses, whose sides were formed of ledges of granite, nearly perpendicular." * * * "This ravine around Sinai becomes a deep and impassable gorge, with perpendicular walls, as it enters Wady Leja, passing through the high neck connecting Sinai with the mountain further south. Descending into el-Leja, under the rocky precipice of Sinai, we found the Wady narrow, and choked up with huge blocks of granite, which had tumbled from the sides of the adjacent mountains. We could now see the olive grove of the deserted convent el-Arbain."

It is unnecessary to point out the inconsistency of all this, with the idea of setting bounds around the mount, lest the people should go up or touch it; and also with their standing "at the nether part of the mount;" Ex. 19, 12. 17.

One other point may be noticed. It would appear, that Moses ascended the mountain in the presence of the people, Ex. 19, 20; and the bounds were set, in part, lest the people should, like him, "go up into" the mount; Ex. 19, 12. 24. Now the peak of Jebel Mûsa, on its southern side, is perfectly inaccessible; nor can it be ascended from any point further south than the convents in the valleys on each side; out of sight of any space or tract on the south of the mountain. But from the plain er-Râhah, a ravine leading up through the steep face of es-Sûfsâfeh affords a way of ascent directly in sight of the whole plain. This is not improbably the *Derb el-Serieh* of Pococke; Descr. of the East, I. p. 144. Ritter Erdk. XIV. p. 542.

See generally, Biblioth. Sac. 1849, p. 381–386.

Note XV.—Page 115.

Manna. For the insect which occasions the manna, *Coccus maniparus*, see Ehrenberg's Symbola Physica, *Insecta*, Dec. I. Tab. 10. For a representation of the tamarisk, with the insects and manna upon it, see the same work, *Plantæ*, Dec. I. Tab. 1, 2. See also a full article upon the tamarisk by the same writer, in Schlechtendal's *Linnæa*, Journal für die Botanik, Bd. II. p. 241. Berlin 1827.

A chemical analysis by Prof. Mitscherlich of Berlin, showed that the manna of the tamarisk of Sinai contains no *Mannin* susceptible of crystallization; but is merely au inspissated sugar (Schleimzucker). Linnæa, ibid. p. 282.

Josephus speaks of manna as existing at Sinai in his day; Antiq. 3. 1. 6. A similar substance is found on different trees in various countries of the east; see Niebuhr's Beschr. von Arab. p. 145. Hardwicke in Asiat. Researches, XIV. p. 182 sq. Winer Bibl. Realw. art. *Manna*.

Note XVI.—Page 118.

Serbal. Since the first publication of this work, the idea has been brought forward by Lepsius, and strenuously urged, that Jebel Serbâl is to be regarded as the Sinai of Scripture. See his Reise nach der Halbinsel des Sinai, 1846; also Breife aus Aegypten, 1852, p. 340 sq. 417 sq. See also the argument stated in Bartlett's Forty Days in the Desert, p. 55 sq.

The main argument urged in behalf of Serbâl, is the fact, that the adjacent Wady Feirân is, and always was, well watered and fruitful; while the region around Jebel Mûsa is an inhospitable desert. Hence the former is the only fit spot in the peninsula for the supply of the Israelites with water and sustenance; and as such must have been known to Moses, and selected by him. See Lepsius Reise, p. 20–22. Breife p. 341 sq. Bartlett l. c. p. 56.

This argument leaves out of view two important points in the question; *first*, that there is around Serbâl no open spot or ground corresponding to the historical account of Israel before Sinai; and *secondly*, that the supply of water for the host at Sinai was miraculous.

Wady Feirân runs for a time parallel to Serbâl. In it for about four miles there is a constant succession of gardens and plantations of palm trees; there are fountains, and in almost every garden a well; but the water is hard; and the valley is not more than a hundred paces across, with high mountains on each side. (Burckhardt, Trav. in Syr. p. 603 sq.) From about the middle of Serbâl, the Wady 'Aleiyât comes down nearly at right angles to Wady Feirân, forming the direct and usual mode of access to Serbâl. These two valleys contain the only open ground, which can be taken into the account. It needs but a glance at the maps of Lepsius himself (Reise), and the sketch of Bartlett (p. 57), to perceive that they do not correspond to the circumstances of the scriptural narrative.

It is admitted, that the main encampment of the host must have been in Wady Feirân itself; from which the summit of Serbâl is only here and there visible. The base of the mountain is reached by the

Wady 'Aleiyat, after a walk of *about an hour;* Bartlett p. 57. This latter valley, according to Bartlett, is an unfit, if not impracticable spot for the encampment of any great number of people; the ground is rugged and rocky,—towards the base of the mountain exceedingly so; pp. 57, 58, comp. p. 62. Beyond the fountain all path soon ceases; and the course thence to the base of the mountain is over a wilderness of loose blocks, which it is no easy matter to cross without slipping; ibid. p. 62.

I need not stop to show how utterly incompatible all this is with the narrative in Exodus; where it is said, the people *stood at the nether part of the mount,* Ex. 19, 17; and Moses was directed to *set bounds round about,* lest the people should go up into the mount or *touch the border* of it; Ex. 19, 12.

The testimony of Scripture, that the supply of water for the host was miraculous, removes the objection made against the present Sinai. At Rephidim the people having murmured for water, the Lord commanded Moses to smite the rock *in Horeb,* and water should flow out; and Moses did so; Ex. 17, 5. 6. If Rephidim, as I have elsewhere supposed (p. 120) was near the entrance to the central granite region, then Horeb was near; and it is easy to see how the miraculous fountain might supply water for the host during their sojourn at Sinai. But if their main encampment was in Wady Feirân, in which water was always plenty, where was the necessity for a miracle at all? and especially in Serbâl (the Sinai and Horeb of Lepsius), which was but an hour distant from the well watered encampment.

I have elsewhere suggested, that the stations of the Israelites, as enumerated, refer perhaps rather to the head-quarters of Moses and the elders, with a portion of the people who kept near them; while other portions preceded or followed them at various distances, as the convenience of water and pasturage might dictate; pp. 72, 73. Thus, during the long sojourn at Sinai, it is not at all improbable, that a part of the people with their flocks may have been encamped in the fertile Wady Feirân. Yet, on the other hand, it seems no less obvious, on the great occasion, when the Lord descended on Sinai and gave the ten commandments, that the whole congregation, even all the people, were assembled before the mount. Ex. 19, 9. 11. 16, etc.

It is singular that Lepsius (Breife p. 421 sq.) should quote the authority of Mr Bartlett as an advocate of his views. Mr B. presents the argument indeed, not however as his own, but expressly as that of those who "adopt a rationalist interpretation, and consider the Bible account as a legendary or mythical amplification of a slender historical foundation." P. 55.

NOTE XVII.—Page 120.

HOREB AND SINAI. The same view respecting the use of Horeb as the general name, and Sinai as the specific one, is adopted by Hengstenberg, Authentic des Pent. II. p. 396. Berl. 1839.—The mountain is first mentioned only as *Horeb,* Ex. 3, 1; then Ex. 17, 6; and the same is necessarily implied Ex. 3, 12. 4, 28. 18, 5. *Sinai* is first used Ex. 19, 1. 2, where the Israelites are said to have departed from Rephidim and come to the "desert of Sinai." From this time, with one exception

(Ex. 23, 6), during their whole sojourn in the vicinity, Sinai alone is spoken of, Ex. 19, 11. 18. 23. 24, 16. 31, 18. 34, 29. 32. Lev. 7, 38. 25, 1. 26, 46. 27, 34. Num. 1, 1. 3, 1. 14. In Num. 10, 12, they break up from *Sinai;* and in the list of stations, Num. 33, 15, Sinai also naturally appears. But elsewhere after their departure, and through the whole book of Deuteronomy, (except in the song of Moses, 33, 2,) *Horeb* alone is named; and the same events are spoken of as occurring on Horeb, which were before described as taking place on Sinai; Deut. 1, 2. 6. 19. 4, 10. 15. 5, 2. 9, 8. 18, 16. 28, 69. [29, 1.] Later sacred writers employ both names; e. g. *Horeb,* 1 K. 8, 9. 19, 8. 2 Chr. 5, 10. Ps. 106, 19. Mal. 3, 22. [4, 4.] *Sinai,* Judg. 5, 5. Ps. 68, 9. 18. [8. 17.] In the New Testament, Sinai alone is read, and had then apparently become a general name, as at the present day; Acts 7. 30. 38. Gal. 4, 24. 25. The same is the case throughout in the writings of Josephus. About the end of the sixth century, according to the Itinerary of Antoninus Martyr, the name Horeb was specially applied to the present mountain of the Cross, east of the valley in which the convent stands.

In more modern times, and ever since the crusades, the application of the names Sinai and Horeb to the particular mountains or peaks has varied greatly among travellers. Sir John Maundeville after A. D. 1322, uses Sinai as a general name, including Jebel Mûsa and St. Catharine; but says the part where the chapel of Elias stands, is called Horeb, corresponding nearly to the present common usage. Ludolf de Suchem, A. D. 1336-50, gives the specific name Sinai to Jebel Mûsa only; and applies that of Horeb apparently to St. Catharine.—Tucher of Nürnberg in A. D. 1479 speaks of Jebel Mûsa as Horeb, and St. Catharine as Sinai; and this nomenclature is followed by Breydenbach and Fabri in A. D. 1484, and very distinctly by Baumgarten A. D. 1507; lib. I. c. 24.—Afterwards Sinai is employed only as a general name, and Horeb still appropriated to Jebel Mûsa; so Belon A. D. 1546, Löwenstein and Wormbser A. D. 1562, and Troilo so late as A. D. 1667. But already in A. D. 1565, Helffrich speaks of Jebel Mûsa as Sinai specifically; and so Monconys A. D. 1647.—In A. D. 1722, the present monkish usage, which applies the name Sinai to Jebel Mûsa, and Horeb to the northern part of the same ridge, had already become established; as appears from the Journal of the Prefect of the Franciscans in that year, and also from Van Egmond and Heyman about the same time; Reizen, etc. II. p. 174. Since that period there has been no change, so far as I know; until Rüppell strangely again assumes St. Catharine to be Horeb. Reise in Abyss. I. p. 120.

Note XVIII.—Page 126.

PHARAN. FEIRAN. Edrîsi about A. D. 1150, and Makrizi about A. D. 1400, both speak of Feirân as a city; and the description of it by the latter is quoted in full by Burckhardt, p. 617. Laborde has given a view of the ruins in his original work, which is not included in the English compilation. So too Bartlett in his Forty Days in the Desert, p. 52 sq.

It is barely possible that this is the Pharan or Paran of Ptolemy, westward of Ailah. Most probably it is that of Eusebius and Jerome; which they however place to the eastward of Ailah, either from a mistaken theory or some confusion of names. Jerome says expressly, that the desert of Pharan joins on Horeb. See Cellarius Not. Orb. II. p. 582. Euseb. et Hieron. Onomast. arts. Φαράν, *Faran; Χωρήβ, Choreb.*—The valley of Pharan mentioned by Josephus (B. J. 4. 9. 4) is obviously a different place, somewhere in the vicinity of the Dead Sea; perhaps connected with the mountain and desert of Paran, so often spoken of in the Old Testament, adjacent to Kadesh. Num. 13, 26.

The Peutinger Tables have a Paran fifty Roman miles from Ailah towards Clysma, apparently on the direct route. This would agree better with the Pharan of Ptolemy.

Note XIX.—Page 129.

Sinaitic Inscriptions. These inscriptions are mentioned first by Cosmas, as cited in the text; and then by several of the early travellers; as Neitzschitz, p. 149; Monconys I. p. 245; also by Pococke, I. p. 148, and Niebuhr in his *Reisebeschr.* I. p. 250. Professed copies of some of them are given by Kircher, in his Prodromus Coptus; and also by Pococke and Niebuhr; but they are very imperfect. Those of Seetzen are better; and some of those made by Burckhardt seemed on a comparison with the originals, to be tolerably accurate. A large number of them have been copied and published by Mr. Grey, in the *Transactions of the Royal Society of Literature,* Vol. III. Pt. I. Lond. 1832; consisting of one hundred and seventy-seven in the unknown character, nine in Greek, and one in Latin.

The remarks of Gesenius upon the Sinaitic inscriptions are found in a note to the German edition of Burckhardt's Travels; *Reisen in Syrien,* Weimar 1824, p. 1071.

The inscriptions have been first deciphered only within the present year (1839) by Prof. Beer of the University of Leipzig. This distinguished palæographist had already occupied himself with them so long ago as A. D. 1833; but without success. See his tract entitled: *Inscriptiones et Papyri veteres Semitici quotquot, etc.* Partic. I. 4to. Lips. 1833. In the winter of 1838–9, his attention was again turned to the inscriptions, in connection perhaps with our reports and the residence of my companion for a time in Leipzig; and after several months of the most persevering and painful application, he succeeded in making out the alphabet, and was enabled to read all the inscriptions which have been copied with any good degree of accuracy. The results at which he has arrived are already prepared for publication, and the various tables engraved; so that his work may not improbably appear before these sheets leave the press.

By the kind permission of Prof. Beer, I am able to give here a summary of these results. I ought perhaps to remark, that all those palæographists to whom they have been communicated, are satisfied of the correctness of the proposed alphabet and readings; and that especially some of the most distinguished, as Gesenius, have expressed to me in conversation their decided approbation of Beer's labours.

The *characters* of the Sinaitic inscriptions, Prof. Beer finds to belong to a distinct and independent alphabet. Some of the letters are wholly peculiar; the others have more or less affinity with the Palmyrene, and particularly with the Estrangelo and Cufic. Indeed, their affinity with the latter is so great, as to lead to the supposition, that the Cufic was afterwards developed from this alphabet. They are written from right to left. In their form, several of the letters much resemble each other, as is the case in other ancient alphabets. This sometimes creates considerable difficulty in deciphering an inscription; though not more than in the Cufic. But the difficulty is here increased by the negligence of the copyists; who have often not noticed the slight difference that actually exists. This is apparent from the different copies of the same inscription, which exist in several instances.

The *contents* of the inscriptions, so far as Prof. Beer has yet proceeded, consist only of proper names; preceded by a word which is usually שלם *peace ;* but sometimes דכיר *memoriatus sit;* and in a very few cases ברוך *blessed.* Between the names, the word בר or בן *son* often occurs; and they are sometimes followed by one or two words at the end; thus the word כהן *priest* occurs twice as a title. In one or two instances the name is followed by a phrase or sentence, which has not yet been deciphered. The names are those common in Arabic; but have this peculiarity, that most of those which are single, end in a Vav (ו), whether they are in the nominative or genitive case; while the compound names end in Yodh (י). Thus we have כלבי, אישי, עודו, זידו, עמרו; and also כבד אלבכלי, איש אלהי, כבד אלהי, כבד אלהי, אלבכקרו. The Arabic article is frequent in the names; but has not always the Alef (א) when in composition.—It is a remarkable fact, that not one Jewish or Christian name has yet been found. The words which are not proper names, seem rather to belong to an Aramæan dialect. A language of this kind, Prof. Beer supposes to have been spoken by the inhabitants of Arabia Petræa, in other words by the Nabathæans, before the present Arabic language spread itself over those parts; and of that language and writing, these inscriptions he regards as the only monuments now known to exist.

The question as to the *writers* of the inscriptions receives very little light from their contents. A word at the end of some of them, may be so read as to affirm that they were *pilgrims;* and this opinion Beer also adopts. But this reading is not certain; and the opinion is to be supported chiefly from the fact, that the inscriptions are found only on the great routes leading from Suez to Mount Sinai. The multitude of them in Wady Mukatteb and around Serbâl may be accounted for, by supposing that mountain or some spot in its vicinity to have been regarded as a holy place; though probably not as Sinai.—That the writers were *Christians,* seems apparent from the crosses connected with many of the inscriptions. The same inscription is in several instances found in more than one place, once with the cross and again without it. The crosses are of such a shape, that they could not well be accidental nor unmeaning, e. g. ⅄, ✝, ⚶.

The *age* also of the inscriptions receives no light from their contents; as no date has yet been read. On palæographic grounds, Prof. Beer supposes the greater part of them could not have been written earlier than the fourth century. Had they been written later, some tradition respecting them would probably have existed in the time of Cosmas. The character of the writing also forbids this supposition.

Thus far Prof. Beer; and thus far all is sufficiently clear. But there still remain some historical points of difficult solution. These Christian pilgrims, who were they? and whence did they come? The fact that all the inscriptions are found only on the great routes from Egypt, would seem to imply that they came from that country, or at least from the western side of the gulf of Suez. But if so, how comes it that not a trace of this alphabet and language is found in Egypt or its vicinity? Egypt too, we know, was full of Jews and Christians in the early centuries; how comes it then that no Jewish nor Christian names are found among the inscriptions? It is true that the heathen proper names continued to be used long after the introduction of Christianity; as we see from the names of the early fathers and bishops; but this will not account for the entire absence of Christian and Jewish names among such hosts of pilgrims coming from Egypt.

On the other hand, were these pilgrims Nabathæans, Ishmaelites, Saracens, the native inhabitants of the peninsula and of Arabia Petræa in general? The heathen names and the language and writing would lead to this conclusion. But then, how comes it that all the inscriptions are on the western side of the peninsula, and not one upon the eastern? Besides, there is no historical evidence, that any *native* Christian population existed in or around the peninsula in the early centuries; but rather the contrary, as we have seen in the text; p. 122 sq. The Christian exiles from Egypt, and the hermits of these mountains, lived in constant exposure to slavery or death from the heathen around them.

Again; how comes it that in the time of Cosmas, about A. D. 530, all knowledge of this alphabet and language had already perished among the Christians of the peninsula, and no tradition remained respecting the inscriptions?

So far the note in the former edition. The work of Prof. Beer, entitled *Studia Asiatica*, Fascic. I, was printed in 1840; but was not published until the next year, about the time of the lamented author's decease. It contains his explanation of the alphabet, and his reading of many of the inscriptions; as also his general historical views as above described.

The work of Beer was reviewed by Credner, in the *Heidelberger Jahrbücher*, 1841, p. 908 sq. He gave to the historical question a new direction; and was the first to bring forward the important passage from Diodorus Siculus, referred to below.

In the Journal of the German Oriental Society for 1849, (Zeitschr. d. morg. Ges. III. p. 129–215,) there appeared a paper by Prof. Tuch of Leipzig, containing the results of his investigations on the general subject, and an exposition of twenty-one inscriptions. In respect to Beer's explanation of the alphabet this writer remarks, that after the keenest scrutiny, he has found nothing to change; p. 130. In respect to the historical inquiry, his main results are the following.

The *dialect* of the inscriptions is neither Aramæan nor Nabathæan, as held by Gesenius and Beer; but Arabic. This appears from the flexion, grammatical structure, stock of words, and the proper names; p. 136 sq.

The *authors* of the inscriptions were therefore Arabs, ancient Tawarah, inhabiting the peninsula, and known to us centuries before the rise of Muhammedanism by their hostilities towards the early Christian settlers; see text p. 122 sq. All the circumstances go to show that they were heathen; as also the fact that no Jewish or Christian name has yet been found in the inscriptions; p. 145 sq. 159 sq.

Pilgrimages to some holy place were the *occasion* of the inscriptions; as represented by the authors themselves. Such sacred places were not unusual among the Arabs in the times before Muhammedanism; one indeed existed in Mecca itself. And according to *Diodorus Siculus* (3. 42, 43), there was in his day and earlier a spot of the like kind in the peninsula of Sinai, a luxuriant palm grove with fountains and streams, an oasis in the midst of a desert region, otherwise without water or shade, and with a southern exposure. Here was an altar of hard stone with an inscription in ancient unknown characters. Hither the people, who dwelt round about, were accustomed to repair once in five years, to celebrate a festival, sacrifice hecatombs of camels, and carry home a supply of water from the sacred fountains. (See also Strabo from Artemidorus, 16. 4. 18.) Whether this palm grove was at Feirân, or perhaps at Tûr, is not clear; though more probably it was at Feirân; see Lepsius, Briefe p. 442 sq. A heathen altar is likewise mentioned by Antoninus Martyr in the sixth century, as on the mountain of the Cross; see text p. 125; and not improbably there may have been others in the peninsula. The tomb of Sheikh Sâlih is not very different at the present day. It was on occasion of these religious festivals, when the people collected around these sacred spots, that the pilgrims on their way to or from them, or in their loiterings, recorded their journeys in these inscriptions; as do Christian pilgrims in and around the convent at the present day.

The *epoch* of the inscriptions reaches back beyond the time of Diodorus Siculus, when the characters were already ancient; of course one or more centuries before Christ; and is probably to be extended down to the third or fourth century after Christ; pp. 171, 174.

The *crosses* found in connection with some of the inscriptions, are regarded by Tuch as ornamental rather than symbolical; like the many other figures everywhere intermingled; p. 154 sq. Comp. text p. 182.

Such is the present state of the inquiry respecting the inscriptions. It is understood, that since the date of Prof. Tuch's paper, a large number of the inscriptions have been accurately copied by a French traveller; but nothing further has yet been published.

The work of Mr Foster on this subject, is too visionary to require notice here.

In the Travels of Irby and Mangles, a fact is mentioned which deserves further examination from travellers. In the vicinity of Wady Mûsa, on the left hand side of the track leading to the village of Dibdiba on the north, this party found upon a tomb, with a large front and four attached columns, an oblong tablet containing an inscription "in five long lines, and immediately underneath, a single figure on a large scale, probably the date." They describe the letters as "well cut, and in a wonderful state of preservation, owing to the shelter which they receive from the projection of cornices and an eastern aspect. None of the party had ever seen these characters before, excepting Mr Bankes; who, upon comparing them, found them to be exactly similar to those which he had seen scratched on the rocks in the Wady Mukatteb, and about the foot of Mount Sinai." This inscription they copied; but it has never been made public. See Travels of Irby and Mangles, pp. 411, 413. [126.]

When we were at Wady Mûsa, I was not aware of the position of this inscription; and the circumstances in which we were there placed, prevented our finding it; nor does it appear to have been discovered by any later traveller. But the same Journal for 1855 (Zeitschr. d. morg. Ges. IX. p. 230 sq.) has an article by Blau, giving an account of three short Sinaitic inscriptions found in or near Petra, by Mr Ross, an English traveller. They seem however to have no connection with the one above described.

In Cairo I was told that similar inscriptions exist in the immense ancient quarries back of Tûra just above Cairo; and also in the granite quarries of Aswân. Lepsius however testifies, that in none of these quarries is there any trace of the Sinaitic characters; and the report doubtless arose from confounding with them the Egyptian demotic characters, which are found in the quarries. Zeitschr. der morg. Ges. III. p. 146.

NOTE XX.—Pages 125, 135.

THE CONVENT AND ITS SERFS. The following passage from the Arabic Annals of Eutychius, (Sa'id Ibn el-Batrik,) Patriarch of Alexandria in the latter half of the ninth century, has been hitherto apparently overlooked; and seems of sufficient importance to be inserted here in a translation. It is found in Eutychii Annales, Tom. II. p. 160 sq. Oxon. 1658.

" But when the monks of Mount Sinai heard of the clemency of the emperor Justinian, and that he delighted to build churches and found convents, they made a journey to him and complained, how the wandering sons of Ishmael were wont to attack them suddenly, eat up their provisions, desolate the place, enter their cells and carry off every thing; and how they also broke into the church and devoured even the holy wafers. Then the emperor Justinian said to them, 'What do ye desire?' And they said, 'We ask of thee, O emperor, that thou wouldst build for us a convent which may be a strong hold.' For before this time there was no convent in Mount Sinai common to all the monks; they lived scattered upon the mountains and in the valleys round about the bush, out of which God (his name be praised!) spoke with Moses. Above the bush they had a great tower, which remains to this day, and in it was the church of St. Mary. And when danger was near, the monks fled into this tower and fortified themselves in it. The emperor dismissed them, and sent with them a legate furnished with a great sum of money; and he wrote to his prefect in Egypt, to supply the legate with money, as much as he needed, and also with men, and to see that he likewise received corn from Egypt. And he commanded the legate to build a church at Kolzum, and the convent Râyeh (Raithu?), and a convent in Mount Sinai; and to build this so strong, that in all the world there should not be found one stronger ; and so secure, that from no quarter should there be any harm to fear, either for the monks or the convent.

"And the legate came to Kolzum, and built there the church of St. Athanasius ; and he built also the convent Ràyeh. Then he came to Mount Sinai ; and found there the bush in a narrow place between two mountains, and the tower near by, and fountains of water springing up ; but the monks were dispersed in the valleys. At first he thought to build the convent high above upon the mountain, and far from the bush and tower. But he gave up this purpose on account of water ; for there was no water above upon the mountain. He built therefore the convent near the bush on the place of the tower, including the tower in the convent ; in the narrow place between two mountains. So that any one on the top of the northern mountain, might throw down a stone into the midst of the convent and injure the monks. And he built the convent in this place, because here was the bush, and other celebrated monuments, and water. And he built a chapel on the top of the mountain, on the spot where Moses received the law. The name of the prior of the convent was Daula.

"Then the legate returned back to the emperor Justinian, and told him of the churches and convents he had built, and described to him how he had built the convent of Mount Sinai. And the emperor said unto him, 'Thou hast done wrong, and hast injured the monks ; for thou hast delivered them into the hand of their enemies. Wherefore hast thou not built the convent on the top of the mountain ?' And the legate said to him, 'I have built the convent near by the bush, and near water. Had I built it above on the top of the mountain, the monks would have been without water ; so that if ever they had been besieged, and cut off from the water, they must have died of thirst. Also the bush would have been far distant from them.' Then the emperor said, 'Thou oughtest then at least to have levelled to the ground the northern mountain ; so that from it no one could do the monks any harm.' The legate said to him, 'Had we laid out all the treasures of Egypt and Rome and Syria upon it, we could not have made an end of this mountain.' Then the emperor was wroth, and commanded to strike off his head.

"Thereupon he sent another legate, and with him a hundred slaves out of the slaves of Rome, with their wives and children ; and commanded him also to take from Egypt another hundred slaves out of the slaves of Rome, with their wives and children ; and to build for them dwellings outside of Mount Sinai, wherein they might dwell, and so guard the convent and the monks ; and also to provide for their sustenance, and to see that a supply of corn was furnished to them and to the convent from Egypt. When now the legate had come to Sinai, he built many dwellings outside of the convent towards the east, and fortified them, and placed in them the slaves, to guard and protect the convent. And the place is called unto this day *Deir el-'Abid*, 'Convent of the Slaves.'

"But when after a long time many children were born unto them, and they were multiplied, and the religion of Muhammed was spread abroad, (this took place under the Khalif Abd el-Melek Ibn Merwân,) then they fell upon one another and killed each other. And many were slain, and many fled, and others embraced the Muhammedan religion. And to this day their posterity in the convents profess this religion, and are called *Benu Sâlih*, and are also named Children (Servants) of the Convent. Among them are the Lakhmiyîn. But the monks destroyed the dwellings of the slaves, after they had embraced the religion of Muhammed; so that no one could any more dwell therein. And they remain desolate unto this day."

Note XXI.—Page 168.

Tezkirah, *or Passport of the Governor of 'Akabah.* " The reason of writing it is, that when it was Wednesday the 10th of Muhurram, year 1254, there came to us Mr Robinson, and with him two others, having an *answer* from the Council to us. This answer he gave to us, and we have read it and understood what is in it. In it we are informed, that they need Arabs and camels to take them to the Wady Mûsa. Now we have found no camels in our neighbourhood, all the Arabs being in Syria. Therefore we said to them, ' How is your opinion? We have no Arabs nor camels. We will send for you to Hussein.' They said, ' We shall be detained.' And we said, ' Consult your views; that we may be at ease, both we and you.' And they said, ' We will go to Gaza; Wady Mûsa is not necessary; we will go to Gaza.' So we gave them Arabs of the Tawarah, and one guide to conduct them as far as Wady el-Abyad. And they went towards Gaza, with the peace of God most High.

" We have written this answer, to prevent interference with them; and no one must interfere with them."

Dated the 10th of   } (Signed)   Othman,
  Muhurram, year '54. }   Governor of the Castle of 'Akabah.
                (L. S.)

Note XXII.—Page 172.

Haj Stations. The following is a list of the stations on the Haj route from Cairo as far as Muweilih, with the portions of the road for which the various tribes of Arabs are responsible and furnish a convoy.

Stations.

1. Birket el-Haj.	8. eth-Themed.
2. Dâr el-Hûmra; no water.	9. Râs en-Nûkb; no water.
3. *'Ajrûd.*	10. *el-'Akabah.*
4. en-Nawatir; water at Mab'ûk.	11. Hakl.
5. Jebeil Hasan; no water.	12. Râs esh-Shûraf; no water.
6. *Nûkhl.*	13. el-Beda'.
7. Wady el-Kureis.	14. *Muweilih.*

Between el-Beda' and Muweilih, Rüppel inserts another station, Ainune as he calls it, the Eynunah of Moresby's chart. Reisen in Nubien, etc. p. 218.

Convoys. The route from Cairo to 'Ajrûd is free. The *Tawarah* are then responsible for it from 'Ajrûd to Nûkhl. But ever since they plundered a caravan several years ago, and were punished for it by the Pasha, they have been deprived of their tolls from the Haj; though it is still their duty to furnish an escort, and they are still responsible for the safety of the caravan on this part of the route.—The *Tiyahah* are responsible only at Nûkhl.—The *Haiwât* from Nûkhl to Râs en-Nûkb.—The *'Alawin*, from Râs en-Nûkb to 'Akabah.   The *'Amrân* from 'Akabah to el-Beda'.—The *Huweitât* from el-Beda' to Muweilih, etc.—All these tribes, except the Tawarah, receive tolls.

A list of stations on the route of the Syrian Haj, from Damascus to Mecca, is given in the Appendix to Burckhardt's Travels in Syria, p. 656 sq.

Note XXIII.—Page 194.

'Abdeh, Eboda. Our 'Amrân guides knew these ruins only under the name of 'Aujeh. Tuweileb called them 'Abdeh ; but told us afterwards, that he knew this name only from M. Linant, who had visited the place a few years before.   In Hebron we were asked, whether we had been at 'Abdeh, which was said to be three days distant from that town. From what was there told us, we were for some time in doubt, whether the place we had visited was the 'Abdeh of the Arabs. For a long time we could get no definite information, nor find any person who had been there. Some said it lay nearer to the 'Arabah, eastward of el-Birein. It was not till after our return from Wady Musa in June, that we became satisfied on this point. We then found in Hebron a very intelligent owner of camels, who himself had travelled through all Syria and the adjacent countries, and had been at 'Abdeh. He described to us the route he had taken, and gave a minute account of the ruins and their situation; mentioning expressly that they lay northwest of el-Birein. His account tallied so exactly with what we had ourselves seen, that we no longer had any doubt on the subject.

These ruins have not been described by any traveller ; nor am I sure that they have been visited by any one, except M. Linant, as above mentioned. Sir F. Henniker, indeed, in crossing the desert from the convent to Gaza, speaks of having seen somewhere in this quarter, " two large stone buildings, having the appearance of fortresses, and situate on the edge of a lofty rock." (Notes, etc. p. 253.) This language and the circumstances of the case, would lead to the conclusion that 'Abdeh was here meant; but the other details of his account are so totally at variance with what we saw, that I must distrust either this conclusion, or the accuracy of the writer. Seetzen, in 1807, travelled direct from the vicinity of Gaza to Sinai.   On the third day he came to a place called 'Abdeh, of which he before had heard much; but he found only a "town whose houses all lay in ruins, and exhibited nothing worth seeing." (Zach's Monatl. Corr. XVII. p. 144. Reisen III. p. 43.) This could not well have been the 'Abdeh that we saw ; though he speaks of the ruins of a church. M. Callier also, in passing in 1834 among the mountains bordering on the 'Arabah, where the Wadys run towards the Dead Sea, speaks of visiting the ruins of an *Abdé*, which were near ; but he does not describe them. (Journal des Savans, Jan. 1836, p. 47.) This location does not correspond at all to the 'Abdeh we visited.—I am inclined to suppose, that both these latter travellers were misinformed by their Arab guides. They had both heard of 'Abdeh, and naturally inquired for it; and the Arabs in their usual manner answered at random, and pointed out any spot that happened first to come to hand. There can be no question, that the ruins we saw, are on or near the ancient Roman road, and answer to the position of Eboda in the Peutinger Tables.

NOTE XXIV.—Page 199.

ROUTES FROM MOUNT SINAI, ACROSS THE DESERT TO GAZA AND HEBRON.

I. *Chief Route from the convent to Gaza, over the Pass el-Mureikhy. Ten days.*

1st Day.	Convent to
	'Ain el-Akhdar, in the Wady of the same name. See page 85.
2d Day.	el-Mureikhy, the Pass.
	'Ammâr es-Sâlimeh, a plain.
3d Day.	er-Rejîm, a spring of water in Wady el-'Arîsh, near its head.
4th Day.	Hûmâdet el-Berbery, a plain. Here the route No. II comes in.
	el-Jûghâmileh, a spring of bitter water in W' el-'Arîsh, a little off the road.
	Themâil Um es-Sa'ideh, pits of bitter water.
5th Day.	Wady el-Hamdh.
6th Day.	Wady el-'Arîsh. The path crosses the Wady and keeps along more to the east.
	Jebel Ikhrimm; see p. 184.
	Wady el-Kureiyeh; see p. 184.
	esh-Shureif.

7th Day.   Wady el-Lussân ⎫ at points to the left of our route; see
           W' Jerâr   ⎬ pp. 187, 188, 189.
           W' Jâifeh   ⎭

        el-Muweilih, with brackish water, near W' el-'Ain; see p. 190.

8th Day.	Wady es-Serâm (head). Here this route falls into ours. See p. 191.
9th Day.	er-Ruhaibeh. Route the same as ours.
10th Day.	Nûttâr Abu Sûmâr, where the Bedawîn have store-houses for grain.
	Wady esh-Sheri'ah, running to the sea.
	Ghûzzeh (Gaza).

This appears to be the route taken by Seetzen in 1807, from near Gaza to the Convent. Zach's Monatl. Corresp. XVII. p. 142 sq.

II. *Route by the Western Pass, er-Râkineh. Ten days.*

1st Day.	Convent to
	Wady Berâh. See page 84.
2d Day.	el-Mûrâk, at the foot of et-Tîh. See p. 77.
3d Day.	er-Râkineh, the Pass.

Abu Nuteighineh, with good water.

4th Day. Húmádet el-Berbery in No. I.

Hence, as before, to Gaza.

III. *Branch Route from Nos.* I *and* II, *by way of Nukhl. Eleven days to Gaza*

3 Days to er-Rejìm as in No. I; or to Abu Nuteighineh as in No. II.

4th Day. Abu-Ulejàn.

5th Day. Núkhl, fortress on the Haj road.

6th Day. Wady er-Rawàk. (Comp. Burckhardt, p. 449.)

7th Day. esh-Shureif, in No. I.

Hence, as before, to Gaza.

Sir F. Henniker passed by er-Rákineh and Núkhl; Notes etc. pp. 246, 247. Russegger, a few months after our journey, crossed the Tíh by the Pass el-Mureikhy, and then went by Núkhl to Ruhaibeh and Hebron. See Berghaus' Annalen der Erdkunde, März 1839, p. 427 sq.

IV. *Eastern route by el-'Ain, etc. Ten days to Gaza.*

2 Days from the Convent to the head of Wady ez-Zúlakah; see page 148.

3d Day. el-'Ain; living water.

4th Day. Wady el-'Atîyeh, running to Wady Wetir.

5th Day. Pass of et-Tíh, northern ridge, near the head of Wady el-Jeráfeh.

eth-Themed; water. See p. 176.

6th Day. el-Mushch-hem. Comp. in No. VII.

7th Day. Wady el-Mâyein on our road.

Hence, the same route as ours.

V. *Branch Route from Nos.* I *and* II, *direct to Gaza along the western side of Wady el-'Arish.*

From the Convent to

Wady el-Hamdh, 5 days, as in No. I, or No. II.

Múktùl edh-Dhuleim.

Wady el-Hasana. Comp. in No. VI.

el-Burkein.

Mukrih el-Ibna.

Jebel el-Helàl. See p. 185.

el-Kàsaby; here the route crosses W' el-'Arîsh.

el-Khùbarah. See p. 202.

el-Bawâty.

el-Minyày.

Ghúzzeh (Gaza).

This appears to have been the route of the pilgrims in the 15th and 16th centuries. See the next page.

VI. *Route between Suez or 'Ajrùd and Hebron.*

From Suez or 'Ajrùd to

el-Mab'ùk, wells just south of the Haj route.

Feràshât esh-Shîh.